太 玄 經

THE CANON OF SUPREME MYSTERY
BY YANG HSIUNG

SUNY Series in Chinese Philosophy and Culture
David L. Hall and Roger T. Ames, Editors

太玄經

THE CANON OF
SUPREME MYSTERY

BY YANG HSIUNG

*A Translation with Commentary
of the* T'AI HSÜAN CHING
by Michael Nylan

STATE UNIVERSITY OF NEW YORK PRESS

Published by
State University of New York Press, Albany

© 1993 State University of New York

This publication has been supported by a grant from the National
Endowment for the Humanities, an independent federal agency.

Printed in the United States of America

For information, address State University of New York Press,
State University Plaza, Albany, N.Y., 12246

Production by Cathleen Collins
Marketing by Lynne Lekakis

Library of Congress Cataloging in Publication Data

Yang, Hsiung, 53 B.C.-18 A.D.
    [T'ai hsüan ching, English]
    The Canon of supreme mystery / by Yang Hsiung; with translation
and commentary by Michael Nylan.
       p. cm.—(SUNY series in Chinese philosophy and culture)
    Translation of: T'ai hsüan ching.
    Includes bibliographical references and index.
    ISBN 0-7914-1395-0 (alk. paper).
    1. Divination—China. 2. Cosmology, Chinese. I. Nylan, Michael.
II. Title. III. Series.
BF1770.C5Y3613 1993
181'.112—dc20   92-8631
                                              CIP

10 9 8 7 6 5 4 3 2 1

To Nathan Sivin and Paul Serruys

Contents

PREFACE	xi
INTRODUCTION	1
General Introduction to the Mystery *Text*	1
On the Term "Mystery"	2
A Capsule Biography of Yang Hsiung	5
The *Mystery* in the Tradition of the *Changes*	6
The Arrangement of the *Mystery*	9
Significant Structure in the *Mystery*	14
The First Seven Heads	18
No. 1. Center – 18, No. 2. Full Circle – 19,	
No. 3. Mired – 19, No. 4. Barrier – 19, No. 5. Small – 20,	
No. 6. Contrariety – 20, No. 7. Ascent – 21	
Every Tenth Head	22
No. 1. Center – 22, No. 11. Divergence – 22,	
No. 21. Release – 22, No. 31. Packing – 23,	
No. 41. Response – 23, No. 51. Constancy – 24,	
No. 61. Embellishment – 24, No. 71. Stoppage – 25,	
No. 81. Nurturing – 25, General Commentary – 26	
Method of Divination of the *Mystery*	27
Interpretation Following Divination	29
On Luck and Divination in the Mystery	33
The *Mystery* as Divination Classic	33
Early Notions of *Ming*: The Historical Background to the Problem of Fate	35
Yang Hsiung's Solution to the Problem of *Ming*	39
Propositions About Time, Luck, and Virtue	47
The Intellectual Debts of Yang's New Classic	55
Yang's *Mystery* as a Chinese *Summa*	57
Contra the Relativists	58
Contra the Immortality Seekers	59
Contra the Proponents of "Change as the Only Constant"	59
Contra Predestination	60
Contra the Mantic Specialists	60
Conclusion	61
Key Terms	63
The Five Classics of Confucianism	63
On *Ch'i*	63
Yin/yang Five Phases Theory: Correlative Thought	65
Self-Cultivation	68
"Center Heart"	69

Ritual 70
The Meaning of *Chen* 71
On the Style of the Book 73
Glossary for the Introductory Sections 75
Names of People 75
Concepts and Terms 76
TRANSLATION OF THE *T'AI HSÜAN CHING* 80
List of Tetragrams 80
No. 1. Center 84
No. 2. Full Circle 95
No. 3. Mired 102
No. 4. Barrier 107
No. 5. Keeping Small 113
No. 6. Contrariety 118
No. 7. Ascent 125
No. 8. Opposition 130
No. 9. Branching Out 135
No. 10. Defectiveness/
            Distortion 140
No. 11. Divergence 144
No. 12. Youthfulness 148
No. 13. Increase 152
No. 14. Penetration 156
No. 15. Reach 161
No. 16. Contact 165
No. 17. Holding Back 170
No. 18. Waiting 174
No. 19. Following 178
No. 20. Advance 182
No. 21. Release 186
No. 22. Resistance 189
No. 23. Ease 193
No. 24. Joy 197
No. 25. Contention 201
No. 26. Endeavor 206
No. 27. Duties 210
No. 28. Change 214
No. 29. Decisiveness 218
No. 30. Bold Resolution 222
No. 31. Packing 226
No. 32. Legion 230
No. 33. Closeness 234
No. 34. Kinship 239
No. 35. Gathering 243
No. 36. Strength 247
No. 37. Purity 251
No. 38. Fullness 254
No. 39. Residence 258
No. 40. Law/Model 262
No. 41. Response 266
No. 42. Going To Meet 272
No. 43. Encounters 276
No. 44. Stove 280
No. 45. Greatness 286
No. 46. Enlargement 290
No. 47. Pattern 294
No. 48. Ritual 300
No. 49. Flight 306
No. 50. Vastness/Wasting 310
No. 51. Constancy 314
No. 52. Measure 318
No. 53. Eternity 323
No. 54. Unity 327
No. 55. Diminishment 331
No. 56. Closed Mouth 335
No. 57. Guardedness 339
No. 58. Closing In 343
No. 59. Massing 347
No. 60. Accumulation 351
No. 61. Embellishment 355
No. 62. Doubt 359
No. 63. Watch 362
No. 64. Sinking 365
No. 65. Inner 368
No. 66. Departure 372
No. 67. Darkening 375
No. 68. Dimming 379
No. 69. Exhaustion 381
No. 70. Severance 385

Contents

No. 71. Stoppage 388

No. 72. Hardness 392

No. 73. Completion 395

No. 74. Closure 398

No. 75. Failure 401

No. 76. Aggravation 403

No. 77. Compliance 406

No. 78. On the Verge 410

No. 79. Difficulties 413

No. 80. Laboring 415

No. 81. Fostering 418

Leap Year Differentials 421

AUTOCOMMENTARIES   423

Polar Oppositions of the Mystery: *Hsüan ch'ung*   423

Interplay of Opposites in the Mystery: *Hsüan ts'o*   426

Evolution of the Mystery: *Hsüan li*   428

Illumination of the Mystery: *Hsüan ying*   433

Numbers of the Mystery: *Hsüan shu*   438

Elaboration of the Mystery: *Hsüan wen*   448

Representations of the Mystery: *Hsüan yi*   453

Diagram of the Mystery: *Hsüan t'u*   456

Revelation of the Mystery: *Hsüan kao*   461

NOTES   465

BIBLIOGRAPHY   629

PARTIAL INDEX OF COMMON IMAGES   655

INDEX   661

Preface

As the first grand synthesis of classic Chinese thought, Yang Hsiung's *Canon of Supreme Mystery* (ca. 4 B.C.) occupies a place in all of Chinese intellectual history roughly comparable to that of the *Summa Theologica* of Thomas Aquinas in the West. As one of the few original works by a recognized philosophical master to have survived from the formative Han period (contemporaneous with and analogous to the Roman empire), the *Mystery* provides us today with the single best remaining clue to early attempts to situate the individual in family, state bureaucracy, and cosmos. As one of the first systematic responses to the *Book of Changes* (*Yi ching*), the divination manual *cum* philosophical treatise, the *Mystery* can also help us reconstruct the original imagery, structure, and meaning of that sacred canon in relation to other classics, such as the *Book of Documents* and the *Book of Odes*.

Despite its obvious importance, the *Mystery* is the only masterwork of early Chinese philosophy that has not been translated into any Western language; its only "modern" scholarly translation is a Japanese rendering that tends to gloss over problematic passages. Still, the *Mystery* offers much to the modern reader. It is a divination manual that suggests a complex interaction between time and virtue in unfolding human destiny. It is also one of the great philosophic poems of world literature, assessing the rival claims on human attention of fame, power, and physical immortality, while situating human endeavor within the larger framework of cosmic energies. The symbols system of the *Mystery* is unsurpassed in its richness in the Chinese language. At the same time, the *Mystery* serves as a repository of early Chinese scientific, philosophical, and technical knowledge.

An accessible (and wherever possible, literal) translation into English is offered here for the complete text of the *Canon of Supreme Mystery* and its ten autocommentaries. Following Chinese tradition (reflected somewhat in the Wilhelm translation of the *Yi ching*), supplementary comments are appended to each block of translation in order to indicate the main lines of interpretation for the passage suggested by earlier scoliasts. In addition, these commentaries supply background information about literary allusions and historical facts where pertinent, in the hopes that the modern reader may experience the text in a fashion not unlike Yang's earlier readers. Included in the translator's introduction are short essays dedicated to each of several key terms employed by Yang Hsiung. No translation can ever hope to fully suggest the intricate beauty of the original text by Yang Hsiung. My hope is simply that this study will revive interest in this important thinker. It is an invitation to others to enter into the pleasures of Han philosophy.

A BRIEF NOTE ON THE TRANSLATION AND COMMENTARIES

Modern literary theory argues that phrases or lines when repeated take on new meanings in view of their new context. The frequent repetition of Appraisal lines in the Fathomings has therefore presented me with an unusual opportunity to clarify, expand, or shade the translation given in the Appraisal. Accordingly, readers of classical Chinese will find that the same Chinese character in related lines is not always rendered as a single English equivalent. Since Yang Hsiung emphasized the changing values of actions and entities in varying situations, I suspect that he would have preferred this to a more rigid approach to translation.

The commentary that follows each section of poetry gives the reader a synopsis of the commentary tradition attached to the *Mystery*. When all the commentators agree on the basic meaning of the poetry, as often happens, I have not thought it necessary to supply a footnote to indicate this general consensus. When one or more commentators offer variant interpretations, a note directs the reader to the appropriate material. In the very few cases where I have gone beyond the Chinese commentators in my interpretation or speculation, I have tried to indicate this in a note.

ACKNOWLEDGEMENTS

Many people have helped with the *Canon of Supreme Mystery*. First among them was Nathan Sivin. Shortly after I finished my Ph.D. dissertation at Princeton in 1982, Professor Sivin offered me the opportunity to coauthor an introductory article on Yang Hsiung's book. That opportunity, along with Professor Sivin's support through the years, encouraged me to continue work on Yang Hsiung. Despite his busy schedule, Professor Sivin often took the time to keep my writing "honest." When my translations were poor or my generalizations sloppy, Professor Sivin made constructive suggestions for their improvement. Where the style is clear and the argument tight in the the text I offer here, much of the credit should go to Nathan Sivin. Where there are obvious failings, they reflect my own inability to adequately (in the Chinese phrase) "pair" his lucid mind. For all of his help, I am most grateful.

Some three years into the project, I happened to meet Father Paul Leo-Mary Serruys, whose 1959 dissertation focused on Yang Hsiung's dialect dictionary, the *Fang yen*. Fortunately, Father Serruys soon became interested in the *T'ai hsüan* text. Over the course of the next few years, using the *T'ai hsüan* as a sort of textbook, Father Serruys instructed me in the fundamental principles of early Chinese linguistics. Father Serruys and I discussed nearly every line of the translation offered here. Often we argued. No series of footnotes, however extensive, could adequately convey the magnitude of my intellectual debt to him. As with Professor

Sivin, I only hope Father Serruys will be pleased with the result, despite my many errors and omissions.

It was Michael Loewe who introduced me to both the rigors and pleasures of Han thought nearly twenty years ago. More recently, I have benefited from the careful consideration he and Professors Victor Mair and Alan K. Ch'an gave the introduction, the translation, and the appendices. These fine scholars queried certain inconsistencies, suggested further readings, and in general made me think much harder about the claims I was making. Professor Ch'en Shun-cheng of Taiwan National University patiently read through much of the *T'ai hsüan* text with me, explaining etymologies and allusions along the way. A friend at Bryn Mawr, Stephen Salkever, also deserves special thanks for helping me to refine my reflections and broaden my reading in comparative texts from the Western tradition. Another colleague at Bryn Mawr, Ty Cunningham, helped me devise a simplified method of divination for the popular version of this translation. And an old friend in Classics, William Mullen, used part of his precious leave time to point out ambiguities and infelicities in the introductory chapter, as well as parallels to Yang Hsiung's thought in world philosophy.

At various points, when I was particularly discouraged about the *T'ai hsüan* project, my esteemed colleagues Sue Glover, Mary Erbaugh, Andrew Plaks, Kathleen Wright, and Raoul Birnbaum all took a look at various parts of the draft and cheered me on. At one stage, when I was in a panic over the loss of a draft version of the introductory chapter, Hans Bielenstein, John Chaffee, Robert Hymes, John Meskill, Martin Amster, and John Reese, as coparticipants in the Columbia Seminar on Traditional China, generously helped me to locate an early draft of a paper given on the "Mystery." Gerry Boswell talked to me of the varieties of mysticism. And Matthew Portal also deserves credit for his advice on a grant application supporting this project. Robert Jay Litz, one of the best writers around and also my best friend, read and reread every line of poetry and prose, pointing out euphonious alternatives to my own clumsy attempts. He can have no idea how much that meant to me.

Various friends from my Princeton circle offered physical assistance in addition to moral support. The staff of Gest Library responded to all my questions with unfailing good humor. Yang Chiu (Joanne Chiang to her Princeton students) and Nancy Norton Tomasko wrote the Chinese characters for the version submitted to SUNY Press for initial consideration. Yang Chiu was responsible for the elegant characters found in the revised version submitted to SUNY. Mr. Qian-shen Bai, now studying at Yale University, generously agreed to write the "clerical script" characters for the book cover. He also cut the seal that will grace the front cover. Nancy Norton Tomasko spent days checking my bibliography and footnotes for errors. Virginia Bower devoted no fewer than three mornings to taking the slides and photographs needed for the illustrations. Sharon Rodgers, Hannah Kaufmann, Toby Paff, Bertrand Lin, and John Elliott contributed to solutions for my seemingly perennial computing problems. J. J. Astley Tracy and Ilene Cohen, two fine editors, offered their suggestions on an early draft of the introductory chapter. When I was pressed for time, Anna Canavan typed swiftly and accurately part of the commentaries.

I thank William Eastman, Director of SUNY Press, for having the courage to take on this risky project. SUNY provided me with an excellent editor, Ed Levy, who caught many awkward constructions in my prose. Cathleen Collins cheerfully answered all questions about the production of the book.

Last, but not least, I wish to thank several institutions for their monetary assistance. Over the course of several drafts, the project was funded by a postdoctoral fellowship from the American Council of Learned Societies, by a Mellon Postdoctoral Grant, and by a National Endowment for the Humanities Summer Stipend.

Introduction

General Introduction to the *Mystery* Text

Yang Hsiung (53 B.C.–A.D. 18) initially won fame under Emperor Ch'eng (r. 33–7 B.C.) for long prose-poems (*fu*) whose satirical content was cloaked in lush imagery, hyperbole, and allusion.[1] By the reign of Emperor Ai (r. 7–1 B.C.), however, Yang Hsiung had redirected his considerable talents to the writing of two philosophical works, the *Fa yen* (*Model Sayings*) and the *T'ai hsüan ching* (*Canon of Supreme Mystery*).[2] The *Model Sayings*, by employing the same dialogue form found in the *Analects* of the sage-master Confucius (551–479 B.C.), evaluates the conflicting claims of immortality, fame, power, and scholarship, while briefly characterizing the essential points of previous thinkers; in the process, it provides a relatively straightforward catechism for the would-be sage. The *Mystery* is a far more difficult text. Like its prototype, the *Yi ching* (*Book of Changes*), the *Mystery* suggests the significant patterns of the universe through different combinations of solid and broken lines accompanied by text.[3] Yang Hsiung also composed ten autocommentaries (all still extant) as counterparts to the "Ten Wings" commentaries appended to the *Changes*. According to two sources, Yang (apparently in an irreverent mood) even composed "commentaries by chapter and verse" (*chang chü*) in the style of the Han scholastics, though these are now lost.[4]

The impact of Yang Hsiung's philosophy on later Chinese thought is undeniable. The historian Pan Ku revered Yang Hsiung as one of the three great Confucian philosophers of Western Han, in company with Liu Hsiang and Liu Hsin.[5] Pan Ku's opinion was shared by the leading Eastern Han thinkers, including Huan T'an, Wang Ch'ung, Chang Heng, Ying Shao, and Sung Chung, all of whom appreciated the breadth and critical acumen of Yang Hsiung's writings.[6] Through them, the *T'ai hsüan* provided inspiration and vocabulary for the *Hsüan hsüeh* movement (in

Chinese, "Mystery Learning") of the post-Han period. The *Mystery*, in fact, continued to greatly influence Chinese thought for a millennium, until prominent Sung thinkers like Su Hsün (1009–1066) and Chu Hsi (1130–1200) applied contemporary standards retroactively to Yang Hsiung, thereby discrediting him on three counts: (a) his service at the court of the "usurper" Wang Mang (r. 9–23);[7] (b) his outright rejection of the theory of human nature proposed by the Confucian master Mencius (?371–?289); and (c) his supposed presumption in composing "classics" in imitation of the sages.[8] Despite counterarguments posed by equally famous Confucians like Ssu-ma Kuang (1018–86), these aspersions cast upon Yang's character resulted in the eventual demotion of the *Mystery* from the highly selective category of "[orthodox] Confucian text" (Ju) to that of "numerology" in the famous *Ssu k'u ch'üan shu* catalogue of 1782.[9] Combined with the inherent difficulties of the text, they also account for the relative paucity of later studies on Yang Hsiung's philosophy.[10]

ON THE TERM "MYSTERY"

The term translated as "Mystery" (*hsüan*) carries a range of meaning from "black" to "darkness" to "hidden" to "mystery." Its overtones are "stillness," "isolation," "nondifferentiation," and "inaccessibility by purely rational processes." In early Chinese thought[11] such ideas bear no unpleasant connotations. They express that dimension of experience that can be known only by quiet and deep contemplation, or by illumination. Yang Hsiung uses *hsüan* in his book title to indicate the profound stage of darkness, silence, ambiguity, and indefiniteness out of which creation springs. In the cosmogonic scheme, it is the undifferentiated stage out of which yin/yang,* then the Five Phases, and ultimately the myriad phenomena of the experiential world develop.[12] In Nature as humans perceive it, it is the latency out of which individual things are born spontaneously and out of which events shape themselves. In the sage— that is, the ideal human being, the perfect student of the *Mystery*—*hsüan* is the spiritual inwardness that precedes conscious decision and action, ensuring that they will be in harmony with the divine process known as "the Way." It is, in other words, the creative aspect of the Tao wherever it is manifested. A description of it drawn from an earlier philosophical classic, the *Lao tzu*, speaks of *hsüan* in this way:

> The way that can be told is not the common way.
> The name that can be named is not the common name.

---

* See Key Terms, page 63

> What has no name is the beginning of Heaven and Earth.
> What has a name is the mother of the myriad creatures.
> Those without desires contemplate its secrets.
> Those who have desires contemplate its periphery.
> These two emerge together, but differ in name.
> Being together, they are called "Mystery."
> Mystery upon mystery,
> Gateway to the myriad secrets.[13]

Although it would be unrealistic to expect general agreement on the meaning of this poem, most who take it as serious philosophy believe it discerns the mystic Tao in two different aspects: as the ineffable fountainhead outside of and prior to phenomenal experience, and as the immanent process that differentiates things and events out of potentiality. Joining these two mysteries is the never-broken connection between the change we see and the unchanging ground of all process. The cosmogonic language of this passage describes every aspect of continuous creation in the cosmos, including that which takes place in the heart/mind of the sage.

The *Mystery* by Yang Hsiung reflects this same vision of *hsüan* in the opening lines to one of its chapters:

> The Mystery of which we speak in hidden places unfolds the myriad
> species, without revealing a form of its own. It fashions the stuff of
> Emptiness and Formlessness, giving birth to the regulations. Tied to
> the gods in Heaven and the spirits on Earth, it fixes the models. It
> pervades and assimilates past and present, originating all categories. It
> unfolds and intersperses yin and yang, generating the *ch'i.** Now
> severed, now conjoined, [through the interaction of yin and yang *ch'i*,
> the various aspects of] Heaven-and-Earth are indeed fully provided.[14]

Yang Hsiung's vision of the Mystery, like that put forward by Lao tzu, bridges the gap between cosmos and consciousness, between the inexpressible and the concrete. Yang attempts to express this again in a second chapter:

> The Way of Heaven is a perfect compass. The Way of Earth is a per-
> fect carpenter's square. The compass in motion describes a complete
> circle through the sites. The square, unmoving, secures things [in their
> proper place]. Circling through the sites makes divine light possible.
> Securing things makes congregation by types possible. . . . Now the
> "Mystery" is the Way of Heaven, the Way of Earth, and the Way of
> Man.[15]

---

*See Key Terms, page 63

In sum, the Mystery includes not only the yin matrix of fecundity and nurturing but the yang impetus toward form. Yang Hsiung makes this explicit through his concern with the energy or vitality (*ch'i*) that shapes individual configurations.

As is typical for Han, Yang combined his borrowed cosmogonic language with the ethical system espoused by early Confucian tradition. Though Yang freely acknowledged his philosophic debt to Lao tzu,[16] he explicitly rejects the earlier philosopher's disdain for "Goodness and Duty, ritual* and study."[17] The *Lao tzu* had assumed that ultimate value lay in the chaos prior to phenomenal existence; therefore, the best human relations imitated Tao in their unstructured and undirected nature. Yang Hsiung took issue with this un-Confucian vision. In emphasizing the immanent and formative aspects of the Mystery, Yang made a fundamental shift toward accommodation with Confucian ideals. Though without visible form, the Mystery in Yang's *Mystery* contains unseen all the myriad forms, patterns, and categories that underlie process and interaction. For Yang, then, the model of the Mystery is violated when human beings fail to realize proper distinctions in rank and function as reinforced by ritual precepts, sumptuary regulations, and the penal code.[18] This explains why Yang Hsiung not only insisted upon the absolute need for the traditional Five Constant Relations, but in fact emphasized those of father/son and ruler/subject which the *Lao tzu* singled out for special condemnation.[19] Yang also questioned the Taoist stress on "nonpurposive activity" (*wu wei*), emphasizing instead the need for conscious adjustment of one's actions to one's position in time.[20]

For Yang Hsiung, traditional Confucian doctrine alone can provide a sufficient key to the true nature of the ineffable Mystery, for it alone is comparably comprehensive. He sees the Five Confucian Classics* as an inexhaustible repository of cosmic wisdom:

> Among the explanations of Heaven, there is none more discerning in its language than that of the *Changes*. Among the explanations for events, there is none more discerning than that of the *Documents*. Among the explanations for the outward embodiment [of virtue], there is none more discerning than that of the *Rites*. Among the explanations for intent, there is none more discerning than that of the *Odes*. Among the explanations for inherent pattern, there is none more discerning than that of the *Chronicles*. Except in the case of these [Five Classics], discerning language is wasted upon petty subjects.[21]

---

*See Key Terms, page 63

Yang assimilated the figure of Confucius himself to the cosmic Mystery. For Yang Hsiung, it is the genius of Confucius that makes it possible for his disciples centuries later to "daily hear what cannot be heard and see what cannot be seen" by some mysterious process rooted in the Tao.[22] Once human beings learn through the Master's teachings to appreciate both the fundamental unity of the Way and the multiplicity of its manifestations, they are ready to become full partners in the triad of Heaven-Earth-Man.[23]

Yang departed, however, from early Confucian models in at least three ways: First, he was openly eclectic, finding support for his interpretation of canonical teachings even in earlier opponents of Confucianism. Prior to the imperial sponsorship of Confucianism as state religion in 135 B.C., citation of texts like the *Lao tzu* tended to imply affiliation with or an intellectual commitment to a single tradition of teaching. But Yang, like many Han thinkers, treated a whole host of competing theories as common intellectual property. Second, Yang systematically incorporated contemporary cosmological theories in his restatement of the basic Confucian message. Finally, Yang adapted to his philosophic discourses the rhythmic cadences, the richly descriptive language, and the multivalent meanings peculiar to the Han prose-poem. For example, one image in the *Mystery*, has an empty stove signifying empty—that is undeserved—reputation, by analogy with the *Changes* Hexagram 50. The passage then says the stove "lacks firewood," with the character for "firewood" conveying its extended meanings of "official salary" and "talent."[24] The complex beauty of the language employed by Yang, no less than the philosophic importance of the *Mystery*, has helped to ensure its transmission through the years.

A CAPSULE BIOGRAPHY OF YANG HSIUNG

Yang Hsiung was born in 53 B.C., in Ch'eng-tu, in the province of Szechwan.[25] In 24 B.C., he completed his first long prose-poem. Some four years later, he traveled to Ch'ang-an (modern Xian), then the Western Han capital, where he was given a junior appointment. In 11 B.C., he composed four lengthy prose-poems, ostensibly in celebration of various state sacrifices, imperial excursions, and ceremonial hunts. In reality, the poems criticize the extravagance, ostentation, and cruelty of court life, implicitly contrasting them with the simple humanity credited to the sage-rulers of the distant past, as Yang's own autobiography (the basis for his official biography) hastens to tell us. This magnificent burst of creative energy was rewarded one year later by a minor promotion to the post of Gentleman-in-Waiting.

In his later years Yang Hsiung took a dramatic turn away from literary composition, on the grounds that his poetry only encouraged the court to engage in greater follies. By then, his autobiography tells us, Yang Hsiung had virtually decided to withdraw from court activities, lest he become embroiled in factional politics. He also wished to retire to mourn the untimely death of a son who had shown great promise.[26] His mature works attempt to discern the inherent patterns underlying language, culture, and cosmos. A cautious "Admonition against Wine" was followed around 2 B.C. by a draft of the *Mystery*, which focuses upon larger questions of fate. Next came two lengthy prose-poems aimed against critics of the *Mystery*: "Dispelling Ridicule" and "Dispelling Objections." In A.D. 5, Yang finished his compilation of scholarly annotations on an earlier abecederarium.[27] Two years later he produced his *Regional Phrases*, China's first dialect dictionary. Three years later, in A.D. 10, Yang Hsiung, still only a minor official at court, was falsely implicated in a plot against the usurper Wang Mang (r. 9–23). In desperation, Yang leapt from the top of a palace tower. His suicide attempt failed. Soon after, a rhymed epigram circulated in the capital:

> Only still and silent,
> He threw himself from the tower.
> At this pure and tranquil,
> He composed a portent text.[28]

After being absolved of all charges through Wang Mang's personal intervention, he went on to finish his second great philosophical work, the *Model Sayings*. During the two-year period from A.D. 13 to 14, he wrote two panegyrics in praise of Wang Mang's maternal relative and the Hsin dynasty founded by Wang, though Yang Hsiung's autobiography omits any mention of either poem.[29] Four years later, Yang died of natural causes.

THE *MYSTERY* IN THE TRADITION OF THE *CHANGES*

The *Mystery* is perhaps the most famous of the companions to the *Changes*,[30] yet it is a great deal more than a slavish imitation. One obvious rationale for Yang Hsiung's neoclassical creation lay in the inherent difficulties faced by contemporary interpreters of the *Changes* tradition. We now believe that the *Changes* is a jumbled and heterogeneous compilation of omens, rhymed proverbs, riddles, paradoxes, and snatches of song and story, drawn from popular lore and at least one technical manual for divination.[31] By the second century B.C., when the *Changes* had been incorporated into the canon of Confucian scriptures,[32] the simple and direct sense of most of these elements could no longer be clearly understood, partly because their once universally shared significance had been lost as Chinese culture evolved, partly because of changes in the language over time, and partly because the message of the original text had been radically reinterpreted in order to reflect later Confucian concepts as yet unknown at the time the *Changes* classic was first compiled.[33]

Confucians of the Western Han dynasty (206 B.C.–A.D. 8) presumed philosophical consistency in the *Changes* text for several reasons. Tradition told them that the *Changes* had originated in a set of cosmic emblems (three-line graphs called "trigrams") invented by the first culture-hero, and then expanded by successive great sages of hoary antiquity into the well-known six-line graphs ("hexagrams"), which are 64 in number.[34] One popular legend also depicted the mature Confucius diligently studying the *Changes* text to perfect his understanding. For these reasons, Han scholars looked to the *Changes* to express a perfect vision of sagehood and the cosmos. Despite the frustrations occasioned by the incredible diversity of the *Changes* text, Han scholars worked hard to find underlying principles in the sequence of hexagrams and their internal structure. In seeking structure in the *Changes*, they found structure; and where there was none to find, they invented structure to satisfy their need for coherence.

Though the sixty-four hexagrams do not occur in a regular order in the text, they can be grouped by pairs. In most cases, one hexagram can be paired with a second, which appears to be the first turned upside down (for example, ☶ and ☶). In the case of the eight symmetrical hexagrams that would not be changed by inversion, pairs are created by changing broken ("yin") lines to unbroken ("yang") lines. An early group of commentaries attached to the *Changes* as its "Ten Wings" carried this line of inquiry even further. In the "Wings," the sequence of the lines with their various yin/yang associations came to be regarded as the main keys to ascertaining the esoteric meaning of the text. Thanks to the increasing elaboration of this tradition by Han masters, it was possible for intelligent students of the *Changes* to sustain the belief that the sacred classic concealed within itself a comprehensive moral vision. Scholars became convinced that the complicated and ambiguous ideas in the text would eventually be resolved by careful analysis into simple images and concepts associated in a regular way with the individual lines and trigrams making up the corresponding six-line hexagram. Hidden within the words of each text, they reasoned, there must be an order identical with that of the corresponding hexagram. Then, in turn, the order of these six-line binary symbols must determine in·some subtle way the words of the "Judgment" and "Line texts" attached to them. Only if this construction were true could the *Book of Changes* be really worthy of inclusion in the set of canonical texts whose correct transmission was sponsored by, and in turn lent legitimacy to, the Han ruling house.[35] Through the Han masters' unflagging efforts and tortuous manipulations, the *Changes* had become by the first century A.D. the longed-for infallible guide to foresight and self-discovery.

Not surprisingly, the *T'ai hsüan* neatly confirms the existence of the comprehensive moral order expected by Han thinkers. But Yang Hsiung was not content to construct further lengthy commentaries to the *Changes*, either to remedy apparent inconsistencies in its text or to slip in new terminology and ideas. Rather than pile lengthy interpretation upon interpretation, as ingenious commentators like Ching Fang (77–37 B.C.)[36] and Meng Hsi (fl. 69 B.C.) determined to do, Yang took the bold step of writing his own *Mystery*.[37]

The *Mystery* is, paradoxically, a completely new book in which the general approach of the *Changes* tradition is freshly embodied in a systematic way. The basic text with its ten autocommentaries employs the most advanced philosophic concepts of Yang's time. Associations derived from Yin/yang Five Phases theory* are used explicitly throughout, and an attempt is made to fully integrate contemporary systems of knowledge, including those of astrology, numerology, music, and logic. Continual reference is also made to the latest form of Confucian orthodoxy, which, by a process not at all self-evident, had come to give the relation of Man to Nature a place as conspicuous as that of man to man.

This new synthesis of beliefs prevalent among Han thinkers drew on every contemporary current of thought, weaving them together so inextricably that from the first century B.C. (in mid-Western Han) it makes no sense to speak of Taoists, Legalists, or even Yin/yang Five Phases cosmologists as distinct groups. Han orthodoxy saw a single underlying pattern governing orderly change in Nature, in the realm of social and political relationships, and in individual experience. Guided by the Confucian Classics, the man of virtue engaged in the arduous process of realizing his full human potential (the Chinese call this "self-cultivation"*)[38] aimed at encompassing all three realms of Heaven-Earth-Man. The virtuous man's goal was sagehood, since only the charismatic power of sagely example could overcome social disorder, create a stable field for personal relationships, and provide psychic ease, all at the same time. The few simple patterns exemplified by the sage manifested the single cosmic Way and informed all well-ordered activity, whether in the phenomenal world of Heaven-and-Earth, in the body, in the recesses of the human heart, in the conscientious action of the individual, or in the ceremonies of the empire. According to this view, there was an identity between cosmic pattern and human goodness.

---

* See Key Terms, page 63

Yang Hsiung's innovations seem to be conscious responses to Han philosophical advances. In his *Mystery*, Yang set out to defend the esoteric meaning of the *Changes*—and by extension, the entire Confucian tradition as it was then articulated—against its principal detractors: those who argued that Heaven was indifferent to the affairs of men, those who found adherence to ritual to be of no practical value, and those who insisted upon a kind of moral relativism. Both the structure and content of his *Mystery* demonstrate the innate superiority of what is fundamental (i.e., the eternal patterns as interpreted by the tradition of the sages) over secondary manifestations: the temporary changes and dislocations resulting from the interplay of those constant laws. The "Great Commentary" to the *Changes* had claimed that the archaic scripture, despite its miscellaneous literary character, could encompass every phenomenon in the realms of Heaven-Earth-Man.[39] As we will see below, the *Mystery*, not at all miscellaneous in character, made concrete this ideal conception of the *Changes*. In doing so, the *Mystery* became more than mere description. It functioned as a perfect model of the mysterious cosmic process itself.

THE ARRANGEMENT OF THE *MYSTERY*

The structure of the *Mystery* is best understood by comparing it with that of the *Changes*. By the first century B.C., the latter consisted of a set of 64 six-line hexagrams, in which each line might be solid (signifying yang *ch'i*)* or broken (signifying yin). Under each hexagram, there appeared six assigned texts, each of which corresponded to one graphic line of the hexagram (hence, the name "Line texts"). The appended commentaries to the *Changes* related these Line texts to the moral, cosmological, and epistemological convictions of their authors, who were shaping a new orthodoxy around Confucianism in the last centuries B.C.

The *Mystery* had the advantage of being created during a single time period by a single author. Therefore, the structure and content of the *Mystery* could be integrated in a fashion that imitates, yet improves upon the coherence found in the *Changes*. The core text of the *Mystery*, like that of its prototype, the *Changes*, presents a series of linear complexes. In contrast to the *Changes*, however, where lines are categorized either as yin (broken) or yang (unbroken), manipulation of the yarrow stalks according to Yang's explicit directions yields three possibilities for each line of the graph: (1) an unbroken line (correlated with Heaven); (2) a line broken once (representing Earth); or (3) a line broken twice (symbolizing Man as one of the triadic realms, living between Heaven and Earth). For the six-line complex of the *Changes*, the *Mystery* substitutes a

---

*See Key Terms, page 63

four-line graph (the "tetragram"), whose component parts are read from top to bottom (that is, in the opposite order from the *Changes*). Four lines, each with 3 possibilities, mean that there are 81 (3 to the 4th power) possible tetragrams in the *Mystery*, as opposed to the 64 graphs of the *Changes*.[40]

The tetragrams are associated with a hierarchical nest of divisions that is at once geographic and social:

> 3 Regions (*fang*) 方
> 9 Provinces (*chou*) 州
> 27 Departments (*pu*) 部
> 81 Families (*chia*) 家

The cosmogonic Mystery itself—like the emperor—is said to occupy the center of both the universe and the sociopolitical realm, where the three realms of Heaven-Earth-Man come together. Each region is divided into nine provinces, which correspond to the Nine Provinces of the Central Kingdom, China. Each province is then subdivided into three departments, which compare with the Han sub-provincial level. The final division into eighty-one families symbolizes the numerous local units which organize the myriad individual phenomena (in Chinese terms, "the myriad things" [*wan wu*]) of society and nature.

Each graphic symbol is associated with a "Head" (*shou*) text in three parts: a title, an image that refers to yin/yang, and a second image related to the "myriad things" of the universe. The title of the tetragram, a single Chinese character, names one aspect of the comprehensive Mystery, such as Measure (Tetragram 52) or Eternity (Tetragram 53), to which humans respond for good or ill. The sentence following it describes in poetic language the evolution of yang or yin energy during a precise phase in the annual cycle. The remainder of each text describes the effect of that evolution upon things as we know them, an effect presumably catalyzed by the patron cosmic phase said to "rule" the tetragram. Each Head (by which I mean the four-line graph, the tetragram title, and its associated text) corresponds to a stretch of 4 1/2 days in the annual cycle.[41] The first forty-one texts, between the winter and summer solstices, speak either first or exclusively of the ascendant yang *ch'i*, while the succeeding forty detail the process by which yin *ch'i* waxes. Read in succession, they provide a remarkable picture of the finely graded steps of cyclic change. Each of the eighty-one tetragrams is also linked to one of the sixty-four hexagrams of the *Changes* (with some duplication of course) in order to evoke the old meanings and associations.

Yang provides for each Head text a series of supplementary texts, on the model of the extensive commentaries appended to the *Changes*. As far as the interpretation of individual tetragrams is concerned, the most important of these autocommentaries are the nine Appraisals that follow each of the eighty-one Head texts. The Appraisals, like the tetragrams, are correlated with the year, with yin/yang, and with the Five Phases. Each Appraisal, as one-ninth of a tetragram, represents half a day, so that alternating Appraisals are designated either day and night. Through their association with night and day, Appraisals come to be considered as yin (usually inauspicious) or yang (usually auspicious), with the first Appraisal being yang in odd-numbered tetragrams and yin in even-numbered tetragrams. To each Appraisal in turn there is also assigned a direction that aligns it with one of the Five Phases, given in the enumeration order Water-Fire-Wood-Metal-Earth. Two additional Appraisals are not assigned to a specific tetragram or time of day; they exist solely to make up the deficiency of 3/4 of a day between the 364 1/2 days of Yang's basic structure (81 tetragrams x 4 1/2 days) and the 365 1/4 days in the solar year.

These 731 Appraisals are loosely patterned after the Line texts of the *Changes*. The Appraisals differ, however, from the Line texts in ways that increase flexibility of interpretation in the divination. In the *Changes*, each Line text refers to a single line of the hexagram. By contrast, the Appraisals do not directly explain the significance of individual lines in the four-line graphic symbol. Instead, they provide a series of shifting literary images suggesting the multifaceted nature of the main cosmological theme presented in the tetragram. By freeing the Appraisals from the individual lines of his tetragrams (which have their own protocols of interpretation), Yang Hsiung directs the reader's attention to larger questions concerning the effect of eternal cosmic patterns upon the changing circumstances that originally prompted divination. He also suggests the complexity of moral choice, for each aspect of the Supreme Mystery apparently includes within it the potential for both human good and human evil. Strength, for example, as explained in Tetragram 36, is found in both brutish and cultivated individuals. The Appraisals, then, function as a metaphoric bridge between the cyclic dominion of fate and the field of human choice and achievement.

To accomplish this, Yang Hsiung anchored the Appraisals to individual acts of divination in four ways: First, the Appraisals pertain to successive stages in the objective situation inquired about. Appraisals 1–3 describe its commencement; Appraisals 4–6, its maturity; and Appraisals 7–9, its decline. Second, the nine Appraisals situate the individual's present and future securely in the hierarchy of social rank. Appraisal 5 is reserved for the ruler, as in Han commentaries to the *Changes*. Appraisals 4 and 6, which flank the ruler, carry implications for his ministers and ancestral house respectively. Appraisals 1 and 9, those furthest from the Son of Heaven, pertain to the "commoner" in social terms, as well as the "petty man" in moral terms. By this device, Yang ensures that the Appraisals speak to a wide variety of possible social interactions and career moves. Third, the nine Appraisals as a unit mark three successive stages in the reader's subjective response to the developing situation. Appropriately enough, the first set of three Appraisals are categorized as Thought (*ssu*), the initial period of inner reflection that precedes outer-directed action, the second set of three Appraisals detail Good Fortune (*fu*), the period marked by effective action; and the last set of three Appraisals talk of Calamity (*huo*), the failure that tends to follow success because of careless, immoral, or untimely action (see Table 1).

Table 1.

Response	Significance of Appraisal		
Thought	1 = interior	2 = middle	3 = exterior
Good Fortune	4 = small	5 = medium	6 = great
Calamity	7 = nascent	8 = median	9 = maximum

Finally, the Appraisals (unlike the Line texts of the *Changes*) are read according to the time of day when the divination is carried out. To each time of day, three Appraisals are assigned, so that the inquirer can know the short-, middle-, and long-term prospects for the situation queried. If the act of divination is carried out in the morning, Appraisals 1, 5, and 7 of the given tetragram are read and considered; if in the evening, Appraisals 3, 4, and 8; if at the median times, Appraisals 2, 6, and 9. (Since Yang Hsiung did not specify these periods of time more definitely, it is impossible to be certain whether by median he meant the afternoon or the periods centered about noon and midnight. In any case, these periods may have been interpreted with some latitude by users of the book.) Yang has arranged it so that the lucky or unlucky character of these prospects is basically decided by agreement or disagreement between the yin/yang values assigned to the Head text and to each individual Appraisal. If the yin/yang value for the Head and that of the relevant Appraisal is the same, the divination is usually considered lucky. If it is different, the divination is usually considered unlucky. Table 2 shows this correlation of time to luck.

Let us see how Yang's stipulations affect the divination. Consider a divination carried out in the evening, the result of which is an odd-numbered (i.e., yang) Head. This result corresponds to the third line of the table. Only Appraisals 3, 4, and 8 would be read. Appraisal 3, being odd-numbered, corresponds to yang *ch'i*. Its presence in a yang Head makes the outcome auspicious for initial endeavors and for Thought, the special theme of the first three Appraisals. By the very same reasoning,

Table 2.

Divination time	Head-type to be read	Appraisals	Divination obtained (auspicious = +)
Morning	yang	1, 5, 7	+ + +
	yin		− − −
Median	yang	2, 6, 9	− − +
	yin		+ + −
Evening	yang	3, 4, 8	+ − −
	yin		− + +

Appraisals 4 and 8 (assigned to yin because they are even-numbered) are inauspicious. Considering them in turn, the indication for the beginning of the situation is auspicious, but those for its middle period and final decline are inauspicious.

Good and bad tidings, like yin/yang orientations in general, are never absolute, but relational. In the value system of the *Mystery*, a yang affiliation by itself is auspicious, but in practice it rarely can be considered in isolation from other factors. A yang entity in conflict with a yin entity may be baleful; by comparison, two yin entities in accord are likely (but only likely) to presage good fortune. To remind the reader that no single factor such as a yin/yang orientation absolutely determines events, Yang Hsiung ensured that several Appraisals do not accord with the relations in the table. This shows the reader that virtuous action outweighs all else in determining an outcome. As Yang himself states, so long as a man is "inwardly upright and outwardly complaint, always humbling himself before others, . . . the outcome of his actions is good fortune and not calamity."[42] The need to combine subtle reasoning on cosmic trends with sensitivity toward social interaction and individual propensities—in other words, to reintegrate Heaven-Earth-Man—makes divination by the *Mystery* a highly skilled art. The divination process itself integrates science and ethics, sensory acuity, and moral perspicacity.

In addition to the basic text of 81 Heads and 731 Appraisals, Yang provided ten commentaries modeled after the "Ten Wings" of the *Changes*. The "Fathomings" ("Hsüan ts'e"), on the pattern of the "Commentary on the Images" ("Hsiang chuan") appended to the *Changes*, summarize the main significance of each Appraisal. In all extant editions, the Fathomings, unlike the other commentaries, have been dispersed throughout the basic text, so that each follows the Appraisal to which it refers.[43] The "Elaboration" commentary ("Hsüan wen") discusses only the first tetragram as a microcosm of the entire book, just as the "Elaborated Teachings" ("Wen yen") commentary of the *Changes* treats only the first hexagram. The remaining commentaries do not interpret individual texts, but assess or illuminate the *Canon of Supreme Mystery* as a whole. Table 3 lists all ten in order, with the corresponding "Wings" commentary from the *Changes*:[44]

Table 3.

Commentary	Correspondent Ten Wings commentary
Hsüan ts'e 玄測 Fathomings	Hsiang 象 Images
Hsüan ch'ung 玄衝 Polar Oppositions	Hsü kua 序卦 Sequence of the Hexagrams
Hsüan ts'o 玄錯 Interplay of Opposites	Tsa kua 雜卦 Interplay of Opposites
Hsüan li 玄攡 Evolution	Hsi tz'u 繫辭 Appended Texts (also known as Great Commentary)
Hsüan ying 玄瑩 Illumination	also the Hsi tz'u 繫辭
Hsüan shu 玄數 Numbers	Shuo kua 說卦 Discussion of the Trigrams
Hsüan wen 玄文 Elaboration	Wen yen 文言 Elaborated Teachings
Hsüan yi 玄捉 Representations	Hsi tz'u 繫辭
Hsüan t'u 玄圖 Diagram	Hsi tz'u 繫辭
Hsüan kao 玄告 Revelation	Shuo kua 說卦

SIGNIFICANT STRUCTURE IN THE *MYSTERY*

The "Ten Wings" of the *Changes* brilliantly, if speciously, read into the original *Changes* text the fundamental patterns that underlie the triadic realms of Heaven-Earth-Man. Han scholars preoccupied with the question of "timeliness" (*shih*) were continually frustrated because neither the content of the *Changes* texts nor the sequence of the hexagrams is ostensibly related to temporal sequence. Yang Hsiung therefore incorporated temporal cycles into the structure of his *Canon of Supreme Mystery*. Due to its careful construction, the *Mystery* reflects the basic seasonal rhythms, the regular motions of the heavenly bodies, and the yin/yang Five Phases interactions that propel change in the natural world, no less than it reflects the fundamental social relationships (the Five Constant Relations) that pervade the human world.

Yang's structure does this in the following way: Appraisal 1 of Tetragram 1 in the *Mystery* is correlated with the so-called Grand Inception: a midnight which marks simultaneously the winter solstice, the first day of the first lunar month, and the beginning of a sixty-day cycle.[45] Each *Mystery* tetragram describes the waxing and waning of yin and yang *ch'i* and their effect on the phenomenal world of the "myriad things" during the short period of each Head's dominion. When the Head texts are read in sequence, they constitute a finely graded sequence of eighty-one phases in the annual cycle, a virtual cosmic pattern in the form of a metaphysical prose-poem.

Since neither the content nor the structure of the *Changes* implies a temporal sequence, the *Mystery* follows generally a proposed rearrangement of the hexagrams put forward by the Han *Changes* master, Ching Fang (77–33 B.C.).[46] In his so-called Hexagram/Solar Period (*kua ch'i*) plan, Ching assigns hexagrams to solar periods (each 1/24 of the tropical year). With Ching's schema, the twelve months are ruled by twelve hexagrams called the "waxing and waning hexagrams" (*hsiao hsi kua*). These twelve begin with the pure yin hexagram entitled The Receptive, which is assigned to the tenth month containing the winter solstice. As the "waxing and waning hexagrams" proceed through the annual cycle, yang lines grow upward from the bottom (Return ☷, Approach ☷, and so on) month by month until the pure yang hexagram The Creative is produced to govern the summer solstice in the fourth civil month. Yin lines then multiply from the bottom upward until the pattern of The Receptive is restored at the end of the cycle. Each pair of hexagrams separated by six months (for example, Approach and Retreat) are line-by-line polar opposites. Each of these twelve "waxing and waning" hexagrams, along with 48 other hexagrams, also correspond to equal intervals of 6 7/80 days (in other words, 1/60 of the solar year of 365 1/4 days). The remaining four hexagrams found in the *Changes*, called "standard hexagrams," correspond to the solstices and equinoxes and thus to the four cardinal points of the sun's path. They are not segments of the cycle, then, but points fixed in space, which move back and forth in time. The sun may pass through one of them on any day of the lunar month in which it is located. (From the astronomer's point of view, it is the new moons that move back and forth around them.)

Yang Hsiung improved upon Ching Fang's approach to symmetry in the cyclic structure he was creating. He avoided, for example, certain inelegancies of Ching Fang's schema (which involved only 60 hexagrams) when he incorporated references to all 64 hexagrams in his own arrangement of tetragrams. He also substituted the winter solstice for Ching Fang's artificial point of departure (the new moon of the tenth civil month), so that his cycle starts at the point which marked the actual beginning of the tropical year for the Han astronomer. For the present, the formal perfection of the *Mystery*'s plan can be demonstrated by a graphic comparison of the two systems, followed by a selection of Head texts. The first seven are given to exhibit the fineness of gradation from one Head text to the next; then a sequence of every tenth Head is provided to show longer trends. For the sake of the reader new to the *Mystery*, each Head text is given its main correlations with (1) the Five Phases, (2) the relevant solar period(s) of the year (indicated by the beginning date), and (3) the *Changes* hexagram assigned by Ching Fang to roughly the same part of the calendar. The brief commentary after each Head text suggests only the most obvious connections between each Head and its associated hexagram. (More information is supplied in commentaries to the translations of tetragrams 1–81 that follow this Introduction.)

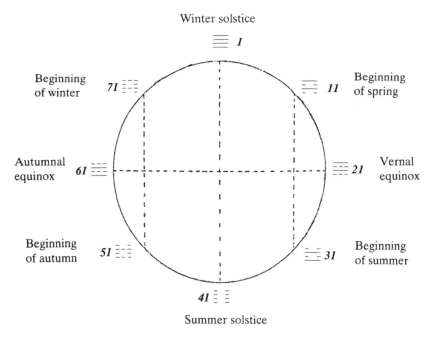

Figure 1. Tetragrams from the T'ai hsuan ching *corresponding to eight major transitions of the solar year. This figure is read clockwise. Reprinted by permission of Hong Kong University Press.*

Tenth month of calendar

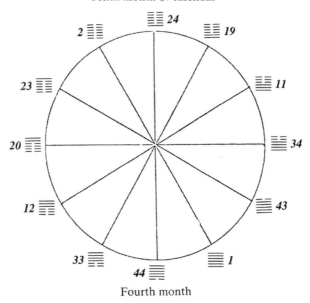

Figure 2. Ching Fang's 'waxing and waning' order for twelve Chou yi *hexagrams. This figure is read clockwise. Reprinted by permission of Hong Kong University Press.*

1. ☰ 中 Center

December 22–December 26 (a.m.)

*Assigned to Water, the Winter Solstice
solar period [begins December 22],
and the* Changes *Hexagram no. 61,
Good Faith at Center*

"Yang *ch'i,* unseen, germinates in the Yellow Palace. Good faith in every case resides at the center."

Tetragram 1 begins with the winter solstice. The Yellow Palace is associated with the phase Earth and with the still center, the balance point between opposing forces, from which creative activity emanates. The second line alludes to the corresponding hexagram in Ching Fang's scheme of temporal associations, which is called Good Faith at Center. The *Changes* commentator Wang Pi (226–49) understands the hexagram title to mean "Faithfulness [to the Tao] issues forth from the center."

A pun gives the word translated as "good faith" (*hsin*) another meaning. *Hsin* occurs in the "Great Commentary" to the *Changes* as a homonymic variant of the character *shen* (meaning "to expand").[47] As future events become present phenomena, they displace previous phenomena into the past, providing the momentum for cyclic processes (see Figures 1 and 2).

> As the sun moves on, the moon comes; as the moon moves on, the sun comes. As sun and moon impel each other, light is produced. . . .
> What moves on contracts; what comes, expands (*hsin*). As what contracts and what expands influence each other, what promotes [productive change] is produced.[48]

The implication in this Head text is that the motive force for the annual cycle is generated in the Yellow Palace through the alternating contraction and expansion of yin and yang. (The pun is repeated in Head no. 41 assigned to the summer solstice.)

Yellow Palace is also a pun of sorts, since any reader would link the term with the *kung* (literally, "palace") musical mode, also known as the Yellow Bell. The Yellow Bell is the origin of all other notes and thus of all the cosmological associations of Chinese harmonics.

2. ䷗ 周 Full Circle
December 26 (p.m.)–December 30

Assigned to Fire, the Winter Solstice solar period, and the Changes *Hexa- am no. 24, Return*

"Yang *ch'i* comes full circle. Divine, it returns to the beginning. Things go on to become their kinds."

The cyclic process continues through the moment of death or complete latency into the rebirth of yang *ch'i*. For this reason, the myriad phenomena endure past their midwinter still point. The imagery of reversion alludes to the associations of the hexagram Return. The word "divine" (*shen*) implies that yang *ch'i*, despite the momentary eclipse of its vitality, is identified with the "godlike forces" (also pronounced *shen*) that draw upon the Mystery to maintain change.[49]

3. ䷂ 礥 Mired
December 31–January 4 (a.m.)

Assigned to Wood, the Winter Solstice solar period, and the Changes *Hexagram no. 3, Difficulty Starting*

"Yang *ch'i* stirs slightly. Though stirred, it is mired [in yin]. 'Mired' refers to the difficulty attending the birth of things."

The first hesitant reawakening of yang vitality is portrayed in language consciously reminiscent of the "Commentary on the Judgments" to the hexagram entitled Difficulty Starting: "When the Hard and Soft couple [i.e., when yin and yang interact] for the first time, there is difficulty in giving birth." Some scholars who comment on this passage in the "Judgments" understand the last clause to mean "hardship is born," but Yang clearly interprets the phrase as "there is difficulty in giving birth."

4. ䷃ 閑 Barrier
January 4 (p.m.)–January 8

Assigned to Metal, the Winter Solstice/ Lesser Cold solar period, [begins roughly January 7] and the Changes *Hexagram no. 3, Difficulty Starting*

"Yang *ch'i* is barred by yin. Mired fast, all things are barred."

19

Since the associated hexagram is the same as that of the preceding Head, this text may be read as more or less continuous with the last. It describes the resistance of yin to yang's stirring, with the consequent effect on phenomena. To remind the reader of the shared hexagram association, this Head text repeats the title from the previous Head.

5. ☷ 少 Small *January 9–January 13 (a.m.)*	*Assigned to Earth, the Lesser Cold* *solar period, and the* Changes *Hexa-* *gram no. 15, Modesty*

"Yang *ch'i*, rippling, spreads through the deep pool. Things like ripplets in its wake can keep themselves very small."

Most commentators paraphrase the first adjective to modify yang *ch'i* as "unmoving" or "quiescent," but it can also refer to the appearance of moving water, in which case "rippling" is more appropriate here. Given this ambiguity of language, it is somewhat unclear whether yang *ch'i* is already in an active state. No doubt, the power of yang vitality over phenomena remains small. Still, its spread throughout the deep (the Yellow Palace, the still center) is emphasized.

The phrase I translate as "like ripplets in its wake" leads to a second wordplay: the same character is employed in the title of the correspondent hexagram, Modesty. Also, in certain editions, the character appears as its variant, meaning "incorruptible."[50]

6. ☲ 戾 Contrariety *January 13 (p.m.)–January 17*	*Assigned to Water, the Lesser Cold* *solar period, and the* Changes *Hexa-* *gram no. 38, Opposition*

"Yang *ch'i*, newly hatched, is very small. Things, each diverging and separating, find their proper categories."

In this Head, corresponding to a period just past mid-January, the segregation of opposites is first manifested in the phenomenal world, despite the continuing weakness of the yang *ch'i*. The name of the Head echoes that of the associated hexagram.

7. ䷭ 上 Ascent
January 18–January 22 (a.m.)

Assigned to Fire, the Lesser Cold/ Greater Cold solar period [begins roughly January 22], and the Changes *hexagram no. 46, Pushing Upward*

"Yang *ch'i* engenders things in a place below. All things shoot through the earth, climbing to a higher place."

The metaphor of plants breaking through the soil applies not only to all natural phenomena but to the yang *ch'i* that impels them, which is no longer immobilized by the strength of its opposite. The annual cycle has just moved (during the dominion of the seventh Appraisal of this tetragram) into Greater Cold, the last solar period of winter. The image of ascent is taken from the title of the *Changes* hexagram.

General Commentary: Heads 1 through 7 represent step by step the hesitant reawakening of yang energy against the opposition of yin, alternating images of nascent activity (Heads 1, 3, 5?, and 7) with reassertions of stasis (Heads 2, 4, and 6).[51] The myriad things, in the grip of yin, are not perceptibly affected until in Head no. 6 there is a subtle indication that they have begun to respond to the push of yang *ch'i*. In Head 7, yang *ch'i* begins to assert itself with unqualified force.

*　　*　　*

Having seen how the first seven Head texts mark fine gradations of change over the course of a little more than a month, let us turn to the broader outline of cyclical change provided in the *Mystery* by examining a sequence constructed from every tenth tetragram.

21

Every Tenth Head Text

1. ䷁ 中 Center
December 22–December 26 (a.m.)

"Yang *ch'i*, unseen, germinates in the Yellow Palace. Good faith in every case resides at the center."

11. ䷽ 差 Divergence
February 5–February 9 (a.m.)

Assigned to Fire, the Spring Onset solar period [begins roughly February 5], and the Changes *Hexagram no. 62, Preponderance of the Small*

"Yang *ch'i*, wriggling, breaks open at the east. Lordly, it emerges from the multitude of obstructions. Things diverge in their appearance."

In Chinese chronology, the solstices and equinoxes occupy the midpoints of seasons, not their beginnings. This Head marks the beginning of spring, the first period under the sovereignty of immature yang. The sun, now moving into the eastern quarter of its annual path, embodies the young yang as it daily crosses the sky. In response to its stimulus, the multiplicity of things become markedly more various in appearance. (Nearer the winter solstice, because most things were only latent, that differentiation was only potential.) Under the beneficial influence of burgeoning yang *ch'i*, differentiation brings cosmic concord. This is reflected in end rhymes on all three lines.

21. ䷧ 釋 Release
March 22–March 26 (a.m.)

Assigned to Wood, the Spring Equinox solar period [begins roughly March 20], and the Changes *Hexagram no. 40, Deliverance*

"Yang *ch'i* to effect harmony strikes open the round casing of yin, warming and releasing things, so that all shed their withered husks and are delivered from their shells."

This unusually concrete description is appropriate to the solar period that begins with the vernal equinox. An early commentator, in an alternate reading based on different punctuation, sees the myriad things responding to the warmth of the spring sun. In either version, the spring stimulates growth and metamorphosis. Once again, the name of the associated hexagram appears in this Head text.

31. ☰☷ 裝 Packing
May 6–May 10 (a.m.)

Assigned to Metal, the Summer Onset solar period [begins roughly May 5], and the Changes *Hexagram no. 56, Sojourner*

"Yang *ch'i* is greatly engaged in affairs. Even so, yin, which is very small, makes its base below. It is packed in readiness, about to depart."

It is now the beginning of summer. Yang has not yet reached its zenith, nor yin its nadir, but this Head is a reminder that the eventual decline of yang *ch'i* is ordained to follow its maturity. Before yang passes on, it will impose its order on the cosmic processes, like a traveler setting his possessions in order before a journey.

The Chinese text, like this translation, does not specify which cosmic agent prepares to depart. Most commentators, however, follow Lu Chi (early third century), who put it, "Yang is packing because its intent is to depart."

41. ☷☷ 應 Response
June 20–June 24 (a.m.)

Assigned to Earth, the Summer Solstice solar period [begins roughly June 21], and the Changes *Hexagram no. 30, Adherence*

"Yang *ch'i* culminates on high. Yin faithfully germinates below. High and low mutually respond."

At the summer solstice, the roles of yin and yang are reversed from their relative positions in Head no. 1, entitled Center. Yang *ch'i* now governs and yin awaits rebirth. As the words "germinates" and "faithfully" signal, however, the two Heads are tightly connected.

51. ䷟ 常 Constancy *August 4–August 8 (a.m.)*	*Assigned to Wood, the Autumn Onset solar period [begins roughly August 7], and the* Changes *Hexagram no. 32, Duration*

"By yin one knows the subject; by yang one knows the lord. The Way of ruler and subject remains unchanged for ten thousand ages."

This Head corresponds to the transition between summer and autumn, the border between yang and yin seasonal dominance. The strength of yang and yin *ch'i* will not be balanced until the equinox, but it is appropriate here (and reminiscent of the corresponding *Changes* hexagram) to assert the fundamental rightness of their eternal hierarchic relationship. The commentator Ssu-ma Kuang (1018–86) remarks in his annotation that this Head is equally "emblematic of autumn's receptivity to summer, of yin's receptivity to yang, and of the subject's receptivity to the lord." The ideal harmony of such relationships is indicated by rhymes in Chinese.

61. ䷺ 餙 Embellishment *September 18–September 22 (a.m.)*	*Assigned to Fire, the Autumn Equinox solar period [begins roughly September 23], and the* Changes *Hexagram no. 45, Ornamental*

"Yin is white while yang is black. Separately they perform their respective tasks. Whether going out or entering in, they are most embellished."

Separating yin and yang in autumn is the equinoctial solar period that marks the transitory balance of yin and yang energies, when primacy is about to pass from yang to yin. The "embellishment" in the Head text reflects the associated *Changes* hexagram. Of its title, the commentator Wang Pi remarks, "*Pi* means embellishment. The Hard and the Soft, the two counterparts [of yang and yin *ch'i*], embellish each other in alternation" because of their balance.[52] Here in this text yin (normally dark) and yang (normally light) reverse their associational colors as yang, by nature superior, relinquishes its ascendancy to yin.

71. ䷗ 止 Stoppage *November 2–November 6 (a.m.)*	*Assigned to Wood, the Winter Onset solar period [begins roughly November 7], and the* Changes *Hexagram no. 52, Resisting*

"Yin, enlarged, stops things above, and yang for its part likewise stops things below. Above and below, together they stop everything."

Winter now begins, with its implications of hibernation, stasis, and latency. Yin *ch'i* clearly has the upper hand. Yang Hsiung expected his readers to recall the "Commentary on the Judgments" to the corresponding hexagram text:

> The title means "stopping." When it is time to stop, then stop. When it is time to act, then act. When movement and rest do not fail to be timely, the Way becomes brilliantly clear.[53]

Cessation is natural, not forced. The beginning of winter is not the time for movement in the cosmos.

81. ䷚ 養 Nurturing *December 17–December 21 (a.m.)*	*Assigned to Metal, the end of the Great Snow solar period [begins roughly December 7], and the* Changes *Hexagram no. 17, Providing Nourishment*

"Yin, like a bow stretched taut, bulges out to the furthest reaches. Yang bathes the myriad things [in its energizing solution], turning them red in the nether regions."

The final Head, Fostering, can be read as continuous with that of Center, the first tetragram, closing the gap between the winter solstice and the new annual cycle. Despite yin's undisputed predominance, the germinating action of yang in both Head texts is associated here—across the gap between the old cycle and the new—with a warmth akin to that of a hen incubating eggs. The rosy flush that yang metaphorically imparts is that of the well-nourished, vital newborn organism—sprout, root, or infant.

General Commentary: In this sample series of equally spaced cuts through the denseness of the *Mystery*, we have passed quickly through nine stages of great significance: the solstices (nos. 1 and 41); the equinoxes (nos. 21 and 61); the four Onsets of seasons, midway between the solstices and the equinoxes (nos. 11, 31, 51, and 71); and the final Head (no. 81). At the solstices, the greatest preponderance of yin or yang vitality is countered by the germinating power of its opposite, weak but relentless. At the equinoxes, yin and yang are momentarily balanced. At the vernal equinox, this balance is implied by the moderation of yang *ch'i*. Looking at the Head texts that immediately surround the two equinoxes, we see that as the dominance of yin or yang fades into equivalence at an equinox, the rise to supremacy of the complementary yang or yin activity is foreordained.

The beginnings of the four seasons not only mediate between, but also echo symbolically the solstices and the equinoxes. The seasons, by contrast, are not moments but quarters of the year, groups of six solar periods each. A single solar period can do no more than represent the transition from one season to another. The Spring Equinox period marks the moment when the greater vitality of yin gives way to that of yang. The Spring Onset, three solar periods earlier, is the transition between the three-month season of mature yin and that of young yang. These two levels of transition, the beginning of spring and the vernal equinox, are reflected in a counterpoint of language and image in Tetragrams no. 11 and 21.

At the borders of the seasons, we find a similar interplay, with the same contrast between present power and future weakness, between relative balance and consequential change. Spring and autumn begin with metaphors of harmony, sovereignty, and stability, but they are immediately followed by other Heads in which one form of cosmic energy "contains" and "repels" the other.[54] In general, summer is the height of growth and activity, and winter, the lowest point. Packing and Stoppage (nos. 31 and 71), which begin the two seasons, reflect this complementarity, but there is a deeper opposition as well. At the beginning of summer, yin appears to be losing its struggle to survive. In contrast, at the beginning of winter (no. 71), the functions of yin and yang in their own spheres are identical. That is because the dominant yang character of summer implies clear distinction; and the dominant yin of winter, indeterminacy and nondifferentiation.

Despite the intricacy of these relations, the overall principle of order is unmistakable: the content of Head texts half a year apart is complementary. This rule holds for all Heads, not merely for the especially significant ones considered above. In most cases, the complementarity of language or image is explicit. In others, it becomes clear when we read each text in the context of the series. The opposition is never that of static symbols, but rather of gradual, ordered processes evoked by symbols.

This selection of Heads, in combination with the charts above, shows briefly how the text of the *Mystery* directly reflects the cyclic character of natural processes. The successive Appraisals attached to the Heads portray the infinite variety of political and psychological processes in light of the Tao. Yang's words, then, describe an evolution, Head by Head and Appraisal by Appraisal. In doing so, they reproduce the annual complementarities and symmetries of time and space.

METHOD OF DIVINATION FOR THE *MYSTERY*

The divination procedure described in the "Numbers" commentary is a point-by-point modification of that given for the *Changes* in its "Great Commentary." There are 36 yarrow stalks in the *T'ai hsüan* set, of which 3 are set aside for symbolic reasons. Later commentaries presume that the 3 supernumerary sticks correspond to the basic triad of Heaven-Earth-Man. They compare, then, with the one stick set aside during the *Changes* divination process, which represents the fundamental cosmic unity.[55] Next, an additional stick is taken into the left hand, possibly to doubly honor the fundamental cosmic unity, as in the *Changes*. The remaining 32 sticks are then divided at random into two piles.[56] The left pile is counted off by threes (rather than by fours as in the *Changes*). This process yields a remainder of 1, 2, or 3, which is then added to the stick in the left hand. The process is then repeated for the right-hand pile. The remainder from the division of the right pile (again, 1, 2, or 3) is similarly added to the growing pile of sticks held in the left hand. At this point, the left hand will hold either 3 or 6 sticks (the sum of the remainders for each pile +1). The entire process (the segregation of one stick, the division into two piles, and the counting off) is then repeated with the 27 or 30 sticks that remain. After that process is completed, 27, 24, or 21 sticks will be left. Dividing this number by 3 will result in 9 (equivalent to the twice-broken line of Man), 8 (the divided line of Earth), or 7 (the solid line of Heaven), with a mathematical probability of approximately 1/9, 4/9, and 4/9 respectively. The top line of the tetragram can now be drawn.

Three more applications of the entire procedure are needed to arrive at a four-line graph, which directs the user to the appropriate Head text.

Yang saw the lines of the tetragram, which are determined by the outcome of divination, as a kind of count. In the "Numbers" autocommentary, he explains how to calculate the number of the Head from the value of each line in the tetragram:

> If the Family line [i.e., the bottom line of the tetragram] is unbroken [i.e., if it corresponds to Heaven], count 1. If it is broken once [corresponding to Earth], count 2. If it is broken twice [corresponding to Man], count 3. If the Department line is unbroken, do not add anything. If it is broken once, add 3. If it is broken twice, add 6. If the Province line is unbroken, do not add anything. If it is broken once, add 9. If it is broken twice, add 18. If the Region line [i.e., the top line of the tetragram] is unbroken, do not add anything. If it is broken once, add 27. If it is broken twice, add 54.[57]

The point of these instructions becomes clear if we apply them to a specific example. Let us take the four-line symbol corresponding to Head no. 48 禮. In that tetragram, the Family line (i.e., the bottom line of the tetragram) is 3. Working upward, we add 0, 18, and 27, making a total of 48. The sequence of Heads, then, is arranged in an arithmetic progression on base 3 to mirror the regular progression of the annual cycle in a way that the *Changes* sequence of hexagrams cannot.[58] The coherent beauty of Yang's mathematical system is designed to instill confidence in the sacred truth of its pronouncements on divination.

Yang not only prescribes the divination procedure itself. He also stipulates the exact conditions under which it is proper to consult the *Mystery*. According to Yang, the sacred efficacy of the divination tool is impaired if the user's mind lacks moral integrity (*ch'eng*), since integrity is the quality that unites the individual with the cosmic order.[59] The inquirer's mind must then be correctly oriented (*chen*).[60] In other words, as in any other Chinese divination procedure, the yarrow stalks of the *Mystery* will yield no useful result unless the divination is carried out when the inquirer is in an appropriately centered spiritual state. Divination is essentially a communion between Man and the divine cosmic processes operating in Heaven-and-Earth, which the yarrow stalks can only facilitate. The divination results are thrown off if true communion is precluded by a fundamental disparity between questioner (Man) and questioned (the spirit realm).[61]

More specifically, the *T'ai hsüan* gives two sorts of prerequisites for communion with the cosmic Mystery. The first is a genuine will to approach the Mystery. The second is single-minded devotion to living its attributes. Of the first prerequisite, Yang Hsiung writes, "Whoever would draw near to the Mystery, the Mystery for its part draws near to him."[62] Emulation of the cosmic Way, as in the relationship of child to parent, naturally accompanies admiration:

> The sage . . . would match his body with Heaven-and-Earth, aim for the numinosity of the ghosts and gods, push his transformations to the limit with yin and yang, and participate in the integrity of the four seasons. Contemplating Heaven, he is Heaven; contemplating Earth, he is Earth; contemplating the divinities, he is divine; contemplating time, he is timely.[63]

The sage achieves identity with the cosmic Way by single-minded concentration on virtue—a discipline as much spiritual as intellectual. As "the gentleman daily strengthens [the aspects of himself that] are deficient and redresses those that are excessive,"[64] he refines his innate powers until they have become perfectly attuned to those of the creative Mystery:

> When one divines with single-minded concentration, the gods prompt the changes [that reveal an answer to the inquiry]. When one deliberates [on this response] with single-minded concentration, one's plans are appropriate. When one establishes the Right with single-minded concentration, no one can overturn it. When one maintains his principles with single-minded concentration, no one can snatch them away.[65]

Yang Hsiung's other requirements also emphasize the sacred character of the divination process:

> The Way of divination consists in this: If you have not attained single-minded concentration, do not divine. If the issue is not in doubt, do not divine. If [your plan] is improper, do not divine. If you will not act in accordance with the outcome [of divination], it is exactly as if you had not divined.[66]

There is little more evidence regarding the *Mystery* as a divination manual, though the usurper Wang Mang is said to have consulted it.[67] Those who studied the book as philosophy evidently also used it for prognostic purposes.[68]

INTERPRETATION FOLLOWING DIVINATION

Drawing upon the elaborate correspondence schemes of Han commentators on the *Changes*, Yang built a coherent and well-wrought system for determining meanings. As he put it in his "Numbers" autocommentary, "In divination, there are four [aspects to consider in interpretation]:[69]

stars (*hsing*), times, numbers, and phrasing." Yang apparently felt that these terms needed no explication. As modern readers, we are dependent upon a late commentator for a clear analysis of these terms. His analysis begins with "stars":

> Suppose it's Tetragram 1, Center. Drawn Ox, the constellation that goes with it, belongs to North (i.e., Water). [That] Water shares the same power with the Water phase of the tetragram. That means that the "stars" are in accord.[70]

As a notion foreign to most modern readers, this idea of "stars" deserves some supplementary explanation: The correlation of Heads and Appraisals with stars (and to some extent with times and numbers) is based on the correspondence of the tetragrams (with their Head texts, of course) to equal divisions of the annual cycle. As stated above, the beginning of the book corresponds to the Grand Inception (*t'ai ch'u*) as defined in the calendar reform of the same name in 104 B.C.: a midnight that simultaneously marks the winter solstice, the first day of the lunar month (when the orbits of sun and moon intersect), and the beginning of the sixty-day cycle. Each of the tetragrams represents 4 1/2 days of the year counted off from this point. All but one of the 731 Appraisals (9 per Head + 2 intercalary Appraisals) are associated with half a day in the round of the year. The second of two intercalary Appraisals is assigned 1/4 of a day.

It is from this equipartition that a great array of correlations follows. At the winter solstice, the sun was by convention located in the first degree of the "lunar lodge" (i.e. the constellation) Oxherd. Since the Oxherd constellation lies at the northernmost point of the celestial equator, all the associations of the phase Water (allied with North in the Han system of correspondences) and of extreme yin come into play. After the winter solstice, the sun moves a Chinese degree each day, each Appraisal applies to an expanse of half a degree, and each Head to four and a half degrees.[71] In Chinese astronomy, the twenty-eight major constellations called lunar lodges are not of equal extent. For example, the first lodge, which is eight degrees long, is succeeded in Appraisal 8 of Tetragram 2 by the Woman constellation, which is twelve degrees in length. Stellar correspondences, each with specific astrological implications, proceed in this way through the round of the sky and the length of the book.

After "stars," the commentary's explication of the three other aspects of interpretation continues:

> "Times" refers to whether the time of divination "conforms with" or "goes against" the solar period a person happens upon [in the outcome

a particular divination]. Suppose it's a divination on the winter solstice. If [the outcome] happens to be a tetragram assigned prior to the tenth month, it is considered "going against." If it's a tetragram after the winter solstice, it is considered "conforming."[72] "Numbers" refers to [the assignment of] numbers to yin/yang and odd/even values. By this, it is fixed whether the outcome happened upon is lucky (Day) or unlucky (Night). "Phrasing" refers to whether or not there is a match between the phrasing of the Nine Appraisals and the ideas prompting the divination.

It is, of course, highly possible that the late commentary attributes to these four important terms a narrower range of meaning than Yang's use of them warrants. "Stars," for example, probably recalled for a thinker of Yang's time an elaborate system of correspondences—astronomical, physical, and even musical—such as Yang cataloged in his autocommentary entitled "Numbers of the Mystery."[73] "Times," "numbers," and "phrasings" may well have directed the reader to consider this matrix of associations (temporal, numerological, and literary) against a background of complex interactions between the Head text and each of the three Appraisals consulted in each individual divination. The inquirer could thus call on a wealth of interconnected entities, each with its own symbolic value, organically connected with every Head and Appraisal (and frequently alluded to in their respective texts). These many dimensions of meaning can converge on the inquirer's question only if the images and associations of the book are rich enough, and if a well-articulated structure makes them accessible.

On the subject of interpretation, a preliminary word concerning the traditional interpretation of the *Mystery* may be in order here. The dynastic history for Western Han clearly states that the draft of the *T'ai hsüan* was completed during the reign of Emperor Ai (r. 7–1 B.C.), when two distaff clans and the catamite Tung Hsien dominated court politics.[74] The concluding encomium in Yang's official biography presents a capsule history of his rather dismal official career designed to defend the philosopher from the charge of sycophancy in general and of partisanship on behalf of the usurper Wang Mang in particular. According to that dynastic history, the composition of the *Mystery* was prompted by Yang Hsiung's decision to "preserve himself" (*tzu shou*), meaning to preserve his life and his integrity, rather than to thrust himself into the limelight during a time of great political upheaval.[75] Such remarks can only mean that soon after Yang's death in A.D. 18, his association with Wang Mang had already become something of a liability to his reputation. Through the years Yang Hsiung's many admirers have risen tirelessly to defend him. Daring interpreters like Ch'en Pen-li (1739–1818), therefore, read into the *Mystery* a veiled satirical attack against all those who undermined Han power at court, especially Wang Mang.

Yang's apologists and detractors have both tended to overlook the basic facts. Unless we credit Yang Hsiung with remarkable prescience, any interpretation of the *Mystery* that focuses on support for or criticism of Wang Mang is patently absurd. During the reign of Emperor Ai, Wang Mang was forced to resign his office. It is doubtful, then, that Yang Hsiung could have predicted Wang's subsequent restoration to power following the untimely death of the young Emperor Ai. Internal evidence from the *Mystery* suggests that Yang Hsiung was a staunch proponent of Han legitimacy and a loyal critic of contemporary abuses, but to read the *Mystery* as political satire is to ignore or distort much of its content. The following section deals with a more important theme of the *Mystery*.

On Luck and Divination in the *Mystery*

THE *MYSTERY* AS DIVINATION CLASSIC

Both the structure and imagery of the *Mystery*, as we have shown, make continual reference to the *Changes*, prompting a basic question: Why did Yang Hsiung choose to model his work upon the only book of divination included among the Five Confucian Classics? In various passages, Yang Hsiung identifies five aspects of the *Changes* that captured his interest: (1) the presumed integrity of the *Changes* text, (2) its breadth of meaning, (3) its abstruse language, (4) its usefulness as a tool for teaching morality, and (5) its thematic treatment of fate. Based on these five qualities, Yang Hsiung "considered the *Changes* to be the greatest of the Classics, and so he composed the *Mystery* [on its model]."[76]

On the first point, Yang Hsiung mistakenly thought the numerical notation[77] of the *Changes* would have prevented significant omissions and interpolations, whether inadvertent or intentional; thus he presumed that the *Changes* text was, among the Five Classics,* the single most reliable guide to antiquity.[78] In addition, the *Changes* was widely believed to be the only one of the Confucian Classics to have survived the famous Burning of the Books order under the previous dynasty of Ch'in.[79]

Second, Yang Hsiung argued that of the Five Classics only the *Changes* was broad enough to answer every moral question put to it, in part because of the different kinds of texts it includes. The *Changes* conveys meaning through the correlation of graphic symbols, verbal images, and classical allusions.[80] The advantage of signs (graphic symbols, verbal images, or allusions) is that their multiple meanings are readily taken in at a single intuitive sweep. Graphic symbols in particular, by avoiding the connotations of words entirely, tend to provide insight into fundamental pattern, for they are at once simple and highly abstract.[81] Metaphors and correspondences can further expand that meaning until a complete universe seems to be refracted through a single point. With lengthy analogies and linked propositions added in the appended commentaries of the Ten Wings, the complete text of the *Changes* appeals simultaneously to human intuition, to the aesthetic sense, and to rigorous categorical logic. Yang Hsiung hoped to imitate this breadth of coverage in the *Mystery*. He writes,

> The *Mystery* . . . is like heaven in its vastness. . . . Were it not economical in its expressions, its points would not be detailed. Were it not compact, its responses would not have universal application. Were it

---

*See Key Terms, page 63

33

not coherent, the events it describes would not be diverse. Were it not deep, its ideas would not reveal anything.[82]

His admirers are right to see in it a mirror of All-under-Heaven designed to "cover many different aspects, though only a few guiding principles underlie it."[83]

Third, Yang Hsiung admitted that he intentionally adopted the abstruse phrasing of the *Changes* to provide himself with some measure of cover in a court rife with intrigue. In his long prose-poem, "Dispelling Ridicule," Yang Hsiung tells of his fear that more forthright criticism might lead to his own execution.

> A guest ridiculed Master Yang, saying, "You silently compose the five-thousand character *Mystery* with its leaves and branches so thickly spread. The explanations alone amount to some 100,000 words. Yet your position is only that of a Gentleman-in-Waiting. In my opinion, your 'dark mystery' is still [insipidly] 'white.' Why else have you been such a miserable failure as an official?"

> Master Yang laughed and replied, "You only wish to vermilion my wheelhubs [i.e., wish to see me with high rank at court]. You do not realize that a single slip could redden my entire clan [through bloodshed]. . . . Those who say anything out of the ordinary are suspect; those who behave unconventionally are penalized for it." [84]

As we will see below, the theory of fate put forth in the *Mystery* directly challenged popular doctrines of legitimacy upon which the Han court rule depended. An unambiguous exposition of this theory would merely have provoked more trouble for Yang.

Fourth, Yang Hsiung knew that a carefully constructed book of divination would engage a wider audience than a conventional guidebook for morality. Ordinary folk (not necessarily the unlettered) tend to consult books of divination in hopes of being told which course of action will benefit them most. According to Yang's own teacher, such people are far more receptive to moral precepts when teachings are disguised as oracular pronouncements sent from the spirit world.[85] The highly sophisticated mind, however, recognizes that something else is at work in the successful divination process: A close identification must be established between the inquirer and the ancient author(s) of the divination text (in Yang's phrase, the individual "immerses" [*ch'ien*] himself in the sages)[86] until the questioner intuits how to apply the cryptic words on the page to his own particular situation. In the quality of that intuition lies the only proof that he has fully "internalized the model"; as Yang writes, "What is divine is not outside [any longer]."[87] In discovering the mind of the sages, then, the inquirer reverently engaged in the divination procedure learns to see into his own heart as well.[88] The enlightened reader perceives divination as the perfect paradigm for all moral acts, which seek to "reanimate the old" through a complex process of identification followed by recreation.[89] The *Mystery* acts in this way, providing illumination for audiences at all levels of awareness. While the ordinary reader finds in it a series of examples outlining in relatively straightforward terms the decided advantages of moral behavior, the truly sympathetic reader engaged in a continuous dialogue with the text gradually uncovers a far more complicated analysis of the effect that individual morality and destiny have in shaping personal experience. In the process, he has received excellent training in the fine art of moral decision-making.[90]

Fifth, Yang expected people to consult books of divination to learn about fate. Since Yang Hsiung particularly wished to address that problem, the neoclassical *Mystery* aptly takes the form of a divination manual.[91] In early China, as in our own culture, numerous debates about fate's role in human life took place in philosophical circles and in society at large. Few problems took intellectual precedence over the question of *ming* (the "Decree" or fate), since classical authorities made a thorough appreciation of it a prerequisite for self-cultivation. Confucius, for example, reportedly said, "He who does not understand *ming* has no way to become a superior man."[92] Similarly, the *Changes* defines the noble man as one who "delights in Heaven and understands *ming*."[93] For this reason, Yang in one chapter explicitly states that the structure and the imagery of his text are designed in such a way as to "exhaustively present the Decree (*ming*)."[94] Yang Hsiung's response to the problem of *ming* produced a vision generally faithful to the ethical norms of the Confucian *Analects* but also responsive to new intellectual concerns about timely opportunity (*shih*) in human life.[95] For this contribution to Confucian thought, he was soon recognized as a "master" in the orthodox tradition. Because Yang's notion of the Decree informs the entire body of his mature work (including the *Model Sayings* and his late prose-poems, as well as the *Mystery*), the material below focuses on that topic.

EARLY NOTIONS OF *MING*: THE HISTORICAL BACKGROUND TO THE PROBLEM OF FATE

Among modern translators, no consensus exists about the proper definition of *ming*; the term is most often rendered as fate or Decree (as in my own introductory remarks), but it is also translated as variously as "duty," "destiny," "predestination," "causal connections and their possibilities," "manifestation of Heaven's will," "the inevitable," "empirical facts," "created world," "lifespan," "objective circumstances," "circumstances beyond human control," and so on.[96] The problem is not simply one of translation.[97] Any Chinese of Yang Hsiung's time would have found a bewildering array of usages for the term, some mutually contradictory. In part, the confusion stemmed from a typical feature of Chinese classical philosophy, in which rival thinkers consciously used the same terminology to articulate significantly different ideas. But there were also unconscious adoptions of meanings through conceptual overlays and etymological extensions as the so-called "Hundred Schools" of philosophy emerged from the earlier religious matrix.[98] Even in the Confucian canon alone, a single passage by the same classical authority may use the one character *ming* to denote two or three different things, since older ideas of *ming* (or Decree) continued to be used alongside newer usages.[99]

As a student of archaic language script,[100] Yang Hsiung was in a better position than most to separate the tangled strands of linguistic convention. He surely knew that early Chou bronze inscriptions used an archaic form of *ming* as an alternate form of the character *ling*, which indicates a superior's orders to his subordinates.[101] Typically, *ming* was associated with the king's decrees of investiture to his inferiors and with Heaven's decree to its chief representative, the king. According to an early Chou formulation, the Decree of Heaven (*T'ien ming*) was a special form of covenant. The covenant essentially stipulated that Heaven agrees to support a certain dynastic line so long as the throne, in return, promotes the well-being of its subject people. Four notable features of this covenant colored all subsequent discussions of *ming*: First and foremost, the Decree of Heaven presupposed a strong connection between Heaven and Man, though the earliest texts are preoccupied with the "One Man," the ruler.[102] Second, the Decree of Heaven implied an impartial reward given for specific acts of "bright virtue."[103] Third, it viewed virtue primarily in terms of obligations to human society, rather than religious duties. Fourth, the Decree of Heaven promised Heaven's support to the recipient(s) for the duration of a fixed (though unspecified) time period, overlooking possible lapses in virtue that might occur while the covenant was in force.[104]

All four aspects of the Decree of Heaven covenant (moral unity of Heaven/Man; reward for virtue; virtue equated with social obligation; and fixed term of contract) continued to form the core of meaning for *ming* over the course of the following several centuries, when the character *ming* came to be extended to other contracts between Heaven (whether seen as supreme god or natural order)[105] and individuals of ever lower rank—first ministers and aristocrats, and finally commoners.[106] Nevertheless, the initial formulation of the Decree of Heaven doctrine became increasingly problematic as the scope of its application dramatically expanded. For one thing, as soon as ordinary people came to be credited with individual decrees, numerous objections were raised about the supposed terms of this unspoken contract, since it was easy to find—and far less dangerous to comment upon—individual cases among the common people in which fate bore no apparent relation to virtue. Moreover, the easy conflation of the accretion of moral goodness with the accumulation of material goods appeared problematic, at least to some. There was also the issue of fairness to be considered if rewards or punishments were really being visited upon distant descendants.[107] Before long, a number of key questions relating to *ming* were put forward. Behind all of them lay a profound "metaphysical doubt as to whether Heaven is after all on the side of human morality."[108] The main questions found in late Chou literature are summarized below:

> What exactly is conferred at birth to humans which makes them essentially different from other living things?

> Since both virtue and wisdom originate in a single deliberative organ (the *hsin* or "heart/mind"), what is the relation between virtue and wisdom?

> Does the granting of motivational impulses and cognitive powers to humans at birth (what later is called the *hsing* or "human nature")[109] include something (maybe the physical *ch'i*?) that predisposes, even determines, the length of lifespan, degree of material success, vocation, and more generally, the quality of life?

> What outside factors, if any, affect the operation of individual *ming*, or is *ming* as part of human nature innate and abiding, impervious to external factors, as certain classical authorities suggest?[110]

> Can a single standard even be established by which to measure an individual's success or failure in human life? What, in other words, is justly called the "good life" (in classical Chinese, the good *ming*)?[111]

> Do acts of either conventional virtue or practical wisdom reap consequent rewards in human life?

> Are rewards and punishments for human conduct meted out by a caring Heaven who speaks through this, or do good and evil acts somehow spontaneously call forth their own responses?

> Which areas are the province of *ming*, since the Confucian *Analects* speaks only of "life and death" in connection with the term, in contrast to later thinkers, who gave it the widest possible construction, listing under its rule "death and life, preservation and ruin, failure and success, poverty and wealth, superior [station] and inferiority, blame and praise, hunger and thirst, cold and heat."[112]

At the heart of this philosophical quagmire lay the eminently practical question: Can individual conduct affect the course of personal fate? There were clear implications for everyday life. And so debate continued.

By the Warring States period (480–222 B.C.), no fewer than five competing theories had evolved concerning the relation of virtue and practical wisdom to chance:

> View no. 1: There is no such thing as *ming*. Consequently, there is no preordained connection between either virtue or practical wisdom and the "good life." Stated another way, no system of cosmic justice operates on behalf of human beings, so that the good are every bit as likely as the wicked to meet with bad fortune.[113]

> View no. 2: *Ming* is determined in exact accordance with virtue or with practical wisdom, so that each separate act results in gain or loss to the doer, whether a conscious Heaven adjusts fate or the acts themselves spontaneously generate good or bad luck. In this view, the individual's Decree can refer simultaneously to externally imposed "fate" or "destiny" and to the internal quality of individual life.

> View no. 3: Individual *ming*, though originally conferred because of virtue, is given for a predetermined length of time, regardless of acts committed in the interval. In its extreme version, this idea opened the way for belief in fixed, interlocking cycles of fortune, like that posited by the cosmologist Tsou Yen (3d c. B.C.) and his adherents.[114]

> View no. 4: *Ming* at birth predestines many, if not all, significant aspects of an individual's life.

> View no. 5: According to a related view, good acts generally make for a good life, though this is *largely* explicable in human terms. Meanwhile some inexplicable inequities exist. The wise man, then, can only do good and "await his fate" with cheerful equanimity.[115]

Never far from people's thoughts in any age, questions about fate acquired a special urgency during the era aptly labelled "Warring States," a period of incessant strife and rapid social change. Still, the notion of the Decree was not the primary focus of debate among recognized masters of Chinese thought in that age. The Hundred School philosophers, sensibly enough, were more preoccupied with questions about the ways a just society would foster the full development of human nature.[116] By definition, a just society, once achieved, would inevitably reveal the true correlation between individual fate, will, and action because it would elevate men of true worth.[117] It was far more practical, then, to try to resolve the many debates on human nature and kingly rule that split even the Confucian camp[118] (especially when philosophical unity was deemed the first step toward the political integration of All-under Heaven),[119] than to try to establish the elusive nature, function, and scope of the Decree.

Shortly before Yang Hsiung's time in the first century B.C., definitions of human nature and the just society had been temporarily laid to rest as important philosophical issues. There were historical reasons for this. By mid-Western Han, the ruling Liu clan had succeeded in establishing its legitimacy, in no small part because of its repeated calls for recommendation of the worthy and its successful identification with the "uncrowned king," Confucius. Meanwhile, Tung Chung-shu (?179–?104 B.C.), "the father of Han Confucianism," had formulated a persuasive synthesis of opposing views of human nature, which accounted for the "mixed" character of human nature (that is, both its good and its evil tendencies) while confirming its origins in Heaven (which most thinkers presumed to be good).[120] Since professional scholars were in rare agreement on these major political and philosophical issues, they turned with renewed enthusiasm[121] in the second century of Western Han to the question of *ming*'s operation of in human existence.

YANG HSIUNG'S SOLUTION TO THE PROBLEM OF *MING*

Yang Hsiung's own solution to the question of *ming* was brilliantly simple and internally coherent. He did, however, leave his followers the difficult task of reconstructing that solution from scattered passages whose allusive (and elusive) tone intentionally imitated archaic Chinese writings produced by the sages rather than the closely reasoned rhetorical arguments of the Warring States philosophers.[122] Since Yang's stated intention in the *Mystery* was to explicate the difficult problem of *ming*, it is at first puzzling that he employed the character only ten times in the entire text of the *Mystery* (three times with the earliest meaning of "[king's] commands").[123] Of course, Yang Hsiung could claim to be emulating the model of Confucius, who "seldom spoke of *ming*," presumably because the most sacred aspects of human existence are taboo.[124] But it is no less likely that Yang's reticence is meant to entice the reader to embark upon that step-by-step immersion in the sage-author's mind that schools the reader in the moral process itself.[125]

Yang Hsiung imbedded the necessary clues to his solution for *ming* in three linked statements. The longest passage begins:

> Someone asked about *ming*. I replied, "*Ming* refers to the decrees of Heaven. It has nothing to do with people's actions." "If people's actions do not constitute *ming*, I beg to ask what about people's actions?" I responded: "By [their actions] they may be preserved or lost; by them they may live or die. [Still,] that is not *ming*. *Ming* refers to what cannot be avoided."[126]

A second passage from the *Mystery* echoes the last line of the preceding statement with one important change; it substitutes "time" for *ming* or the Decree, saying, "Time is what cannot be overcome."[127] And a third passage repeats the association of *ming* with time in defining the Decree as "what is timely or not."[128]

Yang Hsiung's first statement about *ming* suggests that "fate" is an adequate translation for the term if we do not invest it with supernatural overtones. *Ming* in referring to time (meaning "present circumstance" as well as "opportune time") describes the involuntary and imposed part of human existence that will not change through individual effort. (For example, Yang Hsiung came to maturity during an age of misrule and his beloved son died at an early age.) Thus, all three passages emphasize human limitations, for they suggest that any human can fail to meet with suitable opportunities to act. As a general rule, humans, no matter how worthy, can only watch for, not create, individual opportunities, since it is "Heaven that fixes the time."[129] For this reason, one early thinker claimed, "Master Yang taught that to meet or not to meet [with one's desires] is a matter of fate."[130] Naturally enough, such a view of the universe considers skill in ascertaining the opportune time to be at the heart of practical wisdom.[131]

At the same time, numerous statements in the *Mystery* make it clear that for Yang Hsiung *ming* cannot imply total predestination. In the first passage cited above, for example, Yang specifically exempts "preservation and loss, life and death" from the domain of *ming*. Yang Hsiung readily admitted that certain well-defined limits circumscribed human existence: No human, however powerful, is immortal. And only a few will ever win great riches or a throne.[132] These limits are comparatively insignificant, however, once the "preservation and loss" of virtue and the quality of one's "life and death" become the individual's ultimate concerns.[133] One passage in the *Mystery*, therefore, extols the glories attendant upon a virtuous old age,[134] while countless others depict the terrors of a premature fall brought on by a craven dependence upon material pleasure.[135] If we assume philosophical coherence in Yang's mature vision, we can try to reconstruct his most important ideas about the Decree by piecing together general observations on fate and virtue that appear throughout his later works, especially the *Mystery*.

Yang Hsiung clearly demanded that the reader attempt this reconstruction, rather than rest content with fragmentary pronouncements. What are we to make of Yang's initial statement that "preservation and loss, life and death" are exempt from *ming*, especially when we recall that these same four areas are specifically associated with *ming* in the canonical *Analects* attributed to Confucius?[136] It seems that Yang Hsiung wished to challenge his reader, as if he knew that the text can only really teach when it fails to say what we expect it to say; partial truths in obvious conflict are then reexamined, so that a new unitary truth can be established.[137]

Turning to specifics, the *Mystery* depicts four major factors affecting the course and quality of a person's life, though it never groups all four together in a single passage.[138] The four factors to be treated are:

Virtue
Tools
Position
Time

The first notable thing about this list is that Yang reserves *ming* for Time alone, although some early Chinese thinkers loosely viewed all four factors as aspects of *ming* insofar as *ming* may simply refer to the quality of human life. Once we understand the significance of Yang's four factors, this will assume considerable importance.

Elaborating somewhat upon these terms, Virtue refers mainly to the roster of traditional Confucian virtues (among them, filial piety, honesty, loyalty, and modesty). Yang also follows Confucian tradition in making the ritual act virtually synonymous with Goodness since ritual provides the form in which Goodness can be actualized.[139] (For more on ritual, see Key Terms.) For Confucians, ritual is the single mode of behavior capable of fostering necessary social order while satisfying our most basic human needs for beauty and communication. In Yang's writing, however, we also meet newer terms like "cautious watchfulness" and "timely action," associated most often with earlier writings of those very Taoists and Legalists he loved to refute.[140] Such catchwords can be justified in Confucian terms since even the best ritual requires proper timing to promote the common good.[141] Finally, as a committed Confucian, Yang Hsiung believes that Virtue lies within the grasp of each and every human being, though lamentably few may choose to pursue its course.[142]

Under the rubric of Tools, Yang Hsiung puts not only physical artifacts (like jars, stoves, and carts) but also the arts and institutions that civilize society. This single heading, in consequence, houses such disparate items as compass and carpenter's square, the Confucian Classics, the ritual system, supportive friendships, and the family, to the extent that they are civilizing agents.[143] There is, however, one glaring omission from the series. The *Mystery* never mentions the predictive arts touted by certain cosmologists, though the ancient art of divination by milfoil and turtle is often applauded by Yang as a sacred Tool that avails the noble man.[144] Thanks to the legacy of the early sages, all the proper Tools needed for civilization already exist.[145] However, the individual can take full advantage of these available Tools only if he has schooled himself in their proper use; by this training he acquires "practical wisdom" (*chih*).[146] Without such training, the individual either ruins good Tools or chooses Tools that are inadequate or inappropriate to the task.[147] Yang Hsiung provides many comic examples to illustrate his point. In one, a benighted soul lugs a boat overland, then rides a cart into water.[148] By analogy, men who employ Confucian doctrine to acquire wealth, rank, or long life misapply the Tool specifically designed to guide personal self-cultivation and social harmony.[149]

Position refers both to social rank and to the physical location[150] that the individual occupies at the precise moment when action is required.[151] The stock example of good position is that of the ruler, whose greater access to certain resources and opportunities exists (at least while he remains on the throne) regardless of his character; by virtue of his Position, he has what we might call a strategic advantage over others.[152] Being in the right place at the right time, tradition suggests, is at least partly a matter of luck, since even the great sage-master Confucius failed to secure a government position commensurate with his talents.[153] In well-ordered states, however, Virtue helps to secure Position.[154]

Time refers not only to the interlocking cycles of yin/yang and the Five Phases;[155] it also covers the individual cycle of each phenomenon in the cosmos (in Chinese terms, the "myriad things," including Man himself) engaged in a continual process of change.[156] The ancient Chinese viewed Time in a complex fashion; for them,

> there was natural, cyclic time, defined by the alternation of the farming
> seasons and of day and night. Human time reflected the cycles of life
> and the cosmos. Time was not purely cyclic. It was regressive in the
> sense that the perfect social order of archaic times was gone forever.
> But it was also progressive, in the sense that civilization was built out
> of a series of sagely inventions, . . . adaptations of natural patterns to
> human use. These inventions accumulated to let society survive and
> provide scope for its improvement.[157]

For Yang Hsiung, the importance of Time can hardly be overestimated; in a passage cited earlier in this Introduction, Yang places Time in a series that includes Heaven, Earth, and the gods.[158] The Head texts of the *Mystery* depict the annual cycle with its four seasons; the Appraisals reflect the regular alternation of night/day and the sequential operation of the Five Phases. Within the nine Appraisals to each Head, three successive groups of three Appraisals represent the beginning, middle, and end of a specific process or life cycle, each unit of which carries with it its own constraints and benefits. For example, at the age of ninety, women do not bear children, though they may be singularly honored for their accumulated wisdom and experience.[159] For this reason, we can think of Time as synonymous with present [or timely] "opportunity."[160]

If these four factors of Virtue, Tools, Position, and Time together determine the course of individual life, how do they relate to one another? The graphic summary of Yang's comments shown in table 5 will help:

Table 5.

The Mysterious Tao in Operation

ASPECT:	Individual	Society	Heaven (deity or sky)
SCOPE:	With Man	On Earth	In Heaven
FACTOR:	Virtue	Tools, Position	Time (equated with the Decree)

Although oversimplified, the table highlights several important aspects of Yang's solution to *ming*. It shows, for example, that Yang's solution is somewhat more sophisticated than most, in that it accounts for wide variations in individual life by reference to four interdependent factors, rather than in terms of the usual dichotomies of fate-virtue, conduct-reward, Heaven-Man, inner-outer, and so on. It also has Tools and Position playing a mediating role between Virtue and Time. This is true in at least two senses: First, the acquisition of Virtue is entirely determined by the individual human will; "getting the opportune time" for conventional success, by contrast, is completely up to Heaven—in other words, outside human control.[161] (Time is particularly associated with Heaven since the calendar reflects the movements of the heavenly bodies.)[162] Tools and Position, products of civilized society, have been fashioned by sages upon the model of Heaven.[163] Their existence offers the single best proof of the integration of human with cosmic history, of Time with Virtue.[164] Second, while the acquisition of Tools and Position is in some undefinable measure attributable to Virtue,[165] it is Time that determines when Tools and Position can be used.[166] How does this work? According to Yang Hsiung, only the man who identifies completely with the sages can be called virtuous, for only he commands the sympathy, foresight, and dedication necessary to master the creations of the sages fully, so that Tools and Position are ready for use when opportunity arises.[167] Still, despite years of preparation, certain latter-day sages (Confucius among them) have never been called upon to employ the full range of their talents.[168]

Various passages in the *Mystery* place the operations of all four factors (Virtue, Tools, Position, and Time) squarely in the realm of change. (Here Yang contradicts some other early texts, which show only *ming* synonymous with change.)[169] And each of the four factors imposes definite limits on the individual. Time constraints are probably the most obvious in Yang's writings:

> [Timely] opportunities come and go,
> The gap between them finer than a hair.[170]

Sheer probability argues against the frequent convergence of all four factors.[171] Unfortunately, the conventionally defined "good life" of longevity, numerous progeny, wealth, high status, and good reputation depends upon the fortuitous coincidence of all four factors affecting humans.[172] To the degree that Tools and Position are variables dependent upon both Time and Virtue, it is true that nothing can stop the individual from success when Time coincides with Virtue.[173] But with Tools and Position a function of Time, bad timing skews the personal equation in the direction of bad luck, so that the wisest of individuals must exercise extreme caution in order simply to survive.[174] In an age of disorder, high position may even make a person more than ordinarily vulnerable to attack.

Given the crucial importance of Time as a factor in human experience, it is all the more regrettable that Time (once again, meaning "present opportunity") is so limited. How much more convenient if Time, presumably regular in its movements, could be predicted or manipulated. That Time was regular, men of Han had no doubt.[175] Poetic diction, as well as the structure of the *Mystery*, reinforces the idea that astronomical Time is the product of the regular alternation of yin/yang and the Five Phases. In the shape of the calendar, Time even comes to symbolize the cosmic norms.[176] Why then does Yang continue to reiterate that Time lies beyond human control?

Respected scholars at the Han court had argued that Time was amenable to human understanding precisely because it was regular. The "father of Han Confucianism," Tung Chung-shu, stated this unequivocally:

> The fact that definite propositions can be made about [the operation of
> the Five Phases aligned with the seasons] means that sage men can get
> to understand them.[177]

The trouble was that it took only a series of small successive steps to move from understanding Time to "knowing" Time (both "understanding" and "knowing," after all, were indicated by the single character *chih*) to wanting to predict, even control its operations. As numerous contemporary references to magicians, astrologers, and diviners attest,[178] many hoped to predict and manipulate the future through "technical arts" (for instance, portent reading and numerology). Though such arts seemed to corroborate the court-sponsored Doctrine of Mutual Interaction between Heaven and Man (*T'ien jen kan ying*) (and by extension, to prove the legitimacy of the Han throne), Yang Hsiung was anxious to disassociate himself from this pseudo-Confucian viewpoint.

The *Mystery* argues that the patterned operations of Time, however regular in the natural world, are not entirely knowable, notwithstanding the claims made by certain Han magicians. Since Time's movements cannot be forecast with absolute accuracy, manipulation of Time's operations is simply out of the question. Yang Hsiung supplies two reasons for this. First, according to Yang, all supremely great entities (a category that includes Heaven, Earth, the Confucian Classics, and Time) remain ultimately shrouded in mystery, because the part cannot fully comprehend the whole.[179] In one passage, he discusses the first three great entities:

> Someone asked whether . . . they cannot be more easily comprehended. I replied, "They cannot. If Heaven suddenly could be measured, then its covering of things would be thin indeed. If Earth suddenly could be fathomed, then its support of things would be superficial indeed. Great is the way Heaven and Earth form the outer wall for the myriad things, while the Five Classics represent the retaining walls for the numerous theories.[180]

Time, the fourth great entity, envelops all space and material change.[181] Therefore, Man as one tiny part of phenomenal existence can never fully comprehend it; as Yang writes, "What is [truly] great has no borders; what changes has no [set] time."[182] Yang was careful to say that even the sages are only "on the point" (*yu*) of fathoming it, since they know— at best—how to estimate (*ni*) the broad outline of the unknowable.[183] Humans intent upon greatness should seek to conform to Time, instead of challenging its manifest superiority, just as they submit to other superiors.[184]

Yang Hsiung bolsters this argument by reference to the most current cosmological theory. To explain apparent anomalies in the sequential operation of the cosmic phases, Yin/yang Five Phases theorists at the Han court had already posited a so-called Principle of Masking. According to the theory, different rates of change among the five cosmic phases interacting in sequential order occasionally produce patterns whose origins are too difficult to read. (I see this as multiple waves reinforcing or canceling one other.)[185] The *Mystery* makes reference to this Principle when it talks of the Five Phases "concealing their actions."[186] Yang then proceeds to incorporate in the *Mystery* a striking parallel to the Principle of Masking. As early as the first tetragram, we find examples of Appraisals assigned yang (i.e., auspicious) values that inexplicably predict certain disaster (in conventional terms, if not always in moral terms) for the individual confronting the particular slice of Time associated with that Appraisal.[187] As all of these anomalies occur in the last few Appraisals assigned to the Head (positions corresponding to the final stage of the human situation or lifespan when Time's limitations become most obvious),[188] the only possible conclusion to be drawn is that the inauspicious character of "human endings" in some few cases can override (or at least mask) the auspicious character of larger coincident cosmic cycles.[189] No explanation is given for what look like random events, perhaps because, according to Yang, the sage "may investigate irregularities but only records the constant sequences."[190] Yang may also intend by this device to indicate the relative weight of humankind in the triadic realms of Heaven-Earth-Man.[191] In any case, Yang adapts the language of the cosmologists to undermine their bloated claims to foreknowledge.

At first glance, Yang's insistence on Time's unpredictability seems to undercut his continual exhortations to undertake timely action. But this is hardly the case. The *Mystery* emphasizes preparation for all eventualities. When trends change, a variety of signs will indicate the proper course of action. The most important of these are so-called "human portents."[192] Given Time's inherent unpredictability, human behavior becomes the most reliable prognostic tool available. The ceremonial participant who oversteps ritual betrays his overweening ambition; the braggart is easily identified as "hollow." Both kinds of individual will surely land in trouble sooner or later. So reliable are these human portents that the wise man, curious about the future, shifts his attention from the stars (i.e., changes in the natural world) to the study of Virtue in society.[193] No wonder so many Appraisal texts in the *Mystery* treat ritual lapses as emblems of profound disorder.

More important, Yang Hsiung's key arguments about the moral life all follow directly from his single statement that Time (as a major determinant in destiny) lies beyond human control. This yields at least seven important corollaries, which appear in various places in his work:

1. Since the course of human existence depends upon various conjunctions of Virtue, Tools, and Position with unpredictable Time, the wise person devotes every effort to advance preparation in case future opportunity should present itself. From this commonsensical observation, Yang Hsiung extracts from the Five Confucian Classics a single underlying theme: the noble man "jealously guards his days" (*ai jih*) in order to make the best possible use of his limited time.

2. Since the principle of *ai jih* demands that one make the best possible use of limited opportunities, the evaluating mind should first determine, and then focus upon, subjects of greatest importance, while turning away from inherently unproductive subjects.

3. Careful investigation shows that ritual practice is the single most important subject amenable to human understanding and beneficial to mankind. Through its study, the wise person is transformed into the good person.

4. The study of ritual allows humans to develop in such a way that the individual can not only become "partner with" or "consort to" Heaven,"[194] but can even partake of eternity itself. Alone among living things, Man has the power to participate in the divine life through Goodness.

5. If ritual acts cause humans to identify with, even partake of, the divine order, the would-be sage will not try to unduly control Tao in its various manifestations (including fate). Instead, he will acquiesce in the divine and mysterious order known as *ming* (in other words, accept all parts of the Heavenly plan).

6. "Understanding" (*chih*) (i.e., "accepting") the Decree invariably brings certain physical and psychological advantages to the individual. In addition, a number of external advantages *incidentally* may derive from submission to fate. In contrast, no *certain* advantage lies in a person's attempt to control his fate or pursue secondary goals such as power or wealth.

7. The most important advantage of Virtue lies in its potential to effect the ideal state of perfect community (Yang calls it "no gap"), which has both psychological and social dimensions.

PROPOSITIONS ABOUT TIME, LUCK, AND VIRTUE

Let us examine these linked propositions in greater detail, beginning with Yang Hsiung's statement identifying the phrase *ai jih* as the single unifying thread running through sagely practice. In descending orders of literalness, *ai jih* means "to love the days," "to be frugal in the [use of one's] time," and "to jealousy guard one's time" in order to make the best possible use of limited chances and resources.[195] Yang's preoccupation with *ai jih* may come as something of a minor shock to a reader of classical Chinese philosophy. Why? Generations have pondered a very different statement by the Master that identified "consideration for others" (*shu*) as the single theme binding together the entirety of the sage's teachings.[196] Surely Yang Hsiung does not intend to challenge the words of the Master?[197]

The two separate "threads" in fact can be seen to complement one another. If the individual lifespan cannot be extended beyond a certain maximum (the Chinese often talked of a hundred years or so), the brevity of human existence creates in us a heightened sense of obligation and care for human life, so that individuals wish to make the best use of Time. Yang Hsiung uses the analogy of the filial son to show how this works. For the filial son, the inevitable nature of his parents' old age and death produces in the son a acute sense of obligation and love.[198] All social relations, by analogy to this fundamental parent-child relation, are infinitely more precious because they are bound by Time, even where death is not an immediate threat. Time's inexorable flow means that mistakes in social relations may cause irreparable harm; for instance, harsh words or meaningless babble cannot be recalled once the sounds have "flown off" into the air.[199] Humans and human creations (including ritual) acquire heightened value precisely because of their fragile, transitory nature. The phrase *ai jih* indicates that human "love" (for others) in combination with the "days" (that is, Time) determines the Confucian focus on social relations.

Someone might object, as Yang Hsiung's opponents did:[200] "How do we know that months and years spent in forging human relations represent the single best use of Time?" After all, human beings wish for a variety of benefits, and all are reasonable goals to the degree that they can increase human "greatness."[201]

Various philosophers in ancient China suggested different methods to achieve human greatness. One definitional problem, of course, concerned the usual confusion of greatness with happiness. The Legalists, for example, had assumed that man can achieve supreme greatness only by the acquisition of political power, which endows a person with a charisma akin to the gods and ensures a kind of immortality through long-lasting reputation. Other thinkers countered that court life in and of itself presents so grave a risk to physical and mental well-being that conventional desires for high position destroy all possibility of true happiness. In that case, can such unhappiness be accounted great? Many thinkers debated the answer to this question. Some advocated detachment as the wisest goal for Man (given his limited resources), while others responded by experimenting with recipes for physical immortality.

Yang carefully analyzes the problem of maximum benefit without reference to the confusing issue of overlapping definitions for human greatness and happiness. By Yang's logic, a goal worth pursuing must satisfy three criteria:

1. Effort expended must result in measurable gain that is both certain and commensurate with the effort.[202]
2. The greater the gain the better.[203]
3. Personal gain is more safely held when benefits are extended to others, just as a wider base gives the wall additional security.[204]

In other words, the logical mind first determines which goals are both worthy and possible, then it finds a way to maximize benefits.[205] Applying these observations, Yang makes short shrift of the usual claims that maximum satisfaction can be derived from the attainment of certain conventional goals, such as wealth, factual knowledge, political power, or physical immortality.[206] He also plays up the continual frustrations experienced by the unlucky majority who can never reach external goals. In effect, he attacks all goals except the study of ritual precepts, arguing that only ritual can satisfy all three requirements for a worthy goal: First, it is possible to perfect oneself in ritual. Second, ritual action facilitates the effective expansion of one's circle of family, friends, and allies. Third, ritual action ensures that others will not resent this extension of personal charismatic power, no matter how great it becomes.[207]

Since man has limited Time (and consequently limited knowledge) at his disposal, he does better to focus on a few principles that he can then apply to numerous situations.[208] Employing ritual, the truly wise man can use Time (which is limited, and so epitomizes change and decline) to offset the ill effects of Time. Such a person secures and sustains the maximum portion of greatness for as long as possible. This works because ritual precepts are limited in number, with only five fundamental paradigms (the Five Constant Relations of father-son, ruler-subject, husband-wife, elder sibling-younger sibling, and friend-friend) to be mastered. In addition, opportunities for the study of ritual are present everywhere. Confucius himself had remarked that they can be found in everyday life as well as in books,[209] so that there is no need to resort to the complicated calculations and expensive instruments used by diviners and astrologers. As an added bonus, the careful analysis of ritual performance (those "human portents") yields more accurate information about prevailing social trends than the finest astrolabes and templates.[210] Finally, the decided advantage of ritual study is that its benefits are certain. At the very least, through ritual performance a person gains a secure sense of himself. In philosophical language, it satisfies deep physical and psychological longings to fulfill one's own potential as human being and to unite with one's fellow man.[211] Ritual also allows a variety of important social institutions to function. And under ideal conditions, powerful ritual binds the entire universe in a voluntary community so tight that "no gap"[212] (that is, no sense of alienation) remains. According to Yang, a man would be a fool to run after possibly unattainable goals while neglecting to pursue a sure thing.[213] For this reason, the prudent individual studies ritual and Virtue.

Yang's claims by no means stop here. According to the *Mystery*, ritual acts allow each individual *in some aspects* to escape the ruinous clutches of Time itself by entering the world of the eternal "constant norms."

Since this argument is key to the *Mystery*, let us examine each of its steps with particular care.

Yang Hsiung describes the characteristic activities of the *Mystery* in the following passage:

> As for the Mystery, . . .
> The polluted it purifies.
> The precipitous it levels. . . .
> The elevated it lowers.
> The low it raises.
> The abundant it takes from.
> The depleted it gives to.
> The bright it tones down.
> The doubtful it clarifies. . . .
>
> In its active mode, the Mystery daily creates what it [the world] lacks and favors what it renews. In its quiescent mode, the Mystery daily depletes what it [the world] has and diminishes what it has completed.[214]

He then asserts that noble man in practicing ritual operates in a fashion analogous to the Mystery.

> If the noble man daily strengthens what is deficient in him [that is, the good] and eliminates what he possesses in surplus [that is, the evil], then the Way of the Mystery is nearly approximated indeed![215]

This means that the good person approaches the Mystery when he applies himself to the study of ritual. Since it is the social virtues, especially modesty and compliance, which are in short supply and actions contrary to ritual which are in oversupply, the good man employs ritual to habituate himself to a life that increases his good impulses and curbs his evil tendencies. In weighing the claims of competing desires within himself, the good man learns to use ritual to effect a balance in ever wider circles within the family and society at large, just as the Tao balances all aspects of Heaven-Earth-Man, thereby achieving true justice for all.[216] The ritual act, we are to conclude, partakes of divinity because it is categorically akin to the sacred Mystery in its operation. As an unseen motive force behind profound social change, the noble man mimics the cosmic Mystery in its catalyzing activity.[217] Through ritual, the noble man takes on divine aspects. The wide range of his abilities and contacts correspond to the vastness of the Tao.[218]

Lest someone object that this picture greatly exaggerates the power of ritual, Yang Hsiung supplies what he considers to be a second proof of the divine quality of human ritual. This proof begins with the general rule that each phenomenon in the world of Heaven-Earth-Man is subject to cyclical decline, as provided for in Yin/yang Five Phases theory. One passage in the *Mystery* says, for example:

> By rule, abundance enters decline and what ends is born again. There is filling up and emptying out. . . . If yang fails to culminate, then yin fails to germinate. If yin fails to culminate, then yang fails to sprout. . . . Back and forth is their [yin/yang] sequence; twisting and turning is their path. . . . At one point there is life, at one point there is death. Day and night alternate. Yin and yang divide the numbers.[219]

Ordinary life, then, is supremely "inconstant."[220] Few of Yang Hsiung's readers would have balked at this vision of the universe. They consulted a divination text precisely because they were all too aware of life's vagaries. But Yang Hsiung proceeds to make the further claim that Virtue, like the mysterious Tao, is also in some sense eternal, for it is in substance "ever new."[221] Virtue, he insists, then becomes the single entity in all of phenomenal existence that is exempt from the time's predations, since its accumulation does not force an inevitable reversal:

> In the Way of Man, it is good fortune to be upright and calamity to be perverse. Therefore, the noble man is inwardly upright and outwardly compliant. . . . This is why the outcome of his actions is good fortune and not calamity. If in good fortune one does not do evil, [good fortune] cannot give rise to calamity. If in calamity, one does not do good, [calamity] cannot become good fortune. Evil and good! Evil and good! Evil and good! These are what ultimately reveal the noble man![222]

This simple argument urging the continuous accumulation of Goodness is far more important than it looks. By the relatively simple act of distinguishing moral attainment from all other attainments, which are subject to cyclical reversal and decline (such as the accumulation of physical *ch'i*, of power, or of money),[223] Yang Hsiung reasserts the primacy of the constant norms enshrined in ritual over other, transitory goals, which are often summed up in the term "the good life." Virtue is seen in some sense as inviolable, eternal, and infinitely great in potential. After all, even death cannot alter or "snatch away" the quality of a man's moral acts. Especially great virtue may even confer upon its possessors a kind of immortality in the form of lasting reputation.[224] Therefore, Virtue becomes the only worthy goal for Man, since it fulfills Yang's criterion for greatness: it reliably brings infinitely great rewards.

Since only the ritual act brings sure and great rewards, serious moral confusion results whenever the conventional "good life" is erroneously held up as a worthy goal for human beings.[225] (In the first place, the adjective "good" should never be applied to *ming* at all, since Time, unlike Virtue, is not a human construction.) In fact, the term "good *ming*" is a misnomer whose continued use threatens to lead men from the productive pursuit of the Way into fruitless pursuits for long life, riches, and so on. As one Appraisal shows, in muddled fashion the typical lout mistakes contingent good luck for the sure rewards of Virtue:

> Circumstance contrives; the faulty seems correct.
> Fortunate men do not deem this a "happy coincidence."
> Wrong, though right by circumstance,
> Means: Good men return to the constants.[226]

To dispel such popular confusion about "good *ming*," Yang Hsiung tries to employ consistent terminology throughout the *Mystery*.[227] "Good luck" and "bad luck" (*chi hsiung*) are used in connection with aspects of the conventional good life, such as wealth, high status, and long life. Since luck is tied to Time, it cannot be won by effort; therefore, it makes no sense to regard it as the supreme goal in life, though good men may sometimes achieve it "incidentally."[228] "Favor" and "blame" (*hsiu ch'iu*) refer to the societal reaction (in the case of blame, this means the social cost) to a particular course of action. Once again, the good opinion of one's contemporaries is ultimately beyond the control of the individual, and so the wise person refuses to rely upon it for psychic, physical, or economic benefits.[229] In contrast, "good fortune" and "calamity" (*fu huo*) refer to the moral and immoral life respectively:

> What Heaven and Earth honors is called "good fortune." What the
> ghosts and spirits bless is called "good fortune." What the Way of Man
> delights in is called "good fortune." Whatever is despised and abhorred
> is called "calamity."[230]

Since the Way of Man (i.e., Virtue through self-cultivation) by definition lies within the grasp of each individual, the individual holds complete responsibility for his own good fortune (that is, morality),[231] disproving the mistaken assumption of "ordinary folk who think that misfortune and good fortune are determined by *ming*."[232]

According to Yang, conventional bad luck may even be welcomed as a boon so long as it brings the individual a better appreciation of his own ritual obligations.[233] Yang Hsiung's famous prose poem "Expelling Poverty" comes close to burlesque when it details the moral and psychic benefits of dire poverty for the individual:

> All others lock themselves in.
> You alone live in the open.
> All others tremble with fear.
> You alone have no apprehensions.[234]

Across the centuries, such statements seem disingenuous or ironic at the very least, if not outright preposterous. But the *Mystery*, Yang's masterwork, adopts a far more serious tone. There Yang does not wish to claim either that "Virtue is its own reward" or that Virtue's rewards are self-evident. He accepts the notion that he must demonstrate the benefits of Virtue if he is to persuade his readers to try it. So he sets out to prove, as he says, that conforming to "the Mystery [as pattern] is the ultimate in utility."[235]

Accordingly, Yang shows that several advantages accrue from virtuous conduct informed by ritual pattern, itself derived from the divine patterns of the Tao. For instance, the good man enjoys *comparative* freedom from certain kinds of anxiety, such as those about material success.[236] Intent only upon accumulating acts of goodness, he disregards his own self and trusts in Heaven's will. At the very least, since he expects nothing from the world, he cannot be harmed by it: in Yang's words, "Calamity is no calamity unless seen as such."[237] Even more important, a sense of psychic and physical well-being flows from the smooth "fit" between cosmic norms and his developed potential (in Chinese terms, between Heaven's Decree and the personal, inborn "decree from Heaven").[238] In this way the good man "is by virtue made secure"—in other words, he avoids the mental and physical costs of evildoing.[239]

Of course, this does not mean that the good person is an incurable optimist. There are things worth worrying about, including the health of parents, the economic and moral state of one's fellow men, and the state of the empire.[240] But once he has acted honorably, he realizes the rest is up to fate. The consequent reduction in stress promotes better physical health. In fact, virtuous action may be the single best way to extend human longevity.[241] Beyond the domain of the internal, the noble man's considerate behavior combined with his practical wisdom also makes him a valued companion. Since he is valued by others, he is likely to be showered with a variety of material benefits and intangible rewards, such as a happy family life and high position at court. Occasionally, such *incidental* rewards for virtue are not forthcoming due to Time's mysterious operations—after all, even the paragon Shun was plagued by evil family members and the sage Confucius was never awarded a responsible post.[242] In that case, the ability to forge lasting associations with like-minded individuals can help to cushion a person from the worst shocks of Time.[243]

Given the manifest advantages associated with goodness, the perceptive man, even if he is not yet perfectly good, may be brought to realize the inherent wisdom of becoming one with the eternal Tao through ritual. Since Tao refuses to draw attention to its unseen cosmic operations, Man himself must learn to shun all self-promotion. Once he is truly moral, he comes to acquiesce in the mysterious plan imposed upon him by the pervasive pattern known as Tao or T'ien. It is true that one cannot know *ming* in its entirety; still, accepting that it operates means learning to accept the inevitable limitations imposed by Time.[244]

Since there are definite limits on the ability of humans to forestall disaster,[245] the individual who is truly "awake"[246] to reality prepares himself for any eventuality. This is what Yang Hsiung means by timely action and by waiting for *ming*. Waiting, then, is by no means passive. Rather, it is the arduous process by which the individual schools himself in the inherent patterns imbedded in divine ritual, moral decision-making, and flexible response to new developments.[247] Only the petty man rails against fate, like an idiot who thinks his defiant shouts will hold back the raging torrents of the Yellow River.[248] Only the petty man puts his trust in magical "arts" or resorts to divination at every turn.[249] (It only seems paradoxical that this advice comes from a divination manual.)[250] Once we embrace Time's unpredictablity, no longer trying to control the uncontrollable, then "unimaginable joy" and "release" inevitably follow.[251]

Yang Hsiung's solution to the problem of *ming*, then, can be summarized as follows: Four factors, Virtue, Tools, Position, and Time, affect the course of a man's life. Of these four factors, one (Time) is completely outside man's control, while two factors (Tools and Position) are partly dependent for their effectiveness upon Virtue, partly upon Time. The wise man prepares best for the opportune Time by pursuing Virtue above all other goals. The possession of Virtue not only brings inner strength and equanimity, it also tends incidentally to secure the Tools and Position necessary for more tangible pleasures and conventional goals, including long life, progeny, power, and fame. More important, since human Virtue is the one aspect of human existence that escapes the ruinous cycles of decay and loss, the noble man at one with sacred ritual partakes of the eternal, mysterious Tao. In this way, human life, though subject to a wide range of limitations (including illness and death), can become fully powerful, constant, and inviolate.

To properly assess Yang's solution to the problem of fate and virtue, we must understand the immediate implications of Yang's insistence upon the ineffable nature of Tao and Time. Yang Hsiung wants to direct human effort away from a detailed examination of the shifting phenomenal world and refocus attention upon the preservation of ritual norms and cultural patterns.[252] (Yang Hsiung, by the way, took his own advice, spending his last years in the study of significant linguistic and cultural patterns.) This puts him firmly in the Confucian fold. Also, his attempt to disengage success from morality is consistent with the traditional Confucian attitude that conventional goals are simply unrelated to the pursuit of Virtue.[253] At the same time, Yang believes that action in conformity with ritual makes Man a participant in the eternal; on this basis, the "gaps" between the triadic realms of Heaven-Earth-Man can be overcome and cosmic community forged. Yang Hsiung, then, uses his exploration of fate to reaffirm the major Confucian doctrines of his age.

THE INTELLECTUAL DEBTS OF YANG'S NEW CLASSIC

In his own works, Yang outlined four standards which he expected others to use when judging the quality of the *Mystery* as a new Confucian classic: two standards drawn from classical authorities and two tests by practical results. By these criteria, the *Mystery* had to (1) reinterpret Confucian tradition for a contemporary audience, (2) be "easy" to understand, (3) promote social order, and (4) refute heterodox doctrines and their proponents successfully. As we will see, the *Mystery* measured up in all four criteria to the standard of a classic.

As to the first criterion, Confucius himself had said that the true test of a Confucian was that his teachings must "reanimate the old" teachings of the sages, making them appear fresh and vital to his contemporaries.[254] This is clear enough as a rule, though hard to apply. Turning to the second criterion, what did the Great Commentary to the *Changes* mean when it insisted that a classic should be "easy to know" and "easy to follow"?[255] In his writings, Yang took a closer look at this characterization of a moral classic. In one passage, an imaginary disciple asks him directly about the puzzling phrase. The disciple argues that morality is a "heavy burden"[256] and the Five Classics are riddled with apparent inconsistencies, so no Confucian text could be accounted either easy to know or easy to follow.[257] Yang answers that "ease" could only mean that the classics "have no treachery or trickery" in them, no internal contradictions or logical pitfalls.[258] To merit the name of classic, a book could explain neither too much nor too little.[259] And as if those were not enough requirements for a single literary composition, Yang further stipulates that a work could not be dubbed a Confucian classic unless it fulfilled two practical functions: it must make for good order in society;[260] and it must promote the Confucian vision by its successful refutation of the most influential of contemporary heresies.

To compose a new classic, then, Yang had to remain faithful to ideas put forth by Confucius (as he understood them through the partially distorting medium of intervening tradition). Equally, he had to incorporate new terminology and new illustrations so as to enlighten contemporary seekers after Tao and refute contemporary corruptors of the Confucian Way. Yang himself was aware of the danger of lapsing into facile eclecticism. His stated goal was to promote Confucianism while steering clear of what was *tsa* ("mixed," "hybrid," "heterogenous," "heterodox").[261]

Only his success in meeting all these criteria would earn him the title of Confucian Master.

While Yang Hsiung's discussion of fate goes far beyond that presented in the *Analects* of Confucius, his characterization of *ming* as an outside imposition upon Man is true to the Master. According to the *Analects*, Confucius seldom spoke of *ming* and never clearly defined it,[262] though he uses the term to suggest a force beyond human capabilities affecting human existence for good or ill. As it is said, "Whether the Way will prevail" depends upon *ming*, as do poverty, disgrace, illness, and death.[263] Heaven's Decree accordingly is to be feared.[264] The proper attitude to maintain toward it is one of trusting acceptance. Yang Hsiung also presumes that he follows Confucius when he focuses on issues of time in considering fate.[265]

Yang Hsiung's problem, then, is to expand those teachings without departing from the Master's few pronouncements on *ming*. In this, Yang borrowed from Mencius (?371–?289) and Hsün tzu (?298–?238), two rival masters of the Confucian tradition. From Mencius, he took the clear contrast between *ming* as beyond human control and virtue as within human control.[266] He also adopted the Mencian characterization of the good man as quietly "awaiting his fate" (*hou ming*)[267] by cultivating virtue, in hopes that future opportunities may come. From Hsün tzu, the borrowings are even more explicit, since, as far as can be asserted, it is Hsün tzu who first defined fate in terms of Time,[268] which is clearly understood as an ordering principle specifically assigned to Heaven.

Despite such borrowings, Yang's carefully phrased language on the topic of *ming* addresses certain logical problems arising from the works of Mencius and Hsün tzu.[269] Mencius' writings fail abysmally to account for the origin of evil. Since beneficent Heaven is the origin of all that is good (including the heart/mind and human nature), where would a "bad" fate come from? And if ties between Heaven and Man are so close, how is it that an individual's fate might come to be strong enough to prevent the heart/mind and human nature from perfect functioning? Mencius seems unable to focus on internal constraints to goodness (though Yang Hsiung assumes they exist).[270] What's more, Mencius' idealism about the infinite power of charismatic virtue directly contradicts his emphasis on the "external" (i.e., uncontrollable) nature of *ming*.[271]

Half a century later, Hsün tzu attributed all the logical difficulties of the Mencian discourse to Mencius' identification of human community with natural order. Hsün tzu drastically set about severing many of the significant ties linking Heaven to Man, by generally limiting the term Heaven (T'ien) to a physical entity, the sky (or heavens), whose model has limited applicability to any human dilemma. This redefinition of T'ien broke the necessary connection between virtue (as Man's preserve) and timely opportunity (as Heaven's domain). In the process, however, Hsün tzu's logic only succeeded in creating yet another difficulty. Since virtuous conduct gave no certain advantage to the individual,[272] Hsün tzu could supply no real motivation to undertake the arduous course of self-cultivation.[273]

Yang Hsiung reaffirms the close connection between Man and Tao for two main reasons, one practical and one theoretical.[274] First, he knew that the ordinary fellow is much more likely to try ritual if persuaded that T'ien (acting either as deliberate Heaven or spontaneous Nature) will reward him for good behavior. But for the more subtle mind, Yang fashioned a more subtle appeal: Heaven and Virtue are linked through the human propensity to interact, rather than through any initial disposition toward good or evil.[275] As Yang writes, "The Way of Man is to make contact."[276] Naturally, the human potential for interaction is severely limited if Man cannot derive his models from the world of Heaven-and-Earth around him. Then no chance remains for individual goodness to partake of the Eternal. That explains why

> Heaven, were it not for Man, would have nothing to cleave to. Man, were it not for Heaven, would not complete anything."[277]

Yang Hsiung constructed a plausible account of human existence, avoiding all duplicity about human probability (which would discredit that account in the eyes of the intelligent reader) while promising the "average reader" a probable payoff for good conduct in terms of material success.

YANG'S *MYSTERY* AS A CHINESE *SUMMA*

The consummate mastery of the *Mystery* does not end with Yang's solution to the problem of fate. Yang's writings in the *Mystery* are also carefully designed to implicitly refute a number of popular beliefs and philosophical concepts that impugn traditional Confucian truths. In his second philosophical classic, called *Model Sayings*, the attacks on rival theories are quite explicit, with Yang naming names. The *Mystery* works in far less obvious ways. Thanks to its broad scope and coherent vision, the main tenets of Confucian orthodoxy appear as one eternal verity. Since its main task is integrative, it rises above mere polemic. Therefore, Yang's refutations in the *Mystery* are imbedded in the very fabric of the imagery, which makes them seem all the more inevitable and incontrovertible. Still, the *Mystery* ably shows that mistaken or partial views are held by at least five other groups of thinkers: (1) the relativists, (2) the seekers after immortality, (3) the proponents of "Change as the only Constant," (4) the portent specialists, and (5) the proponents of predestination.

Contra the Relativists

The "Appended Texts" commentary to the *Changes* opens with the lines,

> Heaven is of high rank and earth of low. Thus yin and yang are fixed!
> With low and high set out, the noble and debased are positioned![278]

The passage suggests that both social hierarchy and distinction-making (i.e., constructing hierarchies of value) are based on natural models; therefore, they are entirely appropriate for mankind. Many passages in the *Mystery* reiterate this idea.[279] This picture of the natural order runs directly counter to an appealing vision put forward by Chuang tzu and others, who see Man's evaluating impulse as the antithesis of the natural spontaneity of Heaven-and-Earth. The *Mystery* supplies its readers with excellent reasons for not "seeing all things as equal":

1. Humans can be "like" Heaven-and-Earth in certain aspects but humans cannot hope to ever fully imitate the ultimate, unitary, and eternal *Mystery*.[280]
2. Like every other species that has sprung from undifferentiated chaos, humans are to congregate "according to type."[281]
3. Humans come together successfully, however, only when there is hierarchy, for without it strife exists in the world and in the mind.[282] It is our task as humans to bridge those yawning gaps, not to try to return to undifferentiated chaos.
4. Humans who lack a hierarchy of values can see no inherent reason to use Positions, Tools, or Virtue, since they have no particular predisposition for any specific action.[283] But without social hierarchy and prioritized values (for example, a sense of "gain" and "ruin" or "noble" and "base"), ritual in particular loses both its ability to inform our minds and its inducements to mold our conduct.[284]
5. Unless humans fully employ the great civilizing inventions of the sages, most[285] will be condemned at best to mediocrity and at worst to danger or death. Ordinary individuals need to utilize the sages' institutions if they are to improve upon the decidedly "mixed" endowment of good and evil impulses received at birth.[286]
6. The evaluating mind and sense perception, both part of the original endowment from Heaven, make it possible for humans to take full advantage of the good models provided by the sages.[287] To reject using the evaluating mind, then, is not only the height of folly but also an affront to Heaven.[288]

Therefore, one main theme of the *Mystery* can be summed up in the phrase, "Let there be no confusion [of ranks and values]."[289]

Contra the Immortality Seekers

By Yang Hsiung's time, many assumed that good deeds would lead to longevity.[290] A growing body of tradition, however, went much further, claiming that certain acts could ensure physical immortality. Yang Hsiung's utter disdain for such claims occasions his first statement on *ming*: "Time cannot be overcome."[291] Yang assumes that the phenomenal world is ruled by change: According to his argument, "Whatever has a birth must have a death; whatever has a beginning must have an end. This is the Way of Spontaneous Nature . . . [Immortality] is not something that human beings may achieve."[292] The sage "does not take the immortal as master; his techniques are different."[293] Even the ritual act, the greatest of human actions, must operate in the realm of the transitory, though its own eternal character remains undiminished. Therefore, human life cannot be extended by any practices or arts—especially those entailing a physical and mental separation from the community. To create such a gap "of no advantage"[294] is antithetical to ritual norms. It is true that immortality-seekers tend to congratulate themselves on their decision to devote their lives to a "real" (i.e., tangible) good, rather than an abstract good like morality. But, Yang replies, "to be ashamed that a single day goes unlived . . . is in reality [a kind of] death."[295] Since *ming* ultimately controls both length of lifespan and access to position, they risk health and wealth to obtain a goal that is really a function of luck.

Contra the Proponents of "Change as the Only Constant"

Prominent thinkers identified with several of the Hundred Schools operated on the assumption that change itself is the only constant in the physical and social world. This initial premise leads them to argue that man himself is "unnatural" when he tries to cling to one or more fixed principles of conduct. In one passage, Yang raises the rhetorical question, "Is there any stable pattern to virtue in changing times?"[296] He answers a resounding yes:

> Ages differ, events change,
> But the Way of Man never varies.
> The Way of Man is to make contact.[297]

In short, Yang pictures a world where the unchanging Mystery is the hidden source for all phenomenal change, just as ritual contact is the unchanging wellspring of all productive human activity. Since the constant is inherently more valuable than the transitory, adherence to ritual norms is more important than innovation, which Yang specifically condemns as dangerous.[298] Yang concedes a certain need for flexibility, since the eternal cosmic Way operates through change. Still, flexibility can never be a sufficient model of the Tao.

Contra Predestination

Certain thinkers denied that even a weak correlation exists between virtue and individual destiny. By a process none too clear to intellectual historians today, this view, attributed to the followers of Confucius early on in the pre-Han period, came to be associated with critics of the Confucians around Yang's time.[299] To those who believe that all is predetermined at birth (presumably in the original endowment of *ch'i* allotted to each individual or "in the stars"),[300] Yang insists that important human events are not entirely attributable to either Heaven or Man.[301] Yang shows that goodness does in fact provide what we would call a "statistically greater chance" of securing conventional rewards. In fact, as we have seen, Yang Hsiung takes some trouble to show that moral action will "pay" in a more reliable fashion than will other pursuits. Some, though not all, of these advantages can be explained prosaically as advantages that the larger cohesive social unit inherently holds over the isolated individual.

Contra the Mantic Specialists

Above all, Yang Hsiung wished to dispute the official view that moral behavior inevitably elicits its own reward, while immoral behavior always brings its own punishment. This idea, with its unquestionable appeal, had enjoyed a long history in Chinese tradition. Ultimately it could be traced back to the early Chou Decree of Heaven (*T'ien-ming*) doctrine, though it was only many centuries later that it came to be applied to the common people as well as to kings. Taken up by the Mohists (and possibly promoted by certain followers of Mencius under the banner of "establishing *ming*"),[302] it was propagated further in Yang Hsiung's own era by prominent portent specialists elaborating Yin/yang Five Phases correlative theory.[303] Yang Hsiung's theory of *ming* undercuts the three main ideas promoted by mantic technicians:

> That time cycles are predictable and therefore manipulatable.
> That the wise man takes Time as his main subject for study.
> That Goodness is always rewarded by material or physical goods.

To Yang Hsiung, the newest version of portent theory was probably the most objectionable. It portrayed the acquisition of a certain kind of technical expertise (watching the stars, calculating numbers for number magic, devising portent manuals based on ever more elaborated series of correlations, consulting almanacs for lucky and unlucky days) as a kind of moral virtue.[304] This is not the conduct of a true Confucian, Yang protested, but rather that of a "technician"; narrow specialization of any sort was an affront to the comprehensive nature of the Mystery. Also, any preoccupation with compiling data distracted the person from the more important task of "immersing the self" in the example of the perfect sages. This means that the specialist may comprehend the workings of Heaven-and-Earth, but cannot apprehend the ultimate mysteries of life.[305] Such technicians, Yang Hsiung disdained:

> The astrologers use Heaven to predict Man. [In contrast,] sages use Man to predict Heaven['s course]. What counts is Virtue, not the stars.[306]

In effect, Yang Hsiung intended to redirect human efforts to the study of Man (though he himself was an amateur astronomer).[307] In part, he relied on frequent reiterations of the traditional claim that the phenomena of transition are too subtle to be reduced to any empirical formula or theoretical model through mere technical expertise; the first stirrings of change are perceptible only to the divine intuition or illumination of the perfected sage[308] who has fully immersed himself in the complex interactions of cosmos and society. In part, Yang argued by using the basic precepts of correlative thought to refute the claims of the specialists. Moral goodness and temporal goods, he suggested, are not, logically speaking, categorical analogues; this is patently obvious since a variety of external factors may affect the rewards meted out to a man during his lifetime, but no external factor can affect man's potential for Virtue.[309]

Yang Hsiung exhibited considerable bravery in arguing against a one-to-one correspondence between Virtue and conventional success. In the first place, he was challenging the theory by which many high officials had made their reputation at court. This may well account for the treatment he suffered at the hands of certain prominent Confucians among his contemporaries, including Liu Hsin. Certainly, by Yang's own account, the *Mystery* "annoyed scholars."[310]

Far greater danger threatened, however, if Yang Hsiung's theory were to be construed as a direct challenge to the legitimacy of the Han throne, which claimed to rule by the ancient doctrine of Heaven's Decree and by the modern omen theories. Any challenge to the throne invariably ended in execution for the offender. Perhaps this accounts for Yang's reluctance to submit his work to the throne for inclusion in the royal library. Yang was inclined to attribute the success of Han as much to human efforts, as to the gods' protection, at a time of growing pretensions to divine favor by members of the royal circle.[311]

CONCLUSION

I suggest that the *Mystery* has endured because it divulges complex truths with disarming simplicity. Yang's arguments, once decoded, may appear commonsensical, even pedestrian, at points. But their wording is finely gauged so as to be sufficiently—but not overly—exact. In this, Yang generally eschews the technical language favored by the scholastics and composers of the apocrypha of his era.[312] It would be fair, then, to characterize Yang Hsiung's solution of the problem of *ming* as "easy." Yang selectively borrowed key terminology and compelling metaphors from all schools (as he readily admits) to devise a unified theory sufficient to answer all challenges.

Yang Hsiung's work, then, fulfills the various criteria for a new classic: It reanimates old teachings. It is internally consistent. It works to promote social order. It persuades men to return to the main tenets of early Confucianism, while addressing the great questions of man's place in the world order. On all these grounds, Yang Hsiung's *Mystery* is indisputably a Confucian classic. Not surprisingly, upon completion the *Mystery* was soon hailed as such by Yang Hsiung's younger contemporaries like Huan T'an. Doubtless this was in part because of its solution to the perennial problem of fate.

Many modern readers will want to know the answer to the question, Is it "original"?[313] Certainly what a man says gains significance—or finds its significance altered—according to the context within which he speaks. It is true that in the *Mystery* innovative points are set within the framework of the received body of Confucian teachings, rather than in conscious opposition to it. Originality, in fact, was never Yang Hsiung's fundamental goal. Traditional Chinese in general were prudently suspicious of innovation for its own sake.[314] Equally to the point, originality can never be the main goal for any conscientious interpreter of a sacred text in any tradition, ancient or modern, Western or Eastern. To assume that Yang Hsiung's philosophical borrowings make him a second-rate or derivative thinker is to apply anachronistic, inappropriate, and possibly meaningless standards to his text. Even though Yang's brilliant reformulation of the age-old problem of luck and virtue looked at the problem in a new way, Yang Hsiung's primary goal was always to reproduce the original intent of the sages as he understood them. Our job as faithful readers, then, is to fully appreciate the reasons by which Yang was accorded the coveted title of Confucian Master.

According to Yang Hsiung, models that are easy last long.[315] Yang Hsiung's writings have stood the test of time. When one of his rivals snidely predicted that the text of the *Mystery* would soon be relegated to the kitchen, where it would be used as scrap "to cover soy sauce pots," Yang Hsiung only "smiled and said nothing."[316] As successive generations of readers find many observations preserved in the *Mystery* fresh and ever new, perhaps Yang Hsiung has had the last laugh, after all.

Key Terms

THE FIVE CLASSICS OF CONFUCIANISM

The Five Classics of Confucianism are the *Book of Odes*, the *Documents*, the *Chronicles* (usually called the *Spring and Autumn Annals*), the *Book of Changes*, and the *Rituals*. (A sixth classic, devoted to music, is thought to have been lost or incorporated into one of the ritual texts.) The Classics are "Confucian" in two senses Confucius (551–479 B.C.) and his followers used some of them as texts for moral instruction, much as the Greek pedagogues once used Homer.[1] Also, tradition ascribed to Confucius the tasks of compiling, editing, and in some few cases composing the works in this repository of wisdom, although modern scholarship disputes the pious legend that Confucius had a hand in forming the collection. The interpretive problem shared by both early disciples and modern scholars alike is that the Five Classics contain extremely heterogeneous material of different subjects, styles, dates, and points of view. The *Odes* is a collection of songs and hymns that reflect everyday life in court and countryside during the period 800–600 B.C. The *Documents* purports to be a collection of archival materials that preserves important edicts and memorials outlining the responsibilities of the ruling elite. The *Chronicles* reads like a court diary for the rulers of the small state of Lu during the years 722–484 B.C.[2] A divination manual eventually converted for use as a philosophical treatise, the *Changes* attempts to reproduce through graphic symbols and attached texts the multiplicity of changing phenomena produced by the single cosmic Tao. And the three separate volumes of ritual texts are said to include some three thousands discrete rules of conduct, as well as a description of ideal government structure.

Confucian orthodoxy presumed that a single message underlay all Five Classics, despite the variety of materials included therein. But it should come as no surprise that scholars have often been frustrated in their attempts to find in this corpus a unified vision of the world. In the Han dynasty (206 B.C.–A.D. 220), an ongoing literary debate focused on inconsistencies in the Five Classics.[3] Nevertheless, during the two millennia from 134 B.C. to A.D. 1905, the Five Classics provided the basic curriculum for training in proper literary styles and served as the core material tested in civil service exams. From China, the influence of this collection eventually expanded into Japan, Korea, and Vietnam, so that it came to occupy for all East Asia a position roughly analogous to that of the Bible in the West.

ON *CH'I* 氣

The origin of the term is unknown. No Shang or early Chou graphs can be conclusively identified with the concept.[4] The character we now use for *ch'i* shows clouds of steam rising over cooked rice.[5] The graphic form suggests what bubbles or boils over, what fumes, what is agitated; it may also imply some kind of nourishment. In fact, the root meaning of *ch'i* appears to be "vapor" or "breath." Like early Greek, Indian, Latin, and Hebrew philosophy,[6] early Chinese belief presumes a "life breath" that vitalizes as it circulates through bodies or the air. Undifferentiated *ch'i* is the dynamic universal stuff out of which all the disparate things of the cosmos condense (at birth) and into which they dissolve (at death). Like breath, *ch'i* typically operates in rhythmic, floodlike pulses, as it alternates between inhalation (expansion) and exhalation (contraction) in regular cycles. Only bad *ch'i* is blocked or stagnant.[7]

Perhaps the closest English equivalent to *ch'i* is "vitality." As latent energy stored in the Tao, *ch'i* is undifferentiated, but as vital energy operating in the universe, *ch'i* is definable in quality and characteristic in its configurations.[8] By some mysterious process the originally undifferentiated *ch'i* makes for distinctive entities. *Ch'i* can be congealed or compacted in liquid and solid forms. *Ch'i* comes in different grades. The lowest grade of *ch'i* (called "muddy") leads to various malfunctions, including physical deformity, muddled thinking, and excessive desire. The purest refined *ch'i* (the "quintessential" or *ching*) is reserved for two kinds of light-giving entities: the luminous heavenly bodies and the enlightened minds of the sages. Very important, then, is the notion that *ch'i*, as the basic stuff that informs the entire cosmos and binds all humans to the rest of phenomenal existence in Heaven-and-Earth, precludes an absolute dividing line between humans and things. Understandably, the notion of *ch'i* has also worked against the development of the transcendent/immanent dichotomy presumed by many Western thinkers. At the same time, *ch'i* functions as the physical medium that allows sympathetic "mutual response" to take place between categorically related entities. Therefore, *ch'i* theory from earliest times has been preoccupied with the nature and significance of macrocosmic influences on microcosmic processes.[9]

In Master Yang Hsiung's time, the single term *ch'i* signified both the "material stuff" in continual process on Heaven-and-Earth and the underlying dynamism predisposing that stuff to assume specific form, though Sung neo-Confucians a millennium later were to draw a neater conceptual line between *li* ("internal principle") and *ch'i* ("material stuff").[10] We must remember that for the early Chinese, human *ch'i*, despite its obvious physicality,[11] had a definite moral dimension as well. In the properly functioning heart/mind, for example, *ch'i* is said to gather at "the spirit abode."[12] What's more, the will to do good is said to be "commander over the *ch'i*."

In the case of humans, a finite store of *ch'i* endowed at birth is somehow passed down from parents to the child. The birth of a human being, in effect, represents an accumulation of *ch'i*. Over the course of an individual lifespan, the *ch'i* tends to become less active. Physical overexertion may cause it to "block." Tension and stress equally frustrate it. Immoral acts also are said to "abuse the *ch'i*" to the degree that they engender shame, anxiety, and restlessness, for these emotional states produce certain physical symptoms, such as constricted breathing and palpitations of the heart.[13] Human beings, then, have some measure of control over the rate at which their original *ch'i* stagnates or is depleted. Balance in the mental and emotional spheres can be induced by the process dubbed "self-cultivation." Various techniques designed to retain (and ideally augment) the *ch'i*'s activity include both moral and physical "arts": moderation in daily habits, adjustment of posture, meditation as "inward training,"[14] habituation to goodness, and a calm acceptance of fate. The philosopher Mencius (?371–?289), for example, tells his disciples simply that "the way to make *ch'i*" is to "nourish it with integrity."

Master Han Fei (d. 233 B.C.) links the conservation of *ch'i*'s vitality with the acquisition of political power and material wealth.[15] Extending his imagery, I think of *ch'i* as operating like money in the bank: An individual can deposit or withdraw *ch'i* from his fund. What's more, he can inherit a sum or bequeath it to his descendants. Like great reserves of wealth, a great reserve of vital *ch'i* represents the potential to influence others. *Ch'i* thus provides the basis for the charismatic power of the virtuous man. All Confucians insist that each newborn is credited with sufficient *ch'i* to realize the full human potential for sagehood,[16] even though few are wise enough to exercise their innate capacities.

In summation, early Chinese thinkers view all cosmic change in terms of the dynamic process inherent in vital *ch'i*. *Ch'i* is substance, activity, and vitality.

YIN/YANG FIVE PHASES THEORY: CORRELATIVE THOUGHT

The Chinese cosmological system, which assumed its definite shape in China no later than the third century B.C.,[17] envisioned the world in terms of two interlocking systems: yin/yang and the Five Phases (often translated, less accurately, as the Five Agents or the Five Elements).[18] This is sometimes known as correlative thought, or categorical thinking.

According to the theory, there evolved out of primordial chaos one cosmic pattern with dual aspects known as yin and yang. All of phenomenal existence reflects this pattern. The myriad things can be categorized as either male or female, light or dark, day or night, hot or cold, superior or inferior, and so on. This duality is one of the constant norms of the universe, as illustrated by the regular alternation of day and night, of summer and winter. Yin and yang, though opposing, are also complementary in that one can never act independently of the other; the waxing of one invariably entails the waning of the other. Taking an example from nature, the summer solstice is the longest day of the year but, in another sense, it also marks the onset of winter; subsequently, the days grow ever shorter and colder until the winter solstice. The familiar figural representation of yin/yang emphasizes this fluid symbiotic relation. The curvilinear areas of dark and light enfold each other within a perfect circle that knows no beginning or end; the tiny seeds of each are discovered in the swelling contours of its opposite. At the culmination of one, its opposite is born, and on and on, in a constant process of advance and retreat, making and unmaking. In this way, "movement back" becomes "the Way of the Tao."[19] Men of virtue in studying the cosmic patterns infer from this that in victory lies defeat, and in humility, greatness.

Yin/yang may not seem so alien to us, since our language predisposes us to think in terms of positive/negative. But it is far more difficult for us to conceptualize cosmic process in terms of the Five Phases. The list of the Five Phases invariably includes Water, Fire, Wood, Metal, and Earth, though different orders of enumeration are preferred by various classical authorities. The Phases are essentially five different types of process. According to one early authority, "water goes down, fire goes up, wood is pliable," and so on.[20] Each Phase is said to "rule" (i.e., to predominate) a certain period of time (a dynasty, a season, a set of hours), before it gives way to the next phase. This connection with time resulted in conceptual overlays between systems of yin/yang and the Five Phases, as in the following chart (table 6).

Table 6.

Rising Yang		yields to	Rising Yin	
Wood	Fire	Earth	Metal	Water
Spring	Summer	transition	Autumn	Winter
East	South	Center	West	North
Green	Red	Yellow	White	Black

The Chinese soon set about classifying all known entities into groups of fives, constructing exhaustive lists which they hoped would elicit order from the seeming chaos of the world.[21] Yang Hsiung lists all the major correlations in his autocommentary chapter entitled "Numbers of the *Mystery.*"[22] By laws of sympathy and repulsion, things accounted as categorically alike (i.e., correlated with the same Phase) were said to be drawn to one another while things which were categorically different purportedly repelled each other. Again, according to the same theory, careful "inference by analogy from objects of the same kind" (*t'ui lei* 推類)

could facilitate the intuitive apprehension of all parts of the ineffable Tao by some form of indirect communication that is simply not possible through logical argument.[23]

The initial difficulty, of course, lay in determining the exact boundaries of each logical category, so that inferences were not mistakenly drawn. Generations of Chinese scholars, first the early Logicians and later the Han scholastics, devoted a great deal of time and energy to this problem. Due to the occasional rift between logic and language,[24] their first task was to establish formal rules of logic by which to discover the defining characteristics of each entity in the universe, so that essential attributes could be clearly distinguished from accidental attributes. For example, the Logicians determined that a horse must have one head, four legs, and a propensity to run, though it need not be red or black. The color of a horse, then, is a nonessential attribute, something that only accidentally subsists in a particular horse, but does not define the species. While it was relatively simple to agree upon fundamental definitions for animals, shapes, and inanimate objects, the true definition of human nature was a thornier problem, as it touched upon a host of problems which stubbornly resisted solution by the logical method:

> What is the proper definition of human nature?
> What is the proper sphere and existential significance of human activity?
> What can humans reasonably hope to accomplish in this life?

In the Han Confucian synthesis, then, the protoscientist's impulse towards categorization and the logician's search for orderly expression joined forces with the ethical concerns of the traditional scholar. Categorical thinking, inherently preoccupied with the relation of macrocosm to microcosm, came to be applied to many areas of inquiry, most significantly (1) portent theory; (2) the rectification of names; and (3) point-by-point analogies between the human body, the body politic, and the universe. We are familiar enough with body analogies; we often talk of "heads of state," for example. Portent theory and the rectification of names, however, may need some explanation for the modern reader.

Early Chinese portent theory assumed that the king as focus for his state exerts an influence for good or for ill upon those entities that are accounted his categorical analogues: Heaven, because it is high; the Big Dipper, as pivot for the sky; the father, as head of the household; and so on. More specifically, evildoing on the part of man—especially the "One Man," the ruler—provokes dislocations in his counterparts in the natural world. The good ruler, far from decrying these omens, welcomes them as reproofs of his erroneous ways sent by a caring Heaven, compelling him to reform.

To successfully apply categorical thought to happenings in the external world, it was incumbent upon the individual not only to locate himself in a parallel scheme of ethical categories (such as "ruler," "mother," "son," or "court advisor") but also to understand the ethical requirements of the assigned role he currently plays. This led many early Chinese thinkers, including Yang Hsiung, to conflate the earlier Confucian call for a "rectification of names" with the naturalists' talk of Five Phases theory. According to Confucius, greater linguistic precision was required for logical thought and effective action:

> If words are not correct, then speech does not conform [with what was intended]. And if speech does not conform with what was intended, then affairs cannot be completed [properly]. . . . Therefore, let a ruler be a ruler and a father be a father.[25]

For early Confucians, a person failing to fulfill his or her proper societal roles was accounted a "human portent" no less significant than a baleful prodigy in the skies above or earthquakes, floods, and droughts on earth.[26]

The early Chinese assumed that the transition from primordial chaos to civilized order represented successive stages of increasing differentiation. In effect, the Chinese argued that the world as they knew it had evolved by a process analogous to human attempts to identify, demarcate, and name significant geographical, political, social, and religious boundaries.[27] From this they concluded that there existed in the primordial Tao a divine basis for the development of the various human orders. Some Han thinkers even argued that humans engaged in the search for intrinsic categories can further or complete the cosmic processes through their continual ordering and reordering of categories.[28] This helps to explain why categorical thinking and correlative thought figure so largely in Chinese philosophical writings.

SELF-CULTIVATION

"Self-cultivation" refers to the arduous process by which the individual intent on virtue fulfills his own innate potential. This process consists in making second nature the traditional virtues (filial piety, good faith, consideration for others, and so on). For early Confucians, including Yang Hsiung, humans at birth have in their original endowment a host of contradictory impulses and desires, including those for food, sex, and community. Just as the artisan works jade to release its true beauty from rough-hewn pieces, any moral deficiency in the person is polished and carved away until an "elegant and accomplished gentleman"[29] emerges. Time and precision are needed for the process, but complete dedication to the Good is the chief requirement if human nature is to be refined.[30] There are many paths leading to self-cultivation, but the most important is emulation of worthy models past and present, followed by the study of the Five Confucian Classics. Once the noble lessons of various masters, living and dead, have been internalized, the perfectly civilized man emerges.

We can think of moral development as taking place in three successive stages, with self-cultivation the culmination. Stage 1 corresponds to the individual's first awareness of the mix of good and evil impulses, moral and physical desires, inherent in human nature at birth.[31] In Stage 2, the good impulses begin to predominate as a result of moral messages received from a variety of sources: the models presented by family members, oral teachings, and so on. Confucius implied that those who reached this stage of development might be accounted "educated":

> A young man's duty is to behave well to his parents at home and to his elders abroad, to be cautious in giving promises and punctual in keeping them, to have kindly feelings toward everyone, but seek the intimacy of the Good. . . . [As to one who acts thus,] others may say of him that he still lacks education, but I for my part should certainly call him an educated man.[32]

But Confucius also advised his disciples to go on to study the "polite arts" (poetry, archery, and music, for example) when they had energy to spare. In stage 3, then, the polite arts become tools by which members of the moral elite can hope to gain an exquisite sensitivity to the moral patterns embodied in ritual conduct. In effect, the acquisition of new skills reconfigures each individual's perception of structures, values, and imperatives. As the philosopher Hsün tzu remarked, "Once the proper arts are mastered, the mind will follow them."[33]

This notion may sound somewhat familiar to us, for it corresponds to our own own complex definitions of nobility. Still, the Chinese idea of nobility is not entirely equivalent to our own. The European tradition, embracing a more individualistic vision, tends to emphasize noble conduct as a laudable end in itself, while the early Chinese never tired of reminding us that personal self-cultivation is merely the first step in a process of forming harmonious communities in family, town, state, and empire. As Yang Hsiung writes, "Cultivate oneself so that one can later contact others."[34]

"CENTER HEART" (*CHUNG HSIN* 中心)

The phrase *chung hsin* dates back at least as early as the *Odes* (compiled sixth century B.C. from earlier materials).[35] In the *Odes*, the verb-object unit signifies "what centers the heart"; it compares in meaning with the adjective-noun syntactial unit *hsin chung* ("the center of the heart"), though it is strikingly more emphatic.

Since the truest emotions presumably reside at the deepest core of one's being, by a slight extension *chung hsin* came to be equated with the feelings that "are not put on for others to see,"[36] feelings that are completely genuine. After the heart was identified as the seat of the inborn conscience by Mencius, the same expression came to be loosely identified with the evaluating mind.[37] The *Mystery*, for example, insists that "inside there is a ruler."[38] At the same time, the characteristic activity of the evaluating mind is to center the self, in the sense of reestablishing an equilibrium free from emotional bias.[39] Only then can the mind's perceptions hope to "hit the mark,"[40] and so prompt the moral self unerringly.[41] For Yang Hsiung, the way of the sage lies in paying attention to the center heart, in centering the self, and in "hitting the mark" by the correct identification with Confucian tradition. Thus the *Mystery* employs all these associations for the phrase *chung hsin*.

RITUAL

A daughter bows low and eschews the use of her father's personal name. In solemn state ceremonies the emperor periodically offers sacrifices to various protective deities. Imperial ministers wear caps with seven silk pendants but junior officers are allowed only three. The aged and the pious are honored at annual feasts sponsored by the local magistrate. A professional spirit medium on the ridge of the roof calls out "Ho! come back!" to a departing soul, urging it to return to the world of light and life. At the marriage feast, fish are presented to the newly married couple as tokens of fertility. And the rich harmonies of bell and drum exert a powerful effect upon the worlds of Man and nature so that "the common people, the gods, beasts, and birds" happily join in the refrain.[42]

The Han Chinese would consider all these examples of the Confucian ritual system. Though Confucius seems to signify by the term ritual a narrow code of conduct expected of the gentleman, by Han times, the concept embraces many popular religious practices as well. In the Han, ritual meant exhaustive lists of detailed prescriptions governing all aspects of behavior (including physical gestures), as well as an unwritten code of good manners. Sumptuary regulations and taboos, and all manner of ceremonies, formal and informal, at every level of society, were included. At the heart of Han Confucianism lay this body of ritual practice, rather than a logical system. For ritual, as significant pattern, could work to clarify and cohere reality in at least four related ways: First, ritual patterns imitate the character of the unseen sacred Tao, upon which they are modeled. Second, ritual tradition represents the distilled—and therefore, supremely potent—wisdom of the sages throughout history. Third, ritual performance leads the individual to a new understanding about the place of the authentic self in society. Fourth, as if by magic,[43] the correct performance of ritual so pleases observers and co-participants that they devote their best efforts to forging communities, the quintessential human activity. At the heart of effective ritual lay the will to understand others by a process of "likening [others] to oneself," then allowing each his due.[44]

For ritual to prove effective, it was believed, its conventions have to become second nature so that inner disposition combines with outer form in a fitting manner that is understandable to all.[45] This characterization of ritual contrasts sharply with the modern tendency to equate the term with mechanical or repetitive conventions as opposed to the authentic. We can learn much from Han society, where ritual performed a variety of functions: The ritual act could teach even the unlettered the prevailing notions of social hierarchy and intimacy. By "securing men in their position,"[46] ritual also habituated men to the social virtues associated with their station. In effect, it became the glue binding the human community together, mitigating base desires and transmuting them into mutual consideration. At the same time, ritual presupposed the possibility for most, if not all, social acts to become emblematic of the divine cosmic order, thereby closing the gap between the sacred and the mundane.

THE MEANING OF *CHEN* 貞

The character *chen* appears repeatedly in the earliest examples of Chinese writing, the inscriptions on the Shang oracle bones (14th-11th c. B.C.), where it is one of the ten most common graphs. Read from the top down, the original graph is a phonetic compound composed of two parts: an upper portion meaning "to divine" (*pu*) over a lower portion meaning "tripod" (*ting*). (In the modern graph, the lower element meaning "cowrie" [*pei*] is apparently a corrupted form of the tripod graph.)[47] The tripod perhaps signifies both the sacred ritual character and the absolute reliability of the divination process[48] performed by oracle bone specialists at the cauldron site.[49] In any case, *chen* appears in the same word family as the graphs meaning "to determine" (*ting*) and "to make upright or correct" (*cheng*). From this we surmise that the early Chinese envisioned the divination process as one which determined through the testing process[50] the correct action as defined by the wishes of the gods.[51]

In the main text of the *Changes* (complied in late Western Chou), *chen* is the fifth most common graph, almost always occurring as a nominalized verb linked with the characters meaning "good luck" and "benefit" (*chi li*).[52] Apparently, the Shang preoccupation with correct action had subtly shifted in Chou divination to a focus on personal advantage. This focus so pervades the earliest layer of the *Changes* that one specialist has called it the single most important key to understanding the manual.[53] Since divination by that manual preceded all major undertakings at the court, *chen* was identified as the "trunk" (i.e., the reliable source and support) for all affairs.[54]

Several centuries before the composition of the *Mystery*, however, the character *chen* had come to have a wide range of associations beyond the divination process itself. As the root for the graph "favorable omen" (also *chen*),[55] by a kind of shorthand *chen* also often came to mean "good omen."[56] Other changes occurred around the time of Confucius (551–479 B.C.). Chinese language and culture began to exhibit an ethical elaboration and a concomitant deemphasis on sacrifice and divination.[57] Perhaps because young, umblemished animals were offered in sacrifice at the time of divination, *chen* came to be used to describe the males and females of any species who had not yet mated.[58] Particularly with regard to human females, it therefore meant "chaste."[59] In the case of men, it also meant "perseverance" in service of the Right,[60] unswerving loyalty to parents or patrons, and laudable consistency, though early texts were careful to distinguish an unfailing determination to perform one's duty from blind fidelity or stubborn consistency.[61] *Chen* was used as a synonym for "prudence" and "rectitude," since both of these terms imply reliability.[62] In short, *chen* came to stand for gentlemanly conduct exemplifying "perfect correspondence between words and deeds"[63] or absolute alignment with the cosmic norms. Suggested antonyms for *chen* are "out of true," "falsity,"[64] "filthiness," "taint," and "corruptibility" (either physical or moral).

Since Chinese tradition emphasizes that correct behavior can be determined only by reference to one's current role in society, *chen* seems to convey for Yang Hsiung the idea of proper alignment with the prevailing cosmic norms.[65] As Yang writes in prefatory remarks to the *Mystery*, "Only after great *chen* can one *t'ung* ["make it through"]" to establish the three triadic realms of Heaven-Earth-Man, as well as "understand" the cosmic processes.[66] Careless acts liable to land one in trouble are the opposite of *chen*.[67] Depending upon context, I use a variety of terms to translate this graph, including "proven good," "tried and true," "good omen," "stability," "right orientation," and "propriety."

On the Style of the Book

We still know very little about the origin and forms of early Chinese poetry. Only a few samples have come down to us, notably the *Odes* (compiled ca. sixth century B.C. from earlier materials) and the "Songs of Ch'u" (some dated as early as the second country B.C.).[68] Neither do we know the sources of Yang Hsiung's own poetic style. It is safe to say, though, that the core text of the *Mystery* (the nine Appraisals attached to each of the eighty-one Heads) generally borrows a classic form modeled on the ancient *Odes*: rhyming couplets of eight characters (four syllables per line), with each line typically conveying one complete image.[69] Certain lines in the *Mystery*, however, exhibit greater variation in length, with lines ranging from one to six characters. This may have been Yang's way of alluding to the irregular lengths of the Line texts found in the *Book of Changes*.[70] Clearly, Yang's style was affected by the philosophical prototype he chose for the *Mystery*. For example, there is no case where the closing particle *yeh* is used in the Line texts in the *Changes*, but the later "Image" texts consistently use the particle. Faithful to the model, Yang Hsiung's Appraisals, which correspond to the Line texts, do not close with *yeh*, though the Fathomings, Yang's counterpart to the Images, do.

With very few characters defining a typical image, Yang Hsiung's poetry shows extreme compression. Pronouns, demonstratives, adjectives, and adverbs are used sparingly. Simple nouns and verbs predominate. This style of terse simplicity is strikingly different from his earlier prose-poems written for the court, in which long rhythmic passages of dialogue and description employ elaborate parallelism and juxtaposition, extensive enumeration, mythological devices, and striking hyperbole to virtuoso effect. So lean is Yang Hsiung's *Mystery* poetry that if it were not for the frequent rhymes and rhythmic scansion of each line, the Appraisals could be taken for plain, expository speech. No doubt Yang Hsiung intended to impart to his work that air of elegant restraint associated with his antique models.[71] Still, the poetry of the *Mystery* is far from easy to read. There are three main reasons for this: First, the *Mystery* continually evokes whole clusters of meanings in each carefully chosen phrase. Often the full significance of an allusion has been lost, leaving the reader correspondingly impoverished. Two additional problems stem from the nature of early Chinese language itself. Classical Chinese, unlike the Indo-European languages, is what linguists call an "isolating language." In brief, this means that its units are invariable so that their interrelationship is indicated solely by relative positions and connective words, rather than by a clear, well-developed morphology. The same syllabic unit *mu*, for example, can mean "a mother," "the mother," "the mother's," "motherly," "to consider or act as mother," "to be mothered," "mothering," and so on. Also, classical Chinese indicates gender, tense, or number generally by the addition of extra characters (such as those for "female" or "male," "yesterday" or "tomorrow," "ten" or "ten thousand") as modifiers or by specialized graphs (the "particles"). Chinese poetry aims for striking power through a lapidary style. Thus, it tends to omit all redundancies and particles lest the brief lines seem limp or prosaic. In most cases, Yang Hsiung manages to make the compression work *for* him. At its best, his poetry in the *Mystery* is characterized by a measure of fruitful ambiguity, in which each line, even each graph, calls up several different associations. Through such intentional ambiguity Yang Hsiung successfully recreates the multiple layers of meaning that had been imposed on the *Yi ching* text. Rhymes and puns in the *Mystery* serve this polysemy well for they direct the reader's attention to important yet unexpected associations that go beyond the usual linguistic pairings of obvious antonyms and synonyms.[72] Admittedly, at its worst, Yang's poetry verges on the obscure, yet even this vagueness may reflect Yang's decision to use veiled language when touching upon controversial matters.

This ambiguity, of course, can seldom be recreated in English translation because English is an inflected language that embeds highly specific references to gender, number, and case in its nouns, as well as tense and mood in its verbs. The translator is forced to make choices. I have tried above all to preserve a sense of the spareness and seeming simplicity of Yang's poetry, in hopes that the *Mystery* will captivate new generations of readers.

Glossary for the Introductory Sections

NAMES OF PEOPLE

(NOTE: Characters for book titles and authors included in the Bibliography are not repeated here.)

Chang Heng　　張衡

Ch'en Pen-li　　陳本禮

Chiao Kan　　焦贛

Ching Fang　　京房

Chou Tun-yi　　周敦頤

Chu Hsi　　朱熹

Chuang Tsun　　莊遵

Chuang tzu　　莊子

Emperor Ai　　哀帝

Emperor Ch'eng　　成帝

Han Fei　　韓非

Ho Yen　　何宴

Hou Pa　　侯芭

Hsün tzu　　荀子

Hsün Yüeh　　荀悅

Huan T'an　　桓譚

Juan Hsiao-hsü　　阮孝緒

Juan Yüan　　阮元

K'ung An-kuo　　孔安國

Lao tzu　　老子

Liu Hsiang　　劉向

Liu Hsin　　劉歆

Lu K'ai　　陸凱

Mencius　　孟子

Meng Hsi　　孟喜

75

Introduction

Pan Ku   班固

Pao Hsien   包咸

Ssu-ma Kuang   司馬光

Su Hsün   蘇洵

Sung Chung   宋衷

Tsou Yen   鄒衍

Tung Chung-shu   董仲舒

Tung Hsien   董賢

Wang Ch'ung   王充

Wang Mang   王莽

Yang Hsiung   揚雄

Yang Liang   楊倞

Yen Chün-p'ing   嚴君平

CONCEPTS AND TERMS

ai jih ("love the day")   愛日

ch'ang ("constant")   常

chang chü ("chapter and verse commentary")   章句

chen (see Key Terms section)   貞

chen ("favorable omen")   禎

cheng kua ("standard hexagrams")   正卦

cheng ming ("rectification of names")   正名

ch'eng ("integrity")   誠

ch'i (see Key Terms)   氣

chi hsiung ("good luck and ill")   吉凶

chi li ("good luck and benefit")   吉利

chia ("Families" or "house")   家

ch'ien ("immerses")   潛

chih ("practical wisdom")　智

chih ("to know or to understand")　知

chin ("to advance")　進

chih ming ("to know [or understand] *ming*)　知命

ching ("classic" or "canon")　經

ching ("quintessence")　精

ching ("respect")　敬

chou ("Provinces")　州

chung ("center," "centrality")　中

fang ("Regions")　方

fu ("prose poem")　賦

fu huo ("good fortune/bad; morality/immorality")　福禍

hsiao hsi kua ("waxing and waning hexagrams")　消息卦

hsin ("heart/mind")　心

hsin ("good faith")　信

hsing ("human nature")　性

hsing ("stars")　星

hsiu ch'iu ("praise and blame")　休咎

hsüan ("Mystery," "mystery")　玄

hsüan hsüeh ("Mystery Learning")　玄學

hua ("transformation")　化

kua ch'i ("hexagram/solar period")　卦氣

kung ("justice")　公

li ming ("establish fate")　立命

ling ("order")　令

ling ("numinous")　靈

ming ("Decree," "decree")　命

mu ("mother")　母

ni ("to estimate")　擬

pei ("cowry")　貝

pu ("Departments")　部

pu ("to divine by turtle")　卜

shen ("divine")　神

shen ("expansion")　伸

shih ("time," "opportunity")　時

shih ("diviner's board")　式

shou ("Head text")　首

shu ("consideration")　恕

shu chi ("pivot")　樞機

szu ("private")　私

t'ai ch'u ("Grand Inception")　太初

Tao　道

T'ien　天

T'ien jen kan ying ("Mutual Interaction between Heaven and Man")　天人感應

T'ien ming ("Decree of Heaven")　天命

ting ("tripod")　鼎

ting ("to settle")　定

tsa ("mixed")　雜

tsan ("Appraisal")　贊

ts'e ("Fathoming")　測

t'ui lei ("inference by analogy")　推類

tzu shou ("preserve oneself")　自守

wan wu ("myriad things")　萬物

wu ch'ang ("inconstant")　無常

wu hsing ("Five Phases")　五行

wu wei ("non-purposive activity")　無為

Glossary for the Introductory Sections

yin/yang   陰陽

yeh (a particlc)   也

yu ("to be on the point of")   猶

yü pu yü, ming yeh   遇不遇命也

Translation of the *T'ai hsüan ching*

LIST OF TETRAGRAMS

No. 1. Center / Chung 中 ☰ Dec. 22–Dec. 26 (A.M.)	No. 7. Ascent / Shang 上 ☴ Jan. 18–Jan. 22 (A.M.)	No. 13. Increase / Tseng 增 ☵ Feb. 14–Feb. 18 (A.M.)
No. 2. Full Circle / Chou 周 ☰ Dec. 26. (P.M.)–Dec. 30	No. 8. Opposition / Kan 干 ☵ Jan. 22 (P.M.)–Jan. 26	No. 14. Penetration / Jui 銳 ☵ Feb. 18 (P.M.)–Feb. 22
No. 3. Mired / Hsien 礥 ☷ Dec. 31–Jan. 4 (A.M.)	No. 9. Branching Out / Shu 狩 ☷ Jan. 27–Jan. 31 (A.M.)	No. 15. Reach / Ta 達 ☳ Feb. 23–Feb. 27 (A.M.)
No. 4. Barrier / Hsien 閑 ☳ Jan. 4 (P.M.)–Jan. 8	No. 10. Defectiveness / Distortion / Hsien 羨 ☳ Jan. 31 (P.M.)–Feb. 4	No. 16. Contact / Chiao 交 ☵ Feb. 27 (P.M.)–Mar. 3
No. 5. Keeping Small / Shao 少 ☴ Jan. 9–Jan. 13 (A.M.)	No. 11. Divergence / Ch'a 差 ☴ Feb. 5–Feb. 9 (A.M.)	No. 17. Holding Back / Juan 覒 ☴ Mar. 4-Mar. 8 (A.M.)
No. 6. Contrariety / Li 戾 ☷ Jan. 13 (P.M.)–Jan. 17	No. 12. Youthfulness / T'ung 童 ☵ Feb. 9 (P.M.)–Feb. 13	No. 18. Waiting / Hsi 傒 ☷ Mar. 8 (P.M.)–Mar. 12

No. 19. Following / Ts'ung 從 Mar. 13–Mar. 17 (A.M.)	No. 28. Change / Keng 更 Apr. 22 (P.M.)–Apr. 26	No. 37. Purity / Ts'ui 睟 June 2–June 6 (A.M.)
No. 20. Advance / Chin 進 Mar. 17 (P.M.)–Mar. 21	No. 29. Decisiveness / Tuan 斷 Apr. 27–May 1 (A.M.)	No. 38. Fullness / Sheng 盛 June 6 (P.M.)–June 10
No. 21. Release / Shih 釋 Mar. 22–Mar. 26 (A.M.)	No. 30. Bold Resolution / Yi 毅 May 1 (P.M.)–May 5	No. 39. Residence / Chü 居 June 11–June 15 (A.M.)
No. 22. Resistance / Ke 格 Mar. 26 (P.M.)–Mar. 30	No. 31. Packing / Chuang 裝 May 6–May 10 (A.M.)	No. 40. Law/Model / Fa 法 June 15 (P.M.)–June 19
No. 23. Ease / Yi 夷 Mar. 31–Apr. 4 (A.M.)	No. 32. Legion / Chung 衆 May 10 (P.M.)–May 14	No. 41. Response / Ying 應 June 20–June 24 (A.M.)
No. 24. Joy / Le 樂 Apr. 4 (P.M.)–Apr. 8	No. 33. Closeness / Mi 密 May 15–May 19 (A.M.)	No. 42. Going to Meet / Ying 迎 June 24 (P.M.)–June 28
No. 25. Contention / Cheng 爭 Apr. 9–Apr. 13 (A.M.)	No. 34. Kinship / Ch'in 親 May 19 (P.M.)–May 23	No. 43. Encounters / Yü 遇 June 29–July 3 (A.M.)
No. 26. Endeavor / Wu 務 Apr. 13 (P.M.)–Apr 17	No. 35. Gathering / Lien 斂 May 24–May 28 (A.M.)	No. 44. Stove / Tsao 竈 July 3 (P.M.)–July 7
No. 27. Duties / Shih 事 Apr. 18–Apr. 22 (A.M.)	No. 36. Strength / Ch'iang 彊 May 28 (P.M.)–June 1	No. 45. Greatness / Ta 大 July 8–July 12 (A.M.)

No. 46. Enlargement / K'uo	No. 55. Diminishment / Chien	No. 64. Sinking / Ch'en
廓 ䷀	減 ䷀	沈 ䷀
July 12 (P.M.)–July 16	Aug. 22–Aug. 26 (A.M.)	Oct. 1 (P.M.)–Oct. 5
No. 47. Pattern / Wen	No. 56. Closed Mouth / Chin	No. 65. Inner / Nei
文 ䷀	唫 ䷀	内 ䷀
July 17–July 21 (A.M.)	Aug. 26 (P.M.)–Aug. 30	Oct. 6–Oct. 10 (A.M.)
No. 48. Ritual / Li	No. 57. Guardedness / Shou	No. 66. Departure / Ch'ü
禮 ䷀	守 ䷀	去 ䷀
July 21 (P.M.)–July 25	Aug. 31–Sept. 4 (A.M.)	Oct. 10 (P.M.)–Oct. 14
No. 49. Flight / T'ao	No. 58. Closing In / Hsi	No. 67. Darkening / Hui
逃 ䷀	翕 ䷀	晦 ䷀
July 26–July 30 (A.M.)	Sept. 4 (P.M.)–Sept. 8	Oct. 15–oct. 19 (A.M.)
No. 50. Vastness/Wasting / T'ang	No. 59. Massing / Chü	No. 68. Dimming / Meng
唐 ䷀	聚 ䷀	瞢 ䷀
July 30 (P.M.)–Aug. 3	Sept. 9–Sept. 13 (A.M.)	Oct. 19 (P.M.)–Oct. 23
No. 51. Constancy / Ch'ang	No. 60. Accumulation / Chi	No. 69. Exhaustion / Ch'iung
常 ䷀	積 ䷀	窮 ䷀
Aug. 4–Aug. 8 (A.M.)	Sept. 13 (P.M.)–Sept. 17	Oct. 24–Oct. 28 (A.M.)
No. 52. Measure / Tu	No. 61. Embellishment / Shih	No. 70. Severance / Ke
度 ䷀	餙 ䷀	割 ䷀
Aug. 8 (P.M.)–Aug. 12	Sept. 18–Sept. 22 (A.M.)	Oct. 28 (P.M.)–Nov. 1
No. 53. Eternity / Yung	No. 62. Doubt / Yi	No. 71. Stoppage / Chih
永 ䷀	疑 ䷀	止 ䷀
Aug. 13–Aug 17 (A.M.)	Sept. 22 (P.M.)–Sept. 26	Nov. 2–Nov. 6 (A.M.)
No. 54. Unity / K'un	No. 63. Watch / Shih	No. 72. Hardness / Chien
昆 ䷀	視 ䷀	堅 ䷀
Aug. 17 (P.M.)–Aug. 21	Sept. 27–Oct. 1 (A.M.)	Nov. 6 (P.M.)–Nov. 10

No. 73. Completion / Ch'eng	No. 76. Aggravation / Chü	No. 79. Difficulties / Nan
成 ䷕	劇 ䷕	難 ䷕
Nov. 11–Nov. 15 (A.M.)	Nov. 24 (P.M.)–Nov. 28	Dec. 8–Dec. 12 (A.M.)

No. 74. Closure / Chih	No. 77. Compliance / Hsün	No. 80. Laboring / Ch'in
閡 ䷕	馴 ䷕	勤 ䷕
Nov. 15 (P.M.)–Nov. 19	Nov. 29–Dec. 3 (A.M.)	Dec. 12 (P.M.)–Dec. 16

No. 75. Failure / Shih	No. 78. On the Verge / Chiang	No. 81. Fostering / Yang
失 ䷕	將 ䷕	養 ䷕
Nov. 20–Nov. 24 (A.M.)	Dec. 3 (P.M.)–Dec. 7	Dec. 17–Dec. 21 (A.M.)

Intercalary Heads

踦 嬴

Dec. 21 (P.M.) and
Leap Year Feb. 29

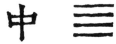

Correlates with Heaven's Mystery;
Yang; *the phase Water; and the* Yi
ching *Hexagram no. 61, Good
Faith at Center; the sun enters the
Drawn Ox constellation, 1st
degree; the dipper points due
north; the musical note is C; the
Winter Solstice solar period begins
with Appraisal 1*

Chung
No. 1. Center
December 22–December 26 (a.m.)

HEAD: Yang *ch'i*, unseen, germinates in the Yellow Palace. Good faith in every case resides at the center.

Though this tetragram is correlated with the Water phase, the Yellow Palace, apparently a term for the shadowy underground realm where the spirits of the dead reside,[1] is associated in the cycle of Five Phases with Earth. Earth symbolizes what is strong and stable; water, what exerts power through ceaseless movement. This tetragram, then, like a still center, represents the balance point between opposing impulses from which creative activity emanates. The second line, with its reference to "good faith" at "center," alludes to the title of the corresponding *Changes* Hexagram no. 61. By a pun, however, the last sentence of the Head text can also read, "Expansion in every case resides at center." By that reading, the Head also refers to the mysterious process by which future events become present phenomena, displacing phenomena into the past and providing the momentum for cyclic processes.[2] As the "Great Commentary" to the *Changes* describes it:

> As the sun moves on, the moon comes. As the moon moves on, the sun comes. As sun and moon impel each other, light is produced. . . . What moves on, contracts. What comes, expands (*hsin*). As what contracts and what expands influence each other, what furthers [activity] is produced.[3]

The first nine Appraisals of Tetragram 1 refer to the first 4 1/2 days immediately following the Winter Solstice. Within that brief period of time, yang begins its struggle to emerge from the domination of yin. Patterns set in these first nine Appraisal texts recapitulate the entire annual cycle covered by all eighty-one tetragrams. At the same time, this "nested" cycle of nine Appraisals stands not only for cosmic process but also for the cycle of human action from initial contemplation to final outcome.

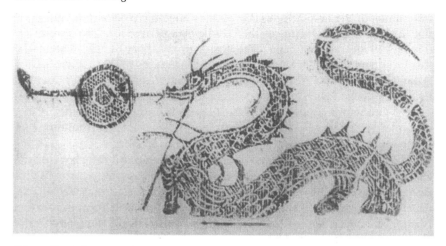

Figure 3. A dragon with a ceremonial jade pi *circlet. Illustration taken from a rubbing from a stone relief, excavated from Hsin-chin, Szechwan (now in the Szechwan Provincial Museum), rubbing 50.5 × 109.5 cm.*

Within the larger cycle of nine Appraisals, smaller cycles operate. Each group of three Appraisals within the nine is a world in miniature that reflects a continuum from incipience to maturation to decline, each with its assigned place in the ninefold scheme. The first three Appraisals, representing the phase of commencement, move from the dark language of nondifferentiation (Appraisal 1) through the polarization of yin/yang within the darkness (Appraisal 2) to the precisely and positively described image of the emergent dragon (Appraisal 3). No image of decline is as yet germane. The second set of three Appraisals, concerned with culmination, begins with a temporally vague, abstract picture of responsiveness and obstruction (Appraisal 4), witnesses the noonday emblem on which the larger series of nine Appraisals pivots (Appraisal 5), and ends with a concrete lunar image of decline played off against renewal (Appraisal 6). The final triplet is entirely related to waning; there is no room at all for new growth. Still, the static situation at first may justly be characterized in terms of ripeness and nurture (Appraisal 7). The central Appraisal 8 provides a picture of decay in which ambiguity gives way to inversion. The last situation (Appraisal 9) dramatically evokes dissolution. But as dissolution ends the larger cycle, various associations imply the eventual beginning of a new one.

The Appraisals work, then, somewhat like a Chinese puzzle. Not only do we find cycle fitted within cycle, but one clue after another ties the series of Appraisals to every microcosm of importance to man. The

Fathoming of the first Appraisal presumes human participation, alongside that of Heaven and Earth, in the cosmic Tao. There are also several reminders of the ages of man. The first Appraisal recalls the womb; the third, the young adult's entry into an official career; the fifth, culminating accomplishment; the seventh, mature stability; and the ninth, natural death in old age. The symbology of administration appears in the apposition of punishment and virtue, as well as in allusions to attributes of the exemplary ruler (in the fifth position) and to his vassals (surrounding him in the fourth and sixth positions correlated with yin *ch'i*).

The appraisals abound in correlates to yin/yang and in echoes of the *Book of Changes*. Images of darkness and moon (associated with Water in Appraisals 1 and 6), of the dragon (Wood, 3) of centering (Earth, 5), and of Fire (Appraisal 7) reflect the significance of each Appraisal in the cosmogonic succession of the Five Phases. Yang Hsiung summarizes the dominant meaning of the Head entitled Center with the aphorism "Integrity, when it occupies the inner part, is preserved in the center."[4] The first Head and its Appraisals, read in the light of Yang's own commentaries, lead the reader to recognize integrity (*ch'eng*) as the central virtue precisely because of its all-encompassing nature. Integrity not only establishes the unity of man with the visible world of Heaven-and-Earth, but it also puts him in touch with the primal Mystery hidden at the cosmic origin (Appraisal 1). The individual may easily fail to attain this integrity if he relies on specious absolutes—for example, the polarization of yin/yang. He will also fail if he is mired in the moral ambiguity (Appraisal 2) that results when an individual disregards his sacred duty to make names (=conceptual categories) correspond to realities (Appraisal 8). Because the petty man ignores the Mystery within him, he is obstructed in both his private desires and public ambitions (Appraisals 4, 6). In contrast, the aspirant to sagehood devotedly imitates the universal, unchanging patterns, and so is led to decisions that make his activities effective (Appraisals 3, 5, 7).

> App. 1: Primal oneness encompasses all.
> It is profound.
> Fath. 1: Primal oneness, all encompassing
> Means: This is the correct state of contemplation.

"Primal oneness"[5] is a set phrase describing the initial cosmic state of nondifferentiation "prior to the appearance of forms."[6] In early Chinese cosmogonies, the world we experience emerges from this initial state through various stages of separation until the perceptible world finally unfolds. The term primal oneness was also associated with both the *axis mundi* and Chuang tzu's Emperor of the Center, who died when the primal unity of his body was violated.[7] The analogous state to primal oneness in what we might call moral psychology is the initial centering of human inwardness that leads to conscious, responsible action. The associations of primal oneness with centering, the theme of this tetragram, are thus multiple.

The term "all-encompassing" is borrowed from the *Chuang tzu*, where it describes that power of the Way acting through the sage that lets him see beyond surface differentiation to the fundamental unity of things, so that he can "merge the myriad things and make them one."[8] The same phrase, however, is glossed by an early commentator as, "in the shape of the earth"; evidently he takes it to mean "swollen and vast."[9] According to the "spheroidal heaven" (*hun-t'ien*) theory of cosmology promoted by Yang, the earth (hemispherical or discoidal in different versions) was centered within the sky like the yolk of an egg. Thus it is natural to juxtapose the phrases all encompassing, with its associations with Earth, and primal oneness, which implies the sky and the cosmic axis.

"Profound," of course, is synonymous with "mystery" insofar as it indicates the creative, yet indeterminate origins of Heaven and Earth, as well as the psychic center within which the sage finds the germs of his future actions. The same character, for obvious reasons, can mean "obscure." The commentator Fan Wang emphasizes the cosmological meaning of the term: In the sky's daily rotation about the central earth, the sun at night is hidden below the horizon and "thus is called 'obscure.'"[10] Yang Hsiung, as his own "Elaboration" autocommentary shows, is not concerned with establishing a single level of meaning. Instead, he would emphasize the strong connection between the Tao, the unity of the cosmos, and the sage's centeredness:

> The worthy man is one with Heaven and Earth [insofar as his] thoughts embrace the many kinds [of being]. [His thoughts] unite them at center but they have not yet taken form outside.[11]

Ssu-ma Kuang fleshes out this theme in his commentary:

> "Primal oneness" is the magnitude of the sky's [starry] images; "all-encompassing" is the breadth of the earth's form. That the heart and mind of man should be able to fathom the immensity of sky and earth surely bespeaks divinity in the operations of heart and mind. Appraisal 1 marks the beginning of contemplation. The heart and mind of the noble man can probe deep and far. He perceives, when he looks up, all that is divine in the sky and, when he looks down, all that is numinous on earth. Neither sky nor earth, nor any thing, can hide their truth from him. Because [at the stage in the process symbolized by Center] his contemplation is not yet formed, it is called "obscure."

The sage is the mediator, discerning the patterns, at once metaphysical and moral, of sky and earth. These perceptions, as the "Great Commentary" to the *Changes* tells us, are the source of the patterns by which the sage orders himself and society.[12] Ssu-ma Kuang does not do violence to the text when he sees in this first Appraisal of the *Mystery* a synthesis of associations that affirms and celebrates human capacities.

In the Fathoming, the "correct [state]" (*chen*)[13] refers to one of the mantic formulae found in the earliest strata of the *Changes*. According to Han interpretations, the term describes the faithful adherence of the sage to the Way of the ancients. By virtue of this orientation, the sage participates in the integrity of the Tao. *Chen* also points to a quality of the cosmos, the dynamic balance that makes its processes equable in every sense. As Fan Wang's cosmological interpretation puts it, the Appraisal is saying that the "revolutions in the sky entirely accord with 'correctness.' "[14]

> App. 2: Spiritual forces war in darkness,
> Deploying yin and yang for battle.
> Fath. 2: Spirits warring in the dark
> Means: There good and evil are juxtaposed.

The earliest texts in China depict the cosmos in terms of binary oppositional phases symbolized by yellow (presumably the light of day) and black (the dark). This helps us to understand the *Changes* imagery, "Dragons battle in the wilds, their blood black and yellow."[15] This oddly anthropomorphic sentiment reflects a strong imbalance in the forces of yin and yang *ch'i*, associated with dark and light respectively.[16] In the Center tetragram, for example, we see solid lines occupying every position in the graphic symbol. Yin and yang, then, challenge each other at a particular point in the cycle when the imbalance is strongest. As the forces for good and evil confront one another in the darkness of primal origin, of midwinter, and of the hidden recesses of the heart and mind, the separation of polarities out of the indeterminate Mystery is bound to be premature and inauspicious.

In the Five Phases correlations, the image of warfare is related to Fire, the patron phase of this Appraisal, which has succeeded the Water found in the preceding Appraisal. Appraisals are alternately yang (day, auspicious) and yin (night, inauspicious) in relation to each other. Yang Hsiung explains this by alternating references to the state of mind of the noble man (aligned with yang) and the petty man (aligned with yin). The pitched battle of Appraisal 2 takes place, he tells us, because "the petty man's heart and mind are undiscriminating," tending to segregate what should be undifferentiated during the first Head's dominance. By contrast, "The worthy man by his actions unites the many kinds [of being]."[17]

> App. 3: The dragon emerges at the center,
> Its head and tail stretch forth,
> Fit for use.
> Fath. 3: Dragon emerging at center
> Means: It reveals its creativity.

Few Chinese images are as rich in associations as that of the dragon. The first Chinese dictionary (ca. A.D. 100) describes the dragon as "chief among the scaly creatures. It can be dark or brilliant, small or large, short or long. At the vernal equinox, it ascends to the sky; at the autumnal equinox, it hides in the deeps."[18] The dragon is protean and timely; it marks two critical points in the annual cycle by its ascent and descent. Thus it is associated with virile yang *ch'i*, with the East and Spring, and with the growth of the myriad things on earth.

In the first hexagram of the *Changes*, a sequence of dragon images portrays the exemplary man in reclusion (the unseen dragon in line 1), in office (the dragon in the fields in line 2), and at the summit of political power (the dragon flying in the sky in line 5). At least this is the way orthodox commentators have explained these enigmatic texts. They argue that the dragon symbolizes the noble man who fulfills his potential by conforming to the present situation.

The dragon found in Appraisal 3, when compared with these pictures of the dragon in the *Changes*, is neither entirely hidden nor fully apparent. With the separation of nascent yang from the primal darkness, the dragon has emerged from the waters barely enough to reveal its head and tail. Yet even before the dragon appears in its full glory, it is recognized as "fit for use," in clear contrast to the hidden dragon in the *Changes*.[19] Why? Another Chinese classic defines "usefulness" in terms of adherence to ritual.[20] Through ritual, Yang's exemplar keeps his integrity (his "exact center"), despite the ups and downs of fortune. Yang equally emphasizes the importance of timeliness:

> What is meant by "dragon emerging at center"? It says that the characteristic virtue of the dragon is apparent for the first time. If the yin has not reached its highest point, then yang will not be born. If disorder has not reached its highest point, then virtue will not assume form. The noble man cultivates virtue, thereby awaiting the proper moment [to act]. He does not rise up before the proper moment, nor draw back after it has already passed. Whether in action or at rest, whether obscure or eminent, he does not stray from the norm. Can this be said of anyone but the noble man? Thus "head and tail are fit for use."[21]

This is Yang's answer to one of the great questions of his time. The best minds of China had accepted the Confucian ideal of government service, but in the declining days of Western Han most men of principle could look forward, if not to rejection, then to blocked careers like Yang's own, or even to disgrace or dismissal. In this Appraisal Yang sees political chaos not as a permanent state but as a precursor to constructive yang activity. His exemplar, in keeping to the exact center,[22] never fails to serve as a norm for others in a social order ideally based upon moral example. Personal virtue is charismatic; eventually it turns disorder into order. Yang Hsiung saw in the disorder of his time a need not for superficial pacification of society ("law and order"), but the reinstitution of a stable, hierarchic society ruled by a moral elite. Once again, Yang appears to be making a play on one word: the dragon's tail is both "truly" (*hsin*) fit for use and "stretched out" (*shen*), ready for action. (For the same pun, see the first Head text above.)

In cosmogony, Appraisal 3 of this tetragram corresponds to a third stage of existence. Following primal chaos (stage 1) and the separation of yin and yang *ch'i* (stage 2), the first emergence of forms (stage 3) foreshadows the proliferation of phenomena in the world as we know it (stage 4).

> App. 4: Lowliness, emptiness, nothingness, compliance—
> Despite a full portion of nature and Decree,
> He is still blocked.
> Fath. 4: Blocked from the lowly and empty
> Means: He cannot receive in full.

Classical Taoism argues that the Way is to be found everywhere, even in the lowest forms of life like "the piss and the dung."[23] The Confucians, of course, object to this provocative characterization of the Way, since they prefer to define it as the paradigm for all patterned behavior. These two rival traditions, however, have more in common than is generally recognized, presumably because both draw from a still more ancient matrix of belief. The two traditions, for example, place equal emphasis on modesty as a necessary attribute of the superior man. The *Analects* explicitly contrasts noble self-deprecation with the pretensions of the petty man:

> I have no hope of seeing an entirely good person. If I could see an entirely constant person that would do. But when doing without pretends to be having, when emptiness pretends to be fullness, when little pretends to be much, it is hard to be constant.[24]

Yang's own explication of this difficult Appraisal uses some of the same vocabulary. Translated tentatively, the "Elaboration" autocommentary reads:

> The petty man cannot find it in his heart to embrace emptiness. . . .
> Although he is debased, he cannot be approached. Although he is

> empty, he cannot be filled. When doing without would be appropriate,
> he is capable of possessing. When compliance would be appropriate,
> he is capable of striking out in an untried direction. Therefore, "despite
> a full portion of nature and Decree," he lacks [the humility] to avoid
> [inappropriate action]. That is why "he is blocked."[25]

As we see, the small man who cannot orient himself to the Way is the complete negation of Confucius' "constant person." On the other hand, the qualities of lowliness, responsiveness, and emptiness which Yang applauds are those most often associated with the exemplars pictured in the *Lao tzu* and *Chuang tzu* texts. And finally, in keeping with the cosmic concerns of Han orthodoxy, we have an indirect reference to the blocked nature of yang *ch'i* at this time of the year. In short, Appraisal 4 represents a perfect example of the Han orthodox synthesis of what had long since ceased to be distinct Confucian, Taoist, and cosmological traditions. The ideals of emptiness, moral rectitude, and yin/yang had learned to live comfortably together.[26]

This Appraisal, of course, presents a mirror image of the preceding and succeeding tetragrams, which alike depict the timely action of the noble man. Here the *Mystery* shows the small man's inability to adapt to time and circumstances in such a way as to fulfill his moral potential and societal obligations (in other words, his "nature and Decree").[27]

> App. 5: When the sun is centered in the sky,
>   Use this time to become a master.
> Fath. 5: Sun centered in the sky
>   Means: The noble man merits his place.

The center represents the mediating balance point between oppositions. In this central Appraisal among the nine, we find a triple coincidence of auspicious "centrality": the name of the Head; the correlation of the Appraisal with Earth,[28] the "center" in the cycle of the Five Phases; and the image of the sun at high noon. Since the good man, like the sun, uses his "light to illumine the entire realm,"[29] the imagery employed here suggests a cosmic analogue of ideal government, which seeks to mediate fairly between the opposing needs and opinions of the subject population. For this reason, the *Mystery*, like contemporary apocryphal writings heralding the Han restoration, makes the centered sun a sign of the Mandate of Heaven.[30] Ssu-ma Kuang comments, "Once a noble man attains the Way he is sure to have his moment; once he has his moment, he is sure to attain his position. From then on, he will be father and mother of the people." The time has come for noble impulses (including yang *ch'i*) to exert themselves.

App. 6: The moon losing its fullness
Is not as good as new light in the west.
Fath. 6: The waning moon
Means: Ignoble men are the first to retreat.

Like the previous text, this Appraisal takes for its theme the light (and therefore, enlightenment).[31] However, by the sixth Appraisal, we already have passed the point of balance. For this reason, as Yang writes, "We contemplate waxing and waning." Here the degree of remaining light is measured through moon imagery,[32] because even-numbered Appraisals in this tetragram are aligned with yin. Since the full moon would correspond to Appraisal 5, we now have the moon moving into its third quarter, no longer quite round. Yang himself defines the moral significance of this image as, "The petty man in the fullness of his powers brings needless ruin upon himself." Unable to maintain a stable position, he begins to retreat.

Neither sun nor moon actually rises in the west. But by roughly the second or third night of each lunar month, the moon has fallen far enough behind the sun to be reborn as the first crescent, just above the western horizon at sunset when the sky is dark enough to make it visible. This configuration is "better" in the sense that the first crescent signals a half-cycle of uninterrupted growth. Half a month later we will have only a half-cycle of decay. Here, as elsewhere, metaphors from Nature teach the reader to distinguish moral alternatives, leading him to choose the good and apprehend the Way.[33]

App. 7: Fully matured:
Fire stores[34] what nurtures.
Water embraces rectitude.
Fath. 7: Embracing the fully ripe[35]
Means: This is the rule for employing subjects.[36]

If the first Head is a microcosm of the eighty-one Heads correlated with the round of the seasons, this Appraisal, speaking of maturity and storage, represents autumn as the balance between Fire and Water, cosmic phases correlated with summer and winter respectively. In Han writings, Fire suggests the nourishing and fructifying activity of summer and, by extension, the use of rewards. Water implies purification, rectitude, and reliance upon judicial punishment in governance. In Yang's writing, fire and water are associated with humaneness (*jen*) and strict attention to duty (*yi*) respectively.[37] Although the punctuation of the Appraisal is problematic, both Appraisal and Fathoming recall the "Great Plan" chapter of the *Book of Documents*, which shows the ideal ruler making a fair distribution of rewards and punishments to elicit the best efforts of his subjects in the service of the state.[38] As we are now in autumn, the season traditionally set aside for legal judgments, the sage must know when and how to impose his will without threatening the well-being of the common people. He must also know how to balance the impulse towards lenience with the promotion of strict standards for behavior.

In his "Elaboration" autocommentary, Yang also ties Fire and Water to the "generosity and tolerance" of the ideal ruler.[39] This statement seems to contradict the usual correlation of Water with punishments. The passage goes on, however, to reiterate the main theme of the "Great Plan," which likens the receptivity of the sage-king to the ability of Heaven and Earth to find room for every phenomenon "except what is not good or not just."[40] In his other philosophical classic, the *Model Sayings*, Yang couples Fire and Water in a slightly different fashion: Only the sage is fit to rule the empire because, like water, his integrity is inexhaustible; and like fire, his actions are bright.[41] These images drawn from other sources also fit this Appraisal, making it an excellent example of Yang's complex use of metaphor.

> App. 8: When yellow is not yellow,
> > It overturns the norms of autumn.
> Fath. 8: That the yellow is not yellow
> > Means: He lacks the virtue of the center.

The point of this Appraisal is spelled out in Yang's "Elaboration" autocommentary: "The petty man fails to model himself on the center." That is, he fails to model himself on the Supreme Mystery, on the proper relation of yin/yang, and on the Mean in human relations. When the nine Appraisals are grouped by threes, Appraisal 8 becomes the center of the final triad. Its centrality associates it with the phase Earth and the color yellow, both emblems of balance between yin and yang. At the same time, in the sequence of nine Appraisals, the eighth is correlated with Wood, with yang's increase, with the color green, and with night. As these two sets of correspondences are at war, what should be yellow (a reference to the turning of the leaves in fall?) in this phase is not. Norms and realities no longer coincide, suggesting the need for a new "rectification of names."[42] It is equally clear that the individual must make readjustments if he is to conform with time. A rhymed quatrain composed by Yang Hsiung underlines the contrast between this inauspicious Appraisal and Appraisal 5:

> When the noble man attains a position, he flourishes.
> When he loses it, he keeps his equanimity.
> When the petty man attains a position, he is tyrannical.
> When he loses it, he perishes.[43]

The petty man, recognizing no constant norms, tends always to excess. Lacking balance, he can gain no lasting merit, despite temporary good fortune. Such misconduct has repercussions in the natural world.

> App. 9: When souls are overturned,
> *Ch'i* and form revert.
> Fath. 9: Overturned souls reverting
> Mean: Time is not overcome.

Death is the separation of *ch'i* and form. What had emerged from undifferentiated *ch'i* now returns to it as the soul breaks down into its constituent parts, which eventually revert to the shadowy bournes of the spirit world.[44] The image of death prefigures the process whereby successive tetragrams evolve from Tetragram 1, as the unbroken lines give way to broken ones. At the same time, we realize that the cycle within Tetragram 1 has now come full circle. Note also that the correlation of Appraisal 9 with the end of the life cycle is so strong that it apparently negates the general rule by which odd-numbered Appraisals in odd-numbered tetragrams are connected with auspicious yang *ch'i*.[45] At the same time, the "Elaboration" autocommentary seeks to temper the unrelievedly inauspicious character of these lines by emphasizing the inevitable nature of cyclical change.

The word translated as "souls" (*ling*) refers to human sentience, an entity powerful enough, according to Chinese legend, to survive even death. What are we, then, to make of this Appraisal's concern with human death and dissolution? In the classic Confucian texts, death is considered a calamity only when it is unnatural. A quiet death following the completion of one's allotted years was generally seen as a blessing—one of the Five Blessings of the "Great Plan" chapter of the *Documents*, as the commentator Ssu-ma Kuang reminds us.[46] Here, "the noble man in his old age" has come to the end of his time.[47] The superior man bows to the inevitable, so as "to conform to his destiny."[48] By definition, he sees his own death in the wider context of ongoing development in the cosmos; therefore he accepts the idea of his own demise.

The Fathoming, translated here as "Time is not overcome," can be also be read as "Time is not bearable." Fan Wang, the only commentator who does not ignore the Fathoming, offers the commonplace observation that the end of life "is [truly] unbearable."[49] He may, however, be reflecting upon the lesson given in the "Elaboration" autocommentary:

> The worthy man grows apprehensive [since he is aware that his demise
> is imminent], where the petty man grows presumptuous [since he uses
> his advanced age to excuse his self-indulgence].[50]

Chou
No. 2. Full Circle
December 26 (p.m.)–December 30

Correlates with Heaven's Mystery;
Yin; the phase Fire; and the Yi
ching *Hexagram no. 24, Return;*
the sun enters the the Drawn Ox
constellation, 5th degree

HEAD: Yang *ch'i* comes full circle. Divine,[1] it returns to the beginning. Things go on to become their kinds.[2]

Just as the center supplemented by circumference describes a complete form, Tetragram 2 expands upon the themes of the first tetragram. Not surprisingly, the Tao as the totality of Being is drawn as a circle, since all the myriad things seamlessly derive from and return to it; in the words of the *Changes*, "All under-Heaven in common return [to it] but by different paths."[3] For the early Chinese, as for the Greeks, the circle is the embodiment of perfection in that nothing can be added to it.[4] Seeking the Tao is also a circular process insofar as any series of correct propositions made about it ultimately leads back to the same solution. Moreover, since all points on the circumference of a circle stand equidistant from its center, the circle may signify equitable treatment.[5] Finally, the circle signifies the eternal and the ineffable in that its path knows no beginning or end. The circle strongly implies renewal, then, a theme that is also found in the hexagram "Return."

Despite these auspicious associations, the notion of coming full circle also spells danger. If there is incomplete closure at the critical juncture where one complete circuit ends and another begins, the necessary cyclical patterns of the cosmos will be interrupted or derailed. For that reason, various texts associate "movement back" with weakness and trouble.[6] This tetragram corresponds to the time right after the winter solstice, a period when special caution is required because of the fragile nature of nascent yang overwhelmed by yin. At this time, according to the *Book of Changes*,

> The kings of antiquity closed the passes at the time of the solstice. Merchants and strangers did not go about, and the ruler did not travel through the provinces.[7]

Since commercial activities were considered secondary (i.e., less essential because nonproductive) as compared with the basic occupations of agriculture and governing, it is easy to see why merchants circulating goods, and strangers making the rounds, found their travels curtailed. Even a royal progress through outlying districts (yet another circuit) was forbidden at this season, despite its crucial function in manifesting imperial power.[8] The king presumably is advised to attend to what is even more basic to his rule: his conformity with the Heaven-ordained Way and his relations with his ministers and the common people.

Through such retreat to the base, much good can be accomplished. In the cosmic realm, it was accepted wisdom that, "if yin is not at the extreme point, yang is not born." It is the periodic return of *ch'i* that promotes its proper circulation throughout the universe, just as a river flows to the sea.[9] In the world of Man, a careful reexamination of fundamental lessons can help to readjust one's actions to the Tao, so that the "flood-like *ch'i*" circulating within the body[10] is strengthened while the chances of conventional success are enhanced.

The Head text shows yang *ch'i* making its divine circuit. While there is no clear demarcation of boundaries in regard to yang's action (a state reminiscent of primal chaos), mysteriously yang *ch'i* prompts each of the myriad things to begin the process of individuation. Humans participate in this process, of course, and can even help to guide it, when they conform with the natural processes as exemplified by ritual. Ritual, like the Tao, establishes a divine balance between community and individuation, thereby insuring the continuity of all life cycles.

Finally, the title of the tetragram probably represents a play upon the name of the Chou dynasty written with the same character. The hexagram Return in Han literature is thought to refer to the defeat of the last evil king of Shang by the founder of the Chou dynasty; by this act, the Chou returned All-under Heaven to the right path.[11] It is the glorious institutions of the early Chou that Yang Hsiung, like Confucius before him, hoped in later times to restore. For,

> The moral power of Chou may, indeed, be called an absolutely perfect moral power.[12]

Both as a committed Confucian and as a descendant of the Chou ruling house, Yang Hsiung would think it his solemn duty to promote such a restoration.[13]

> App. 1: Returning to the heart of Heaven,
> In what virtue does he err?
> The Way is blocked.
> Fath. 1: That the heart's return is blocked
> Means: The center does not reciprocate.

Clearly, no task is more fundamental to the individual than intelligent conformity with the cosmic patterns, so Yang Hsiung appropriately mentions "returning to the heart of Heaven" in Appraisal 1 of this tetragram.

The *Changes* hexagram Return claims to embody the heart of Heaven and Earth in urging a full turn away from error.[14] Despite a vague agreement that "What is received from Heaven should be returned to Heaven,"[15] early thinkers found that the real difficulty lies in ascertaining Heaven's will. Like other Confucian classics, the *Mystery* presumes that Heaven's will can be discerned in at least three ways: 1) in the conscientious decisions made by the individual who has "self-knowledge";[16] 2) in the patterns of civilization transmitted by sage-rulers and preserved in tradition;[17] and 3) in the expressed will of the people, on the assumption that "Heaven sees as the people see."[18] In theory, so long as the state is just, there need never be a conflict between the individual's self-cultivation, his acquiescence in the wisdom of public opinion, and his conformity with societal conventions.

Still, early Chinese philosophers were far too sophisticated to be unaware of the sometimes contradictory lessons conveyed by these three sources. In a benighted age, for example, the superior man's conscience may tell him to rebel against public mores. Yang Hsiung provides a further test to resolve questions of morality: Like Confucius before him,[19] Yang suggests that the advisability of a particular action can be judged on the basis of a single, infallible criterion: Does the action exemplify the virtue of reciprocity? Where there is evil, it is likely to stem from the individual's failure to accord others the same consideration he himself expects. As a result, community is broken.

> App. 2: A pivot set directly center
> Sweeps full circle, not in angles.
> Fath. 2: A pivot placed directly center
> Means: Set your thoughts on the Mean.[20]

Beginning in Chou times, the pivot metaphor appears regularly in discussions regarding the related subjects of astronomy and kingship. In the heavens, the Dipper functions as a pivot around which the various starry configurations revolve. Aligned with the *axis mundi*, it ensures the seamless alternation of night and day.[21] The king is "pivot" or "pole" of All-under-Heaven in at least three senses:[22] First, it is he who steadies and defines the movement of all lesser aspects of creation; the ruler's position and influence are such that his desires constitute the directing force of his subordinates. Second, the ruler is like the pivot in that he alone appears unmoved and inactive (*wu-wei*), while his subjects undergo radical transformations under his influence. Third, the ruler, like the pivot, is impartial in action, so that the sweep of his mind gives equal consideration to all options and candidates. In this, of course, he imitates Heaven's model.[23]

Though all early Chinese thinkers are in agreement that it is by virtue of his pivotal position that the king oversees and informs the full round of activities in his realm, they cannot reach agreement on the best way to "plant" the pivot. The Confucians assert that the ruler's pivotal role depends on his charismatic virtue. As the famous passage in the *Analects* says, "He who rules by moral force is like the pole-star, which remains in its place while all the lesser stars do homage to it."[24] Just as a pivot cannot inscribe a complete circle unless its hinges are correctly and firmly placed,[25] dominion over All-under Heaven will be prevented by improper behavior. Texts associated with the Legalists, in contrast, insist that the ruler acts as pivot for the state either because he occupies the "strategic position"[26] in government or because he employs certain bureaucratic techniques; for the Legalists, calculation, more than character, determines the king's efficacy.

In the Fathoming, we have Yang Hsiung's rebuttal to the Legalist theory. The individual is told to consider the manifest advantages of rule by virtue, as demonstrated by the homely metaphor of the center back seam of a cloak.[27] The center seam gains significance only because it holds the various parts together. The king can hold his subjects to the extent that he embodies the impartial perfection of the Mean. Here, Yang Hsiung repeats the central theme of the "Great Plan" chapter of the *Documents*, which describes the true king in the following manner:

> Have nothing onesided, nothing oblique.
> Follow the king's righteousness.
> Have no predilections, . . . no aversions.
> And follow the king's road. . . .
> Have nothing deflected, nothing perverse.
> The king's way is straight.[28]

The private individual, of course, models himself upon Heaven and the king in his devotion to the Mean. Since Position 2 corresponds to the central one of the three Appraisals devoted to Thought, Yang appropriately emphasizes the center and the Mean at this juncture.

The image of the "pivot" at the same time refers to the Hun-t'ien astronomical theory favored by Yang Hsiung. According to this theory, the sun and the moon are stars moving in a uniform fashion around the North Pole (yet another "center pivot").[29]

> App. 3: What I give out and what I take in
> Are chief factors[30] in good luck or ill.
> Fath. 3: What comes from me, what enters me
> Means: We cannot but take care.

Ssu-ma Kuang assumes that these lines refer to the effect of external situations ("what enters me") upon the thought processes, including motivation, which are then translated into action ("What comes from me"). Certainly this is plausible; it is also consistent with the theme of circularity. Still, in that case the Appraisal would better be phrased as, "What enters me [then] comes from me." For this reason, I suggest an alternate interpretation. The phrase "exit/enter" usually refers to effort or funds expended, compared with the return received (in either the material or spiritual sense).[31] The verses recall a simple truth: As a man sows, so shall he reap. As each action leads to specific consequences, only single-minded devotion to the Way can help to insure good luck. In this way, the individual has a certain degree of control over aspects of his fate.

> App. 4: He is girded by hook and belt,
> On which is tied a ring of jade.[32]
> Fath. 4: Girding his hook and belt
> Means: He shows self-constraint.

The image of circling comes up no fewer than four times in this brief passage: once as a belt encircling the waist, once as a belt looping around its hook, again in the jade ring, and finally, as a man returning to his best self by accepting necessary constraints.[33]

Clothing signifies man's separation from the beasts, as in the Bible. In early China, clothing provided a further ethical demarcation through the ritual system of sumptuary regulations, which stipulated that the official, who presumably exemplifies the Way, is to be distinguished from the commoner by his superior clothing. Such distinctions are entirely praiseworthy, according to Yang, as they promote the social virtues.[34] Here not only the belt and hook,[35] but also the jade ornament suggest that it is a member of the ruling elite who shows laudable "self-constraint"; because of its cost, few outside the ranks of aristocrats could afford jade, even if its use had not been restricted by sumptuary laws.

Jade is highly prized by the Chinese for many reasons. First, human nature is likened to jade in discussions about self-cultivation since the inherent beauty of both is enhanced through polishing.[36] In particular, jade ornaments suspended from the belt symbolize a life regulated by ritual, for their rhythmic tinkling sounds remind the wearer to measure his steps.[37] Second, jade exemplifies the constancy of the superior man because jade is cool to the touch in any weather. Third, since Neolithic times jade has been thought to have unique life-giving properties. For this reason, jade was used for many funeral goods, including the famous jade suits excavated at Man-ch'eng. The jade ring specifically stands for the eternal nature of the life process.[38] All of these associations come neatly into play here, as ritual conduct strengthens the humane official in conformity with the eternal Tao.

App. 5: He dwells at the center of the land,
    And there sets his golden carriage.
    Heaven's[39] warnings increase.
Fath. 5: The dwelling, the gold, the increased warnings
    Means: The petty man does not triumph.

Ssu-ma Kuang gives one interpretation widely followed by other commentators: The individual enjoys a number of advantages and everything seems predisposed to good fortune: "His dwelling is nothing, if not beautiful; his carriage is nothing, if not sturdy. Still, the petty man never can dwell long [in peace] and practice it [virtue]." Therefore, Heaven's warnings increase until both power and possessions are lost.[40] This sounds likely enough. The only problem with Ssu-ma Kuang's analysis is that its connection with the theme of circularity is unclear.

Let us begin with what we know. The Appraisal must be inauspicious. Since Position 5 corresponds to the Son of Heaven, it is likely that the ruler is at fault. There are other indications as well. The dwelling is located in the center of the country, that is, the capital,[41] and there is talk of the carriage, a common metaphor for government.[42] Furthermore, the carriage is made of gold. Only a king could afford such an equipage. But therein lies the trouble.[43] The ruler's fondness for luxury and display eventually undermines the royal house. Expansion is not followed by retrenchment. If it takes a great man to acquire the chariot, it is the "petty man who [by his course of action] tears down his own dwelling."[44] The ideal ruler "remembers danger even in safety."[45]

The Appraisal can also be read as a critique of men returned to private life (reading "dwelling" as "a thatched cottage") after office-holding (the carriage), who refuse to give up the appurtenances of their former station. Many Han works censure men whose official position and social pretensions do not correspond; according to the "Doctrine of the Mean," "The superior man does what is proper to the station he is in; he does not desire to go beyond this."[46] In some cases, the coupling of chariot and dwelling in Han tradition also points to "[official] salary not matched by [the diligent performance of] duties."[47]

App. 6: Good faith encircles his integrity[48]
    And penetrates to Heaven above.
Fath. 6: Good faith sustaining his integrity
    Means: It communicates on high.

The Chinese generally ascribe the virtue of constancy to Heaven, since the fixed stars do not depart from their courses and the seasons alternate in a set pattern without fail.[49] As the good person develops his capacity on Heaven's model for reliability, Heaven is sure to reward him. "Good faith" (*hsin* 信) refers to the social relations, to keeping promises and fulfilling one's duties within the family and in office.[50] The term "integrity" (*ch'eng* 誠), by contrast, usually embraces realms (both inner and cosmic) beyond social relations. It refers to that perfect conformity of the inner mind of man with Heaven's will that insures the integration of the human spirit with the cosmic realm.[51] As one commentator to the *Mystery* put it, "Good faith is the Way of Man; . . . integrity, the Way of Heaven."[52] Yang Hsiung reminds his readers that man's social responsibilities are not only consistent with, but preconditions for conformity with the larger cosmic patterns;[53] good faith and integrity mutually reinforce one another. (This reminder, of course, disputes the claims of certain recluses who insist that societal claims must be abandoned in service to the greater Tao.) Therefore, "Integrity and good faith give birth to what is godlike."[54]

> App. 7: Greatly[55] immoral men, seeing their peers,[56]
> Return to cover.
> Fath. 7: Great excess, seeing friends,
> Means: Association is impossible.

In the *Mystery*, goodness by definition produces community. While Fathoming 6 attests to the power of virtue to forge strong ties between Heaven and Man, here we find vice destroying all possibility of true friendship among men. One main avenue to spiritual enlightenment, instruction by wise and caring friends, is effectively closed.[57]

The Chinese does not specify who returns to cover. Possibly, the evildoer is embarassed to have a true friend (by definition, a good man) witness his actions.[58] Perhaps the evildoer seeks to hide from himself knowledge of his own crimes.[59] A third possibility is that former associates slink away in disgust after they witness wicked acts. Associations based on profit rather than virtue are especially likely to collapse.[60]

> App. 8: Turning out faults[61] from the self,
> Misfortunes will not be great.
> Fath. 8: Ridding himself of faults
> Means: Calamity will not strike.

A failing, if truly repented, need not end in disaster. It is as if the good person "returns from no great distance."[62]

> App. 9: As he returns to ruin,
> Some reject him and walk away.[63]
> Fath. 9: Reverting to ruin
> Means: His way is at an end.

Once again, the final Appraisal of this tetragram pictures complete dissolution—this time, that of the state. He who persists in evil finds that his subjects desert him in droves, bringing an end to the dynasty.[64]

Popular legend provides a famous counterexample in the person of Duke Tan-fu (also called T'ai-wang). The duke was originally ruler of the small state of Pin (in present-day Shensi) when the threat of barbarian invasion forced him to relocate his capital. Despite the hardship involved in the transfer, his loyal subjects followed him to the new state called Chou because of his great virtue. Only three generations later, his grandson succeeded to the position of Son of Heaven.[65]

Hsien
No. 3. Mired
December 31–January 4 (a.m.)

Correlates with Heaven's Mystery; Yang; *the phase Wood; and the* Yi ching *Hexagram; no. 3, Difficulty Starting; the sun enters the* Woman constellation, 2d degree

HEAD: Yang *ch'i* stirs slightly. Though stirred, it is mired [in yin]. "Mired" refers to the difficulty attending the birth of things.

This tetragram explores the difficulty experienced at the start of any initiative. The character used for the title of this tetragram, a *hapax graphomenon* found only in the *Mystery*, is made up of two components: the first means "stone," the second means "firm" or "solid." Cognates for the title character include "to bind tightly or fast," "solidly fixed," "imprisoned," and "unmoving."[1] Clearly, movement is sluggish and weighted down at the beginning.[2] Throughout the tetragram, the title character is played off against the verb, "to pull out,"[3] an action which is always viewed favorably. The title, then, must indicate the lamentable situation in which something is "held fast" or "mired" in some kind of trouble. This definition is supported by the Head text that pictures yang *ch'i* like a child struggling to escape the dark hold of the cosmic womb. (Note the tetragram's correlation with the Woman constellation.)

Like the succeeding tetragram Barrier, this tetragram emphasizes the dangers inherent in premature action. The early Appraisals in particular show the disadvantages of inadequate development, which prevents clean extraction (of the hair from the head, of evil from the self, of the worthy man from obscurity, of the world from its benighted customs). The wise man awaits the proper time in the cycle so that trends favor him, knowing that even yang *ch'i* must wait until spring before manifesting itself in full glory.

In an additive narrative form borrowed from the *Changes*, Appraisals 5–7 skillfully use the metaphor of the journey to suggest the course of potential development from moral ignorance to full appreciation of the Tao.[4] Like the traveler, the person set upon self-cultivation meets various obstacles and detours, but so long as he never swerves from the right path, he will eventually arrive safely at his destination.

The journey metaphor also levels implicit criticism at the Sophists and at Chuang tzu, who used the paradox "Mountain and abyss are level" in arguing for the absolute equivalence of all experience.[5] Following the tradition of the philosopher Hsün tzu, Yang Hsiung insists upon the substantive differences between various courses of action open to the individual. In his verses, then, mountain and abyss are shown to be far more dangerous than hill and gully.

> App. 1: Yellow, pure, and in hiding,[6]
>> Its boundaries are unseen,
>> Stored away, pent-up in the Springs.
> Fath. 1: Yellow, pure, and in hiding
>> Means: Transformations take place in secret.[7]

Since this tetragram corresponds to the second week after the winter solstice, yang *ch'i* remains confined to the watery netherworld of the Yellow Springs.[8] Although its outline is unclear, its potency is signified by the adjectives "yellow" and "pure." Yang *ch'i* is yellow in two senses: It is essential to future development and nourishing like yellow Earth.[9] It is pure in that it is both unadulterated and concentrated, though latent.[10] Here it is poised to feed the roots of future action.

Position 1 is aligned with the Beginning of Thought, as well as with the Water phase. The watery depths symbolize the mind's unseen operations prior to action and may also suggest the suasive potential of the superior man.[11]

> App. 2: The yellow is impure,
>> Bent[12] at the root.
> Fath. 2: That yellow is impure
>> Means: What is central and suitable is lost.[13]

The commentator Fan Wang attributes arrested development to the antagonistic relation between the agent Fire (assigned to Appraisal 2) and the agent Wood (assigned to the full tetragram and to Appraisal 3).[14] But Ssu-ma Kuang seems much closer to the mark: If the base is weak in any way, future growth is sure to be stunted. Our attention is drawn to the petty man whose weak conscience impedes his moral growth.

> App. 3: The rosy babe is lifted up[15]
>> So that original[16] purity
>> Will have its rightful end.
> Fath. 3: Newborn child, lifted and lifted,
>> Means: Father and mother attend to it.

The baby is naked, alerting us to man's original likeness to the beasts.[17] The newborn babe is rosy, with red signifying virile yang *ch'i*, and by extension, perfect potentiality, auspicious coherence, and concentration of the vital powers. The powerful metaphor of the rosy babe is typically employed by early Taoist thinkers to prove the remarkable strength of the inborn capacities.[18] However, the *Mystery* is careful to distinguish the potential for virtue implanted in all of us from its eventual actualization in the noble man. The seeds of inborn goodness are fragile and easily lost. And a return to infantile spontaneity is by no means to be confused with true virtue.[19] Just as the naked child in its highly vulnerable state requires the support of both loving parents,[20] so does full development of the heart/mind depend upon careful training received from moral superiors. This poem praises not the child, but those authorities (living or dead) who guide their subordinates "as if they were tending a newborn babe."[21] As the *Changes* maxim puts it, "To nourish the Right in the young ignoramus is the task of the sage."[22]

Of course, once the extended course of moral training has led the child to realize his full potential for humanity, the son becomes the joy of his parents' old age. That explains why the parents watch over it not only with anxiety, but also with affection and hope.

> App. 4: Pulling out our faults[23]
>> Is not possible by force.
> Fath. 4: Uprooting our faults
>> Means: This goes beyond physical strength.[24]

The Appraisal's correlation with the phase Metal may account for its references to physical force.[25] In any case, by referring to the difficulties of reform, these lines balance Yang's reference to original purity in Appraisal 3. The *Mystery* is careful not to promote an idealistic vision of man in the state of nature. According to Yang Hsiung, the inborn nature at birth is a mixture of good and evil; only those who weed out their evil tendencies can become truly good.[26] But the application of physical force alone cannot produce improvement;[27] as Yang writes elsewhere, "The noble man excels in virtue; the petty man, in physical strength."[28] The best way to correct oneself is to follow the example of moral superiors, either in person or through study of their teachings.

Since the verb "pull out" can also mean "raising someone from obscurity," these verses also conceivably rebuke the ruler for his appointment of officials. This possibility is strengthened by the alignment of Position 4 with ministerial rank. Two commentators (Fan Wang and Ssu-ma Kuang), therefore, offer a second reading for the Appraisal:

> To raise me from obscurity, [despite? because of?] faults,
> By force, one cannot overcome [difficulties].
> To raise me from obscurity, [despite? because of?] faults,
> Force is not up to [the task].

In selecting his officials, the ruler has consciously or inadvertently chosen those who prefer to rule by force.

> App. 5: To pull the chariot
>   Out of mountain or abyss[29]
>   Is a task befitting the great man.
> Fath. 5: Pulling chariots from mountain and abyss
>   Means: This is the strength of the highly placed.

As in the West, the abyss symbolizes desperate situations; the mountain, dangerous heights to be scaled. The term "great man" can refer either to a giant or to the worthy man fit to govern others. If the chariot represents political purchase, the magnitude of the ruler's difficulties is suggested by both the extremely dangerous location of the carriage and its stalled condition. It will take a great man in high places to rescue the stranded state from its precarious position. A fine example of incremental repetition, Appraisals 5–9 follow the chariot on its progress.

> App. 6: Leading his chariot,
>   He enters the ruins.[30]
> Fath. 6: Leading his chariot into the ruins
>   Means: He has not found the Way.

Having just been plucked from extreme danger (either political chaos or the moral abyss), the ruler now sets off in a direction which leads to ultimate destruction. Perhaps he has been poorly advised by his ministers.[31]

> App. 7: Escaping perilous terrain,
>   He ascends the hill.
>   There he is brought an ox.[32]

Fath. 7: To escape the defile, go up the hill
Means: There is no substitute for timely aid.[33]

Although the chariot has not yet reached the safety of the level plain, imminent danger has been avoided. And though the chariot is ill-suited to hilly terrain, this present move has two advantages: first, from the top of a hill, the driver can see the Way all the more clearly;[34] second, the top of the hill is more defensible. Since someone brings an ox, reliable help from outside has been secured. The ultimate source of this valuable aid is indicated by a pun. The graph for hill is also used for the personal name of Confucius, the great sage-master.

App. 8: Failing to pull the chariot free,
He cracks his ribs,[35] cracking axle.
Fath. 8: Failing to pull the chariot free
Means: He harms his own person.

The petty individual who fails to measure his own strength will not be able to pluck himself from danger.[36] Instead, his misguided efforts will simply compound his problems. Here, both his tools and his person suffer. If the carriage stands for the state, both the ruling house and its head are overturned.

App. 9: High mountains tower.
Below, the river breaks in waves.[37]
That man has an oar-drawn ferry.
With him, you can cross.
Fath. 9: High mountains, great rivers
Mean: Without the boat, impossible to cross.

Position 9 represents an extreme situation. Here either course of action seems to present its own dangers. To one side, there are towering mountains; on the other, raging rapids. Extreme caution must be exercised if death (physical or moral) is to be avoided. The wise individual keeps on the alert for outside help in order to survive.

Among the waters, there are great rivers; among the mountains,
there are towering peaks. What is tall or great, ordinary men cannot
cross. . . . Surely it has never happened yet that one discards the boat
to cross the waters. Nor has it ever happened that one discards the Five
Classics [of Confucianism] but is saved in the Way.[38]

For Yang Hsiung, Confucian tradition as recorded in the Classics provides the only vehicle by which to pass through life's vicissitudes.[39]

Hsien

No. 4. Barrier

January 4 (p.m.)–January 8

Correlates with Heaven's Mystery;
Yin*; the phase Metal; and the* Yi
ching *Hexagram no. 3, Difficulty
Starting; the sun enters the
Woman constellation, 6th degree;
the Dipper points NNE*

HEAD: Yang *ch'i* is barred by yin. Mired fast,[1] all things are barred.

As the Winter Solstice solar period gives way to the Lesser Cold with Appraisal 4 of this tetragram, the power of yin *ch'i* grows progressively weaker. Still, yin is sufficiently strong to impede the emergence of yang for now.[2] Since the growth of the myriad things depends upon yang *ch'i*, they feel its predicament keenly and are impeded in their development.

Like Tetragram 3, this tetragram is correlated with the *Changes* hexagram entitled Difficulty Starting. All three texts illustrate human reliance upon a variety of aids, including tools and specialists, in building the civilized order. However, the *Changes* focuses upon carting, wooing, and hunting while Yang Hsiung considers many different barriers in his examination of human response to the outside world.

The single character of the tetragram title refers to a crossbar at an entrance, to separating pens devised for domesticated animals, or to the horse corral. From these root meanings there evolved more abstract ideas of "defense," "obstacle," and "interception." Barriers are good if they prevent outside influences from harming the vital inner core. Earlier, the *Lao tzu* had advised the individual to

> Block the openings,
> Bar the gates,
> And all your life you will not run dry.[3]

Certain physical techniques, including breath control, were designed specifically to stave off the daily depletion of bodily *ch'i* that ended in death. Meanwhile, the early Confucians focused instead on the preservation of integrity. For them, the single best barrier was to be found in the thorough habituation to goodness that obstructs evil impulses: "Use Duty to bar [evil in] oneself. Use the rites to bar it."[4] At the same time, certain barriers admittedly have a negative impact in that they prevent good influences from penetrating. The Logicians used the metaphor of "separating pens" to talk of "restricted viewpoints" that prejudice the individual against the truth.[5]

The primary focus of the *Changes* tradition, of course, was preventing calamities "in advance."[6] It promised the noble man that attention to details and calculation of contemporary trends would allow the circumvention of the usual troubles plaguing humankind. For many early Chinese thinkers, the key lay in the proper and timely use of barriers.

> App. 1: Snakes lurk in the mud.[7]
>> All are female. None are male.
>> None finally receive the gift.[8]
> Fath. 1: The snake in the mud is no hidden dragon.
>> Meaning: The ruler on the dragon throne is no ruler.

Position 1 appropriately mentions the low ground of mud and mire. The hidden dragon in the *Changes* tradition signifies the superior man (especially the ruler) prior to action.[9] Because the dragon is said to bring the rain needed by the agricultural community, it brings to mind many forms of grace that rain down from on high, including the ruler's benefactions to his subjects. Here, however, there is only a poor imitation of the dragon, a snake coiled in the mud. Though the dragon and snake were commonly classified as members of a single genus,[10] crucial differences were said to exist: First, the dragon can transform itself by magic into various forms but the snake can only molt its skin in a superficial change.[11] Second, the dragon mates normally (and indeed, is associated with fertility), but the snake is assumed to be hermaphroditic, and therefore self-generating; this violation of the "constant norm" of sexual reproduction is regarded as highly inauspicious. Third, the dragon endows blessings while the snake merely brings harm to Man by its bite. Where the dragon is welcomed, the snake is feared.

This baleful imagery is intensified by the image of a snake that waits in mud. A contrasting *Changes* passage calls this auspicious,[12] but here, apparently, the snake lies in wait to ambush its victims. This is quite different from the "hidden" dragon (where "hidden" connotes "marvelous" and "mysterious"). Evil is compounded when all males are absent, since this points to an excess of yin *ch'i* associated with death and destruction. Finally, the statement "None receive the gift" suggests a profound degree of disorder. In traditional societies, the orderly exchange of gifts is seen to cement social bonds and self-interest, thereby securing a solid foundation for the community. Once the superior's bounty fails to reach his inferiors, the entire system of hierarchical relations that typifies Chinese society is undermined.[13] Small wonder that "the ruler is no ruler," an obvious contravention of the Confucian injunction to "rectify names."[14] With hierarchical roles so ill-defined, "inferiors assault their superiors."[15]

Since Appraisal 1 corresponds to the period prior to action, there exists an alternate interpretation for the same lines. The "snake" is actually a dragon coiled in mud, one popular image for the good official forced into reclusion until a true ruler ascends the throne. The female (signifying the subordinate, the "good official") exists, but as yet no male (or "true ruler") appears to receive Heaven's mandate, as the nominal king is unfit to bear his title.[16]

> App. 2: Barring his storehouse door,
> He secures the precious treasure.
> Fath. 2: Locking his storehouse
> Means: The center heart is a deep, deep pool.

Man's integrity is his precious treasure. The innermost self (the center heart)* is like a deep pool in at least five respects: First, its source in the Tao is inexhaustible. Second, its source is unseen. Third, water reflects well only if it is clean and still; by analogy, the mind works well only if it is unmoved and clean as a result of daily self-examination.[17] Fourth, water's flow is gradual and cumulative, like progress in self-cultivation.[18] Finally, water's purity insures that, in the words of the *Lao tzu*, "it excels in benefitting without contending".[19]

To retain his integrity, the superior man bent on moral reform must keep himself from destructive outside influences, such as bad companions. Since Position 2 represents low position, the subject of these lines must patiently prepare for some future employment of his talents.

> App. 3: The gate is shut but not bolted.
> The golden key is thrown away.[20]
> Fath. 3: Shut but not locked
> Means: Thieves steal through the gate.

In contrast to Appraisal 2, the individual refuses to take proper precautions to safeguard himself from harm. As the *Changes* states, "To be careless in guarding things only tempts thieves to steal."[21]

> App. 4: Lifting[22] our[23] yoke or collar-bar,
> The gain is slight. It benefits
> Minor expeditions only.
> Fath. 4: Unharnessed from our yoke or collar-bar
> Means: The good man values keeping his word.[24]

The yoke and collar-bar secure draft animals to a vehicle; the yoke is used for larger vehicles; the collar-bar, for smaller ones. But what have they to do with "keeping one's word"? Apparently, Yang Hsiung alludes to a passage from the *Analects*:

---

*See Key Terms, page 63

> I do not see what use a man can be put to, whose word cannot be
> trusted. How can a wagon be made to go if it has no yoke, or a carriage
> if it has no collar-bar?[25]

Just as restraint must be applied before the draft animal can be harnessed
for use, the individual must be willing to abide by his word before he can
be of much service to himself or others. Admittedly, a cart may be pulled
for a short distance without yoke or collar-bar, but this soon proves a
great (and unsustainable) waste of effort. By analogy, when an individual
refuses to be bound by his promises, he is like an animal run amuck. In
the long run, only good faith can sustain both social relations and self-
interest. As Confucius said, "Man's very life is honesty in that, without it,
he will be lucky indeed if he escapes with his life."[26]

> App. 5: Mired in evil, barred from good,
> He tries to pry us from our villainy
> Which is hard as rock though not a rock.
> Danger.
> Fath. 5: Stuck and blocked, like a stone,
> Means: The enemy holds firm.

Position 5 is aligned with Earth; stones are the hardest parts of earth.
Here Position 5, signifying the Son of Heaven, is aligned with inauspicious yin, associated with weakness and decay. For that reason, the ruler
feels his strength is insufficient to root out evil influences (in himself or
others). The "enemy" within, offering stubborn resistance to reform, remains firmly in control, like a rock.[27] As the *Changes* writes, "Weak character coupled with a place of honor . . . seldom escapes disaster."[28]

> App. 6: Safe behind his yellow walls,[29]
> He rests on golden mats.
> Fath. 6: Yellow walls for barricades
> Mean: He is fortified by virtue.

Physical and spiritual barriers here work together. The wise man bars
the entrance to his house with high earthen walls. He then rests safely inside, perhaps meditating or reading in the texts of the ancients. The Confucian Classics advise man to,

> Embrace virtue, your safeguard.
> Let your heirs be your fortress.[30]

The cultivation of virtue promotes the safety of one's home and person.
Virtue provides the best "refuge" and most "peaceful abode."[31]

Taking off from the talk of "heirs" in the *Odes*, the early commentator
Fan Wang sees in the yellow walls and golden mat specific references to

the ancestral temple, whose continued existence depends upon successive acts of virtue in the line of descendants. In view of Yang's own autocommentary, which correlates Appraisal 6 with the ancestors,[32] Fan Wang may well be right. Still, it is just as likely that yellow and gold refer to the pure yang *ch'i* of the centered mind.

> App. 7: Staggering,[33]
>> He is barred from his sleeping mat,
>> While someone sleeps securely in his house.[34]
> Fath. 7: Gates locked to those who stumble
>> Mean: The evil lies at home.[35]

I give one possible interpretation for the verse. The individual, unable to conduct himself properly, finds that ease and security are denied him. Sooner or later, someone else will usurp his place. Death may be imminent, for the Ode says, "You will drop off in death, / And another will enter [your] chamber."[36]

Another reading is offered by Wang Ya, who takes the straw sleeping mats to be "relay stations," a symbol of officialdom. The criticism seems to be leveled against the court, which bars advancement to worthy advisors. Meanwhile, evildoers have wormed their way into the ruler's confidence to such an extent that they lounge even in the inner sanctum of the palace. As Wang writes, this is "to bar the outside, but lose the inside."[37]

A third interpretation offered by three commentators (Fan Wang, Yeh Tzu-ch'i, and Ch'en Pen-li),[38] reads "sleeping mats" with a different determinative to signify the "bloating illness"[39] associated with the arrogant, deformed, and vicious who refuse to yield or bend.[40] Yang's verses are then read in the following fashion:

> Crooked [their conduct].
> Barred [are the good] by the arrogant.
> Some [even] bed down in his home [the palace].
> Barring by the crooked
> Means: The evil lies [close] to home.

A fourth and final solution is offered by the late Ch'ing annotator Yü Yueh:[41]

> With crooked conduct [a man is no safer than if]
> He barred [his door] with a coarse mat,
> Or slept in a thatched cottage.

Yü Yueh's solution is attractive for several reasons: First, it draws upon material from Yang Hsiung's own dialect dictionary, which talks of "coarse straw mats." Second, it contrasts a thatched cottage and coarse mats with the secure fortress and sleeping mats of Appraisal 6. The thatched cottage is no proof against thieves on the lookout for valuable objects; the coarse mat cannot promote a safe rest. Therefore, the individual's most "precious treasure," his integrity, is no longer secure.

> App. 8: The Red Stench spreads to[42] the passes.
>   If the Great King does not bar its way,[43]
>   Contagion will sweep the kingdom
>   And drive his house.
> Fath. 8: The Red Stench reaching the passes
>   Means: He fears it may enter the palace.

Here barriers are clearly needed. Only by blocking the passes can the inner regions of China be protected from the "miasmic vapors" threatening the borders.[44] Careful to recognize the potential danger, the good king promptly takes steps to halt the epidemic at the passes.

A plague, of course, is also an apt metaphor for evil men or evil influences. The "great ruler" bars their entrance to the heart/mind.

> App. 9: Barring gates on an empty house,
>   He keeps it utterly empty.[45]
> Fath. 9: Barring the gates to keep it empty
>   Means: Finally, nothing can fill it.[46]

The term "emptiness" has both good and bad connotations. Emptiness is praiseworthy when it signifies the virtues of humility and receptivity, as in Appraisal 4 of Tetragram 1. Here, however, emptiness portends a poverty of mind and spirit. Perhaps the individual has waited too long to bar the gate (that is, to apply self-restraint), so that none of "his precious treasure" (his integrity) remains.[47] A man devoid of all principle in effect has nothing left to defend. As one Confucian canon rhetorically asks, "If the city is occupied by villainous enemies, then why take pains to wall it?"[48]

These lines could also be read as criticism of strait-laced extremists who have decided to go into reclusion. Certain men of Han took the prescription to refrain from evil contacts too far when they avoided societal contact entirely. One question frequently posed was, "If the noble man 'preserves himself,' how is he to have contact [with others]?"[49] Yang's answer was unequivocal: Since the end of all virtue is the enhancement of community, eremitism by definition leads to a barren existence bereft of true humanity. In the words of the *Changes*, the "sack tied up has no misfortune, [but] neither has it honor."[50] Barriers, if wrongly applied, do more harm than good.

Correlates with Heaven's Mystery;
Yang; the phase Earth; and the Yi
ching *Hexagram no. 15, Modesty;*
the sun enters the Woman
constellation 11th degree

Shao
No. 5. Keeping Small
January 9–January 13 (a.m.)

HEAD: Yang *ch'i*, rippling,[1] spreads through the deep pool. Things like ripplets[2] in its wake can keep themselves very small.

This tetragram describes the initial stirrings of the myriad things within the earth in the wake of yang *ch'i's* first generative pulses. In terms of language it is one of the simplest tetragrams since it borrows almost all of its images directly from the correspondent *Changes* hexagram entitled Modesty. The "Judgment" to that hexagram says:

> It is the way of Heaven to empty the full and increase the modest. It is
> the way of Earth to cramp[3] the full and augment the modest. Spirits
> and gods harm the full and prosper the modest. It is the way of Man to
> hate fullness and love the modest.[4]

In similar language, the *Lao tzu* describes Heaven's Way:

> What is high, it presses down.
> What is low, it lifts up.
> The excessive it takes from,
> The deficient it gives to.[5]

Since the superior man by definition models his behavior on Heaven and Earth at all times, he also acts to "reduce the excessive and augment the deficient."[6] According to the Confucians, he carries out this "godlike" task by implementing ritual in every aspect of his life.[7]

By Han times, humility or self-deprecation (i.e. reducing the excessive) was elevated to one of the major virtues. Whatever his personal circumstances, the good man does not seek to blame others for his own faults; above all, he does not boast of wealth or position. Instead, he creates order precisely by condescending to share credit and resources with his inferiors, an attitude which endears him to them, and makes them accede to his moral and/or political rule.[8] At the same time, the courteous humility of the good man elicits valuable advice from potential allies. For these reasons, whether in humble circumstances or in power, the superior man downplays his own achievements.

This emphasis upon self-deprecation seems to have been a relatively recent invention in Yang's time. More ancient texts, including the *Odes* and the *Documents*, argue that each man should act in a way appropriate to his social station. Inferiors must not arrogate powers to themselves and superiors are expected to display the inherent majesty of their positions by impressive ceremonial display, though swagger and arrogance are always misplaced. It was apparently the late Warring States quietists who elevated self-deprecation to a major virtue, regardless of the individual's status. Eventually, those in high position come to see modesty as a technique useful in circumventing the usual cyclical downturns of fate.[9] In cosmic terms, "reversal is the [characteristic] movement of the Tao," so that each thing falls prey to swift decline immediately after reaching full development. Only "holding fast to the submissive" (keeping away from the apex of florescence)[10] can forestall inexorable devolution within the cyclical process. In purely human terms, excessive brilliance of any type is best hidden lest it awaken the jealousy and enmity of fellow men or the gods. As an earlier book in the *Changes* tradition observes:

Rely [on others] for success
[In that case,] no troubles.
Hide oneself,
Then life is kept intact.[11]

In Yang Hsiung's day, as in our own, great wealth, rather than birth, prompted swaggering arrogance, while poverty could provoke cadging or sometimes, a kind of perverse pride. This, plus Yang's own struggle to come to terms with his comparative poverty, probably accounts for the *Mystery*'s focus on this issue.

App. 1: In darkness,[12] he makes himself small,
        Becoming consummately humble.
Fath. 1: In obscurity, self-deprecation
        Means: He conceals his humility.

All commentators agree that these lines describe the contentment that characterizes the gentleman in humble, even obscure circumstances. He does not seek to have others recognize him, nor does he congratulate himself on his own modesty, being, as the *Changes* says, "modest about his modesty."[13] Confucius used the following description of him:

The good man does not grieve that others do not recognize his merits. His only anxiety is lest he fail to recognize theirs. . . . He does not care about not being in office. All he cares about is having the the qualities that entitle him to office. He does not mind failing to get recognition. He is too busy doing the things that entitle him to recognition.[14]

His willingness to carry out his modesty "to the utmost" makes his character admirable, even "marvelous."[15]

> App. 2: Self-deprecation, less than complete,
>   He clutches his cares to his breast.
> Fath. 2: Self-deprecation failing
>   Means: His humility is imperfect.[16]

The petty man occasionally assumes a mask of humility but in reality he is far too self-absorbed to be really self-forgetful. Not surprisingly, he tends to ignore the needs of others. Once offended, those around him may turn against him.[17]

> App. 3: Modestly done, his actions succeed.
>   He is a model for masters of men.
> Fath. 3: To be modest in success
>   Means: His humility is tried and true.[18]

Position 3 marks the transition from thought to action. So long as the individual remains a model of humility, he can successfully marshal the talents of those around him. The good man tests his modesty in at least three ways: First, he complies with the teachings of the ancients, acknowledging their superiority. Second, he downplays his own attainments while acknowledging his dependence upon friends and advisors. Third, he effects all major changes in minor increments to avoid unduly alarming others.[19] By the gradual accumulation of such modest accomplishments the good man transforms the circle of his acquaintances until they unconsciously imitate his attitude of compliance in their dealings with one another.

Yang Hsiung's language is ambiguous enough to read as praise of laissez-faire government, as a modern commentator suggests.[20] In that case, the poem would read:

> When actions are minimized, [it brings] his success.
> This is the model for the master of men.
> Minimizing, his [way of] getting men['s allegiance].
> Humility is the [method] tried and true.

However, Yang Hsiung frequently denounces proponents of "noninterference" and "non-purposive activity" in his *Model Sayings*.[21] Instead, Yang Hsiung follows the lead of Hsün tzu in emphasizing the long years of reform needed to attain perfect government or true self-cultivation.[22]

> App. 4: Taking penury as poverty,[23]
>   Some recklessly relieve it.[24]

> Fath. 4: Preoccupied with poverty[25]
> Means: He cannot maintain the Right.

Position 4 among the Appraisals corresponds to "lower rank." It is also correlated with the agent Metal. Perhaps this accounts for the concern with wealth.[26] In any case, the subject of these lines has made two distinct errors: Not only is he self-absorbed; he has also chosen profit over righteousness. In contrast, the superior man who "delights in Heaven and recognizes his fate"[27] overcomes ordinary anxieties about low position and poverty.[28] In one way, poverty should even be welcomed, since the poor soon learn to free themselves not only from apprehension about the future but also from dependence upon comfort.[29] As Confucius said:

> If any means of escaping poverty presented itself that did not involve doing wrong, I would adopt it, even though my employment were only that of the gentleman who holds the whip. But so long as it is a question of illegitimate means, I shall continue to pursue what I love more, [righteousness]. . . . Poverty and obscurity are what every man detests, but if they can only be avoided to the detriment of the Way he professes, he must accept them. . . . A gentleman takes as much trouble to discover what is right as lesser men take to discover what will pay.[30]

> App. 5: What the Earth empties[31]
> Runs down to valley streams.
> Fath. 5: The Earth emptying itself
> Means: Men regard this as sagely.

Position 5 corresponds to auspicious Day. Earth, aligned with center, becomes the gathering place for the hundred streams, just as the noble man draws loyal adherents to him "by virtue of his emptiness."[32] Paradoxically, earth's willingness to allow itself to be eroded is a major factor in its endurance. The good man, then, does well to imitate Earth's condescension.

> App. 6: The small cup is filled to the brim.[33]
> Once full, it later topples.
> Fath. 6: The small cup kept full
> Means: How can it be worth filling?

This Appraisal corresponds to a point just after the apex of development. Recognizing the cyclical nature of fortune, the wise man in prosperity keeps himself especially humble, ever "mindful of danger when at peace."[34] Here, however, a vessel of small capacity (symbolizing a man of slight worth) has been filled to the brim (that is, given a job that strains his abilities). When position does not correspond with ability disaster soon results. As the *Lao tzu* says,

> Rather than fill it to the brim . . .
> Better to have stopped in time.[35]

If the commentators are to be trusted, the passage refers to a miraculous vessel purportedly housed in a temple of Chou (or Lu?) which stood in position when empty, but overturned as soon as it was filled.[36] The moral of the story is that humility is all the more necessary for those in honored positions. Note the contrast with the *Odes*, which celebrate the ruler's ability to "keep full."[37]

> App. 7: To examine oneself when poor
> > Helps make riches appear.
> Fath. 7: Self-assessment in poverty
> > Means: This invites great wealth.

When a gentleman meets with bad luck, he searches his own conscience before blaming others. As the *Analects* says, "Attack the evil within oneself. . . . And if you have made a mistake, do not be afraid of admitting the fact and amending your ways."[38] Such humility on the part of the noble man means that other men delight in his company, which, in turn helps to ease his circumstances. What's more, his mental balance allows him to take maximum advantage of future opportunities.[39] All this conduces to great good fortune.

> App. 8: Though poor, he pretends he is not
> > And so no one offers him relief.
> Fath. 8: Poor but not poor
> > Means: How can this be worthy of respect?

The interpretation of this verse depends upon the meaning of the terse phrase "poor not poor" that begins both Appraisal and Fathoming. By my reading, the meaning of the verse is that the individual, though impoverished (in either moral or financial terms), refuses to acknowledge his poverty. In consequence, he is likely to offend others with his wastefulness, pretense, and arrogance.[40]

Among the various commentators, Fan Wang reads the line as, "The [self-proclaimed] poor are not poor"; in other words, those of comparative wealth spend their time poor-mouthing. To Ssu-ma Kuang, the same line conveys the despicable scrabble to escape honorable poverty, which ultimately provokes others' revulsion: "In poverty, not [willing] to be poor." All three readings assume an unwise individual who is unable to work within the constraints of his present social station. For this reason, the individual is unworthy of respect.

> App. 9: Fine rain and drizzle
> Moisten parched gullies.
> In three days, the valley is soaked.
> Fath. 9: Fine rain soaking the valley
> Means: Humility works quietly.[41]

Fine rain signifies the humanizing influences of the sage; the ruler is said, for example, to "moisten"[42] his subordinates by grants and favors. In the sacred imagery of ancient China, the valley symbolizes whatever nourishes and is good.[43] The use of the magic "completion number," three, hints at the miracle involved in producing a thoroughly civilized man through repeated small acts of goodness. With steady application, even the smallest improvements can lead to major accomplishments, just as Aesop suggested in his fable of the tortoise and hare.

Li

No. 6. Contrariety

January 13 (p.m.)–January 17

Correlates with Heaven's Mystery; Yin; the phase Water; and the Yi ching Hexagram no. 38, Opposition; the sun enters the Barrens constellation, 4th degree

HEAD: Yang *ch'i*, newly hatched,[1] is very small. Things, each diverging and separating, find[2] their proper categories.

Although the yang *ch'i* is still weak, under its impetus the myriad things continue to grow, their behavior now slightly more aware and more distinctive than before. In Head no. 2, for example, things "went on to become their kinds." Now, they actively participate in the process of differentiation. The specific phrase "finding their proper categories" alludes to the *Changes*, which describes the evolution of all phenomena from their single origin in the Tao by reference to symbolic number magic and divination procedure.[3] Two fundamental questions of Han thought concern this process of categorization: How do the disparate things relate to one another? And how do the myriad things relate to the mysterious One that spawned them? Correlative thinking (see Key Terms) gave an answer to the first question, an answer subsequently employed in China by mas-

犀

Figure 4. In Chinese mythology, the ssu *and* hsi *are the female and male respectively of a one-horned species. The* hsi *depicted here looks very much like the female* ssu *of popular depictions, except that the* ssu *is shown as less hairy. Illustration from* San ts'ai t'u hui, *an encyclopedia of 1609, "Animals" section, 4/3a.*

Figure 5. Fu Hsi and Nu Wa (deities associated with yang and yin ch'i *respectively) holding the compass and square as symbols of divine order. Illustration from tomb tile, excavated from Chungking, Szechwan (45 × 39 cm.), now in the Szechwan Provincial Museum.*

ters of the various arts of medicine, astrology, and omen prediction. The relation of the One to the many, essence to existence, the unknowable to the knowable, was a question largely left to the poets and philosophers.

To suggest the interconnectedness of disparate parts of the triadic realms of Heaven-Earth-Man, Yang Hsiung gives familiar examples of mutually dependent, but distinctly different entities in this tetragram: back and belly, husband and wife, physical mind and judgment, life and death, substance and application. In each case he concludes that "separate ways" contribute to creative action and civilizing order. In combination, separate functions with distinctive properties ultimately add to a sum greater than their individual parts. In the case of the family, for example, both husband and wife make distinctive contributions, without which children cannot be born or a patrimony (in either the material or moral sense) be built. A just society, the family writ large, cannot exist without the interdependent hierarchies enshrined in the Five Constant Relations. Distinction, then, is undeniably useful.

At the same time, any act of individuation threatens desirable unity. This potential for discord prompted the sages to invent ritual, which makes use of inherent inequalities to teach people to prefer consistency, cohesiveness, and stability over more disruptive alternatives. Ritual also curbs the possible abuses associated with hierarchy; ideally, it binds the entire unequal community by a basic fairness (the Chinese definition of "equality").[4] Hierarchical order constrained and patterned by ritual, then, is the proper model of differentiation among men.

> App. 1: Once the Void is deflected,
>   The heart inclines as well.
> Fath. 1: The Void astray and the heart turned
>   Mean: He embraces what is not upright.

In Yang's schema, Position 1 corresponds to the Beginning of Thought. Appropriately, Yang begins this Appraisal with a reference to the "void," an epithet for the innermost heart/mind, the ruler of the intellect and emotions.[5] In the sage, this core is characterized by a perfect receptivity to shifting events processed by the five senses. However, as soon as the inner mind turns aside from the true Way, thoughts and emotions grow confused. (This is symbolized by the deviation from the strictly vertical or "upright" line.) Inappropriate persons or courses of actions are unduly favored. Based on false assumptions, the individual's judgment will be skewed. When the heart "has inclinations" (in other words, is prejudiced), the heart "inclines" towards a faulty course. Misfortune will quickly follow.

> App. 2: Straightening his belly,
>   Pulling up his back,
>   He achieves[6] proper alignment.
> Fath. 2: A straightened belly
>   Means: The center heart is settled.

Appraisal 2, early in the tetragram, appropriately refers to preliminary training of the heart/mind. All commentators agree that the belly refers to what is inside (and so relatively prior and important); the back, to what is outside.[7] The message of this Appraisal is: Rectify the inner self and good behavior will follow. Once good behavior becomes a habit, inner resolve is so strengthened that upright acts become progressively easier to perform. And so "the center heart is settled." Only then is the gentleman ready to transform others. Inner orientation supports outer reforms of ever greater scope.

App. 3: He twists his belly
       In straightening his back.
Fath. 3: A twisted belly and straight back
        Mean: Inner and outer are at war.

Here is a person who appears to be "straight" (presumably because he self-righteously pretends to virtue), though he is crooked at the core.[8] Position 3 marks the initial transition from Thought to Action. When thought and behavior fail to correspond, harmful tensions arise within the individual. Also, a censorious attitude toward others is likely to elicit their anger. Inevitably, such deceit directed toward the self and others ends in misfortune.

App. 4: Husband and wife take separate ways.
       It is the family they mean to preserve.
Fath. 4: The separate ways of husband and wife
        Mean: Each has a separate sphere.[9]

As in the two preceding Appraisals, inner contrasts with outer. Moving from the site of the physical body, the theme now shifts to the fundamental distinctions underlying a civilized order. In early China, the husband tended to public matters outside the home while the wife managed the domestic sphere inside the family residence. Through this division of responsibilities the family maintained harmony and material welfare. The fruitful nature of male/female complementarity is one theme found in the *Changes*:

> Heaven and Earth are opposites, but their action is concerted. Man and Woman are opposites, but their wills conjoin. The myriad things stand in opposition to one another, but their actions are by type.[10]

App. 5: South by east, he aims at the *ssu*,
       But north by west, his arrow flies.
Fath. 5: Taking aim at the *ssu* in the southeast
        Means: He does not hit its head.[11]

In ancient Chinese myth, the *ssu* is a marvelous beast (occasionally identified as a rhinoceros or a wild ox) easily recognized by the luminescent horn atop its head that renders it visible even at night, while it bathes in deep waters.[12] A rare creature, the *ssu* is considered the sport of kings, and so it appears in Appraisal 5, which is assigned to the Son of Heaven. Southeast China is a land of marshes and river valleys—in other words, the natural habitat for such a water creature.

The arrow aimed southeast flies in the absolutely opposite direction. Since the shining horn of the *ssu* makes it an easy target, even for the untrained archer, this mistake is particularly egregious. Clearly, the individual has lost all sense of moral direction. Intending to go one way, he ends up going the opposite. If he desires to improve his aim, numerous guides, including the Five Classics and the suasive example of good men, exist to instruct him. They are designed to help him straighten his thoughts like an arrow.[13]

Since the *ssu*'s horn points unerringly to the good, kings who hoped to find true merit among the various candidates for office purportedly had drinking cups made from horns of the *ssu*. The merits of applicants for official posts in ancient times were assessed during ceremonial archery contests. Since both the *ssu* and archery are associated with bureaucratic selection, the text also works as oblique criticism of the king's failure to appoint the right men to the appropriate rank.

> App. 6: Level, line, compass, and square:
> Different are their applications.
> Fath. 6: Level, line, compass, and square
> Mean: Divergent are their ways.

All "great instruments"[14] were invented by the ancients to help lesser men "first rule the self and then rule others."[15] Though all are needed in construction, by no means do these tools all work in the same way. Level and line determine straight horizontal and vertical lines, while compass and square are needed to form perfect circles and corners. By analogy, each of the social institutions, including bureaucracy and ritual,[16] has its own function in building civilization, with each addressing a separate human need. It is characteristic of the sage-ruler that he always knows which tool to apply to the specific problem at hand, even when the "tool" is a public servant. Here Yang's verses recall a text from Master Huai-nan (d. 122 B.C.):

> The superior man in his use of men is like the skilled workman in the disposition of his wood. Large pieces are used for boats and beams; small pieces, for oars and joists. Long pieces are used for eaves and rafters; short pieces, for gargoyles and decorative designs. All of these pieces, irrespective of their size, find their niche, and all of the carpenter's instruments and templates have their application.[17]

> App. 7: An unwomanly woman
> Has only herself in mind.[18]
> She overturns her husband's plans.[19]
> Fath. 7: An unwomanly woman
> Means: This is utterly abominable.

According to the text, as yin elements women should be receptive rather than active, and concerned with domestic, rather than public events. In contrast with that ideal, the "unwomanly woman" described here not only has a mind of her own, she even works to undermine her partner's endeavors.

According to the *Odes*, "a woman thinks not of morality" but only of food and children.[20] In part because of this presumed weakness, convention decreed that a woman devote herself to her father before marriage, to her husband after marriage, and to her son when a widow. Though some women in Western Han were well educated and independent,[21] an increasing conservativism led not a few Han thinkers to assume that a woman should have no opinions or cares apart from those of her husband. This depiction of women was not viewed as particularly repressive at the time. It was assumed that each individual, if prompted to express his or her innate potential, will find his or her place (in Chinese, "each achieving its proper role"),[22] in a thoroughly integrated "natural" order.

As yin is to yang and woman to man, so the official is to his ruler. Therefore, this passage equally describes the usurpation of power by an evil official. Early Chinese thinkers repeatedly warned against the confusion of political roles:

> Where the ruler and the minister have different Ways, there is proper order, but where they are the same, there is disorder. If each gets what is appropriate to him and dwells in what is right for him, the one above and those below will know how to deal with each other.[23]

> App. 8: Killing and birthing[24] oppose each other.[25]
>   Harmony and centrality he takes as his way.
> Fath. 8: Killing and birthing, mutually opposed,
>   Mean: Centrality defines the limits.

Killing and birthing seem unalterably opposed, though Heaven participates in both. As Yang writes, Heaven and Earth "at one point give life; at one point give death."[26] By analogy, the state acts both to punish (by the penal code) and to foster (by means of rewards).[27] Each activity is somehow rooted in a single standard derived from cosmic norms. He who acts through ritual to maintain the Mean will know how to apply the norms in each individual case.

It is also possible that Yang Hsiung means to describe the "good death" here. The ancient Chinese defined "the good death" as a natural death faced calmly, if possible in bed surrounded by loved ones. Paradoxically, the good death is inextricably tied to the good life, because acts commanding communal respect are prerequisites for living out one's days in peace. The same pursuit of the Right which shapes an individual's existence defines community boundaries, in both the psychic and social senses.

App. 9: The Green Sprite's wife lives apart
        In a separate house of the sky.
        If the pattern is broken,[28]
        The harvest's bounty fails.
Fath. 9: The female mate of Ts'ang-ling
        Means: Failure brings defeat.

The Green Sprite (or Ts'ang-ling) is the planet Jupiter (allied with Wood and east), whose mate is the planet Venus (allied with Metal and west). In the normal course of events, these planets do not reside in the same lunar lodge.[29] This is probably because their natures are fundamentally opposed: Metal harms Wood. It is, after all, the metal ax which chops wood. A conjunction of the two planets portends evil, especially to vegetation. According to a Han treatise on astrology, floods and periodic crop failures will result. A conjunction of Venus and Jupiter also presages civil war, and more particularly, the rise of a commoner to threaten the imperial throne.[30]

Shang
No. 7. Ascent
January 18–January 22 (a.m.)

Correlates with Heaven's Mystery; Yang; the phase Fire; and the Yi ching Hexagram no. 46, Pushing Upward; the sun enters the Barrens constellation, 8th degree

HEAD: Yang *ch'i* engenders things in a place below. All things[1] shoot through[2] the earth, climbing to a higher place.[3]

This tetragram is aligned with Fire, whose nature is to rise up;[4] hence, the image of Ascent. In the natural world of Heaven-and-Earth, it is now the Lesser Cold solar period, when the shoots of living things first appear, like arrow tips pushing their way through the soil.

In the parallel realm of Man, individuals also begin their upward drive. This ascent may be auspicious or inauspicious, depending on the motive force that propels it. On the one hand, this tetragram decries the misplaced "pushiness" typical of the ambitious individual intent upon securing worldly position or fame at any price. Similarly, in his *Model Sayings*, Yang insists that the use of the synonym "advance" (*chin*) be confined to "advance in the Way," rather than "greedy ambition" for high

Figure 6. A Han dynasty watchtower (130 cm. high). excavated from Ling-pao Prefecture, Honan, tomb no. 3 of Chang Wan.

position and salary.[5] On the other hand, the individual is to be applauded for assiduous attempts at self-cultivation that aim at a higher Good.

Many of the images in this tetragram implicitly consider the appropriate speed of a correct ascent. In most cases, the tetragram assumes a slow pace for gradual reform, following the Image text attached to the correspondent hexagram:

> The image of pushing upward.
> Thus the noble man by compliant virtue
> Heaps up small things
> To achieve the high and great.[6]

In his *Model Sayings*, Yang Hsiung also presumes that the acquisition of virtue needs time:

> Not like a clap of thunder, not like a clap,
> But quietly, so quietly,
> [Virtue] grows greater and greater
> [So that after] a long time, it becomes fuller.[7]

The sluggish rate of visible change is to be expected at this time of year, when the first intimations of spring have only just begun.

> App. 1: Elevating his pure mind,
> He blunts its bit-like sharpness.[8]
> Fath. 1: Elevating his pure mind
> Means: He is harmonious and happy.

In Position 1, which corresponds to the Beginning of Thought, Yang Hsiung refers to the heart/mind's potential for goodness. In learning to ignore the impatient desire for fame and power,[9] the individual develops his best impulses during a slow maturation process. As a result, a stable happiness born of compliance with the cosmic norms replaces the sharpness associated with the clever, restless mind.[10] As the *Lao tzu* advises:

> Blunt the sharpness. . . .
> Let your wheels move only along old ruts.[11]

> App. 2: Rising without roots,
> His thoughts climb to Heaven.
> Falling back,[12] he's stuck in the abyss.
> Fath 2: Rising without roots
> Means: He is unable to sustain himself.[13]

Man's roots lie in the inborn goodness that constitutes a part of his original nature. These fragile roots must be cultivated carefully if they are to survive the stress and strain of daily life. Man's roots are also associated with family and close friends.[14] Here an individual aspires to—or worse—accepts high position without thinking of his own need for self-cultivation or the needs of those in his circle. The climb to Heaven is proverbially "beyond one's reach."[15] A speedy climb is all the more dangerous. This advance is particularly unjustified, so the person is likely to topple, sooner or later, into the "abyss" (destruction or obscurity). The good person, in contrast, is ever mindful of the maxim:

> There is no crime greater than having too many desires.
> There is no disaster greater than not being content.
> There is no misfortune greater than being covetous.
> In being content, one will always have enough.[16]

> App 3: Flying out from dark ravines,
>   He soars to lush trees,
>   Drawn by their rare fruit.[17]
> Fath. 3: Out from ravines, up to the trees,
>   Means: He knows the way to go.

Appraisal 3 refers to Ode 165, in which a bird disturbed by the sound of the woodcutter's blows flies to safety in a stand of tall trees.[18] To any reader trained in the Chinese Classics, the image of a bird escaping a dark ravine would also bring to mind a famous passage from the *Mencius*, which compares coming up into the light with the idea of enlightenment following study of the Classics.[19] With the word for "timber" a pun for "talent,"[20] we find that a man's very security depends upon developing his inborn capacities by following the hallowed precepts of the ancients.

The "rare fruits" (literally, rare grains) sought may be official stipends, which in early Han were customarily paid in grain.[21] Since Yang Hsiung tends to denounce the common preoccupation with material success,[22] it is far more likely that rare fruits signify the "excellent Way," as the commentator Ssu-ma Kuang suggests.

> App. 4: Reaching ever higher, though unaligned,
>   Like a plant, full-flowered without roots,
>   He wraps himself[23] in empty fame.
> Fath. 4: Reaching higher though unaligned
>   Means: He rises recklessly.

Position 4 corresponds to official rank and the turn to action. As the individual considers possible career moves, he should remember that correct alignment with the Way (that is, the determined pursuit of Goodness) is the root of all merit and glory. Though the unscrupulous individual may prosper temporarily, danger lies ahead. Lacking the proper foundation in virtue, his advance soon falters, just as flowers plucked from their roots inevitably wilt. Once his unstable character is unmasked, the disapprobation of others will only hasten his downfall.

App. 5: Rising from the deep marsh, a crane calls,
      Stepping up to Heaven, unashamed.
Fath. 5: A calling crane, unashamed,
      Means: He has what it takes at center.[24]

In China, the crane is associated with longevity. It is also known to fly high.[25] In ancient Chinese imagery, then, the figure of the calling crane symbolizes the superior man whose reputation is well known.[26] This crane is "unashamed," despite the bold daring of its initiative, because its pure heart deserves such swift advance. His call is heard in all directions since virtue compels men to follow its suasive example.

As Position 5 corresponds to the Son of Heaven, one early commentator is quick to see in these lines a celebration of the virtuous commoner's rise from obscurity to the imperial throne.[27]

App. 6: He ascends to the hall,
      His upper and lower garments reversed.
      Men at court are dismayed.[28]
Fath. 6: Ascending to the hall in disarray
      Means: The great masses are lost.

Ode 100 uses clothes in disarray as a stock metaphor to criticize disorder at court.[29] In his haste, an official confuses jacket and skirt, top and bottom. This reversal indicates subversion of the proper hierarchical relations (such as might occur when an official or empress arrogates imperial power). Those who witness this breach in ritual recognize it as an evil omen. Not surprisingly, all onlookers try to distance themselves from the perpetrator. The fault is considered especially grave since it occurs in the formal audience hall where the community gathers for the celebration of solemn rites. Due to the magnitude of error, dissatisfaction soon spreads beyond the inner circles of the court to the masses.

An alternate interpretation draws upon Yang's use of the same metaphor in the *Model Sayings* to suggest the heterodox adherents of the Hundred Schools Philosophers, who reject the Classics associated with Confucius.[30] When critics of Confucius hold sway at court, the common people will suffer, then repudiate the throne.

App. 7: He climbs the rickety[31] tower
      Some prop it with wood.
Fath. 7: Ascending the tower with the aid of props[32]
      Means: His supports hold firm.[33]

The tower points not only to high position but also to the elevated mind, as in the famous T'ang poem:

As daylight fades along the hills
The Yellow River joins the sea

> To gaze unto infinity
> Go mount another storey still.[34]

Despite such good associations, high towers are inherently dangerous structures. Like the Tower of Babel, they can represent overweening ambition. In "great winds" (that is, turbulent eras), they are vulnerable to collapse. The wise individual, recognizing the risks involved in his ascent, makes sure that he is provided with sturdy wooden props to forestall possible disaster. The prop, of course, may be knowledge of the classics, the support of excellent friends and ministers, or the auspicious *ch'i* accruing from virtuous action.[35] The opposite case is presented below.

> App. 8: Scaling the dangerous heights,[36]
>> Someone axes the ladder beneath him.
> Fath. 8: Scaling the peak, his ladder axed,
>> Means: He loses his knights[37] and commonfolk.

Once the individual rises to high position, he must maintain the support of those below. Otherwise, his subordinates will surely undercut him. Nor can safety be assured the individual whose ambitions lead him to rise too precipitously.

> App. 9: Perched on a rotten stump,
>> First he faces ruin, then finds a firmer base.
> Fath. 9: Perched on a stump, then on a firmer base,
>> Means: He later secures good men.

The arrogant individual finally repents his earlier errors, humbling himself in order to win the support of worthy followers. For the throne, worthy officials, in the words of the Odes, are the necessary "base of the state."[38]

Kan
No. 8. Opposition
January 22 (p.m.)–January 26

Correlates with Heaven's Mystery; Yin; the phase Wood; and the Yi ching *Hexagram no. 46, Pushing Upward; the sun enters the Roof constellation, 3rd degree*

HEAD: Yang [*ch'i*][1], supporting things [in their advance],[2] seems to be[3] drilling into solid matter. Thrusting forward like a spear,[4] there is penetration.

The title of this tetragram means "to hit or knock against," "to offend," "to seek," and "to violate." The clearly negative associations are employed by Yang in the unlucky, odd-numbered Appraisals, but the tetragram also celebrates some positive aspects of opposition, especially loyal opposition by worthy advisors at court, which in some sense mimics the bracing effect of yang *ch'i* upon the myriad living things. The calendar indicates the Great Cold, a fifteen-day solar period no less harsh than a remonstrant's stern admonition. Still, thanks to yang *ch'i*, the myriad things will eventually break out of their hard shells to meet the light of day. Similarly, the individual is beholden to loyal critics for the liberation of his thoughts. The fledgling moral conscience, then, depends for its survival on the expert "drilling" of a wiser individual. Inexpert advice, however, further weakens the conscience, just as clumsy probing with a drill damages the base material.

A great many Warring States philosophical texts insist upon the minister's right to remonstrate with his ruler, and under certain circumstances to even depose him.[5] It could even be argued that Confucius authorized such views, for as the Master reportedly said:

> How can he be accounted loyal who refrains from admonishing [the object of his loyalty]?[6]

In general, this tradition was upheld, even strengthened in early Western Han. The *Garden of Sayings* by Yang Hsiung's contemporary, Liu Hsiang (77?–6? B.C.), devotes an entire chapter to ministerial remonstrance, drawing upon numerous historical and pseudohistorical anecdotes.[7] However, certain Confucians (perhaps under Legalist influence) began to argue that forthright remonstrance threatened the dignity of the throne and undercut the principle of strict hierarchy underlying the social order. More conservative texts, then, proposed that "a [good] subject does not admonish in a direct way."[8] By A.D. 79, the scholastics present at the imperially convened White Tiger Hall Discussions on orthodoxy concluded that of five different kinds of remonstrance, "forthright remonstrance is the worst."[9] Yang Hsiung appears to harken back to the Warring States and early Western Han thinkers on this issue. His *Model Sayings* argues that certain kinds of indirect criticism actually encourage, rather than curb evil tendencies.[10] In this tetragram, he advocates "forthright" criticism on the part of the official, so long as the ruler has been adequately prepared.

> App. 1: He cranks[11] the drill,
> > Boring into internal cracks.
> > Danger.
> Fath. 1: The bit boring inside
> > Means: Turning the bit is wrong.

The drill is a metaphor for speech that plays upon the listener's own predispositions for effect. Shang Yang, for example, purportedly knew three techniques by which to "drill" his evil persuasions into Duke Hsiao of Ch'in.[12] The intelligent advisor, like the good artisan, carefully calculates his moves. Just as the drill tip must be applied with extreme care, words of loyal remonstrance must be aimed cautiously, lest further damage result. This is especially true if there are weak spots in the base material (that is, the conscience of the listener).[13] The evil rhetorician, in contrast, purposely preys upon the faults of his audience, until he persuades others to prefer wrong. If this goes on at court, it will soon create havoc in the kingdom.[14]

The early commentator Fan Wang offers an alternate interpretation, reading the first line of the Appraisal as "Wobbling, the drill bit." To Fan, the sharp bit of the drill symbolizes singlemindedness. In that case, the text reproves consciences that shift at will. This is linguistically possible, but somewhat less persuasive in view of the long association of drills with rhetoric.[15]

> App. 2: At the first small signs,[16]
>   Oppose and rectify.
>   Only apply the model decrees.[17]
> Fath. 2: At first small signs, to oppose and rectify
>   Means: He greatly protests small errors.

The most effective remonstrance is leveled at incipient evil for the simple reason that mistakes are far easier to correct before they have become well-established habits. Early reproofs help the person who is basically good "deal with the thing while it is still nothing."[18] All parties then become one in their dedication to applying the model decrees transmitted from the sages.[19]

> App. 3: He gags his mouth with wood,
>   And bolts tight the lock.
>   This is counter to propriety.
> Fath. 3: Gagged and bolted so tightly
>   Means: "Seeking salary is perverse."

The "gag" and "bolt" are slang for the rhetorical devices practiced by unscrupulous advisors.[20] I suspect that the gag describes the clever speaker preventing his opponents from answering his arguments; and the bolt, taking advantage of the listener's prejudices to construct a seemingly airtight argument. One late commentator, however, takes the gag and bolts as synonyms, meaning "to preserve a tactical silence during debate" so as to curry favor with those in authority.[21] In this way, petty men secure their own fortunes while tricking the unwary listener into embarking on disastrous policies. Such scheming makes a mockery of the solemn injunction of the *Odes* to "seek good fortune by no evil ways."[22]

Conceivably both gag and bolt could refer to the evil official's attempt to "block up the people's mouths." One early text argues:

> To block up the people's mouths is even more extreme than blocking up rivers. If a river is obstructed and breaks through, the injury to people will necessarily be great. And so it is with the people. Therefore, those who control the rivers dredge them out, causing them to flow. Those who control the people open channels of communication, causing them to speak.[23]

> App. 4: Critical words cut to the bone
> Because the time is right.
> Fath. 4: The time for sharp criticism
> Means: To be forthright is his way.[24]

The "bones" signify the innermost being. If an admonition "cuts to the bone," it means that it is both "incisive" and "taken to heart."[25] Clearly, the advisor has chosen the right time to level his forthright criticism. Had he spoken at the wrong time, he would have suffered the ill effects of the other's anger without having persuaded him to reform his conduct.

> App. 5: He stupidly seeks a heap of sweets.[26]
> Someone hands him an unfired tile.
> Fath. 5: The striving of an ignorant man
> Means: The gift is not good.

Many commentators see an allusion to a well-known anecdote involving Prince Ch'ung-erh, who later became Duke Wen of Chin (r. 636–628 B.C.). When traveling through Wei, Ch'ung-erh was reduced to begging food from a countryman, who handed him a clod of earth. In his anger, the young prince wished to scourge the giver with his whip, but his aide Tzu-fan rightly identified the gift of soil as a good omen presaging feudal possession of the area.[27] Unfortunately, there is no direct analogy between the two passages. Ch'ung-erh properly sought bare sustenance, not fine delicacies. What's more, the gift to Ch'ung-erh was auspicious. Yang Hsiung's verse, in contrast, is correlated with inauspicious Night. The stories are comparable only insofar as both recount the unexpected fruits of striving.

The heap symbolizes what is high and great; the sweets, whatever is most desirable.[28] If an individual hankers for high position despite his own lack of qualifications, he is likely to meet with misfortune and insult, instead of support.[29] The potsherd symbolizes the stern necessity to perform menial tasks.[30] The subject, reaching too soon for a life of luxury and ease, experiences a life of poverty and hard labor. His singleminded pursuit of material success has deterred him from pursuit of the Way.

App. 6: The trunk[31] reaches to[32] heaven.
 With propriety comes prosperity.[33]
Fath. 6: Properly aligned for the trunk's reach
 Means: Thus is prosperity preserved.[34]

In a yin tetragram, Position 6 represents the apex of the cycle; hence, the image of a tree piercing the sky. The tree trunk usually stands for the staunch friend and advisor, especially the high official who supports his ruler, though it may also symbolize the emperor as *axis mundi* of the universe. If the tree trunk is tall enough to reach to Heaven, it is surely grand enough to support any endeavor on Earth. (Contrast Appraisal 2, Tetragram 7.)

App. 7: When shouldered spears are many,[35]
 Confrontations follow.[36]
Fath. 7: Shouldered spears in great numbers
 Mean: They do not give way.[37]

Spears symbolize a quarrelsome nature. Belligerent individuals tend to meet misfortune because of their warlike proclivities.[38] The final Fathoming line (literally, "not admitted [on?] the Way") is intentionally ambiguous. It can either mean that the bellicose ignore the decided advantages of the Confucian Way of deference, or that the troops on one or both sides do not yield their ground. Both situations prove equally dangerous.

If we assume that this verse concerns not only Opposition but controversial speech, the lines could read:

[Like] spears borne, explication upon explication,
A confrontation.
[Like] spears borne, explication upon explication,
Mean: [The debaters] will not give way.

App. 8: Fiery tongues inflame the city.
 He sprays water from[39] a jar.
Fath. 8: Fiery tongues and water spewed
 Mean: Thus the noble man exorcises evil.[40]

The phrase "fiery tongues" refers to slanderers, whose rumors can fire up an entire city.[41] The significance of the water sprayed is less clear. It probably refers to the exorcist's spitting holy water in all directions from a jar,[42] an apt symbol for the purifying words of the good man. It is also possible that the gentleman spits to express his complete contempt for the slanderer.[43] Since the contents of a single jar of water are hardly enough to quench a raging fire, clearly we witness a miraculously efficacious force.

> App. 9: Reaching for the floating clouds,
>   He forthwith falls from Heaven.
> Fath. 9: Reaching for the floating clouds
>   Means: Only then does Heaven let him fall.

In a passage in the *Analects*, Confucius claims that the thought of accepting ill-gotten gains is as remote from him as clouds floating overhead.[44] Overreaching ambitions end in the individual's downfall, especially when cosmic trends are unfavorable, as they are in the final Appraisal 9. As a Chinese proverb says, "The higher the climb, the harder the fall."[45]

If the verses continue the theme of remonstrance, the lines may also describe the man who launches into an elaborate speech without considering his audience. Such a would-be reformer might as well be punching air. Small wonder that he falls from high position.

Shu

No. 9. Branching Out
January 27–January 31 (a.m.)

Correlates with Heaven's Mystery;
Yang; *the phase Metal; and the* Yi ching *Hexagram no. 19, Approach; the sun enters the Roof constellation, 7th degree*

HEAD: Yang *ch'i* is strong within, but weak without. All things, branching out, advance to greatness.[1]

Although yang *ch'i* appears weak outside, it grows strong within, providing a base for the continued growth, proliferation, and differentiation of the myriad things. This tetragram signifies the initial stage of advance for things; as one commentator writes, "[Things] advance, but still have not reached florescence."[2] Like the first tentative branching and leafing out of vegetation in early spring, the myriad things under the beneficient influence of yang *ch'i* spread out to cover the face of the earth.

The title character, a *hapax graphomenon*, means "to advance slowly" or "to advance until it is pervasive."[3] Advance is auspicious so long as it is done with care; advance brings misfortune if it is driven by overweening ambition or intemperate desire.

> App. 1: From the time I crawled,
>   I have loved this hidden[4] virtue.
> Fath. 1: Crawling toward hidden virtue
>   Means: It is as though I had not walked.

These lines aptly suggest the frustration occasionally experienced by the individual who desires to "walk in the Way." Impatient to achieve self-cultivation, it seems virtually impossible to reach the stage where virtue seems an easy path. At best, the newcomer to self-cultivation can hope for slow and steady progress. For this reason, she is likened to the small baby creeping towards an elusive ("hidden") goal. The phrase "from the time I crawled" emphasizes her consistent devotion to following the Way.[5]

The commentators offer variations on and refinements of this reading. Fan Wang, for example, applies the lines to the theme of slow advancement of the virtuous commoner up the bureaucratic ladder. In any reading, virtue remains "hidden," either because the stupid masses fail to recognize it[6] or because the superior man dislikes drawing attention to himself. The true man of virtue prefers to stay low ("crawling"), downplaying his abilities ("as though I had not [adequately] walked"). Alternately, the last line of the Fathoming may show that the individual has reached such a high stage of development that Goodness becomes effortless.[7]

> App. 2: Dazzled,[8] his all-consuming greed[9]
>   Does not help him gain his goals.
> Fath. 2: Deluded by ever-greater greed
>   Means: With many desires, he proceeds.

Position 2 marks the Middle of Thought. This tetragram takes "slow advance" as its theme.[10] Here, however, thoughts grow frenzied as the individual plunges forward in pursuit of his desires, like hounds moving towards the kill.[11] We know those desires to be unworthy, for "dazzling" has bad connotations in classical Chinese; it brings to mind delusion and blindness.[12] The individual's perceptions are clouded by cupidity. The only glint in his eye is that provoked by enticing and elusive objects of desire. Driven by an overwhelming urge to fulfill his desires, the greedy individual cannot begin to progress in the Way or achieve its long-term benefits. Paradoxically, real satisfaction eludes him, as his attempts to satisfy desire merely feed the creation of ever greater needs. Only a consistent effort to dampen desire can bring true happiness.[13]

Since this Appraisal is aligned with inauspicious night, two commentators suggest an alternate reading for the entire poem, with a night hunt as subject:[14]

> [By] the glittering light [of the torch], the hunt.
> [Dogs fight over the game] greedily.
> Going forward to no profit.[15]

> [By] the glittering light, the [night] hunt
> [Dogs fight over the game] greedily.
> [Driven by] increased desires, they go forward,
> [To bite the hand of their master.]

In this interpretation, bloodthirsty masters in their stupidity fail to realize the appetites they have created in those in their service. It is true that Yang Hsiung's prose-poems often deplore the waste and extravagance of imperial hunts, but the most famous night hunt was associated with virtuous King Wen of Chou.[16]

> App. 3: Warmed,[17] the low grasses spread
>   Up mounds and hills, as they should.
> Fath. 3: Warm grasses on mounds and hills
>   Means: The short look down on the tall.

When short grasses cover the hills, their vantage point allows them to overlook the highest of trees. This simple fact underlines the manifest advantages attached to "standing on the shoulders" of the ancient sages. The verse recalls a passage from the *Hsün tzu*:

> In the west there is a plant named "servant's cane," with a stalk no more than four inches long. It grows atop high mountains, from whence it looks down upon pools a hundred fathoms deep. It is not that it can grow [to such a height]; it is simply the place where it stands.[18]

By analogy, the ordinary individual can make use of what is great (defined as ritual and social duty, as outlined in the Confucian Classics)[19] to outperform others who are naturally more talented.

> App. 4: Pouncing on wine and food,[20]
>   He battens but gains no renown.
> Fath. 4: Coveting wine and food
>   Means: In serving, he lacks direction.[21]

Appraisal 4 signifies the official. Here a highly placed person neglects the responsibilities of his position. Lacking sufficient self-cultivation to check impulses toward luxury and self-indulgence, he cares only for the perquisites of his rank. Overindulgence in food and drink is a particular offense against virtue since their consumption is regulated by ritual.[22]

In ancient China, as in most cultures where the majority live at subsistence level, plumpness was often associated with enviable comfort. Where the official's paunch betokens greed, rather than the ease that comes with Goodness, it is no wonder that the state is poorly served. The subject of these lines is a slave to his desires, rather than master of them.

> App. 5: For branching out, there is enough
> If he trusts his sturdy carriage.[23]
> Fath. 5: That there's enough for branching out
> Means: His position is just as it should be.

The phrase "there is enough" suggests that the ruler, as subject of Appraisal 5, is well equipped to proceed along the Way of goodness.[24] Moreover, the chariot (signifying political leverage gained through the loyal support of subordinates) is at hand. With its help, the king can hope to extend his influence in every direction. Virtue and position combine to make this an auspicious forecast.

> App. 6: Branching out alone by leaps and bounds[25]
> Is good for small things, but not for great.
> Fath. 6: Expanding alone by leaps and bounds
> Means: This cannot be turned to something great.

"Alone" is the crucial word in these verses. While American tradition often celebrates the romantic loner, Confucian tradition is generally suspicious of the would-be self-made man. In contrast to the subject of Appraisal 5, who uses all available help to extend his influence, the subject of these verses acts independently. If a man intends to go far, he should seek like-minded companions of virtue, who will both further his cause and restrain his conduct. Without such help, who can hope to progress far?

> App. 7: In old age,[26] the time comes[27]
> To bring to fruition what has been learned.[28]
> Fath. 7: White-haired, to meet the time
> Means: In old age, he gets his chance.

Position 7, being past the midpoint of the tetragram, symbolizes aging and decay. So does the color white, which is aligned with autumn and the west, the region where the sun declines. Still, the Appraisal is aligned with yang *ch'i*, making it, on balance, lucky. Though the man of virtue, like the sun, approaches the hour of his demise, his accomplishments appear most brilliantly in old age, just as the light of the sun is most dazzling in late afternoon. Once the good man finally succeeds to a position of considerable power, reform among the people will quickly follow, securing his reputation forever.

> App. 8: He is overrun with fleas and lice.
> Danger.
> Fath. 8: The spread of fleas and lice
> Means: Parasites are not worth trusting.[29]

Lice do far more than make their host uncomfortable; as parasites, they sap his vitality.[30] In this, they are like bad companions or backbiting officials at court. Such men depend for their livelihood upon the "host," but it is certain that the host cannot depend on them in return. Once they have weakened him sufficiently, they move on. They fail to operate by reciprocity, a fundamental Confucian virtue. Good men avoid them at all costs.

> App. 9: Throughout, he proceeds as if[31]
> On the edge of an abyss,
> Bound head and foot.
> Fath. 9: Bound throughout the entire advance
> Means: He fears to meet with harm.[32]

Position 9 completes the characteristic activity of the tetragram, in this case slow "spreading out." In some sense, the limited movement in Position 9 brings us full circle to the crawling of Position 1.[33] That may account in part for the curious use of the image of a man (or an animal?) bound head to tail. Here the bound figure conveys the idea of caution from beginning to end ("head to foot") in the face of dangerous entanglements. The wise person follows the injunction to "be as careful at the end as at the beginning,"[34] never forgetting that, "beneath good fortune disaster crouches."[35] After all,

> The noble man fears the will of Heaven, fears great men, and fears the words of the divine sages. [Only] the small man does not know the will of Heaven and so does not fear it.[36]

Thanks to such wariness, good fortune prevails.

The early commentator Fan Wang reads the character meaning "bound" as its cognate, meaning "to look upon something with affection."[37] The poem then serves to describe the good man who reviews an entire range of activities (his own or that of the cosmos?), from first to last:

> Completing the spread,
> To look upon it from beginning to end,
> When approaching the abyss [the cosmic origin? death?].[38]

> Looking while completing the spread,
> Means: He fears to meet with harm.

Hsien

No. 10. Defectiveness or Distortion
January 31 (p.m.)–February 4

Correlates with Heaven's Mystery; Yin; the phase Water; and the Yi ching Hexagram no. 62, Minor Error;[1] the sun enters the Roof constellation, 12th degree

---

HEAD: Yang *ch'i*, assisting things that are still in obscurity,[2] pushes against the wrapping [of yin *ch'i*,][3] distorting the shapes of things,[4] so that they are not yet able to walk perfectly upright.

The generative action of yang *ch'i*, usually considered good, initially has mixed results as it operates on the growth of the myriad things. Since yang *ch'i* is not quite strong enough to break yin's influence at one stroke, yang must force the hard casing constructed by yin *ch'i* in order to free the germinating embryos. In the process, the shapes of things are somewhat distorted, both by the pressure exerted on them and by their own wriggling out of narrow cells of confinement. The uneven quality of weather in early spring, which grows hot and cold by turns, is attributed to this deviation from the earlier perfection of the circle.[5]

> App. 1: Starting off wrong,
>   The path winds thereafter.
> Fath. 1: Defective at the beginning
>   Means: Later it is hard to correct.[6]

Yang Hsiung's language is reminiscent of the *Book of Changes* tradition:

> Rectify the base and the myriad things will be in good order. But if you are off by a hair's breadth [at the beginning], you will miss by a thousand *li* [at the end]. . . . Thus to conduct his affairs the noble man carefully considers the beginning.[7]

Like the *Changes*, the *Mystery* emphasizes the ease with which a minor deviation from the Way leads over time to ever greater errors. As the proverb goes, "There is nothing better than preventing depravity at its inception."[8]

The same lines, of course, fit a second topic, that of logical argument, equally well, with the early Chinese equating illogic with a "turn off course."[9] Since Position 1 represents the Beginning of Thought, the reader is urged not to stray from rational discourse. Below, the same metaphor works in Appraisal 2, the pair to this position.

> App. 2: From small defects he can return.
>> He can be taken as model.
> Fath. 2: That minor defects can then be turned
>> Means: He need not go far to set things right.

The *Changes* equates the return with the recovery of the true self through the admission and correction of one's failings.[10] It also identifies the superior Way with "taking great care at the beginning" of any transaction.[11] Clearly, error can be corrected with relative ease in the early stages, before it has taken hold of the heart/mind.

> App. 3: Swerving from the path,[12]
>> He cannot go straight.
> Fath. 3: On a crooked path[13]
>> Means: A straight course is impossible.

The individual blindly proceeds further down the path of error. His own sense of direction may be faulty; he may also choose a winding road over the shortest route, which by definition is straight and open. Like a lost traveler, he persists in the mistaken belief that the wrong way represents a "return."

> App. 4: The circumstance contrives; the faulty seems correct.[14]
>> Lucky men[15] do not deem this "happy coincidence."[16]
> Fath. 4: Wrong, but right by circumstance
>> Means: The good return to the constants.[17]

The general rule is that wickedness ends in calamity. While luck may follow wrongdoing in some few cases, not to act by the "constant" rule is to gamble with one's security, even with one's life. As Chinese tradition observes, "The noble man lives at his ease, awaiting his fate, while the petty man courts dangers, looking for lucky coincidences. . . . The superior man does not mistake lucky coincidences for something reliable."[18] That explains why the bad person finds that "riches are his ruin."[19]

The majority of commentators, however, find a very different argument in Appraisal 4: The noble man at certain points in his career may feel that he has no alternative but to deviate from conventional morality in order to promote a greater good. For example, the good man may reasonably conclude that he needs to preserve his own life in order to make future contributions to society;[20] he may also believe that a single deviant act (such as an assassination) can turn the ethical balance of the community in favor of the Right. Similarly, a loyal minister may assume power temporarily if a regency is required to save the state.[21] In support of this interpretation, the commentators cite various anecdotes about Confucius; in one, Confucius decides to break an oath since it had been forced on him.[22] If this line of interpretation is followed, the last line of the Fathoming must read, "Good [though] contrary to constants." In light of Appraisal 1, the utility of moral compromise seems questionable, especially before the end of the cycle.

> App. 5: The great Way is level,
> > But narrow byways
> > Distress the grand carriage.
> Fath. 5: That the great Way is level
> > Means: Why not follow it?

The same character is used for both the "great" highway and the surname of Confucius.[23] Therefore, Yang uses the image of the journey to demonstrate the inferiority of other philosophical schools when compared with the moral teachings of Confucius. Other thinkers may have their use, admittedly, but their vision is partial and inadequate. Only Confucian teachings are comprehensive enough to offer guidance in every circumstance to all persons, including the leader symbolized by the grand carriage.[24] It is distressing, then, that men of ordinary vision, including those in the high places, continue to prefer the partial truths offered by the Hundred Schools. As Lao tzu wrote, "The great Way is level, / [But] the people prefer the bypaths."[25]

> App. 6: When the Great Void strays,[26]
> > Some right it, some help it
> > Get back on course.[27]
> > He finds men straight as arrows.
> Fath. 6: When the mind strays, arrow-like men
> > Mean: He obtains worthy officials.

As in Appraisal 1 of Tetragram 6, the Great Void is an epithet for the heart/mind. Mistaken perceptions leading to faulty conduct can be corrected by a concerted effort under the direction of good men. The honest criticism of loyal supporters constrains the weak conscience to undertake much-needed reform.[28] The commentaries supply examples of loyal ministers from history, the most famous of which are Kuan Chung (d. 645 B.C.) and Yen tzu (d. ca. 500 B.C.).

> App. 7: To bend old[29] truths[30]
> > Is to wander the road
> > And go along with danger.[31]
> Fath. 7: Bending the old
> > Means: He only acts to initiate ideas.

As Confucius says, "He who sets to work upon a different strand destroys the whole fabric."[32] Though he changes the metaphor, Yang Hsiung similarly attacks "innovation" and "eclecticism" (*tsa*), two tendencies he decries elsewhere in his work.[33] Those who deviate from the "way of the ancients" manipulate hallowed texts to justify their own corrupt readings. In the *Analects*, the supreme sage Confucius spoke of himself as "a transmittor, not a creator."[34] How, then, can lesser minds at a later date arrogate to themselves the task of creating new philosophies?[35] What is it in humans that leads them to prefer novelty over the tried and true ways of the past? Innovators induce, rather than dispel confusion on key ethical issues. As the philosopher Mencius (4th c. B.C.) wrote, "There has never been one who could straighten others by bending himself."[36]

> App. 8: Though twisting his foot,[37]
>> He saves himself from a fall in the ditch.
>> Now he faces the proper way.
> Fath. 8: Twisting his foot
>> Means: He avoids unlucky events.

Appraisal 8 comes near the end of the cycle. Due to its situation, only partial success is possible even when the verse, as here, is aligned with auspicious Day. The ditch is made of dirt; therefore, it stands for filth and corruption in general. In ancient China, the ditch also symbolizes ignominious poverty, sickness, and death, for in times of famine or plague, corpses were hurled into wayside ditches without benefit of formal funerals.[38] To dodge ultimate disaster ("the ditch"), the individual jerks aside, risking injury to his foot (a mere appendage, after all).[39] Though he is injured in the process, at least he redirects his life to avoid future disasters. Henceforth, he constrains himself to conform to the Way.[40]

> App. 9: The carriage axle breaks,
>> The yoke snaps.
>> The team of four tangles in its traces.[41]
>> Men in high places spit blood.
> Fath. 9: The axle breaks, they spit blood.
>> Meaning: In the end, it's too late for regrets.

A dramatic scene of collapse and chaos ends the tetragram. In the middle of a journey or a battle, the conveyance belonging to a great man (the ruler?) collapses. The four horses hitched to the vehicle, their traces hopelessly entangled, struggle in vain to free themselves from the wreckage. With his chariot destroyed and his own person critically wounded, the great man has no way to flee. At the scene, he slowly bleeds to death.

The reason for this calamity is clear, thanks to earlier Appraisals. Once the man in high places departs from the true Path, he strays on dangerous bypaths, experimenting with heterodox ideas. His former supporters may try to desert his service, though many are equally caught up in the disaster. Naturally, the leader loses his power or even his life ("the blood"). It is now too late to reform.

The Ch'ing commentator Ch'en Pen-li applies the entire description to the failed attempts by loyal officials to reform the court. As those in the imperial service (symbolized by the traces?) have no power to affect the corrupt ruler, they spit blood in anger and frustration.[42]

Correlates with Heaven's Mystery; Yang; the phase Fire; and the Yi ching Hexagram no. 62, Minor Error; the sun enters the Roof constellation, 16th degree; the Dipper points ENE; the musical note is B^1

Ch'a
No. 11. Divergence
February 5–February 9 (a.m.)

HEAD: Yang *ch'i*, wriggling, breaks open at the east. Lordly, it emerges from the multitude of obstructions.[2] Things diverge in their appearance.[3]

This tetragram is aligned with the Spring Onset solar period. Accordingly, all images in the Head suggest the coming of the new season. With east as the direction of spring, it is only natural that yang *ch'i* should make its first appearance there. Even the particular wriggling form that yang takes (*ch'un* in Chinese) is synonymous with activity in the spring (also *ch'un*);[4] like a young insect working its way out of its chrysalis, yang frees itself from the confinement of dark earth and yin *ch'i*. Yang *ch'i* is masterful, even godlike, in its promotion of the universal patterns that result in cosmic harmony.[5] For that reason, it is called "lordly."[6]

The tetragram title implies "divergence," "deviation," "variety," "discrepancy," "inequality,"[7] and "distinction." At this juncture, the myriad things diverge further in their characteristic appearances and activities, less threatened by the ill winds of winter. Divergence can lead to fault and error, but distinction is to be applauded insofar as it underlies man's ability to make ethical judgments.

> App. 1: Failing in small things,
> Attack them yourself
> At the source.[8]

> Fath. 1: Attacking minor failings oneself
> Means: As yet, others do not know.

Continuing the argument of the previous tetragram, Appraisal 1 asserts the wisdom of correcting one's faults when they first appear so that error never grows obvious enough to become a source of shame.

> App. 2: Being steeped in his desires,[9]
> He brings about what he abhors.
> Fath. 2: Steeped in his desires
> Means: He is gradually led to error.

The indiscriminate pursuit of pleasure usually ends in disaster. The wise person, then, moderates his desires lest he gradually become a slave to them and reduce his chances of future happiness.

One oft-quoted anecdote beautifully illustrates the progressive errors that evolve from a single false step. The chief minister to the last king of Shang wept bitterly when his ruler decided to acquire a single pair of ivory chopsticks. When asked why he lamented so innocuous an act, the minister replied:

> Chopsticks are not be used with pottery but with cups made of jade or rhinoceros. Those do not go with vegetarian stews but with the meat of long-haired buffalos and unborn leopards. And those who eat such meats do not wear short hemp clothes or eat in a thatched house. Instead, they put on nine layers of embroidered dresses and move to live in magnificent mansions with lofty terraces. Afraid of the ending, I cannot help trembling with fear at the beginning.[10]

> App. 3: "Might there be ruin? Oh, might there be?"[11]
> Thus he is led to the bright light.
> Fath. 3: "Oh, ruin, such ruin!"
> Means: Shocked, he protects himself.

The worthy man weighs each action carefully, knowing full well that even minor mistakes may lead to his eventual downfall. In consequence, it is the prospect of ruin that prompts continued self-examination and speedy reform. Measuring his failings by the hard light of day (the "bright light"), the prudent individual goes on to win a reputation (a second "bright light"). That explains why, as the proverb goes, "In security the noble man is mindful of danger."[12]

> App. 4: Passing over[13] small acts of goodness,
> He will not overcome.
> Fath. 4: Foregoing small acts of goodness
> Means: He cannot reach greatness.

The *Changes* tells us that

> the petty man considers the small good to be of no advantage, so he makes no effort. He thinks the small sin does no harm, and so he does not give it up. . . . If good does not accumulate, it will not be enough to make a man's name.[14]

Another Chinese classic, the *Documents*, concurs:

> If you do not attend zealously to small acts, the result will affect your virtue in great ones.[15]

Self-cultivation is a slow process of learning, whereby the individual becomes practiced in discerning and performing the good act. If the individual is either too arrogant or too careless to make a habit of small acts of nobility, great virtue cannot be attained. Like the philosopher Hsün tzu before him, Yang Hsiung emphasizes the importance of gradual habituation to the Good.

Ssu-ma Kuang, however, reads this Appraisal as a critique of those who "go too far" in small acts of kindness or conscience while ignoring the greater good. He offers examples from Chinese tradition, including that of Wei Sheng:[16] Wei Sheng had arranged to meet his lady love under a bridge. The lady failed to show. When heavy rains came, Wei Sheng refused to leave the spot, lest he break his word, and so drowned under the bridge. The moral of the story is, those who are overly concerned with small points lose sight of the greater goal.

> App. 5: Having passed the gate, he returns[17]
> To enter, gaining that center court.
> Fath. 5: Having missed the gate, turning to enter
> Means: Before going too far,[18] he reverses his course.

The gate marks an easy access to home. By extension, it symbolizes whatever facilitates an easy entrance to understanding.[19] For this reason, the teachings of Confucius are frequently identified as the gates to learning. The center courtyard or lightwell is an integral part of the ancient Chinese house, providing free access to the gods inhabiting the open air above, as well as light and rainwater for the benefit of the inhabitants.[20] As the inner sanctum of the house, it also stands for the innermost thoughts of the individual and, by a pun,[21] for "conduct according to the Mean."

In these verses, the individual awakens to the magnitude of his error, then reforms his conduct in conformity with the Mean. His safe arrival at the inner sanctum, despite initial confusion and physical barriers, suggests that he has achieved moral perfection.

App. 6: In a great hurry,[22] he misses his gate
  And fails to enter his house.
Fath. 6: That in a rush, he does not enter
  Means: Truly, this is cause for grief.

In contrast to the subject of the preceding Appraisal, this individual is so muddled that he fails to realize his error. Perhaps other enticements or heterodox teachings have overwhelmed plain good sense. Confucius said:

> If a man finds he has made a mistake, then he must not be afraid of admitting the fact and amending his ways. . . . To have faults and make no effort to amend them is to have faults indeed![23]

App. 7: As with a pile of eggs,
  He acts with great caution.
  From fear comes propriety, then safety.
Fath. 7: Precarious as a pile of eggs
  Means: From his own danger, he creates safety.[24]

A "pile of eggs" is a popular metaphor in early China for critical danger.[25] If one approaches any serious problem with due caution, it may be possible to save the situation. The greater the caution, the greater the likelihood of success.

App. 8: He stumbles forth[26] on fettered feet.
  His jaw is branded, his eyebrows destroyed.
Fath. 8: The fettered feet
  Mean: From one step into calamity, no return.

A variety of punishments, each more dangerous than the last, is likely to befall the individual who does not mend his ways. The specific nature of those punishments, however, is a subject of dispute among the commentators. One commentator, for example, says that the evildoer is made to "bear the cangue" rather than suffer branding on the face.[27] In light of a parallel passage in the *Changes*, the verses may also be read:

> Feet fettered, he lurches forward,
> [To deep water] just up to the area over his eyes,
> Submerging his eyebrows.[28]

Certainly, the second reading emphasizes the imminent nature of the danger.

App. 9: Passing decrepit city walls, he finds
  Verdant shoots rising from stumps.[29]
Fath. 9: Passing the decrepit walls of his city
  Means: Through self-reform, life is renewed.

Since neolithic times, city walls in China have been constructed of wooden pillars packed with wattle-and-daub or tamped earth.[30] Since the city wall encloses its inhabitants, defining the community and insuring physical safety, city walls in good repair signify security on the psychic, physical, and political levels. Accordingly, their upkeep is a top priority for stable administrations. Here the city walls are in utter disrepair. Either the city is deserted or its government mismanaged. Intruders can easily breach the city's defenses. Still, there are some signs of hope: from nearby fallen trees or the wooden supports in the wall itself, young shoots have begun to sprout.[31] In the midst of death, renewal occurs. By analogy, even the most hardened of criminals can learn to recover his best self.

T'ung
No. 12. Youthfulness
February 9 (p.m.)–February 13

Correlates with Heaven's Mystery; Yin; the phase Wood; and the Yi ching *Hexagram no. 4, Youthful Folly; the sun enters the House constellation, 4th degree*

HEAD: Yang *ch'i* is first spied. Things like callow youths all still lack understanding.

This tetragram, like the previous one, is assigned to the Spring Onset solar period when plants and animals are expected to first emerge from their winter homes. The title character describes young animals whose horns have still not grown, the land still barren of vegetation, and youths of either sex who still lack the characteristic development of the heart/mind that makes people truly "human." The first signs of maturity now start to appear. So long as lack of development is primarily a function of time, we can anticipate the future happily. However, many promising trends may be nipped in the bud if they are not nurtured by trained caretakers.

For this reason, this tetragram advises the youth (or one who is new to any endeavor) to look for good teachers to guide the maturation process. Certain mistakes are particularly associated with youth (such as impetuosity and faulty judgment or indecision due to lack of experience). Unless an appropriate master is found, such faults tend to multiply over time, especially when the individual is intelligent.[1] If a person fails to locate a good teacher, "then if his studying has no direction and his mind lacks penetration, he himself is to blame."[2] As Yang Hsiung states categorically in his other "classic," the *Model Sayings*:

> To work at study is not as good as to work at finding a teacher. A teacher is a model for others. . . . Just as within a single noisy marketplace there are countless different ideas, within a book of a single chapter there are countless different theories. For the marketplace, a balance must be set up [to determine correct weight and value], so for each book, a teacher must be set up.[3]

In contrast to the corresponding *Changes* hexagram, which praises certain childlike qualities, the *Mystery* censures the puerile.[4]

> App. 1: The fatuous youth is not awake.
> Meeting us,[5] he is blind[6] and dim.[7]
> Fath. 1: A loutish youth who is unaware
> Means: We fear he'll be "dark" 'til the end.

Appraisal 1 corresponds to the Beginning of Thought. The most important task for the immature youth is to find a good teacher to train his heart/mind.[8] A Chinese pun identifies the teacher as "the first-awakened one"[9] who leads others to the Way. Here, unfortunately, Position 1 corresponds to inauspicious night and so Yang Hsiung speaks of darkness: Either the inane youth selects teachers who are equally ignorant ("He meets us, who are [also] blind and dim.") or the immature youth fails to heed his good teachers' words ("[Even after] meeting us, he is blind and dim.") Under such conditions, no pupil can hope to gain enlightenment. Unless he changes his ways, he is likely to remain doubly in the dark in that he will be both "unenlightened" and "in obscurity."

> App. 2: He casts the sacred milfoil.
> He fires the turtle's shell.
> Leaving the muck, he enters the anointed.
> Fath. 2: Casting milfoil, firing the turtle,
> Means: He approaches the path of glory.

As Confucius tells us, the better part of wisdom is to recognize what you do not know.[10] For that reason, the youth in search of greater understanding uses divination procedures to resolve cases of grave doubt. (Their sacred character precludes casual use.) Divination by milfoil (also called yarrow) and by turtle are the two ancient forms of prognostication hallowed by Chinese tradition. Significantly, each of these instruments for communication with the divine represents accumulated age and experience: the graph for milfoil contains the character for "old" within it,[11] while the marvelous capacities of the turtle are attributed to its fabled longevity. By implication, if the ancients are consulted in every doubtful case, a miracle will take place: the individual will emerge from obscurity and muddleheadedness (the "muck") to gain enlightenment and honor (an "anointment").[12]

> App. 3: The Eastern Star already shines,[13]
> Yet he cannot proceed by its light.
> Fath. 3: The Eastern Star already shining
> Means: Why not go?

Appraisal 3 marks the transition from Thought to Action. The necessary preconditions for enlightenment are present since the Eastern Star already shines. In other words, good teachers are available, the classics have been promulgated, and all the various tools of civilization (including divination) have been provided. For some reason, the individual fails to take advantage of the opportunities for moral growth, assuming himself to be incapable of maturity. In reality, he lacks sufficient will to follow in the Way.[14] The *Analects* condemns those who "hear of duty, yet do not move toward it."[15]

> App. 4: Some follow those in front.
> Those ahead light their way.[16]
> Fath. 4: Following the ones in front
> Means: Great is the light of those who lead.

In contrast to Appraisal 3, Appraisal 4 praises individuals who take full advantage of the illumination provided by moral exemplars of the past.[17] Given the penetrating power of those exemplars, even those who follow at some distance in time and space can find their Way by the light. This contention implicitly refutes Chuang tzu's belief that the Classics represent only the "dregs" of the former sages' teachings.[18]

> App. 5: If in thick brush he seeks the *ssu*,
> He finds a prize less valued.[19]
> Fath. 5: Hunting the *ssu* in the brush
> Means: The catch is not worth the praise.

The hunter lays a trap to catch a female *ssu*. (Probably a wild ox is indicated, though the prey may be a rhinoceros or some other marvelous beast.) The thick brush (that literally "covers" or "conceals") may function in several ways: Perhaps it keeps the hunter from finding his prey. Perhaps it conceals the hunter stalking his catch. Perhaps it hides a trap in the underbrush. In any case, there is no doubt that the hunter ignores important ritual rules which dictate that the female of the species is to be spared in the general slaughter. As one commentator remarks, the hunter "stops at nothing to get the game."[20] Such obsessive behavior not only diverts the hunter's attention from proper pursuits[21] while weakening his sense of scruples; it also diminishes future stocks of game. Despite the "catch," the man himself may be "caught" short in the short-term (if he is gored by his prey) or in the long-term (when stocks are depleted). This is an excellent example of the Chinese propensity to address concerns from both moral and practical considerations.

This portrait of an evil hunter contrasts with stories told of the legendary sage-kings of antiquity. Good King T'ang, for example, purportedly constructed a special trap open on three sides so that beasts could easily escape it. In the same way, T'ang framed his laws in such a way that his subjects found it easy to avoid being "framed" for criminal activities.[22] All men of virtue display a profound empathy for living things; as leader of this group, the Son of Heaven in Appraisal 5 never takes unfair advantage of the weak and helpless.

> App. 6: Open wide the tent,
> > Inviting guests from every quarter.
> Fath. 6: Throwing the tent open
> > Means: He sees the many lights.

We tend to think of Chinese rulers as closeted in "forbidden palaces," but early tradition made it incumbent upon every good ruler to conduct royal progresses throughout the land so that he could consult widely with candidates for public office.[23] Here the ruler opens his private quarters to all comers, as a public sign of his avid desire for the moral enlightenment provided by the "leading lights" of his kingdom. With the tent flaps up, the night sky comes into view.[24] The ruler is equally receptive to the constant norms illustrated by the starry firmament in its divine orbit (again, the "lights"). In consequence, the multitude of the ruler's subjects are transformed under his suasive example, yet a third instance of "many lights."

> App. 7: Cultivating the puny
> > He becomes a runt.[25]
> Fath. 7: Making the puny grow
> > Means: There is nothing to be achieved.

If the individual lacks the acuity and commitment to greatness that properly define the mature adult, we compare his stunted intellectual and moral growth to the crippled form of a dwarf. Greatness is equated with strict adherence to the Confucian Way, since virtue represents the supreme human goal on practical, as well as moral grounds.[26] And "development" must be defined in terms of strengthening the discerning mind that knows greatness, rather than nurturing the lesser, even bestial parts of human nature.[27] Physical development alone can hardly be considered a major accomplishment.

App. 8: Some beat him, some prod him.
He polishes the mysterious mirror of his mind
And so changes.
Fath. 8: Beating and prodding him
Means: In that way, his errors decline.

As the situation nears the end of its cycle, the individual finally responds to repeated and severe criticisms with a sincere attempt at moral reform. The wise individual is grateful for harsh criticism, since personal improvement usually depends on it. As the *Changes* writes, "To make immature fools develop, it helps to punish people."[28]

The heart/mind is a mirror in that it reflects all sensory impressions, however fleeting. By clearing away all misguided notions and intellectual baggage, the individual restores the pristine clarity of that organ, "polishing his mysterious mirror" so that it functions properly.[29] It is never too late to begin this process, although years of accumulated dust may complicate the task.

App. 9: The young buck butts the wild ox,
Cracking its own skull.
Fath. 9: The buck butting the ox
Means: In return, it harms itself.[30]

The immature deer still lacks horns, so it lacks the brute strength, the experience, and the skills necessary to defeat a dangerous opponent. In a serious miscalculation of its capacities, the fawn takes on the powerful wild ox (or possibly rhinoceros) known for its tough hide. It can neither fend off an attack by such a fearsome rival nor launch a counterattack. Inevitably, the fawn is gored or trampled by the ox. By analogy, the immature individual would do well to avoid all premature engagements with formidable adversaries. It is often pride that leads one foolishly into the fray.

Correlates with Heaven's Mystery; Yang; the phase Metal; and the Yi ching *Hexagram no. 42, Increase; the sun enters the House constellation, 8th degree*

Tseng
No. 13. Increase
February 14–February 18 (a.m.)

HEAD: Yang *ch'i* is burgeoning.[1] Things accordingly pile up and increase. Daily manifesting [their energy],[2] they grow.

As yang *ch'i* daily increases, under its protection all things prosper. This is a odd-numbered (i.e., yang) Head with an auspicious title, so the tetragram is lucky in its main theme: An increase in moral acuity is based on a sound ethical foundation. This increase, of course, mimics yang *ch'i*, which productively expands only after building a solid inner base in Tetragram 9. Head 13 represents a major step forward from the immaturity discussed in the previous tetragram.[3]

> App. 1: Hearing aright, and increasingly silent,
>   Outsiders fail to notice.
> Fath. 1: Hearing aright, ever more silent,
>   Means: He discerns what is inside.[4]

Appraisal 1, signifying the Beginning of Thought, here is associated with auspicious Day. The first response of the gentleman to hearing the Way is to contemplate it in silence. Temporarily distracted from mundane existence, the good man may even appear stupid to those of lesser understanding;[5] true virtue is recognized only by an inner circle of accomplished individuals.[6] Having no desire to show off his knowledge of the Way,[7] he considers in awed silence the miraculous patterns of the cosmos. Eventually, he quietly applies what he has learned to the "inside," the inner workings of the universe and the seeds of Goodness deep within himself.[8] As the *Lao tzu* says:

> He who knows others is clever
> He who knows himself has discernment.[9]

> App. 2: To increase his search for glory
>   Without squaring his inner life[10]
>   Is benighted.
> Fath. 2: Not increasing his "squareness"
>   Means: He only embellishes the outside.[11]

The contrast between internal and external continues. Squareness refers to "directional" behavior aimed at the Tao. It implies "squaring" thoughts and deeds,[12] as well as acting within well-established bounds.[13] The good person, then, takes it as a duty to make the outer life square with inner constraints.[14] A true increase in virtue works against artifice[15] and pretension, but the petty person focuses on external adornment, hoping to fool others by superficial changes. Yang Hsiung puts a spin on the famous question posed by the *Lao tzu*, "Which is dearer, your name or your life?"[16] Yang asks instead, "Which is dearer, the inner life or outer glory?" External brilliance cannot conceal inner confusion for long.[17]

> App. 3: Trees stay put,
>   And so steadily grow.

> Fath. 3: Rooted trees, gradual increase,
> Means: They cannot be suppressed.[18]

Wood comes up for two reasons: Appraisal 3 is assigned to agent Wood in the *Mystery*'s schema of correlations. At the same time, the Judgment attached to the correspondent *Changes* hexagram associates the "way of wood" with increase, success, and the promise of "daily advance without limit."[19] Trees support extensive (if gradual) growth above to the extent that they are firmly rooted below. They become the model for acquiring virtue.[20]

> App. 4: His waist cannot bear the load,
> Yet others add to the weight on top.[21]
> Fath. 4: That the center cannot hold
> Means: He can be defeated.

The poem depends upon a neat *double entendre*, with the same word meaning "waist" and "what is central" or "essential."[22] As the fulcrum of the body, the waist bears the major portion of weight in any beast of burden, including man. With the physical center too weak to bear the initial burden, one can only imagine the damage that will result when additional weight is heaped on. By analogy, when the essential core of one's being is inadequate to deal with life's daily challenges, an extra crisis may send the person into complete collapse. The essential core, however, can be strengthened by various techniques of self-cultivation.

> App. 5: In marshes, being low makes for capacity.[23]
> Many waters converge there.
> Fath. 5: That the low marsh holds much
> Means: From self-effacement springs greatness.[24]

The *Lao tzu* explains, "The reason why the river and the sea are able to be kings of the Hundred Valleys is that they excel in taking the lower position."[25] Modesty and self-effacement make for true greatness in that they compel the support of others. Appraisal 5 corresponds to the ruler. Clearly, the single most important attribute that qualifies the emperor to head the state is his ability to humble himself, as demonstrated by the courteous treatment of subordinates and a willingness to accept harsh criticism. Acting thus, the ruler becomes the figure around whom "the myriad blessings converge."[26] This, of course, is the central argument of the influential "Great Plan" chapter of the *Book of Documents*.

> App. 6: Like a torch, the Red Chariot spreads its light.[27]
> One day increases our lists by three thousand.[28]
> The noble man wins praise.
> The petty man takes wounds.

> Fath. 6: By the Red Chariot, daily increasing,
>   Means: The petty man is no match for the noble.[29]

The Red Chariot probably refers to the sun in its daily round. The sun, in turn, suggests the good ruler in two ways: First, the beneficent presence of the sage-king acts like the sun to enlighten, fostering peace and harmony wherever it goes. And second, the wise leader's favors are distributed fairly to all men of worth, just as the sun shines equally on every region of the earth. But what has this to do with an "increase of three thousand"?[30] Literary convention associates the founding of the Chou dynasty (correlated with Red and Fire in the Chinese schema)[31] with just such an increase. After all, legend tells us that good King Wu in 1122 B.C. was able to muster three thousand troops in a few days' time to defeat the last evil tyrant of the Shang-Yin dynasty.[32] As the philosopher Mencius (4th. c. B.C.) says, "So long as the ruler of a state is drawn to benevolence, he will have *no match* in the empire."[33]

One commentator, however, sees these verses as a kind of shorthand description of the high official's life. In his public life, the official employs munificent "red chariots"; in his private life at home, he enjoys the warm glow of torchlight. His retainers daily increase in numbers. The man of virtue merits this rapid rise in salary and position. The same promotions, however, prove disastrous for the ambitious man who lacks virtue.[34]

> App. 7: With height increased,
>   Cut back its peak
>   To make the mountain stable.
> Fath. 7: Increased height and graded peak
>   Mean: With loss, all is accomplished.

Paradoxically, the *Changes* associates final "expansion" with "decrease."[35] The individual who trims his own desires for aggrandizement increases his chances of accomplishing his goals. Therefore, the wise person acts to curb himself in order to assure his own security, preferring to keep his growth in balance with a solid base of support. Nothing is more dangerous than unimpeded or unsupported increase,[36] here symbolized by a mountain precipice. After all, the higher the position attained, the harder the fall.

> App. 8: Enslaved by a handful of cowries,[37]
>   Past profits shave future gain.[38]
> Fath. 8: Enslaved for a handful of cash
>   Means: First happiness, then ruin.[39]

The cowry, one of the earliest forms of currency in China, signifies wealth. The individual becomes a willing slave in return for material advancement. In his greed for cash, he accepts utter debasement, indicated here by the word "shaved," which refers to the tonsure of the indentured servant, the slave, or the convict.[40] As in the New Testament story of Judas Iscariot, the paltry sums gained are contrasted with the magnitude of the moral loss.

> App. 9: Jagged peaks do not collapse
> When they lean on their foothills.
> Fath. 9: That rocky crags do not collapse
> Means: Many knights give firm support.[41]

Appraisal 9 represents the extremities. In the case of mountains, the peak or precipice is the part most vulnerable to collapse. However, if the dizzying heights are supported by a firm base, they will not topple over even under the greatest stress. Likewise, if the ruler is supported by many worthy followers, his reign cannot be overturned.

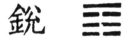

Jui

No. 14. Penetration
February 18 (p.m.)–February 22

Correlates with Heaven's Mystery; Yin;[1] the phase Earth; and the Yi ching *Hexagram no. 53, Advance; the sun enters the House constellation, 13th degree*

HEAD: Yang *ch'i*, like a high hill,[2] penetrates [upward].[3] That means the birth of things. All concentrate on oneness and avoid duality.[4]

This tetragram witnesses the transition from the Spring Onset to the Rainfall solar period, usually sometime in late February. Things in their early stages typically show little differentiation as they focus on internal growth. For example, the tips of vegetation just now pushing through the surface of the soil are so tightly furled that one plant is barely distinguishable from another. Perhaps from them Yang Hsiung takes his title, meaning "sharp tip" or "point" or "penetration." Succeeding Appraisals play out the full range of the title's meaning. Because a point or tip is sharp, the same term conveys mental or moral acuity; whatever is piercing, zealous, or focused; whatever is penetrating, or pointing in a particular direction.[5] The same character also refers to what is comparatively trifling or insignificant, as in the English expression "the tip of the iceberg."

Nearly all these meanings are employed below, requiring different translations for the same character. In many cases, the antonym for the title character is "duality" associated with moral confusion,[6] as the Head already suggests.

The tetragram presents oneness as its main theme, in the two senses of individual wholeness and social cohesion. But if those kinds of oneness are the proper goals of the individual, single-minded devotion—a third kind of oneness—is the means. As Hsün tzu, the Confucian master, wrote:

> If you pile up earth to make a mountain, wind and rain will rise up
> from it. If you pile up water to make a deep pool, dragons of all kinds
> will appear. If you pile up enough good deeds to make your charisma-
> tic virtue whole, a godlike understanding will come of itself and the
> sagelike mind will be perfected. And so, unless you pile up little steps,
> you will never be able to journey a thousand *li*; unless you pile up tiny
> streams, you will have no way to fill a river or a sea. . . . Achievement
> consists in never giving up.[7]

Only the focused mind can hope to discern the unifying principle behind the institutions and arts of civilization. For this reason, the Confucian Classics advise, "Carry forever the single mind."[8] As the saying goes, "No weapon is as piercing as a fixed purpose."[9] Accomplishment in all areas, then, is tied to the penetrating mind that depends on oneness.[10]

> App. 1: The crab skitters side-to-side, lagging
> Behind the worm in the Yellow Springs.[11]
> Fath. 1: The crab skittering side-to-side
> Means: His heart is not one.

The crab has six legs; the earthworm, none. Still, when the crab walks, it skitters from side to side, incapable of walking in a straight line, suggesting that its mind moves in many directions at once. Because it is unable to concentrate, it never learns how to make its own home; it must look for an empty hole dug by a snake or water serpent. Despite the apparent handicap of having no legs, the earthworm tunnels quickly to its destination by inserting the tip of its body. The verse undoubtedly refers to a passage in the *Hsün tzu*:

> An earthworm has no sharp claws or teeth, no strong muscles or
> bones, and yet above ground it feasts on mud and below it drinks at the
> Yellow Springs. This is because it keeps its mind on one thing. The
> crab has six legs and two pincers, but unless it can find an empty hole
> dug by a snake or a water serpent, the crab has no place to lodge. This
> is because the crab allows its mind to go off in all directions.[12]

If a race were to be conducted in the Yellow Springs below ground, the earthworm would surely beat the crab. This Chinese version of the tortoise and hare fable conveys a different moral than that put forward by Aesop, however. The problem here is not the crab's arrogance, though elsewhere Yang Hsiung inveighs against that attitude; instead, the problem is a superfluity of talents (e.g., too many legs) combined with aimless busywork, which distract the crab from the fundamental tasks at hand.

> App. 2: Focus on the One,[13]
>   Then nothing is unattainable.
> Fath. 2: Attainments from focus on the One
>   Mean: His grasp of the Way is sure.

The unlimited achievements that can be attained by anyone in single-minded pursuit of the Way present a direct contrast to the undirected activity of the crab. If the crab's progress is negligible, the advantages of "concentrating the mind, and unifying the will"[14] are manifold. Unswerving devotion to learning finally enables the individual to "contact the spirits, becoming a partner in the triad with Heaven and Earth."[15] As one text writes:

> To be one with phenomena and be able to see their underlying continuity is called "godlike"; to be one with affairs and be able to transform [them] is called "wisdom." . . . Only the noble man who holds on to the One can attain to this.[16]

> App. 3: Agitated, his focus[17] is erratic.
> Fath. 3: Pointing madly in his agitation
>   Means: He cannot dwell in the One.[18]

The adverb "madly,"[19] as in our own language, denotes inconstancy, irregularity, the excessively emotional, and any deviation from what is proper. The individual certainly displays sufficient emotional intensity. Unfortunately, there is no particular commitment to steady advance along a single path of Goodness. Given the individual's frequent vacillations, no achievement is possible. The *Changes* aptly compares this haphazard course to the frenetic movements of the hamster.[20]

> App. 4: If acute in timing,[21]
>   Nothing is not benefited.
> Fath. 4: To be sharp about time
>   Means: He gains what he can from the moment.

Development in any of the three triadic realms of Heaven-Earth Man can occur only when it is timely.[22] As men of Han observed, even the sage-master Confucius could not overcome the limitations imposed by time to become ruler of the empire, so lesser men can hardly hope to prevail. The gentleman moves when an opportunity for advancement presents itself, but wisely refrains from action when the time is not yet ripe, lest he endanger himself. Because he rides on prevailing trends to further his own goals, he is likely to benefit himself and others.[23]

App. 5: Penetrating[24] East, he forgets the West.
Watching his back, he overlooks his heart.
Fath. 5: Advancing East, ignoring the West
Means: Unable to reverse, he cannot escape.

As the center of the tetragram, Position 5 presents the main argument against onesidedness,[25] which holds for military strategists and philosophers alike: In becoming obsessed by a small corner of the truth, most men fail to comprehend general principles.[26] In devising his strategy for living, the wise person considers all factors, just as the general preparing for battle considers all possible avenues of attack and retreat. It is the stupid person who concerns himself only with superficial, immediate gratification (the "back"), without weighing the fundamental risks (the "heart"). Having made no provision to extricate himself from difficulties, he now faces certain ruin; in effect, he has become his own worst enemy. The concentration applauded in Appraisal 3 here has turned into blind onesidedness.

App. 6: Acute in categories,[27]
He holds within[28] the Five Gauges[29]
And Ten Thousand Measures.[30]
He is tried and true.
Fath. 6: Acute as to categories
Means: Riches and rank[31] without measure.[32]

My translation is tentative, as most of the key terms in this poem are open to a variety of interpretations; I suspect intentionally ambiguous language has been used to enrich the portrait of the sage. The heart/mind of the sage is acute in regard to categorical (i.e., correlative) thinking and responsive to the needs of the masses.[33] It also has sufficient capacity to embrace every conceivable thing within itself; it can "hold Ten Thousands Measures," as Yang Hsiung says.[34] The sagely *hsin* operates by strict standards, derived from cosmic norms (taking the Five Gauges as an epithet for the five cosmic phases of Water, Fire, Wood, Metal and Earth).[35] Because of his unfailing utility, the sage is employed in high, even royal office, where he is given "riches and rank without measure" (another Ten Thousands Measures?) sufficient to "match his charismatic virtue."[36] Once in office, he propagates moral standards (more Gauges) and bestows material aid (more Measures) to all below.[37] He also standardizes weights and measures while improving communications (here the Gauges would refer to roadways), acts associated with unification of the empire under the good emperor.[38] As a result of such policies, the breadth and weight of the ruler's influence extends far and wide (a final possibility, perhaps, for the Five Gauges and Ten Thousand Measures).

> App. 7: Sharp for profit,
> Dishonor and hatred set in.[39]
> Fath. 7: Focused on profit
> Means: Disgrace lies in being onesided.

Early Chinese texts, whether Confucian or Taoist, typically warn the individual against a preoccupation with getting rich. Profit-seeking tends to blunt one's appreciation of moral distinctions. Excess in any one direction, in fact, tends to lead one astray, bringing on his downfall. The good man devotes himself to cultivating the true Way and trusts to Heaven for the rest.

> App. 8: Sharp when he ought to be sharp,
> He saves himself from his own defeat.
> Fath. 8: Focused when he should be
> Means: In fear, he turns the cause of calamity around.

Coming near the end of the tetragram, Appraisal 8 represents potential disaster. Still, the superior man can turn calamity to his own advantage if he applies his penetrating mind to the problem at hand. This proves the rule that "he who is conscious of danger creates security for himself,"[40] snatching victory from the jaws of defeat.

> App. 9: High peak and steep bank
> Come tumbling down.
> Fath. 9: High peaks, steep banks
> Mean: With extreme sharpness, inevitable collapse.

High mountains, majestic in appearance, seem ultrastable and so eternal. Steep banks seem equally unassailable. Still, if "reversal is the movement of the Tao," any extreme situation is likely to revert to its opposite. The highest is made low.

In their splendor tall mountains often stand for the ruler, and convention compares the ruler's death to the collapse of a mountain peak. In the case of the emperor, overweening ambition and self-aggrandizement fed by incessant wars and exploitation of the common people spell the final collapse of the dynasty. If the mountains stand for ordinary individuals, they symbolize another lesson about sharp advance:

He who advances sharply falls back rapidly.[41]

*Correlates with Heaven's
Mystery;* Yang; *the phase
Water; and the* Yi *ching
Hexagram no. 11, Greatness;
the sun enters the Wall
constellation, 1st degree*

Ta
No. 15. Reach
February 23–February 27 (a.m.)

HEAD: Yang *ch'i* emerges, limb to branch to twig. There is nothing that does not reach its full extension.[1]

The language used in this Head text is particularly beautiful. The luxuriant growth of trees suggests the burgeoning presence of yang *ch'i*. With its energy reaching out to ever smaller units, the web of yang's influence grows increasingly comprehensive until each aspect of the cosmos is profoundly affected.[2] This impulse towards progressive differentiation is analogous to the mind's ability to make ever finer distinctions, so that the tetragram Reach symbolizes mental "perceptiveness" that "comprehends" as well, which are two other possible translations for the title. In a third application of Reach, the gracious condescension that yang *ch'i* displays towards phenomenal existence becomes the model for the good ruler in his dealings with the masses. These three kinds of reaching (physical, mental, and political) are treated below, with many of the Appraisals reading on all three levels simultaneously. Finally, one of the commentators interprets the tetragram title as Success, following standard usage in the *Odes*.[3] The greater one's acuity and contacts, the more likely conventional types of success are to come within one's reach.

> App. 1: Though hidden, the center, on its own
> Comprehends, pushing through, undeterred.[4]
> Fath. 1: That the hidden center alone reaches
> Means: Inner clarity is boundless.

The innermost heart/mind of the superior man with its heightened powers of comprehension penetrates each problem in turn until it assimilates the daimonic powers of Heaven-and-Earth and the sages.[5] If such marvelous powers are to be realized, great persistence is needed, as indicated by the repetition of images emphasizing the "push through." That process is hidden not only because of the depth of the individual's soul,[6] but also because the mind's latent power is held in reserve prior to the decision to take action, which is addressed in later Appraisals.[7]

App. 2: Misleading the belly
Affects[8] the eye.
Fath. 2: That the belly's delusions reach the eye
Means: It makes the Way unclear.[9]

The theme is the interdependence of inner and outer. As in many early Chinese texts, the belly (the internal organ which stands for sensory desire and "gut" reactions) is contrasted with the outer eye (the discriminating mind that makes contact with the outer world).[10] If the belly is confused, the eye cannot hope to evaluate various courses of action properly. For this reason, the individual will confuse the Way. As one Chinese master cautions, "Do not let the senses confuse the mind."[11]

App. 3: Only by sweeping down can the green wood's[12]
Excellence reach melons and gourds.[13]
Fath. 3: Only by its condescension
Means: Reciprocity within becomes the measure.[14]

Gracious condescension is suggested in terms reminiscent of the Head text. To the Chinese reader, the downward sweep of verdant branches in spring inevitably recalls the flowing robes of the sage-kings of old. The great tree offers support and protection to lesser living things, just like the sage-king; here it allows the lowly but useful melons and gourds to wind their vines around its majestic form.[15] Similarly, the man of great virtue does not avoid all contact with lesser individuals. Instead, he fosters others' development by a sympathetic understanding of their essential needs and natures. As a result, the lives of his subordinates are made secure.[16] Consideration for others, in short, becomes the true measure of nobility.

App. 4: Petty wit has little reach.[17]
Greatly misled by the narrow and small,[18]
He never[19] will be saved.[20]
Fath. 4: Keen in small things, confused in great
Means: He only knows one corner of the problem.

As teacher, Confucius looked for one attribute in his disciples: the ability, "given one corner of a problem," to correctly surmise the other three.[21] As Confucius argues, a gentleman is defined by the comprehensive nature of his view.[22] The sage, then, is "all-seeing."[23] A smattering of knowledge often leads to complacency, which in turn provokes disaster.[24] For this reason, many passages in the early Chinese classics inveigh against petty onesidedness.[25] As Appraisal 4 corresponds to lower rank, Yang Hsiung discusses the typical failures of minor bureaucrats. The great/small contrast is also found in the correspondent *Changes* hexagram.

> App. 5: Having reached the Central Crossroad,
>   Neither small nor great misleads him.
> Fath. 5: Reaching the place where all paths converge
>   Means: The way is open in all four directions.

Appraisal 5 is said to rule the tetragram as center. The lines are correlated with yang *ch'i* in a yang tetragram; hence, their auspicious character. The pursuit of Goodness is like a journey down a path. Once the individual fully assimilates the idea of the Mean, all roads lie open to him; regardless of which course is chosen, every action is consistent with morality. In the case of the temporal ruler, every move meets with immediate success. This imagery offers a direct contrast to that of Tetragram 31, Appraisal 6.

> App. 6: A great reach has no bounds,
>   It does not stop at center.[26]
>   Barriers[27] create obstacles.[28]
> Fath. 6: A great reach, without bounds,
>   Means: It should not continue on one side only.

Any reading of these lines depends upon the moral weight given the first phrase in the Appraisal and Fathoming: "great reach without bounds." Is this a description of morality or immorality? Early evidence may be cited to support either view. One commentator argues:

> The Great Way ought to reach every single place. It is not right to stop
> it in mid-course. If someone builds raised earth embankments [i.e.,
> barriers between fields], that is to create a place where something does
> not get through, to create an obstruction.[29]

It is true that unimpeded reach is the quality attributed to the superior man in Han texts. Nevertheless, certain commentators, including Ssu-ma Kuang, are not entirely unjustified in equating the phrase "no bounds" with "dangerous license."[30] In that case, the poem says:

> A great reach without bounds,
> [If] not stopped at center and regulated by ditches,
> Is evil.
>
> A great reach without bounds
> Means: Not right to let it continue on all sides.[31]

In the rice fields, embankments are necessary if the fields are to be worked productively. In the human realm, the institutionalization of various restraints is needed for the beneficial functioning of society. Otherwise, an unimpeded flow of emotions and ambitions will prove no less damaging to society than floodwaters are to new crops.[32] The implied cultivation of the fields also suggests the cultivation of the mind, which depends upon the acceptance of a set of limits embodied in ritual. Without such constraints, the mind ranges so freely that its undeveloped powers will fail to hit upon significant pattern in the triadic realms of Heaven-Earth-Man.[33] When the worthy man restrains himself and others, he follows the example of the early sage-king and flood-queller Yü, the first to set up boundaries.[34]

> App. 7: Reached by the flint probe's cut:
> With early loss comes later gain.
> Fath. 7: The scalpel reaching the affected spot
> Means: By this means, in the end, he is not disabled.[35]

Early Chinese texts frequently compare the strictures of early training to unpleasant medicine or painful surgery forced upon the patient by the conscientious doctor. As the proverb says, "Good medicine is bitter to the tongue."[36] Similarly, the harsh necessity of the penal code is likened to the flint probe employed in acupuncture.[37] Early correction, however traumatic, results in future benefit. Once the old, diseased area is cut away, there is a chance for new healthy growth to take its place.[38]

> App. 8: Misleading the eye
> Affects the belly.
> Fath. 8: That the eye's delusions reach the belly
> Means: The outer deceives the inner.

Following Appraisal 2 above, this verse reiterates the interdependence of mind and body, inner and outer. If the eye as the mind's receptor for outward impressions becomes confused for any reason, the resulting mistakes, sooner or later, are bound to affect the innermost self. For example, a half-starved man may reach for chalk to eat, rather than rice, or a well-dressed man may think himself a gentleman.[39] Such outer mistakes inevitably cause physical and moral damage to the inner self.

> App. 9: Perceiving his blame, he rights himself
> And in the end, he wins renown.
> Fath. 9: Comprehending blame, final renown,
> Means: He's good at using the Way to retreat.[40]

Though Appraisal 9 represents the final stage of calamity, here it is aligned with auspicious Day (see Table 2, page 00). The superior individual, recognizing the justice of society's complaints about his conduct, amends his ways and retreats from evil, thereby securing a good name for himself.

Correlates with Heaven's Mystery;
Yin; the phase Fire; and the Yi
ching Hexagram no. 11, Greatness;
the sun enters the Wall constel-
lation, 6th degree; the musical note
is B¹

Chiao
No. 16. Contact
February 27 (p.m.)–Mar 3

HEAD: Yang makes contact with yin; and yin with yang. Things ascend to the Hall of Light, fully emergent and flourishing.[2]

According to Chinese ways of thinking, the ideal human state is one of sustained, mutually beneficial contact between two or more parties. As Yang Hsiung says in his other philosophical classic, "It is the Way of Man to make contact."[3] No less explicit is Confucius' emphasis on humaneness (*jen*), the virtue that cannot exist outside of social relations (and one that is, not coincidentally, correlated with the warm and expansive spring season now upon us). In the "golden age" of the past, communities purportedly served the legitimate interests of all while maintaining the dignity of each.[4] Stable hierarchical relations wove elements of society together in a complex web of mutual obligation, but reciprocity (implying not only mutual obligation but also an empathetic "likening to oneself")[5] was also needed to temper the possible ill effects of unmediated power relations. The perfect community, therefore, was thought to be equally dependent upon hierarchy and reciprocity. As such, the perfect community is modeled upon the cosmos, where yang *ch'i* acts as ruler, defining the patterns of growth, while yin acts as subject, responding appropriately. This tetragram celebrates such ideal contact, which, the Head text promises, makes the good individual both resplendent as the sun and powerful as the king in his sacred audience hall.

The Hall of Light,[6] according to early commentators, refers simply to the region above ground in the light of day, as contrasted with the Yellow Springs below ground. But the same binome is used to describe the sacred site where the king makes ritual contact with the gods.[7] Its use suggests that all things are sanctified by contact with the Mystery.

This tetragram is correlated with the Rainfall solar period. Rain symbolizes beneficent grace and germinating influence, whether the reference is to sexual contact or to political relations. Consequently, the general tone of this tetragram is lucky, except in those few cases where "stimulus and response" occurs between categorically dissimilar partners, prompting repulsion and disaster.

Figure 7. A scene of cosmic harmony, with birds, and animals, and humans in perfect accord. Illustration from rubbing of a stone relief from Kang-tzu, Kiangsu (65 × 118 cm).

App. 1: In the dark[8] he contacts the gods.
He fasts but fails to use propriety.
Fath. 1: Dark contact, improper,[9]
Means: He harbors wrong, holding shame within.

Appraisal 1, corresponding to the Beginning of Thought, is aligned here with inauspicious Night. In approaching the unseen gods, an attitude of extreme reverence must be adopted. Fasting is a spiritual exercise designed to concentrate the spirit, focusing it upon intimations of the divine implanted in our nature. The ordinary unthinking individual may perform this purification perfunctorily, assuming that the mere performance of ritual works effective magic, regardless of intent; this is to operate on the mistaken notion that fasting alone, without a profound realignment of the self, is enough to please the gods. Conversely, the unreflective person may become overly preoccupied with the supernatural; in his anxiety to please the gods, he may neglect to maintain fundamental social relations,

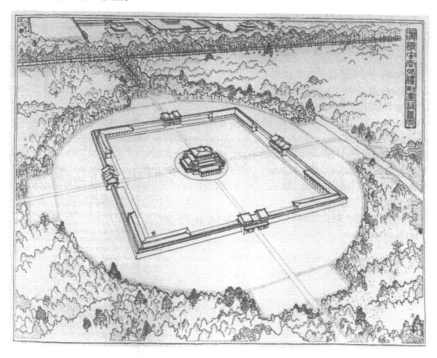

Figure 8. The "Hall of Light" illustration reflects a recent archaeological reconstruction of the site.

the root of all Goodness. Perhaps he assumes that the dark provides sufficient cover for his "dark" errors anyway.[10] But sacred ritual, incorrectly practiced, is worse than useless. Far from conferring blessings, it promotes evil and results in shame.[11]

> App. 2: Dark contact, when based on trust,
>> Grows luminous.
> Fath. 2: Trust behind dark contact
>> Means: In good faith he meets the gods and spirits.

By definition, the divine is located wherever perceptible change is effected by an unseen cause.[12] Though the Tao itself remains forever shrouded in mystery, the results of its operations are abundantly clear to all. In this set of verses, mutual trust prevails between gods and man since a community of shared interests has been forged through correct ritual practice. The truly good person, whose charismatic virtue is luminous, even daemonically compelling,[13] can hope to attract the blessings of the unseen world.

167

App. 3: He contacts wood and stone.
Fath. 3: Befriending wood and stone
    Means: He cannot turn to other men.[14]

Stone epitomizes whatever is hard; wood, that which is pliable. Things in different categories repel each other, creating a disastrous response, as in the antagonistic relation between wood (i.e., any kind of vegetation) and stone (i.e., axes or scythes).[15] Knowing this, the wise person seeks alliances with those who are fully developed human beings. Meanwhile, the benighted individual looks to make meaningful contact with those who are less than fully human—those who are no better than "wood and stone." The Confucian *Analects* cautions us, "Have no friends unequal to yourself."[16] Under the influence of "unequal friends," we soon become no better than inanimate objects. Certainly we cannot then hope to influence others.[17]

App. 4: Contact, back and forth,
    With fragrant smoke rising.[18]
    This is the gate of gain and ruin.
Fath. 4: Mutual contact, harmonious,
    Means: He acts in concert with the gods.[19]

Appraisal 4 represents the Beginning of Good Fortune; hence, this sketch of satisfactory relations between the gods and humans. The fragrant fumes of burning sacrificial meats give the ritual participant intense satisfaction. The depth of his pleasure, as he well knows, derives from a fundamental correspondence between his inner commitment to perfect integrity and its visible expression in solemn sacrifice.[20] When inner and outer are in perfect accord, the individual joins the gods in the execution of the divine plan. Whether or not that plan will prevail among men is thus determined largely by individual choice.[21]

App. 5: Contacting parrot and ape,
    He fails to garner his glory.
Fath. 5: Befriending parrot and ape
    Means: He goes the way of bird and beast.

In general, both parrots and apes exhibit a high degree of intelligence and curiosity, steady habits, and the capacity for speech.[22] Yet despite their strong resemblance to human beings, neither parrot nor ape possesses the single most important characteristic of humans: the capacity for moral action framed by ritual.[23] Unless a person observes the rules of propriety, his heart is no better than that of a bird or beast.[24] What is more, it is precisely such "bestial" persons who tend to ignore the rules and treat others rudely, as if they were mere parrots and apes.[25]

The parrot may also stand more specifically for flatterers and sycophants (since the bird only repeats its master's words); the ape traditionally stands for pompous blusterers (since it is given to dramatic beatings of its chest).[26] The wise person avoids contact with lesser, bestial men, lest he be influenced for the worse.[27]

> App. 6: How vast the great state![28]
>> With it small states seek contact.
>> "The sacred meats that we possess
>> We gladly share with you."
> Fath. 6: Contact between great and small
>> Means: In treating worthies well, glory blazes forth.

Great states encourage minor states to enter into formal tributary relations; through ritual, the prestige of both parties is enhanced. Similarly, the wise leader encourages the best candidates to join the government by sharing his profits with them. In the end, all benefit. As the *Changes* says, "I have a good goblet/ Which I will share with you."[29]

> App. 7: He befriends bird and rat,
>> Wasting his store of millet.
> Fath. 7: Contact with bird and rat
>> Means: Nothing but waste!

Echoing the images in Appraisal 5 above, this poem again exhorts the reader to learn to distinguish bestial men from the worthy. Clearly, the situation is now worse: Contact is made with animals that do not bear the slightest resemblance to human beings. In fact, bird and rat are two of the most notorious enemies of man, since their continual predations threaten the basic food stores of society.[30] An individual has lost all powers of evaluation when he befriends bird and rat.

Applied to statecraft, the king has utterly failed to distinguish worthy men in office from social parasites and evil sycophants intent upon plundering the treasury for their own profit.[31]

> App. 8: Ax and lance fly back and forth.
>> Using his propriety, he will not rue the day.
> Fath. 8: Ax and lance, blow for blow,
>> Mean: In campaigns,[32] he is invincible.[33]

The use of force, properly employed in the defense of morality, is sanctioned here, and its ultimate success is guaranteed so long as the individual remains steadfast in his virtue. Though succeeding Appraisals qualify this sanction, certain Chinese tended to regard nobility and war as antithetical. Therefore, one late commentator reinterprets the poem to mean, "[Friends] use their propriety to intervene [in a peaceful way] so that the regrettable acts of aggression are finally discontinued."[34]

App. 9: He unrightly joins in battle.[35]
　　　　And so is routed at the city wall.[36]
　　　　Since he is cruel, he is devoured.[37]
Fath. 9: Cut down in the battle fray
　　　　Means: How could he ever succeed?

In antiquity, the two great affairs of state were said to be sacrifice and war.[38] Throughout this tetragram, the *Mystery* reminds us that no major project should be undertaken without the proper mental disposition. Even when an individual commands a force, its deployment will redound to his glory only if he acts for the Good and avoids unnecessary violence. Insatiable greed, ambition or cruelty invariably backfire. The belligerent loses first part, then all of his territory. Those in power should reserve their arms to punish recalcitrant evildoers on behalf of the entire society, rather than to seek private gain. This Appraisal directly counters certain Legalist writings, which applaud annexation by force.

Correlates with Heaven's Mystery; Yang; the phase Wood; and the Yi ching *Hexagram no. 5, Waiting; the sun enters the Straddler constellation, 1st degree; the Dipper points due east; musical note is E-flat*[1]

Juan
No. 17. Holding Back
March 4–March 8 (a.m.)

HEAD: Yang *ch'i* can be firm, can be pliant, can be active or at rest. Seeing difficulty, it shrinks back.

This tetragram begins the "Startled from Hibernation" solar period. Since yin still reigns supreme, the myriad things continue to experience difficulties, but yang *ch'i* is by turns firm or flexible, at work or at ease. Avoiding direct confrontation with the stronger forces of yin, it handily survives to nourish all of Heaven-and-Earth. The overall pattern of increasing warmth in mid-spring testifies to its general effectiveness. This tetragram, then, celebrates acts of pliancy, tentativeness, timidity, reticence, and even weakness that ultimately lead to greater strength. Many technical arts and ritual acts are based on this principle.

This tetragram's alignment with Wood is significant since the primary characteristic of wood, according to the early Chinese, is its pliability. At the same time, wood is strong enough to support the weight of roofs and walls, even in the most munificent of palace structures. The *Mystery* applauds the combination of pliancy and strength that Wood represents.

> App. 1: Ruddy shoots, with tips now sharp—[2]
> Their advances profit by retreat.
> Fath. 1: Ruddy tips now tightly furled
> Mean: Retreat in order to move ahead.

In mid-spring, the tightly furled tips of various plants emerge from the surface of the soil. Although these points may appear extremely fragile, their compressed conelike shape works well to protect them while facilitating their steady upward thrust into the light. If the leaves were to unfurl too soon, before all danger of frost has passed, advance might well prove hazardous. By analogy, the wise person yields to others, especially when the time is not yet right to advance his ideas. His reticence gains him the friends and supporters necessary to win high rank and renown in the dangerous world outside.

> App. 2: Shrinking his heart
> Makes for infirmity.
> Fath. 2: Holding back his mind
> Means: The center lacks all courage.

Tactical retreat may be required in certain situations, as the previous verse makes plain. However, due caution should not be confused with cowardice. The man of virtue must not waver when confronted with necessary moral decisions; neither should he shrink from proper commitments. Should his moral courage fail him,[3] he is in danger of losing what distinguishes him. For this reason, the *Tso Commentary* says, "The person who is humane but not armed has no ability to succeed."[4]

> App. 3: Drawing in his knees,
> He protects his joints.
> Though not unconstrained,[5]
> There is no offense in the end.[6]
> Fath. 3: Pulling back his knees
> Means: It is improper for limbs to sprawl.[7]

The poem hinges on a single pun: the word for "body joints" means "moderation" as well.[8] The man of virtue at times may choose to draw back in order to protect his principles.[9] At first glance, this decision seems to restrict his sphere of activity, but in the end the adoption of certain self-imposed limits saves him from greater harm. It also allows him to bide his time until he can be of real use to others.[10] This verse reminds us that there is no exact equivalent in early China to our notion of positive freedom. Lack of constraints tends to imply wicked license contrary to the Constant Way.[11]

Ssu-ma Kuang finds more trenchant criticism here. Of the subject of the poem, he writes, "Although he cannot himself act with license, in the end he does not attain the Constant Way." My comparatively positive reading depends upon this Appraisal's alignment with auspicious Day.

> App. 4: Holding back his outbursts,[12]
> In three years, not a single peep.[13]
> Fath. 4: Outbursts suppressed, with nary a peep
> Mean: The right time is repeatedly missed.

Building on Appraisal 2, this poem chides the individual who fails to speak out against present evils. Because of his lack of courage, numerous opportunities for reform are missed. According to Confucius, this unwillingness to speak up when speech is appropriate is a typical bureaucratic failing.[14] Appraisal 4, of course, corresponds to official rank.

> App. 5: The golden mushroom does not grow.
> It awaits the propitious cloud.
> Fath. 5: That mushrooms of immortality do not grow
> Means: They wait to be joined by their mates.

Golden fungi and felicitous clouds are auspicious omens that herald the rise of a sagely universal ruler.[15] The golden fungus is also associated with immortality cults and the generative powers of spring.[16] As in the *Book of Changes*, the very fact that portents—good or bad—exist demonstrates Heaven's continuing concern for Man, for Heaven-sent signs guide those in pursuit of the Way. The golden fungus, then, is eagerly awaited for many reasons. But to the Chinese, good things ideally come in pairs: official and ruler, husband and wife, and so on, with each partner joined in mutual reliance and benefit. Therefore, the golden fungus can appear only when its fitting match is found. Position 5 as ruler of the tetragram tells us that a true leader cannot arise without worthy supporters. Good "ministers" (*ch'ing*) would be one "propitious" (*ch'ing*) sign of a true leader, as a pun makes clear.[17]

> App. 6: Recoiling, he misses the time.
> Perhaps disaster follows him.[18]
> Fath. 6: Drawing back, missing the moment,
> Means: Jail then flight come later.

Having missed the opportunity to advance the cause of morality, the individual must seize the moment to draw back in the face of clear and present danger, lest he risk offending those in power, who will then accuse him of various crimes. The moral coward, however, hesitates even now to act. As an autocommentary to the *Mystery* puts it:

> The noble man cultivating virtue, awaits the proper moment. He does not set out before the right moment, nor draw back after it has already passed. . . . Can this be said of anyone but the noble man?[19]

App. 7: Tempering his moderation.[20]
      Holding fast his principles,[21]
      He offers his life for the cause.[22]
Fath. 7: Less moderate, offering to die,
      Means: There is a ruler within him.

Appraisal 7, marking the Beginning of Calamity, depicts a brave man who is willing to offer up his life, if need be, in order to promote the Way. A long tradition in China glorifies the hero willing to "exhaust himself in the service of Heaven."[23] A wiser person, however, might have been able to avoid such dramatic self-sacrifice. Confucius labeled courage without canniness "mere foolhardiness."

App. 8: The crown[24] of a hollow,[25] dried-out tree
      Is struck by gusts which shake its limbs.
      The petty man has reason to hang back.
      Thrice he retreats before he is snagged.
Fath. 8: The quaking of hollow trees
      Means: The petty man suffers disgrace.[26]

The hollow tree and the petty man are alike in not having a strong inner core. Without any inner resources, the petty man is also dry and lifeless. And finally, because he emphasizes secondary considerations over fundamental values, he resembles the crown of the tree, rather than its roots. Such an individual inevitably quails in the face of stronger force.[27] Unable to stand firm, he is seriously shaken. Knowing his own weaknesses, the clever (if immoral) individual refuses to take a stand on any issue, hoping thereby to elude danger. After all, such accomodation comes far more easily to him than undertaking the arduous task of self-reform. Still, his plan ultimately fails; in the end the petty man finds himself trapped by his own weaknesses.

The wording is vague enough to admit a second comparison, in which the petty man is compared to a small animal perched on a limb of a rotten tree. When a storm arises, the animal is too scared to escape. Trapped on a shaky limb, it faces certain death.

App. 9: He regrets withdrawing.[28]
The past leaves, the future returns.
Fath. 9: Returns from regretted withdrawals
Mean: Gain lies in the future.

In this last Appraisal, the individual comes to realize that his previous compromises and accomodations have been ill-timed, ill-advised, or immoral. He changes his course, returning to the Right, and in the end achieves his goal—so very great is the "return" for Virtue. Appraisal 9 marks the end of the cycle. Having gone as far in Holding Back as possible, the individual's moral sensibilities finally begin to reassert themselves.

Hsi

No. 18. Waiting
March 8 (p.m.)–March 12

Correlates with Heaven's Mystery; Yin; the phase Metal; and the Yi ching *Hexagram no. 5, Waiting; the sun enters the Straddler constellation, 6th degree*

HEAD: Yang *ch'i* has what it waits for. When it is permissible to advance, it advances, so that things all achieve their desires.

This tetragram is the twin of the previous one in two senses: Both are correlated with the same hexagram in the *Changes* and the same solar period, "Startled from Hibernation." For this reason, the Appraisals of Tetragram 18 largely reiterate the theme of Tetragram 17; once again, we are told that it is necessary to acquiesce in Heaven's patterns, waiting for the proper time to act. The propriety of this is proven by the natural world, where the myriad things patiently await warmer days to complete their separate destinies. The Head, however, registers a slight but significant change in the terms of waiting: In the previous tetragram, there was still a tendency to recoil in the face of danger. Now there is a sense of quiet strength that can bide its time until the right time to act.[1]

App. 1: Those whose villainy is hidden
Await bad luck from Heaven.
Fath. 1: The wait by secret villains
Means: No time is propitious.[2]

By convention Heaven is omniscient; by definition, then, no evil can truly be hidden from it. Even if Heaven is understood simply as "the Way things are," the evildoer is inevitably unmasked by circumstances.[3] It is true that a crime may well seem hidden if knowledge of it is kept from one's fellow men. Perhaps the intended crime has not yet been perpetrated, since Appraisal 1 corresponds to the Beginning of Thought. Still, cosmic operations invariably ensure that nothing goes right for the criminal. That hidden villainy meets with Heaven's retribution is, in fact, one proof of the interconnectedness of Heaven-Earth-Man.

> App. 2: Those whose virtue is hidden
> Await prosperity[4] from Heaven.
> Fath. 2: The wait by men of hidden virtue
> Means: Bright are the coming days.[5]

In contrast to the previous Appraisal, the good person "piles up virtue in secret, then is showered with good fortune, plain as day," as Ssu-ma Kuang, the commentator, writes. The hidden criminal waits uneasily, fearing Heaven's displeasure; secret virtue, in contrast, confidently anticipates Heaven's manifest rewards. Prospects are truly "bright" for such a person.

> App. 3: He awaits a later date.
> Fath. 3: Waiting until too late
> Means: He is remiss.

Since timely action is a key factor in success, the wise person is always on the lookout for opportune moments to further the Good. But here the individual has overlooked the right time to act. As Yang's autocommentary says, "The noble man cultivates virtue, thereby awaiting the proper moment. He does not rise up before the proper moment, nor draw back after it has already passed."[6]

> App. 4: Retracting his horn, righting his foot:
> Only by this he awaits the good.[7]
> Fath. 4: The horn retracted and the straightened foot
> Means: He is not contrary[8] or perverse.[9]

The horn symbolizes aggressiveness. Because it is hard, it also signifies stubbornness. To retract the horn, then, means to withdraw from quarrels and competitiveness. The "straightened foot" walks in the right direction following the one true Way. Peaceable and reliable, the noble man quietly lives out his days, trusting to his reward. Perhaps the reward will come in the form of official salary, since the poem employs grain to suggest the good.

Due to the terse character of Yang Hsiung's language, the very same verse is read by one commentator, Ch'en Pen-li, as a condemnation of Yang's contemporaries in the Han bureaucracy. Evil officials are derelict in their duties; they neither remonstrate with their ruler (they retract their horns), nor put in the required effort (they straighten [i.e., rest] their feet). Meanwhile, they continue to draw their salaries quietly. By this reading, the Fathoming complains, "They do not oppose or stab [others in need of reform]."[10] Since by Yang's schema this Appraisal should be auspicious, the first interpretation is more likely, in that it celebrates a wise decision.

> App. 5: Great ranks flock to serve the palace,
> Meanly the petty men wait in vain.
> Fath. 5: Ranks in palace employ
> Mean: Rank cannot be got for nothing.

The palace of the Son of Heaven, the seat of central government, ideally functions as a kind of *axis mundi* around which matters of state revolve. When a just society exists, men of virtue are induced by their leader's charismatic virtue to enter his service, where they are duly honored with high rank.[11] Meanwhile, petty men of inferior virtue wait in vain for posts.

The character for rank also means sparrow. By a pun, the first line of the Appraisal reads, "In great flocks, sparrows alight on palace walls."[12] This, however, would be an ill omen. Palace walls are the wrong place for birds to seek nourishment; by the same token, petty men should not congregate at court, expecting rewards where none is deserved.[13] The *Changes* warns of killing in connection with "hawks alighting on palace walls."[14] Danger may come.

> App. 6: Awaiting good fortune, properly aligned,[15]
> He will partake of gold.
> Fath. 6: Awaiting good fortune with utmost propriety
> Means: Rectitude can be taken like tonic.

The good person trusts to Heaven and awaits his fate, knowing that he has made every effort to cultivate the seeds of virtue within himself. At the very least, virtue invigorates like a tonic. It may well win the individual "golden" fortune and fame. It can even secure him a kind of immortality. In this, virtue far excels the concoctions of potable gold touted by quacks. Once again, Yang Hsiung insists upon the practical benefits of Confucian morality.

Ssu-ma Kuang's commentary is rather curious. Reading the character as metal instead of gold, he extols the courage of the superior man who is willing to endure any hardship, even "eating metal," in order to carry out rectitude.[16]

App. 7: He recklessly awaits misfortune.[17]
    This is the station of ill-omened men.[18]
Fath. 7: Awaiting misfortune recklessly
    Means: He makes a date with calamity.

Evildoers know that they will probably be punished for their crimes. In their hearts, they cannot help but be somewhat apprehensive about future retribution. But they feign complete unconcern and invite calamity by their reckless disregard for the Good. Their own deeds condemn them to perpetual unhappiness.

App. 8: Discounting the calamitous in present calamity,
    We wait for Heaven to keep us alive.
Fath. 8: Calamity is no calamity unless seen as such.[19]
    Meaning: It is not Heaven that faults us.[20]

When his luck is down, the superior man trusts Heaven to keep him alive, secure in the knowledge that if "on looking within he finds no taint,"[21] there can be no reason to grieve or fear. He is also wise enough to see that to turn away from virtue is the only real disaster. Just as the natural world awaits spring's renewal, the good person perseveres in the Way and calmly awaits Heaven's vindication.[22] Should calamity continue, he can take comfort in the belief that an impersonal fate has hurt him. His "unmoved mind" in any case will bring him subtle psychological and physical benefits. For this reason, "only the noble man can be oppressed without losing his sense of joy."[23]

App. 9: Waiting, twisted up like a cripple,[24]
    Heaven strikes his forehead.
Fath. 9: That the waiting cripple is struck
    Means: In the end, he is incurable.

Due to his spinal deformity, the cripple afflicted by the *wang* disease[25] always appears to look defiantly at Heaven. In his arrogance, the moral cripple with his deformed soul also challenges Heaven to punish him. When Heaven moves to smite him, so devastating is the blow that he can never recover.[26] With the face turned toward Heaven, the forehead is particularly vulnerable to these blows.

Ts'ung

No. 19. Following

March 13–March 17 (a.m.)

Correlates with Heaven's Mystery;
Yang; *the phase Water; and the* Yi
ching *Hexagram no. 17, Pursuit;
the sun enters the Straddler constellation, 10th degree*

HEAD: Yang leaps into pools, into marshes, into fields, into mountains. Things are all poised[1] to follow.

The yang *ch'i* grows steadily stronger, making itself felt in every portion of the land in All-under-Heaven; its presence is now in evidence everywhere, as it moves from the lowest to the highest places. No longer confined to the nether regions, yang *ch'i* expresses its newfound freedom with a joy conveyed by the verb "leap," usually reserved for activities associated with good fortune, with energy and health, with "feeling one's oats," with eager and lively spirits. For their part, the myriad things look forward to yang's coming in happy expectation of the growing period of spring and summer; their only desire is to develop further by following yang *ch'i*.

As yang is to the myriad things, so the noble man is to the common people. Lesser mortals "crane their necks" and "stand on tiptoe" to catch a glimpse of him, anxious to express their loyalty and to become like him.[2] In the triadic realms of Heaven-Earth-Man, then, all are ready to obey the Good; hence, the tetragram's title.

> App. 1: The sun, unseen, espouses it.[3]
> > The moon, in darkness, follows it.[4]
> > This is the foundation.
> Fath. 1: The sun takes a wife, the moon follows.
> > Meaning: The subordinate's response is the base.

Appropriately enough, Appraisal 1 describes the "marriage" of sun and moon that takes place on the first day of the lunar calendar when sun and moon are conjoined.[5] Immediately after this union, on the succeeding days of the lunar month, the moon (when viewed from stationary Earth) appears to follow the sun faithfully in its westerly course.[6] This provides the model for a wife's submission to her husband, or a subject's to his ruler. To further the simile, the moon, like a self-effacing wife who walks slightly behind her husband, seems to lag somewhat behind the sun until the new marriage at the beginning of the next lunar month. The

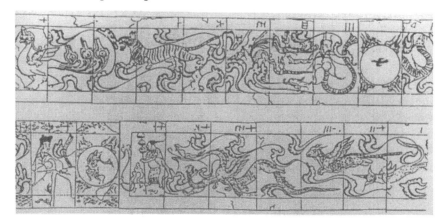

Figure 9. The sun and moon from a Han dynasty depiction. The sun is identified by the black crow; the moon, by its resident frog. Illustration from the excavation report on the tomb of Pu Ch'ien-ch'iu, Loyang, Honan province, dated to the first century B.C. The swirling cloud forms are meant to represent the Milky Way ("Heaven's Barge" or the "Silver River" in Chinese), which is mentioned in Appraisal 77.

natural accord between yin and yang, leader and follower, represents an eternal constant, which in turn serves as the basis of all social relations. Though its ultimate motive force remains shrouded in mystery ("in darkness"),[7] we know that compliance cannot result from coercion by the superior (= yang, male, sun, ruler), but from a recognition of shared goals.

> App. 2: In dawn's first light, things barely emerge.[8]
> Pairing, following, they gather by type.[9]
> Fath. 2: Barely emerging, following by pairs
> Means: They do not know their destination.

Han literary convention typically employs the new dawn to signify auspicious beginnings.[10] By the same token, the *Changes* phrase, "things following their own kind"[11] usually celebrates the orderly division of cosmos and society into successive related units. However, these lines (correlated with yin) are clearly inauspicious. Perhaps the dim light of dawn is too feeble to provide sufficient illumination.[12] Therefore, the myriad things confusedly pick partners (and by extension, directions in life) without ever really understanding the choices before them.[13]

App. 3: Men do not attack him.
   They are drawn to follow.[14]
Fath. 3: That men do not attack him
   Means: This, in itself, is proof of Virtue's power.[15]

The good person appears inviolable, since good manners and self-deprecation forestall the attacks of others. Insofar as he "leads himself to follow" the Right, others are drawn to follow, thanks to the force of his charismatic example (literally, "They themselves are drawn to follow him."). The comparative ease with which the good person confronts life's difficulties is compelling proof of Heaven's favor and virtue's efficacy.

App. 4: The call to follow is improper.
   A woman takes his bloodied basket.[16]
   Lost.
Fath. 4: Loss following the call
   Means: How can theirs be a worthy match?

A passage in the *Changes* reads:

The woman holds out the basket,
But there are no fruits in it.
The knight stabs the sheep,
But there is no blood.
There is nothing which this favors.[17]

In the *Mystery*, matters are, if anything, worse, due to the reversal of traditional male/female roles: The woman, rather than the man, tries to offer the blood sacrifice, although it is her place to offer fruit only.[18] What, we may ask, is lost in consequence? Husband and wife may both have lost the ritual proper to the service of the gods (the basket, then, "is lost").[19] Otherwise, it is possible that the woman keenly feels the loss of her husband, for the blood-soaked basket signifies death, perhaps after a disastrous military expedition.[20] Clearly, the earlier "cries to follow" were inappropriate or ineffective. Unfortunately, those lacking in virtue often seek to hide their own shame by inducing others to emulate their bad example. Only the noble man will find that others follow him without bloodshed since he is in perfect compliance with ritual at all times.[21]

A criticism of Dowager Empress Wang may be embedded in these lines, with the second part of the Appraisal reading, "There is a woman who carries on [the line with the product of] her bloody basket (i.e., the pelvic region from which menstrual blood and birth fluids flow)./ Lost [is the dynasty]."[22]

> App. 5: Follow the example of water
> Which goes to fill the hollows.[23]
> Fath. 5: To follow water filling the holes
> Means: He does not overstep himself.

Readers are enjoined to follow the pattern provided by water, which seeks the low places, moving on only after the hollows have been completely filled. These lines clearly allude to the philosopher Mencius, who says:

> Flowing water is such that it does not go further forward until it has filled all the hollows. A gentleman in his pursuit of the Way does not proceed unless he achieves a beautiful pattern.[24]

By following ritual patterns, the good person molds himself until he is in perfect conformity with the Good, just as water meets the outline of the hollow. In that way, he reaches a stage where he can act without overstepping moral boundaries or infringing upon others. Self-cultivation, like water's flow, is gradual and modest, but effective.[25]

> App. 6: Following his eye,
> He loses his belly.
> Fath. 6: The eye followed, the belly lost,
> Means: He indulges his desires to excess.[26]

As in earlier tetragrams, the eye stands for what is outer; the belly, for what is inner ("inner virtue," according to one commentator). Also, the eye stands for intellectual appreciation or sensual desire, as opposed to the belly, which stands for the instinctual gratification of basic needs for food, sex, and true community.[27] Here desire develops at the expense of the body's basic instinct for self-preservation.[28] The desire for novelty, for example, may cause the individual to choose bubblegum ice cream or the latest theory over more nourishing fare for the mind and body. This fundamental inability to set the right priorities in life can only end in disaster; at the very least, it will end in the individual's loss of moral potential.[29]

> App. 7: Shaking off the foul in him,
> He allows the good[30] to grow:[31]
> Realgar eats away the flesh.
> Fath. 7: Shaking corruption, following the pure,
> Means: He is saved from bad luck.

Traditionally, Chinese doctors applied disulphide of arsenic (realgar) to "corrupt flesh" (including carbuncles and sores) on the principle that "poison eats poison."[32] Healing could then take place. By analogy, harsh self-criticism permits self-renewal to occur. With Appraisal 7 near the end of the tetragram, relatively drastic measures are needed if the patient's prognosis is to improve.

> App. 8: The tainted is allowed.[33]
> > Calamity, flying out, cannot be contained.[34]
> Fath. 8: Following corruption
> > Means: Calamity cannot be argued away.

This individual follows evil companions or an evil course of action willingly; no reform is attempted. Like the evils in Pandora's box, calamity soon flies out beyond his control. All are deaf to his pleas for help.

> App. 9: Follow what is most commendable.
> > Then and only then will he climb the stairs,
> > Ascending to the proper end.[35]
> Fath. 9: Following the model of perfection
> > Means: Later, he gets results.[36]

Ideally, education trains youths to emulate what is most admirable (Confucian tradition and the example of the ancient sages). The cultivated individual can then embark upon a distinguished career in public service (signified by the flight of steps) which will benefit the entire community. This image leads naturally to the following tetragram, entitled Advance.

Chin
No. 20. Advance
March 17 (p.m.)–March 21

Correlates with Heaven's Mystery; Yin; *the phase Fire; and the* Yi ching *Hexagram no. 35, Progress; the sun enters the Straddler constellation, 15th degree*

HEAD: Yang, attracting things,[1] advances.[2] Things emerge most prolifically.[3] Like morning light opening,[4] they go forward.

We are approaching the vernal equinox, the first time in the annual cycle when the strength of yang *ch'i* is equal to that of yin. (After the vernal equinox, yang will dominate until the autumn equinox.) Under the beneficent influence of yang *ch'i*, the myriad things, including Man, find their growth enhanced. As the days lengthen and the light improves, all things develop. In the human realm, true advance means "advance in the Way,"[5] predicated on tireless effort,[6] but leading to profound personal and societal transformation. Conventional desires for advancement sparked by overweening ambition and arrogant pride, however, result in reckless acts.

> App. 1: In darkness[7] he advances. Obstructions[8]
> Act as the mother of retreat.[9]
> Fath. 1: The dark advance obstructed
> Means: Deflection breeds retreat.

The first Appraisal correlates with the Water phase, whose color is black. But there are additional reasons for darkness here: First, any new endeavor in its initial phase is uncharted. Second, the advance takes place in secret since it is improper. The unmitigated darkness prevents the individual from finding his proper path. Somewhere along the Way, he meets with one or more obstructions, then veers off in the wrong direction. The greater the advance, the greater the retreat from Goodness. In this way, the first obstruction becomes the "mother" of defeat.[10]

> App. 2: To advance using the model of centrality:
> The singular perspicacity of the Great Man.[11]
> Fath. 2: Advancing by the Mean
> Means: The model must be internalized.[12]

Several Confucian Classics emphasize the importance of "centrality."[13] In private life, centrality means keeping to the ideal Mean of good conduct (an idea similar to the Aristotelian mean). In the public sphere, centrality implies the unique position held by the ruler as focus for his subjects' talents and aspirations.[14] Any noble act is prompted by the fully developed conscience, which internalizes the model of the sages, so individual "centeredness" cannot be counted as something external.[15]

Appraisal 2 is usually assigned to commoners, yet here the *Mystery* speaks of the Great Man. The theme of this tetragram is advance. Through sustained efforts to embody the Mean, any person can advance to become a sage.[16]

> App. 3: Impetuous and most presumptuous,
> He cannot find the center path.
> Fath. 3: That he is wildly unstable[17]
> Means: His advance is not centered.

Appraisal 3 marks the transition from Thought to Action. Aligned here with inauspicious Night, it describes reckless advance in disregard of the conventions. Confucius advocated moderation ("the center path") to his headstrong disciples.[18]

> App. 4: The sun in its flight dispels darkness.[19]
>   The myriad things are suffused with joy.[20]
> Fath. 4: That the sun's flight dispels darkness
>   Means: The way of the ruler flourishes.[21]

The sun (often called the Red Bird) is compared to a gigantic bird whose flight through the heavens brings light and warmth to regions that would otherwise languish in darkness. The sun, of course, symbolizes the able ruler for several reasons: Their positions are correspondingly high. Both shine equally on all regions as they progress through their respective realms. Both bring light and enlightenment to those below. As the good ruler's suasive example helps subjects who would otherwise remain benighted, so he may also be said to "dispel darkness." Responding to such beneficent influences, all the myriad things of the cosmos reach a state of perfect harmony.

> App. 5: He advances by patronage.[22]
>   Some support him like a crutch.
> Fath. 5: Advancement by connection
>   Means: He is constrained by his patron's house.[23]

Appraisal 5, in its central position, is ruler (i.e., dominant image) of the tetragram. In a yin (even-numbered) tetragram such as this, a yang line is unlucky. An angry complaint is lodged against the most common means of advancement at the Han court: patronage and factionalism.[24] Not only were true worthies discouraged from offering their candidacy. Also, those who had won their posts unfairly often tendered poor advice to the throne, since they felt constrained by loyalty to their own patrons. Perhaps Yang Hsiung ruefully reflects upon his own situation, for he was pressed to write fulsome praise in honour of his patron Wang Mang.[25] One commentator, however, sees here a veiled prediction of the downfall of the powerful Wang clan, in which older officials expunge ("comb out") the "filth" from the court so as to recover a just political order:

> Advancing with fine-toothed combs [in hand],[26]
> Some lean on them [the experienced officials] as props.
> Advancing with fine-toothed combs [in hand],
> They restrain[27] those in honoured positions.[28]

> App. 6: Advancing by the high and bright,
>   He garners blessings without bounds.

> Fath. 6: Advancing by the high and bright
> Means: His Way is far-reaching.[29]

The deserving person advances because he imitates the lofty and illustrious way of the ancient sages embodied in ritual. His efforts are repaid by high position and extraordinary blessings. (In an alternate reading of the Appraisal line, "he advances and so is lofty and illustrious.") Thus, his influence becomes far-reaching in at least two senses: First, his moral influence permeates every aspect of contemporary society. Second, his descendants will receive the benefits of this vast store of accumulated *ch'i* for generations to come.[30]

> App. 7: He cannot sustain his advance.[31]
> Hearing blame, he stops up his ears.[32]
> Fath. 7: Advance perverted
> Means: Detractions grow ever more obvious.

In the *Mystery* schema, Position 7 is the Beginning of Calamity. This benighted individual, whose advance has come at the expense of the greater good, finally meets severe criticism. Incapable of reform, he can only expect disparaging remarks and disaffection to increase.

> App. 8: Advancing into a deep pool,
> The noble man uses a boat.
> Fath. 8: To advance in pools by using a boat
> Means: He proceeds by the Way.

The boat stands for all the civilizing inventions of the sage kings of antiquity, whose utility stems from their imitation of fundamental cosmic patterns.[33] The wise individual who faces potential danger (= the deep water) strictly follows the tradition of the sages as outlined in the Classics. Otherwise, progress becomes difficult, due to moral ineptitude.

> App. 9: Heading upstream, barefoot over mountains:
> In three long years he has not returned.
> Fath. 9: Climbing against current and crag
> Means: In the end, it cannot be prolonged.[34]

In a contrast to the preceding verse, the subject of this final Appraisal sets himself a series of nearly impossible tasks, possibly out of blind perversity or a regrettable love of physical daring.[35] Unfortunately, he does not know enough to employ the tools at hand to his advantage. Though great effort is expended, few, if any gains result. His failure is all the more regrettable in that it is completely unnecessary. A wiser individual uses available resources, like the classics, to persevere in the Way.

Shih

No. 21. Release
March 22–March 26 (a.m.)

Correlates with Heaven's Mystery;
Yang; *the phase Wood; and the* Yi
ching *Hexagram no. 40, Deliver-*
ance; the sun enters the Wall con-
stellation, 3d degree; the Dipper
points due east;[1] the musical note is
E-flat; the Spring Equinox solar
period begins with Appraisal 3

HEAD: Yang *ch'i* to effect harmony strikes open[2] the round casing of yin,[3] warming and releasing things, so that all shed their withered husks and are delivered from their shells.

Previous tetragrams, including the Head text of Tetragram 10, consistently associate yin with what encircles, encases, or wraps around things, thereby hampering their growth; hence, my translation. However, this Head text could also read, "Yang *ch'i* harmoniously catalyzes. Round and warm, [like the sun it] releases the things so that all shed their withered husks. . . ."[4] Either version emphasizes the generative influence of yang *ch'i* at the transitional vernal equinox. Once yin and yang have come into balance, yang *ch'i* is strong enough to break yin's hold on the myriad things. Like thunder, the "release of Heaven-and-Earth," yang *ch'i* catalyzes productive growth so that seed pods now break open;[5] animals and insects, shaking off hibernation, begin to stir. As a host of creatures emerge from their shells, husks, and moltings to the clear light of day, we may expect moral renewal in mankind as well. A boundless potential for good opens up, with a focus on lightening the burdens of others. Inappropriate release entailing careless or remiss behavior, however, leads inevitably to loss.[6]

> App. 1: Movement, though nameless,
> Leads to achievement.[7]
> Fath. 1: Moving, but without a name
> Means: Indescribable are its glories.

Appraisal 1 representing the Beginning of Thought is here aligned with auspicious yang. By convention, both the Tao and the sage are "nameless" in the sense that their greatness cannot be reduced to one or more discrete attributes. The virtue of the ancient sage-king Yao, for example, was "so boundless that the people could not find a name for it."[8] And though the patterns they establish help lesser creatures realize their innate potential, both the Tao and the sage prefer to operate behind the scenes, without drawing attention to themselves. In consequence, few among us can fully recognize, let alone articulate the extent of their innate power.[9] They are at once "extraordinary" and "ordinary" (because existence without them seems impossible). No wonder their achievements cannot be adequately described.

> App. 2: Movement yields echo and shadow.[10]
> Fath. 2: Movement yielding only echo and shadow
>   Means: It is not worth noting.[11]

Echo and shadow usually symbolize the mysterious but powerful attraction between things in categorical sympathy. These same images can also suggest the close conformity of the superior man to cosmic norms, of inferiors to true superiors, and so on.[12] Here, however, the point is decidedly different: While the unseen Tao produces manifest achievements, self-important operators produce no tangible benefit, either because their nature is fundamentally derivative (like echo and shadow),[13] or because they pursue transitory goals of no greater substance than an echo or shadow.[14] As the Chinese proverb says, "They chase the wind and catch the shadow." A return to the basic and substantial, rather than the secondary and shifting, would lead men back to the Tao.[15]

> App. 3: The wind moves and thunder rouses.
>   Follow their lofty and exalted natures.
> Fath. 3: Wind moving, thunder rousing
>   Means: Their movements have purpose.

Appraisal 3 corresponds to the Wood phase, to East, and to spring. Since antiquity, the Chinese have assumed that spring thunderstorms stimulate the proper growth of things. The good leader is like a force of nature in that his catalyzing activity seems no less irresistible.[16] In contrast to the Taoist sage, who practices "nonaction," the Confucian sage works with the purpose of improving and elevating others.

> App. 4: In moving to the highlands,[17]
>   He loses friends from the lowlands.[18]
> Fath. 4: Moving to the highlands
>   Means: He is in danger of losing his base.[19]

Appraisal 4 marks the Beginning of Good Fortune; unfortunately, here it is aligned with inauspicious night. In climbing from a low post to a high one, the individual neglects his old base, whether it be former allies, the support of followers, the teachings of the Confucian masters, or simply the attachment to right conduct. For this reason, he is likely to be toppled from his position of prominence.[20]

This poem may also serve as a comment on the wily chief minister who flatters the ruler above while oppressing the common people below.[21] In that case, not only the individual but the dynasty faces extinction.

> App. 5: Like healing salves, the ruler's virtue[22]
> Soothes the Four States.
> Fath. 5: The salves that smooth and release
> Mean: The people's joy knows no bounds.

A standard metaphor compares precious unguents to the ruler's gracious virtue. Just as unguents smooth and heal broken skin, the ruler's right conduct restores life to the body politic and obviates political friction,[23] even beyond the borders of the Central Kingdom.[24] For this reason, the ruler's subjects can look forward to a period of unparalleled peace and joy.

> App. 6: Thunder at court
> Destroys harmony and propriety.
> Fath. 6: Thunder at court
> Means: Both harmony and rectitude are lost.

Thunderclaps express divine anger and, by extension, the wrath of the Son of Heaven.[25] They also suggest new developments, which tend to frighten, rather than soothe.[26] Finally, repeated thunderclaps may symbolize self-promoting ministers who make the people quail as they abuse the authority of their offices.[27] Anger, innovations, and arrogance are all out of place at court. For this reason, "harmony and rectitude are lost."[28]

> App. 7: Thunder crashes, again and again,[29]
> Washing away his shame.
> Fath. 7: Repeated thunderclaps, no disgrace,
> Means: Shame is excised from everywhere.[30]

In the *Changes,* repeated thunderclaps convey a salutary shock to the system:

> Thunder repeated: the image of shock. In fear and trembling, the
> noble man sets his life in order and examines himself.[31]

The right response to bad omens is to resolve upon self-reform. Then, paradoxically, "shock will bring success."[32] These same lines, however, according to certain commentators, describe the righteous indignation felt by the superior individual towards those who dare to blame or insult him. Whatever their charges, he remains unsullied as anger purges the shame.[33]

> App. 8: Driven by profit, he falls
> Flat on his face, then dies.
> Fath. 8: To be driven by profit
> Means: He walks together with death.[34]

Conventional wisdom equates the "good life" with the acquistion of wealth, but running after profit all too often ends in the death of the soul. It may also cause physical death, since "those whose measures are dictated by mere expediency arouse continual resentment."[35] For this reason, Confucius derided lesser men who go to a great deal of trouble "to discover what will pay."[36]

> App. 9: Today accused,[37] tomorrow blessed.[38]
> In the end, he's freed from his chains.[39]
> Fath. 9: Today accused, tomorrow blessed
> Means: By that, he's released from calamity.

As one Chinese philosopher noted, "It is never anyone's proper destiny to die in chains."[40] Appraisal 9 is the last Appraisal; hence, the reference to a final release from danger. The vague wording of the end line of the Fathoming tends to focus the reader's attention on the question, "What can one use to release oneself from calamity?" A passage in the *Changes* supplies the answer: Strict adherence to moral standards obviates the need for most constraints, physical and mental, used to train or curb lesser men.[41] And "proof" of the blessings associated with morality is supplied by the story of good King Wen of Chou, who was released from jail even under the evil last king of the Shang dynasty.[42]

Ke
No. 22. Resistance
March 26 (p.m.)–March 30

Correlates with Heaven's Mystery; Yin; the phase Metal; and the Yi ching Hexagram no. 34, Greatly Strong;[1] the sun enters the Wall constellation, 8th degree

HEAD: Yang *ch'i*, internally strong, can offer resistance to the many manifestations of yin.[2] Repelling them, it forces them to withdraw.

As the first tetragram following the vernal equinox, Resistance signals a dramatic shift in the cosmic balance. For the first time in the lunar year, yang *ch'i* is slightly stronger than yin, though yin's influence is still manifest. Yang *ch'i* begins its assault on yin, propelled perhaps by the tetragram's alignment with Metal, the stuff of weapons. Still, at this point in the annual cycle yang *ch'i* is merely "internally strong." Only in later tetragrams will yang confront yin externally. The relative weakness of yang *ch'i* is not the primary reason, however, why the Appraisals below do not celebrate warlike postures. As the *Changes* tells us, "The petty person uses his strength, but the noble man does not act in this way."[3] True resistance entails perseverance, not brute force. Developing strength and power in these early stages depends on distancing oneself from impropriety while staying close to integrity.

The character used for the title depicts a length of wooden board which demarcates space and separates objects. Footboards and backboards in carriages, window sills, cupboards, animal enclosures, and fences use the same word. In the texts that follow, appropriate separation, distancing, and resistance are dominant themes.

> App. 1: Sealing off inner goodness,[4]
> Propriety fails, goodness is lost.[5]
> Fath. 1: Sealing off inner goodness
> Means: The center cannot assimilate the good.[6]

The first position, which marks the Beginning of Thought, depicts the inner workings of the heart/mind, where seeds of goodness are implanted, as well as impulses toward evil.[7] If an individual assiduously works to develop the good within, he will grow in moral strength as his evil impulses wane. If, however, the individual fails to develop his potential for Good, his inner resistance to evil impulses will break down. As his mind increasingly fails to distinguish right from wrong, he will lose all appreciation of "the time-tested categories."[8] The conscience as moral center will no longer review his conduct daily,[9] nor will it be able to "assimilate the good" by imitation of the ancients. In that case, the individual loses all chance to cultivate his humaneness, the virtue that distinguishes him from the brutes.

> App. 2: Sealing off internal evil
> Makes propriety profound.[10]
> Fath. 2: Sealing off internal evil
> Means: Hidden propriety is marvelous.

In a contrast to the preceding verses, this poem presents a good person, who steadfastly contains his evil impulses, lest his moral courage be sapped. As the individual becomes more fully human, he finally achieves that mysterious charisma associated with the ancient sage-kings. The most significant acts of resistance, then, often take place in the hidden recesses of the heart and mind.

> App. 3: Shunning belt and hook,[11]
> He is as loose as his garments.[12]
> Fath. 3: No belt or hook for his trousers
> Means: There are no means of restraint.

In Chinese ways of thinking, personal appearance (including the disposition of one's garments) reflects the inner self. If an individual refuses to accept the customary restraints upon his person (i.e., the belt and hook) that also serve to enhance his looks,[13] inevitably the beauty and order embodied in ritual patterns are disturbed. A breakdown of the all-important Five Relations (ruler/subject, father/son, husband/wife, elder sibling/ younger sibling, and friend/friend) ensues. With relations shattered, chaos follows.

> App. 4: The net deters.[14]
> There is a right way to capture birds.
> Fath. 4: That the net prevents capture
> Means: Rectify the role of law.[15]

With both Appraisal and Tetragram allied with Metal and punishments, the penal code is subject of these verses. Using the stock metaphor of "the net" of the law, the constructive aspects of the legal system are considered: The net confines birds of prey (i.e., the evildoers in human society), keeping them away from the innocent. The very presence of a net may also act as deterrent to ward off potentially destructive animals, obviating the need for any future action against them.[16] Equally important, the net allows the hunter to catch birds without harming their feathers, breaking their eggs, or overturning their nests.[17] If the law functions in this careful way, criminals are captured and the innocent protected. Ideally, the law has nothing to do with revenge.[18]

> App. 5: If glue and lacquer loosen,
> The bow does not shoot,
> For horn and wood have split.
> Fath. 5: That glue and lacquer loosen
> Means: Promises do not stick.

One early commentator[19] offers a complicated explication of the images employed here: The loosening of the lacquer symbolizes the indiscretions of the ruler; the wooden bow stands for the subordinate; the horn, for the king's own person. In that case, the text means, "If the ruler is indiscreet, he loses his official."[20]

Though Appraisal 5 signifies the ruler, the poem may simply describe any situation in which the bonds of mutual trust have been broken.[21] Just as the failure of the glue renders the bow unusable, lack of good faith undermines the utility of all social institutions. Clearly, the primary responsibility for establishing group cohesion rests with the elite, whose members must continually and publicly reaffirm their absolute commitment to justice and the common good. It is this attitude that works as "social glue."[22]

> App. 6: Waxing metal,[23] waning stone.
> What's gone is small; what comes is great.
> Fath. 6: Waxing metal and waning stone
> Mean: Excellence daily grows greater.

Though metal and stone are both aligned with West and autumn in the Han system of correspondences, here they clearly function as opposites. After all, there are certain important differences between the two materials: Metal shines, while unpolished stone is dull; metal alone suggests glory and enlightenment.[24] Metal is also more "productive" and valuable;[25] most would ascribe greater beauty to it. Finally, metal seems almost indestructible, while stone can erode. (This may be germane, since Appraisal 6 correlates with Water.) In short, "Good is named metal, and evil, stone,"[26] so an increase in good, rather than in evil, is predicted.

> App. 7: In rejecting his most valued men,
> Seal and sash are endangered.
> Fath. 7: Rejecting his most valued men
> Means: He loses the means to correct the self.

Seal and sash are emblems of political authority; ideally they derive from inner integrity and a strong commitment to the public good. Since the empire is not "one man's possession," its ruler must consult widely with others to learn how best to promote a community of interests. Here, the emperor endangers the state by ignoring good counsel.

> App. 8: Reluctant to fasten tight that belt,
> The superior man finds timely opportunity.
> The petty man, aggrieved,[27] is blocked.
> Fath. 8: Reluctance to cinch that belt
> Means: It is fitting that he cannot act.

The same act, a refusal to gird the self, may have different implications when carried out by the immoral individual (as in Appraisal 3) or by the moral superior (as here).[28] The leather belt specifically signifies officeholding, with all its implied constraints. On principle, the superior man delays assuming office until he is prepared and the time is right. (Perhaps the good man avoids court for a time because the bureaucracy is ruled by factionalism or headed by a bad ruler.)[29] Faced with the prospect of onerous duties and routine, the inferior man also hesitates to take up office. Since his refusal stems from simple selfishness or mindless nonconformity rather than good sense, he will find his career blocked.

> App. 9: It widens its eyes, raises its horn,
> And so its unlowered body is struck.
> Fath. 9: Widened eyes and a raised horn
> Mean: It brings harm back on itself.[30]

With Appraisal 9, which corresponds to the extreme point of resistance, the situation moves far beyond righteous indignation. The eyes are wide with a desire for revenge. The horn is raised, signifying an eagerness for conflict. Here, in the extreme situation, the emotions rule, rather than conscience or good sense. With more humane solutions available, offensive and arrogant stances stubbornly maintained (despite the possible consequences) can only bring harm to oneself in the end.

Yi

No. 23. Ease

March 31–April 4 (a.m.)

Correlates with Heaven's Mystery; Yang; the phase Earth; and the Yi ching Hexagram no. 34, Greatly Strong;[1] the sun enters the Wall constellation, 12th degree

HEAD: Yang *ch'i* injures and cuts off[2] yin so that it succumbs to[3] a debilitating illness. Things as a rule are balanced and at ease.

Continuing its assault on yin, yang *ch'i* seriously weakens yin; as yin can no longer hope to save itself, it reluctantly releases its hold on the myriad things, which now escape its ruinous clutches.[4] Both the initial injury and the resultant ease are suggested by the character chosen for the title, which has three main meanings: (1) "to injure or harm," (2) "to level" (both in the sense of "to put in balance" and "to flatten by force"), and (3) "to ease." The Appraisals below suggest the complicated ties that relate ease and injury.[5]

> App. 1: At first, secretly of two minds,
> He grasps what eases his inner self.[6]

Fath. 1: Initial confusion, then equanimity
   Means: This relieves[7] his inner self.

The phrase "to be of two minds"[8] is sometimes a synonym for duplicitous. More often, however, it suggests the conflicting impulses to uphold social duty and to serve self-interest. The notion of divided allegiances can also be applied to a subordinate serving two masters. All these situations stem from the mind's secret struggle over priorities. If wise and good, the individual orders his goals, ranking inner happiness above conventional goods[9] and communal needs above selfish desires. A calm, yet resolute mind is the key to the internal equilibrium that promotes the healthful circulation of the "ever-flowing *ch'i.*"[10]

App. 2: Secretly injured,
   He blunders into Heaven's net.
Fath. 2: Secretly hurt, crashing into the net
   Means: "Though loosely woven, it does not fail."

"Heaven's net" is the conventional phrase for "cosmic retribution," the Chinese counterpart to the recording angel of the Judeo-Christian tradition. The coarse mesh of the net signifies Heaven's desire for leniency. Yet justice demands that the net catch every wicked individual, so that virtue and fate will roughly correspond. As the *Lao tzu* says:

The net of heaven is cast wide. Though the mesh is not fine, nothing ever slips through.[11]

For the Chinese, talk of Heaven does not necessarily imply a transcendent being as judge. Perhaps the evildoer is naturally caught in entanglements of his own creation, as his lies and cruelty isolate him from the community.

App. 3: After three days of wailing,
   The frail infant is far from hoarse.[12]
Fath. 3: The infant's continuous wails
   Mean: The center heart is in harmony.

Another image from the *Lao tzu* proves the invincible nature of inner oneness by the well-known example:

The newborn baby howls all the day without its voice cracking once. This is because it is harmony at its height.[13]

The *Mystery* agrees with Lao tzu on two points: First, external weakness is not always an accurate indicator of internal weakness. Second, inner peace of mind gives the individual a mysterious power. Still, neither point seems a sufficient reason to advocate a complete rejection of civilization, of maturity, or of social duty.[14]

> App. 4: After grinding flat his teeth,
>   Some try to feed him dirt.[15]
> Fath. 4: That his teeth are leveled
>   Means: Food no longer appeals.

The teeth are ground down, either by repeated acts of gluttony[16] or by "chomping at the bit" for riches and high rank. Once the teeth are gone, the individual lacks a basic tool for survival. No longer whole himself, the individual is soon devalued by others. Paradoxically, then, self-indulgence ultimately creates a situation where certain basic desires (such as those for food and community) can never be satisfied.[17]

> App. 5: With inner ease, nothing but profit.
> Fath. 5: The benefits of inner ease
>   Mean: Its paths are many.

The person who is dedicated to the Way maintains peace of mind; as a result, his mind is calm enough to consider the utility of all options. Just as the one Tao spawns the myriad things, single-mindedness leads to many ways for several reasons: After the arduous task of building a broad moral foundation, acquiring the expertise needed for a specific task is relatively easy. The moral person has already developed the self-discipline needed for lesser tasks. What's more, inner wholeness attunes the individual to the Tao, so that he is particularly sensitive to changing scenes and unfolding situations. As the *Changes* promises:

> By means of what is easy and simple, we grasp the order of All-under-Heaven.[18]

> App. 6: He is injured in the hut.
>   His house stands empty as a mound.
> Fath. 6: Injured at the hut
>   Means: His virtue is lost.[19]

Confucians argue that the virtue of humaneness provides the only secure and happy dwelling for mankind.[20] Those who abandon the struggle to follow the true path of Goodness leave themselves unprotected. Here, the individual is "injured." An alternate reading of the Appraisal suggests that his own misbehavior has ended in another's "levelling his dwelling." With "his virtue lost," he can only wander among the "hills and ruins," seeking a makeshift home. Both readings yield much the same lesson: Once the individual lays waste to his virtue, all true security evaporates.

App. 7: The trunk is pliable and weak,[21]
Yet wood in contact dulls the metal saw.[22]
Such is leveling.

Fath. 7: That the trunk is weak
Means: "The weak overcome the strong."

To the Chinese, wood is known for its pliability while metal exemplifies durability and strength.[23] In language reminiscent of the *Lao tzu*,[24] the *Mystery* reminds readers of a paradoxical truth: The softer wood dulls the metal saw. By analogy, gentle virtue is more compelling than brute force. Appraisal 7 in its message underscores the lesson of Appraisal 3.

Ssu-ma Kuang reads the verses differently:

The [well] bar is pliable,
The bar is weak.
[The rope] splits the wood.
[The whetstone] sharpens metal.
[Examples of] leveling.

The [well] bar is pliable.
Meaning: "The weak overcome the strong."[25]

A rope wears into wood, just as a whetstone sharpens knives. Ssu-ma Kuang, then, gives two more good examples of the power of "the weak."

App. 8: In wearing down its horn
There is danger.[26]

Fath. 8: Injuring his horn[27]
Means: He is wounded by the use of awesome force.

The animal's horn symbolizes brute strength and aggressive behavior. Here the horn has been worn down by overfrequent use until the animal can no longer defend itself.

App. 9: The benefits of ease[28] in old age:
It is right to be respected when aged and infirm.[29]

Fath. 9: The propriety of ease in old age
Means: Retired, he hangs his carriage at home.[30]

Since Appraisal 9 represents extreme ease, it properly addresses the subject of old age and retirement. After years of loyal service, the aged official is allowed to retire quietly to his native place, where his official carriage hangs on the wall, no longer in use. The old man wants only to live out his days in peace and honor; he makes no effort to influence others by flaunting his former position. The *Documents* labels the last of life's blessings "coming to a good end." Here, the individual has clearly accomplished this.[31]

Correlates with Heaven's Mystery; Yin; the phase Water; and the Yi ching Hexagram no. 16, Amusement;[1] the sun enters the Stomach constellation, 5th degree; the Dipper points ESE; the musical note is E

Le
No. 24. Joy
April 4 (p.m.)–April 8

HEAD: Yang begins to emerge from obscurity.[2] Unrolling what had been folded up,[3] it thereby gains harmony and ease so that all things are filled with joy.[4]

Once again the expansive nature of yang *ch'i* contrasts with yin's propensity to cramp things under its influence. As the gentle spring rains begin, yang *ch'i* not only "begins to emerge from obscurity," but also, according to an alternate reading of one part of the Head text, "begins to put forth warmth."[5] Warmth unfurls the tightly curled leaves of vegetation and prompts hibernating animals to stretch their limbs in preparation for leaving their dens. In fact, the warmth of spring elicits expansive feelings of delight in all living creatures. Since many of these feelings are spontaneously expressed in ecstatic cries, including mating calls, the tetragram is equally associated with music, which functions as outlet for and moderating influence on the emotions.[6] (It is worth recalling that both "joy" and "music" are written with the same graph in Chinese.) According to one of his own disciples, Yang Hsiung never learned to fully appreciate music.[7] This may explain why Yang's references to music appear conventional, if not hackneyed. Still, as one of the foremost classicists of his time, Yang Hsiung clearly knew the pertinent texts. All the general ideas found in the Appraisals and many of his specific images are drawn from two chapters: the "Record on Music" chapter in the *Record of Ritual* and Hsün tzu's "Discussion on Music."

Given the tetragram title, the reader might expect this tetragram to be full of happy overtones, but Yang Hsiung also uses the Joy theme to portray the evil consequences of overindulgence in pleasure. In this he follows the imagery of the correspondent hexagram, which cautions against enthusiasms that bring misfortune and remorse.[8] As the Odes say, "Let us not be wild in our love of enjoyment."[9] True happiness, as the *Changes* shows, depends upon integrity, perseverance, and adherence to ritual.

App. 1: Solitary pleasure is pleasure confined.[10]
          Its reach does not reach far.
Fath. 1: Solitary pleasure is pleasure confined.
          Meaning: It dissipates his inner self.[11]

Though the commentators quarrel over the right pejorative to characterize solitary enjoyment, the general message is clear: To the Chinese, pleasure is essentially a social feeling. The inner soul is ultimately destroyed by solitary pleasures, which neither enhance mutual regard between individuals nor promote communion with the great men of the past (through appreciation of their painting or calligraphy, for example). In short, personal greatness can only be achieved through interaction with others. As one Confucian master wrote:

> It was by sharing their enjoyments with the people that [the ideal] men of antiquity were able to enjoy themselves. . . . There is just one thing in which the ancients greatly surpassed others, and that is the way they extended what they did.[12]

The noble person "does not keep what he desires for himself"[13] for practical as well as moral reasons. The *ch'i* aroused by pleasurable emotions must find suitable outlets in ritual and music (both essentially public activities) if it is not to harm the body.[14] Also, taking the Tao as model, the noble person makes every effort to encourage others to reach their full potential.[15] As a result of these two factors, communal happiness soon replaces solitary enjoyment. In contrast, by definition the petty person is too selfish to afford others the same opportunity for pleasure that he enjoys.[16]

App. 2: The time for unimaginable joy[17]
          Is set in Heaven.
Fath. 2: Joy that is unimaginable
          Means: Use the seasons and the year.

It is in the individual's best interests to adjust his actions to prevailing cosmic trends, thereby multiplying the efficacy of his own labors. Having done that, he can look forward to success. The joy he will receive is "unimaginable" in two senses: first, it exceeds all expectations,[18] and second, its ultimate source cannot be located.[19]

Three commentators would have us relate these lines to the Mencian program of "virtuous government."[20] According to Mencius, the ruler should employ the people in *corveé* labor and military service only during slack agricultural seasons. In this way, state service will never threaten the people's livelihood. While the state grows rich from taxes, the people grow content, without ever giving it much thought. After all, "The best of all rulers is but a shadowy presence to his subjects."[21]

> App. 3: All composure is gone.[22]
>> Weeping, howling, wailing figures
>> Lean in doorways.
> Fath. 3: Not at ease or refined
>> Means: Rites and music have been abolished.[23]

The Appraisal uses no fewer than six onomatopoeic characters, whose meanings are disputed.[24] All six may be read as mournful sounds, but some or all may also convey "sounds of merriment."[25] In a sense, it hardly matters what particular emotion each character signifies. The unmistakable impression is one of a babble of incoherent and distressing noises. Such excessive displays of emotion directly contravene the rites; uncontrolled outbursts can only end in disgrace. Therefore, the Appraisal ends with "leaning in doorways." This can mean misfortune is at one's very doorstep.[26] Otherwise, it probably refers either to public expressions of bereavement,[27] or to the age-old posture adopted by degraded women selling their bodies.[28]

> App. 4: Discarding his ties,
>> Severing his bonds,
>> He eases his godlike[29] heart.
> Fath. 4: Breaking free of ties and bonds
>> Means: The heart truly rejoices.[30]

Contrary to popular belief, steadfast adherence to the Way need not cause the principled person to feel constrained by duty. Rather, the good person finds compliance with ritual eminently satisfying for both aesthetic and practical reasons. Free at last of ungovernable desire for external objects,[31] the individual is finally in control of the "unmoved" heart/mind.[32] He can rest content, having achieved inner equanimity.[33]

> App. 5: Rich harmonies of bell and drum,[34]
>> Then mournful[35] pipes and strings—
>> For them, decline may follow.
> Fath. 5: Bell and drum sounding in unison
>> Means: After joy comes grief.

The proverb says, "With extreme pleasure, sorrow arises."[36] In typical court performances bell and drum, with their bracing airs, are followed by the thin whine of pipes and strings, which tend to arouse uneasy longings, even depravity in the listener. Here the petty person (be he emperor or commoner) indulges his senses,[37] courting disaster. For one thing, an overpreoccupation with pleasure precludes proper participation in social and political activity. It will also weaken the body.[38] Yang Hsiung may have had in mind a famous anecdote regarding two dukes of the sixth century B.C. who found "strange music their chief delight." After they insisted on successive performances of increasingly mournful music, they were afflicted by droughts and curious illnesses.[39]

> App. 6: Let joy and music swell, filling every gap,[40]
> To the delight of commonfolk and gods and birds.
> Fath. 6: Great joy and music filling every space
> Means: Joy embraces all and every thing.[41]

In even-numbered tetragrams, Appraisal 6 corresponds to the Son ot Heaven; hence, this classic description of the joy that pervades the kingdom ruled by a sage. In contrast to Appraisal 1, which describes the misguided individual (possibly the ruler) who refuses to extend his pleasures to the people, here the benefits of sagely rule accrue not only to human subjects, but to all living creatures. By the end, each thing in the triadic realms of Heaven-Earth-Man is joined in ecstatic union; no absolute barrier separates Man from the rest of creation.[42] Equally important, the gap is closed between the human order as it ought to be and as it actually is.[43] This is proof that the charismatic individual's influence pervades all the cosmos. It is also proof that "it is possible to enjoy harmonious pleasure without any abandoned behavior."[44]

> App. 7: People sigh,[45] ghosts sigh
> Over limitations fixed by Heaven.
> Fath. 7: Ghosts and people sighing
> Means: They proclaim the end of happiness.[46]

The preceding Appraisal posits the fundamental unity of all things. Now the otherworldly and human realms are joined in sorrow, rather than in joy. The operation of cosmic cycles may undercut the best laid plans. Evildoers, who have temporarily eluded cosmic retribution, must now accept their punishment. Those who are good meanwhile face old age and death. The very presence of ghosts indicates some kind of cosmic imbalance in the Chinese mind.[47]

According to several commentators, the first line of the Appraisal and Fathoming read, "People laugh, and ghosts laugh." In that case, an unthinking outburst of laughter suggests the failure to regulate emotions that inevitably leads to calamity. As the *Changes* writes, "When the wife and children laugh 'tee-hee'/ It will end in distress."[48]

> App. 8: Heaving sigh after sigh,[49] fearing his own faults,[50]
> He forgets the errors and deceptions[51] of others.[52]

Fath. 8: Sigh after sigh, he fears the self.
Meaning: In the end,[53] he protects himself.

The subject of the previous Appraisal wastes time bemoaning his fate, but here the protagonist works hard to overcome his own faults in order to insure his own protection. So intent is he upon self-improvement that he comes to ignore the faults of others, a sure sign of the gentleman.[54] Meanwhile, such good conduct replenishes the individual's store of the life-giving *ch'i.*[55]

Some commentators reinterpret the onomatopoeic graphs so that the first line of the Appraisal and Fathoming reads, "Even in the midst of laughing tee-hee."[56] The wise man is equally careful in good times and in bad to correct his own mistakes.[57]

App. 9: His joy nearly complete,
Grief comes before day is done.
He[58] sighs and snivels as he weeps and wails.[59]
Fath. 9: Nearly absolute joy
Means: Truly, this is cause for regret.

Appraisal 9 marks both the culmination and the end of Joy. With it, comes danger,[60] so that ultimately the uncautious individual is plunged into great sorrow, with "sighing and sobbing, snivel and snot."[61]

Correlates with Heaven's Mystery; Yang; the phase Fire; and the Yi ching Hexagram no. 6, Conflict; the sun enters the Stomach constellation, 9th degree

Cheng
No. 25. Contention
April 9–April 13 (a.m.)

HEAD: Yang *ch'i* overflows everywhere. It is "neither onesided, nor partial," so that things vie against one another in competition,[1] with each one following its own proper model.[2]

Yang *ch'i* functions like the true king described in the canonical "Great Plan" chapter of the *Documents*: It is "neither onesided nor partial"[3] in its dealings with subordinates, for "to show no favoritism" is divine.[4] Early Chinese thought generally assumes that the Tao and the good ruler are alike in allowing each thing to develop its distinctive nature. That each thing "follows its own model," then, is one accepted proof of good rule, not a condemnation of lesser creatures. Consequently, "At the birth of the myriad things/ Each gets what is suitable for it."[5] In gratitude for this impartial treatment, the myriad things, like the subjects of a good king, are eager to transform themselves through yang's good graces. The Head text, then, celebrates the benefits of equality in Confucian terms: "fair treatment as determined by social roles" (not the modern Western notion of equal civil rights for all).[6]

Since each creature, if fairly treated, is inspired to act according to its better nature, the tetragram is considered generally auspicious, despite its title. That the tetragram phase is Fire, no doubt, accounts for the raging conflict found in the following Appraisals. Still, just as the Joy Appraisals were less happy than might be expected, those in Contention are less evil than the title suggests. Under certain conditions, conflict and contention play a positive role, whether in the law courts or on the battlefield.[7] In some cases, punishment, even war, represents the only viable way to suppress evil and advance the cycle. In making this argument, the *Mystery* shifts the emphasis from the correspondent *Changes* hexagram, which usually condemns contention and conflict.

> App. 1: Contend best by not contending.
>   Retire to obscurity.
> Fath. 1: In contending, not contending
>   Means: This is the normal course[8] of the Way.[9]

The opening line of both Appraisal and Fathoming literally reads, "Contend not contend." The commentators give four possible interpretations of the line: (1) "Contend before the occasion for contention becomes apparent to obviate the need for obvious contention";[10] (2) "Contend best by not being quarrelsome";[11] (3) "To fight on incontestable ground" (i.e., on the basis of the Confucian Classics), so that "nothing can overcome [him]";[12] and (4) "Able to fight, but choosing not to fight," a reading that emphasizes the latent power of the good person.[13]

The first interpretation clearly draws upon early Taoist and Legalist texts, which enjoin the superior man to solve problems before they become apparent. This fits well with Appraisal 1, since it focuses on the beginning of the cycle. The second reading recalls the nature of Water (the Appraisal's correlation), by showing it to be soft yet forceful in eroding other things. The ritual act, which always exemplifies courtesy and humility, makes the actor equally gentle yet compelling. Since courtesy and ritual constitute "the normal course of the Way," paradoxically "the gentlest gamester is the soonest victor."[14]

App. 2: A weakling tries to shout back the River.[15]
Fath. 2: A weakling shooing the Yellow River
 Means: How can such a man be relied upon?

The weakling, seriously miscalculating his strength, thinks he can intimidate the Yellow River simply by his shouts.[16] (Presumably, the threat to the River comes because this Appraisal corresponds to Fire, Water's enemy.) The futility of the act should be obvious to all, though the weakling is blithely unaware of his own incapacities. What's more, the Yellow River is seen as a storehouse of blessings by agrarian China, since it is the mighty fountainhead of all the rivers in the North China plain that bring life-giving water to the crops. The weakling's posturing against it, then, could hardly be more inappropriate[17] or self-defeating. Compare the *Chuang tzu* story where a stupid owl tries to "shoo away" a spirit-bird:

> In the south there is a bird called the Yüan-ch'u . . . [which] rises up
> from the South Sea and flies to the North Sea, and it will rest on
> nothing but the [marvelous] Wu-t'ung tree, eat nothing but the fruit of
> the Lien, and drink only from springs of sweet water. Once there was
> an owl who had gotten hold of a half-rotten old rat. As the Yüan-ch'u
> passed by, the owl raised its head, looked up at the Yüan-ch'u, and
> said, "Shoo!"[18]

Both the poem and the story mock ludicrous acts of physical courage. As Confucius said, "The man who is ready to 'beard a tiger or rush a river' . . . that is the sort of man I would not take."[19]

App. 3: Archers amiably[20] contend.
Fath. 3: Amiably contending in archery
 Means: The noble man yields to his neighbor.

Confucius remarked:

> Gentlemen never contend. You will say that in archery they do so. But
> even then they bow and make way for one another in going up to the
> archery-ground, when they are coming down, and at the subsequent
> drinking bout. Thus even when competing, they still remain
> gentlemen.[21]

Ritual archery contests, in fact, provided a public arena for the display of gentlemanly conduct. The superior man competes, but his way of contending takes a completely different form from that of a lesser man. Even though his fellow competitors may not recognize it, the true gentleman is only concerned lest he be unable to compete with others in Goodness.[22] The noble man therefore yields graciously to his neighbor, unlike the petty person, who is intent on success at any price.

App. 4: Those who battle for petty profit
Never achieve propriety.[23]
Fath. 4: Attached to petty profit
Means: The Right Way is then obscured.[24]

Though desire for wealth and rank is perfectly natural, as even the most strait-laced Confucians admit,[25] it should not override righteousness in cases of conflicting goods. What does it profit a man to win wealth if the Way of true humanity is lost?

App. 5: Taking a stand at the crossroads,
Yields benefit on every side.
Fath. 5: Contending at the crossroads
Means: The place to fight is the center.

The best policy is not predisposed towards any particular line (though it faithfully follows the Good); good policy responds flexibly to each contingency as it arises, thereby achieving the Mean.[26] The crossroads represents the central junction of some nine major highways. Since the king customarily locates his capital at the crossroads, it signifies the king's central and centralizing role in his kingdom.[27] It also suggests that consensus should be reached after all arguments regarding specific policy proposals have been submitted to the king and debated at court.[28] As a result of state-wide cooperation and consensus, the king's subjects gravitate to him.[29] The ruler, then, secures his own strategic advantage by being equally open to all sides. Meanwhile, his subjects benefit no less by the process.[30]

App. 6: Biceps and forearms as thick as shanks,[31]
Bloated thighs and calves:
These are bodily ailments indeed.
Fath. 6: Shank-like upper arms and lower limbs
Mean: They treat the superior[32] as servant.[33]

The early Han statesman Chia Yi (200–168 B.C.) described the disproportionate strength of the feudal kingdoms vis-à-vis the imperial domain:

> The empire suffers from a kind of bloating illness, in which the shin is nearly as big as the waist, and the finger nearly as big as the thigh.[34]

In others words, the trunk (the emperor) is weak when compared with the secondary appendages (the feudal lords). With the power of the feudal kingdoms broken long before Yang Hsiung's time, the chief threats to the throne were posed by chief ministers (conventionally known as "forearms and thighs," in the same way we might say, "right-hand men") and imperial relatives by marriage.[35] Adapting the metaphor of Master Chia, Yang warns the emperor about the disproportionate strength of certain factions at court. More generally, the *Mystery* inveighs against any subordinate who usurps his leader's power. Also, all secondary goals (e.g., those for wealth, position, and fame) should be abandoned in favor of the primary goal of keeping to the Way. Why? In the words of one Han philosopher:

> The small is properly adjunct to the large. . . . The important and the large should have the means to control the unimportant and the small.[36]

App. 7: Contend with shield and lance and helmet,
      But place them in the king's heralds' service.[37]
Fath. 7: Contending with shield and lance
      Means: They protect the ruler's person.

Weapons are properly employed when used for the public good; their use for selfish gain or for revenge is strictly forbidden. The king's advance riders protect the royal person as he makes his progress through the empire, so their martial spirit is rightly celebrated.[38] The *Odes* praise "the lead chariot of the king's host" and "the commander. . . who is a pattern to all the states."[39]

App. 8: The wolf fills its mouth
      With the arrow at its back.
Fath. 8: The wolf cramming its mouth
      Means: He does not turn to see the harm.

Wolves epitomize all that is wicked and rapacious to the sedentary farmers of north and central China. Here greed comes at the expense of wisdom. So intent is the wolf upon devouring its prey that it fails to notice the angry hunter or bow. (The image probably comes from the Chinese constellations, where the Wooden Bow lies directly behind the Wolf.[40] Certainly, talk of greed is also appropriate to the Stomach constellation aligned with this tetragram.)[41]

The moral is clear: Greed is risky, since it works against one's long-term interests. As the Han proverb says, "In carrying out early matters, don't forget the later ones."[42] Or, in the words of Aesop, "False confidence is the forerunner of misfortune."[43]

App. 9: Two tigers, teeth bared.[44]
      Whichever holds back survives.
Fath. 9: Two tigers, teeth bared,
      Means: The victor knows what to restrain.[45]

Appraisal 9 represents extreme Contention. Two tigers face off, poised for the attack. Fully cognizant of the gravity of the situation, the wilier of the two opponents chooses retreat, for a vicious mauling means certain death. In this, the cunning tiger follows military strategy, which advises, "When pitted against an equal, better retire."[46] After all, "Which is dearer, your name or your life?[47]

Wu
No. 26. Endeavor
April 13 (p.m.)–April 17

Correlates with Heaven's Mystery; Yin; the phase Wood; and the Yi ching Hexagram no. 18, Undertakings;[1] the sun enters the Stomach constellation, 14th degree

HEAD: Yang *ch'i* exerts itself in the task [of completing things].[2] All things, conforming their hearts, take control of[3] their own affairs.

Two aspects of yang *ch'i*, both alluded to in the Head text, appear at first glance to be somewhat antithetical: the single-mindedness of yang *ch'i*[4] and its fostering of individuality in the myriad things. (The One fostering the Many is a theme that is found in both Confucian and Taoist teachings.)[5] The good leader, of course, imitates both aspects of yang *ch'i*. His unswerving devotion to the public good is absolute. So, too, is his determination to provide economic security and social mobility sufficient to insure that each subordinate can fulfill his own potential.[6] Only in that way can the realm of Man become as richly varied as the phenomenal world of Heaven-and-Earth. The success of all endeavors ultimately rests on united efforts drawing upon collective strengths; with proper direction, seemingly miraculous feats can be accomplished.

> App. 1: First endeavors find no focus.
> > The petty man is useless after all.[7]
> Fath. 1: Undirected first endeavors
> > Mean: Order is not the province of the petty man.[8]

To initiate a project is an act of creation.[9] In large part, the success of the project will depend upon its sponsor's complete dedication to a fixed vision. By definition, however, the petty person lacks singlemindedness. Whatever thing passes before his eyes, he desires; whatever ambition crosses his mind, he pursues. Since sustained effort and a sense of direction are missing, no significant achievement is possible. The petty person may pride himself on his flexibility, but in reality his priorities are confused. Assigning proper relative value to personal goals is the first step toward establishing human order for the early Confucians. Small wonder, then, that the petty person only increases disorder.

> App. 2: Seeking for himself the new and fresh,
>   Its fragrance pure, refined, and rare—
>   Such is the conduct of the noble man.
> Fath. 2: For himself, seeking the new and fresh
>   Means: Light and glory suffuse the self.[10]

Many ancient Chinese texts enjoin the would-be sage to "daily renew his virtue"[11] by self-assessment and reform. The good person is also one who seeks to renew the hallowed tradition of the sages by applying their general principles to the specifics of his life.[12] Through this process of cultivation, he comes to epitomize all that is new and fresh, rare and refined. This kind of moral brilliance, it should be noted, stems from hard work, not from luck or innate genius. With his dedication to morality, he is not one who "seeks great blessings [only] for himself."[13] Over time, the individual's "fragrance" enhances (i.e., "perfumes") the quality of life in his entire community.[14]

> App. 3: If neither fettered nor constrained,
>   Men's[15] minds rot and spoil.
> Fath. 3: Neither fettered nor restrained
>   Means: Their bodies are not intact.

The Taoist classics at points espouse a return to primitivism and a sublime disdain for conventions and cultural baggage. The *Mystery* directly contradicts them on these points: Without the restraints imposed by education and training in ritual, the discriminating mind remains too undisciplined to develop its capacities fully.[16] When the mind malfunctions, its judgment is clouded; before long the body will succumb to a variety of ills: "Their bodies are not intact."[17] Self-abuse, mutilating punishments, even execution may be in store for the future.

Since Appraisal 3 is aligned with Wood, one commentator sees a description of a tree infested with vermin[18] or insects ("Its core rots and spoils"). If the tree is to survive, the affected branches must be lopped off. By analogy, the would-be sage ruthlessly cuts off that part of himself which is liable to rot.[19]

    App. 4: The arrow seems to fly itself
          With the help[20] of feathers.[21]
          The canopy is borne aloft, the cart conveys it.
    Fath. 4: The arrow and canopied chariot
          Mean: Their Way is exemplary.[22]

Using standard metaphors of his time, Yang Hsiung suggests the benefits of proper alliance and high position.[23] Though the arrow appears to rise "by itself," it cannot fly unless the feathers on its central shaft are strong and properly arranged. Similarly, the canopy (symbol of political authority)[24] will shade the chariot only if it is connected with a sturdy carriage pole. The lesson is clear: No man, however worthy, can expect to succeed if he fails either to make staunch allies or to position himself correctly. For this reason, friends and associates must be chosen with extreme care.[25]

Perhaps the reader is also meant to consider the role of the unseen wind in connection with both arrow and canopy. The wind symbolizes suasive example by charismatic virtue.[26] In that case, the arrow shaft might represent the king's policy; the feathers, his officials;[27] and the air, the invisible yet transforming effect of kingly virtue on the people. As for the canopy, only the currents of the wind keep it fully open so that it adequately protects those below.[28]

    App. 5: All the spider's arduous labor
          Cannot match the silkworm's cloth.[29]
    Fath. 5: The spider's endeavor
          Means: There is no benefit to man.

Both the spider and the silkworm spin marvelous threads of equal strength, durability, and beauty, but only the silkworm's products are of use to mankind. In addition, the spider's web is designed to destroy, while the silkworm's cocoon fosters its own development.[30] Industry, however admirable, is not equivalent to Goodness. As a passage from the *Documents* says:

    Avoid doing whatever is of no benefit if it injures that which benefits.
    Only then will [merit] be complete.[31]

    App. 6: When blossom and fruit smell sweetest,
          That is the time to use them best.
    Fath. 6: Fragrant blossoms put to good use
          Means: They benefit the present year.[32]

Flowers and fruits when fully ripe are pleasing to smell and to taste. That is the time they should be eaten. By analogy, the person of true cultivation gives off a kind of fragrance because he is both "refined and of substance" (a pun in Chinese for the binome translated "blossom and fruit").[33] He also should be put to immediate use by his superiors.

App. 7: Once its fragrance is lost,
There is no place to go.[34]
Fath. 7: Losing his fragrance
Means: Virtue thereby fades.

Here the fragrance of self-cultivation is destroyed. The individual lacks all sense of moral direction, as in Appraisal 1. But since the time is later, this now matters more. Decay proceeds from the inner core.[35] It is equally distressing to watch this in an exquisite flower or in a human being.

App. 8: Yellow Center: he escapes calamity
Because he is properly aligned.[36]
Fath. 8: Yellow Center, avoiding calamity,
Means: He is attuned and thus upright.

Appraisal 8 occupies the central position in the unit of Appraisals 7–9 assigned to Calamity; hence, centrality is played off against calamity. Yellow, of course, is the color assigned to the center; it is said to harmonize and balance its counterparts. For this reason, the yellow center signifies inner virtue directed by the Mean, which works to establish an equilibrium among the emotions. Calamity may be avoided if we stick to the path of moderation and mediation, even at the perilous end of the cycle.

App. 9: The task complete, he defeats himself.
Raindrops form,[37] only to fall.
Fath. 9: The task complete, self-defeat
Means: This is not Heaven's Decree.[38]

With Appraisal 9, "endeavor" reaches its culmination. The rainclouds symbolize futile tasks, for as soon as individual raindrops accumulate, they disperse in a shower. When the individual finds that his hard work has accomplished nothing, he should not blame his failure on Heaven or on fate or on some inherent flaw in human beings. Clearly, the fault lies within himself. Perhaps he tends to arrogance or excess; perhaps he unwisely ignores prevailing conditions;[39] perhaps success has gone to his head. Apparently, he ignores the proverb, "When the task is accomplished, the Way of Heaven lies in retreat."[40]

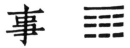

Shih

No. 27. Duties

April 18–April 22 (a.m.)

Correlates with Heaven's Mystery;
Yang; *the phase Metal; and the*
Yi ching *Hexagram no. 18, Under-*
takings; the sun enters the Mane
constellation, 4th degree

HEAD: Yang *ch'i* greatly stimulates[1] and shed lights on the duties [of the myriad things].[2] Things expand and expand[3] according to rule, each one exerting its own strength to the fullest.

Yang *ch'i* waxes ever greater, imparting strength and intelligence to all the myriad things, so that each fulfills its intended role. As yang *ch'i* is to phenomenal things, so the ruler is to the masses. The common people learn their social duties through the suasive encouragement of the ruler. Since a single hexagram provides the prototype for both this tetragram and the preceding one, Tetragrams 26 and 27 are generally similar in message. There is, however, a subtle shift in emphasis: In Endeavor, the focus was on regulating action; in Duty, the main theme is the proper division of social responsibilities.[4]

> App. 1: Service, without serving narrow ends
> Leaves nothing left unserved.
> Fath. 1: Serving with impartial service
> Means: He proceeds by the Way.

Most commentators read the first line of Appraisal and Fathoming (literally, "Serve without serving") as a celebration of *wu wei* ("non-purposive activity") in Nature. In support, they cite the famous *Lao tzu* passage, "The Way does not act, yet nothing is left undone."[5] Still, Yang Hsiung's *Model Sayings* strongly objects to *wu wei* in government (what we might call laissez-faire), arguing that *wu wei* can only work in an already perfect society.[6] For that reason, I offer a different reading, one which emphasizes the impartial nature of Goodness. As Confucius said, the good man refuses to align himself with a particular faction or cause; instead, he only sides with the Right.[7] The same lines, however, could also mean that the superior man does not take credit for his merits (serving without claiming to serve).[8] Or, that the gentleman acts with such mastery of ritual (in the words of the *Changes*, he is "simple" and "easy") that he serves without seeming to serve.[9]

App. 2: If, when outcomes hinge on choice,[10]
He refuses counsel or advice,
He forfeits any token[11] of his wit.[12]
Fath. 2: Seeking neither counsel nor advice
Means: His comprehension is lost.

A single decision could swing the course of events either way; hence, the metaphor of the pivot. At such critical junctures, the wise person consults widely among friends and advisors to devise the correct policy. The Confucian Classics credit the sage-kings of the golden past with culling advice from a wide spectrum of subjects, from humble woodcutters and fishermen as well as worthy ministers. The famous "Great Plan," for example, tells the ruler to confer with no fewer than four separate classes of advisors: the sacred beings (through turtle and milfoil divination), the chief ministers, the minor officials, and the common people.[13] After all, "He who likes to ask becomes enlarged. He who only uses himself grows small."[14] Confucius himself set an example of "inquiring about every matter."[15] Despite these models, the petty person is too arrogant or too impatient to consult others, even at a crucial turning point in affairs. Not surprisingly, his plans go wildly awry.

App. 3: Opportunities come and go,
The gap between them finer than a hair.
Fath. 3: Time goes and comes,
Meaning: He hastens, lest he fail.

Appraisal 3 marks the transition from thought to action. By definition, all transitions should be "timely"[16] insofar as time is envisioned as a series of distinct moments separated by imperceptible breaks. Past and future, after all, are divided by that single instant we call the present, whose duration is no greater than a hair is wide. The wise and cultivated person lays the groundwork for swift action that "seizes the moment" when he carefully analyzes the main categorical relations in the cosmos. As timely opportunity approaches, "he hastens, lest he fail," knowing that either premature or belated action may be fatal to the success of his plans.[17] This poem gives a new twist to the Han proverb: "Off by a hair's breadth,/ Missed by a thousand miles."[18]

App. 4: Though men do women's work,[19]
They cannot substitute[20] in suckling.
Fath. 4: That a man does women's work
Means: He negates his duty.

In early China, hierarchical relations were based chiefly on age, gender, and educational attainments, though wealth, of course, played its part. An outrageous example, that of men suckling children, is meant to prove the natural basis for the social law of strict separation in gender roles, and by extension, all aspects of the social hierarchy. Here, with "men doing women's work," humans consciously overturn the fundamental yin/yang values operating in the cosmos. In consequence, the society has no hope of attaining that ideal state where "each attains his or her proper role" by maximizing the individual's innate potential. The *Tso Commentary* laments any case where

> the woman has her husband's house, and the man, his wife's chamber. . . . Any deviation is sure to lead to ruin.[21]

App. 5: Serving as duty demands,[22]
      The king grants[23] him provisions.[24]
Fath. 5: Doing his duty
      Means: He fulfills the burdens of his office.[25]

Appraisal 5 refers to the ruler. It is the ruler's prerogative and duty to dispense rewards, punishments, and ritual foods to his subjects and allies in order to maximize good order in the state.[26] After the ruler tasted the sacrificial meats offered to the gods, it was customary to distribute portions to officials of proven merit. Every ritual act represents an exchange. Officials reconfirmed their allegiance to the ruling house in return for receiving the physical and spiritual benefits presumably derived from supping on the sacred offerings. The ruler, for his part, must take great care to ascertain the true mettle of his men, lest the gods be insulted and the state be ruined by unworthy officials.

App. 6: Though the burden is great, he shoulders it alone,
      Beset by[27] unresolved problems.[28]
Fath. 6: Grave responsibilities, acting alone
      Means: How can this be borne?

The good and wise leader never makes a major policy decision without consulting his subordinates. Since changes in policy affect so many others, those in power should not try to bear the responsibility alone. The more the participants in the decision-making process, the fewer the stupid decisions that will be made, for the good reason that "many heads are better than one." And if the best-laid plans still go awry, at least the positive sense of community engendered by the consultative process will offset some of the disintegrating effects of political failure.[29]

App. 7: The grown man supports the orphan child.
      The young boy lifts a jar.
Fath. 7: The grown man raising the orphan
      Means: The child knows what to do.[30]

The social structure in China is underpinned by reciprocal, yet hierarchical relations. The doctrine of filial piety stipulates that the child's obligations to its parents are nearly absolute; it is said that the child can never adequately repay his parents for the gift of life. Here an older member of the clan decides to rear an orphan. This implies that he will feed, protect, and educate the young boy. In such a case, the orphan's obligations exceed even the normal demands of filial piety. As if to acknowledge his debt, the young boy raises the jar, accepting his duty to feed his protector and act as willing servant. When each member of the family acknowledges his debts to the others, each responds by making his or her separate contribution to the unit. The ideal ruler/official relation is analogous. The ruler agrees to provide economic security, physical protection, and a suasive example for his subjects; in return, the subordinates offer loyalty and taxes. Reciprocity is the essential root of Chinese hierarchy.

The Ch'ing scholar Yü Yüeh believes that "orphan" is a misprint for "bow";[31] the elder lifts the bow as the younger raises the wine-jar. Again, the lesson would be that each age has its characteristic activities and appropriate responsibilities. The elder protects while the younger serves.

> App. 8: When women do men's work,[32]
>   After ten years, they're still unteachable.[33]
> Fath. 8: That a woman does a man's work
>   Means: Finally the family will not prosper.[34]

The poem reverses the situation presented in Appraisal 4, though the moral is much the same: men and women should not change roles, lest family harmony and prosperity be undermined. If a young woman were to take the position of family head, she would become unteachable in two senses: first, she would find herself ignoring the advice given by those who were considered to be her natural superiors (adult males in the family, including her husband and father-in-law, and women of the previous generation): second, her initiatives would represent a fundamental challenge to the most basic of what were held to be "natural" laws by the Chinese. Similarly, the appointed official should never presume to usurp his ruler's position.

> App. 9: It offends the ear but sets the toe on track.
>   The matter will go right.[35]
> Fath. 9: Offended ears, compliant toes
>   Mean: Contrary talk makes for obedient conduct.[36]

The poetry in Chinese is vivid in its sharp juxtaposition of three verbs of position. Here we see an individual who, after overhearing unpleasant truths about himself, finally corrects his behavior and follows in the footsteps of the sage-rulers. Displeasing talk ultimately brings marked advantages, as "Loyal words offend the ears but benefit conduct."[37] After all, strong medicine must be bitter if it is to effect the cure.

Keng
No. 28. Change
April 22 (p.m.)–April 26

Correlates with Earth's Mystery; Yin;[1] the phase Water; and the Yi ching *Hexagram no. 49, Molting [and so Renewal]; the sun enters the Mane constellation, 9th degree;[2] the Clear Brightness solar period*

HEAD: Yang *ch'i*, already flying up,[3] alters tendencies and shifts forms. Things change with regard to their spirit potencies.[4]

In Yang's schema, Tetragram 28 begins the second of three divisions of the *Mystery*, corresponding to the triadic realm of Earth. Earth is, of course, aligned with center both in the triad Heaven-Earth-Man and in the five directions and Phases. According to the *Changes*, "What establishes the Way of Earth is [the interaction between] weakness and firmness."[5] The *Yi ching* goes on to argue, "Only through change and transformation can all things come to perfection."[6]

Yang Hsiung's own autocommentaries give "making new" as the main theme of Change.[7] Perhaps Yang was thinking of the the Han Lustration festival, precursor of the familiar Ch'ing-ming festival, which celebrated this possibility of renewed life after the earth has escaped the ruinous clutches of winter.[8] The days lengthen, vegetation turns verdant green, and migrating birds return as harbingers of spring.

No doubt such welcome changes are supported by the growth of auspicious yang. The upward thrust of yang *ch'i* leads many things to rise above their old selves (literally and figuratively), yet the metamorphosis is accomplished naturally, without overt chaos, destruction, or coercion. Tradition says that this is the time when scorpions become dragonflies, field mice turn into quail, and crow's feet are changed into butterflies. In the world of Man, the upward flight occurs through self-cultivation. And just as flight depends upon the interaction of structural patterns (in the wing) and unseen currents (in the wind), the human potential for moral elevation relies upon the interaction of structural patterns in society and unseen tendencies in the spirit.

This tetragram shows life resurgent and moral life retrieved from evil habits. Though change of any kind calls for caution, change at this time opens the way for generally positive developments.[9]

> App. 1: Having evolved in darkness,
>   It is not right.
>   Impropriety seems like nature.[10]
> Fath. 1: Darkly changed, proprieties blocked,
>   Means: In youth,[11] he alters his course.

Deep at the core of his being,[12] the individual has neglected to develop the potential for goodness that is endowed with human nature. As he accustoms himself to evil, it becomes his second nature. Such a basic distortion of human nature can seem natural enough, especially when changes are carried out gradually over the years.[13] As one Han philosopher observed:

> Whatever is completed during one's youth seems like the human nature sent by Heaven. Whatever is customary comes to seem "natural."[14]

Still, the implications of such changes could not be more profound. Through his failure to develop his innate potential for Goodness, the petty person loses the only characteristic that truly distinguishes him from the beasts. It is especially important, then, to take care at the beginning and attend to the base.

> App. 2: The time is Seven, the time is Nine.
>   The carriage rolls on its way.[15]
> Fath. 2: Timely seven times, timely nine times
>   Means: Without fail, he faces change.

By convention, both 7 and 9 as odd numbers symbolize yang *ch'i*. In a nine-part cycle, they would correspond to maturity and decline. There may also be number magic at work here: Since $2 + 7 = 9$, Fire (Phase for Appraisal nos. 2 and 7) and Metal (Phase for no. 9) are in direct opposition, and so change occurs.[16] Still, the *Mystery* seldom discusses maturity, let alone irrevocable decline this early in its sequence of Appraisals. Probably 7 and 9 merely stand for repetitive change. Like the carriage wheel, life moves inexorably on in its journey. The moral person makes sufficient preparation to insure that the trip goes as smoothly as possible. He also adjusts his conduct continually along the road, the better to conform with everchanging cosmic, political, and personal cycles.[17] Then, whether faced with prosperity or material failure, he is able respond appropriately to circumstances, and better able to uphold the constant norms underlying phenomenal change. Since the sage is not fixated on a single mode of operation, he can experience endless transformations without damaging the self. In other words, the sage can also be "timely seven times, timely nine times."[18]

> App. 3: White things in mud
> Turn black.
> Fath. 3: Changing white in mud
> Means: Change does not enlighten.

A popular metaphor compares human nature at birth to undyed silk, which is then colored by training and experience.[19] Moral improvement should work to turn evil into good, black into white. Here, by contrast, material of pristine purity is steeped in filth. This suggests the effect on the soul of bad companions[20] or bad customs. That no good can come from this is clearly shown in a pun by which "black" also means "calamity."[21]

> App. 4: With each change, slight gain;
> In use, nothing but profit.
> Fath. 4: In change, slight gain
> Means: This is what the people look to.[22]

Appraisal 4 marks the Beginning of Good Fortune. Several types of good fortune may be predicted by these lines. In one reading, the incremental political and cultural changes instituted by the sage-ruler eventually lead to marked social improvements, though the reforms largely go unnoticed by the subject population.[23] (Certainly Yang Hsiung strongly opposed Legalist measures on grounds that they instituted massive changes of no real benefit to the common people.)[24] Or, perhaps the good ruler's lack of greed lets him rest content with slight personal gain so long as his policies benefit the common people.[25]

In another reading, the gradual accrual of seemingly inconsequential acts of courtesy and consideration develops the human character capable of forging strong community so that "not a use but profits."[26]

> App. 5: Oxen without horns or horses with them
> Exist neither in the past or present.
> Fath. 5: Hornless ox, horse with horns
> Means: A change in Heaven's constants.

A mature ox always has horns while a horse is always without them. So undisputably clear is this distinction that early Chinese Logicians used the figures of horse and ox as stock examples to demonstrate absolutely separate logical categories.[27] Here eternal constants are overturned, which can only have disastrous implications for human society. With the eternal verities ignored or disputed, society enters a state of chaos, in which few can hope to realize their full potential.[28]

> App. 6: In water, they ride on carts,
> Out of water, they go by boat.
> True kings rightly reverse them.[29]
> Fath. 6: Carts and boats, in and out,
> Means: His way is change.[30]

The *Changes* in its Great Commentary celebrates the sage king's invention of various tools, including carts and boats, in imitation of sacred images in Heaven-and-Earth. Thanks to such inventions, mankind has moved from primitive existence to advanced forms of social life. It would be foolish, even dangerous to ignore the inspired nature of the sages' inventions and try to reinvent the wheel. By the same token, thoughtless changes in customary laws and institutions prove worse than useless, even positively destructive.

> Nothing is as good as a boat for crossing water, nothing as good as a cart for crossing land. Though a boat will get you over water, if you try to push it across land, you may push till your dying day and hardly move it any distance at all. . . .[31]

Effort is wasted and culture disrupted. The sage-ruler acts to restore the perfect harmony between the human and nonhuman worlds.

> App. 7: Though change they should, they don't,[32]
> And thus create the ill.[33]
> Fath. 7: Change unchanged
> Means: They cannot improve themselves.[34]

Appraisal 7 corresponds to the Beginning of Calamity; presumably, some measure of adjustment is needed in these later phases of the cosmic cycle if the balance is to be maintained. In the political world, men should consider the warning of the Confucian master, Tung Chung-shu (?179–?104 B.C.): "To make government policy and then not carry it out is very serious."[35] As one passage in the famous *Chronicles of Mr. Lü* argues:

> As times change, it is fitting to change the laws. It is like the good doctor. As an illness goes through ten thousand changes, so his drugs must make ten thousand changes. . . . The one who makes changes in the law must make changes on the basis of contemporary conditions.[36]

Though the translation follows the reading favored by the commentators, given the linguistic compression of the first line (literally, "Change not change"), the Appraisal could also mean:

> To change what should not be changed.
> And so to create infirmity.
> To change what should not be changed
> Means: Unable to improve oneself.

In this second reading, the foolish ruler meddles with just policies or the foolish individual works to change those qualities (like loyalty and good faith) that are worth preserving.

> App. 8: When a team of four won't budge,[37]
> One can always change the driver.
> Fath. 8: That the team of four won't budge
> Means: Changing the driver will help.[38]

The driver is a stock metaphor for the ruler of the state.[39] When the current ruling house cannot ease societal friction and solve stubborn problems, Heaven's Mandate may soon be transferred to a new dynastic line. Note that the people (in the poem, the team of four) are not blamed for their disloyalty. It is the drivers who are blamed for misrule in the state. The ruler must take full responsibility for his subjects' welfare.[40]

> App. 9: If he does not persist in virtue,[41]
> In three years, he'll be replaced.
> Fath. 9: Flagging virtue replaced[42]
> Means: An inability to endure.

Chinese tradition recognizes the need for three years to effect a major change.[43] By the end of this trial period, we see the individual entering the climactic final stages of failure occasioned by his inability or disinclination to reform. If he persists in error, he will lose his authority, possibly even his life.

Correlates with Earth's Mystery; Yang; the phase Fire; and the Yi ching Hexagram no. 43, Breaking Through [and so, Resolution]; the sun enters the Net constellation, 3d degree

Tuan

No. 29. Decisiveness
April 27–May 1 (a.m.)

HEAD: Yang *ch'i* is strong within and firm without[1] so that in acting there can be a decisive breakthrough.

218

Tetragram 9 earlier in the year spoke of yang *ch'i* as "strong within but weak outside." Now that we are in the latter half of the spring season, the balance between yin and yang that obtained at the vernal equinox has given way to the clear supremacy of yang *ch'i*. With yang in full command of its powers, it also works to "strengthen what is within and firm the outside" of the myriad things, spurring on their development.[2] All this is inherently auspicious, especially because of the perfect correspondence between inner and outer. As the *Changes* tells us, inner integrity, strength, and steadfastness are preconditions for growth in the direction of brilliance.[3]

The Appraisals play upon the full range of meanings associated with the characters in the title of this tetragram and with the correspondent *Changes* hexagram no. 43. The title character for this tetragram means "to cut" and, by extension, "to decide" or "to act resolutely." The same graph can describe the "incisive mind." The graph used for the hexagram title has the root meaning of "to open a passage." From this it has the extended meanings of "to cut off or open," and "decisiveness." It also relates to calls to arms, weapons, captives of war, and cries of alarm, all of which are mentioned below.

> App. 1: His resolute heart destroys an ax,
>   Still he keeps his square and chalk-line hidden.
> Fath. 1: The decisive heart destroying the ax
>   Means: The self is ruled from within.[4]

Since this poem marks an auspicious Beginning of Thought, it indicates a heart that discerns right from wrong, though its standards remain hidden.[5] The will is properly set on the Good, as we see in the reference to a carpenter's chalk-line and square, which both symbolize the ability to apply principles of good order to the tasks at hand. Still, the *Mystery* does not entirely clarify the relation of heart to ax.[6] In this translation,[7] the *Mystery* claims that the cutting edge of the well-ordered mind is far more powerful and incisive than the blade of the ax. Certainly, the Chinese are fond of proverbs where an intangible activity easily vanquishes strong objects, for example, "The mouths of the masses [i.e., their wagging tongues] [are corrosive enough to] melt metal."[8] Still, the first line of Appraisal and Fathoming could also read, "The decisive heart, the destructive ax," implying a parallel between heart and ax. Do heart and ax act in concert or do they work in opposition? If the ax stands for interdiction or punishment, the ax may be the external counterpart to the internal conscience.[9] When the internalization of ritual guidelines is incomplete for any reason, a good penal code and the threat of punishment may motivate the heart to clarify right from wrong. Future punishments may then be avoided.[10] In other words, so long as the discerning mind polices its own activity, the body can avoid future harm.[11]

App. 2: When dark decisions breed adversity,[12]
    The fault lies in[13] stopping up the ears.
Fath. 2: Obscure decisions obstructing
    Means: The center heart[14] is uncertain.

Western philosophy often assumes that the senses undermine the mind's functioning.[15] Prior to the coming of Buddhism, early Chinese philosophy, by contrast, assumes that perceptual knowledge derived from the five senses is absolutely crucial to the correct operation of the heart/mind.[16] Here one of the five sensory receptors, the ear, has been blocked. In early Chinese tradition, the ear is particularly associated with moral development.[17] When insufficient or distorted information is received by the mind, its powers of discrimination are severely hampered. The mind is thrown into confusion so that its decisions are faulty or it lacks decisiveness. It would be highly dangerous to proceed.

On another level, good advisors act as "ears" to the ruler. The poem may describe, then, the failure of the ruler to follow the excellent advice of his counselors.[18]

App. 3: Clearing[19] his blocked-up ears and nose[20]
    Will help to cure the corruption.
Fath. 3: Clearing his obstructions
    Means: Whatever plans he has will benefit.[21]

Those "having plans" are worthy candidates for office who desire to have the ruler implement their ideas.[22] The ruler rids himself of bad advisors,[23] especially those who wish to block the career paths of better candidates. Or, he excises his own worst impulses, so that he is more receptive to good counsel.[24] Once inner and outer corruption have been cleared, all can benefit from the advice.

App. 4: If he wrongly decides about us,
    His undeserved wages bring shame.[25]
Fath. 4: Wrong decisions about us
    Means: Drawing his salary is shameful.

Appraisal 4 in Yang Hsiung's schema is reserved for the ranks of officials; here it also corresponds to inauspicious night. This official is incapable of devising correct policy.[26] Therefore, he should be ashamed to draw his salary; he should submit his resignation. As the Odes say, "Oh, that gentleman!/ He would not eat the bread of idleness."[27]

App. 5: Once the belly is resolved,
    The legs[28] are free to act.[29]
    With the noble man decisive,[30]
    The little guy survives.

Fath. 5: Set free through great gutsy resolve
Means: In decisiveness, order is attained.

Appraisal 5 corresponds to the ruler. Since the belly is both the center of the body and its storehouse of energy, it symbolizes the ruler. The thighs stand for his chief ministers, though we would talk of "right-hand men" instead.[31] The limbs depend upon the belly, just as the ministers depend upon the ruler for guidance; the belly functions as the seat of moral courage while the thighs act to carry out the "great resolve."[32] Since this Appraisal is auspicious, belly and thigh act in concert to insure the survival and security of the common man through just government policy.[33] No subject of the state need fear wrongful imprisonment. And since the ruler's own resolution influences his subordinates for the good, they themselves develop a strong moral sense.[34]

App. 6: Deciding not to decide
With your enemies nearby
Later attracts the battle ax.[35]
Fath. 6: Deciding not to decide
Means: Crime overtakes his person.

The large battle ax is reserved for the decapitation of criminals or enemies; it is never employed in peaceful activities, such as agriculture. The individual who fails to distinguish the right course of action in a timely fashion risks his rank, and possibly even his life, as his foes will quickly seize upon his hesitation. His own downfall then occurs with relative ease, either indirectly (because the continued presence of evildoers in society weakens its very fabric) or directly (because his enemies launch a campaign to wrest power from him).

App. 7: When *keng* cuts through *chia*,[36]
My heart is steady.[37]
Later the glory is ours.[38]
Fath. 7: *Keng* cutting through *chia*
Means: Duty cuts through human feeling.

In the complex system of Yin/yang Five Phases correlations that link the directions, the calendar, and the virtues, *keng* (allied with Metal, the west, social duty, and punishments) conquers *chia* (allied with Wood, the east, humaneness, and suasive example). Since Appraisal 7 represents the mature phase of the cycle (tied to yin *ch'i*, harvests, and punishments), *keng* is properly in ascendancy.

Humaneness describes acts that acknowledge what is due all men by virtue of their humanity. Social duty, by contrast, refers to the fulfillment of "graded" obligations determined by variations in social and kinship ranks, gender, and seniority.[39] The era has passed when compassion and empathy is appropriate; it has been succeeded by the use of somewhat sterner standards of justice. The *Mystery* probably alludes to a passage in the classic *Book of Documents*: "When sternness overcomes his love, then things are surely brought to a successful conclusion."[40]

> App. 8: He attacks valiant dwarfs,[41]
> But graciously pardons highwaymen.[42]
> Fath. 8: Decisions favoring highwaymen
> Means: He makes decisions recklessly.

The corrupt or incompetent official oppresses the "little man," who may run afoul of the law through ignorance,[43] while he lets the worst offenders go free. Though this official is admittedly decisive, his actions subvert the good society.

> App. 9: The finely honed[44] blade of the ax
> Is the sign of the carpenter.[45]
> Fath. 9: The ax so shiny bright
> Means: It is good for attacking chaos.

Appraisal 9 represents the End or Extreme of Calamity. Though society is already to some degree in chaos, control can still be reasserted, given the availability of proper tools. The blade symbolizes both the army and the penal code, since both entail the use of weapons.[46] That it is highly polished (or, possibly curved) is significant, since that allows it to sever cleanly without slipping.[47] Luckily, the ruler is heir to various good tools, including social institutions and Confucian tradition, which will help restore order among miscreants without unduly disrupting the lives of the innocent. However, it would have been better to have used such tools at an earlier stage to forestall evil.

Correlates with Earth's Mystery; Yin; the phase Wood; and the Yi ching Hexagram no. 43, Breaking Through [and so, Resolution]; the sun enters the Net constellation, 7th degree

Yi
No. 30. Bold Resolution
May 1 (p.m.)–May 5

HEAD: Yang *ch'i* just now[1] comes into its own.[2] Resolutely, it dares to act so that things develop[3] their goals.[4]

This tetragram is associated with east, with Wood, and with spring through its assigned constellation, patron Phase, and season of the year. The conjunction of Wood/east/spring proves so compelling that the last barriers to yang *ch'i*'s beneficial action are removed.[5] Yang *ch'i* now flourishes, with no real impediments to its catalyzing activities. Like Tao, it operates in such a way as to allow each of the myriad things to fulfill its potential on its own distinctive pattern.

The tetragram title, Bold Resolution, suggests gutsy courage that takes the initiative. This is a direct contrast to the usual characterization of Wood, which emphasizes slow growth and pliability. Why such a sudden burst of resolution at this juncture in the spring? Perhaps the *Changes* supplies the answer when it argues, "A breakthrough results from steady increase."[6] Prior to this, there has been a steady increase in the power of yang *ch'i*. Finally, it is time for yang and the myriad things under its protection to break through yin's obstacles in a display of courage. Wood, after all, is coupled with the virtue of steadfast resolution in early Chinese tradition.[7] Any breakthrough, however, depends upon two preconditions covered by the correspondent Hexagram 43: The first is the need for truthful communication between superior and inferior.[8] The second is the obligation of the leader to "dispense emoluments to inferiors and refrain from resting [only] on his charisma."[9] Both preconditions associate "resolution" with "filling up" [with information, with riches]; hence, the imagery employed in some of the Appraisals below. The attempts in Tetragram 30 to redefine the notion of courage are also noteworthy. One component of the graph for the tetragram title depicts an enraged wild boar, yet the *Mystery* despises brute, physical courage uninformed by moral courage. As Yang Hsiung's other neoclassic, the *Model Sayings*, emphasizes, the courage of sages like Mencius far surpasses that of mere men of arms.[10]

> App. 1: Harboring what is awesome,[11]
>   Emptiness fills him nonetheless.[12]
> Fath. 1: An all-consuming love of power
>   Means: The Way and its Power are lost.

The individual's preoccupation with external displays of force or grandeur leads him to neglect the cultivation of his inner life and virtue.[13] Self-importance fills the mind (conventionally termed the Void) with what is inherently empty. Since he fails to develop either his innate capacity for Goodness or his concern for the masses, he is a prime example of the wrong kind of resolution, just like the knight errants of old.[14] Any disparity between his public and private personae is inherently dangerous, both to him and to society.

App. 2: Resolute in mind and belly,
   He is the model of stability.[15]
Fath. 2: Resolute in mind and belly
   Means: He is strong and firm within.

If mind and body are equally resolved upon pursuit of the Good, its attainment is assured. As Confucius said, "If we really wanted Goodness, we would find that it was by our very side."[16]

App. 3: A crown of power fills his head.[17]
   The noble man thinks, "This is not enough."
   The petty man thinks, "More than enough."
Fath. 3: Flaunting power, a swollen head
   Means: Only a petty man finds this superior.

The truly moral person is not content with the external trappings of power. With his singular desire for moral community, he recognizes the magnitude of the task before him: he must wisely employ his authority to transform the daily habits of his subordinates.[18] In the words of Confucius, the good ruler is modest; he "inspires awe, but is not ferocious; and he is proud, without being insolent."[19] The petty man, in contrast, worships rank and title. In his arrogance,[20] he parades his symbols of authority, mistaking them for moral authority itself. Lacking inner resources, he relies upon harsh punishments since these appear more "impressive" than rule by benevolence.[21] All the while, unlike his moral betters, he is supremely confident that he is more than capable of governing well.[22] Self-delusion leads to the collapse of power.

App. 4: The noble man makes a tool of speech.[23]
   His words[24] are gentle yet resolute.
Fath. 4: The noble man's tool of speech
   Means: There is method in his words.

Appraisal 4 is aligned with Metal in Chinese tradition: In the cycle of Phases, Metal corresponds to the mouth and tongue in the body; hence, the reference to speech. The proper balance between gentility and courageous resolution is analogous to the balance implied here between Wood (patron phase for the tetragram) and Metal (patron phase for the Appraisal). Since Appraisal 4 also corresponds to officialdom, the poem probably describes the duties of the advisor: Specifically, both honest criticism and loyal obedience are to be offered to the leader.[25] Numerous Han texts instructed the official to suit his style of remonstrance to the situation at court;[26] the most effective reproofs, they argued, use "indirect speech," which warns the ruler while saving him from public humiliation. Yang Hsiung worried that indirect criticism was easily misunderstood; then it only encouraged the ruler in his follies.[27] The good advisor should be "conciliatory, but not accomodating."[28]

> App. 5: Not working the field, but eating the yield,
>   He boldly seeks a sinecure.[29]
> Fath. 5: Not tilling, but reaping
>   Means: The wage is not matched by worth.

Despite an obvious lack of cultivation (the pun is intentional), the subject of the poem assumes a high rank and salary. In this, he is like the farmer who expects to gather a bountiful harvest without planting his fields.[30] Only hard work can lead to just rewards. Especially in the service of the state, the good man is "Intent upon the task,/ Not bent upon the pay."[31] The *Odes* characterizes the lazy or incompetent man in power by the following critique:

> Since you neither sow nor till,
> How can you take the produce of 300 farms?[32]

> App. 6: Resolved to serve as ridgepole and pillar,
>   He helps secure his great master's place.[33]
> Fath. 6: Resolved to be pillar and pole
>   Means: His strength bears the burdens of state.[34]

Using a stock metaphor, the structural supports of the house are equated with the main supports of the ruling house. The ridgepole stands for the ruler; the pillars, for his high officials. Just as the stability of the house depends upon the strength and placement of its constituent materials, the security of the dynastic house relies upon the development of human resources coupled with the placement of good men in appropriate positions of trust.[35]

> App. 7: The big ram may be headstrong
>   But its bleat is less than bold.[36]
> Fath. 7: The stubborn resolve of a ram
>   Means: Its speech is no model.

Despite its size and strength, the ram is not regarded as an ideal role model. Like the billy goat of Western anecdote, it appears to be unduly stubborn and ill-tempered, even downright contentious.[37] It is undiscriminating in its eating habits.[38] And its shrill screech, which is unlikely to win any admirers, has no staying power or depth.[39] From this we learn that size and strength alone do not constitute true excellence;[40] one's manner is crucial. The model sages, it is said, "got things by being cordial, frank, courteous, temperate, and deferential."[41] The ancient sages provide the only adequate model for human behavior.[42]

App. 8: Bold in the face of calamity, so steady![43]
This is the base of a noble man's fame.
Fath. 8: Resolute and steady in facing calamity
Means: His virtue[44] cannot be concealed.

The superior man calmly faces adversity, "delighting in Heaven and recognizing his fate,"[45] for real integrity provides a strong sense of security.[46] Since he can maintain his equanimity, chances are good that he will eventually find a way to extricate himself from present calamity. But should misfortune continue, he can at least hope that human memory or the annals of history will take note of his exemplary moral courage.[47]

App. 9: The boar's resolve lies in its tusks,
Which entice[48] the archer's outstretched bow.
Fath. 9: The boar's brashness in its tusks
Means: That is what the petty officer[49] hunts.

Appraisal 7 presented a case of physical courage that was distinctly unappealing. By Appraisal 9, the situation is far worse: displays of bravado now wreak destruction. The boar's tusks are rustic symbols for bravery. Therefore, every local strongman is intent upon securing a set for himself, the better to advertise his own ferocity.[50] Angry farmers may also take up arms to stop the boar from destroying their crops or goring their animals. Ironically, the source of the boar's courage, the strong tusks that make the boar consider itself invincible, prove to be its downfall. By analogy, the petty individual relies on the appurtenances of power to make himself invulnerable to attack but his attitude only makes him more liable to assault. As he harms others, so he is harmed.[51]

Chuang
No. 31. Packing
May 6–May 10 (a.m.)

Correlates with Earth's Mystery;
Yang; the phase Metal; and the
Yi ching Hexagram no. 56,
Traveling; the sun enters the
Net[1] constellation, 11th degree[2]

HEAD: Yang *ch'i* is greatly engaged in affairs. Even so yin, which is very small,[3] makes its base below. It is packed in readiness, about to depart.[4]

The second appraisal of this tetragram marks the beginning of the Summer Onset solar period. Paradoxically, just as yang *ch'i* seems ready to take off, we learn of yin's first preparations to rise again. After the summer solstice, yang *ch'i*'s power, though seemingly invincible, will start to wane in the face of growing yin *ch'i*, for "whatever has exhausted its greatness must lose its home."[5] Like the sage, yang *ch'i* recognizes the coming trend, so it wisely begins preparations for its departure.[6] The tetragram Packing, therefore, celebrates providence and farsightedness, rather than travel per se. (Only in modern times, of course, are the delights of travel celebrated.) In general, the early Chinese regarded the sedentary life as the basis of their society. The *Changes*, for example, associates wandering with carelessness, lack of discernment, and neglect of the all-important social bonds.[7]

> App. 1: Packing in secret,
> None see him go.[8]
> Fath. 1: Packing in secret, so that no one sees
> Means: The mind is already directed outward.

Appraisal 1 describes the Beginning of Thought. Thought, in contrast to action, is typically hidden from sight. The noble person begins preparations to go out into the world. In his heart, he is set upon going.[9] Also, he knows where to go, since he anticipates future trends. At this early stage, others largely ignore him,[10] in part because he is williing to "hide himself" until he is fully ready to act.[11] (This is an apt portrayal of yang *ch'i* at this time.)

> App. 2: Honking geese[12] mourn the coming ice.
> Setting wings to that southward wind[13]
> They yearn for their mates in their hearts.[14]
> Fath. 2: Grief of the wild geese
> Means: No joy for hearts filled with sorrow.[15]

As water birds, wild geese cannot survive in bitterly cold regions.[16] Therefore, at the first hint of winter, they fly south to warmer climes in search of food. Geese and ducks are said to be monogamous creatures, for when a goose has lost its mate, it is reluctant to abandon it, even when it must do so in order to survive. The goose confronts the most difficult of human dilemmas: to give up one's desire or to give up life itself.

At first reading, the scene appears to symbolize the faithfulness of devoted marriage partners cruelly separated by adversity or death. A classical treatise on mourning rites cites the reluctance of certain birds and beasts to leave their mates in death as proof of the natural and inevitable character of family feelings.[17] But here the goose may have gone too far, for emotional attachment clouds its judgment.[18] The wise person knows when to leave and harbors no regrets.[19] The *Changes* warns the petty person: "In waiting to escape, there is affliction. Danger."[20]

> App. 3: Moving on toward[21] his goal,
>   Happiness may well ensue.[22]
> Fath. 3: Moving on toward his goal
>   Means: He meets what he rejoices in.[23]

Despite our empathy for the wild goose in the preceding Appraisal, a less emotional person would realize that the goose should never be deterred from its proper course. So long as the will is fixed on proper goals, it will make progress. Happiness, not sorrow, will follow.

> App. 4: *K'un* birds fly out at dawn,[24]
>   Flocking together up north.
>   "Ying-ying," they call back and forth,
>   And never stop singing to feed.[25]
> Fath. 4: The dawn flight of the *k'un*
>   Means: How can they live on so little?[26]

The *k'un* is a mythical bird akin to the roc or phoenix of Western tradition. (Like the phoenix, it is associated with the sun,[27] although some tales identify it as the pet of the immortal Queen Mother of the West.) According to Chinese myth, the *k'un* is distinguished by its enormous size and flying speed. Here a flock of *k'un* birds flies north, though the *k'un*'s natural habitat is the south.[28] Although they sing in harmony,[29] they ignore their own basic natures and needs; for this reason, they fail to feed themselves. Their initial difficulty, caused by lack of direction, is made worse once they are content to remain in an untenable position. Their profound willfulness is clear; perhaps they are also too lazy to change direction. It is even sadder that they encourage each other in fruitless pursuits.[30]

Given the pun on "dawn" and "court," it is tempting to read in the poem a warning against great official(s) (usually assigned to Appraisal 4) "who fly high at court," and then go on to build factions in the north. Having lost their sense of direction, they now are only dedicated to amassing greater wealth through higher salaries: "They never stop feeding" (an alternate reading for the last line) on the state's resources. Such officials are unreliable supports for the king.[31]

> App. 5: The wild swan packs for the Tz'u[32]
>   Where food and drink are plentiful.[33]
> Fath. 5: The swan packing for the River Tz'u
>   Means: It fully intends to attain its goal.

The wild swan, the third water bird in this series of Appraisals, is provident, unlike the previously mentioned goose and *k'un*. At this propitious time, the swan makes plans to go to the Tz'u River (in present-day

Shantung Province), a body of fresh water too large to freeze; food and drink will be available throughout the winter. So it will "eat and drink in concord," becoming a symbol of "good fortune."[34]

The same graph used for "wild swan" means "great" as well. Obviously, these lines apply to the morally "great," who are farsighted enough to anticipate future needs.[35]

> App. 6: Through six junctions and round nine roads,
>   No limits on their course, they ply their trade.
> Fath. 6: Through six junctions
>   Means: Itinerant merchants conduct their business.

Americans often label untrammeled freedom and reckless individuality as romantic and desirable; the Frontier Myth is still powerful for us. Early Chinese tradition would not have understood this facile equation of physical mobility with happiness and self-fulfillment; even the "free and easy wandering" advocated by Chuang tzu referred to travel by the mind, not the body.[36] The Confucians in particular felt that human development itself depended on siting the developing individual firmly within a nested series of social relations that would teach him basic moral lessons. True self-cultivation means learning to realize the full moral potential inherent in each of the many societal roles played by one person during the course of a life. "How truly limiting is the prospect of being able to go absolutely anywhere," one commentator perceptively remarks.[37] The very rootlessness of the merchant precludes his learning to become truly moral. Should he feel the desire to do good, he is unlikely to be in one place long enough to sustain that desire through practice. Should he do wrong in his desire for profit,[38] his wanderings will make it that much harder to apprehend and punish him, even when the corrective would be salutary. In the worst case scenario, the merchant roams highways and byways, his restlessness and lack of restraint matched only by his unbounded desire for profit. To the Confucians, whose ethical standards reflect a society economically based in sedentary agriculture, the merchant's only "good" is to exploit others.

> App. 7: Packing without a partner:
>   Better to attack the wicked unencumbered.[39]
> Fath. 7: Packing without a partner
>   Means: Calamity is imminent.

The meaning of this poem is far from obvious. (The commentators are little help.)[40] Chinese tradition assumes that morality is charismatic. A lack of likeminded companions ("no partner") usually suggests evildoing.[41] Since by Yang Hsiung's schema an odd-numbered Appraisal in an odd-numbered Tetragram should be auspicious, my translation tries to wrest a somewhat happier meaning from the text. The tentative translation therefore adds the word "unencumbered." Previous Appraisals have criticized the misguided impulse to flock together. Here the truly good person will brave it alone if it is necessary to save the situation.

> App. 8: The young,[42] strewn like grain 'cross rutted paths,[43]
> Weep at sacrifices offered to the Road.[44]
> With these they send them on their way.
> Fath. 8: The young scattered on the road
> Means: They dispatch them to their deaths.

Yang Hsiung's language is somewhat unclear at points, but the general idea is clear enough: Here packing is associated with the tearful preparations for war. The youngest and middle children from many families gather at the crossroads, to witness the sacrifice to the Road. As their elder brothers (and possibly their fathers) go off, all realize that they may never return. This Appraisal prefigures Tetragram 32, whose main theme is war.

> App. 9: He packs at dusk.
> Fath. 9: Packing at dusk
> Means: He can still escape the worst.[45]

Appraisal 9, of course, corresponds to Extreme Calamity. Still, at dusk there is just enough light by which to execute a last-minute change in plans. It is preferable, of course, to set out on a journey at dawn so as to make as much progress as possible. Though there is little to be gained by a late start (especially in moral development), at least this individual escapes to relative safety.

Chung
No. 32. Legion
May 10 (p.m.)–May 14

*Correlates with Earth's Mystery;
Yin; the phase Earth; and the Yi
ching Hexagram no. 7, Troops;
the sun enters the Triaster
constellation[1]*

HEAD: Yang *ch'i* expands to[2] the heights, embracing all equally[3] so that the myriad things everywhere grow bright.[4] Beautiful[5] and large they grow, multiplying into legions.

Like its *Changes* counterpart, this tetragram plays off two separate meanings of "legion": "the multitudes" [i.e., the masses] and "the military unit." The Head text focuses on yang *ch'i*'s role in fostering the growth of many things and an increase in their numbers.[6] The Appraisals consider the masses' role in warfare: small farmers are conscripted into infantry divisions, only to die in bloody pitched battles. After the unification of the Chinese empire in 221 B.C., civil virtues slowly came to be favored over the martial. As a later proverb goes, "No good iron should be used to make a weapon; no good man should be used to make a soldier." This process was not much advanced in Western Han, however, as successful military campaigns expanded the influence of the Chinese empire deep into Central Asia. The *Mystery*, following ancient precedent, can envision the just war, but more often than not it deplores the devastation visited upon the common people.

> App. 1: Secretly the war begins.
> > Like fire the news spreads.[7]
> > Farming stops. Grain goes to war-horses.[8]
> > Soon[9] corpses will litter[10] the fields.
> Fath. 1: The beginning of the dark war
> > Means: Once begun, it only gets worse.

Few are able to identify the factors that will lead to war; initial preparations for war are state secrets. But once war flares up, the effect is all too clear: The alarm is sounded. The news spreads like wildfire.[11] Farmers abandon their fields. The able-bodied are conscripted into the army. Those left behind may have to flee their homes in the face of advancing enemy troops. Surplus grain is fed to the war horses, rather than to humans, so food supplies dwindle dangerously. In short, death reigns where life should be; corpses litter the rice fields. No end can justify disruption of the natural order of things. The *Lao tzu* presents the contrasting case "when the Way prevails in the empire": "Fleet-footed horses are relegated to ploughing the fields."[12]

Certain Han thinkers vehemently opposed mutilating punishments and wars under any circumstances, arguing that the perfectly good ruler can induce order without ever resorting to tools of destruction.[13] Yang's view is not so extreme. Like Mencius, he principally objects to war because it destroys the common people's emotional and financial security, which are the surest foundations for their moral action.

> App. 2: Weapons have no blades.[14]
> > No armies are deployed.
> > Even the gentle unicorn[15] submits
> > To serve[16] the gentle ruler.[17]

Fath. 2: That no blades clash
  Means: Virtue conquers every quarter.

"Arms are instruments of ill omen, not the instruments of the gentleman. . . . One who exults in the killing of men will never have his way in the empire."[18] The conquest of men's hearts by virtue is far superior to the conquest of their bodies by war. This is proven by the marvelous unicorn. Its sharp horn makes it capable of fighting, yet according to myth, it refuses to attack other animals.[19] The appearance of the unicorn heralds the rise of a true king who prefers rule by charismatic virtue to war, despite his reserve of power and authority. As the *Lao tzu* says, "One who excels in defeating his enemies does not join issue."[20]

App. 3: As conscripts load the carts
  A soldier[21] pushes wife and child[22] away.
  While rifts inside grow wider.[23]
Fath. 3: That some in the army load carts
  Means: Councils of war draw harm within.[24]

Carts are being loaded, but we do not know their contents. Are they filled with grain in preparation for war? With corpses? Or with captured prisoners?[25] Since Appraisal 3 marks the transition from thought to action, most likely battle plans have been drawn up, but no engagement has yet been fought. Why does the paterfamilias push his wife and child away? Perhaps through him we glimpse the state's misguided eagerness for war. Perhaps we are led to consider the way in which the ruler ("father and mother" to his people) can bring harm to his "children" (i.e., his subjects) by war.[26] Perhaps the action mirrors the rifts inside the war room between contending strategists. A bellicose ruler and discord among the generals is enough to spell defeat for the entire state. Hierarchical relations are subverted. Chaos threatens. The portents of disaster are clear.[27]

App. 4: The tiger's roar rouses them to battle.[28]
  The leopard rears,[29] its selfish fears
  Suppressed.[30]
Fath. 4: The awesome roar of the tiger
  Means: Swift and sure as a hawk in flight.[31]

The *Mystery* celebrates the martial virtue[32] of good leaders. That much is clear. But any analysis of the poem hinges on whether tiger and leopard are seen as enemies or allies. In my translation, the tiger's roar not only strikes terror into the hearts of its enemies; it also serves to alert its allies to join the fray. The leopard responds by leaping up to volunteer, now that it has overcome its own selfish desires. True martial spirit requires self-restraint and self-sacrifice on others' behalf.[33] Those who take up arms in this spirit find that nothing can withstand their sure and swift advance.

However, two later commentators, reading variant characters, view the leopard as symbol of the petty person; by definition, then, the leopard becomes the tiger's enemy or its inferior.[34] In their readings, the leopard aggressively "raises the shaft" of its lance in a display of mere bravado.[35] It wrongly trusts brute strength alone to enforce its will.

> App. 5: Pitched battles[36] to the din of bell and drum:[37]
> Like bears, like demons they clash.
> Fath. 5: Locked in combat, clash! clash!
> Means: He is king by brute force alone.

The bad ruler relies upon physical strength alone to enforce his will. Forsaking virtue, he and his men are no better than animals.[38]

> App. 6: The army of the great king
> Thunders in their ears.
> Its only use is to subdue men's hearts.[39]
> Fath. 6: Armies like thunderbolts
> Mean: Almighty is their awesome strike.

Ancient metaphor compares the awesome quality of the king's presence to thunder.[40] The true king employs his crack troops in order to make men submit to the Good, not to wreak destruction. Sure in his purpose, he moves swiftly, stunning his enemies, who can only cower in anticipation of the impending crash.[41] With such moral force at his command, the ruler seldom needs to resort to arms to enforce his will; his mighty presence alone acts as a deterrent to evil.

> App. 7: A confusion of pennants and flags,[42]
> Shields and lances in disarray.[43]
> Army wives with child[44] bemoan their loss.[45]
> Wailing, they cast scathing glances
> At the king.[46]
> Fath. 7: A confusion of pennants and flags
> Means: He incites a great resentment in the people.[47]

The army has suffered a devastating defeat. The dead must now be gathered for burial. The blame for all this rightly rests with the ruler, who ordered his people into war. So resentful are the ruler's subjects that rebellion is likely to follow. He who resorts to war may find himself destroyed by it.

App. 8: The king's armies grow weaker.[48]
   Once he sees their ravaged state
   No more tumbrels[49] will be seen.
Fath. 8: The decimated ranks of his army
   Mean: No longer will they bloody their blades.

"Carriages full of corpses" are a sure sign of lack of merit, according to the *Changes.*[50] The wise ruler recognizes when his army is too ill, too poorly provisioned, or too dispirited to continue the fight. Recalling his troops from the field, the good ruler turns his attention to domestic reforms that will ensure the safety and security of his people. The truly great ruler goes one step further: never again does he resort to warfare.[51]

App. 9: The battle-ax blade is broken,[52]
   Its handle is cracked.
   It is right to stop, wrong to attack.[53]
   The advance will be bloody.
Fath. 9: Blade broken and handle cracked
   Means: There is not enough to go on.[54]

The man who presses forward despite inadequate tools (where tools may also suggest prior training) will meet with calamity. Reckless courage, after all, is of little use in any great endeavor.[55] Appraisal 9 represents the Extreme of Calamity. Here we witness the folly of continued aggression.

Correlates with Earth's Mystery;
Yang; the phase Water; and the Yi
ching Hexagram no. 8, Holding
Together; the sun enters the
Triaster constellation, 3d degree

Mi
No. 33. Closeness
May 15–May 19 (a.m.)

HEAD: Yang *ch'i* draws near[1] to Heaven. The myriad things, budding and flowering,[2] are all closely packed together, with no intervening gaps.

The previous tetragram describes yang *ch'i* merely "expanding to the heights."[3] Now culminating yang begins to "draw near to Heaven," which emphasizes its increased power and fundamental kinship with Heaven. As "the two become one,"[4] the bond between yang *ch'i* and Heaven be-

Figure 10. "Peeking through the gap." Illustration from a rubbing on a tomb relief, excavated from Lu-shan, Szechwan (48 × 65 cm.). Apparently a winged divinity is holding the incription here.

comes a fit symbol for suitably intimate relations of all kinds,[5] especially the primary bonds within the family and between ruler and official. The myriad things for their part unconsciously imitate these tight psychic bonds by physical proximity. As they grow larger and more numerous, they crowd against one another until no space is left between.

Tetragram 33 variously applies the idea of "no gap" to cosmogonic stages (where it describes the undifferentiated chaos of primordial *ch'i*); to spatial relations; to unbroken feelings of good fellowship; to political alliances and kinship ties; and to a perfect "fit" between perceptual knowledge and external reality, between human potential and its actuality. "No gap" may also refer to absolute correspondence between ascribed social roles and individual acts, another "fit" usually identified by the catchword "rectification of names" (*cheng ming*). In all these cases, wherever no gap prevails, the individual, society, and cosmos operate in perfect harmony.[6]

The graph used for the tetragram title conveys "closeness," "fineness" [of weave, for example], and "density." In certain cases, the same graph also means "close-mouthed" or "discreet."[7] The Chinese presume a connection between the two sets of meanings. A prudent disinclination to talk promotes perfect "closeness" in the community.

App. 1: He seeks a glimpse of the Great Unknown,
     But there is no gap in the Gate.
Fath. 1: Peering into it, that there is no gap
     Means: It is shut up tight on every side.[8]

The "Gate" probably refers to the border between potential and actual existence, between life and death, between tangible experience and the ineffable.[9] Behind our everyday world lies the inchoate source we call the Tao, from which all patterned and particulate matter eventually emerges. And since Appraisal 1 represents the Beginning of Thought, we imagine a similar barrier behind which hide thoughts which are as yet unformulated or unrevealed.[10] The Tao prefers to hide its origins. Similarly, the gentleperson dislikes advertising his thoughts,[11] in part because "things nearly complete, if not handled with absolute discretion, as a rule will be harmed in their completion."[12] No one has the power to peer either into prior existence or into another's innermost mind, despite a strong desire to do so. Still, the very metaphor of the gate holds out the hope that eventually we can pass beyond the barrier to enter the Great Unknown[13]—perhaps at death or by a flash of sudden illumination. Until then, we know at least that the ineffable Tao informs and animates our present life, while the unseen mind rules our conduct.

App. 2: If he fails to draw us close,
     Our[14] hearts stray far from home.[15]
Fath. 2: Not close, not friendly,
     Means: He turns away from his proper place.[16]

The original poem is careful not to specify who is to be blamed for the psychic distance that prevails, though many commentators see these lines as a warning to the ruler who fails to act as "father and mother" to his subjects.[17] The poem also works as a critique of the individual whose restless ambition or search for novelty cause him to neglect the proper cultivation of what is near to hand (for example, loyal officials or even his own conscience).[18] Eventually, this kind of petty person finds himself exposed.[19]

App. 3: Being close to our parents
     Helps us gain true humanity.
Fath. 3: Being close to kin
     Means: We act to promote the good.

According to the ancient Confucians, the development of humane impulses depends upon the quality of the home environment. To them, it is natural for the child to love the parents, and only by appropriately extending this affection to others can the individual learn to take part in society in a truly human way.[20] Given the all-important nature of the parent-child bond, the *Classic of Filial Piety* insists, "Not to love one's kin . . . is a perversion of virtue."[21] Should the family for any reason fail to instill habits of filial piety and devotion in the child, the growing child will find it very difficult to commit to close relations with others. What is more, it is only the unusually gifted child who will look beyond the family circle to learn that fine balance between openheartedness and discrimination the Chinese identified with the moral life.[22]

> App. 4: Three days close to putrid flesh,
>   And he fails to notice the stench.[23]
> Fath. 4: Being close to stink and rot
>   Means: Minor evils are pervasive.[24]

Ordinarily, the rank smell of rotting flesh turns the stomach, but human beings seem to have a remarkable capacity, given enough time, to accustom themselves to anything. Therefore, the person who consorts with evil companions soon "fails to notice the stench." The *Mystery* alludes to an anecdote in which Confucius compares "living with a bad man" to "being with a rotten carp."[25] These lines implicitly criticize Taoist doctrine, which assumes that man's ability to adapt to uncomfortable and unpleasant situations is one proof of the natural equality of all experiences.

> App. 5: Intimacy unimpaired,
>   You are Heaven's chosen consort.
> Fath. 5: A tight fit and no rift.
>   Means: Merit lies in being close to Heaven.

In early Chou, the good ruler was commonly identified as Heaven's consort, mate, or analogue; in other words, the match between Heaven and ruler was thought to be so close that the only suitable metaphor was sexual. Here the ideal leader perfectly conforms to Heaven's designs, thereby completing its work on earth.[26] Those of merit find their virtue recognized by the state and rewarded with high position.[27] As greater numbers are influenced by these models of perfection, harmony comes to prevail in the entire community.[28]

> App. 6: Associating with great evil,
>   His miseries may increase.
> Fath. 6: Being close to great evil
>   Means: Joining the errant, he becomes the same.

Past the halfway mark in the cycle, Appraisal 6 tends towards decline unless it is assigned to auspicious yang *ch'i*. The minor evils associated with bad companions in Appraisal 4 have now become great evils since the allies of the wicked quickly are schooled in evil.[29] Soon the associates are unable to distinguish between aberrant and correct behavior.[30]

> App. 7: In the net's fine mesh is a tear
> As small as the gill of a fish.[31]
> Great is the ruler who prevents its recurrence.[32]
> Fath. 7: A fine opening, small as a gill,
> Means: We rely on the ruler for repairs.[33]

If the smallest rift occurs between various groups in society, the great ruler first repairs it, and then hastens to prevent its recurrence.[34]

> App. 8: Having filed his teeth, he is left with gums.[35]
> In three years, he will no longer rule.[36]
> Fath. 8: Teeth filed, depending on gums
> Means: The ruler uproots himself.

The teeth rely on their base in the gums, just as hard yang *ch'i* rests on softer yin.[37] But if the teeth are ground down to the level of the gums (presumably because of overaggression or self-destructive impulses), they become dysfunctional. The adult loses all the advantages of maturity, reverting to the helpless state of a mewling infant. How will he ever manage to keep his strength on a diet of gruel? His large frame inevitably weakens, until the gums and even vital organs are debilitated.[38]

By analogy, the individual who wears down his staunch supporters, or a state that weakens its own allies, loses the last line of defense.[39] By extension, the state that places a child on the throne is also in grave danger.[40]

> App. 9: In the face of repeated disasters,[41]
> He first bows low, then honorably dies.
> Fath. 9: Faced with calamity upon calamity
> Means: Finally, he cannot be deprived of honor.[42]

Appraisal 9 is open to many different readings. It should describe the ultimate state of Closeness. Despite its talk of death, it is aligned with auspicious yang *ch'i*. In my reading, the individual in the face of serial calamities bows to his fate, but remains steadfast in his devotion to the Way.

Reading the same passage in a slightly different way ("close in repeated disasters"),[43] one commentator remarks that true gentlemen remain close allies even in hard times. This is for two reasons, he says: first, each is willing to humble himself before others; and second, each is equally committed to the Way.

It could also be the case that the subject of the poem is demoted from office and executed, despite his loyalty and innocence. Though his life can be taken away by an unjust authority, his honor is not so easily snatched away.[44] Still another reading would have the individual recognizing his own moral failings (the inner disasters that have led to visible disasters) shortly before death. Wiser now, the individual humbles himself and reforms his conduct so that he wrests from life an honorable end.[45] Finally, one commentator reads the poem as a description of the ruler who willingly condescends to his subordinates, thereby winning their absolute loyalty.

> In the face of repeated disasters.
> First, he humbles himself, then later gets
> Men willing to die for him.
>
> Faced with frequent disaster
> Means: Til the end, he cannot be deprived of support.[46]

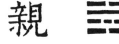

Ch'in
No. 34. Kinship
May 19 (p.m.)–May 23

Correlates with Earth's Mystery; Yin; the phase Fire; and the Yi ching Hexagram no. 8, Holding Together; the sun enters the Triaster constellation, 7th degree;[1] the Dipper points SSE; the musical note is F[2]

HEAD: Yang in every direction is humane and loving. It is completely true, generous,[3] and trustworthy so that things all feel a kinship and are at peace.

By the end of this tetragram, summer is in full force. As yang *ch'i* grows stronger and the days noticeably lengthen, the myriad things bask in its warmth. Since there is more than enough yang *ch'i* to foster growth for all, there is no need for contention among living things. Things consequently are drawn to yang and to each other; in their harmonious union, they come to imitate the perfection of yang *ch'i*.[4]

This tetragram, like its predecessor, is paired with Hexagram 8, called Holding Together. The Appraisals suggest that the habit of according one's own kin proper treatment is the first, crucial step towards forming close bonds with all others (whether in friendships, in political alliances, or in wider family circles). On the other hand, as the *Odes* say, "If you keep your own at a distance,/ The people all act thus [to you]!"[5] The second step is to follow Heaven's example in "treating the virtuous as kin."[6]

> App. 1: If kin are not close,[7] their wills
>   Grate like teeth in an uneven bite.
> Fath. 1: That kin are not as close as skin
>   Means: The center heart is closed off.

Unlike the Christian tradition, Confucian tradition does not expect the individual to love each and every other person as himself. Instead, Confucianism asserts that each person owes the greatest loyalty and devotion to family members (and by analogy, to the ruler who truly acts as "father and mother" of the people). These feelings of responsibility are then to be extended, but in ever decreasing measure, to wider circles outside the family into the village and kingdom. This poem is perfectly ambiguous in that it gives two different, if related messages: (1) Unless the habit of respect and love is engendered in the family, the capacities of the innermost heart/mind probably will fail to develop sufficiently, and (2) "If those treated as kin are not of his skin [i.e., his family], / Their ideas grate like teeth in a bad bite" (an alternate reading for the Appraisal).[8] Surrogate family relations, then, can never be an adequate substitute for real kinship ties. Differing temperaments and interests inevitably lead to wrangling,[9] weakening the bonds between unrelated parties.[10]

> App. 2: Trusting ties of flesh and blood,[11]
>   To meet their goals they rely on[12] kin.
> Fath. 2: Trusting flesh and blood
>   Means: No one can come between them.[13]

This Appraisal elaborates the moral of Appraisal 1. The wise person realizes that a tight family unit provides the single best base of support from which an individual can develop. Having learned certain fundamental lessons within the family context (including a good sense of priorities), the individual can then go on to make a mark upon society at large.

> App. 3: The mulberry fly abandons its young.[14]
>   The wasp that takes them on
>   Does not meet with disgrace.[15]
> Fath. 3: That the fly ignores its relations
>   Means: It fails its own body.

The *Mystery* alludes to Ode 196, which says:

> The mulberry insect has young.
> The sphex wasp rears them.
> Teach and train your sons
> So they will try to be good like it.[16]

The mulberry fly fails to protect its own larvae adequately; instead of housing them in a safe place, the mulberry fly shows no particular familial affection towards its young, leaving them to be preyed upon by its enemies. According to legend, the sphex does not devour the mulberry fly larvae. Rather, acting as surrogate parent, it introduces the mulberry larvae into its own nest, where over time they metamorphose into young wasps. The mulberry fly shows unusual lack of foresight, since its careless behavior deprives it of descendants to carry on the family line.[17] The Ode, then, seems to chastise parents whose lack of care may end in their young identifying more with the interests of others. The havoc this could wreak in the family should be an important consideration to any right-thinking individual. In other writings, Yang Hsiung employs the same metaphor to prove the relative importance of nurture over nature in the socialization process.[18]

> App. 4: Guests feel like kin in sharing the rites
> When food and drink are properly measured.[19]
> Fath. 4: That in rites guests feel like kin
> Means: Host and guest come together.

The moral superior uses ritual activity to forge good relations with others. Feelings of good fellowship engendered by the feast promote lasting social ties. Food and drink, then, become the tools, not the goals of ceremony, which is carefully designed to induce conduct that exemplifies the Mean. As host and guest come together in mutual esteem, those who participate in the feast are "fed virtue" as well as ordinary food.[20] This will induce the gods to participate.[21]

> App. 5: Slighting those who deserve his care,
> His closest friends shall run away.
> Fath. 5: Slighting those who deserve his care
> Means: On every side,[22] he alienates good men.

Relatives "should not treat each other coldly," the Classics say.[23] If a man cannot bring himself to bestow affection and gratitude where it is due, why shouldn't his allies and subordinates desert him, reasoning that "he who slights those he ought to treat well will slight all others, whoever they may be."[24] In contrast, the moral superior graciously condescends even to those with the most distant claims to consideration.[25]

App. 6: Caring for those who deserve it,
     The noble man grasps the Dipper.
Fath. 6: Generous to those who deserve it
     Means: He attracts good men from every side.

The leader may be said to grasp the Dipper in two senses: First, he ladles out food and wine to honor his guests at ritual feasts. Second, by virtue of his suasive example he like the Dipper (the constellation that is symbol of kingly rule) in the sense that "all the lesser lights will revolve" around him happily.[26]

App. 7: However high and lofty his rank,
     He is base in conducting affairs.
Fath. 7: Rank high but conduct base
     Means: His character is inadequate.

Appraisal 7 corresponds to the Beginning of Calamity. Well past the midpoint of the cycle, decline begins to set in. The immoral public servant no longer fulfills his duties well. The gross disparity between rank and character makes this leader's position all the more precarious. Should trouble arise, he will not be able to save himself.

App. 8: Dried meat shared with close kin:[27]
     Flawlessly, the noble man performs his duty
     To act as trunk of the family tree.[28]
Fath. 8: Doing his duty by kin
     Means: He claims no credit for himself.[29]

Family obligation is the "trunk of goodness,"[30] and the family head is "trunk" of the family tree. The ideal family head is careful to fulfill his obligations towards inferiors, dependents, and kinsmen. On appropriate occasions, he sends gifts of dried meat to nourish individual family members[31] and strengthen the bonds between them. As Confucius notes, "When gentlemen are punctilious in regard to their own kin, the people are encouraged to be humane."[32] On the other hand, to neglect such proprieties would be to risk internal dissension within the clan. As the *Odes* warn, "Loss of kindly feeling may arise from faults in [dispensing] dried meat."[33]

App. 9: Immature yet close: ill-omened.
Fath. 9: A childish intimacy untested[34]
     Means: It turns on its very own roots.[35]

If immaturity is allowed to persist so late in the cycle, the relations built upon it are fundamentally flawed. "Immature, benighted people never love the Right," as one commentator remarks.[36] For that reason, such intimacy cannot stand the test of time.

Lien

No. 35. Gathering
May 24–May 28 (a.m.)

Correlates with Earth's Mystery;
Yang; *the phase Wood; and the* Yi
Hexagram no. 9, Small Levies;[1]
the sun enters the Well constel-
lation, 3 degree

HEAD: Yang *ch'i* swells[2] hugely, filling out to the very outer edges. Minute yin[3] on a small scale gathers its forces on the inside.[4]

At this point in high summer, the position of yang *ch'i* seems unassailable, yet nascent yin has already begun to gather its forces below. Thus does the cosmic cycle alternate between full and empty. With yang *ch'i* swelling out to the edges, yin takes advantage of the hollow space left behind at center to build a base of strength. The myriad things mirror this activity, since much "growth on the outside necessarily leads to hollowness within."[5] Given the danger implied by this imbalance between inner and outer, the moral person is especially careful in how she proceeds. As yin begins to gather force, she finds it most effective to take precautions "at the beginning," before trouble of any kind looms large.

The tetragram's title suggests a gradual increase in the accumulation of yin *ch'i* in the cosmic cycle. It also implies that yin will bide its time, "gathering its forces" until it is powerful enough to launch a full-scale attack on yang. The same graph means "savings" or "stores" (as in money or harvests) and "government levies" or "taxes"—still another kind of transfer from a greater "outside" to a smaller reserve "inside." The outer/inner and big/little parallel dichotomies lie at the heart of the *Mystery's* portrayal of benevolent government. According to hallowed Confucian tradition, taxes should not exceed a tithe on the value of the harvest.[6] Early Chinese rulers were also told not to overtax their subjects by repeated wars and extraordinary levies or by exacting corvée labor for massive construction projects. Once it has lost the support of the commoners, a bloated empire will find itself, like yang *ch'i* at this juncture, hollow at the core. In any case, the best method by which the ruler can come to command vast reserves of wealth and power is not through taxes, but through keeping the people's absolute loyalty. In effect, the ruler stores his possessions in the granaries and barns of his subjects.[7]

>   App. 1: Small taxes kept the same,[8]
>   Help the common people feel secure
>   And rectify the state.
>   Fath. 1: Small taxes kept the same
>   Means: His way is fitting.

According to legend, in the golden age of antiquity the highest tax exacted by a ruler in years of plenty was 1/10th of the yield; the only permissible variation occurred in times of famine, when taxes were reduced or forgiven, depending on local conditions. The state is made secure when it provides for the economic security of its people. The government should never extort unfair exactions from its people; after all, it was founded initially to prevent the strong from bullying the weak.[9]

> App. 2: Greedy[10] hoarding, bit by bit,[11]
>   Steeps us in impropriety.
> Fath. 2: Black hoarding, bit by bit,
>   Means: This is not the way to glory.

To squirrel away petty profit is one sure way of habituating oneself to evil. Minor covetous acts may seem inconsequential at the outset, but they result in a slow but steady erosion of one's moral faculties.

> App. 3: Seeing it is small, he eschews its use
>   So that we may fully develop.
> Fath. 3: Seeing the small, he does not use it.
>   Meaning: He waits for us to grow big.

Ritual precepts forbid the use of young animals for sacrifice.[12] Such prohibitions teach an important lesson (already known to hunters, fishermen, and farmers): Young and fragile things must be patiently fostered until they mature enough to be put to use. Only an idiot pulls his rice-sprouts out of the ground, on the mistaken notion that he can thereby hasten the growth process.[13] By analogy, the person who hopes to cultivate his virtue does not prematurely test himself;[14] nor does the wise leader squeeze those followers who cannot yet make significant contributions.[15] Should the ruler extort the last coin from his subjects, his indigent population will never accumulate sufficient wealth to support his expansionist dreams.[16]

> App. 4: In gathering profit and reducing punishment,
>   Small is the advance and great the retreat.
> Fath. 4: Gathering profits, reducing punishments,
>   Means: His government is in retreat.

Chinese tradition presumes that ordinary people will look to their ruler for their values. Here, the government gives them mixed messages. On the one hand, to reduce punishments suggests that generosity is good. On the other, to raise taxes shows that profit is valued over humaneness. Is it any wonder that the common people are left in utter confusion, and that this government lacks a secure foundation?

These poems may criticize Emperor Wu of early Western Han

(r. 140–87 B.C.) specifically. To support his foreign wars, Emperor Wu encouraged the institution of government monopolies while selling exemptions from punishments, all over vigorous protests from Confucian scholars at court. Conceivably, these lines could also represent a general warning to the state *not* to reduce punishments so long as the common people are engaged in the "secondary," commercial occupations. After all, profit-seekers tend to be lawbreakers as well.[17] Finally, the poem could describe the petty man, who willingly risks breaking the law for the sake of minor gain. He "gathers profits, [then] minor punishments./ Making a small advance but a big retreat./ . . . His rectitude retreats."[18] In all these cases, short-term gains ultimately spell defeat.

> App. 5: Livestock propagate contentedly,[19]
> Snowy white[20] cocoons blanket the fields.
> Fath. 5: Happy livestock and white cocoons
> Mean: The state does not "steal their time."

Domestic animals (especially the ox) and the silkworm are said to be especially pleasing to the gods of Earth, the patron Phase for the central Appraisal 5.[21] Both agriculture (as men's work) and sericulture (as women's work) appear in this scene of idyllic productivity. Food and clothing, the basic necessities of life, are provided. What's more, there is silk for the aged and for ritual. Such good order results when the people stick to the "basic" occupations, rather than the merchant or artisan trades.[22] But the Fathoming offers the main reason for this material prosperity: the wise ruler, acceding to the natural rhythms of the universe, is careful not to "steal the time." In other words, from spring planting through the autumn harvest, the state should not employ the common people in war or corvée.[23]

> App. 6: Though small and weak at first,[24]
> Something big begins to grow.[25]
> The petty man fails to take heed.
> Fath. 6: Warnings about the sick and weak
> Means: He is oblivious to the first small signs of change.

The "Great Commentary" to the *Changes* defines the gentleman in terms of his superb sensitivity to the practical and ethical implications of the unfolding situation, long before it has fully evolved.[26] As tradition states, it is advantageous to

> Contemplate difficulty when it is still easy.
> Manage a great affair when it is still small.[27]

In contrast, the petty man, in his self-absorption, lacks awareness of the obvious or the inevitable, even when it lies right under his nose.

Alternately, these verses could describe the common people, who despite their individual weakness, collectively form the only secure basis for the state:

> Pitiable and weak [are the common people]
> [Yet] they make the great origin [of the state].
> Petty men [in power] do not take heed.

> Warnings about the pitiable and weak
> Mean: They fail to discern the [power of the] small.[28]

App. 7: The husband pulls in the cart shafts.
     His wife peels wild and bitter herbs.[29]
     What benefits the king's paternal aunts
     Does nothing for the common run of men.[30]
     An affliction.
Fath. 7: Pulling in harness and peeling herbs
     Means: Wealth is collected from them.

In the *Mystery*'s regular alternation of Day and Night, yin and yang, this Appraisal should be lucky. This appears to be an exception. Both husband and wife are employed in lowly jobs entailing a vast expenditure in energy for very little profit.[31] In happier circumstances, draft animals replace human beings in the traces, and the main meal is grain, not bitter herbs. The tiny sums extorted from the working poor could never fund the state adequately, especially when they are siphoned off by the great families of the realm.

However, an auspicious reading is possible: If the commonfolk find ways to survive these harsh and troubled times, their strength represents a great resource for the state. Persistence and courage is to be valued.

App. 8: Heavy taxes bring down the state.
Fath. 8: Great downfalls from great levies
     Mean: Such collections are wrong.

By Appraisal 8, we are already in the Middle of Calamity. Those in power, rapacious in their demands for taxes, have secured their own downfall. Even the most cynical of rulers, if wise, should realize the advantage of accepting a lower standard of living in return for the security of his throne.

App. 9: Taxing in season
     Helps forestall[32] utter ruin.
Fath. 9: Collecting taxes when timely
     Means: How could disaster be imminent?[33]

In good harvest years, the wise ruler orders a significant proportion of tax receipts reserved as a hedge against bad times. In times of natural disaster or famine, these reserves are redistributed among the common people. He only levies public service during the slack agricultural seasons. And he demands no payment before the harvest. Because he has taken account of the cyclical rhythms of Heaven-and-Earth, he will find that the people have more than enough to support him and themselves in comparative luxury. As Mencius wrote:

> So long as you do not interfere with the busy seasons in the fields, then there will be more grain than the people can eat. . . . This is the first step along the Kingly Way. . . .[34]

Ch'iang
No. 36. Strength
May 28 (p.m.)–June 1

Correlates with Earth's Mystery; Yin; the phase Metal; and the Yi ching Hexagram no. 1, Masculine; the sun enters the Well constellation, 7th degree

HEAD: Yang *ch'i* is pure[1] and hard, dry and firm.[2] Each and every one of the myriad things is strengthened.

Strength can be good or bad, depending on the situation. The first hints of future trouble for yang *ch'i* appeared in the Head text of Tetragram 35. Although pure yang *ch'i*, like Heaven, is "strong and untiring,"[3] things that grow too strong under its influence tend to be overbearing and unbending.[4] Also, things that grow too "dry and firm" suggest stiff corpses.[5] As if to ease our apprehensions about present developments, this Head text treats only the most positive effects of yang's uninterrupted growth on the myriad things.

> App. 1: To be hardheaded is not right.[6]
>   It makes him utterly useless.
> Fath. 1: To be hard at center
>   Means: One cannot confer with him.

The petty person tends to be stubborn and unyielding, overbearing and inflexible. Basic cooperation is not an option, let alone a fruitful

Figure 11. Mt. T'ai, a sacred mountain of China. illus. from a rubbing, Chinese
Rubbings from the Field Museum *no. 32 (110 × 62 cm.), of unknown date (probably Ch'ing dynasty).*

working relation. The Master himself said, "It is useless to take counsel with those who follow a different way [than ritual]."[7] By contrast, the ideal friend and ally is both flexible and upright; for that reason, people seek his advice.[8] Strength is a necessary, but not a sufficient cause of greatness.

> App. 2: The phoenix spreads its wings in flight.
> Noble men approach the proper time:
> No one can ever hold them back.
> Fath. 2: A phoenix in flight
> Means: Opportunity comes to the noble man.

A truly moral person is like a phoenix. With regard to their respective species, both are equally rare.[9] The patterns of both are pleasing. (The phoenix is famous for its exquisite plumage and fastidious habits. In humans, ritual acts provide the pleasing patterns.) Both are endowed with unusual strength. In taking flight, the phoenix spreads its wings (*hsiu*) to catch the wind (*feng*). By a pun,[10] the truly moral person cultivates himself (*hsiu*) to extend his influence to others (also *feng*). So long as adequate preparations have been made, and the time is right, both the phoenix and the moral person will soar far above their peers.[11]

> App. 3: If pillars are uncentered and beams not high,
> The great mansion is laid low.
> Fath. 3: Pillars not centered
> Mean: They cannot set the foundation straight.

In both Chinese and Indian conventions, the ruler's chief ministers were called his "pillars" and "beams." A house will be stable only if its pillars and beams are measured and positioned correctly. If we follow this architectural metaphor, the ruling house can only remain strong if its chief ministers are selected and employed wisely. In the state, as in architecture, the effect of the whole depends upon the balance between numerous structural parts, but a firm foundation is crucial for both.[12]

> App. 4: Keen of eye and ear, there and over there,[13]
> His attendants, left and right,
> Offer him staunch support.[14]
> Fath. 4: Perceptive aides all around[15]
> Mean: From every side, many knights approach.[16]

The ideal man in office is said to be "perceptive in ear and eye."[17] The good ruler must use all available evidence to judge candidates for office. He is bound to select those who, like him, are keen of eye and ear. The talented, therefore, flock to court, where they can put their perceptiveness to good use in service of the king.[18] Their support strengthens the ruling house.

> App. 5: Noble men, when strong, use virtue.
> Petty men, when strong, use force.
> Fath. 5: That the petty man is strong
> Means: His faults increase as he gains rank.

Given the charisma associated with rank and riches, it may seem difficult at first to judge a person of position or wealth impartially.[19] But the petty person who has finagled his way into office becomes more overbearing as his arrogance and pride increase. In contrast, the moral superior upon attaining high rank becomes even more conscious of his responsibility to lead others along the path of virtue.[20]

> App. 6: Using my strength to "overcome myself,"[21]
> The sky is the limit to what I can do.[22]
> Fath. 6: Strength in overcoming myself
> Means: Great excellence has no limits.[23]

True excellence depends upon the individual overcoming his own selfish, biased, or arrogant tendencies.[24] He may also decide to "overcome his own strength" (an alternate reading of the first Appraisal line), as he recognizes the wisdom of yielding in many situations.[25] Paradoxically, then, strength comes from conquering the self.[26]

> App. 7: Metal is strong but flesh is weak.
> Blood flows in the fields.
> Fath. 7: Strong metal and weak flesh
> Mean: The laws cause great harm.

Not even the strongest man can withstand a blow by weapons. Knowing the irreparable harm that weapons can wreak, the good leader runs his state in such a way as to minimize the need for harsh punishments.[27] Here blood flows even in the rice fields, suggesting the tyrannous nature of this regime and its laws. It is the Legalists, not good Confucians, who resort to arms to solve problems. Legend has it that the first Legalist master Shang Yang executed so many in the field that the Wei River ran red with their blood.[28]

> App. 8: He strengthens where he fails,[29]
> Making an effort where he is weak.
> Fath. 8: Strong after failure
> Means: He works hard to make himself strong.

The moral superior learns to recognize and reform his failings. The best way to do this is to immerse himself in the model of the sages.[30]

App. 9: He uproots Mount T'ai,
　　　He snaps pillars and beams.
　　　Such men stumble and fall.
Fath. 9: Mountains uprooted and beams snapped
　　　Mean: In the end, he's undone by violence.[31]

Proverbial strongmen are said to be able to pull Mount T'ai (the "Great Mountain," located in present Shantung province) out from its roots, and still go on to chop whole beams in two, like matchsticks. Unfortunately, those who develop their own physical strength to this degree seldom devote equal time to moral self-cultivation.[32] Since their character is relatively unformed, they invite disaster upon themselves.[33]

T'ai-shan usually points to the ruler, as that mountain symbolizes what is of greatest weight and solidity. Perhaps Yang Hsiung criticizes the evil First Emperor of Ch'in, whose tyranny undermined the dynasty.

Correlates with Earth's Mystery; Yang; the phase Water; and the Yi ching Hexagram no. 1, Masculine; the sun enters the Well constellation, 11th degree

Ts'ui
No. 37. Purity
June 2–June 6 (a.m.)

HEAD: Yang *ch'i* is uniformly pure, clear, and bright, so that things all are doubly illuminated[1] and protected by its shining light.

As yang *ch'i* approaches its culmination at the summer solstice, yin *ch'i* appears quiescent (though we know from an earlier Head text that it is gathering its forces quietly below).[2] As pure yang *ch'i* bathes each of the myriad things in its cleansing and energizing light, each thing comes to epitomize that particular form of brilliance consistent with its nature.[3] In human society, men ideally achieve the luster associated with unadulterated virtue.[4]

App. 1: Pure within,[5]
　　　He is clear, without stain.
Fath. 1: Pure within
　　　Means: Clear, without a stain.

As if to reiterate the singular perfection of the individual, the Appraisal's description has been repeated word for word in the Fathoming. Appraisal 1, tied to the Water phase, suggests that the human heart/mind in its original state at birth is pure and limpid as Water. As adults, we can return to that original purity as soon as we wish for Goodness above all else since that heartfelt wish rids our *hsin* of inappropriate desire.[6] Since the first graph used in the poem has two meanings, "to gaze" and "to be pure," the poem could also be read:

> Gazing within, he finds
> Clarity without corruption.
> Looking within.
> [His conscience] is clear and incorrupt.[7]

App. 2: Tainted secretly while feigning[8] purity,
    He is shamed to the center of his self.
Fath. 2: A dark mix pretending to be pure
    Means: The center buries itself.

In a direct contrast to Appraisal 1, this poem describes an individual who feigns integrity though he is plagued by divided loyalties and contradictory impulses. Though others may be taken in by the pretense, his conscience suffers greatly.[9] He is like "a wolf in sheep's clothing."[10]

App. 3: He lifts his eyes up to Heaven.
    He lowers his ears to the depths.
    Such is reverence.[11]
Fath. 3: Eyes raised and ears lowered
    Means: His powers of perception investigate the limits.

The sacred cosmic patterns of Heaven-and-Earth are perceptible to Man so long as he maintains a reverential attitude towards them.[12] These patterns may be adapted to the human order as needed. The *Changes* begins its description of the culture heroes of antiquity, therefore, with the following passage:

> When in early antiquity Pao Hsi ruled the world, he looked up and contemplated the images in the heavens. He looked down and contemplated the models on earth. He contemplated the markings of birds and beasts and their suitability [to particular environments] on earth. Near to hand he took them [patterns] from his own person; farther way, he took them from [other] things. And so he invented the Eight Trigrams [of the *Changes* on the cosmic model] to establish contact with the charismatic power of the gods and to categorize the actual conditions of the myriad things.[13]

The latter-day seeker after wisdom has two additional ways of perceiving the fundamental cosmic patterns. He can "look up" the Classics composed by the sages; he can "look down" by consulting widely with others, even with the humblest members of society.[14] Once he has carried out his investigations reverently, he can establish fundamental truths for the good of the human race. Then he himself will be worthy of respect.

> App. 4: The petty man envies the pure,
>   And so loses rank and propriety.[15]
> Fath. 4: That small men envy the pure
>   Means: The Way is not attained.

The petty man, instead of working hard to emulate the pure goodness of the sages, simply envies his moral superiors. In consequence, he fails to reform himself. He may even try to impede the rise of good men. Though sooner or later he forfeits his influence,[16] his misconduct impedes the course of the Way.

> App. 5: Pure to the hidden "yellow" core:
>   Supremely[17] stable, he knows no bounds.[18]
> Fath. 5: Pure in the hidden "yellow" mind
>   Means: His model is the rectifying Earth.[19]

The phrase "hidden yellow" appears in Tetragram 1, where it signifies the deepest (hidden) recesses of the mind of the centered individual (yellow = the color of the center). The yellow center is associated with Earth, which epitomizes the related virtues of fairness (presumably because all points on its surface lie equidistant from its core), of humility (since the earth is content to lie below our feet), of stability (since the earth never moves beneath our feet),[20] and of openness (since the earth is vast). The man who exemplifies all these virtues is hidden in another sense: the full extent of his brilliance will never be known by ordinary mortals.[21]

> App. 6: Great purity gives way to error,
>   And so there is change.
> Fath. 6: Perfect purity succeeded by error
>   Means: The petty man is overcome.

A state or an individual fails to sustain its earlier virtue. Change and defeat ensue. The only remedy lies in the Confucian prescription to "conquer oneself and return to ritual."[22]

> App. 7: In his purity, he sees his faults in time.[23]
>   The noble man moves to repair them.

Fath. 7: Pure because of timely fault-finding[24]
Means: He is good at mending errors.

Though Appraisal 7 corresponds to the Beginning of Calamity, the individual here fortunately manages to correct his faults before it is too late. Perhaps good advisors assist him in reform.[25]

App. 8: Pure evil, without a trace of good.
Fath. 8: Pure evil, without a trace of good
Means: Finally, he cannot be helped.

According to Yang Hsiung's theory of human nature, human beings at birth generally fall into three types: the very good; the very bad; and the vast majority, who are "mixed" (partly good and partly bad). According to Yang, neither the very good nor the very bad are much affected by education.[26] As Confucius remarked, "The very wisest and the very stupidest [in moral terms] are the only ones who cannot change."[27] For the truly evil, punitive measures may be necessary.

App. 9: Pure to the end and forever new,[28]
He is propriety[29] exemplified.
Fath. 9: Propriety that is pure to the end
Means: Truly, this is cause for celebration.

The truly moral person monitors his own conduct each day in order to preserve his hard-won perfection. He is "ever new" because he returns to his roots in filial piety and love of the ancients. He also invokes the eternal timelessness of sacred realm through daily ritual, which brings the primordial mythical time into the present.[30] His moral example untarnished, he deserves the praise of all.

Sheng
No. 38. Fullness
June 6 (p.m.)–June 10

Correlates with Earth's Mystery; Yin; the phase Fire; and the Yi ching *Hexagram no. 14, Great Possessions; the sun enters the Well constellation, 16th degree*[1]

HEAD: Yang *ch'i*, high and full, fills and stops up every space so that things completely[2] fulfill its[3] intentions.

With summer in full swing, yang *ch'i* approaches the height of its powers. As yang fills up every nook and cranny of the cosmos, it animates all living things so that each becomes "replete with virtue."[4] Animals grow heavy with maturity; many are ripe with child.[5] Fruits grow heavy on the vine. In the world of Man, the moral person brimming with virtue is ready to "curb evil and foster good."[6] Misfortune comes, however, to those bloated by arrogance or by unhealthy desires for profit or position.

> App. 1: He prospers, but not by the line.[7]
>
> > He loses secret[8] virtue.
>
> Fath. 1: Prosperous but unprincipled
>
> > Means: At center, he fails to conquer himself.

That already in Appraisal 1 there is talk of prosperity reflects the fullness of yang *ch'i* at this time of the year. Unfortunately, the individual, once so self-effacing, tends to grow careless with prosperity; self-satisfied, he slips from quiet virtue into immodesty or even garrulousness.[9] If he is not careful, such errors will grow. For this reason, as the proverb says, "Prosperity is the beginning of decline."[10]

> App. 2: Acts that do not depend on reward[11]
>
> > Can lead to great riches.[12]
>
> Fath. 2: Acts independent of ends
>
> > Mean: This we call "Mysterious Power."

The *Lao tzu* praises the Tao, saying that it

> Gives birth, but does not take possesion.
> Benefits, but does not depend.
> Acts as steward, but does not take control.
> This is called "Mysterious Power."[13]

The *Mystery* describes the good person, who in imitation of the Tao pursues the moral course without thought of reward or recognition.[14] His focus on Goodness should be enough to achieve great virtue (one kind of riches).[15] In the process, the individual is likely to also attain material success. As Confucius once remarked, "The person who seldom gets into trouble . . . will be sure in the process to get his reward."[16] At the very least, lacking any desire to lord it over others, he will probably make no enemies as he goes through life.[17]

> App. 3: Love of profit fills the breast.
>
> > It does not profit the common good.
>
> Fath. 3: Love of profit swelling the breast
>
> > Means: It builds[18] private gates.

According to most ancient works of Chinese philosophy, the common good should take precedence over private benefits in areas of moral conflict. For this reason, the Chinese language has no exact equivalent for our modern Western notion of privacy.[19] The term translated as "private" (*szu*) carries the perjorative sense of "selfishness." Those who love profit serve the interests of private "gates" (for example, private patrons or heterodox schools of philosophy), rather than the common good, which calls for selfless devotion to duty.

> App. 4: With slight prosperity, subservience[20]
>   Functions as gateway for great men.[21]
> Fath. 4: Minor prosperity, proper subservience,
>   Means: He serves the worthy and humane.[22]

The theme of subservience appears appropriately in Appraisal 4, assigned to members of the bureaucracy. The Chinese graph for "subservience" shows a figure with the head bowed low and the eye turned in. The individual is fit for office only after humility, obedience, and the powers of self-reflection have been developed. In the desire to discharge his obligations to others, the individual comes to disregard his own prosperity.[23] But others, coming to admire this unselfishness, propel him to higher position. Paradoxically, the individual who humbles himself attains still greater success.[24]

> App. 5: Failing to bear good fortune lightly,
>   He picks up ill and is then ensnared.[25]
> Fath. 5: Bearing good fortune and raising ill
>   Means: Such is the way of the petty man.[26]

Good and bad fortune are frequently intertwined. As good fortune becomes a heavy burden, calamity is "picked up" or "raised." There are two ways to account for this: If the leader parades his own wealth and power,[27] the envy and malice of all around him are excited. Or perhaps the individual is not up to the job; in other words, "his shoulders are not broad enough" to bear weighty responsibilities.

> App. 6: Granting him glory, Heaven
>   Opens wide all borders to him.
>   In[28] modesty, there are rewards.[29]
> Fath. 6: That Heaven grants him glory
>   Means: Modesty increases what he has.[30]

Appraisal 6 in an even-numbered tetragram corresponds to the Son of Heaven as recipient of Heaven's mandate. So long as the ruler conforms to Heaven's will with due modesty, there are no theoretical limitations on his power and authority.

> App. 7: As summer's fiery heat mounts up,
>   It calls forth winter's icy springs.
> Fath. 7: With mounting fires, that springs grow cold
>   Means: Calamity is not far away.

Appraisal 7 represents a triple conjunction of Fire, it is the second Fire line in a Fire tetragram. Appraisal 7 is also the Beginning of Calamity. The line, then, follows tradition in predicting that an excess of fiery yang *ch'i* at the summer solstice must give way to the waxing power of destructive yin.[31] (The cold springs of winter bring to mind the Yellow Springs, the underground region inhabited by the shades after death.)

> App. 8: He damps down[32] the full blaze[33]
>   As collapse is about to begin.[34]
> Fath. 8: Drawing off from the brim
>   Means: He barely escapes from danger.[35]

One Han figure of speech compares the immoral person to a fool asleep on a lighted pile of wood.[36] A fire in full blaze is dazzling in its beauty, but it can also be dangerous—especially when the beauty of the fire disguises its essentially destructive nature.[37] The wise individual always withdraws to a safe distance in the presence of danger. The conscious decision not to "play with fire" makes good sense at any time.[38] Here, however, the individual saves himself only at the last moment. Still, even then additional benefits come from damping down the fire: The fire is put out with water from the jar. And since the jar is now less than full, the water no longer spills so easily.[39]

> App. 9: The greatest prosperity does not save.
>   Calamity is sent down from Heaven.
> Fath. 9: That extreme fullness has no power to save[40]
>   Means: Heaven's Way is reversion.[41]

Lacking the will to be good, the individual is prey to all the traps that success brings to mind and body. Calamity strikes at the height of prosperity, revealing the hollow nature of material success. As always, the root of the problem lies within the self; Heaven cannot be blamed when Man chooses to disobey the cosmic laws.[42]

Correlates with Earth's Mystery;
Yang; *the phase Wood; and the* Yi
ching *Hexagram no. 37, Family
Members; the sun enters the Well
constellation, 21st degree*

Chü

No. 39. Residence

June 11–June 15 (a.m.)

HEAD: Yang[1] on all sides occupies the outer rim.[2] Awesome and formidable,[3] it serves as the inner and outer walls for things so that all the myriad things get its protective frame.[4]

Yang *ch'i* moves to take up residence at the outside of things. Like a frame or shelter or city wall, it surrounds and protects things, strengthening their defenses so that all things feel "safe at home" under its influence.[5] As the *Changes* states, "When the house is set in order, the world is set on a firm course."[6] Until yin grows stronger, the potential for Good seems unlimited.

At the same time, the architectural metaphor suggests that yang *ch'i* will soon reach its natural limits. Walls and frames are useful constructions, but their firm structure works against open-ended potential. Also, wide outer frames by definition are inherently weaker than the inner core, where strength can be concentrated.[7] As yang *ch'i* moves to a position at the outer rim, it empties out from the core of Being, leaving behind a vacuum to be filled by yin *ch'i*. (Compare the description of male as "outer" and female as "inner" in the *Changes*.)[8] Danger lies in neglecting what is fundamental (or inner) while attending to the secondary (or outer).

> App. 1: Not giving or receiving praise or blame,[9]
> He thus preserves his house.
> Fath. 1: No praise or blame
> Means: His Way is constant.

Appraisal 1 is associated with the Water phase, with silence, and with the tranquil inner mind. Only those who are self-motivated are single-minded enough to pursue the Good. Unconcerned with others' praise or blame,[10] the good person follows the Right assiduously, acting with equal nobility in public and in private. At the same time, he may aptly be called a conformist in that he bends his will to the constant norms enshrined in the Confucian tradition. Preoccupied with his own moral quest, he has absolutely no desire to criticize others,[11] so nothing makes him stand out from the crowd. In this way, he preserves his family line.[12]

> App. 2: The household has no flasks.
>> The wife supplants her elders.[13]
>> She errs,[14] washing them in mud.[15]
> Fath. 2: A house without flasks
>> Means: It lacks the means to carry on.

Family rituals preserved in the Confucian canon are designed to balance hierarchy with reciprocity, so that both respect and love, as well as order and intimacy, prevail in the home. This household has no flasks for water and wine, so neither mundane tasks (like drawing water from the well)[16] nor ritual duties can be carried out properly. Worse, in utter disregard of Chinese custom, the young wife refuses to defer to the senior women of her husband's household;[17] instead, she tries to take over the household management in a virtual usurpation of her elders' power. Misrule reigns in the family; even ordinary values are overturned as muddy water is mistaken for clean.

It is tempting to read the graph meaning "flask" as a misprint for a second character signifying the proper seclusion and internal order of the women's quarters.[18] In that case, the *Mystery* reminds us that strict segregation of the sexes is the rule within the family. This reading, however, would violate Yang Hsiung's rhyme scheme.

> App. 3: With young and old in proper order,
>> The son can sustain the father.
> Fath. 3: Sons carrying their fathers
>> Means: Only then can there be renewal.

The fundamental paradox of Chinese hierarchy is that its very survival depends upon adequate provision for mobility and change within that hierarchy. Before his parents' death, the filial son is subject (with very few reservations) to the will of his parents. Upon the death of his father, however, he succeeds to a higher position as paterfamilias.[19] Households and individuals survive only when they take into account both eternal constants and changing realities.

> App. 4: A pig appears in the audience hall,
>> With a puppy following its tracks.[20]
> Fath. 4: A pig in the audience hall
>> Means: Their presence[21] is unlucky.

In any private residence, the audience hall as the main public room serves a variety of important functions. The ancestral tablets are arranged on an altar in that room, making one corner of the hall a kind of chapel dedicated to the dead. The audience hall also serves as a living room, where family, friends, and guests gather for meals and other ritual occasions.

The Chinese graph for "house" (*chia*) depicts a pig under a roof; as wealth "on the hoof," the pig should reside somewhere inside the family compound. But the pig is dirty and smelly, despite its long domestication. Such a creature has no place in the most sacred room of the house. Still less should the dog be there. Though European—especially English—tradition has elevated the dog to man's best friend, in China the dog has remained a lowly watchdog, whose rightful post is outside the main gate.[22] Even worse, the dog is in hot pursuit of the pig. Once the dog catches up with it, there is sure to be a tussle. According to Chinese divination texts, a fight between a dog and a pig is a bad omen signifying lack of discipline in the household, especially in sexual matters.[23]

> App. 5: Rudders and oars steady the ride.[24]
>   They are good for riches and stability.
> Fath. 5: Peace and harmony through rudder and oar
>   Means: The ride is smooth to the borders.

The boat is a miraculous conveyance since it combines the convenience and safety of an earth-bound residence with the capacity for travel on water.[25] This image, then, emphasizes stability in the midst of change. Top and bottom, rudder and oar, work in concert, just as higher and lower ranks[26] must cooperate to create a just and safe state. Safety in the boat depends in equal measure on the initial construction of the boat and the skills of its captain. By analogy, the just society requires both good institutions and a capable ruler.[27] Once it is properly launched and piloted, the heavy frame of the ship glides easily over the waves, just as the ship of state "rides on" the masses.[28] Riches and security come to all who avail themselves of it.

> App. 6: He who sets his well and stove apart,
>   In three years, only sees his family's back.
> Fath. 6: To put out well and stove
>   Means: In three years, no feasts are enjoyed.[29]

To set the well and stove apart signifies the decision to split the extended family household into separate units based on the nuclear family—a decision often forced upon the extended family by members of the younger generation.[30] Each time a member of the new, smaller household unit goes to its own separate well and stove to fetch water and cook, it reinforces the group's refusal to cooperate. Discord in the family predictably ends in three related disasters: First, family elders, who usually counsel against a split, are increasingly ignored by the rebellious younger generation.[31] Family elders and ancestors may even suffer neglect (so they only "see the backs" of their insubordinate family members).[32] Second, the initial division of communal family property generates even more mutual antipathy. Third, the property division works against future cooperation between family members, no matter how mutually advantageous such cooperation might be. A single act of rebellion makes the entire community suffer.

> App. 7: The old man pulls a cart.[33]
> The young girl raises a jar.
> Both benefit the ancestral house.
> Fath. 7: An old fellow pulling a cart
> Means: Only then do their bodies grow strong.

The old man is apparently still vigorous enough to pull the cart by a large rope looped around his arm. The elder's job, as he sees it, is to "carry the young," both physically and emotionally, until they are old enough to assume some responsibility for themselves. The younger members of the family feel solicitous towards the family head, despite his evident strength. In this way, they demonstrate their willingness to fulfill family obligations. Conscientious in her tasks, with no mind to dally,[34] the young girl here hastens to raise a wine or water jar to the old man's lips in a gentle gesture of good will. The lesson is clear: the major responsibility for the family is given to the male elders, while those who are young, weak, or female repay their elders with respect and love. Since the generations behave well toward each other, the family line is likely to prosper; the advantages of a tight family unit become obvious when each performs his or her role.

> App. 8: His stools upended, his ladles in pairs:[35]
> His household is no good.
> Fath. 8: Overturned stools, too many ladles by twice,
> Mean: Family usage is not right.

In early China, the Chinese sat on mats placed on the ground, though a stool was provided for the elderly as a mark of respect.[36] (The chair was a Western import that gained popularity in T'ang times.) An upended stool signifies disrespect for the aged.

At the supper table, a single ladle was commonly reserved for the host's use when serving soups or stews. To double the number of large spoons implies one of three conditions, all undesirable: unwonted luxury in the household,[37] a strong challenge to the prerogatives of the paterfamilias,[38] or the doubling of the women in the household (presumably because of the age-old comparison of the spoon to the womb).[39] Since all respect and probity has been undermined, the family cannot continue strong.

> App. 9: If the stump produces new shoots,
>   Its kind is not cut off.
> Fath. 9: A stump producing new shoots
>   Means: Only then does its type last long.

After a tree is felled, new shoots sprout from the stump. By analogy, after the demise of the head of the household, the birth of one or more sons promises new life for the genealogical line.

Correlates with Earth's Mystery;
Yin; the phase Metal; and the Yi
ching Hexagram no. 48, The Well;
the sun enters the Well constella-

Fa

tion, 25th degree[1]

No. 40. Law or Model

June 15 (p.m.)–June 19

HEAD: Yang suspends its law on high. Things [in response] lift their gaze to their own models so that each and every one takes on[2] pattern.

With the next tetragram arrives the summer solstice, the annual culminating point for yang *ch'i*, which accounts for the repeated references to yang's high position. With yang *ch'i* providing a model of perfection, all things come to measure and adapt themselves according to cosmic law. As the *Odes* assure us, "Heaven produces the teeming multitudes,/ As there are things, there must be norms and laws [for them]."[3] This tetragram's title refers to models and patterns of any kind (even ritual pattern), as well as to the penal code.[4] In the earlier Appraisals, which we would expect to be more auspicious, the focus is on various models hallowed in Confucian tradition: the ruler's model by suasive example, the model provided by the Confucian Classics, the sagely model of the culture-heroes of antiquity. But in the first yin line past the midway point, when the power of inauspicious yin is growing, the Appraisals shift to consider the place of penal law (allied with yin and with Metal in Han correlations). In general, Confucianism admits that even sages may be forced to apply the penal code to particularly recalcitrant cases, though suasive example is preferable in dealing with most humans, both because it is more humane and because it is more effective.[5] In comparing the law to the well of Hexagram 48, this tetragram tries to emphasize one aspect of the law: Like the well, the law should not change; only if the law is known to all and equitably applied will it serve the community adequately.[6]

> App. 1: The model he builds is an unfit model.
> Fath. 1: That the model built is no model
> Means: It is not worth using.

Yang Hsiung's other neoclassical text, the *Model Sayings*, laments the fact that "there are many such cases where a model which is not a fit model, and a pattern is not a fit pattern."[7] Unsuitable models prove worse than useless for the individual or society, for they convey the wrong values or techniques. One example might be that of an evil father, who sets a pattern of inattention or even abuse for his children, which is then replicated in succeeding generations. Another example pertains to the workings of the mind since Appraisal 1 corresponds to Beginning Thought. As these lines caution, the mind that uses the wrong mental construct to view a certain situation will make inappropriate decisions. Both the world of Heaven-and-Earth and the Confucian Classics provide sufficent models of correct thought and behavior.[8] Any departure from these preordained, natural patterns inevitably creates disorder.

> App. 2: He copies the model by centering,
> And so he overcomes.[9]
> Fath. 2: To pattern oneself on the Mean
> Means: Being revered by all the masses.[10]

The cosmic model has been reproduced in the social institutions, ritual precepts, and practical inventions of the sage-kings of antiquity, whose conduct provides the correct model for Man. All these models teach the individual to center himself by keeping to the Mean.[11]

> App. 3: Failure to start with[12] level and line,
> Ruins his settings of compass and square.
> Fath. 3: Level and line not at the start
> Means: It is their use that is at fault.

A Han proverb laments the ease with which we compound initial errors: "Off by a hair's breadth [at the beginning], you'll miss by a thousand miles [in the end]."[13] Any initial miscalculation, however slight, is multiplied with each subsequent measurement. To stray ever so slightly from the Way, then, is to risk grave moral error. The metaphor implies that there is nothing wrong with the base material; the problem arises when the individual decides he need not use available tools. By analogy, there is nothing inherently wrong with human nature; we fail to be good when we fail to use the tools provided by the sages.[14]

> App. 4: Level, line, compass, square—
> None work against our applications.
> Fath. 4: Level, line, compass, and square
> Mean: They each proceed from the self.

A worthy man in office (since Appraisal 4 corresponds to the bureaucracy) uses great care to ensure that each plan he devises is in exact conformity with the models presented by the sages of antiquity. In this, he is like the good carpenter who continually checks his own constructs against level and line, compass and square. When such precautions are taken over a period of time, the correct models are fully internalized. Then the official is self-disciplined enough to rule others.[15]

> App. 5: The well rope is short, too short.[16]
> The water jar is full.
> Though the well is deep and wide,
> In the end, it cannot slake our thirst.
> Fath. 5: That the jar is already full
> Means: This is not the way to study.

The proper source of all learning is the Confucian Classics, which are profound as a deep well, and as refreshing and vitalizing as clean water.[17] To avail himself of the Classics, however, the individual must adopt the proper attitude to learning. First, the individual must apply himself to the task of how best to plumb the depths; in other words, he had better master the use of the rope. Second, the individual must devote his entire attention to Confucianism. If the individual has drunk too deeply of heterodox texts, there will be no room left in his mind for the teachings of the sages. In other words, he will be like a jar that is full to the brim. The *Mystery* counters criticisms of Confucianism by arguing that its doctrines are sufficient for all human purposes, just as water from the well is sufficient to slake any thirst. The trouble is, we petty persons do not know how to use the resources at our disposal.[18]

> App. 6: In the lead thread, in the guide rope
> Propriety's glories are shown.
> Fath. 6: Lead thread and guide rope
> Mean: The Grand Rule is made clear to us.

The ruler exemplifies for his people the underlying principles of the integrated cosmic and social fabrics (in Chinese terms, the lead thread and the guide rope).[19] Once the good ruler orders his person and his clan, he proceeds to institute the Grand Rule,[20] an ideal state in which all humans develop in their social roles. The orderly reign redounds to his glory; his name goes down in history as a sage.

> App. 7: If fine nets are cast on deep pools,
>   This does not benefit the fish.
> Fath. 7: Fine nets on deep pools
>   Mean: Tyrannical laws spread wider.

In this first yin line past the midpoint of the cycle, the *Mystery* turns to consider the penal code in society. The fine net refers to penal law that is unusually harsh; a wider mesh would allow the "small fish" to escape.[21] Those who give it any thought know that if all the fish are taken, none will be left for later. The moral is, unmitigated severity destroys the very thing it intends to preserve. When very minor infractions of the law are punished severely, the people are less likely to become good.

> App. 8: He corrects those of us with faults
>   Until we have no depravity.[22]
> Fath. 8: Righting those faults
>   Means: He drives us on to perfection.

The true moral superior continually corrects his inferiors until they attain perfection. Ideally, as one Confucian Classic says, "Through punishments there may come to be no punishments."[23]

> App. 9: If the well has no rail,
>   Water spills straight over.[24]
>   With no valley or gorge,[25]
>   It will end in a flood.[26]
> Fath. 9: Wells without railings
>   Mean: Laws are unduly excessive.[27]

Water's propensity to flow beyond the confines of the well is compared to the potential of a harsh penal code to engulf all in its ruinous flood. Two remedies exist: the first is to strictly circumscribe the operation of the law (the metaphorical equivalent to putting a railing or collar around the well), so that it does not wreak havoc in the community; the second is to provide as a backup an alternate outlet to drain away any excess (an equivalent to the valley or gorge).[28] In human society, the single most important outlet for excessive desires is the ritual system. Over-reliance on law only leads to greater lawlessness.[29]

Ying

No. 41. Response
June 20–June 24 (a.m.)

Correlates with Earth's Mystery; Yang; the phase Earth; and the Yi ching Hexagram no. 30, Adherence;[1] the sun enters the Well constellation, 29th degree; the Dipper points due south; the musical note is F-sharp;[2] the Summer Solstice solar period begins with Appraisal 5

HEAD: Yang *ch'i* culminates on high. Yin faithfully[3] germinates below.[4] High and low mutually respond.

Tetragram 41 corresponds with the summer solstice,[5] one of two "centers" of the lunar year. As if to emphasize this quality of centredness, Yang Hsiung has arranged the *Mystery* in such a fashion that Tetragram 41 represents a triple conjunction of centers:[6] With 81 tetragrams as his total, Yang Hsiung assigned the first 27 tetragrams to Heaven, the second group of 27 to Earth, and the final third to Man. Tetragram 41 is assigned to the exact center of the "Earth Mystery" (Tetragrams 28–54), which itself holds the center position in the triadic realms of Heaven-Earth-Man. This tetragram is also assigned in the sequence of the Five Phases to the cosmic agent Earth, said to occupy the center of the four points of the compass. So much centredness cannot help but promote the Good.

The title character Response conveys four related meanings: (1) to respond or react, (2) the right or inevitable response in a specific case, (3) conformity to natural patterns in the cosmos and in society, and (4) harmonious union. The Appraisals, playing upon the full range of these associations, generally focus upon the paradigmatic relations between Heaven and Earth, ruler and subject. According to Yang, conformity with the Way is a necessary precondition for successful interaction. Once Man conforms with the Tao,

> Heaven and Earth will unite
> And the sweet dew will fall.
> The people will be equitable,
> Though no one so decrees.[7]

Each of Yang's texts also refers to one or more of the glosses given by Han scholastics for the title of the correspondent hexagram no. 30:[8] (1) "adherence," (2) "jointure," (3) "brilliant light," (4) "enlightenment," (5) "dispersal/separation," or (6) "nets" [for hunting and fishing]. Given the auspicious nature of most of these associations, it should come as no surprise that even the Appraisals assigned to inauspicious Night seem somewhat less dire in their warnings. Still, Yang cautions us about the dangers inherent in florescence. At the very point of yang's culmination, the summer solstice, the contrary power of yin begins to grow. By analogy, we know that the roots of decay are often planted in present prosperity.

Yang's characterization of yin *ch'i* is crucial to our analysis of the larger cyclic patterns at work. Yang chooses to describe yin's activity as *hsin*, a graph which can be understood in at least three ways: *Hsin* may mean "faithfully" (i.e., without fail), as in my translation. The climax of yang *ch'i* above "without fail" spontaneously provokes the birth of yin *ch'i* below. This definition underscores the regularity and inevitability of cosmic response, a theme emphasized by the Head text of Tetragram 1 assigned to the winter solstice. But assuming that Yang's language plays off both Tetragram 1 and the *Changes*, we may also wish to read *hsin* as "expanding."[9] Those texts remind us that the alternating expansion and contraction of yin and yang *ch'i* provides the momentum for all phenomenal change through time and space. Finally, there is the curious gloss offered by the Sung commentator Ssu-ma Kuang.[10] In the absence of any context, it may point to colloquial usage by which *hsin* refers to the fuse of the firecracker.[11] A fuse is an excellent metaphor for the catalyzing properties of nascent yin *ch'i*, for its modest start will in time produce the most startling of changes. Like most Han thinkers, Yang Hsiung subscribed to prevailing beliefs about the sacred origins of language; for him, moral connections are often revealed by homonyms. It is tempting, then, to apply all three descriptions to yin's activity in reading the following texts.

> App. 1: Six, as trunk, sets the pattern,
>   Making Five, the branches, well-arranged.[12]
> Fath. 1: Six, as trunk, setting patterns
>   Means: He adheres to the ruler.[13]

The number symbolism used here is somewhat confusing.[14] According to the "Great Commentary" to the *Changes*, the number 6 corresponds to yin and Earth, while 5 is assigned to yang and Heaven.[15] If we assume that Yang adopts the *Changes* numerology, then we might read these lines as proof of Yang's eclectic philosophy, for they make yin *ch'i* the ineffable fountainhead of all the various yang manifestations, as in classical Taoist philosophy.

The orthodox Confucian objection is given by the Ch'ing scholar, Ch'en Pen-li:

> Heaven's number is five; Earth's is six. The trunk is assigned to yang;
> the branches, to yin. In a discussion employing the numbers of Heaven
> and Earth, the trunk, then, ought to be called "five" and the branches
> "six." Now, in contrast, [the passage] says, "Six, the trunk . . . five, the
> branches . . ." This, then, is a case of yin and yang mixed, [which por-
> tends] the reversal of the positions of ruler and minister.[16]

Unfortunately, Appraisal 1 in an odd-numbered tetragram is always
correlated with auspicious yang *ch'i*; this makes it highly unlikely that
Yang's verses should offer veiled criticism.

I suggest a simple solution: Each Appraisal in the tetragram is
assigned to one of the Five Phases in succession. Six, then, represents the
higher One—a kind of internal pun for the ruler (of Heaven or of Earth),
as it does with many other Han writers.[17] Yang Hsiung can be said to
typify Han classicism in his preference for divine Oneness over that which
is varied or multiplicitous.[18] Here the one ruler's influence spreads
throughout the empire, transforming it. Only the ruler, the One Man as
he is called, can accomplish this, since he alone provides a unifying vision
of the Way to counter multiple claims based on self-interest. So long as
the ruler's influence addresses the needs of his people, they will respond
by offering him their complete allegiance. In this way, the branches depend upon the trunk in the same way that subjects depend upon the
ruler.[19]

Because Appraisal 1 is assigned to the cosmic agent Water, another
observation springs to mind: The superiority of the Way over other techniques of rule is like the supremacy of the great ocean to the small
streams crossing the land.[20]

> App. 2: The calendar lays it out above,
> > Below, the pitchpipes are attuned to it.
> > If not, the union of spheres is blocked.
> Fath. 2: What is set out above is harmonized below.
> > Meaning: Otherwise, how could we think them correct?[21]

The commentator Fan Wang explains the meaning of these verses in
the following way:

> The calendar is used to regulate the year; the pitch standards, to
> harmonize the notes. Issued to the Hundred Clans, the common people
> uphold them in order to complete their appointed tasks. Should they
> remain unstandardized, they prove to be impediments [to the ruler's
> civilizing influence].[22]

The calendar and pitch standards suggest the full range of inventions,
cultural patterns, and institutions bestowed by the sage-rulers upon hu-

man society. The calendar regulates agricultural and ritual activity. Music allows men to express their emotions in a socially productive manner that fully satisfies their inborn natures. Since the calendar is tied to movements in Heaven's course and the pitchpipes are tuned by earthly configurations,[23] the sage-ruler clearly models himself upon the constant patterns of Heaven-and-Earth.[24] Each ruler has the solemn responsibility to interpret cosmic norms for the benefit of the common people through wise and natural government policies and institutions. Should he ignore that responsibility, he does not deserve, nor will he win the support of the common people.[25]

> App. 3: In length and in breadth,
> Heaven's Net is vast.
> Fath. 3: In length and breadth
> Means: Warp and woof are properly placed.

The phrase Heavenly Net refers to the tightly woven social fabric, to the cosmic fabric, and more particularly, to divine justice.[26] Yang Hsiung's writings are preoccupied with the society/fabric analogy. Both society and fabric function by holding together a variety of disparate strands in harmonious pattern. The social fabric depends, of course, on hierarchy, just as the lead rope of the net pulls the secondary lines.[27]

According to the Han Doctrine of Mutual Interaction Between Heaven and Man, the cosmic Net also provides each individual with external checks upon his conduct, which come in the form of portents. With the combined help of the Classics and such omens, the man intent upon self-reform should have no trouble learning to conform to the divine Way. All potential for social and cosmic harmony, however, is ravaged by the disruptive penal system mentioned in Appraisal 4 below.

> App. 4: Setting nets and snares to catch us,[28]
> Entangling lines stretch to the wilds.[29]
> Fath. 4: Laying traps for us
> Means: He is incapable of ruling humanely.

Appraisal 3, allied with the Wood Phase and the virtue of humaneness, emphasized the supportive structure of the social fabric provided by benevolent Heaven in concert with the sage-kings of old. With Appraisal 4 allied with Metal (signifying war and harsh laws), Yang denounces the tyrannical ruler's overreliance upon punishments to effect his will. Legend says that good King T'ang purportedly constructed hunting nets open on three sides in order to give every wild animal the maximum opportunity to escape. On the same principle, he made his laws intentionally easy to follow, so that the common people would not run afoul of them through ignorance.[30] Confucius insisted that punishments alone cannot effect good order:

> Govern the people by regulations, keep order among them by chastisements, and they will flee from you and lose all self respect. Govern them by moral force, keep order among them by ritual and they will keep their self-respect and come to you of their own accord. . . . If it is really possible to govern countries by ritual and yielding, there is no more to be said.[31]

Unfortunately, the ruler portrayed in this Appraisal has decided to forego rule by humaneness—with disastrous results.

It is interesting that some later commentators read these verses as a justification for harsh authoritarian rule:

> [The good king] leads us [by] traps and snares,
> And casts the net over the uncivilized.
> [Fortunately, his net] reaches.

Such an interpretation is anachronistic for the early Han period.

> App. 5: The dragon, in soaring to Heaven,
>   Rightly[32] fears for its scales.[33]
> Fath. 5: The fear of the soaring dragon[34]
>   Means: At the peak, it fears a fall.

Appraisal 5 in the tetragram represents the apogee of development, especially when it is correlated with auspicious Day. Typically, it is assigned to the Son of Heaven. As in Tetragram 1, the dragon symbolizes the ruler for three reasons: first, both dragon and ruler are said to be formed of the essence of yang *ch'i*; second, the dragon brings fructifying rain to the crops below, just as the ruler showers blessings on his lowly subjects; third, the dragon in flight rides invisible currents of wind, just as the ruler "rides" the intangible support of the common people. At the height of his powers, the good and wise ruler continually checks popular reaction to his policies, for fear of finding himself without support. In this he follows the *Changes* injunction to be mindful of danger in the midst of security.[35] The most efficient way for the leader to assess the security of his position is to examine his own conduct in light of the constant patterns of Heaven-and-Earth. Once this self-examination and necessary corrections have been completed, the leader can continue to soar unimpeded. Should he fail to reform himself, however, he will fall like Icarus, due to his own arrogance.

> App. 6: Blazing heat is sustained[36] in Heaven,
>   While icy yin germinates in Earth.

> Fath. 6: Sustained in heaven, germinating in earth,
> Means: Yang begins its retreat.

With Appraisal 6, we pass the day of the summer solstice. These verses reverse the description of the germinating yang *ch'i* found in Tetragram 1, which was assigned to the winter solstice. Although yin *ch'i* appears to be completely vanquished by the strength of yang, it begins gathering its strength deep in the recesses of earth below.[37] As mirror images, Tetragrams 1 and 41 remind us of the absolute complementarity of yin and yang *ch'i*, which then provide a pattern for reciprocal relations among men. Still, we cannot call these verses entirely auspicious, since light and enlightenment are now in retreat. As Ssu-ma Kuang writes, "The way of the petty man waxes; that of the gentleman, declines. . . . The first subtle hint of caution and warning is fully laid out in this [set of verses]."

> App. 7: Each day he overcomes his faults.[38]
> Good omens increase in response.[39]
> Fath. 7: Daily stronger where once he was weak
> Means: He hates whatever defeats the good.[40]

The Appraisal describes the good person's determination to correct himself;[41] the Fathoming, his abhorrence of unworthy men[42] or evil impulses capable of subverting his concerted efforts. According to tradition, "If the gentleman can daily overcome his failings, then those who respond to him will be numerous."[43] Daily renewal is sure to bring prosperity.[44]

> App. 8: Culminating yang summons[45] yin.
> In less than a day, it responds.
> Fath. 8: That extreme yang summons yin
> Means: In response,[46] it emerges.

Like Appraisal 6, this poem is designed to show that responsiveness does not in every case necessarily tend toward the good. Once again, sober reference is made to the growth of yin *ch'i*, which paradoxically begins just at the point when yang reaches its apogee. Given the inauspicious associations of yin, some might wish that it were slower to respond to yang's cyclic activity. If we apply the metaphor to human existence, we learn that any manifest success contains the seeds of its own destruction, for success tends to breed arrogance and recklessness. This may explain the precipitate rise and fall of dynasties, families, or individuals.

> App. 9: With a culmination of great light,[47]
> The noble man responds with Grand Decline.
> Fath. 9: The culmination of great light
> Means: It would not be right to stay[48] this process.[49]

Appraisal 9 aptly describes an extreme Response. Fortunately, it correlates here with auspicious Day. The earliest commentators tend to see in this poem a reference to the selfless leader ceding his throne to a worthy disciple in order to prolong an era of supreme brilliance (the great light) beyond his own allotted lifespan.[50]

Despite the auspicious character of this Appraisal, later commentators (beginning with Ssu-ma Kuang) read into the verses a far less rosy picture: The gentleman is forced to tender his resignation in the face of a corrupt court.[51] In this interpretation, the position can be called lucky only in some limited sense: the gentleman remembers his duty and performs it gracefully.

I suggest that the lines may, in fact, have no political import at all. The *Changes* includes a striking image, in which

> men either beat the pot and sing or loudly bewail the approach of old age in the shimmering light of the setting sun.[52]

Human mortality stands in stark contrast to the regular, eternal movements of the universe. As the poet Catullus wrote, "Suns may set and rise again. For us, when the short light has once set, there remains to be slept the sleep of one unbroken night." The petty man feels ill-used by Time. The superior man, in contrast, is defined by his ability to respond productively to the entire range of changing situations. He is wise enough to accept his old age and impending demise as part of the larger eternal pattern. Rather than railing against the inevitable, he uses the precious time that remains to him to benefit society. In this way, he exemplifies psychic equilibrium and inner peace.

Ying
No. 42. Going to Meet
June 24 (p.m.)–June 28

Correlates with Earth's Mystery; Yin; the phase Water; and the Yi ching *Hexagram no. 31, Influence; the sun enters the Ghost constellation, 1st degree*

HEAD: Yin *ch'i* takes shape below. Things all turn toward [it][1] to welcome it.

This tetragram begins the second half of the *Mystery*, which is assigned to the latter half of the calendar year. In this period, yin *ch'i* grows stronger every day. In contrast with Head texts of the preceding forty-one tetragrams, therefore, each Head text from now on will open with the phrase "yin *ch'i*." Still, aside from this, there are few indications in this season of late summer that yang *ch'i* is losing control. For a while longer, yang will seem to continue at the height of its powers. The myriad things, in consequence, must go against the apparent prevailing trend in order to align themselves with this new cosmic trend as they come to maturity; hence, the reference to "turning" to welcome yin *ch'i*.[2]

This tetragram, like its predecessor, considers the themes of "stimulus," "response," and "mutual influence"; it presumes that by simple laws of mutual attraction and mutual repulsion change in one part of the universe immediately alters all other entities that are categorically related to it. (See Key Terms on correlative thinking.)[3] Here the *Mystery* mainly focuses upon aspects of physical and political responsiveness, which correspond to two paradigms of strong sympathetic response: sexual relations between husband and wife and the mutual dependence of ruler and subject. While the spread of mutual influence is often slow, as the imagery emphasizes, such influence is eventually pervasive.

> App. 1: Meeting another, he does not respond.[4]
> Lacking the good, he is perverse.[5]
> Fath. 1: In meeting another, not responding
> Means: He is not one whom you should join.

For some reason, a preliminary meeting between potential partners fails to induce a climate of mutual sympathy. At least one of the parties must be at fault since a true meeting of the minds depends on virtue.[6] It would be counterproductive, as well as wrong, to form an alliance with an evil person. The gentleperson is careful to make friends only with people of his or her own sort.

> App. 2: The scaly dragon, plunging to[7] the depths
> Induces its eggs on the heights to quicken.[8]
> Though some men talk in darkness,
> The Hundred Clans respond to them.
> Fath. 2: Transformations by dragons in hiding
> Mean: The center essence is integrity.

According to legend, the female scaly dragon leaves her watery home in the abyss to deposit her eggs on a mountainside before returning to deep waters. Miraculously, at the right time the eggs hatch spontaneously, revealing in each a tiny, but fully individuated dragonlet—all without direct intervention by their mother.[9] A second legend says that the egg of the scaly dragon is produced from the mating of snake and pheasant. The egg is then drawn irresistibly to watery pools, where the egg metamorphoses into a dragon.[10] Both traditions reflect the Chinese notion of mutual interaction by category, by which transformations over time and space take place by laws of mutual sympathy, rather than Newtonian laws of cause-and-effect.

The dragon, of course, stands for the moral superior, especially the ruler; the egg, for the less developed human being. Though both parties seem to inhabit entirely different spheres, the moral superior miraculously affects others, who learn by suasive influence to develop properly into full human beings.[11]

> App. 3: The quintessential stuff of things
>> Travels subtly back and forth.[12]
>> Ill omens precede the quickest senses.[13]
> Fath. 3: The essence, all unseen, goes back and forth.
>> Meaning: Evil omens are proof of blame.[14]

Since each of the myriad things is composed of numinous *ch'i*,[15] in some sense all parts of the cosmos can resonate with others because of their underlying sympathy. The gods and spirits are only the most exquisitely sensitive (and therefore, reactive) members of the universe since their constitutive *ch'i* is particularly subtle and concentrated ("quintessential"). By definition, the sage has acquired similar divine powers of perception. Omen theory tells us that the gods, spirits, and sages react immediately to the slightest moral shift on the part of other human beings. Even such swift reactions, however, lag behind the spontaneous production of portents in the cosmos. The merest inclination towards evil on the part of those in power, for example, produces serious dislocations in the starry heavens. In this Appraisal, dedicated to the transition from thought to action, we are reminded that our innermost thoughts soon prompt visible reactions. We must take special care, then, not to depart from the Way, lest we disorder the entire cosmic fabric.[16]

> App. 4: For trousers, there are always tops,
>> And for men with eyes shiny as pearls,
>> Women with lashes curving like hooks.[17]
>> This is right and good.
> Fath. 4: Trousers matched to tops
>> Mean: Yin stimulates yang.

Sexual attraction is proper and natural, so long as the partners are suitably mated; without it, the human race could not continue.[18] Here, the luminously clear pupils of the man's eyes indicate his upright character,[19] while the gentle curve of the woman's lashes suggests her willingness to respond sexually.[20] Several points in the poem should be noted. Trousers and tops point to penis and breasts, but the Chinese assumed that it is the woman who often plays the role of sexual initiator.

Then comes the play upon pearls and fishhooks: both belong to the watery realm, and sexual intercourse promotes the production of watery fluids. Finally, the fishhook is used to catch fish and oysters, while the seductive curve of the eyelashes "hooks" a man.

> App. 5: When yellow rides high,[21]
> It obstructs the good.
> Fath. 5: That yellow's rise bodes ill
> Means: One cannot make friends with it.

Yellow as the color assigned to the center is usually auspicious. Here, the problem is that yellow mounts to the top position. (This may refer to the increasing ascendancy of yin *ch'i* following the summer solstice.) Yellow no longer knows its place, so its characteristic virtues of self-abnegation, loyalty, and good faith fail utterly. Perhaps a trusted subordinate intends to usurp his superior's position,[22] for the word "rises" also means "to bully." Those with great ambitions make the worst allies.

> App. 6: Black Heaven meets Yellow Earth.[23]
> Their ideas interact, one upon the other.[24]
> Fath. 6: Black and yellow meeting
> Means: They respond by type.

Black is the color of Heaven; yellow, that of Earth. The interaction of these two cosmic powers is said to produce timely wind and rain,[25] which all the myriad things depend upon for life. As the *Changes* says:

> Heaven and Earth[26] come together, and the myriad things are transformed in pristine form. Male and female blend their essences, and the myriad things are transformed and engendered.[27]

All successful relations between partners are modelled on these momentous cosmic meetings. Since all things respond by type, the good person cannot attract evil friends, any more than the mating call of a warbler could attract a hawk.[28]

> App. 7: From a distance, he glares in anger.
> Coming nearer, he knocks him down.
> To meet with a father should be happy.[29]
> Fath. 7: Glaring from afar, striking when near,
> Means: He has lost the idea of "father."

By rights, the bond between parent and child should be the most intimate of all human relations.[30] Here instead, father and son are estranged, presumably because of the son's lack of virtue. (A truly virtuous son would continue to esteem even the worst father, as the ancient sage-king Shun is said to have done.) So serious is the estrangement that a blow is struck, though by Chinese law a child who struck a parent faced the death penalty.[31] This injustice indicates the bitter opposition that prevails between superior and inferior at all levels.[32]

> App. 8: Seeing blood pour through the gates,
> He keeps it away from center court.[33]
> Fath. 8: Seeing blood enter the gates
> Means: By worthiness he protects himself.

Trouble appears on the scene. The wise person prevents more pervasive disaster (the inner courtyard symbolizes the inmost self and the core of any social unit) by virtuous action and the reliance on good advisors (i.e., by using one's own worth and that of others).[34]

> App. 9: Damp that meets the foot of the bed
> Seeps into[35] the adjoining room.
> Fath. 9: Damp meeting the foot of the bed
> Means: The collapse occurs within.

Like damp spreading throughout the house, contagion is now pervasive. Since the problem is water (aligned with yin *ch'i*), the problem may well have arisen because of evil women or subordinates. Though the change has been gradual, by the end of the cycle in Appraisal 9, the inner bases of self and society are so completely rotten that evil cannot be easily destroyed. Such ruin is "total" in that it involves all parts, both high and low;[36] the imminent collapse will soon engulf all members of society.

Correlates with Earth's Mystery; Yang; the phase Fire; and the Yi ching Hexagram no. 44, Encountering; the sun enters the Willow constellation, 1st degree

Yü

No. 43. Encounters
June 29–July 3 (a.m.)

HEAD: As yin *ch'i* starts to come, yang *ch'i* starts to go. Going and coming, they encounter each other on the way.

Shortly after the summer solstice we see yin *ch'i* begin to wax in power (that is, it "comes"),[1] although much of its activity still goes largely unnoticed. Remember, as early as Tetragram 31, entitled "Packing," yang *ch'i* had been making preparations to depart. One commentator attributes yang's earlier dilatory action to its increasing enfeeblement, but now it is forced to leave under pressure from its opponent, yin *ch'i*.[2] On the model of yin and yang, certain kinds of imbalance, if mediated by ritual, can lead to productive situations: for example, the ruler condescends to humble himself before his officials, and the groom abases himself in welcoming his new bride to the household. However, imbalance that ignores ritual is inherently unlucky; hence, the Appraisal depicts various encounters with all types of evil men, including bullies, slanderers, and unfilial children.

> App. 1: Meeting the gods in darkness[3]
> Until even dreams instruct,[4]
> This is a good sign.
> Fath. 1: Meeting the gods in secret
> Means: Thoughts attain the proper pattern.

Appraisal 1 often describes hidden or formless thoughts that have not as yet been translated into action. Dreams clearly reveal the hidden preoccupations of the heart and mind.[5] For most of us, our dreams seem wild and disordered, since we fail to perceive the fundamental patterns underlying phenomenal existence. But dreams of the truly good reflect an intuitive knowledge of cosmic order, leading one to further careful consideration of the Way. As one early text asks:

> Can you concentrate? Can you adhere to the Unity of Nature? . . .
> Think about it! Think about it! And think of it again! Then the ghosts and gods will teach it. It is not actually that the gods and gods will teach it, but that it reflects the culminating development of the essential *ch'i*.[6]

The Ch'ing scholar Yü Yüeh reads the Appraisal text differently:

> In darkness, to meet the gods.
> Dreams of blind men.
> Rectitude.

On the basis of other passages in the *Mystery*, Yü Yüeh believes that the reader is directed to consider the special gifts of the blind music masters of old. Such men were regularly favored by the gods with special communications, even though (or possibly, because?) they lacked the normal faculty of sight.

> App. 2: To come upon a conceited[7] child,
> Who rejects teachings prescribed for him.[8]
> Fath. 2: Encountering the fractious child
> Means: He is an unworthy son.

Immature, truculent and conceited, the youth knows nothing, yet he resists all attempts at instruction. How can he prove himself worthy to carry on the family name? The moral foundation of the adult is built by proper molding of the child within the family circle.[9]

> App. 3: They neither meet illicitly
> > Nor do they think at all of gain.[10]
> > Such is good conduct for knights and ladies.
> Fath. 3: Neither going nor seeking
> > Means: This is the rule for gentlefolk.

Ritual dictates that the gentleman cannot act as his own matchmaker, nor can he promote himself at court. Similarly, a real lady does not seek out her own husband. This reticence stems from three causes: First, it would appear arrogant to put forward for consideration one's own claims to merit.[11] Second, most adult relations are strictly ruled by hierarchies of gender, age, and status; self-promotion undercuts those necessary orders. Third, the truly superior person devotes his or her whole self to Goodness, rather than to external accomplishment.[12]

> App. 4: Utterly exhausted,[13] the "opener,"[14]
> > Having brought the rain, is endangered.
> Fath. 4: That the "opener" encounters rain
> > Means: It turns out he harms himself.[15]

In ancient China, in times of drought it was customary to force important religious leaders (magicians and sometimes even kings) to expose themselves in a courtyard or square. The theory was that the gods, taking pity on their wretched naked state, would shower rain down upon them.[16] It was also the custom for magicians and shamanesses to perform rain dances. Paradoxically, perhaps, the one who forces the skies to open may harm himself in the process: either the frenzied dancing works so well that a cold shower of rain ends in giving the dancer a bad chill, or the "opener" deludes himself into thinking that by his own actions he can command the gods. The opener, then, could symbolize two different flawed personality types. The first secures his own downfall by acting without sufficient forethought.[17] The second mistakenly takes undeserved, even coincidental success as a mark of his own inherent superiority.[18]

> App. 5: Out hunting, he comes upon game.
> > None forbid his taking it.
> Fath. 5: That the hunter chances upon game
> > Means: It truly is encouraging.

In a yang tetragram, Appraisal 5 depicts the culmination of good fortune. The hunter inadvertently stumbles across his prey. No one would prevent him from taking advantage of his good fortune. By analogy, the truly good person in single-minded pursuit of the Way may somehow stumble upon high office and riches in the process of self-cultivation. Though the good person does not make material success his primary goal,[19] all right-thinking men take pleasure in cases where virtue is rewarded.

> App. 6: The lowly[20] spider, in weaving its web,
>   Comes upon a wasp.
>   However great the profit,
>   It cannot follow through.
> Fath. 6: The lowly spider's web
>   Means: Harm is not far away.

Obviously, the spider weaves its web to catch small insects. However, a wasp in the web spells trouble, partly because of its disproportionate size,[21] and partly because of its stinger. Since the spider cannot disarm its victim without risking injury to itself, the spider's very success leads to its possible destruction. The lesson is clear: do not be indiscriminate in the pursuit of profit; otherwise, your initially successful schemes may have unwonted consequences.

> App. 7: He brandishes his horn, eager to defend
>   Ruler and father from further insult,
>   Though such a fate is undeserved.[22]
> Fath. 7: Raising his horn
>   Means: Straight on the Way he proceeds.[23]

The image of "brandishing the horn" comes from the correspondent hexagram in the *Changes*:

> Coming to meet with his horns. Humiliation. No blame. . . . At the
> top, utter humiliation.[24]

Appraisal 7 marks the Beginning of Calamity, but in this tetragram it is aligned with auspicious day; once again, we can expect no blame. Righteous anger is displayed in the defense of worthy superiors. Though the loyal subordinate faces possible death, he never swerves from duty.[25] In this dire prospect, we detect the growing influence of yin *ch'i*, associated with decline and sorrow.

> App. 8: Two wild oxen clash in battle.
>   The one that loses its horn
>   Will not conquer death.[26]

Fath. 8: Two locked in mortal combat
    Means: Lost weapons spell certain death.

The strength of the wild ox or rhinoceros (early texts do not clearly distinguish between the two) resides in its horn; that's what gives it sufficient confidence to engage its foes in battle. Here two opponents, evenly matched at the outset, meet in bloody battle until the loss of one animal's horn renders it completely defenseless in the fray.[27] Certain death follows for the loser. From this we learn that it is dangerous to miscalculate either our strength or that of an opponent.[28] We are also cautioned against entering crucial battles in which the outcome depends solely on a single advantage or tool.

App. 9: The enemy's blow, though deflected,[29]
    Hits lower by chance, wounding the foot.[30]
Fath. 9: Fending off its horn
    Means: How can one escape unscathed?[31]

Near the end of the cycle, a person is lucky if he manages to escape total destruction. An attack aimed at the highest levels is only partially deflected.[32]

Correlates with Earth's Mystery;
Yin; the phase Wood; and the Yi
ching Hexagram no. 50, Tripod;
the sun enters the Willow constel-
lation, 6th degree; the Dipper
points SSW; the musical note is G^1

Tsao
No. 44. Stove
July 3 (p.m.)–July 7

HEAD: Though yin, being moist, would sprinkle them, yang, still hot, would blend them.[2]

Appraisal 7 of this tetragram sees the end of the Summer Solstice solar period. The influence of yin *ch'i* steadily waxes while that of yang continually wanes. Still, at this point, the heat of yang is so intense that it apparently continues to affect the growth of the myriad things, despite yin's counterimpulses. The stove is the place where flavors are blended. In Chinese terms, flavors are characterized as cold or hot, by analogy

周
史
頌
鼎

Figure 12. A tripod. Illustration from Hsi ch'ing ku chien *3/21a. Similar bronze tripods are frequently depicted in Han art. One tripod carved on the ceiling at Wu-liang-ts'e is identified by a cartouche as, "a divine tripod, which cooks without fire and produces the five flavours spontaneously." The* Mo tzu *talks of magical tripods "that boil, though they have not been fired, that put themselves in storage, though they have not been lifted, that transport themselves, though they have not been moved."*

with yin/yang. The stove serves, then, as an apt symbol for the characteristic mixing of yin and yang that now occurs. The stove also signifies the
harmony and material wealth associated with the extended family unit.
Finally, in certain early texts, the master of the stove, the knowledgeable
chef, becomes a metaphor for the good teacher and perfect ruler.[3] This
metaphor presumes the *Changes's* remark that cooking has two main purposes: to prepare sacrifices to the gods and to feast worthy officials at
court.[4] Accordingly, this tetragram examines the true king's care of
worthy officials, though it omits all explicit reference to state religion.

In the Chinese mind, the tripod and the stove on which it sits are inextricably connected. (Compare the title of the correspondent *Changes*
hexagram.) Out of the tripod come marvelous, even demonic things, as
out of a great primordial soup.[5] Along with its ancient religious significance, the tripod also represents the conferral of legitimate political authority, as in the famous Nine Cauldrons of the legendary sage ruler Yü.
Cast bronze, of course, was a luxury good whose use was reserved for the
political elite. But bronze cauldrons in their technical perfection also symbolized the full range of social and legal institutions provided by the sages
to enable many different types of people to coexist successfully.[6] Ultimately, bronze ritual vessels suggest close cooperation between the ruler
and the gods, ancestors, and common people, while the three legs of the
tripod specifically recall the interdependence of the triadic realms of
Heaven-Earth-Man and the king's three chief ministers.[7] Finally, the
circular forms of the tripod's looped handles promise eternity through
cyclical renewal; for this reason, the "tripod means taking up the new."[8]
Each of these associations comes into play in the Appraisals below.

> App. 1: When there is no food in the stove,[9]
> He begs from neighbors.
> Fath. 1: The empty stove
> Means: He bears an empty reputation.

The interpretation of this poem depends upon a pun: the Chinese
character for "food" also means "substance" or "authentic nature." Since
the sole function of a stove is to cook food, a stove that lacks food is like
a person who lacks fundamental integrity and merit.[10] The sole function
of Man, after all, is to realize his inherent potential for Goodness, turning
his "uncooked" or "raw" capacities into a finished person of self-cultivation. Therefore, a person who appears to be human but lacks true
humanity is no less dysfunctional than a stove without food. Though the
individual may win material wealth or high position, he holds an empty,
borrowed reputation. No help from friends or allies can do him any
permanent good. Bad luck surely follows, as in the related omen of the

basket with no fruit in it.[11] Only the person who hungers to be filled may improve over time.[12]

> App. 2: The golden[13] tripod is immense,[14]
>> Its center bowl matches its size.[15]
>> Still, they do not eat nor do they drink.
>> Truly, there is no harm.
> Fath. 2: An immense golden tripod
>> Means: At center, incorruptible and good.[16]

In antiquity, the polished bronze tripod was reserved for luxury items, such as meat stews or warmed wine, to be consumed either by the gods or by high-ranking members of the court. The tripod may be compared to the charismatic virtue of a good person in that it represents an inexhaustible store of riches, always ready for use, that sustains others. So mysterious and great, in fact, are the tripod's powers (and those of Goodness, by analogy) that ordinary individuals need not actively resort to it to receives its benefits. Advantages multiply throughout society precisely because the good person conforms to the wisdom of the ages no less perfectly than the bowl of the tripod conforms to its outer shape.

Still, the exact connotation of the line, "They do not drink, nor do they eat," may be debated. At least we know it cannot imply praise of asceticism *per se*, since that is an idea foreign to pre-Buddhist China.[17] Since Appraisal 2 corresponds to those of low rank not yet in service, perhaps they "do not dare to eat"[18] (of official salary) because the time is still too early. According to this reading, the good and humble person, despite enormous talents (akin to the bowl's great capacity), patiently develops his capacities, awaiting later opportunities for action; foregoing all present claims to recognition, he is happy to offer the use of his many talents to those above. In this reading, the empty bowl hints at the gentleperson's propensity for nurturing the virtue of "inner emptiness."[19] In an alternate reading, an incorruptible official of great capacity chooses "not to eat" (i.e., accept court salary) under an evil regime.[20]

> App. 3: There is no firewood in the stove.
>> The golden vessel is set aside.[21]
> Fath. 3: That the stove lacks wood
>> Means: What one has cannot be used.

Here the *Mystery* plays upon another pun, with a synonym for firewood meaning "talent" or "capacity."[22] Even the best of rulers must depend upon worthy officials to disseminate his policies among the common people. In this, the ruler is like the stove, which requires firewood to function, no matter how fine it is.

App. 4: Eating food from the tripod steamer,[23]
    He gains the strength to toil.[24]
Fath. 4: Eating the steamer's food
    Means: It is offered to us in time.[25]

In contrast to Appraisal 3, here the wise individual has properly prepared and used his cooking utensils. Seeds have been planted, food harvested, and brushwood gathered to make a fire. When the proper time comes to employ his strength, the individual will not only experience no difficulty in securing his just deserts; he will also find that he has grown from his efforts, just as rice doubles or triples in size when cooked.[26] The moral person can expect good results when following the Way of the sages.[27]

App. 5: The large tripod can be used as goblet[28]
    But this is neither pious nor dignified.
Fath. 5: The large tripod serving as goblet
    Means: The feast then lacks all meaning.

Appraisal 5 describes the Son of Heaven. In antiquity, Heaven conferred upon the emperor a set of nine Great Tripods as symbols of legitimate authority. When the Son of Heaven in turn wished to confer special favors upon his vassal lords, he also had ritual vessels cast in commemoration of his subordinates' meritorious service.[29] The bronze tripod, then, as a mark of supreme favor and legitimate appointment is reserved for the most sacred of ceremonies; it should not be used for more mundane purposes[30] by those who are "neither pious nor dignified." In this case, those in power may be besotted with drink.[31] Certainly, they fail to understand the critical importance of making distinctions; if they mistake a tripod for a goblet, they are likely to mistake great for small in moral and political matters as well.

App. 6: The Five Tastes are blended properly,
    The flavors are balanced and fine.
    A feast fit for the great man.[32]
Fath. 6: A feast where flavors are harmonized
    Means: This is the duty of ministers.

The pot stands for society or the state. The Five Tastes are its various components. "Great man" is a term used either for the ruler or for the noble men in his service.[33] By a pun[34] the chief minister of the state acts as chef-manager for the feast.

Numerous classical texts urge the ruler to seek out worthy candidates for office, who can aid him in the difficult enterprise of ruling. The day-today job of coordinating the diverse talents of these great men shifted from the emperor to the prime minister by late Western Han, as increasing conservatism required the ruler to distance himself from mundane administrative affairs.[35]

> App. 7: The fattened ox is perfectly plump
> But if cooked in an unwashed pot,
> Retching and gagging[36] result.
> Fath. 7: A fattened ox, then retching
> Means: Impure are their goals.

Animal fat imparts tenderness and flavor to the dish. Here the animal has been prepared for the feast, but the cook ignores simple precautions in its preparation. As a result, sickness, rather than satiety and good health, follows. Since no flaw exists in the basic material, one's actions must be at fault. If one's intentions are bad, even a ritual gift will provoke revulsion. Extreme caution must be exercised when offerings are prepared, lest bodily harm result.

The metaphor applies to the political sphere as well. Rulers can secure the help of worthy candidates for office only if they first make sufficient preparations in self-cultivation.[37] High salary alone cannot induce good men to put up with a ruler whose conduct disgusts them.[38]

> App. 8: If he eats what he has stored,[39]
> Despite an outcry, no harm[40] is done.
> Fath. 8: Eating what he has stored
> Means: He is lavished with his ruler's favor.

Stored grain implies the prosperity and security brought about by providential behavior. The good farmer need not want for anything so long as he consumes only what he has earned. Similarly, the good official enjoys his ruler's favor because of his hard work. Though others, acting out of envy, may object to his high rank and salary, it is no more than the good official deserves.

Several of the commentators offer a different reading, however:

> He has eaten his commission.
> Despite his outcry [at the ruler's faults],
> [The ruler] does not think [him] slanderous.
> Eating his commission
> Means: He is lavished with his [ruler's] favor.[41]

The good official, having taken a salary from his ruler, hastens to remonstrate against any faults of his superior. The wise ruler in return recognizes his official's loyalty and showers him with awards and appointments.

App. 9: Once the fire in the stove is put out,
   Nothing but disaster comes to the house.
Fath. 9: That the stove's fire is extinguished
   Means: It takes away from the state.

Traditionally, when a family line was destroyed, its stove was dismantled. And when a dynastic line was destroyed, its conqueror laid waste to the altar sites where burnt offerings had once been made to the patron gods of the former ruling house. Destruction of the stove represents final death for the family and state; no hope for revival remains. It is now far too late to apply the earlier, relatively simple solution of "using firewood" (i.e., worthy talent) to fire up the stove.

Correlates with Earth's Mystery;
Yang; *the phase Metal; and the*
Yi ching *Hexagram no. 55,*
Abundance; the sun enters the
Willow constellation, 10th degree

Ta
No. 45. Greatness
July 8–July 12 (a.m.)

HEAD: While yin[1] empties out what is inside,[2] yang increases[3] what is outside. Things are like basins and canopies.[4]

Despite its apparent strength outside, yang *ch'i* is steadily drained by yin's inexorable increase. The particular form of the interaction between yin and yang *ch'i* mimics, as it happens, the archaic character meaning "to join" 合, which shows a covered vessel. The universe itself is envisioned as a canopy or inverted basin, with the broad sweep of the late summer sky sheltering the blasted earth below. The myriad things in imitation grow hollow inside and overextended outside.

Such images may be important for several reasons: First, Hexagram 55 in the *Changes*, the counterpart to this tetragram, repeatedly mentions things (such as curtains and underbrush) which screen off the light,[5] thereby obscuring heavenly patterns. The canopy in particular, of course, is an apt symbol for late summer, since heat and glare prompt its frequent use. Second, insofar as the myriad things' functioning depends on maintaining Tao as center, they are like a canopy that revolves around a central fixed point. Third, the Kai-t'ien ("Cover Heaven") astronomical theory originally favored by Yang Hsiung imagined the heavens as a giant canopy arched over the earth, with the cosmic axis as handle;[6] once again, this cover extending over emptiness is positioned by its center.[7] Not surprisingly, centrality and emptiness, then, become two of the main themes of the Appraisals. The sophisticated reader will also note the Appraisals' play on several cognate characters, all of which have "small" imbedded in the graph.[8] As we learn from the correspondent *Changes* hexagram, true greatness is defined in terms of "attaining a place at which one is at home." The gentleman makes the Tao his home.

> App. 1: The pool so deep and broad
>   Cradles all sides in darkness.[9]
> Fath. 1: The deep, broad pool
>   Means: It envelops an infinity of things.

Appraisal 1 corresponds to Water; hence, the metaphor of the pool. It also signifies beginnings: on the personal level, the Beginning of Thought, and on the cosmic level, the primordial *ch'i* of the mysterious Tao from which all forms evolve. Since the pool (the mind, the Tao) is infinitely vast and deep, its lifegiving substance can nourish all living things; it can never run dry. Yet it draws no attention to itself.[10]

> App. 2: In enlarging its ambitions[11]
>   The self grinds itself down.[12]
> Fath. 2: His growing ambitions
>   Means: He is harmed by his thoughts.

Appraisal 2 describes the ordinary fellow, who in his egotism considers his own mind to be a wondrous pool infinitely "deep and broad." Unfortunately, his actual abilities and rank are inadequate for his grand schemes; he is incapable of handling even the situation at hand. For this reason, the petty man wears himself down in vain attempts to grasp power or solve problems on his own.[13] He would do better to devote his time to study and then apply the ancient models of good behavior to himself. As Confucius remarked, "To think without studying [the Way of the former kings] is dangerous."[14]

Convention compares the process of self-cultivation to the grinding, polishing, and carving of fine jade, which only enhance the value of the already precious material.[15] The petty person who intends to refashion his life never learns to use the right tools if he fails to imitate the inherent modesty of the sages. Like the careless jadecutter, he gouges himself. Inexperience and ineptitude can only harm the self.[16]

> App. 3: Treating the small as great
>   Helps in becoming great.

Fath. 3: Making great use of the small
    Means: He takes the small as the base.

The first lines of Appraisal and Fathoming read literally, "Great not great." Obviously, these lines are open to interpretation. Appraisal 3 marks the transition from thought to action, so probably the *Mystery* intends to teach a familiar lesson: by definition the truly wise pay close attention to the first small signs of change, since no one has sufficient strength to singlehandedly defeat a well-developed trend. The sage looks at small details overlooked by lesser men, making them the secure foundation of his visionary rule.

The commentators unanimously prefer a different reading, however:

The great do not view themselves as great.
It helps to use [this way] to become great.
The great do not view themselves as great,
Meaning: They use "keeping small" as the base.

Either reading is possible. (Compare with Appraisal 6 below.)

App. 4: Though failing to get the knife he needs,
    He enlarges his gates outside the city.[17]
    Such fame is empty.
Fath. 4: Enlarging his gates in suburbs
    Means: As real worth goes, the name comes.

Position 4 corresponds to official rank. Chinese sumptuary rules limit the construction and enlargement of high gates to those honored with high rank by the emperor.[18] Enlargement of the gates, then, constitutes public display of enhanced status. The petty man typically disregards internal reform, concentrating instead on advertising himself. In this, he fails to focus on what is fundamental. That his preoccupations are far from central is indicated by the gate's location out in the country.[19]

The greatness of any house lies in its ability to concentrate its resources. The sharp knife symbolizes the sharp mind able to frame good decisions which benefit the community.[20] The knife also symbolizes money since certain coins were minted in its image.[21] Here the house lacks either the incisive thinking or the material resources it needs to flourish. How long can it sustain itself? Before too long, its reputation will be shown to be hollow.

App. 5: By using the Mean, he draws the outlands[22]
    Into his realm, and so is victorious.[23]
Fath. 5: Bringing them in by centering
    Means: He oversees the Nine Barbarians.

Position 5 is aligned with Earth, with the center, and with humaneness, the binding agent for society. As such, it represents the virtue of Centrality, or "keeping to the Mean." By epitomizing what is central, the true sage eventually gains power and authority over all four corners of the earth.[24] The ruler functions as *axis mundi* around which other things revolve. In return, all peoples are shielded from harm by the royal presence.

> App. 6: The great fail because of the small;[25]
> The many, because of the few.[26]
> Fath. 6: The great failing in the small
> Means: The seemingly insignificant breeds disaster.

If the individual neglects what appear to be only the insignificant beginnings of contrary trends, those unfortunate tendencies will eventually grow to overwhelm present prosperity, much as a large wave overwhelms tiny ripples. The true sage is on the lookout for the first signs of disruption; by taking immediate steps to remedy the situation, he can both adapt to and manipulate the situation for the benefit of the Good. This is no less true in the private world of the soul[27] than in the public world of the court.

> App. 7: Great self-indulgence has led him astray.
> When he limits his cups of wine,
> Others may increase his portion.[28]
> Fath. 7: Indulging to excess, then depriving himself
> Means: He is able to fault himself.[29]

This individual is drunk on wine or on self-importance.[30] To counteract the self-indulgence which clouds his judgment, he must sternly take himself in hand. When he curbs his own vices, he is bound to find others happy to reward him.

> App. 8: When the immense wall with a narrow base
> Goes three years without repairs,
> It collapses.
> Fath. 8: A narrow base for the big wall
> Means: Collapse is not long in coming.

This individual has high rank and considerable fame. Unfortunately, he lacks sufficient moral cultivation to acquit himself honorably. Inevitably, the individual who lacks a strong moral base comes to ruin. To maintain his safety in such a precarious situation, continual care is needed, just as earthen walls must be rebuilt at regular intervals, especially if they are large.[31] "Three years" means "after the cycle is complete," since three is the completion number. "Repair" refers to moral reform. "Collapse" is a customary euphemism for the ruler's demise.

> App. 9: A Great End gained by self-denigration.[32]
> Evil is driven beyond the heavens.
> Fath. 9: Great Ends gained by abnegation
> Mean: Modesty is the stuff of greatness.

The Great End may refer either to a good end (i.e., an honorable death) or to the attainment of life's central ambition. Any person can achieve either of these desirable ends only if he is willing to yield when appropriate, rather than thrust himself forward regardless of consequences.[33] Paradoxically, the greatest goods come to the person who minimizes his own pretensions and claims to understanding.[34]

K'uo
No. 46. Enlargement
July 12 (p.m.)–July 16

Correlates with Earth's Mystery; Yin; the phase Water; and the Yi ching *Hexagram no. 55, Abundance; the sun enters the Willow constellation, 15th degree*

HEAD: Yin *ch'i*, concealed,[1] gathers them in.[2] Yang, still enlarging, opens them up.[3]

Despite its growing strength, yin *ch'i* is still too weak to prevent a final burst of activity and development by the myriad things. Yang *ch'i* in late summer still operates with relative freedom, so that the myriad things enlarge until harvest or hibernation time. Yin *ch'i*, then, is pictured as a kind of "unmoved mover," which acts to counter all tendencies towards proliferation and expansion. The early commentaries in no way object to yin's activities, seeing them as part of the normal cyclical processes, but the later commentaries tend to argue the evils of yin. One commentator says, for example, that yin "hiding [its evil, pretends to] harmonize with and conform to" yang's activity, despite its intention to suck the strength from yang at a later point.[4]

The character used for the tetragram title originally referred to the outer city walls built for defense; hence, the Appraisals' repeated references to architectural forms. It was typical in ancient China to construct the outer city walls first, allowing room for later population growth. For this reason, the tetragram talks of large, even bloated forms encasing empty spaces. Not surprisingly, classical texts use the same graph to describe that individual who combines self-aggrandizement with ignorance.[5] The proverb tells us that, "The largest vessel fills most slowly."[6] That means, rapid expansion often undermines internal solidity. Such lessons apply to the self-cultivation of the individual, of course, as well as to issues of statecraft.

> App. 1: He enlarges and extends it,
>   But the base was not built straight.
> Fath. 1: Enlarging and extending it
>   Means: From the first, the base leans.

The classical *Doctrine of the Mean* stipulates a fixed order for reform: The individual must first rectify himself, then the household, then the state, and finally All-under-Heaven.[7] Here the individual enlarges his power base before achieving full mastery of the Way. Since his base is not "straight" (i.e., in accord with Tao), whatever security he builds is likely to collapse under pressure, just as the physical structure constructed on a faulty foundation is sure to collapse.[8]

> App. 2: Gold posts and jade props
>   Stand large in inner city walls.
> Fath. 2: Gold posts and jade props
>   Means: Many are the supports and uprights.[9]

Posts and props[10] are structural units required in the construction of the strong tamped-earth walls used in all major public works projects in early China, including palace complexes. The excellent material employed in their construction insures durability, strength, and impregnability.[11] The presence of rare gold and jade also points to the singular importance of the site and structure. We should also note the reference here to the inner defensive walls. Primary attention is focused on internal, rather than external matters. From this we see that the wise person intent on constructing a strictly upright moral life is absolutely dependent upon "golden" advice from the sages, whose collective wisdom will help him secure and enhance his position. As Fan Wang writes, "One uses the city wall to guard oneself, just as one employs worthies [as models and as advisors] to protect oneself."[12]

> App. 3: Though enlarging, she bears no son.
>   He beds[13] a barren wife.
> Fath. 3: Great but not with child
>   Means: How can he get descendants?

In Appraisal 3, the transition from thought to action, the individual seeks to enlarge his power base, but lacks the means to bring his plans to completion. The metaphor used is easily understood: The husband, intent upon producing an heir, mistakenly weds a "stone wife," a term which can refer to a barren woman[14] or possibly (more literally) to a stone sculpture carved to commemorate chaste wives. Two lessons are taught here: first, initial miscalculations about one's capacity may preclude final fruition, no matter how many attempts are made; second, apparent capacity should not be confused with real capacity.

> App. 4: Enlarging his gates and doors,
>   He protects himself from robbers and rogues.[15]
> Fath. 4: Enlarging the gates and doors
>   Means: He extends what he plans and builds.[16]

Since the height of gates and doors is strictly regulated by sumptuary laws, raising the height implies a significant improvement in both the resources and the status of the household. At the same time, an enlarged entry implies increased contact with the outside world.[17] Such contact can continue in safety so long as the basic structural elements of the house are strong. By analogy, so long as the good person is strongly committed to the Way, he is able to realize future plans without endangering himself.[18] The gate may also indicate the capital (specifically, the palace complex), while the doors stand for the common people.[19] Merit serves a protective function, increasing support at court and among the populace.[20]

> App. 5: Heaven's gate is opened wide,
>   Extending the steps of its hall.[21]
>   This may give rise to error.
> Fath. 5: That Heaven's gate is opened wide
>   Means: Virtue cannot fill the sacred hall.

Heaven wishes to favor those below, especially the ruling elite, so its gate is opened wide to promote free communication with those on earth. That the steps extend straight to its formal audience hall signifies the relative ease with which the ruler should be able to achieve the fundamental task of bridging Heaven-and-Man by self-cultivation. Unfortunately, the ruler here lacks the requisite virtue to act as partner to Heaven;[22] ignoring Heaven's manifest desire to help, the ruler makes no effort to grow in wisdom and in truth. Instead, the bad ruler views every natural advantage and possible opportunity as a way to increase his hold over others. Sooner or later, it will become obvious that he cannot hope to measure up in terms of virtue. Rulers like this, even though they may have "ascended to the hall," have "not entered the inner sanctum."[23]

> App. 6: With plenty the norm, how lofty his reign [24]
>   The Hundred Lords[25] give staunch support.[26]
>   This is what his virtue begets.[27]

> Fath. 6: That all is abundance and all is lofty
> Means: This is what we call the Great Peace.

The good ruler consolidates his political power through the exercise of his charismatic virtue. He provides material abundance for his many subjects (The Hundred Lords are his feudal lords.); his grace is also abundant enough to induce their moral transformation. He is lofty in three related senses: First, he exemplifies the tradition handed down from the great sage kings of yore. Second, he strengthens ties between Man, the gods, and the ancestors in Heaven. Third, he is far superior to all others in moral and political terms. Such a wise emperor is supported by other noble men (defined by either birth or virtue). As his policies take effect throughout the land, the perfect social order known as the Great Peace is ushered in.

> App. 7: Outside he is high and mighty.[28]
> At center, though, he fails.
> The noble man is sent to the wilds,
> While petty men enter his chambers.
> Fath. 7: That the outside is high and mighty
> Means: At center, he has no men worthy of the name.

The phrase "no men" traditionally refers to a dearth of loyal supporters, rather than the complete absence of subjects. Mencius writes:

> As a rule, a state without law-abiding families and reliable officials
> . . . will perish.[29]

Position 7 marks the Beginning of Calamity. The evil king may appear all-powerful to others, but his rule will ultimately fail since he exiles worthy men from court and surrounds himself with petty sycophants. In his crazed desire for increased power, he has neglected what is crucial to the maintenance of that power. Nothing could be worse for the state.

> App. 8: Enlarging their outside, hollowing their inside
> Is best for drums and signal-bells.[30]
> Fath. 8: Enlarging the outside, emptying the inside
> Means: Only then can one be heard.

Yang Hsiung occasionally likes to upset conventional expectations. Most of the Appraisals for this tetragram warn against enlarging the exterior while ignoring the crucial foundation of the interior. But then, just as we are tempted to make a hard and fast rule on this point, Yang reminds us to measure all conduct against the specific case at hand. In some instances, like that of the ritual bell and drum, the effectiveness of an object depends entirely on the combination of a large outside with an empty inside.[31] And so we are led to a more subtle understanding of the terms "greatness" and "emptiness": Greatness implies power, but power can either derive from virtue or from misguided self-aggrandizement. Emptiness can convey either receptivity to the Tao or empty-headed unconcern for the one true Way.

Since bells and drums are a necessary part of ritual life (at home, on the battlefield, and at court), they suggest that the good man's influence grows wider the more he relies on the unseen and the empty (i.e., the humble heart). Because bells and drums set the beat, their rhythms also signify the moderation and self-restraint required of the truly moral individual.

> App. 9: He builds the largest of very high walls.[32]
>> In three years, he has no servants.
> App. 9: Maximizing the size of the wall
>> Means: In the end, none are willing to serve.

Position 9 corresponds to the Height of Calamity, so Yang Hsiung depicts an extreme situation in which the ruler forfeits his throne. The imagery here suggests the ruler's multiple failures in knowing when to stop.[33] Perhaps Yang Hsiung is criticizing the megalomaniacal construction projects favored by the First Emperor of Ch'in and Emperor Wu of Han. Perhaps the wall construction signals the ruler's unwillingness to preserve lines of communication between the throne and its subjects.[34] (External signs of political power, after all, are less crucial in determining the strength of the empire than the ruler's ability to secure the loyalty of his people.) Finally, the high protective walls may alert us to the poverty of the corrupt ruler's inner soul.[35] The *Changes* warns, "To be in high position, yet lack the people's support, . . . that man will have cause for regret at every turn."[36]

Wen
No. 47. Pattern
July 17–July 21 (a.m.)

Correlates with Earth's Mystery;
Yang; *the phase Fire; and the* Yi
ching *Hexagram no. 59, Dispersal;*[1] *the sun enters the Star constellation, 4th degree*

HEAD: As yin gathers their plainness to itself, yang disperses their patterns. "The plain and the patterned are interspersed"[2] so that the myriad things grow bright and beautiful.

The Head text explores one of the most fundamental patterns in the Chinese universe: yin is associated with the unadorned, hidden, inner core, while yang is tied to the multiplicity of forms that evolve from it. Pattern (especially, the relation between the societal patterns we call "culture," the behavioral patterns we call "conduct," and the cosmic patterns we call "portents") is perhaps the single most important preoccupation of Han thinkers. Even thought itself is basically conceived of as the process whereby underlying, significant patterns are extracted from the many disparate bits of information fed to the heart/mind by the sensory organs.[3] This process produces an evaluating mind able to judge proper moral direction. Once each phenomenon is assigned its correct categorical (or correlative) value, events and things are seen to operate by invariable cosmic patterns. Many early Chinese thinkers were intent upon discovering the cosmic laws in order to find ways of manipulating the course of future events, but the *Mystery* focuses upon a series of statements drawn from the Confucian Classics that relate pattern to culture and sagehood.

Four passages are most important to understanding this tetragram. The first characterizes ritual in terms of pattern:

> Tzu-hsia asked the meaning of the poem:
>
>> Oh the sweet smile dimpling.
>> The lovely eyes so black and white!
>> Plain silk that you would take
>> For coloured stuff.
>
> The Master said, "The painting comes after the plain groundwork."
> Tzu-hsia said, "Then ritual comes afterwards?" The Master replied,
> "Ah, . . . At last I have someone with whom I can discuss the Odes."[4]

The second quotation describes the noble man as one who (not unlike the cosmos) represents a balance between the plain and the patterned:

> When natural substance prevails over ornamentation, you get the boorishness of the rustic. When ornamentation prevails over substance, you get the pedantry of the scribe. Only when ornamentation and substance are duly blended do you get the true gentleman.[5]

A third passage compares the gentleman to two marvelous animals known for both beauty and strength:

> [He who effects] great change is like a tiger, his patterns distinctive. . . . The superior man changes like a leopard, his markings fine. The small man [merely] changes his spots.[6]

The fourth depicts the sage as one who has fully internalized the cosmic patterns and so is able to induce societal order among his fellow men:

[Only the sage] could copy it [the patterned nature of Heaven]. . . .
Sublime are his achievements, dazzling the manifestations of his [internal] pattern.[7]

This series of four quotations reveals a kind of progression, which mirrors the development of the individual soul. Achievement necessarily begins with attention to the "plain groundwork," that is, building a solid basis in integrity. Next comes the pattern, for "a gentleman in his pursuit of the Way does not get there unless he manages to exemplify a beautiful pattern."[8] If the human being goes on to fully develop his innate potential by imitation of the Ancients,[9] we have the brilliance of the sage, who draws his inspiration for cultural patterns from the regular movements of Nature. The course of humanity is, thus, to "first cultivate the self and later make it pervade [the outer world]."[10]

These quotations, however, do not provide an answer to the fundamental question, "How can a person distinguish the right patterns of the moral superior from the deceptively pleasing patterns of the petty individual?" Part of the *Mystery's* answer can be gleaned from the arrangement of the Appraisals. In general, the vigor of the early lines is associated with plainness. As the tetragram moves towards the end of the cycle, ornate pattern takes over, becoming ever more complicated until it threatens to obscure the basic substance entirely. This has implications for the development of the heart/mind, of course, but also for court policy as well.[11] The Appraisals suggest that the court forego excessive expenditure on finery and palace carvings, both to conserve wealth for more important uses and to set a proper example for its subjects.[12]

App. 1: For collar and lapel, why use undyed silk?
     For its jade-like purity.
Fath. 1: For collar and lapel, why the undyed silk?
     Meaning: Its pattern lies within.

Appraisal 1 typically describes the shadowy, undeveloped inner core of the human being. Here it contrasts the undyed silk used for interfacing with the figured silk preferred for the outer clothing. Plain raw silk is like the unadorned substance in human nature at birth. The subtle patterns of the silk that lie within the lining material give shape to the whole, though the surface patterns of dyed silk are much more obvious. By analogy, the good person builds upon the innate potential for Goodness when striving to internalize the pattern of the sages; later, plain thoughts can be translated into the brilliant insignia of culture. As the anecdote about Tzu-hsia shows, just as the painting comes after the groundwork, so does ritual come after the proper internal attitude is established.[13]

The traditional commentators, however, interpret the lines in light of the following passage from the "Doctrine of the Mean":

> Over the embroidered robe she puts a plain singlet, suggesting a dislike of the obvious display of pattern found in the robe. . . . [Similarly,] the gentleman works for the concealment of his virtue.[14]

The poem then would read:

> The embroidered[15] collar[16] is covered
> With undyed silk as pure as jade.
> Undyed silk on embroidered collar
> Means: The pattern lies within.

Both interpretations emphasize the superior man's integrity over external marks of culture. Either reading is linguistically possible, but the first provides a better contrast with Appraisal 2. Also, the second reading seems to pertain to a time later in the cycle.

> App. 2: The pattern is richly figured,
>   But the base material is bad.
> Fath. 2: Embellishments without substance
>   Mean: Both cannot be equally fine.

Confucius once said of a lazy student, "Rotten wood cannot be carved nor a wall of dry dung trowelled."[17] Outward embellishment cannot hide a lack of inner quality. Real cultivation (defined as attaining the pattern of true humanity) is possible only when it develops from a firm core of integrity. "Embellishment that lacks substance provokes resentment,"[18] so danger lies ahead. This is a different point from that made by Lao tzu and Chuang tzu, who suspect embellishment in all its forms, preferring the unadorned, which they associate with spontaneous Nature, to the "artificial" products of society.

> App. 3: The greater the pattern, the simpler it seems.
>   The great[19] seems truly inadequate.
> Fath. 3: In patterns, plainer is greater.[20]
>   Meaning: It has more than enough substance.

This lucky set of verses presents a paradoxical truth: The greater the man, the simpler he appears to be. By extension, the greater the institution or tool, the more naturally it appears to function. For this reason, "vast virtue seems inadequate."[21] The average person fails to appreciate the miraculous nature of either the sage or sagely institutions. This is both because the inherent modesty of the sage prevents him from parading his achievements, and because the petty mind mistakenly assumes that great tasks and talents require extraordinary complexity. Confucius himself confessed to a similar misapprehension when assessing the character of his best disciple, Yen Hui:

> The Master said, "I can talk to Yen Hui a whole day without his ever differing from me. One would think he was stupid. But if I inquire into his private conduct when he is not with me, I find that it fully demonstrates what I have taught him. No, Hui is by no means stupid."[22]

App. 4: Ornate patterns and overembellished:
    If tiger and leopard were patterned thus,
    It would not please Heaven; it would be bad.
Fath. 4: That ornament obstructs
    Means: How is it worthy of praise?[23]

One passage in the *Changes* (cited above) compares the distinctive markings of the tiger and leopard to the superior patterns of cultivation displayed by the truly noble person.[24] If their bold markings, so easily seen,[25] were indistinguishable from those of lesser beasts, the tiger and leopard would no longer be fit analogues to the superior person. Overly ornate patterns, in fact, recall the petty man, who is hardly worthy of praise.

This reading differs from that proposed by the commentators:

> Ornate patterns, highly embellished.
> Tiger and leopard are patterned thus.
> Unless they tend toward Heaven,[26]
> They are no good.

The commentators offer the following analysis: The tiger and the leopard, despite the value of their ornamental skins, are not employed in sacrifices for two reasons: First, only solid-color animals are offered to the gods, demonstrating the god's preference for plain substance over pattern. Second, both tiger and leopard are beasts of prey. Since the ancient Chinese equated moral action with deeds which forge strong community, the tiger and leopard are hardly fit offerings to the gods. However beautiful and rare, mere pattern alone cannot suffice to please the gods or win renown in the world of Man. Excessive emphasis on surface embellishment may in fact create many problems for oneself and others.[27] After all, it is because of their patterns that tiger and leopard are hunted down.[28]

App. 5: Bright and bold:
    Brilliant the patterns that are upheld
    When chariots and robes are fully used.[29]
Fath. 5: What is bold is on high.
    Meaning: Heaven's patterns are most bright.

In the very first chapter of the *Documents*, the ancient sage-king Shun bestows upon various officials "chariots and robes according to their services."[30] Sumptuary regulations and liberal rewards were considered important tools of good government in China. Through them, the government hoped to teach its subjects the relative worth of various contributions to society; by making virtue and duty "the root of profitable action,"[31] the court strove to encourage good behavior and discourage the bad. In theory, once each shining model of good behavior receives munificent awards of chariots and robes, even the lowest type of person may wish to emulate his good example. Therefore, the ruler of true cultivation employs sumptuary regulations (one pattern) bestowed in court ceremonies (another pattern) to enforce cultural values (still another pattern) derived from Heaven (the ultimate source of divine pattern).[32]

> App. 6: The pattern of wild geese in flight
> Is no model for man.
> They fly as they wish toward the river.[33]
> Fath. 6: No rule to the patterns of geese
> Means: They go wherever they please.

In China, as in the West, migratory birds are thought to be portents, due to their uncanny ability to predict the onset of cold weather. However, the wild goose often breaks rank as it flies south, stopping off at river banks. Thus, no "great pattern"[34] marks its behavior. In this it is like the individual of some talent whose desires lead him to disregard proper social constraints.

> App. 7: While pheasants win no favor,
> Chickens are lavished with grain.[35]
> Fath. 7: That pheasants win no support
> Means: It is hard to feed those in hiding.[36]

Because of its patterned plumage and rich taste, the pheasant should be valued far above the lowly chicken. Nevertheless, the pheasant's refusal to be domesticated makes it an unreliable source of food or feathers.[37] Given this, it is hardly surprising that the inherently less valuable but domesticated bird is offered the grain.

Since official salary was paid in grain, the verse is a thinly veiled comment on political life. The two birds, of course, symbolize the worthy and the mediocre candidate for office. If noble men avoid government service, only mediocre talents will be left for the ruler to appoint.[38] For this reason, the good man should not regard himself as too pure to accept patronage from others, nor should he forsake the court in periods of decline. (We are now, after all, in Position 7.)[39] In return, the wise ruler will reward him for his contributions to society.

App. 8: Intricate carving and grain-patterned cloth[40]
   Squander the farmers' time.[41]
   With patterns, then chaos.
Fath. 8: Patterns of intricate carving
   Mean: They only waste their days.

The *Mystery* encapsulates the famous argument made by an earlier Confucian master, Chia Yi (200–168 B.C.), in a memorial to the throne: The production of each and every single luxury item represents a severe loss to the state, since it diverts necessary manpower from the production of such basic goods as grain and plaincloth.[42]

App. 9: Extremely complex patterns:
   Changed to the bolder ax-and-stripe.[43]
Fath. 9: That the ultrapatterned is exchanged
   Means: They match it to the substance.[44]

Appraisal 9 as the last poem of the tetragram reflects extreme patternization. The auspicious character of the line correlated with yang *ch'i* requires a retreat from extreme embellishment and a return to greater simplicity of pattern. Accordingly, the sacrificial robes are patterned with bold figures rendered in dramatic colors. This change in clothing signifies a fundamental change of heart. The private person returns to ritual as the basis of self-cultivation. Meanwhile, high officials restore the essentials of government, including an emphasis on ritual and agriculture.

Correlates with Earth's Mystery; Yin; the phase Wood; and the Yi ching *Hexagram no. 10, Step; the sun enters the Spread constellation, 2d degree; the Dipper points SSW; the musical note is* G^1

Li

No. 48. Ritual
July 21 (p.m.)–July 25

HEAD: Yin is in the low regions while yang is on high. If high and low right [their] bodies, things join in having ritual.

The Great Heat solar period, when yang *ch'i* blazes most fiercely, opens with Appraisal 3 of this tetragram. Even so, the decline of yang ch'i has already begun. Yin is poised below in the lower regions, ready to advance, while yang, still on high, prepares to leave.[2] Thus, the two complementary configurations of energy now appear in a dancelike counterpoint of rhythm and pattern. In the world of Man, this pattern of interdependence and complimentarity finds its analogy in the delicately balanced rituals that rule relations between host and guest.[3] On that model, all significant exchanges (for example, the exchange of gifts or of verbal communications) take on correct ritual postures appropriate to their times.

"Ritual" (li) is the word the Chinese gave to any symbolic act that marks a significant interaction between two or more parties (for example, between the gods and man). According to Confucius, the physical enactment of ritual becomes fully compelling only if it reflects a profound integrity of the spirit; it is this perfect harmony of form and heart that infuses each gesture with dignity and direction. Perfunctory ceremony or mechanical gestures, even if they mimic ritual, are unworthy of the name.[4] Insofar as ritual implies spiritual wholeness, the graph for ritual relates to the cognate graph "body," which describes corporeal completeness.[5]

The word for ritual takes on ever wider associations under the influence of the Warring States philosopher Hsün tzu.[6] In many ways, it comes to embrace not only all "rules for living," but also all cosmic interactions. In short, it comes to be synonymous with Tao. For this reason, the Head text can speak of the myriad things participating in ritual activity in company with human beings.

Correct ritual performance makes for good community and fair government.[7] It also intimates the ineffable that would remain otherwise unknown, while it provides numerous opportunities for aesthetic and moral appreciation. However, the forms of ritual—at least initially—place fundamental constraints on the heart/mind and the body. Long hours of disciplined study and intensive training are required if one is to truly master them and make them "second nature." The Changes hexagram aligned with this tetragram speaks of conditions "subject to restraint."[8] The Mystery will develop that theme below.

> App. 1: Stepping on tiptoe,
>> He leaves his forebears[9] behind.
> Fath. 1: Raising his heels
>> Means: He makes his own family retreat.

Because of a phonetic identity between the two graphs, many early dictionaries define ritual (li) in terms of behavioral "steps" (also li).[10] To readers in the West, stepping on tiptoe often indicates extreme deference, on the presumption that a mincing step minimizes the obtrusive character of a person advancing. (Of course, stepping on tiptoe can also indicate a certain degree of furtiveness.) In China, however, "stepping on tiptoes" is equated with "high-stepping"; it is the outer expression of inner arrogance since the desire to raise the heel reveals a person's ambitions to "force to a high point what is [naturally] positioned below."[11] For this reason, such a step becomes "a symbol of the usurpation of a superior's [place]."[12] Here, arrogance and ambition threaten the entire family hierarchy, for the youngster has forgotten even the most basic filial duties owed the living and the dead.

In ancient China, those who looked toward the future with eager anticipation were also said to "stand on tiptoe."[13] So much attention directed to the future can lead one to forget the past. That this individual forgets even the ancestors, from whom life itself derives, is clear proof of self-absorption.[14] At Appraisal 1, which indicates either the beginning of a cycle or very low social position, the individual already congratulates himself on being a self-made man. Such a fundamental mistake can only spell trouble for the future. As one text predicts, "He who tiptoes cannot stand."[15]

> App. 2: With a gaze most deferential,[16]
> With reverential steps,
> Only then is he shot through with integrity.
>
> Fath. 2: Most deferential, most grave
> Means: Respect issues from the heart.

The *Analects* of Confucius repeatedly identifies respect as the first, crucial step on the road to moral perfection. Inevitably, a reverential attitude toward one's superiors results in outward displays of virtue. Here inner and outer correspond perfectly; eye and step, intention and act, move easily in ritual forms.

The poem literally says that the noble man is "pierced through with jujube [wood]," a phrase that may puzzle the Western reader, but not the Chinese. No fewer than twenty poems in the *Book of Odes* refer to the thorny jujube, whose red core symbolizes the compassion, wisdom, tenderness, and honesty of the individual.[17] In later texts, the jujube especially stands for the good minister, who must be "thorny" at times in order to remonstrate with the ruler, despite his absolute integrity and loyalty to the throne (his "red core").[18] Loyalty and trustworthiness, then, become the basis of ritual.[19]

> App. 3: The portrait is perfect in form,
> But in truth, it lacks perfection.
>
> Fath. 3: The portrait, perfect in form,
> Means: It is not true to its source.[20]

As in English, in Chinese the words for "faithful" and "true" denote both the accuracy with which an artist's image reproduces reality and the integrity of one's inner psychic state.[21] A painting—however good—can never really come to life; it is two-dimensional, even curiously flat, rather than multifaceted.[22] In that, it is fundamentally different from the real object on which it is modeled. Only very stupid people would confuse the painted representation with the real thing. No less benighted are those who presume that the outer forms of ritual constitute the "real thing" in its totality. Only those who intend to convey true humanity through the forms infuse each ritual act with a sacred character; it is this inner commitment to Goodness, not the mechanical imitation of certain prescribed gestures, that endows the ritual with power. Simply going through the motions teaches nothing, nor does it forge true community.[23] How, then, can it be equated with true ritual? As the Confucian Classics say, "In small particulars, he practices deportment as if that were all important. Is that not far from saying that he knows ritual?"[24]

This verse does not criticize imitation *per se*. Faithful imitation of the ancients' intentions lies at the heart of good ritual.[25]

> App. 4: The stately demeanor of peacock and goose
> Helps when mounting the steps.
> Fath. 4: The decorum of peacock and wild goose
> Means: They can be used as models.

Both the peacock and the wild goose are rare birds. In both species, the plumage of the males is brilliantly colored in intricate patterns. Therefore, in ancient times, their beautiful feathers were used in the insignia of rank on ceremonial caps. The wild goose was admired for its uncanny ability to fly at the correct time in orderly fashion; the peacock, for the stately sweep of its majestic walk.[26] For all these reasons, the two species were associated with impressive ceremony. From this poem we learn that the wise leader "on the rise," if sufficiently schooled in correct ritual pattern, can lead his followers to a profound moral transformation.

> App. 5: Harboring his rebellious intent,
> He smashes his ladles in error,[27]
> Then ruins the gift of Nine Arrows.[28]
> Fath. 5: Rebelliously breaking ladles
> Means: He reduces his own dignity.[29]

Appraisal 5 corresponds to the ruler. In the ritual enfeoffment of his vassal lords, the Son of Heaven confers upon his chief supporters nine symbolic gifts of investiture (the so-called Nine Conferrals),[30] including a bundle of arrows, sacrificial wine, and ceremonial clothing, all of which symbolize the ruler's absolute trust in his subordinates. For example, trustworthy officials are said to be "straight as arrows"; hence, the gift of arrows.[31] Such important gifts are presumably reserved for those who, mindful of ancient precedents and family honor, can be depended upon to sacrifice their very lives to protect the ancestral house.[32] After all, the classics tell us that, "The purpose of ritual is to secure men in their positions."[33]

Here, the disrespect shown the Son of Heaven by one or more enfeoffed lords is evident. The subordinate who lacks virtue rises up in revolt. The outward sign of his inner rebellion is his willful destruction of the ritual gifts received at his appointment. Rebellious subordinates soon lose their "dignity," which in archaic usage refers to high rank and a generous stipend. "This is to lose the empire through inhumanity."[34]

> App. 6: Having ranked them in order like fishscales,[35]
> Only then does he grant them largesse.[36]
> By this, like a lord, he rises to Heaven.[37]
> Fath. 6: Serried ranks like fishscales
> Mean: Noble and base take their places.

Ideally, the imperial bureaucracy is a tight, orderly formation that functions as one, though ritual stipulates that separate duties and prerogatives be assigned to each official grade. Therefore, many early Chinese writers compare the bureaucracy to the overlapping scales of a fish.[38] Careful gradations in rank supported by ritual prerogatives clarify proper standards of conduct for All-under-Heaven. Ritual pattern, by its very integrity and cohesiveness, makes usurpation unthinkable and unworkable. The most important task of the sage-ruler, then, is to employ ritual to make appropriate distinctions between his many subordinates, so that each person receives a rank commensurate with his ability and merit.

> App. 7: Overstepping ritual:
> "One who knows no fear enters fearsome situations."
> Fath. 7: Fearlessly overstepping ritual
> Means: This is what other men reject.

Ritual is the root of all productive social activity, for ritual is the most effective means to secure the goodwill of family and friends. To abandon ritual is to turn to "rule by punishments," a policy which ultimately undermines state order, according to the Confucians. On the other hand, to go beyond ritual (in other words, to be overelaborate in one's practices) is to muddy the clear message ritual normally conveys. Excessive ritual also represents an unjust burden in terms of time and money. For this reason, in the case of ritual, "to go too far is as bad as not to go far enough."[39] Whoever ignores due consideration for others, as expressed in ritual, can expect to be abandoned by those for whom he has demonstrated contempt. As the *Documents* says, "One who knows no fear enters fearsome situations."[40]

> App. 8: His cap is full of holes,
>   His shoes are in good repair.[41]
> Fath. 8: That the cap is full of holes
>   Means: Clearly the cap must go on top.[42]

Those who occupy the top positions have failed, while those below still perform their jobs admirably. Despite the better condition of the shoes (i.e., those below), shoes cannot be worn atop the head. In other words, bad rulers cannot be easily overthrown by good subjects.[43] The metaphor suggests that social status and political position are to some extent predetermined for some fixed period of time by the Mandate of Heaven. Just because an inferior demonstrates marked ability, it does not follow that he can immediately challenge his superiors. Instead, he should patiently await Heaven's commands.

The commentator Ch'en Pen-li gives a slightly different reading based upon variant characters:

> A cap of plaited rushes[44]
> Shoes of fine brocade.[45]
> Cap of plaited rushes,
> Clearly, [this man] cannot but be set right.[46]

To wear luxurious clothing while in mourning represents the height of un-filiality. How can such a person, whose basic values are wrong, possibly be entrusted with public office? Lapses in ritual suggest an unsuitable, even an unseemly situation.

> App. 9: He wears a hat, but has no head.
>   Of what use is high rank[47] to him?
> Fath. 9: Having no head, he wears it still.
>   Meaning: Where is he going to go?

Appraisal 9 always describes extremes, and so we hear of the head. If the ruler has no head for ruling, what does it matter that he wears the crown as symbol of his authority? And if the ruler loses his head through his own ineptitude, still less will the crown or rank matter.[48]

One commentator finds in these lines a veiled attack on Wang Mang for his alleged assassination of Emperor P'ing in A.D. 6.[49] But Ssu-ma Kuang argues for a different interpretation. In ritual, even the emperor learns to humble himself. Only an evil ruler assumes that no higher authority exists. Such a ruler learns nothing from the example of the ancients; he also ignores useful advice from his contemporaries. Oblivious to the reverence that underlies ritual, he indulges all his worst, arrogant impulses. Ultimate destruction follows.

Correlates with Earth's Mystery;
Yang; *the phase Metal; and the* Yi
ching *Hexagram no. 33, Retreat;*
the sun enters the Spread constella-
tion, 6th degree

T'ao

No. 49. Flight
July 26–July 30 (a.m.)

HEAD: Yin *ch'i* manifests its strength.[1] Yang *ch'i* plunges into[2] retreat. The myriad things are about to be destroyed.

It may seem premature to predict the death of the myriad things immediately following the Great Heat solar period of late summer, but this tetragram is allied with Metal, the "killing" or "punishing" Phase; hence, the imagery of battle. The tetragram's title, Flight, predicts a quick retreat by yang *ch'i* as soon as yin *ch'i* reveals its strength.[3] In response, the myriad things will be destroyed. After all, as the *Changes* reminds us, "Things cannot abide forever in their place."[4]

Since the Head text characterizes initial retreat as the first important step toward ultimate destruction, it is notable that the *Mystery* talks of flight as both auspicious and inauspicious in the Appraisals. Enforced flight is inherently dangerous because it leaves one's flanks exposed, but voluntary retreat from a position (as, for example, in certain acts of courtesy) can actually prove of benefit to the superior man.

> App. 1: Retreating waters as they level
> Obliterate the tracks they made.[5]
> Fath. 1: Leveled by retreating waters
> Means: The tracks are not recut.[6]

Appraisal 1, at the beginning of the cycle, is allied with the Water Phase. It is the property of water to level through erosion and flooding. The poem must be auspicious, since it is allied with Day and yang *ch'i*. In this translation, escape becomes possible once the fugitives have fled through water, which erases all evidence of their flight. By analogy, self-cultivation acts like water to cleanse the self of all traces of one's former bestial impulses. The same poem also works as a description of the mysterious Tao, which erases the present moment as the future unfolds. Were Yang Hsiung more firmly in the camp of the Taoists, it would be tempting to read these lines as criticism of human civilization, which must be cleansed by the natural action of the waters, so that it can return to the desired original state of blankness.[7]

Many commentators, however, would read the first line of both

Appraisal and Fathoming as, "The leveling of [tracks made by animals] that have fled [to] water" at the first sign of a fire.[8] The poem then demonstrates the ability of the noble man to foresee and quickly respond to disaster before complete devastation occurs.[9]

> App. 2: Preoccupied with worries,[10]
> He fails to notice the ditch,
> Though shod in golden slippers.
> Fath. 2: The very troubled mind
> Means: Righteousness does not advance.[11]

Not unlike Freud, the ancient Chinese insisted that unconscious or inadvertent slips reveal our innermost state of mind. In the vast majority of cases, they reasoned, luckless individuals simply needed to exercise greater caution to improve their fate. The most famous anecdote illustrating this is that of music master Tzu-ch'un, who stubbed his toe one day. Tzu-ch'un responded to the minor accident by retreating to his bedroom for an entire month to consider the possible disgrace that might result from similar acts of carelessness.[12]

Heedless of his finery, the hapless subject of this poem pitches headlong into a drainage ditch, sullying his shoes. His lapse in judgment seems more serious when we remember that golden shoes indicate high rank and status.

The commentators Fan Wang and Ssu-ma Kuang interpret these lines somewhat differently, however. To Fan Wang, the golden slippers symbolize the petty person's stubborn determination to remain in office at all costs, rather than to retire into seclusion when danger is at hand. The failure to keep in mind the ditch, to Fan Wang, signifies the bad official's adamant refusal to suffer hardship for the sake of righteousness. (Apparently, in this version, the official shies away from taking the expected plunge into the ditch.) Fan Wang writes, that such a person is not willing to go through the ditch himself (an alternate reading for the second Appraisal line.)[13]

Ssu-ma Kuang agrees that it is this combination of great danger and high stakes which makes the petty man turn skittish:

> The petty man, although he sees that calamity is about to arrive, is so terrified that he cannot use his sense of duty [as his guide] in making a decision. [Instead,] clinging to his favors and salary, he tarries rather than leaves. He does not realize that the ditch lies at [his very] feet. Suddenly, he topples forward. Confucius said, "Having seen one's duty, to fail to act is to lack courage."[14] Therefore, it says, "Righteousness does not advance."

App. 3: Clenching his thighs,[15] whipping his horse,
　　　　With bandits watching his door,
　　　　It's best for him to flee.
Fath. 3: Kneeing and whipping the horse's rump
　　　　Means: He sees what's coming.[16]

Appraisal 3 marks the transition from thought to action. The horse's owner, seeing robbers case his house, recognizes the danger he is in. Salutary fear galvanizes him into action. Fortunately, he has a means of escape. He flees on horseback, digging his knee into the horse's haunches and wielding his whip to make the horse run faster. Thanks to his quick response, he manages to slip away, though his escape is narrow.

App. 4: The tall[17] trees are but tips at top.[18]
　　　　As birds in flight pass over them,
　　　　Some stop and then alight.[19]
Fath. 4: Birds in the tall trees
　　　　Means: Wanting to stop, they drop down.

One popular anecdote of Han times tells of a flock of birds in flight that decide to rest in what appears to be an inviting grove of tall trees.[20] But when the birds alight on the trees, the fragile treetops cannot support their weight, and the boughs swing down under them. Some plunge to their deaths. Others die when the tips snap back, stunning the birds, which are then easily picked off by crafty hunters. It is also possible that the lush forest conceals hunters' traps.[21] This cautionary tale teaches two main lessons: first, we must all learn to distinguish external appearance from internal substance; second, we must never be seduced by unsuitable but alluring prospects and desires, especially in midcourse.[22]

Since Appraisal 4 corresponds to court officials, the subject may well be the king's officials. Perhaps they find the king's support less than adequate.[23] Or perhaps the petty person, ambitious for high rank, forgets the inherent danger of "living at the top."[24]

App. 5: Falcons are seen massing[25] in woods,
　　　　Otters plunge into deepest pools.
　　　　An attack is imminent.[26]
Fath. 5: The sight of falcons and otters
　　　　Means: To flee bad luck, hide in the deep.

When great danger looms, the superior man knows enough to retreat.[27] Falcons and otters often signify cruelty since both prey on smaller creatures.[28] In this case, however, even strong falcons and otters scurry away rather than face impending doom.[29]

App. 6: With so many fields unploughed,[30]
     He wastes the work we put into footpaths.[31]
Fath. 6: Many fields, as yet unplowed,
     Mean: He wastes strength and loses merit.[32]

The early mention of "many fields" leaves the reader to expect great wealth and vast territories, such as might belong to members of the ruling elite. Initial preparations for a good harvest have been made. A group of conscientious farmers have constructed raised footpaths between fields. These footpaths, which look like low dikes flattened at the top, serve two main functions: Water collects between them, facilitating the irrigation process. They also allow the farmer to tend his crops without trampling tender shoots underfoot. Despite these preparations, the farmer in this poem fails to hitch his oxen to plough the fields. From seed sown in unploughed fields, he can hardly expect great profits, even with his vast holdings.[33] The fields, in effect, become a dead loss; the vast labor already expended fails to further production.

With regard to self-cultivation, a man cannot expect to develop his talents unless he is willing to harrow his soul.[34] This poem may also apply to the ruler who, in ignoring hardworking advisors (symbolized by the farmer's oxen), ultimately fails to use his kingdom's resources to the full.[35] Finally, two commentators apparently interpret the verses as a critique of careless hunters who destroy the farmer's fields as they pursue sport.[36]

App. 7: By keeping an eye on the fowler's net,
     Later the bird can fly.
Fath. 7: Keeping the rope in sight
     Means: It is not quite high enough.[37]

The wise individual keeps danger in sight, so that he can effect an escape if necessary. Like the bird, this individual nearly fails to fly high enough to escape harm's way. Luckily, the rope is not thrown quite high enough to snare the bird.

App. 8: The neck is pierced by an arrow[38]
     And the wings are bound by its string.[39]
Fath. 8: The neck hit, the wings bound,
     Means: Do not struggle in vain.

The hunter attaches a string to his arrow because it helps him locate his prey after the hit. The string also serves to bind the catch. The bird, if shot, may still have sufficient strength to flap its wings. But once its wings are bound, it can never hope to fly off to safety. As the poem indicates, all further struggle is futile.[40]

App. 9: It's best to flee, even on calloused feet[41]
When bands of thieves[42] surround the city walls.
Fath. 9: That thieves and knaves besiege the walls
Means: Where on earth can a person flee?

Appraisal 9, though aligned with auspicious Day, also represents the culmination of Flight. The individual realizes he is under seige since evil men now surround his stronghold. Despite his evident panic, he manages, after much travail, to escape with his life, though there is no promise of a more secure future.

唐 ䷠

Correlates with Earth's Mystery; Yin; the phase Earth; and the Yi ching Hexagram no. 33, Retreat; the sun enters the Spread constellation, 11th degree

T'ang

No. 50. Vastness or Wasting

July 30 (p.m.)–August 3

HEAD: Yin *ch'i* increasingly[1] comes; yang *ch'i* increasingly goes. Things are on the verge of dissipation.[2]

At this point in the yearly cycle, autumn will soon be upon us. Things move inexorably past ripeness to spoilage. The range of meaning found in the title for this tetragram admirably bridges the transition from laudable maturity to first decay, for its associations are both good and bad. On the one hand, the title can mean "vast" or "great," especially with reference to capacity (in both senses). But closely related to vastness is the idea of "what is wasted."[3] By a series of small extensions, the same graph comes to mean "to flee," "to drift," "to toss about aimlessly,"[4] "to feel unsettled," "to experience loss or failure," "to act in vain," "to suffer decay,"[5] and "to be emptied or exhausted." The same graph signifies the wanton and dissipated, the exaggerated and the unrestrained;[6] therefore, it is used in connection with abrupt, boastful, rude, or preposterous acts that defy ritual.

App. 1: When inner restraints[7] are absent,[8]
Do not act. Danger.[9]
Fath. 1: Unrestrained within
Means: He holds to no principle.

Figure 13. Shooting arrows at birds. Illustration from a rubbing of a pottery tomb relief unearthed from Peng County, Szechwan (26 × 44 cm.), dated to the Eastern Han dynasty.

Appraisal 1 corresponds to the beginning of the cycle and to first thoughts; hence, the focus on the inner workings of the mind. The mind of the unprincipled individual will not direct the body properly. Surely this is dangerous.

> App. 2: When adrift and in the dark,
>   It helps to set out for the East.
> Fath. 2: Help for drifting in the dark[10]
>   Means: The bright path is beneficial.

Dark and light are contrasted here. After the sun rises each morning from the vast, dark pool located beneath the horizon, the myriad things, formerly condemned to darkness, are flooded with brilliant light. If we wish our minds to be similarly enlightened, we must move in the direction of an equally bright path, the Way, as embodied in the Confucian Classics.

> App. 3: To be oversimple is improper.[11]
>   Lost is that rhythmic sound of jade.[12]
> Fath. 3: That there is no measured sound of jade
>   Means: He is not your haven.[13]

One who overvalues rustic simplicity cannot provide a sure model for others seeking the refinements of civilized life.

> App. 4: Broadminded, with no predilections,[14]
>   The Way and the Right are his lords.

Figure 14. Shooting arrows at birds and harvesting the fields. Illustration from a pottery tomb tile unearthed from Chengdu, Szechwan (39.5 × 48 cm.), dated to the Eastern Han period (now in the Chengdu Museum).

> Fath. 4: To be greatly without bias[15]
>> Means: He sides only with righteousness.[16]

A famous passage in the Confucian *Analects* says that the truly superior person is simply "on the side of what is right," and so is without particular predispositions. Similarly, the "Great Plan" chapter of the *Documents* identifies this fairmindedness with the King's Way.[18]

> App. 5: He sets the deer to running
>> While clasping a mouse to his breast.
>> What he gained has no value.
> Fath. 5: A deer on the run and a mouse at the breast
>> Means: This is not enough for merit.

Because of a pun, the deer represents any piece of great good fortune.[19] Attaining the throne in early slang became "catching the deer."[20] A wise man always foregoes petty profit for the sake of a larger gain.[21] Here, however, we see a foolish person, who wastes time and effort in vain pursuits, ignoring great opportunities.[22] If we consider study, for example, the only learning worth pursuing is the Confucian Way associated with the ancient sage-kings. If we consider official appointments instead, only virtuous candidates are worth pursuing.[23] Were it not so tragic, such marked inability to distinguish good from bad would be ludicrous.

> App. 6: The great do not hoard their sufficiencies.[24]
> Like Heaven, they disperse their wealth.
> Fath. 6: That the great do not hoard
> Means: No trace of selfishness marks their faces.[25]

In general, Confucian philosophers were suspicious of acting alone rather than in concert with family or friends. To monopolize resources, to be independent-minded, or to claim to be a self-made man, all these acts represented challenges to societal cohesion. This is one reason why the *Analects* holds that "virtue never dwells alone."[26] According to the Chinese texts, all human beings, even the emperor, must acknowledge their dependence upon others. The emperor, for example, should acknowledge his dependence on able ministers, the common people, and his ancestors. (Position 6 corresponds to the ancestral temple.) Far from begrudging the expenditure of treasury funds on such people, the truly great leader realizes that by rewarding each subject with a rank and salary consistent with his merits, the emperor multiplies his eyes and ears, and at the same time ensures the transmission of his suasive example down to the lowest rungs of society. The security and well-being of society, then, ultimately rest upon the ruler's willingness to share his wealth with others. As the *Mencius* says, "It was by sharing their pleasure with the people that the men of antiquity were able to enjoy themselves."[27]

> App. 7: Shooting one arrow at three birds in flight:
> Though he sets forth by dawn's first light,[28]
> At day's end, he has not returned:
> Lost.
> Fath. 7: One shot for three birds
> Means: He strikes out aimlessly.[29]

These verses demonstrate the utter uselessness of unfocused or misguided activity. Though an entire day has been spent in frenzied pursuit of a goal, no obvious gain results, despite many opportunities. Alternately, the same lines can describe a hunter who loses himself in the pleasures of the chase.[30] Far better "to concentrate the mind and unify the will"[31] in a single-minded search for the Way, since this holds out the promise of success.

App. 8: The great accept[32] official posts,
   Ghosts at the shrine cease wailing.
   Some gain their blessings.[33]
Fath. 8: That the great accept posts
   Means: They restore what had been lost.[34]

The main theme of the verses is clear, though the identity of "the great" is open to question. Once good leaders take up (or, are restored to) office, the local patron gods cease their weeping and wailing, in expectation of renewed good rule and the reinstitution of regular sacrifices. The common people also expect to benefit from their administration, and so "some gain their blessings." Both the gods above and the people below rejoice in the ability of the truly great to restore what had been lost.

App. 9: Bright pearls used for birdshot.
   Even if flesh by chance is struck,
   It will not repay the outlay.[35]
Fath. 9: Lustrous pearls used for shot
   Means: The expense is not recouped.

Pebbles would work as well as pearls in shooting game birds. What's more, pebbles, when compared with pearls, are of relatively little value. Therefore, the hunter can afford to lose a certain number of pebbles, though he can't afford to lose a single pearl. Once again, the reader is urged to carefully consider which acts are truly worthwhile.[36] The *Mystery* suggests that when precious human life is to be employed, only the Way represents a goal sufficiently great to aim for. Unfortunately, the petty person typically pursues the vastly inferior goals of fame, fortune, and sex.

Correlates with Earth's Mystery;
Yang; the phase Water and the Yi
ching Hexagram no. 32, Duration;
the sun enters the Spread constella-
tion, 15th degree; the Dipper points
Ch'ang
WSW; the musical note is G-sharp[1]
No. 51. Constancy
August 4–August 8 (a.m.)

HEAD: By yin one knows the subject; by yang one knows the lord. The Way of ruler and subject remains unchanged for ten thousand ages.[2]

The Autumn Onset solar period, usually regarded as the juncture between summer and autumn, begins with Appraisal 6 of this tetragram. Here, then, we have another critical meeting point between yin and yang. Since this is the last opportunity yang will have to "lord" it over yin, it is appropriate that Yang Hsiung should discuss the relations of the ruler (whose correlate is yang) and the subordinate (identified with yin). That autumn follows summer is an invariable rule of nature. Following this immutable pattern, all subjects, including court officials, must follow the ruler. Hierarchy functions as the necessary basis for enduring and productive relations; as the *Changes* argues, the four seasons keep to their constant course only when the "strong is above and the weak below."[3] Not surprisingly, the need to recognize one's proper place in the hierarchy is a theme of this tetragram. So long as hierarchy is preserved, the worst calamities associated with yin *ch'i* may be avoided. This may explain why the penal code associated with the autumn season is represented in a positive, rather than a negative light.

> App. 1: Holding up the ink-line of the gods,[4]
> He follows the sacred model.
> Using the One to pair ten thousand,
> To the end, his light does not fade.[5]
> Fath. 1: Upholding divine measure
> Means: He embodies the form of the One.[6]

Because its primal Oneness produces the myriad things, the Tao in its totality lies essentially beyond mere human comprehension. Certain broad patterns of cosmic activity, however, are discernible to Man. For example, the superior man takes primal oneness as his model when dealing with others. Single-minded in his pursuit of moral understanding and unshakeable in his integrity, he "holds fast to the One"[7] Way. Applying the single tool of categorical logic to the entire universe, he comes to grasp all the myriad things within his mind,[8] so all-encompassing is his understanding. Conformity with such sacred norms gains him charismatic power[9] that will work to effect a perfect union of all the myriad things in the cosmos.[10] Above and below,[11] inner unity brings the union of all.[12]

> App. 2: Little[13] constancy within:
> Female chastity in danger.[14]
> Fath. 2: Inner constants undeveloped
> Mean: The women are not upright.

"Inner" often refers to women or the women's quarters, since only men participated in "outer" [i.e., public and social] lives. The husband/wife relation was viewed as one of the great, constant patterns in human relationships. Like the ruler-subject relation, it presumed a hierarchical structure tempered by mutuality. It was believed that the entire hierarchy would collapse, however, if women were unchaste before or after marriage.[15] Clear lines of patrilineal descent had to be assured for both religious and economic reasons. Unfortunately, bastard males passed off as legitimate heirs would participate as adults in sacrifices to ancestors in the patrilineal line. Since tradition insisted that the ancestors would accept no sacrifices from those of different surnames, the prosperity of the clan might be jeopardized for generations by a single illicit liaison. Furthermore, female infidelity demonstrated a fundamentally rebellious attitude toward husbands, to whom women owed their loyalty. Such a cavalier attitude could ultimately infect the rest of society. Since women who were less than "upright" undermined the "eternally correct" social structure, female sexual and political intrigue was a source of considerable concern to strict Confucian scholars.

> App. 3: The sun makes its virtue constant
>   By not eclipsing for three years.
> Fath. 3: The sun, making its virtue constant,
>   Means: The Way of the Ruler shines forth.[16]

Appraisal 1 compared the truly good person to a sun that never sets. Appraisal 3 presents a variation on this astronomical motif. In Han omen literature, eclipses of the sun and moon were thought to presage disorder in the apartments of the king and queen respectively.[17] Often the solar eclipse portended usurpation of the royal power (yang) by ministers or consorts (both of whom were yin). In folk tradition, "three" stands for "many." If no eclipse occurs for many years in succession, the sun's uninterrupted light will shine brilliantly on all below. The charismatic ruler, by analogy, enlightens others, with no fear that he will be eclipsed since he has made his virtue constant.[18]

> App. 4: The moon is inconstant.
>   She sometimes strays from her course.[19]
> Fath. 4: The inconstant moon
>   Means: The minister errs in his course.

The moon symbolizes the minister for several reasons: First, the moon's light entirely depends upon the sun for its brightness, just as the minister's authority derives entirely from his ruler. Second, the moon shines less brightly than the sun, just as the minister is less glorious than his ruler. Third, the moon, even to the naked eye, appears to wobble occasionally in its course.[20] The Chinese took this irregular motion of the moon to mean that an evil minister wavers in his loyalty to the throne.[21] One early astrological text predicts:

> When the state is controlled by ministers . . . the movement [of the moon] inclines sometimes toward the south and sometimes toward the north. Irregular motion of the moon, whether fast or slow, indicates excessive power held by relatives of the empress.[22]

App. 5: Whether up, down, or sideways in his course,[23]
    He takes Heaven and Earth as his constants.
Fath. 5: His vertical, his horizontal
    Means: The order of ruler and official is constant.

The early commentator Fan Wang says, "Heaven is vertical; Earth, horizontal. This is the constant way." Man moving in horizontal and vertical directions suggests the fundamental interconnectedness of the three realms of Heaven-Earth-Man.[24] Elaborate patterns in the night sky and geological configurations are studied by the sage intent upon devising models for human culture;[25] the sage hopes to recreate in human society that marvelous interdependence that proves so productive in the phenomenal world. Patterns in Heaven and Earth, then, suggest the norm for ruler and official.

App. 6: Having reached Seven, he tends toward Nine.[26]
    Weakness stirs in what was once firm.
    He cannot overcome the rule for him.
Fath. 6: Getting Seven and becoming Nine
    Means: Abundance is left as he rides to decay.

Why this talk of Seven and Nine in Appraisal 6, which marks the transition from beneficial Action to Calamity?[27] Beneficial yang ch'i is said to culminate by the seventh position, and to decline by the ninth. Yin, of course, is "weak" while yang is traditionally characterized as "firm." Given the ongoing cycles of the constant, yet everchanging Tao, whoever grasps at good luck ("abundance") finds bad luck later in the cycle. Only the wise individual who knows when to stop is likely to maintain his present position. He contentedly cultivates his virtue while regarding material success with an unmoved mind.[28]

App. 7: Back and forth, forever it flows.
    Those most constant, coming together,[29]
    Can carry on in propriety.
Fath. 7: Ever flowing, back and forth,
    Means: He takes the Right to confront the wrong.[30]

In this auspicious Appraisal aligned with Day, the flowing water calls to mind the desirable qualities of flood-like ch'i[31] associated with integrity, a power at once gentle and inexorable in its effect. At the same time, the flow suggests the passage of time.[32] When good men come together, early errors give way to rectitude.

> App. 8: Constant illness not seen as ill:
> Blame is complete, yet uncondemned.
> Fath. 8: Chronic illness not seen as such
> Means: He is unable to cure himself.

The individual's persistent evildoing is likened to a chronic illness. The individual who has grown accustomed to moral or physical disease forgets what health was like. No cure is possible if the individual fails to see himself as sick.[33] As the *Lao tzu* advises:

> One must be sick of illness
> If one is to recover from illness.[34]

> App. 9: Seeing his illness as illness,
> Magician-healers will not fail.
> Fath. 9: Seeing the illness for what it is
> Means: He can serve as his own doctor.

In contrast to Appraisal 8, this individual does not gloss over the serious nature of his chronic lapses. Once he has diagnosed himself correctly, he can certainly effect a cure. Good advisors and the Confucian Classics, after all, exist to help in the process of healing the soul.[35]

Tu

No. 52. Measure
August 8 (p.m.)–August 12

Correlates with Earth's Mystery; Yin; the phase Fire; and the Yi ching Hexagram no. 60, Regulation; the sun enters the Wing constellation, 2d degree

HEAD: Yin *ch'i* daily[1] leaps up. Yang *ch'i* daily yields ground.[2] Leaping and more leaping, receding and more receding,[3] each attains its proper measure.

At this point of the year, yin *ch'i* leaps into prominence above ground, while yang hastens its retreat. In effect, yin's rapid advance has stopped the progress of yang *ch'i*.[4] Since waxing and waning occur in proper measure, the continuation of the eternal cycle is assured.

*Figure 15. Tamping earth (*hang-t'u*) in order to provide a secure foundation for major public buildings. Illustration from* Erh ya *2/6b.*

This tetragram and its allied *Changes* hexagram (Regulation) applaud "stopping in an appropriate place," "recognizing one's place," "remaining central," and "accepting the superior's position above."[5] In Chinese political theory (Confucian or Legalist), "measure" refers to the institutions by which the ruler maintains good order and unifies his empire. By tradition, fixing standardized weights and measures throughout the land was viewed as the first step in the establishment of standardized morality. As seen below, the successful construction of a city (especially the capital) was also seen as proof of the king's ability to correctly appraise situations in accordance with natural and human requirements. The capital recreates on a human scale the significant features of the cosmos—the better to convey to the populace the king's charismatic sway over the triadic realms of Heaven-Earth-Man. Therefore, the well-designed capital illustrates the true king's capacity to take the proper measure not only of mankind, but also of the universe.[6]

App. 1: He consistently fails[7]
    To measure by the Mean.
Fath. 1: That measures at center only fail
    Means: There can be no success.

The measures at center point to the individual conscience, which uses the Mean as its standard. As soon as the conscience fails to distinguish right from wrong, the individual cannot possibly attain full Goodness. For this reason, the classics advise us to conduct our internal measurements with extreme care:

> Be like the forester, who when he has adjusted the spring, goes to examine the end of the arrow to see whether it is placed according to rule, and only then lets it go.[8]

> App. 2: Like waters[9] that do not recede,
>   The center measure is hidden.
> Fath. 2: Waters not receding
>   Mean: Only then can there be rectitude.

Here the individual conscience is likened to a stream whose strong yet reliable flow brings health and refreshment to all who take advantage of it. That the wellspring is hidden far away in the inner recesses only testifies to the depth and purity of its source. In moral development, the person intent upon improving himself through assiduous study of the classics[10] will discover that his unseen conscience never fails him, and that blessings will wash down on him in one continous flow.

> App. 3: Each small measure,
>   Slightly more off than the last:
>   Steps toward great disaster.[11]
> Fath. 3: Small errors in measurement[12]
>   Mean: Great calculations are overturned.

An initial miscalculation eventually leads to disastrous departures from the Way. As an oft-quoted Han proverb has it:

> Off by a hair's breadth [in the beginning],
> Missed by a thousand miles [in the end].[13]

Therefore, even "a small oversight leads to major damage."[14] Since Appraisal 3 marks the transition from thought to action, this is a timely warning.

> App. 4: Post and upright help in building walls.
> Fath. 4: The benefits of post and upright
>   Means: These benefit the building.[15]

In ancient Chinese architecture, sturdy posts and uprights are used first to compress and mold, then to support the tamped earth used in major construction works, including palace complexes. Walls serve several crucial functions. They protect the inhabitants from the elements and from intruders. By enclosing space they provide a focus for the community, thereby strengthening the bonds between men. In teaching men how to make crucial divisions of space, they also signal the civilized need for less tangible demarcations like hierarchy. Secure city walls, therefore, make the entire state secure.

If the wall stands for the state, the sturdy posts and uprights represent the ministerial advisors to the king. They help the ruler both to bear the crushing weight of his responsibilities and to construct wise policies. Just as the wise builder checks that he has enough material for construction, the good ruler makes sure that he has an adequate provision of good advisors.[16] If the wall is a symbol for civilization as a whole, posts and uprights stand for ritual.[17]

> App. 5: If the posts do not act as posts,
> > It spells disaster for building.
> Fath. 5: That posts are not posts
> > Means: There can be no security.

Appraisal 5 corresponds to the Son of Heaven. Once again, the ruler's posts are his close advisors, drawn from his chief ministers and close relations. If their talents[18] are inadequate to the task, the entire ruling house will collapse (literally and figuratively), in part because the example of the ruling elite is imitated by all the king's subjects. As errors multiply throughout the kingdom, its peace and security are destroyed. For this reason, the wise ruler is careful to select the best possible material for government service.[19]

> App. 6: Examine great measures again and again.[20]
> > In heaven, the images are revealed.
> > Elicit the models from them.
> Fath. 6: Great measurements taken with great care
> > Mean: The images drawn down are reliable guides.

The sages are said to apply cosmic standards to human predicaments.[21] In the heavens, the greatest of all measures is the Big Dipper,[22] symbol of the ruling house and focus of the entire night sky of constellations and planets. Heaven displays this image to suggest the natural character of hierarchical patterns. With these to guide him in the dark, man can build correct social relations. As the *Changes* describes the sages:

> Looking upward, they contemplated the images in the Heavens.
> Looking downward, they examined the Earth's patterns. . . . From
> the heavens there hang images that reveal [the correct models for
> mankind]. The sages imitate them.[23]

Without such guides, the fragile seeds of morality innate in each person can never develop along the lines of Heaven's manifest intentions for the world.

> App. 7: To draw guidelines without measuring[24]
> Brings down the instant ridicule[25] of ghosts.
> Fath. 7: Unmeasured guidelines
> Mean: Those with keen sight[26] only laugh.

Those who fail either to take the proper measure of a situation or to apply the guidelines of the sages to a problem deserve blame. Ghosts represent the shadowy spirit world. With their special insight into human affairs, they are able to discern such failures more quickly than ordinary individuals. As all perceptive persons withdraw their support from the individual who refuses to reform, disaster surely follows.

> App. 8: Red from the stone[27] cannot be pried apart.
> Equally ingrained is the knight's integrity.[28]
> Fath. 8: The indelible nature of the stone's red
> Means: Covenants are possible with him.[29]

Like certain medieval scholastics, the early Chinese Logicians were intrigued by the relation of the separate attributes of a thing (for example, the color of a stone) to the essential nature of the thing. Playing off the language of the Logicians, the *Mystery* uses this familiar vocabulary to imply the priority of certain Confucian values. If redness is an integral part of the stone, good character equally defines the essential nature of the ideal *shih* in office.[30] Stone is known for its firmness and durability, two desirable qualities in candidates for office. The color red often signifies good faith and loyalty.[31] (The most famous red stone in China, of course, was cinnabar, a chemical base for the production of the elixir of immortality. Perhaps the *Mystery* reminds us that good character can win us lasting fame, which is a type of immortality.)[32]

> App. 9: When error[33] comes from repeated faults,[34]
> Ten years[35] is too short to restore true measure.
> Fath. 9: Those cumulative mistakes
> Mean: Constructive action is precluded.[36]

Appraisal 9 signifies action that comes too late in the cycle.[37] As faults are compounded over time, the person is led ever further from the True Path. The *Changes* says of such a situation:

> He misses the return. Misfortune. There will be disaster. . . . For ten
> years, it will not be possible to go forward again. . . . Such is the
> opposition to the way of the noble man.[38]

Yung
No. 53. Eternity
August 13–August 17 (a.m.)

Correlates with Earth's Mystery;
Yang; *the phase Wood; and the*
Yi ching Hexagram no. 32, Duration;[1] *the sun enters the Wing constellation, 6th degree*

HEAD: Yin seizes by force of arms. Yang endows by civil means.[2] The Way can be made to last forever.

In Han thinking, yin *ch'i* is allied with punishments and war, while yang is associated with the gentler rule of suasive example that gradually habituates lesser creatures to the norms of civilization. Since autumn has begun, the Head refers to the killing power of yin *ch'i* associated with the harvest. (Until now, the warmth of yang has promoted only growth and renewal.) As the Head text makes plain, cosmic balance requires both yang and yin *ch'i*, spring/summer and autumn/winter, suasive example and punishments, give and take. Certain Confucians of a particularly idealistic stamp had been known to dispute this idea; they argued instead that the good ruler's example over time obviates the need for any punishments by the sage-ruler.[3]

An equally significant aspect of Tetragram 53 is the identification of "eternal rules" that "make [things] endure"[4] with traditional hierarchy in the family and state. The Appraisals therefore discuss patrilineal succession and the so-called Three Guide Lines of ruler-subject, father-child, and husband-wife. These hierarchies are said to be eternal in at least two senses: first, they are are modeled upon preordained cosmic patterns that operate throughout all time; second, adherence to these norms creates an orderly society that can attain lasting peace.

> App. 1: Not to demote the heir or fault his claim,[5]
>   Choosing the eldest son is the constant rule.[6]
> Fath. 1: Neither deposing nor faulting
>   Means: To preserve forever the ancestral line.

In commoner families in ancient China, the principle was equal inheritance among the sons. At the imperial court, however, one important controversy focused on the best way to decide the apppointment of the heir apparent. Many Confucian scholars argued that the eldest son, regardless of his mother's status in the hierarchy of the back palace, should inherit the title and responsibilities of his father; his mother's eventual elevation to the rank of empress would naturally be arranged "on account of the son."[7] However, other scholars, equally eminent, defined the eldest son quite differently. For them, only the eldest son of the principal wife could become the legitimate heir, regardless of his age relative to other royal sons. Only a few scholars argued that the most meritorious of the royal sons should be appointed heir, in imitation of practices attributed to the Golden Age of the past.[8]

Yang Hsiung's talk of the eldest son clearly opposes the principle of imperial succession based on merit. The absence of strict guidelines for the succession led to competition between brothers during the ruler's lifetime; often it led to chaos after his death, when rival factions put forward different candidates for the throne. Merit is, after all, in the eyes of the beholder. Rules for succession should always adhere to age as the chief criterion, lest the entire royal court be plagued by internal disputes.[9] This naturally implies the father's responsibility to see to it that his eldest son is so well schooled in the moral and practical arts that there can be no real objection to his installation as heir. Only in this way can the direct patrilineal line from the ancestors be preserved and its multiple functions (religious, social, and economic) be carried out.

The verses offer criticism of the late Western Han court's inept handling of various succession crises. When Emperor P'ing died in A.D. 5, for example, the appointment of his successor sparked considerable controversy. On the pretext that the selection of an older candidate would confuse generational lines, Wang Mang allegedly chose the youngest possible candidate; it was rumored that Wang intended to build a secure power base during the long regency needed for a infant emperor.[10]

> App. 2: He longs to demote the heir and fault his claim.
>   Forever lost are propriety's blessings.
> Fath. 2: Longing within to demote or find fault
>   Means: How can the line be made to last?

Here, Yang Hsiung criticizes the benighted family head who disinherits the eldest son, thereby overturning the natural preordained order of succession. With such a negative example, how can the royal house be expected to maintain its power for long?[11]

> App. 3: Eternal is his Way.
>   A blameless state is achieved.[12]
> Fath. 3: Eternal is his Way,
>   Meaning: Truly, this can be preserved.

The *Analects* insists, "It is not the Way which makes human beings great, but human beings who make the Way great."[13] Here the individual has dedicated himself to absolute conformity with the Way. Because he is good, he avoids unlucky blame (the enmity of his fellow men). Through his steady accumulation of virtue he himself partakes of the eternal nature of the Tao. Worldly success, however, is by no means assured.[14]

> App. 4: The succession order is set aside.
> To favor secondary wives[15]
> Means eternal loss for rightful masters.
> Fath. 4: That the order of sons is disordered
> Means: This is no way to make it eternal.

The disruption of the natural order of succession undermines the fundamental principles embodied in sacred ritual. Though a favorite may persuade the ruler to name her son as heir, such an unlawful appointment spells lasting trouble for the entire family.

All extant commentaries read the lines somewhat differently:

> The order of sons is disordered.
> When the guest goes first, the host is lost forever.
> The order of sons is disordered,
> Meaning: This is not the method [to insure] eternity.

In this reading, disorder inside the family finds its parallel in discourteous relations between guest and host. After all, the conventions are equally ignored when the guest takes the lead in a ceremony and when a younger son claims the title of heir.

> App. 5: The Three Guide Lines attain Center Perfection.[16]
> Heaven makes its good fortune eternal.
> Fath. 5: Eternal through the Three Guide Lines[17]
> Means: Their Way lasts forever.

At least since the time of Tung Chung-shu (176?–104? B.C.), the term "Three Guide Lines" has been used to signify the all-important social relations between ruler/subject, father/child, and husband/wife, which in theory balance rights and responsibilities to the mutual benefit of all parties.[18] The fundamental importance of these three social relations is suggested in two ways: first, their collective name identifies them as what gives shape to the social fabric; second, the relations are treated here in Appraisal 5, the central position of the tetragram. Through repeated ritual acts the wise ruler promotes the values embodied in the Guide Lines. By the time all have learned to emulate his example, the ruler himself has reached that state of godlike perfection called *chung-chi* ("Center Perfection"), so that he henceforth functions as *axis mundi* for the entire universe.[19] Harmony and good fortune will prevail, with mutual obligations supported by ritual behavior.

App. 6: The great presume good fortune eternal.[20]
Returning to an empty court, he enters
The great darkness he brought on himself.[21]
Fath. 6: In greatness, thinking good fortune eternal
Means: Good fortune turns to ruin.

Like its prototype, the *Book of Changes*, the *Mystery* cautions all fortunate people to proceed with great care, lest they bring about their own downfall by arrogant behavior. There is only one sure way for the great to extend their good fortune and protect themselves against ruin: that way is to pile up more virtue through ritual observances (the only secure kind of good fortune).[22] Those less fortunate will then respond with love and respect, rather than with hate and fear. The subject of these verses forgets this simple lesson. Thus he is totally unprepared for the calamity that he has brought upon himself.[23] That his courtyard (his mind? his physical home?) is empty suggests that he deserves to have no loyal adherents.[24] His life is also empty in that it lacks lasting achievements. Had he only upheld the eternal standards embodied in the Three Guide Lines, ignominious defeat could have been avoided.

App. 7: By the old tree new sprouts grow,
Which eternally twine its hollows.[25]
Fath. 7: That an old tree grows the "time"
Means: Eternal is its body.

Appraisal 7, well past the halfway mark, depicts an old tree well past its prime. Fortunately, the Appraisal corresponds to auspicious Day, so we can expect some kind of restoration. Either new sprouts spring from old wood, as many commentators assume, or the green tendrils of the "time plant"[26] wind round the old wood, binding its hollows together, and extending its lifespan. The support of the young gives the old a new lease on life.[27]

App. 8: Permanent lapses lead to ill fortune,[28]
Bringing ruin down on one's heirs.
Fath. 8: Persisting in error
Means: His decree[29] is cut by half.

Repeatedly the petty man leaves the path of Goodness. His persistent errors can only lead to ruin, since no lasting good fortune can come from abandoning the Way of the ancients. Repeated evil acts, however, not only affect the present life of the wicked individual, but they also damage the lives of his descendants. Besides transmitting a bad example to junior members of the family, parental misbehavior depletes the portion of vital life-force available to descendants in their patrimony.[30] Thus the sins of the father are likely to be visited upon the sons, according to the Chinese notion of collective responsibility.

> App. 9: Always, at the end, conform to the beginning.
> Fath. 9: Ends that always conform to beginnings
> Mean: He prolongs joy and true ease.[31]

Appraisal 9 marks the end of the cycle, yet, in a seeming paradox, the *Mystery* writes of the joys associated with new beginnings. The truly moral person feels a kind of inner strength and vitality akin to that of youth, even when facing his own end.[32] This strength, of course, comes from continual efforts at self-improvement. He takes care to act to follow the ancient injunction:

> You should make your virtue ever new. At the last, as at first, have
> this as your one object: daily self-renewal.[33]

As he takes care to orient himself by the Way, itself the origin of all things, he returns to the beginning, even at the end.[34]

昆 ☰☰

K'un
No. 54. Unity
August 17 (p.m.)–August 21

Correlates with Earth's Mystery; Yin; the phase Metal; and the Yi ching Hexagram no. 13, Fellowship with Men; the sun enters the Wing constellation, 11th degree

HEAD: Yin is about to divide them, but yang still unifies them. The Way of Unity exalts[1] sympathetic union.[2]

In general, it is the physical *ch'i* that allows the multiple properties of a thing to cohere; it is also *ch'i* that contains the properties that differentiate one thing from another. The *Mystery* credits yang *ch'i* with the nurturing impulse to keep things intact, which counters the disintegrating impulses identified with yin *ch'i*.[3] At this point in the annual cycle, just prior to the Autumn Equinox, yin and yang are almost in balance.[4] A kind of stasis has been achieved, which makes for cohesion, at least temporarily. Since unity by definition is entirely good, according to the *Mystery*, the Appraisals must depart from their usual format designed to illustrate both good and bad connotations of the term employed for the tetragram's title.

Yang *ch'i* epitomizes undifferentiated love in the cosmos.[5] Like a good ruler, yang fosters a strong sense of community in fragmented things as it responds to their needs, forging an effective whole. Specifically, in the realm of Man, the Appraisals suggest that three main factors contribute to unity: (1) the elite's empathy for those in trouble,[6] (2) a necessary consensus on morality, and (3) an equitable government policy in the public interest. Once achieved, unity becomes the single most important factor in stabilizing dynastic rule.[7] With a true meeting of all minds, unity and good fellowship can reign supreme.

> App. 1: United with the black,
>   He does not know the white.
> Fath. 1: At one with the black
>   Means: He is not fit to be called "human."

For the good Confucian, it is the potential to be Good that distinguishes the human being from the beast.[8] This potential develops when the powers of discrimination basic to the heart/mind are habitually employed. Most commentators, therefore, apply these lines to benighted individuals who fail to distinguish good (= the white, the pure, and knowledge) from bad (= the black, the impure, and stupidity),[9] even when confronted with glaring examples. In embracing the wicked, such individuals lose any vestige of true humanity. The *Model Sayings* identifies "following ritual and duty" as the ideal practice for those who wish to avoid beastliness.[10]

The contrast between black and white, however, need not only refer to morality.[11] The lines function equally well as critical comments on predetermined views or onesidedness.[12] Only an openminded person "who sees a question from all sides"[13] is fit to be called "human."

> App. 2: White and black intermingle.[14]
>   Three birds, one beak, same tail.
> Fath. 2: For three birds, one beak
>   Means: There is no harm in their hearts.

Confucius said:

> The noble man, though in harmony [with others], does not [necessarily] agree [with them].[15]

That white and black coexist means that the gentleman can live among lesser mortals without being sullied himself.[16] Moral superiors may also sometimes find it expedient to join with lesser men in defense of life and property. (In terms of the metaphor, they may use the same beak.) This reading, unfortunately, does little to explain the final line of the Fathoming.[17]

However, one commentator imagines a better society in which, "[Their] forms may differ but [their] heart's desires are the same."[18] But if social harmony is not to be undercut by such variety, those in the group must believe that they share a common foundation and goals (here, a common beak and tail).[19] This sharing strengthens the communal bonds between men, so that they flock together as naturally as birds.[20]

> App. 3: United with the white,
>   Lost from not being black.[21]
>   No point of connection.[22]
>   For one tail, three beaks.
> Fath. 3: Joining the white, not with the black
>   Means: Neither feels kin to the other.

As the commentators offer no convincing explanation for these lines, my translation is necessarily tentative. For one single end (the tail), there are numerous approaches (the beak). Apparently, no single meeting point can be found between various groups in opposition. Such uncompromising attitudes naturally preclude the formation of real community.

In an alternate reading, the individual who initially joins with the white comes to congratulate himself on simply not being "black," and so makes no real effort to improve himself. Insofar as he remains uncultivated, his efforts will be scattered.

> App. 4: Birds trust their nests to the thickets.[23]
>   Men trust their fates to just regimes.
> Fath. 4: Birds entrusting their nests
>   Mean: Where there is justice, there are no poor.

Good government acting in the public interest unifies the community. Such governments act to protect their fragile subjects from economic ills, just as the sturdy thicket serves to protect fragile bird nests from the elements. In return for this support, the common people give their allegiance to the ruler.[24]

> App. 5: The hub is no hub[25]
>   With spokes unevenly spaced.
>   Many hairline cracks ruin the jade.
> Fath. 5: Hubs with spokes unevenly spaced
>   Mean: How could they ever be even enough?

As luxury items, both carriages and jade objects are reserved for members of the ruling elite. Appraisal 5 usually refers to the Son of Heaven as center of the state. The carriage wheel is a particularly apt symbol for state unity, since it can only function well if many different parts (the spokes) come together in a single focus.[26] The ruler is like the wheel hub in that all his subjects must revolve around him; it is he, in turn, who gives shape to their efforts.[27] The ruler's person can provide a focus for his subjects' many talents, however, only to the degree that the ruler is evenhanded in his treatment.[28] Should the ruler distribute his favors unfairly, the state will break down.[29] In effect, this breakdown will result from the many rifts between ruler and individual subject, each seemingly unimportant at the time. The analogy is to the numerous hairline cracks that mar an otherwise valuable piece of jade.[30]

> App. 6: Uniform measures for well and market;
> Writing made standard, and also the carts.
> Fath. 6: Uniform measures at well and market
> Mean: All share a single order.[31]

Wells and markets, writing and carts, are four institutions created by the sages according to divine cosmic patterns. The well and market both exemplify the interdependence of various groups in a good society, since these are places where villagers tend to congregate. In an ordered society, farmers (the well) and merchants (the market) meet to exchange basic commodities.

The sage-kings are said to have perfected material culture by a series of other inventions, including the writing system and the cart. After their inventions, wise rulers of later times mandated a single writing system and a standardized system of weights and measures (which regulated even the length of cart axles so that roads and wheel ruts would be of uniform width).[32] Culture is likely to advance only if the writing system is unified; economic and cultural exchange are likely to flourish only if transportation improves; and cardinal virtues like honesty will prevail only if a single pricing structure is introduced. Though such reforms represent major changes in government policy, the common people do not regard these changes as unwelcome interference in their lives; instead, they find them natural.[33] Thus is the ideal community fostered.

> App. 7: Off on the side, covers don't cover,
> Nor can they shield him [34] from evening rain.[35]
> Fath 7: That canopies askew do not cover
> Means: The disposition is not equal.

Virtue acts like a canopy to shield one from calamity. Onesided prejudice, however, leaves the individual open to disaster. For this reason, the wise ruler protects himself and his people by his equitable treatment.

Several commentators disagree with this reading. For them, both the canopy and the rain signify the ruler. Like the ruler, the canopy shelters those below; like the ruler's favors, the rain showers down. Here, however, the canopy provides inadequate shelter. Similarly, the evening rains are in some way "too inadequate" to save the crops from destruction (An alternate interpretation of Line 2 would be, "The evening rains do not save.")[36] All these failings suggest the ruler's stinginess in dispensing gifts and appointments. Neither reading bodes well for the health of the body politic.

> App. 8: He joins in danger and disaster,
>   Then defeats them, making it safe.
> Fath. 8: Safety from danger and disaster
>   Means: Throughout he extends humankindness.

Paradoxically, whoever is willing to risk his life to help others will find that this insures his own safety. Because of his real concern for his fellow man, he snatches moral victory from danger and defeat. At the same time, the good man can be trusted to return good for evil, so his enemies are dissuaded from causing further harm.

> App. 9: Uniting with death,
>   He leaves to bandits all that is left.[37]
> Fath. 9: Joining with death
>   Means: Giving up on his heaven-sent person.[38]

Though the *Mystery* does not tell us his motives, it makes it perfectly clear that this individual has thrown away his life. Perhaps suicide is the only course open to him, either because he has acted despicably or because he has valued his own life so little that he put himself in peril.[39] Had he only acted more prudently, he may never have needed to waste the precious gift of life, endowed by Heaven and bestowed by his parents.[40]

Correlates with Human's Mystery; Yang; *the phase Metal; and the* Yi ching *Hexagram no. 41, Decrease; the sun enters the Wing constellation, 15th degree; the Dipper points WSW; the musical note is A-flat*[1]

Chien
No. 55. Diminishment
August 22–August 26 (a.m.)

HEAD: Yin *ch'i* waxes; yang *ch'i* wanes. Yin prospers; yang declines. The myriad things by this [process] are made very, very small.

This tetragram opens the third and final phase in the triadic Mystery of Heaven-Earth-Man. Not surprisingly, in view of man's many imperfections, this final phase of the *Mystery* generally marks the least auspicious of the three phases. Many of the verses belonging to Tetragrams 54–81 assigned to Man specifically address individual human responsibility in the face of contrary trends and an unhappy fate.

It is autumn. The decline of the myriad things is increasingly evident. In the midst of growing troubles, the wise person does well to remember that there is "a time for decrease. . . and a time for increase. In decreasing and in increasing, . . . one must go with the time."[2] Self-restraint, perseverance in the Good, and "a decrease in faults" are advised by the *Changes*.[3] Only by such methods can one hope to escape the downward course associated with the end (whether the end be the end of the annual cycle, the end of a lifespan, or the end of a project).

> App. 1: Good at diminishing, and so undiminished.
> A mystery deep and dark.[4]
> Fath. 1: That good diminishing does not diminish
> Means: Constantly he empties himself.[5]

Appraisal 1 corresponds to first thoughts, the Water phase, and to the lowest social rank. Individuals should imitate water, whose nature it is to seek low places. By shunning the limelight and cleansing the self of egotistical impulses, the individual can avoid the calamities that result from arrogance and notoriety. Paradoxically, such decrease brings only increase in the end. As the *Lao tzu* writes:

> He does not show himself
> And so is conspicuous.
> He does not consider himself right
> And so is illustrious.
> He does not brag
> And so has merit.
> He does not boast
> And so endures.[6]

> App. 2: A heart diminished will strike itself
> So as to punish[7] his own person.
> Fath. 2: That a heart reduced inflicts the self
> Means: He confines it at center.

Evil acts that ignore the conscience diminish the heart. As the moral will is weakened over time, the body's physical store of *ch'i* is gradually depleted. Once hidden inner weaknesses affect the entire body, the damage they have wrought becomes obvious to all.[8] Then "what truly is inside takes form on the outside."[9] Though the petty man tries to attribute his failing powers to an innate incapacity for Good, the truth is that he himself has stunted his own development by hampering his conscience.[10]

> App. 3: Decreasing his decorum[11]
> > Helps to bring light to the steps.
> Fath. 3: Decreasing ceremony
> > Means: He wishes to restrain himself.[12]

In most cases, decorum and ceremony have positive connotations in ancient China, but here the *Mystery* calls for a decrease in pomp and ceremony. The steps symbolize advancement in the official bureaucracy. Therefore, the verses may decry those in high position who use elaborate ceremony simply to distance themselves from those below.[13] Or, they may warn those who want to advance further against excessive pomp and display. For members of the ruling elite, a desire for less formality (the initial act of self-restraint) may lead eventually to even greater and more widespread self-restraint, as "higher-ups" accept the frank remonstrances of those below. If they respond by working to reform themselves, their advance in the Way (and often, incidentally, in their careers) proceeds quickly.

Occasionally, the graph translated as "ceremony" means "canons" or "rules." It is conceivable, then, that Yang Hsiung makes a second argument: laws should be promulgated only when they demonstrably keep the population from committing evil actions. When laws are kept to a minimum, men will work to restrain themselves. This will lead to social order and the glory of the dynastic house.

> App. 4: Good order diminished[14]
> > Reduces his position.
> Fath. 4: Decreasing order
> > Means: This is no way to control the masses.

State control is justified insofar as it relieves the masses from crippling insecurities (such as those prompted by crime or natural disasters). If the government cannot insure good order, it no longer deserves the support of the masses.[15] Here the petty man in high office can neither control disorder nor hold onto his own position. How, then, could he hope to transform the masses through the suasive force of his moral example?

> App. 5: Decrease: the proven good of Yellow Earth.
> > When the low receives from the high: true peace.
> Fath. 5: Decrease as Yellow's virtue
> > Means: The subordinate's Way is now proper.[16]

Appraisal 5, of course, corresponds to the Son of Heaven. Yellow (or gold) is the color identified with desirable centrality and with Earth. The good king acts as the center for his kingdom provided that he distributes his favors fairly among his subjects, in effect downplaying his own elevated position. In this, he mimics Earth's own propensity to level itself. In return for his humility, he wins the maximum cooperation from those below.[17] This makes for peace and social order.

> App. 6: Obscuring what was clear,[18]
> > He amasses but never reduces,
> > Ungiving as a stone.
> App. 6: Obscuring, ungiving
> > Means: His favors do not bring balance.[19]

The wise ruler distributes just rewards to those below, with several aims in mind: (1) he wishes to focus attention on examples of model conduct, (2) he wishes to "share his pleasures" with the common people, and (3) he wishes to teach them the virtues of cooperation.[20] The stupid ruler confuses the mere accumulation of land and goods with the accumulation of charismatic authority.[21] Such an individual, intent only on adding to his coffers, fails to reduce taxes or bestow bounties on the subject population.[22] Since the stingy ruler fails to teach his people the benefits of generosity, they, not unreasonably, feel they owe him no more loyalty than they do a stone.

> App. 7: Decreasing his infirmities,[23]
> > And so diminishing his cares,
> > The danger thus is stayed.
> Fath. 7: Decreasing his infirmities
> > Means: He brings no danger on himself.

In the *Changes*, the phrase "decreasing his infirmities" signifies the noble man's reformation of his faults.[24] Through continual reform, the individual is brought to the state where his health (moral, mental, and perhaps physical) improves. Now in his prime, the individual is strong enough to withstand difficulty; thus, he avoids danger.

> App. 8: Its flowing out in floods[25]
> > Brings loss to life's root.
> Fath. 8: Flowing, ever flowing
> > Means: The living root is destroyed.

In living plants, vigorous growth depends upon strong, healthy roots. If the sap gushes out from the plant, the death of the plant inevitably follows. By analogy, in the individual conscience, the roots of moral action must be nourished by repeated noble acts. If violence is done to the conscience, it is soon destroyed.[26]

App. 9: Decrease at the end
    Helps in ascending West Mountain
    And overseeing Great River.
Fath. 9: Ascent by decrease at the end
    Means: Truly this can be done.

Climbing moutains to oversee great rivers is "using the tall to oversee what is low."[27] West Mountain is said to be the site of the Chou royal family's ancestral tombs; as such, it represents their great patrimony of charismatic virtue.[28] In popular tradition, West Mountain is also said to be the sacred abode of the immortals under their Queen Mother.[29] Finally, West Mountain is the home to which the sun daily returns after it sinks below the horizon. The mountain, therefore, links immortality with constant virtue, especially at this time of completion. The Great River is apparently no less sacred. The *Changes* literature calls it a place "beneficial to cross."[30] Perhaps it is the river that separates life from death; perhaps it refers to the waters that lie below the surface of the earth.[31]

In several works, Yang Hsiung explicitly denies the possibility of immortality.[32] The good person, in acknowledging the larger cycles operating in the universe, comes to calmly accept his own impending death, trusting that his virtue may secure him a kind of immortality.[33]

Chin
No. 56. Closed Mouth
August 26 (p.m.)–August 30

Correlates with Human's Mystery; Yin; the phase Fire; and the Yi ching Hexagram no. 12, Obstruction; the sun enters the Axletree constellation, 3d degree

HEAD: Yin does not transform it; yang does not bestow it.[1] The myriad things are each[2] closed shut.

The closed mouth can symbolize many different types of closedness, including the unwillingness to engage in orderly social intercourse, or the inability to speak or eat. More positively, it may refer to reservoirs of any kind (for example, those of *ch'i*, blood, or water). Since the *Mystery* equates human achievement with making contact, closed entities are generally regarded as unlucky. In the natural world of Heaven-and-Earth, the normal process of growth depends upon the comingling of yin and yang. The myriad things seem all but dead at this point in the year, though we know that the minimal presence of generative yang *ch'i* held in reserve (itself "closed shut") guarantees their continued existence. Not surprisingly, then, the tetragram emphasizes the inherent dangers of too much separateness. Turning to the world of Man, tradition describes the noble man as "silent, but not close-mouthed."[3] After all, so long as unity is the chief ideal, communication is its necessary vehicle. Only when disorder reigns will the moral superior sometimes need to turn away from others and "fall back upon his inner worth in order to escape difficulties," hoping that obstruction will finally revert to good fortune.[4]

> App. 1: Close-mouthed and ungiving,[5]
> The husband takes the wife's place.[6]
> Fath. 1: Close-mouthed, ungiving
> Means: This is what men find abhorrent.

There is probably both a sexual and a social metaphor here. According to Han notions of sexuality. "The man [has intercourse] in order to make the woman's *ch'i* arrive to himself; the woman, in order to expel illness."[7] The completion of the sexual act, which required the comingling of distinct fluids from both male and female, was known to regulate the blood circulation and to relax the nervous system, with the added benefit that children might be produced. Here the male fails to to bestow his yang fluids on a female partner.[8] (Possibly he is impotent, with the result that no fluids are exchanged. Possibly he hoards his seminal fluids, thereby weakening his female partner.[9] Possibly he is only interested in taking male partners into his bed.) Such an "ungiving male" becomes like a woman in the sense that his penile opening (one "mouth") does no more to release yang *ch'i* into the vagina (the female "mouth") than that of a female would. This departure from proper conjugal roles recalls the overturned norms of the winter season, when yin seems to dominate while yang shrinks back.

These same lines equally describe a man who prefers seclusion within the home (traditionally, the woman's place) to fulfilling his masculine responsibilities as public representative of the household.[10] As the *Changes* writes, "Not to venture outside the gate and courtyard is unlucky."[11] Failure to uphold one's natural societal role is abhorrent to others, because it is an offense against the human order.

> App. 2: The blood, if closed off,[12]
> Nourishes dry bones.
> Fath. 2: The closed system of blood
> Means: The emaciated body grows fat on its own.

Once again, the lines refer to ancient Chinese medical concepts that recognize the life-giving properties of blood. If the individual by various techniques can learn to direct internal blood circulation, he can restore vigor to his entire system, rather than succumb to the progressive desiccation of the bones, body, and spirit associated with old age. In effect, the individual learns how to "keep the self whole and nourish oneself."[13] By analogy, the moral superior learns to revitalize his spirit through mastery of the Confucian Way. As the "Great Learning" says, "Riches enrich the house; virtue enriches one's person."[14]

> App. 3: His demeanor is standoffish,[15]
> He stammers at the mouth.[16]
> Closed off, he has no words.
> Fath. 3: Disengaged from others[17]
> Means: The Way of Man is slighted.

Human beings have an unusual facility to create a meaningful community through the vehicle of speech. The individual described here refuses to use that gift. Though Han recluses claimed that they served higher goals than mere social cohesion, insofar as their conduct undercut the very basis of society, it was less than human.[18]

> App. 4: Shutting up his stores of grain,
> He defies custom by failing to save[19]
> Even the old and members of his clan.
> Fath. 4: Closing off his grain
> Means: They cannot look to each other with hope.

According to Yang's schema, this set of verses should be auspicious. Therefore, some interpretations of the Appraisal depict a providential head of the household who prudently decides to reserve stores of grain for those deserving of special consideration: the aged and fellow clan members. For "not to relieve would not be customary, as it would affect the aged even of the clan" (an alternate reading of the second and third line of the Appraisal). Unfortunately, the Fathoming line then makes no sense.

Another commentator appears to argue that the verses describe the good ruler who punishes ("putting in bonds")[20] even his close relatives if they do not conform to custom. Their pleas for special treatment are justly ignored since responsibility to the state properly overrides family considerations.[21] At least this explanation has the merit of explaining the Fathoming.

My translation offers an internally consistent, though inauspicious reading.[22] See the following Appraisal for another treatment of the miser.

> App. 5: Keeping neither to center nor Mean,
> He harvests rotten vermin.[23]

Fath. 5: Neither centered nor moderate
Means: His close-mouthedness is wrong.

The evil man commits one of two errors (both indicated by Yang's ambiguous phrasing). Either he hoards grain so long that all he finds in his storehouse are the rotted corpses of the rats who feasted on his stores of grain. Or, in his inveterate stinginess, the miser himself becomes a "rat." Whoever hoards his resources, in fact, turns out to be his own worst enemy.[24] He has forgotten that the sole purpose of accumulation is to permit the later dispersal of grain and goods to promote the Good. By contrast, "though the superior man accumulates, he is also able to disperse."[25]

App. 6: The spring at its source, full to overflowing,
Is held in reserve on the hill in the park.[26]
App. 6: The closing off of the source of the spring[27]
Means: It cannot be criticized.

Appraisal 6 corresponds to the Water phase; hence, the spring is used as metaphor. The swelling waters indicate the abundant force of Water. Water is like the "ever-flowing *ch'i*" that endows the body with physical and moral strength. The source of the *ch'i*'s flow is the conscience, which keeps to the high moral ground.[18] The hill specifically described is a high mound depressed at top so that it forms a natural reservoir. Just as deep waters may collect until they are needed, the good conscience quietly gathers strength, awaiting the time when it will be put to use.[29] In this case, to be closed at the mouth is praiseworthy.

App. 7: If closed off in the limbs,[30]
The Yellow Flesh decays.
Fath. 7: Blocked in the four limbs
Means: Bones and flesh are harmed.

Appraisal 7 represents decay. The color yellow always refers to what is central, suggesting the marrow, the innermost muscles, or possibly the vital organs.[31] If the circulating *ch'i* and blood are held up in the appendages,[32] the center body cannot be nourished adequately. If this metaphor is applied to the body politic, all resources of the state are siphoned off by secondary figures, so that the people's welfare is neglected.[33] If the metaphor applies to family relations, lesser figures grab much needed resources for themselves.[34]

App. 8: Blocked and confronting calamity,
He offers an ox to expiate blame.
Fath. 8: Blocked and facing calamity
Means: The great expense is justified.

The wise man who meets with calamity takes immediate steps to remedy the situation. First, he acknowledges his faults, then he tries to make reparation for his crimes. Finally, he reverently makes sacrifices to the gods, sparing no expense, in order to expiate his sins. Generosity, reverence, and ritual can counter the miserable "closed-mouthedness" associated with miserly spirits.[35]

> App. 9: Closed skies do not rain.
> Dried meat is dried out more.[36]
> Fath. 9: Blocked and no rain
> Means: What can one hope for?

Rain signifies a balance between yin and yang.[37] If a drought lasts for weeks on end, a serious cosmic imbalance exists. Since fructifying rainfall symbolizes the ruler's grace and favors, drought indicates that the "king's favors have dried up, so that people and things are exhausted."[38] Once his subjects no longer look to him with hope and love, their conduct is marked by increasing desperation.[39]

Shou
No. 57. Guardedness
August 31–September 4 (a.m.)

Correlates with Human's Mystery; Yang; the phase Wood; and the Yi ching Hexagram no. 12, Obstruction; the sun enters the Axletree constellation, 6th degree

HEAD: Yin guards the door; yang guards the gate. No things make contact.

Yin guards what is relatively inside; yang takes care of what is comparatively outside. Thus, yin may be said to keep watch over earth, while yang watches Heaven.[1] Since yin and yang are each at their separate stations, apparently defending their own territories, there can be no mutual contact. With the marvelous capacity for interaction lost to the myriad things, no thing can germinate or grow.

> App. 1: Shut the double windows
> To guard first possessions.
> Fath. 1: Shutting the double windows
> Means: He is good at keeping what he has.

Figure 16. The tilt-hammer (sometimes called the treadle) used in pounding rice. Illustration from San ts'ai tu h'ui, *an encyclopedia of 1609, "Utensils" section, 11/39b.*

Since Appraisal 1 refers to the Beginning of Thought, the "double windows" most likely refer to the eyes and ears as primary vehicles for sensory contact with the outside world. In general, Han philosophy does not celebrate denial of the senses for its own sake. At the same time, many texts recognize that sensation-seeking deters one from reverent attention to social duty. Driven by desire, a person "is agitated, with his thoughts helter-skelter."[2] One classical text says:

> The people are born good. It is because of [desires for] external things that they change.[3]

If this is so, then to preserve Man's original potential for Goodness, the individual must learn to lessen desire.[4] The good man keeps unnecessary distractions at bay, the better to dedicate himself to pursuit of the Way.

Three commentators read the poem quite differently. The windows stand for ways to view the world outside. That the windows are double suggests "factionalism among friends."[5] Thus the good official, if he is to remain principled, must avoid viewing the world through the biases of his faction.[6]

> App. 2: To blindly preserve the self
> Is not as good as "maintaining the One."[7]
> Fath. 2: Blindly bent on self-preservation
> Means: At center, he lacks a way to sustain himself.[8]

In Confucian terms, to abandon moral considerations in order to save one's own person demonstrates a kind of blindness. Paradoxically, in the desire to save himself, the individual loses all sense of self. He knows that his principles will be thrown to the winds as soon as real or imagined danger appears. The individual would do better in moral and practical terms to keep a steady course of action, in which he "firmly grasps the One"[9] by single-minded devotion to the One Way.

> App. 3: Neither losing nor gaining,
> He comes and goes in silence.
> Fath. 3: Neither losing nor gaining
> Means: He maintains his original state.

The *Changes* associates "neither losing nor gaining" with good order.[10] The noble man disregards material gain or loss, praise or blame, since he only cares for the Way.[11] This insures that he maintains his original potential for Goodness endowed by Heaven.

> App. 4: Images of snarling dogs[12] on guard.
> Fath. 4: Guarded by a make-believe dog
> Means: Integrity[13] has nothing to rely upon.[14]

To scare away thieves, Han dynasty buildings were frequently decorated with painted or sculpted images of guard dogs. (Door knockers, for example, were made in this shape.) Such models prove ineffective since even the stupidest of robbers can easily tell the difference between an image of a dog and the real thing. The poem mocks those who believe that others cannot see behind their public masks to their true intentions and character.[15] The poem may also mock those who rely on false friends as allies.

    App. 5: Guarding center by harmony[16]
        In covenants with marquises,
        He is tried and true.[17]
    Fath. 5: Holding the center by harmony
        Means: The feudal lords turn to him.

Appraisal 5 represents the Son of Heaven and center. According to Han readings of the "Great Plan" chapter of the *Documents*, the emperor holds fast to the Way of Centrality and Harmony through ritual action. As his word can be trusted, the feudal lords will acknowledge his sovereignty through various covenants.

    App. 6: The carriage rests on the block.
        The jade tablet and disc gather dust.
    Fath. 6: The carriage on the block
        Means: He fails to contact his neighbors.

The carriage symbolizes contact through trade, war, and diplomacy. The jade tablet and round *pi* disc are associated with both state sacrifice and high office. Though the two most important affairs of state are sacrifice and war,[18] here the state neglects its functions. No meetings are held; no tokens of good faith are exchanged. Ritual obligations (both public and private) are ignored. Since the ruler no longer extends his civilizing influence to others, neighboring fiefs no longer benefit from his proximity. While Lao tzu celebrates states that express no interest in their neighbors,[19] the *Mystery* equates lack of contact with calamity.

    App. 7: The many yang greatly[20] defend
        The male offspring's propriety.
    Fath. 7: The defense by various yang
        Means: He guards propriety and good faith.

The commentators offer little help here. It seems that the active nature of male yang (as opposed to the quiescent nature of yin) leads it to defend (while yin tends to thwart.)[21] The Head text talks of yang guarding the gate. Images of guarded passageways appear also in Appraisals 1 and 4. As the male heir moves out into the public world, his proper sphere, his acts of virtue will summon the vitality, strength, and creativity of yang *ch'i* in its many aspects to protect him.

> App. 8: The mortar lacks a pestle.
> His treadle is raised.[22]
> The sky clouds over but no rain falls:
> Glaring sun and blazing heat.
> Fath. 8: To be without a pestle
> Means: What he preserves is poverty.

The basic tools to secure a livelihood are lacking: even the mortar lacks a pestle. What's more, even the tools at hand are used improperly: the treadle is raised rather than rammed down. At the very least, the individual is confused. Perhaps he is also lazy. Such a person can expect no help from Heaven. Without Heaven's help, a drought will blast the crops, so that only poverty is preserved.

> App. 9: Joining the white-haired in their principles,[23]
> He rejects the young with their coal-black hair.
> He is not in danger.
> Fath. 9: Joining the aged in having principles
> Means: The old excel[24] the new.

In China, men of experience tend to be valued over strapping youths. One chapter of the *Documents* has a wise ruler saying:

> Henceforth I shall take advice from the aged and then be free from error. Those white-haired officers whose physical strength is failing, I would rather have. Those dashing brave officers, who are faultless in shooting and charioteering, I would rather not have.[25]

Correlates with Human's Mystery; Yin; the phase Metal; and the Yi ching *Hexagram no. 57, The Penetrating; the sun enters the Axletree constellation, 11th degree; the Dipper points due west; the musical note is A*[1]

Hsi
No. 58. Closing In
September 4 (p.m.)–September 8

HEAD: Yin as it comes moves against change; yang as it goes adapts to transformation.[2] Things, retreating, descend below to gather together.

At this time of the year, yin waxes while yang wanes. Since yin *ch'i* rises from below (contrary to the action of its allied Phase Water, which flows downward), it may be said to go against natural change.[3] It can also be said to move against change insofar as it harms other things.[4] Yang *ch'i* now descends from on high, another action in opposition to the characteristic activity of its allied phase, Fire, whose nature is to rise up. Still, yang may be said to adapt to transformation, either because it continues to foster growth or, as seems more likely, because it accedes to yin's temporary rule.[5]

One of Yang Hsiung's autocommentaries takes "entering" as a gloss for the tetragram's title.[6] Some read the title as "joining."[7] As the harvest is gathered in, things shut down, after which they hibernate or withdraw into their shells. After closing in, then, all join together in entering a state of rest.[8]

> App. 1: Wildly they clash[9] in the dark,
> Closing on their goals.[10]
> Though they wish to wander freely,[11]
> Heaven does not foster them.[12]
> Fath. 1: Thrashing in the dark
> Means: Heaven is not yet with them.

Appraisal 1 usually describes first thought. Here various conflicting desires and ambitions contend for dominance in the hidden recesses of the mind. With the individual confused, personal goals are somehow constrained, so that the person is hampered from seeing self-cultivation as the only goal worthy of his efforts. Just when the season calls for "gathering in" (i.e., conserving rather than expending valuable resources), the mind wastes itself on undirected activity. Heaven frowns upon the individual's lack of direction and restraint.[13] Such profound ignorance of Heaven's patterns does not augur well. Only minds with a unified vision in accord with cosmic laws can hope to succeed.

> App. 2: Closing in at the dark center,
> He aims for what is tried and true.[14]
> Fath. 2: Into the dark center
> Means: He corrects the self.[15]

The individual maximizes his own charismatic force by focusing on his "dark center," the hidden conscience, wellspring of all good action that reflects the dark center of phenomenal existence, the Tao. Once his thoughts focus on the Way, succeeding actions will not go astray, just as a careful aim in archery insures an accurate shot. This directed devotion to the Right contrasts with the aimless activity described in Appraisal 1.

> App. 3: All intent on eating, gobble gobble.
> Fath. 3: Intent on gobbling
> Means: Profit for him is like a ritual dance.[16]

Appraisal 3 describes the person who is "advancing." The individual's desires and ambitions are insatiable, as indicated by his hasty gobbling of the food put before him. As one commentator remarks, "[This is] an image of one who will go absolutely anywhere [in avid pursuit of profit]."[17] In contrast, the true gentleperson who eagerly follows the rituals "never goes on eating until he is sated"; from ritual he learns useful self-restraint.[18]

> App. 4: Closing its wings
> Helps it to rise.
> Fath. 4: Closing in on what makes him rise[19]
> Means: This is the aid of true friends.

In Chinese, as in English, "raising" or "rising up" is associated with elevation in official rank no less than with physical movements. The graph for "wings" is cognate with that for "protection" or "support";[20] for this reason, it often appears in the titles for the king's officers. Chinese tradition suspects the self-made man, arguing that a man of true virtue attracts worthy friends to support and protect him.[21] The wings folded in, therefore, symbolize the good man's rise to power through the concerted efforts of true friends.

> App. 5: He draws in his belly
> To avoid[22] the grain.[23]
> Fath. 5: Collapsing the belly
> Means: This is no way to build a reputation.[24]

The belly is commonly identified in Chinese philosophy as the seat of the physical appetites for food and sex. These lines probably mock the benighted individual who denies himself various human pleasures in the vain hope of attaining immortality through a strict regimen.[25] No enduring reputation can be gained by either asceticism or eremitism since both defy the ritual norms.

> App. 6: A golden[26] heart and vast wings
> Draw in to Heaven.
> Fath. 6: The golden heart and vast wings
> Means: They help to get support.

The golden heart, of course, refers to the heart/mind of one who exemplifies good faith, the virtue associated with Yellow and Center. The vast wings suggest unusual strength that may be employed to shield others from harm. If the heart refers to the king, the wings are his worthy officials.[27] It is equally possible, however, that perfect virtue and great strength are here conjoined in a single individual, whose efforts will be blessed.

> App. 7: Drawn in the arrow's string—[28]
> > Ah, how pitiable!
> Fath. 7: Grief from the string drawn in
> > Means: He is caught in the net of harm.[29]

The hunter ties a string to his arrow for three good reasons: first, the fallen prey is then more easily located by the hunter; second, the arrow is then preserved for future use; and third, the string comes in handy when the hunter goes to pin back the pitiful wings that still struggle to fly. The bird shot down in midflight is effortlessly pulled towards the archer, who easily binds its wings, making escape impossible. By analogy, the person in midcareer is easily felled by a calculating enemy, who renders his prey utterly helpless.

> App. 8: He shakes off the net,
> > Breaking its meshes:
> > A close call.
> Fath. 8: Shaking nets and cutting cords
> > Means: In danger, he manages to go on.[30]

Though the hunter's prey is already ensnared, it manages to struggle free. Such a narrow escape must strike the victim's heart with fear. If the individual is thereby inspired to reform his behavior, initial calamity can end in good fortune.

> App. 9: He brandishes his horn,
> > Using it only to attack[31] his kin.
> Fath. 9: Brandishing its horn
> > Means: He exterminates his own kind.[32]

Provocative acts often bring down destruction not only upon oneself, but upon one's relatives.[33] This was especially true in ancient China, where the law assumed collective responsibility for all serious crimes. The violent criminal may find his entire clan exterminated and his ancestors forever deprived of sacrifices. In this way, evil persons draw disaster into their own homes.

Chu
No. 59. Massing
September 9 (p.m.)–September 13

Correlates with Human's Mystery;
Yang; *the phase Earth; and the* Yi
ching *Hexagram no. 45, Gathering
Together; the sun enters the Axletree constellation, 15th degree*[1]

HEAD: Yin *ch'i* is gathering and amassing. Yang does not prohibit or prevent [anything], so things together peak[2] in their accumulation.

At this time of the year, the myriad things begin to mass together, either because they are stored together after harvest or because they huddle together in the face of harsh winter. In this, they follow the model of now dominant yin *ch'i*, which is tied to contraction, rather than expansion.[3] Interestingly, Yang Hsiung associates massing with ghosts and spirits, although in other passages of his works Yang Hsiung explicitly states that he doubts their existence.[4] Most likely, he is following the tradition of the correlate *Changes* hexagram, which is filled with talk of ghosts and ancestral spirits.[5] The *Changes* shows the wise ruler offering sacrifices to the spirits gathered at the ancestral temple, so that he may prepare for "the unforeseen"[6] and forestall confusion. Unity of mind and will is no less important in religious practice than in the conduct of war.

> App. 1: Ghosts and gods use the formless,[7]
> So numinous are they.[8]
> Fath. 1: Ghosts and gods, formless and numinous,
> Mean: Their forms are unseen.

Appraisal 1 is aligned with Water, whose source and power are invisible. Also hidden at this time of year are the myriad things, as they burrow down, retreat, or die. With all "things reverting to their base," the discussion naturally shifts to the ghosts and gods, whose operations are by definition unseen, though the results of their operations are manifest to all.[9] Apparently, the perfect efficacy of ghosts and spirits depends upon this unseen quality, for paradoxically "Whatever has form has limits. . . ."[10] For this reason, the superior man chooses to operate as much as possible behind the scenes to effect his will.

> App. 2: At the banquet they gather,
> Titter, titter.
> Fath. 2: Laughter at banquet gatherings
> Means: In their pleasure, they go to excess.[11]

Figure 17. A Han dynasty banquet. Note that the guests are seated on the floor. Chairs, which were imported from the West, became popular only in the T'ang dynasty (618–906). Illustration from rubbing of tomb relief excavated from Ch'eng-tu, Szechwan, Ting chia yao tien (46 × 42 cm).

The ordinary person wants to meet with boon companions in the pursuit of pleasure. Ignoring the constraints of ritual, he easily lapses into vacuous laughter and appalling excess. It could also be that his mediocrity prompts the ridicule of others.[12]

> App. 3: He reveres his own elders
> As gateway to the many ghosts.[13]
> Fath. 3: To revere one's own elders
> Means: The ghosts await respect.

For the ancient Chinese, piety towards living and dead forebears was the foundation of all morality.[14] Family feeling should inform the ritual

348

act so that the individual is naturally schooled in the properly reverential attitude, an attitude that could be extended to other authority figures. Many also regarded ancestor worship as a prerequisite for good fortune, since a man's ancestors could intercede on his behalf in the spirit world, thereby securing the favor of the gods in heaven. Here the *Mystery* shows the aged to be one step away from the ancestors; a single barrier (the gate of death) separates the living from the dead. Members of the household should treat their elders with respect, then, for both practical and moral reasons.[15]

> App. 4: Leading sheep to show to the thicket god,[16]
> Extending the left thigh, tablet in hand.[17]
> Both are uncouth.
> Fath. 4: Leading sheeps to thickets
> Means: This is hardly worth glorifying.[18]

The Fathoming offers severe criticism, but the commentators cannot agree on the specific nature of the ritual lapses cited here. Apparently, the right thigh, rather than the left, should be extended when bowing to the emperor during a formal audience.[19] But it is less clear what is wrong with "leading the sheep." Ssu-ma Kuang believes that it is inappropriate to offer the sacrifice of a sheep to the god of the soil, represented by a thicket of trees. Perhaps an ox should have been slaughtered, rather than the lowly sheep.[20] A modern commentator, Cheng Keng-wang, finds an additional flaw in the proceedings: No blood sacrifice is offered; the gods are only "shown" a sheep.[21] In any case, when mistakes mar the rituals, they are of no use to man or the gods; no good can come from them.[22]

> App. 5: With *yu* herbs in the tripod's blood[23]
> Good ties for nine degrees of kin,[24]
> Only then does real trust exist.
> Fath. 5: The *yu* in the tripod
> Means: There is trust[25] in the king's decree.

Appraisal 5 corresponds to the Son of Heaven, who mixes an herbal infusion in the tripod with the bloody meats as an offering to the ancestors.[26] This ceremony concludes the pact between members of the king's clan, who partake of his charismatic authority as they share the sacrificial meats.[27] Through a single ritual act, then, the entire political structure is cemented and the king's power extended.

> App. 6: Fearing his ghosts, honoring their rites,
> Wanton acts cause benightedness.
> By excess, he will be ruined.[28]

Fath. 6: Reckless acts in fearing ghosts
   Means: He goes beyond what is right for him.[29]

Many Han thinkers explicitly denounce the popular fear of ghosts, arguing that excessive sacrifices and weird cults both deplete household funds and disorder human relations.[30] As the *Tso Commentary* writes:

> When a country is about to rise, it listens to its worthy men. When the country is about to fall, it listens to the spirits.[31]

Similarly, the *Record of Ritual* warns that "excessive sacrifices bring no good fortune."[32] Those who merely fear the unknown show little inclination to embrace the sacred cosmic norms. They splurge on sacrifices, presumptuously apply for help from gods above their own station, and neglect their regular duties. All such activities would anger, rather than satisfy the inhabitants of the otherworld. Real love and honor inject an element of solemn restraint into the ritual process. In actuality, these cowards cheat the dead out of the true devotion that is their due.

App. 7: Duly reverent, they gather at the hillside grave.
Fath. 7: Reverently gathering at the hillside grave
   Means: Ritual is not forsaken.

The grave sited on a hill is regarded as especially favorable by geomantic specialists, who see in the grave a symbol both of individual death and family continuity. Here sacrifices to the dead ancestors proceed with the utmost reverence. As one treats the dead, so is one likely to treat the living members of one's family and, by extension, other figures of authority. We may expect good fortune to result.

App. 8: Owls and pigeons[33] in the forest
   Scare off[34] many other birds.
Fath. 8: Owls and pigeons in the forest
   Mean: This is frightening to many.

The Chinese consider the owl and the pigeon "robber birds"[35] since they feed upon smaller birds, fledglings, and eggs purloined from nests. Defenseless birds of other species are afraid to enter the forest, lest they be killed. By analogy, in the world of Man the vicious or violent individual (especially the slanderer) may cause widespread panic.[36]

App. 9: Snivel dripping collects at the nose.
   The family gathers[37] together.
Fath. 9: Snivel dripping and collecting at noses
   Means: A timely fate is cut off.

According to Yang's own schema, these lines should be auspicious; they should also convey an extreme example of "massing." For this reason, Fan Wang attempts a tortuous explication of the metaphors. It is more natural, however, to read this as a description of mourners gathered for a funeral. Death itself gives an extreme example of Massing; in death, the body collapses, pulling in on itself. The lines are auspicious only insofar as death rituals bring the kinship community together.[38]

Chi
No. 60. Accumulation
September 13 (p.m.)–September 17

Correlates with Human's Mystery; Yin; the phase Water; and the Yi ching Hexagram no. 26, Great Provisioning;[1] the sun enters the Horn constellation, 3d degree

HEAD: Yin is about to largely close things. Yang is still slightly opening things.[2] Mountains, valleys, wetlands, and marshes, to them the myriad things return.

Creatures return to their nests or lairs in preparation for the approach of winter. In the world of Man, it is now time for humans to consider their center,[3] their conscience. As the days darken and inauspicious yin *ch'i* accumulates, the psychic journey "home" (i.e., to one's conscience) becomes at least as important as any physical retreat. Periodic returns to the inner self are necessary for the proper functioning of each and every living thing. At the same time, continuous accumulation that knows no retrenchment tends to be fraught with danger. (The single exception is provided by virtue, the steady acquisition of which promotes physical safety and psychic security.) A good example is provided by the heedless accumulation of various luxury items like jade and silk. Not only are such luxuries easily lost to thieves or robbers; their very possession may threaten the soul. More is not necessarily better, then, despite the Legalists' tendency to link the development of charismatic power with the accretion of physical *ch'i* and the accumulation of material goods.[4]

> App. 1: Accumulating evil[5] in the dark
> > Creates the basis for what will be clear.[6]
> Fath. 1: Darkly hoarding evil
> > Means: Putting oneself in the wrong from the first.

Though the petty person repeatedly does wrong in secret, the ill effects of his crimes will soon become obvious to all.[7]

Figure 18. Illustration from a rubbing of a pottery tomb relief excavated from Chengdu, Szechwan (40 × 49 cm.), now in the Chengdu Museum. While the illustrated carriage is enclosed on three sides, a carriage "with ears" has two large side panels, but none in back. These "ears" shield the occupants of the carriage from curious eyes. Insofar as they create a visual separation, they assert the occupants' privileged status. In an ideal Confucian world, such privilege is reserved for those of special merit and virtue. A good example of a carriage "with ears" may be found at Wu-liang-ts'e (Shangtung province) in the scene where the sage Confucius meets the sage Lao tzu. See Édouard Chavannes, Mission archeologique dans la Chine septentrionale *(Paris, 1913), vol. 2, plate 71, no. 137.*

> App. 2: Accumulating the useless
> > And so coming to great use:
> > Such is the stout heart[8] of the noble man.
> Fath. 2: Amassing the useless
> > Means: He cannot be circumscribed.

Early Taoist texts extol the "usefulness of being useless." According to their arguments, only the truly useless can avoid relentless exploitation by others. The *Mystery*, however, subtly shifts the connotations of the phrase so that the poem means something like:

> Accumulating [virtue, though] it is unuscd.[9]
> And so to come to be of great use:
> Such is the stout heart of the noble man.
> Accumulating the [temporarily] unused
> Means: It cannot be circumscribed [so great is it].[10]

Unlike the petty person, the morally superior person accumulates wisdom and experience long before his appointment (i.e., when such knowledge is apparently useless), to better serve his ruler and the common people in the future.

> App. 3: Collecting stones he does not eat
>   Wastes his efforts and strength.
> Fath. 3: Piling stones that none will eat
>   Means: Nothing can be harvested.

The wise individual makes sure that his energies are expended to secure certain benefit. It only makes sense, then, for him to invest his time and effort in ways that are most likely to bring a sure return. Only the accumulation of merit carries with it an inevitable reward. Acquisition for its own sake profits the individual nothing.

> App. 4: Piling up good, the noble man
>   Gains a carriage with "ears."
> Fath. 4: Nobility amassing good
>   Means: And so he comes to prosper.[11]

The superior man grows gradually in wisdom and truth until his reputation for virtue insures an appointment to public office under a good king.[12] The carriage with "ears" (i.e., side panels) indicates high rank and imperial favor; the panels remind us that virtue acts like a screen insofar as it protects the individual from corruption.[13]

> App. 5: When stores are not full,
>   Theft brings no gain.[14]
> Fath. 5: Full stores and robbers in full supply
>   Means: As it turns out, it harms the self.[15]

Appraisal 5 corresponds to the Son of Heaven, so the failure of central government is likely to be the subject here. Because of puns, however, there are no fewer than three related ways to understand these lines. The first reading criticizes the bad ruler who exploits his subjects through taxation and corvée labor, never understanding that his interests are identical with those of the common people: "[The common people's] stores are not full./, [Yet the ruler] steals what is in short supply."[16] A second reading advises the ruler to share his wealth with the

common people to forestall all attempts at usurpation, for "when stores
are not full, / Stealing is no gain."[17] A third reading emphasizes that the
ruling elite's obsession with material goods not only depletes the treasury,
but also attracts thieves to court: "When [the ruler's] stores are not full,
robbers are few./. . . . When stores are full, robbers are many."[18] The
sage master Confucius once told a local ruler that the best way to rid himself of burglars was to excise his own thieving tendencies: "If only you
yourself were free from desire, they would not steal even if you paid them
to."[19] As the bad ruler soon learns, "Too much stored/ Ends in immense
loss."[20] Only the ruler's lack of cupidity sets a proper suasive example for
his subjects.[21]

> App. 6: Great and full he grandly disperses,[22]
> So in getting men, he has no peer.[23]
> Fath. 6: Great, full, grand, and giving
> Means: He is the one to whom all men come.[24]

Han scholars defined the king as "he to whom men gravitate."[25]
Having accumulated sufficient charismatic power, the true king disperses
goods and favors to worthy subjects, both to improve the caliber of his
bureaucracy and to incite the common people to virtue:

> The humane [ruler] employs his wealth to distinguish himself. The in-
> humane [ruler] employs his person to accumulate wealth. . . . Virtue is
> the root; wealth is secondary. If [the ruler] makes the root a secondary
> goal, he will only compete with the people and promote thievery.[26]

> App. 7: How grand the display[27]
> With jade and silk arrayed!
> Desires cut loose[28] only summon[29] thieves.
> Fath. 7: "How grand his display!"
> Means: Thieves it attracts.

Numerous Warring States and Han thinkers inveighed against lavish
display of any kind (even in the case of funeral rites), reasoning that any
conspicuous display of wealth provokes greed and violence.[30]

> App. 8: Though he piles up good,
> The hour is calamitous,
> Only because of his forebears' crimes.[31]
> Fath. 8: Accumulated good and calamitous times
> Means: It is not his fault.

The Chinese were hard pressed to provide a reasonable explanation
for cases in which the good individual meets with a bad fate. The *Mystery*

falls back upon one standard solution to the problem of evil: the family is collectively responsible for individual fate. After all, as the *Changes* says:

> The house that accumulates good is sure to have a surplus of blessings; the house that accumulates evil is sure to have a surplus of ills. When a subordinate assassinates his ruler or a son his father, it is not a matter of a single day's or night's events. The root causes build up gradually.[32]

> App. 9: Petty men's accumulated wrongs
>   Are brought home to their progeny.
> Fath. 9: Piling up evil in the petty
>   Means: They are perverted by calamity.[33]

Appraisal 9 represents Extreme Calamity. Surely evil is extreme when it blights not only the individual's own life, but also the lives of his descendants as well.

Correlates with Human's Myster; Yang; the phase Fire; and the Yi ching Hexagram no. 45, "Ornamental";[1] the sun enters the Horn constellation, 7th degree; the Dipper points due west; the musical note is A;[2] the Autumn Equinox solar period begins with Appraisal 6

Shih

No. 61. Embellishment
September 18–September 22 (a.m.)

HEAD: Yin is white while yang is black. Separately they perform their respective tasks.[3] Whether going out or entering in, they are most embellished.[4]

This tetragram marks the autumn equinox, when yin and yang, equally strong, are in exact opposition to one another. The *Mystery* conveys this stark contrast through the colors black and white. Given the Han system of correspondences, where winter (as a time of extreme yin) is symbolized by black while autumn (a time when yang is relatively greater) is white, the commentators clearly feel the need for some explication of

Yang's color symbolism. The late Eastern Han exegete Sung Chung (d. A.D. 219) reasons that yin now begins to come out into the clear light of day, while yang retreats below into shadowy realms; therefore, yin is white and yang is black. His near contemporary Lu Chi (d. ca. A.D. 250) adds, "Yin *ch'i* rules the west; hence, the talk of white [the color associated with the west in Five Phases thought]. Yang retreats to the north; hence, it is said to be black. . . ." A third commentator suggests that white refers to what is seen now and black to what is hidden.[5] A final exegesis is given by a late commentator, who suggests that in this time of yin's dominance, yang *ch'i* attempts to take on the protective coloration of yin.

It is also possible that the black and white color scheme is used to recall the elaborate patterning of certain court robes used in antique ceremonies. Ornamentation in general fulfilled an important function in ancient Chinese society. Strictly regulated by sumptuary laws, ornamentation was thought to promote good order since it drew attention to the secure social status of those singled out as moral exemplars.[6]

> App. 1: Speaking by not speaking,[7]
>   He does not use speech.
> Fath. 1: Speaking by not speaking
>   Means: Being silent, he is to be trusted.

In one sense, we regard speech as a characteristic ornament of human existence. On the other hand, early Chinese philosophers emphasized the impossibility of capturing in words the ineffable nature of Tao or Heaven. The true sage, then, models himself upon Heaven, which "does not speak" but reveals itself in deeds.[8] Confucian texts in particular tend to be wary of speech for an additional reason: Grand words ring especially false when they do not translate into brave deeds.[9] The wise person does not boast of his talents, bray about his accomplishments, or promise more than he can carry out.[10]

> App. 2: The ornament lacks substance.[11]
>   With pattern put first, faulty robes follow.[12]
> Fath. 2: Without substance, emphasizing pattern
>   Means: He loses all propriety.[13]

Numerous debates appear in early Chinese philosophy about the proper balance between ornamentation and substance. (See No. 47, page 296.) Classical Taoist thinkers often argued that the plain and the rustic most nearly approach the "natural" Way,[14] but thinkers associated with the Confucian school tended to equate the Way with schematized patterns, including ritual activity. True Confucians, however, also insisted that ornamentation should not prevail over substance, since that would be to prefer the secondary over the fundamental;[15] as Confucius taught, "the pattern comes *after* the plain groundwork."[16] To illustrate this principle, the *Mystery* employs clothing as a visible sign of inner character.[17]

> App. 3: Sticking out yellow[18] tongues
> And grasping golden brushes
> Help reveal the men of wisdom.
> Fath. 3: The benefits of tongue and brush[19]
> Mean: They help us see the men who know.

It is easy to estimate the true moral worth of a person by what he says in person or on paper. For,

> Speech is the music of the heart. Writing is the painting of the heart. Once the musical notes and paintings take form, the [difference between] the noble and the petty person is apparent.[20]

Here speech and writing "express the beauty within,"[21] as a golden yellow signifies what is good, central, and in accord with the Mean.

> App. 4: Sharp tongues[22] toady for profit.[23]
> This is a sure sign of merchants.
> Fath. 4: The sure sign of toadies
> Means: This is profit to business.

Love of profit often interferes with pursuit of the Right.[24] Merchants succeed best when they use smooth but "twisty" speech that flatters the customer. The would-be sage, however, finds the merchant's glib disregard for truth abhorrent.

> App. 5: Humble words are like water,
> And true to Heaven's Female.[25]
> Fath. 5: A flow of humble words
> Means: He is able to empty himself.

The ruler is advised to act like a female. In other words, he should condescend to his subordinates and humbly ask their advice. A modest stance may indeed secure greatness.

> App. 6: Pointless speech, when suppressed,
> Still goes flying off.
> The great man shakes the wind.
> Fath. 6: Speech that runs on
> Means: Suppressed, it rises up again.

A Chinese proverb says, "No team of four horses can overtake a word once it has flown out." Ironically, the empty speech of the petty man often "flies" better than the weightier speeches given by a truly noble person. But in these lines we see the virtuous person about to blast the idle prattler from the scene.

> App. 7: Talk of current affairs is taboo.[26]
> Fine subtlety in phrasing, though,
> Shows suspect points to those on high.[27]
> Fath. 7: Times when one should not speak[28]
> Mean: How else can it be clarified?[29]

There may be times when the loyal subject is forced to speak on forbidden topics. Since this is likely to irritate the mediocre ruler (let alone the bad ruler), the wise advisor takes special care in his phrasing so that he conveys all his points successfully without drawing the ruler's ire down upon himself. (Interestingly enough, the text leaves open whether subtle phrasing refers to allusive indirection or just finely crafted rhetoric.)[30]

> App. 8: The cicada cries *yung yung*,[31]
> As blood spurts from its mouth.
> Fath. 8: The shrill cry of the cicada
> Means: The mouth wounds itself.

However loyal the remonstrant, he would be unwise to harp upon the ruler's faults or to adopt a shrill tone of voice in his accusations. Otherwise, his voice may soon come to seem no less irritating than the din of the cicadas. When the angry ruler moves to punish him, he will learn that the mouth can harm itself.

> App. 9: The white tongue that labored[32]
> Is drawn back to its roots
> When noble men are not trusted.
> Fath. 9: A plain tongue that presses on
> Means: Integrity can be prolonged.[33]

Two commentators assume that the white (i.e., "clear" and "honest") tongue belongs to the truly good person, who in better times would hasten to offer loyal advice. In a benighted age, however, such a person checks his tongue since remonstrance, however loyal, would prove useless. As the *Changes* says, "When what is said is not believed, those who value talk are confounded."[34]

However, there are two other possible explanations for the poem. Perhaps the white tongue symbolizes slander, since white is the color assigned to the Metal Phase and metal slashes mercilessly. Or perhaps the tongue is white because it is too "bare" (i.e., obvious) in its speech.[35] Then the poem would read:

> The "white" tongue that goes on and on
> Is pushed back to its root

No. 62. Doubt / Yi

When noble men do not believe [a word of it].
The white tongue belaboring
Means: Truly, it can be seen as [too] long.

In this reading, the superior wisdom of the moral man prevents him from being taken in by others' speeches.

Correlates with Human's Mystery; Yin; the phase Wood; and the Yi ching Hexagram no. 57, Laying the Offering;[1] *the sun enters the Horn constellation, 12th degree*

Yi
No. 62. Doubt
September 22 (p.m.)–September 26

HEAD: Yin and yang grind against one other. Things all wither,[2] then disperse.[3] Some seem to be right, some seem to be wrong.[4]

By midautumn, open hostility between yin and yang *ch'i* brings on the withering and decay of the myriad things, despite the beauties of fall mentioned in the previous tetragram.[5] All of creation at the autumn equinox is evenly divided between yin and yang, night and day, right and wrong;[6] this confusing situation may well account for increasing doubt. Yin's cyclical rise to prominence seems to undercut the true and natural state of things, in which yang should take the lead;[7] this also leads to doubt. And finally, there is the doubt expressed by yin: Though it now holds sway, yin *ch'i* is suspicious about yang's future course. Will it continue to cower in submission or does it only await a future opportunity to undermine yin's dominion?[8]

App. 1: In doubt and confusion,[9]
He loses what is tried and straight.[10]
Fath. 1: To lose the Right in perplexity
Means: How could it be settled in his mind?

If it is to function properly, the mind must be calm. The individual beset with doubts about the proper course of action can never hope to act effectively. All doubts can be resolved, however, by applying the Way of the sage-kings to present-day problems.

App. 2: In doubt, return to the self.[11]
In truth, it is no distance.[12]

359

Fath. 2: In times of doubt, reversing the self
Means: Return to what is clear and still.

This set of verses advises those in doubt to "return to the self" in three related stages: (1) to recover one's inherent goodness by a process of (2) self-examination that ends in a decision (3) to reverse one's previous course of action. By this act of will, the individual consciously rejoins the larger cosmic Tao, which is "clear and still."[13] His mind, reflecting the Tao, becomes perfectly lucid and unmoved (meaning both unflappable and unbiased). For this reason, one early philosopher, Mencius, defines "supreme courage" in terms of this ability to "return to the self."[14]

App. 3: Doubts overcome clarity.
He suffers mounting distress.[15]
In his heart it advances.[16]
Fath. 3: Doubts stronger than clarity
Mean: The center heart grows dim.

An earlier clarity of the heart/mind succumbs to doubt. As a result, the conscience weakens.[17]

App. 4: In cases of doubt, examine the old
To meet the tried and true.
Fath. 4: In cases of doubt, to examine the old
Means: First ask.

Chinese tradition emphasizes the unassuming nature of the true gentleperson. Confucius himself, though an expert on ritual matters, was always careful to "ask for information" from local elders[18] and other potential instructors.[19] Because such behavior obviates unnecessary mistakes, "he who likes to ask is blessed as a rule."[20]

App. 5: Mistaken hopes that orpiment[21]
Holds gold at center.
Fath. 5: Doubts about the center[22]
Means: Crooks steal from the upright.

Orpiment (arsenic trisulfide, also called pigment of gold) is a yellow crystal of pearly lustre[23] frequently found in gold and silver mines. Though somewhat like gold in appearance, its properties are quite different. Gold is harder than orpiment. Gold also has no cleavage, unlike orpiment, which has perfect cleavage in one direction. Gold is insoluble in acids (except for aqua regia) while orpiment is soluble in sulphuric acid or potassium nitrate. Thanks to early alchemical experiments, much of this was known to the early Chinese.[24] Any learned person, then, who looked beyond the surface would be expected to see the difference between real gold and its imitator. Those of little discernment, however, mistake the base for the precious. Since Appraisal 5 describes the leader, it is evidently the ruler's failure to distinguish good from evil men that is particularly decried.[25] (More pointedly, this poem may criticize members of the elite, including many emperors, who favored alchemists and immortality-seekers over sober scholars.)

> App. 6: Honest oaths are fit to be heard.
>> In cases of doubt, they preserve the truth.[26]
> Fath. 6: Proper oaths worth hearing
>> Mean: They are decrees of enlightened kings.[27]

As written or verbal compacts, oaths provide a standard by which all doubts may be resolved to the satisfaction of the parties concerned.[28] Wise rulers learn early to be careful in how they frame their words. A well-known story recorded in the *Garden of Sayings* speaks to this: King Ch'eng of Chou (tradit. r. 1115–1079) as a child was out playing with a friend. In jest, he cut a leaf from a pawlownia tree, then announced, "I use this to enfeoff you." Later, when the story was reported to the regent, the regent insisted that the king's word must be kept; therefore, the king's playmate was duly awarded a fief.[29]

> App. 7: "Are there ghostly souls[30]
>> That sigh and sough?"[31]
>> The arrow shot at crows in trees[32]
>> Strikes at the fox in its lair.
>> To overturn the eye and ear brings danger.[33]
> Fath. 7: Doubts about ghostly souls
>> Mean: Truly, they cannot be believed.

Imagine a late autumn evening. (After all, the tetragram is allied with autumn; this Appraisal, with night.) Will-o'-the wisps dance by; the wind rustles the trees and whistles through caves, making weird keening sounds.[34] Perhaps the anxious hunter mistakes the sound of woodland creatures for a ghost. Frightened by the prospect of a haunting, he takes up his weapons to kill the phantoms, since they portend evil.[35] He may be so rattled that he confuses the fox and crow, though the size, coloration, and habitat of the two animals are completely different.[36] In any case, he shoots by sound, rather than by sight. With both the eye and ear fooled, the mind can no longer be sure of what is real and what is not. With one stroke, Yang Hsiung neatly suggests both the unreliability of sense perception and the danger of preconceived notions.[37]

> App. 8: Confounded by doubts, yet[38]
>> So able are the clients he meets
>> That three years hence, he's still not tired.

Fath. 8: Confounding doubts by receiving guests
 Means: This is very much worth our respect.

The wise leader makes every effort to resolve his doubts by seeking experts who can enlighten him. Having found good counselors, he is delighted to talk with them and take their advice. The host who recognizes the value of wise guests or clients merits our respect.

App. 9: In the final appraisal,[39] doubt without trust.
 Drawing the bow, the deer—presumed there—is not.
Fath. 9: Final doubts but no faith
 Means: He never has what it takes for fame.

By a pun, to "aim at the deer" means to "aim for good luck" or even for imperial office.[40] Efforts are wasted when the goal is misplaced. An atmosphere of suspicion and doubt can never lead to a secure reputation.

Correlates with Human's Mystery;
Yang; *the phase Metal; and the* Yi ching *Hexagram no. 20, Contemplation; the sun enters the Gullet constellation, 4th degree*

Shih
No. 63. Watch
September 27–October 1 (a.m.)

HEAD: Yin forms the corporeal soul while yang forms its dying counterpart.[1] All the external forms and appearances of things can be observed.

After the autumn equinox, yin *ch'i* shows its true corporeal form; it takes the lead, while yang, now relatively less powerful, retreats quietly.[2] Yin's robust appearance contrasts with yang's present frailty.[3] Though all things appear in their mature form, soon, following yang, they will become hollow shells of their former selves and die. Under the dim half-light cast by a midautumn moon wreathed in clouds, "roving souls act to make changes."[4]

App. 1: Keeping his light within,
 He does not use its brilliance.
Fath. 1: Keeping his light within
 Means: His eyes peer into the depths.

The noble man is by definition engaged in a continual process of self-examination.[5] He does not focus his inner light on others' foibles; he prefers to correct his own. As a result of this process, he achieves a state of full enlightenment. Once enlightened, he does not advertise his achievement;[6] he is content to hide his inner light, especially in a troubled age or when a display of talent would be premature.[7] But thanks to his powers of self-perception, he need not seek for the sometimes feeble outside light provided by others' opinions.[8]

> App. 2: The noble man looks to the inside.
> The petty man looks to the outside.
> Fath. 2: The petty man watching externals
> Means: He is incapable of seeing the heart.

Two important differences between noble and petty people are suggested here. First, when mistakes are made, the moral person first examines his own heart to see if he has failed; the petty man, in contrast, blames others for his failure.[9] Second, in judging others, the moral person looks beyond surface appearances to the inner heart, while the petty man, like Shakespeare's Polonius, focuses on outward appearance.[10]

> App. 3: Making his virtue seen,
> He is fit to support[11]
> The realm of the king.
> Fath. 3: Supports whose virtues are revealed
> Mean: Only then can perfection exist.

Appraisal 3 represents completed thought about to be translated into action; it also symbolizes advancement. Inner virtue, having been perfected,[12] is now properly revealed to one's superiors, so that it can be used for the benefit of the realm.[13]

> App. 4: He powders his forehead and cheeks.[14]
> It rains on his dyed beard:[15]
> A sight utterly lacking in charm.
> Fath. 4: Powdered heads with rained-on beards
> Mean: One cannot bear to look.

Pale powder washes down this man's face, possibly because of a rainshower,[16] turning his beard white, the color of old age, death, and mourning. Perhaps the black from his dyed beard also runs, so that he soon becomes a hideous sight. By analogy, the petty man attends only to the externals (the "powdering" and the "dyeing"). As soon as he meets with even a minor mishap, he is shown in his true colors. No wonder others turn away from him in disgust.

> App. 5: *Luan* and *feng* in great numbers,
> 　　　Their virtue is dazzling.
> Fath. 5: Many magical birds in pairs
> 　　　Mean: Virtue's light is dazzling bright.

The *luan* and *feng* (male and female of the same species of marvelous birds), like the phoenix in Western culture, are said to possess extraordinary powers. Highly discriminating in their habits, these birds alight "only where the light of virtue shines."[17] Their beauty dazzles the beholder, demonstrating the compelling aspect of charismatic virtue. Such auspicious omens occur in great numbers only at the court of an enlightened ruler to whom good advisors flock.

> App. 6: A plain cart with a canopy
> 　　　Of kingfisher feathers—
> 　　　Just to see it harms propriety.
> Fath. 6: A feathered cover for a cart that's plain
> 　　　Means: There is only love of externals.

According to Chinese sumptuary regulations, the commoner rode in an undecorated carriage, while great officials, who presumably exemplified the highest virtue, rode along in a carriage decorated with a canopy constructed from the brilliant blue-green feathers of the kingfisher bird. The owner of this cart is common, even base at heart, but he pretends to virtue and high rank.

> App. 7: Looking to his flaws,
> 　　　He finds no taint.
> Fath. 7: Seeing to his flaws
> 　　　Means: He can correct himself.

The good person attends to his own cultivation.

> App. 8: Kingfishers in flight
> 　　　Have their wings ensnared.[18]
> 　　　The furs of fox and sable
> 　　　Rob their very selves of life.
> Fath. 8: Kingfisher, fox, and sable
> 　　　Mean: What is loved makes for blame.

Were the kingfisher's feathers less brilliantly colored, no nets would be set to trap it. Were the furs of the fox and sable less warm and lustrous, no traps would be laid to catch them. It is, paradoxically, our love for them that endangers them.

> App. 9: The rays of the setting sun
> 　　　Flood the eastern sky with light.[19]
> 　　　By this we watch its beginning.

Fath. 9: That the sinking sun sets the east alight
　　Means: At the end, look back to beginnings.

Appraisal 9 marks the end of the cycle. As dusk falls, the eastern sky is flooded with light cast back by the setting sun. This warm light at sunset prefigures the brilliant rays cast by the rising sun on a new day. A good end points to the new beginning.

Ch'en

No. 64. Sinking
October 1 (p.m.)–October 5

Correlates with Human's Mystery; Yin; the phase Water; and the Yi ching Hexagram no. 20, Contemplation;[1] the sun enters the Gullet constellation, 7th degree[2]

HEAD: Yin is held to the bosom of[3] yang, and yang is held to the bosom of yin. Their wills are set upon the Mysterious Palace.

The verb "to hold to the bosom" conveys a sense of the inextricable bonds between yin and yang *ch'i*, whose patterns of development are mutually dependent. At this point in late autumn, yin and yang "have gone their separate ways for a long time."[4] At the autumn equinox their powers were evenly balanced; now each feels the loss of the other. Both anticipate their eventual reunion at the Mystery Palace, the location where yang is born and yin achieves its maximum effect.[5]

The title of Tetragram 64 apparently refers to "sinking the gaze" to look below.[6] Like the preceding tetragram, Tetragram 64 in its Appraisals makes reference to various birds, but this time they are ominous birds of prey, whose actions symbolize the increasing depradations of inauspicious yin *ch'i* upon helpless yang.

App. 1: Inclining an ear to the women's rooms,
　　He does not hear the good.[7]
Fath. 1: Immersing himself in back rooms
　　Means: He loses what embodies virtue.

Some early Chinese thinkers assumed that women were inferior in virtue. Others explained women's supposed propensity for gossip, intrigue, and trivial pursuits as the inevitable result of their confinement within the women's quarters. However, there was an absolute need for chaste women to provide an heir to carry on the religious and economic activites of the family. To this end, the rites stipulated the strict segregation of the sexes except in the conjugal bedchamber.[8] Given women's general exclusion from public affairs, the man who preferred to "incline an ear" to the women's ward (by eavesdropping, engaging the women in idle chatter, or participating in feminine pursuits) could never hope to learn enough about public affairs. At best, he would remain as ill-informed or weak as a woman.[9] At worst, his overindulgence in these yin activities might lead to poor health, insanity, or even death. For this reason, the *Record of Ritual* insists that "what is said within the women's quarters shall not become known outside; what is said among men outside shall not be divulged to the women."[10]

> App. 2: Sinking his gaze
> > To see himself better
> > Is wiser than the skew[11]
> > Of one blind in one eye.
> Fath. 2: A deeply penetrating look
> > Means: He gets to be upright and fine.

The good person examines his conscience daily. In contrast, the petty person only perceives the faults of others and fails to see his own. In this he is like a half-blind man who looks askance at others.[12]

> App. 3: He sinks into beauty,
> > Losing the tried and straight.
> Fath. 3: Immersed in beauty
> > Means: This makes us deaf and blind.

To sink into beauty is to be hopelessly enthralled by beautiful women and sensuous music. As *Lao tzu* writes:

> The Five Colors make people blind in the eye.
> The Five Notes make people deaf in the ear.[13]

With the mind besotted with sensory delights, no time or energy remains for the "tried and straight" Way transmitted from the Ancients. Adherence to the Tao eventually yields more reliable pleasures for the individual. To be oblivious to the greater moral good makes us in effect deaf and blind to its advantages.

> App. 4: The *wan-ch'u* lowers its gaze,
> > Eating the bitter bamboo, as is right.
> Fath. 4: A fledgling phoenix drops down to look.
> > Meaning: This is the way it selects its food.

The singular purity of the mythical *wan-ch'u* is proven in Chinese tradition by its unerring taste for the finest. It is said:

> In the south there is a bird called the Wan-ch'u, which alights only on
> the rarest of trees, eats nothing but the fruit of the Lien, and drinks
> only from springs of sweet water.[14]

The moral person is equally choosy when it comes to selecting who and
what will sustain him.

> App. 5: Eagle and hawk soar high
>   But sink their bellies low.
>   They prefer newhatched things,[15]
>   Disdaining good rice gruel.[16]
> Fath. 5: That eagle and hawk soar high
>   Means: They fasten on rotten stuff.

The eagle and hawk are among the most majestic of birds. Due to the
power and size of their wings, they easily soar high above ordinary birds.
In this, they are like the person ambitious for high position. Unfortunately, high position is no guarantee of right conduct. In certain cases, a propensity for "high-flying" is coupled with a vicious or perverse nature. The
eagle and hawk prefer carrion to the rice gruel fed to domesticated fowl.
They are like evil leaders who use their positions to advance the equally
corrupt or to steal from the common people.[17]

> App. 6: He views each kernel as a pile,[18]
>   Clear on profit and right for king.[19]
> Fath. 6: Seeing the kernel as a pile
>   Means: His Way is clear.

The virtuous person considers each kernel (and by analogy, every
minor event or insignificant person) as a thing of enormous importance.
The good ruler, therefore, weighs each and every thing he exacts from his
people with the utmost seriousness. An overly indulgent attitude, by contrast, would certainly lead to great troubles.

> App. 7: Like nets, like snares,[20]
>   Red flesh spells danger for kites and owls.[21]
> Fath. 7: Nets and snares, bloody flesh,
>   Mean: They eat what is unclean.

Nets and snares are baited with red meat to catch evil birds of prey.
Greed overcomes good sense when the lure of bloody flesh overcomes the
birds' survival instincts. The moral is, the compulsion to satisfy one's
worst desires is in itself a deadly trap.

> App. 8: He hopes[22] to get his medicine
>   To help in corrective campaigns.

Fath. 8: Looking for his medicine
  Means: This is good for campaign marches.

The punitive campaign and the march symbolize the individual's crusade for moral righteousness. The individual decides to cure his own illnesses first, the better to improve his defenses against the many evils outside.

App. 9: Bloodstained,[23] the hard steel[24]
  Sinks into the forehead.
  First a master, but later ruined.
Fath. 9: Bloody steel sunk in the head
  Means: In the end, defeated by greed.

Blood has the dual associations of desire and death. The ruthless individual eventually is undone by his own greed for power.

Nei

No. 65. Inner

October 6–October 10 (a.m.)

Correlates with Human's Mystery; Yang; the phase Fire; and the Yi ching Hexagram no. 54, The Marrying Maiden; the sun enters the Base constellation, 4th degree[1]

HEAD: Yin, leaving its inside, goes to stay on the outside. Yang, leaving its outside, goes to stay on the inside. The myriad things come to completion.

With Appraisal no. 3, the Cold Dew solar period begins. As yin *ch'i* completely fills Heaven and Earth, and yang returns below,[2] transition becomes an appropriate theme for the tetragram. In particular, this tetragram focuses on one transition point, marriage, which parallels yin's current position as it experiences the onset of full maturity. Marriage, as the *Changes* tells us, is simultaneously end and beginning, transitory yet eternal.[3] Rituals often acknowledge the confusion of such transitional times by reversing some aspects of customary order. In both the betrothal and nuptial ceremonies of ancient China, for example, when the bride is introduced to the groom's house, she finds her future husband giving precedence to her.[4] In all human relations (whose basic model is husband

and wife), there is a need for such periodic reversals if one wishes to establish great harmony and productivity.

The reversals begin in the Head text, which shows yin *ch'i* (usually associated with what is hidden or inside) moving into an outside (i.e., visible) position, while exhausted yang *ch'i* retreats to some place out of sight. The myriad things now approach completion, in which full maturity leads to death or hibernation. With yin now clearly dominant, the tetragram considers the rightful place of women, aligned with yin and the inner (or private) worlds, contrasting it with men's outer (or public) selves.

> App. 1: Careful about consorts:[5]
> To be chaste at first
> Makes for later peace.
> Fath. 1: Careful about his consorts
> Means: He begins with women of proven worth.[6]

Along with filial piety, female chastity was one of the main supports of the patriarchal system in China, since a single act of infidelity could confuse the direct line of patrilineal descent ever after. All order requires self-restraint exercised in the interests of the larger community; therefore, good order in the household is an important first step toward order in the community, and even toward cosmic order.[7] For these reasons, a woman chaste in both mind and spirit is needed for the "inner apartments" if harmony is to prevail after marriage. If care is taken at the start of any marriage, the end is likely to be good.[8]

> App. 2: Depraved is his wife.
> He puts her away from that Yellow Couch.
> Fath. 2: Depravity in the inner chambers
> Means: He is far from at peace in his mind.[9]

The Yellow Couch usually refers to the imperial couch, although it may simply be a flowery term for the conjugal bed in the inner apartments.[10] But yellow, of course, also signifies the central virtues of moderation and humility, while the couch symbolizes ease and harmony,[11] as well as conjugal love. The principal wife ignores proper conjugal relations, which are to be ruled by moderation, and wallows in depravity. (Perhaps the text hints at the occult arts popular in Han times to suppress rivals in love or to secure an heir. It is also possible that the woman here is licentious or jealous.[12] In either case, she is ruled by her passions.) Lest her behavior infect the entire household, the husband shuns her, thereby insuring peace in the household. The husband is acutely aware of the distance between the present reality and the ideal family situation.

App. 3: Despite your courtesy,[13] she grieves
       That she approaches[14] our western steps.
Fath. 3: Your decorum and her sorrow
        Mean: This is how it feels to replace a mother.

In the ancient Chinese marriage ceremony, the future mother-in-law descends the western steps to indicate that she will soon give way to the younger generation. The bride then mounts the steps of the ancestral hall to show that she and her progeny will ultimately replace the older generation.[15] Thoughtful newlyweds cannot but feel some sorrow at the implications of their marriage ceremony. The joyful prospect of new children to continue the ancestral line is offset by an acute awareness of the increasing age and approaching death of the present family heads. Marriage typifies times of transition, which are usually marked by mingled joy and sorrow.[16]

App. 4: Loving the petty, loving the perils,
       Losing even his cloak of hemp.[17]
       Danger.
Fath. 4: Preferring the petty and perilous
        Means: This is not worth glorifying.

Warm clothes are one of the basic necessities of life. As winter approaches, the wise person is provident enough to prepare sufficient food and clothing to sustain his family over time. In contrast, the petty person, having flirted with danger, loses every single possession, even the coarsest of cloaks. (Is there a hint of a sexual adventure here?) Such improvidence will surely ruin the entire family.

App. 5: The dragon lowers itself to the mud.
       Noble men profit in taking on wives[18]
       When meeting by custom as equals.[19]
Fath. 5: A dragon descends to the mud.
        Meaning: Yang goes below yin.

The dragon, of course, may refer to the dragon ruler, the Son of Heaven who flies high above the common run of men. But the dragon is also a symbol of the virile male at the height of his powers. As winter (aligned with yin and the female) draws near, the soaring dragon is said to burrow into the mud. Clearly, a concerted effort to level differences is required for harmonious union and mutual benefit.[20] This is true not only for male-female relations but for those between leader and subordinate.[21]

App. 6: At dusk in mid-flight,
       He draws in his wings.[22]

> Though he wants the palace full,
> He will not see his woman.[23]

Fath. 6: In the yellow dusk, drawing in his wings
    Means: He is unable to restrain himself.

The winged creature (possibly a dragon?) suggests any "high flyer" of power and ambition. In the half-light of dusk,[24] his thoughts turn towards home. Sexual desire fills his breast; he wishes his home were full of luscious beauties.[25] But it is this very preoccupation with sex, ironically enough, that prevents him from finding a suitable mate with whom he could find true satisfaction.

> App. 7: A crumbling wall grows foxtail shoots.
>   When grizzled heads[26] bring home young wives,
>   Their wives are soon with child.[27]

Fath. 7: That a crumbling wall grows foxtail shoots
    Means: This is a sign[28] of felicitous things.[29]

The *Changes* epitomizes great prosperity by "an old fellow taking a young woman to wife."[30] Appraisal 7 typically marks the onset of old age, but here a fruitful marriage brightens prospects for the future.

> App. 8: Inside, not to subdue one's wife
>   Lays waste to home and even the state:
>   Wading through depths unfathomably deep.

Fath. 8: Women inside who are uncontrolled
    Mean: These are calamities for the state.

The wife, who is "inner," should submit to her husband, who is "outer." If the wife insists on taking her pleasures where she chooses, in utter defiance of her husband and her sacred duty, her promiscuity spells ruin for the family line, whether she is a commoner or a member of the royal line. To allow her to produce illegitimate children[31] is a self-destructive impulse, like wading into a deep body of water. This poem recalls a famous couplet from the *Odes*:

> Disorder does not come down from Heaven.
> It is produced by the woman.[32]

> App. 9: Rain falls onto the land.
>   It cannot stop, it cannot exceed.

Fath. 9: Rain falling down on the land
    Means: Favor comes in goodly measure.

The fertility of the loess soil in the Central Plain region of China depends upon abundant rainfall. In consequence, the pouring rain comes to symbolize all types of favors bestowed, including the king's benefactions to his subjects and the husband's gift of semen to his conjugal partner. Here rain (= grace and favor, even semen) showers down from above upon a yin figure (Earth = yin; women relative to men; and subordinates relative to their leader.) Grace in proper measure imparts new life.

Ch'ü

No. 66. Departure
October 10 (p.m.)–October 14

Correlates with Human's Mystery; Yin; the phase Wood;[1] and the Yi ching *Hexagram no. 25, Nothing to Look Forward To;[2] the sun enters the Base constellation, 9th degree*

HEAD: Yang takes leave from its yin. Yin takes leave from its yang. All things are disappointed and perturbed [with no sense of belonging to either].[3]

In the previous tetragram, yin and yang quit their usual bases. Now, in this tetragram, they abandon their partnership. No chance remains for harmonious union. The myriad things feel despair, for they are left without a sense of belonging or direction. The tetragram is correlated with a *Changes* hexagram, whose title was interpreted by Han Confucians to mean "no hope" or "no expectations," and whose theme was the loss that accrues from "reckless behavior." This tetragram's assignment to Wood underscores the contrast between the present desiccated condition of all things and their former luxuriance. Given the unfavorable trends of the time, the wise person accounts it good if he is able to extricate himself from complete disaster.

> App. 1: He leaves this Numen Pool
> To dwell in that withered garden.
> Fath. 1: Quitting this Numen Pool
> Means: He does not proceed with modesty.

Appraisal 1 corresponds to Water; hence, the reference to restorative waters. The exact meaning of the term Numen Pool is not certain. King Wen of Chou constructed in his domain a number of sites with "numen" in the title (for example, the Numen Terrace and Numen Park).[4] The Numen Pool may belong to a sage whose charisma reflects a deep, even inexhaustible source of wisdom and grace. Most likely, however, the pool is simply an epithet for the innermost heart-mind, that marvelous reservoir of thought and the conscience. The withered garden, apparently on high ground,[5] presents a striking contrast. The garden lacks moisture (a symbol for fecundity and grace), so it provides nothing to the community. By analogy, the petty man, ever intent on climbing high in the social and political worlds, fails to cultivate those virtues, in particular humility, that would yield good fruit.

> App. 2: He leaves that withered garden
>   To dwell below in the Numen Pool.
> Fath. 2: Dwelling in the Numen Pool below
>   Means: Such is the light of humility's Way.

Appraisal 2 clearly reverses the preceding verses. Humility and a well-kept conscience provide the best preparation for future glories.

> App. 3: Raising high his step
>   In going to the hall,
>   He is somewhat exposed.
> Fath. 3: High steps and exposure
>   Mean: He proceeds wantonly.

For the ancient Chinese, as for Freud, physical gestures indicate inner states of mind. "Highstepping," for example, betokens overweening political ambition.[6] The final Appraisal line then gives a compound term, which can be construed either as "There is dew" or as "There is [something] revealed."[7] If dew soaks the hem, we know that the individual has taken insufficient care of his person.[8] However, dew may also soak the road, signifying that the path to power is a slippery one.[9] In any case, the wicked individual now finds his evil intentions exposed to others.

> App. 4: Quitting as son,
>   He becomes a father.
>   Quitting as subject,
>   He becomes a ruler.
> Fath. 4: Leaving as son to become the father
>   Means: It is not what he had hoped for.

In this tentative translation,[10] the lines illustrate the unsought, but appropriate changes in status that inevitably occur with increased maturity.[11] Such changes parallel yang's temporary abdication to yin at this season of the year. However, the Sung commentator Ssu-ma Kuang reads the Appraisal as, "Leaving the son to go to the father, Leaving the subject to go to the ruler." To him, this suggests a proper understanding of and acquiescence in hierarchical order. Such model behavior is rewarded, he argues, "beyond his wildest dreams" (an alternate reading for the final Fathoming line).

App. 5: Hiking up his skirt
        He goes to the court,
        Where wild grasses grow.[12]
Fath. 5: Hoisting his robes where grasses grow
        Means: They, for their part, should also be feared.

Appraisal 5 plays upon Appraisal 3. Once again, the subject of the verses raises something (here, the hem of his robe).[13] But once he is out in the courtyard, he discovers wild grasses and brambles that threaten to snag his robes or his flesh. The courtyard (and the court) should be more orderly; the individual (a high official, judging from his long robes) should have taken greater care. Perhaps he has been exiled to the wastelands because of depraved behavior?[14] By any reading, this image spells disaster.

App. 6: He freely[15] leaves his achievements behind.
        Heaven will grant him its name.
Fath. 6: Willing to leave his success behind
        Means: He declines to occupy a position.

The Taoist sage Lao tzu equates Heaven's Way with "retreating when the task is accomplished."[16] Chinese tradition in general praises wise men who readily give up their positions once their objectives have been achieved. The best example was provided by the illustrious Duke of Chou (tradit. llth c. B.C.), who stepped down as regent once his young charge, King Ch'eng,[17] was mature enough to take up his responsibilities. The texts celebrate those "without prideful presumption" or "contentious desire"[18] for reputation. History (or "Heaven") will reward them.

App. 7: Having left his virtue and propriety,
        Even three deaths do not clear his name.
Fath. 7: Departing from virtue and propriety
        Means: In the end, he dies an ugly death.

The number three signifies "many" deaths.[19] Here death comes first to virtue, and then to one's person and reputation. The evil that men do lives on in popular memory and historical record.

App. 8: The moon is a crescent on high
        And Fire is about to[20] descend.[21]
        He cannot use them to move
        For in movement, lies fault.
Fath. 8: Crescent moon and hanging Fire
        Means: He fears to suffer blame.

The crescent moon appears in the final third of the lunar month. The Fire Star (Antares, the central star of the Chinese Heart constellation),[22] is suspended just above the horizon in the tenth month, near the end of the year. Both indicators, then, point to the end of the phase and the inevitable dying of the light. The proper time for initiatives has already passed. The wise individual avoids all precipitate action, lest he fall into error; the noble man waits for Heaven to improve the situation, knowing that he himself is powerless.

> App. 9: He seeks me with no success
> Since my turn to the northwest.
> Fath. 9: Seeking, but not getting me
> Means: How can it last long?

Weak yang *ch'i* makes a turn northwest, the direction of yin's maximum activity. But the northwest is also the direction of yang's rebirth, according to tradition. This suggests that of the many changes brought about by the cycle, some may usher in welcome events. Yin's domination, for example, seems absolute now, but it will not last. Soon nascent yang will reappear, giving hope to all.[23]

Hui
No. 67. Darkening
October 15–October 19 (a.m.)

Correlates with Human's Mystery; Yang; the phase Metal; and the Yi ching Hexagram no. 36, The Light Injured;[1] the sun enters the Base constellation, 13th degree

HEAD: Yin ascends to yang['s usual position]; yang descends to yin['s]. Things all are losing light.

The *Changes* hexagram correlated with this tetragram sets the tone for the Head and Appraisals:

> "Darkening" means "damage," "injury." . . . Expansion will certainly encounter resistance and injury. . . .[2]

The Image text attached to the same hexagram tells us that the primary technique the noble man uses to deal with such situations is to "veil his light" (i.e., hide his superiority) in order to live out his days unharmed among the benighted.[3]

In the natural world, there remains only the gloomy crepuscular light of winter. The myriad things, which depended on yang *ch'i* for their light and vitality, are in decline now that yang retreats far below earth.[4]

App. 1: Together in the dark,[5] he alone sees.
   Seclusion is proper.[6]
Fath. 1: In common dark, the only one to see
   Means: At center, he is singularly brilliant.

In a benighted age,[7] when all seem equally in the dark regarding moral values, enlightenment is still possible for the individual intent upon Goodness. However, the humane person who is out of step with his neighbors may choose to temporarily hide his light, in order to preserve himself in a time of chaos. Only an inner light shines forth in all its brilliance.[8] After all, in Appraisal 1, it is still too early for action that may reform the world.[9]

App. 2: Blindly forging ahead, he meets obstructions.

Fath. 2: Blindly marching into obstacles[10]
   Means: Clearly, he does not see the Way.[11]

The rash individual forges ahead, oblivious to all the difficulties that lie ahead. But in reality, he is no better able to see the one true Way than a "blind man tapping his cane to find the road."[12] Only study of the Ancients can provide sufficient guidance for life, yet this individual claims to know it all.

By a series of puns, the same lines describe the topsy-turvy situation in which the blind music masters of old taught recalcitrant rulers how "to see" basic moral truths:

The blind fight against wrong.
It is the sighted who do not see the Way.

App. 3: Yin proceeds while yang follows:
   Good for making what is not bad luck.
Fath. 3: Yin proceeding with yang following
   Means: The matter must go outside.[13]

Appraisal 3 marks the transition from thought to action. Normally, yang initiates activities to which yin responds. However, by this time of the year, their characteristic activities have been reversed. In certain circumstances, the priority of yin is now accounted good. For example, a good woman may lead her husband to virtue.[14] In another case, the conscience (= yin, because it is inner) motivates the individual's action (= yang, because it is outer). In all such cases, appropriate internal change will have its external effect.[15]

>App. 4: Confusing his categories,[16]
>>He loses the golden casket.
>Fath. 4: Dim about categories
>>Means: Laws and institutions decline.

In early Chinese thought, categorical thinking provides the key to all logic. If a suitable analogy to the sage-rulers' precepts can be found, then complicated moral issues can be untangled with ease. The wise individual, therefore, closely guards the "golden casket,"[17] the precious strongbox where important records and state documents are kept.[18] But woe to the individual who "confuses the categories," who reasons, in other words, by improper analogy. Such muddleheaded thought undermines legal, institutional, and ethical systems, whose very existence requires a body of precedents.

>App. 5: With the sun at noon[19]
>>And the moon quite full,
>>The noble man dims himself
>>So as not to enter extremes.
>Fath. 5: The noon sun and the full moon
>>Mean: Bright, he fears extermination.

Appraisal 5, midpoint of the tetragram cycle, corresponds to the sun at high noon and the moon in midmonth. (Such brilliant light may recall the Son of Heaven, usually assigned to this Position.) But the forces of darkness will soon prevail. The noble man at the height of his powers should consider "hiding his light" in order to preserve himself as the cycle begins its downturn. He should take for his model the ancient sage Chi tzu, who feigned madness rather than serve the evil last king of Shang.[20] By reclusion, either physical or psychic, the moral superior can evade the decline that typically follows great florescence. One who is truly "brilliant" would never endanger the self by pressing for further growth or advantage at the wrong time.

>App. 6: The Dark Bird is filled with worry
>>As the light slips down into hiding.
>Fath. 6: The Dark Bird filled with grief
>>Means: He is about to descend to the dark.

The Dark Bird usually refers to either the swallow or the crane, migratory birds thought to "worry" at winter's approach.[21] Here, however, given the word-plays on light and enlightenment, darkness and moral benightedness,[22] the Dark Bird may refer to the black crow, symbol of the sun. As the sun's light recedes, the noble man is filled with sorrow. Nature's darkening has brought to mind the increasing number of souls who have left the light to slip into the dark.[23]

> App. 7: In darkest night,[24] a light is raised.
>   Some follow it and go forth.
> Fath. 7: Raising a light at darkest night
>   Means: Virtue will soon go forth.[25]

The gentleman "raises a light" for his fellow men, either by the force of his example or by recommending worthy candidates for office. Some, following his lead, embark on the path of Virtue, so that enlightenment eventually spreads throughout the land.[26]

The modern scholar Yü Yüeh reads the poem differently, so that it depicts the ability of even the imperfect individual to lead others to the Good:

> Squinting,[27] he makes out the light.
> Some, following him, go forth.

> App. 8: Seeing what is not his truth[28]
>   Harms his own right eye.[29]
>   It destroys the state and ruins his house.
> Fath. 8: That seeing wrong harms the eye
>   Means: By this, the state is lost.

This ruler fails to discern the difference between true and false. Acting on false assumptions ("seeing what is unreal"), his judgment is hampered. Perhaps he also injures his chief advisors, who would have acted as his "right" eyes, thereby bringing ruin to the state and royal house.[30]

> App. 9: In the last dark days,[31] seeing dimness for itself[32]
>   Helps him stay true in an unenlightened age.[33]
> Fath. 9: The benefits of dimming in the last dark days
>   Mean: It is no use to be brilliant alone.[34]

Like Chi tzu,[35] who "veiled his light" (by feigning madness) in order to escape execution by the last evil ruler of the Shang dynasty, the gentleman faced with insoluble difficulties in a benighted age at the end of a dynastic cycle recognizes his own inability to induce an immediate improvement;[36] one enlightened person cannot light the whole world.[37] Rather than draw attention to himself, which might prove dangerous, he bides his time, cultivating his virtue, until such time as he can act more effectively. Seeing dimness for what it is, then, may lead to greater enlightenment.

Correlates with Human's Mystery;
Yin; the phase Earth; and the Yi
ching *Hexagram no. 36, The Light*
Injured; the sun enters the Cham-
ber constellation, 3d degree; the
Dipper points WNW; the musical
note is A-sharp[1]

Meng
No. 68. Dimming
October 19 (p.m.)–October 23

HEAD: Yin marches to the south. Yang marches to the north. Things lose light and proper orientation.[2] Not a one but grows increasingly dim.

This tetragram is the twin of the previous one, since it is paired with the same *Changes* hexagram; therefore, the images of darkening and damage continue.[3] Yin and yang *ch'i* have reversed their usual orientation, with yin in the south and yang in the north. Confusion reigns as the Winter Dew solar period yields to Frostfall. All sentient beings grow dim and feeble as the light fails. Human hearts as a result become ignorant of or insensible to the value of tradition. All things enter that dream-like state where reality and illusion are confused.[4]

> App. 1: The belly dim, he glimpses Heaven,
> But fails to see its borders.
> Fath. 1: Dim-bellied and sky-glimpsing
> Means: He lacks all ability to see.

The "belly" refers to the seat of the emotions (elsewhere located in the heart-mind).[5] With its powers of perception clouded,[6] the self cannot hope to imagine the full range of marvelous reality. Even a brief glimpse of the divine cannot support full illumination. Ignorance and insensitivity continue to reign.

> App. 2: Lucid at heart, he glimpses Heaven,
> Seeing clear its very roots.
> Fath. 2: Bright-bellied and sky-glimpsing
> Means: At center, exceptional brilliance.

This Appraisal reverses the message of the previous Appraisal, predicting the most profound insight.[7]

> App. 3: Blind masters: some teach archery
> But fail to hit their target.
> Fath. 3: Instruction by the blind
> Means: They lack the means to discriminate.

Appraisal 3 marks the transition from thought to action. Lacking sufficient clarity himself, how can a teacher enlighten his pupils? As the philosopher Mencius wrote:

> Men of worth use their light to enlighten. Nowadays some would use their benighted state to enlighten.[8]

App. 4: With Right as his mirror, he does not go astray.
    To others, he is one to rely on.
Fath. 4: The Right reflecting true
    Means: Integrity can be trusted.

Whoever takes the worthy man as model[9] provides contemporaries with a perfect "mirror" of good conduct.

App. 5: Turning his back on what is bright,
    Going against the light,
    He hits enveloping darkness.
Fath. 5: Against the bright, against the light
    Means: This is what others turn against.[10]

Appraisal 5, corresponding to the Son of Heaven, is ruler of the tetragram. The arrogant ruler refuses to take advice from worthy supporters, for he believes himself sufficiently enlightened.[11] It will not be long before his subjects revolt.

App. 6: From the dark going to the light,[12]
    Reluctant to dazzle and charm.[13]
Fath. 6: The dim light of day
    Means: The center is not blinded by light.[14]

In a benighted age, the noble person hides his light, since the world is unused to such brilliance.[15] The commentator Wang Ya, however, offers a completely different reading of the poem:

> From the dark, going to light
> He does not think it right to flicker or be weak.
> From the dark, going to light
> Means: The center does not obscure the light.

By this reading, the noble man is careful not to be like the weak flicker of a small candle. To give out insufficient light will only prove misleading to others.

App. 7: Dimming the good,[16]
    They bring to light what they abhor.[17]
Fath. 7: Evil in obscuring the good[18]
    Means: His unenlightened state is all too clear.

Appraisal 7 reflects the failure of will to do good. The individual's evil propensities grow increasingly obvious over time.

> App. 8: Dusk is a time that benefits the moon.
>> A small good omen, but too soon for stars.
> Fath. 8: That dusk favors the moon
>> Means: Still there is something to be hoped for.

The dim light of dusk as we near the end of the cycle sets the stage for the moon. Sometime soon, the stars will come out. Although the dark age might profit most from the great light provided by the sages, a lesser light can still do some good.[19]

> App. 9: Drawn-out sighs at the time
>> Do not secure the good.
>> The male breaks a hairpin.
>> The wife changes her luck.
> Fath. 9: Not capturing their good
>> Means: The husband dies, his wife sighs.

Death is, after all, the extreme case of dimness and insensibility. When a husband dies, his hairpins are broken to signify that he will no longer be using them. His widow changes her hair ornaments to don mourning, showing all that her luck has changed for the worse. (By a pun, "luck" and "hair ornaments" are read interchangeably in the fourth line of the Appraisal.)[20]

Ch'iung
No. 69. Exhaustion
October 24–October 28 (a.m.)

Correlates with Human's Mystery; Yang; the phase Water; and the Yi ching Hexagram no. 47, Hemmed in; the sun enters the Heart constellation, 2d degree

HEAD: Yin *ch'i* fills the eaves while yang loses its place. The myriad things are exhausted and agitated.[1]

The tetragram title can describe a variety of situations where the individual faces a symbolic or actual dead-end, including the absolute exhaustion of one's physical powers and utter impoverishment. Not surprisingly, the tetragram, like its correlate *Changes* hexagram, is generally inauspicious in tone, with gloomy predictions of "perplexity," "distrust," "losing one's way," physical dangers, and psychic discomforts. However, the same character may be given the more positive meaning of "reaching the culmination." To reach moral perfection is the aim of the would-be sage; nobility of character, in turn, insures that ultimate victory can be snatched from temporary defeat. As the *Changes* tells us, only the noble person "is capable of being in straits without losing the power to succeed"[2] because in times of crisis he is prompted to undertake a thorough-going reform. Consequently, the virtuous individual not only survives present difficulties, but even prospers as soon as the times turn more favorable.

The Head text contains an internal pun.[3] The myriad things are not only agitated and exhausted because they have lost their master, yang *ch'i*,[4] they have also "run out of places" where they can hide. The Appraisal texts focus on examples of those who have no haven to which they can escape. Occasionally, even meritorious individuals find themselves caught up in wider cycles of inauspicious fate.

> App. 1: He sees his limits as limits,
> So people embrace him as center.[5]
> Fath. 1: Recognizing his own limits
> Means: Emotions dwell at the center.

The first lines of the Appraisal and Fathoming talk literally of "seeing his extremity as extremity." One interpretation for the lines (reflected in this translation) presumes that the truly superior human being exerts all his charismatic powers to attract, then utilize talented supporters, who regard him as "center."[6] Given his suasive influence, the people imitate him, letting their emotions also be centered.[7]

Two other interpretations for the same lines are equally possible, however, given such a wide range of meaning for the word "extremity." One alternative has the noble man "seeing the limits of his desperate straits." The moral superior faces present calamity with perfect equanimity,[8] in part because no misfortune exists that can deter a truly determined would-be sage from achieving moral perfection. As the *Analects* says, "The superior man can withstand extreme hardships. It is only the small man who, when faced with them, is swept off his feet."[9] Once the individual approaches the perfection of the sage, he then employs suasive example to rouse others to redirect their attention to the core values that constitute the Good in Confucian tradition.

In yet another reading, the person of virtue "pushes to the very extremes his own limits" so that he daily improves in virtue.[10] Eventually, having realized the full human potential for sagehood, he becomes a much beloved model for the common people.

App. 2: Failing to see his limits as limits,
 The people come to reject him as center.[11]
Fath. 2: Unaware of his limits
 Means: Deceit can be made to flourish.

This verse is the mirror opposite of the preceding one. As with Appraisal 1, there are three possible readings: (1) the evil individual fails to seek guidance since he does not recognize his own limits; (2) the weak person's good intentions are jettisoned in the face of calamity; and (3) the petty man fails to push his potential for humanity to its natural limits. The result of any one of these three failures is the same. The people will "reject him as center."

App. 3: However desperate, his thoughts apprehend.
Fath. 3: Apprehension in desperate straits
 Means: A tutor resides in the heart.

"Apprehending" for proponents of the Confucian school refers to "apprehending the [Confucian] Way," while true "desperation" is measured in terms of distance from the Way.[12] When a superior person faces a crisis, the inner resources of the heart/mind will see him through. Such resources have been developed by a prior intensive study of various classical precedents, rather than by "exhaustive [analytical] thinking."[13]

App. 4: The soil is not sweet.
 Trees wither and lose their leaves.[14]
Fath. 4: A disharmonious earth
 Means: Affliction extends to the common people.

When the earth, symbol of all that nourishes, fails to support luxuriant growth, the common people find themselves without sufficient food to eat. Soon famine and its attendant diseases appear. Wise leaders work hard to remedy this situation, for "if the common people have not enough for their needs, the ruler cannot expect to have enough for his needs."[15]

App. 5: The stew has no ricecakes.[16]
 His belly rumbles *k'an-k'an*, empty as a drum,
 Yet he does not lose his model.
Fath. 5: Cooked dishes without rice
 Mean: Even so, he does not lose the Right.

Appraisal 5 as the ruler of the tetragram depicts the perfect model of upright behavior in poverty. This individual is so poor that he cannot afford to supplement his meager stew of greens with nourishing grains.[17] Nevertheless, he manages to perfectly embody the ancient models of proper behavior. In this he is like Yen Hui, the favorite disciple of Confucius, of whom the Master remarked:

Incomparable indeed was Hui. A handful of rice to eat, a gourdful of water to drink, living in a mean street—others would have found it unendurably depressing, but to Hui's cheerfulness it made no difference at all! . . . Hui was capable of occupying his whole mind for three months on end with no thought but that of Goodness. [18]

App. 6: The mountains have no game.
  The rivers boast no fish.
  Troubles attack the person.
Fath. 6: Mountains without beasts
  Mean: Trouble to the common people.

In early Chinese tradition, the products of the mountains and rivers are reserved for the common people, who use them to supplement their meager diets and incomes. Evil rulers often claimed these areas as their own property, causing a severe reduction in the people's standard of living. Under such conditions, "While some men can get enough to eat,/ Few men can eat their fill."[19] Such exploitation of the people is likely to backfire.[20]

It is also possible that the common people have wrecklessly misused available natural resources; on their own initiative, they have burnt the hillsides to flush out all the game and drained the lakes to catch all the fish. Despite the magnitude of the initial catch, such wasteful exploitation of limited resources destroys all future food sources.[21]

App. 7: Though he straightens his step,
  He lands in[22] prison.
  In three years, he sees a pardon.[23]
Fath. 7: Righting his foot
  Means: The danger gets him peace.

Appraisal 7 ordinarily represents the loss of one's ambition, but here it corresponds to lucky Day. The subject of the poem modifies his conduct in accordance with the Right. Though he is thrown into prison, his case will be reviewed and he will be pardoned. The superior man calmly awaits better times, knowing that ultimately he will be vindicated.

App. 8: He trudges through frost and snow,
  With his neck bound to his knees.
Fath. 8: Bound neck to knee
  Means: After all, life is not worth living.

Frost and snow symbolize danger of all sorts since they are difficult to negotiate in the best of times. Now, bound neck to knee, this person faces additional impediments. Even if he survives this ordeal, the pain will be so great that life will hardly be worth living.

App. 9: Jade circlets are smashed and tablets broken.
   In mortar and stove, frogs breed.
   Calamities from Heaven are loaded on.[24]
Fath. 9: Circlets and tablets, broken and smashed,
   Mean: Chance does not favor him.[25]

The circlet and tablet of jade are signs of enfeoffment bestowed by rulers on their vassal lords. Wanton destruction of these insignia suggests a violent breach in the contractual relations binding superior and inferior. As political upheaval plunges all into chaos, entire communities are laid waste, despite the virtues of some. With the population decimated, the unused mortars and stoves are inhabited by frogs.[26] Little separates the pitiful survivors from wild animals, since no food preparation is possible.

Ke
No. 70. Severance
October 28 (p.m.)–November 1

Correlates with Human's Mystery; Yin; the phase Fire; and the Yi ching Hexagram no. 23, Splitting Apart; the sun enters the Tail constellation, 2d degree

HEAD: Yin *ch'i* cuts away at things. Yang's form is hung[1] and killed.[2] In seven [times seven] days, it will nearly be severed.

This tetragram, like the corresponding hexagram in the *Changes*, equates utter ruin with severed relations: "Splitting apart means ruin."[3] In the phenomenal world, yin and yang *ch'i* are openly antagonistic. With some 49 (7 × 7) days left until the winter solstice, when yang *ch'i* will seem to die under yin's power, the utter extinction of yang seems a real possibility. After all, the destruction of Hun-t'un, symbol of the primeval chaos, is said to have required only seven days.[4] However bloodthirsty yin's action may appear, it ultimately (and paradoxically) provokes a stronger yang *ch'i*. Those of true understanding recognize "the alternation of increase and decrease" as the course of Heaven.[5] They therefore look to patch up serious breaches and estrangements. One good way is for superiors "to give generously to those below," as the *Changes* suggests.[6]

App. 1: Cutting off his ears and eyes
   Affects his mind and belly.
   Danger.

Fath. 1: Cutting off ears and eyes
Means: The center has no outlet.

The ears and eyes supply the inner organs with perceptual evidence, thereby insuring the proper functioning and protection of the center. The individual who is deaf and blind (either literally or metaphorically), finds it difficult to sustain the self, let alone prosper. Danger lies ahead.

This lesson may be applied to affairs at court. Since the ruler seldom leaves the confines of his palace, he depends upon others to gather information for him. Loyal advisors may be likened to the ruler's ears and eyes. Should the ruler punish those who tell him the true state of affairs, he will have destroyed the one tool with which he can correct current policy. In consequence, his throne will be endangered.[7]

App. 2: Cutting off his warts and wens
Helps to make him incorrupt.
Fath. 2: Cutting off warts and tumors
Means: What is loathesome can not grow big.

Warts and tumors symbolize corrupt deeds prompted by greed.[8] When illness pollutes the body, the only hope of a cure may lie in lancing the infected areas. Though hardly pleasant, the benefit of such decisive action is evident: the flesh is no longer plagued by festering corruption. By analogy, the wise individual heals himself by swiftly excising all impurities. The ruler, for his part, expels evil officials from court.

App. 3: Cutting the nose to feed the mouth,
He loses what lets him breathe.
Fath. 3: Cutting the nose and losing the Master
Means: The loss brings no glory.

In great stupidity, this individual feeds one organ (in Chinese, one "Master") to another, forgetting that both are needed if the body is to prosper. Considering the lack of meat on the nose, the act is particularly absurd. Important lessons may be drawn from this. Perhaps the "nose" (i.e., a loyal minister who smells out trouble) is "sacrificed" to the unprincipled ruler.[9] Or, as two commentators suggest, perhaps "those above are hurt in order to feed those below."[10]

App. 4: The butcher hacks meat in even pieces.
Fath. 4: The butcher's even hacking
Means: Perfection can exist.[11]

The good butcher hacks the meat evenly and easily off the bones. In this he is like the chief minister, whose job it is to fairly apportion government positions among suitable candidates.[12] Confucius remarked of this weighty task, "I do not fear [that the state] has few [resources], but I fear unjust distribution."[13]

> App. 5: Cutting off his thighs and arms,
> > He loses the use of his horses in shafts.[14]
> Fath. 5: Cutting off his thighs and arms
> > Means: Gone are the great officials.

Thigh and forearm typically symbolize the ruler's chief ministers; "horses in shafts" probably stands for the common people. The poem tells us that the Son of Heaven cannot hope to extend his influence throughout the realm if he severs good relations with his chief ministers.

> App. 6: Though he cuts it, there is no wound.
> > It satisfies all on all four sides.
> Fath. 6: Cutting without harm
> > Means: The Way can be divided.

With most entities, a cut or division necessarily entails a wound. The case of the Tao, however, is startlingly different. One can apportion courtesy and care to all, without fear of the supply ever running out. Paradoxically, the more generous the gift, the more the giver receives.

> App. 7: Violet rainbows, carnelian clouds
> > Like friends[15] encircle the sun.
> > His affliction is not excised.
> Fath. 7: Violet rainbows and carnelian clouds
> > Mean: He does not know to cut them.

Spectacular rainbows and brightly colored clouds, for all their apparent beauty, lead the eye away from the sun.[16] If brilliant but cunning advisors surround the leader, they may try to compete with him for attention or prevent his light from reaching the common people. Relations with such advisors should be severed.

> App. 8: Cutting out the borers,
> > He gets at our heart's disease.[17]
> Fath. 8: Cutting out the parasites
> > Means: This is good for the state.

The parasite or borer stands for individuals whose beliefs and actions undermine the healthy state. Master Han Fei included Confucians in this category, since good Confucians place loyalty to the family over loyalty to the state.[18] Yang Hsiung turns the metaphor around, attacking adherents of heterodox teachings, including the Legalists. When the state is rid of such parasites, it will flourish once again.

App. 9: Cutting the flesh to get at the bones,
    The crown is drowned in blood.
Fath. 9: To cut the flesh and drown in blood
    Means: He is unable to keep himself whole.

The final Appraisal depicts the harm that comes from too much deep cutting. As muscle and blood vessels are severed, loss of blood and its attendant risk of infection make death almost certain. Applied to the state, the metaphor suggests that the ruler's cruel exploitation of his subjects will end in his own death.

Chih
No. 71. Stoppage
November 2–November 6 (a.m.)

Correlates with Human's Mystery; Yang; the phase Wood; and the Yi ching *Hexagram no. 52, Stopping;*[1] *the sun enters the Tail constellation, 6th degree*

HEAD: Yin, enlarged, stops things above, and yang for its part stops things below.[2] Above and below, together they stop everything.

The Winter Onset solar period begins with the last Appraisal of this tetragram. A seventeenth-century commentator describes cosmic trends in this way:

> At this time, the Frostfall solar period is already past. Hibernating insects all hunker down. The magpies have entered the oceans to become oysters. Whatever fat there is in things has turned to yin; with the shrinking and splitting already complete, there is no way [for yin *ch'i*] to requisition more. Therefore, [yin] quits its tyrannical and bullying rule above, and temporarily stops to calculate [the situation]. Yang likewise stops below in fear of yin's awesome majesty, afraid of its [yin's] destructive [action]. Therefore, it [yang] hides its shadow in the Mystery Palace [far below the earth's surface,] not daring to come out again, hoping in this way to avoid further paring of its [resources].[3]

In essence, yin and yang are cut off from each other, though good fortune depends upon their successful interaction.[4] The myriad things as a result are "each stopped in their tracks, so that they do not proceed"; ob-

Figure 19. Ku *poison being expelled by an exorcist from a victim. Illustration from* Wu-liang-ts'e *(Eastern Han), left chamber, no. 4.*

structed by yin's growth above, they would retreat to yang below.[5] The *Changes* characterizes human relations in much the same language:

> Those above and below are in opposition and have nothing in common. . . . The superior man does not permit his thoughts to go beyond his situation.[6]

With both cosmos and society on the verge of an absolute split, the wise person focuses his or her entire attention upon present dangers and "knows when to stop" taking the initative.[7] Not surprisingly, both this tetragram and its correspondent hexagram tend to focus on the negative aspects of stoppage.

> App. 1: Stopping at the stopping place,
> There is inner light and no blame.
> Fath. 1: Stopping at the right place
> Means: Wisdom enough for enlightenment.

Appraisal 1 corresponds to Water in the cycle of the Five Phases. The cultivated mind, undistracted by inappropriate or excessive desires, reflects virtue with the same degree of accuracy as a still pool of water. As the "Great Learning" teaches us:

Know when to stop and then you can be quiescent. Be quiescent and
then you can be at peace. Be at peace and then you can think. Think
and then you can achieve everything.[8]

App. 2: Braking the cart, he waits
  For the horse to come to a halt.
Fath. 2: The carriage braked, he waits.[9]
  Meaning: He cannot use it to go forward.

Appraisal 2 corresponds to the middle stage of the thought process
and to the status of "commoners." When external constraints are applied,
all movement slowly grinds to a halt. Someone with half-baked plans or
insufficient wisdom[10] now finds himself unable to proceed. At some later
time, it may be safe to continue the journey.[11]

App. 3: Closing his gates and doors,
  By this he stops *ku* madness.[12]
Fath. 3: Closing his gates and doors
  Means: He prevents whatever is not right.

Ku indicates a variety of virulent poisons associated with sexual in-
dulgence and black magic. The pictograph shows three insects, worms, or
reptiles in a bowl, a possible reference to the standard recipe for concoct-
ing the poison: Leave several poisonous insects or reptiles in a covered
jar until one has devoured all the others, then extract the concentrated
poison of the survivor. The poem urges the reader to close his mind to all
dangerous impulses, delusions, and heterodox arguments, all of which
poison the perceptions.[13] Lewd and superstitious men should also be
shunned.[14]

App. 4: They stop at saplings
  To seek their luxuriant fruits.[15]
Fath. 4: Stopping by young trees
  Means: Theirs is a fruitless search.

Appraisal 4 marks the initial transition from thought to action.
However, some prematurely look for perfection and completion.[16]
Should further cultivation of the tree (i.e., the heart/mind) be discontinued, the tree may never bear fruit upon maturity; by analogy, the petty
man rushes towards an ambitious goal, such as high office, before he is
ready.[17]

App. 5: Pillars keep the house in place.[18]
  Canopies shield the carriage.
  Hubs balance the space between.
Fath. 5: Pillars, canopies, and hub
  Mean: They honor the center.

Human civilization depends upon a number of inventions that exemplify the twin principles of "not moving" (i.e., stability) and centrality. The pillars, positioned at regular intervals, bear the weight of the home. The canopy, if properly centered, shelters the entire carriage from the elements. Finally, the hub keeps spokes and axles in place while the wheels move. Likewise, the good ruler knows enough to promote stability with centrality. He steadies the state like a pillar; he shelters the common people like a canopy; he functions as the hub of his kingdom. He alone has the ability to coordinate his subjects' activities so that their efforts converge productively.[19]

> App. 6: Square wheels and angular[20] axles
> Make for bumpy rides in the cart.
> Fath. 6: Square wheels and bumpy roads
> Mean: At every turn, he jolts himself.

The early Chinese believed that the sages of old invented certain fundamental tools like carts and roads to facilitate the development of human civilization. If such tools are wrongly fashioned, clearly their most basic functions, let alone their divine origins in cosmic patterns, are no longer understood. Just like the ill-made cart lurching along, society muddles along uncomfortably and without stability. Smooth progress in the Way becomes impossible.

> App. 7: When the cart has its wheels tied on,[21]
> The horse wears out its hooves.[22]
> To stop is good.
> Fath. 7: Carts tied and horses tired
> Mean: To proceed can be difficult.[23]

Normally, Appraisal 7, though aligned with Defeat, is lucky in an odd-numbered tetragram because it is aligned with auspicious Day. Here, however, the cart is worse than useless. Either it is in such poor repair that its wheels have to be tied on or else its wheels are "tied up" (i.e., clogged) by debris and mud from the road or tangled ropes. Compounding the difficulty, the cart is drawn by an old nag whose hooves are worn thin. The wise person, recognizing the nature of the problem, stops to make major repairs.

> App. 8: Good bows return; so do the bad.
> Good mounts are headstrong; so are the bad.
> Snap the bowstring, smash the cart,
> For this will never stop.[24]
> Fath. 8: Bows that return and headstrong horses
> Mean: In the end, they are unusable.

The bow and horse symbolize man's developed capacities, since a long course of training precedes skilled use of these tools. Even after training, the tools may prove unusable. For example, even the best wooden bow, because of its sensitivity to moisture and heat, may lose its proper tension.[25] Similarly, a spirited horse at times seems unruly. Clearly, poorly made bows and unbroken horses are even less useable.[26] To employ such tools even temporarily may end in disaster.[27] By analogy, a person's mettle must be fully trained and tested if proper use is to be made of him.[28] And even a good person, improperly employed, will make mistakes.[29]

> App. 9: Broken on a tree stump,[30]
>   And snagged on knife-sharp stones,
>   It stops.
> Fath. 9: Broken on trees, snagged on stones
>   Means: This is where the noble man stops.

As successive calamities befall the journey, the noble man, recognizing the hopelessness of his situation, "knows enough to stop."

Chien
No. 72. Hardness
November 6 (p.m.)–November 10

Correlates with Human's Mystery; Yin; the phase Metal; and the Yi ching *Hexagram no. 52, Stopping;[1] the sun enters the Tail constellation, 10th degree*

HEAD: Yin's form is covered with callouses while yang loses its main thread. Things compete in hardening themselves.

The assignment of this tetragram to the patron phase Metal may account for the tetragram's title. The hardness of metal may be reinforced by the mountains mentioned in the correspondent *Changes* hexagram.[2] In any case, as yin *ch'i* builds a tough outer casing, yang grows correspondingly weaker until it loses the main function of its existence (literally, "its main thread"), its propensity for nurturing. In imitation of yin *ch'i*, the myriad things begin to compete with each other for scarce resources under winter's harsh conditions. Their only hope of survival lies in hardening themselves. In the human realm, as in the natural world of Heaven-and-Earth, both advantages and disadvantages accrue from this tendency to hardness. A staunch defense of the Good, of course, is commendable, but stubbornness in pursuit of lesser goals is likely to lead to failure.

> App. 1: The massive stones so hard inside
> Do not change for the good.
> Fath. 1: That massive stones are hard inside
> Means: They cannot be transformed.

Appraisal 1 corresponds to the Beginning of Thought. An obdurate, massive stone symbolizes a stubborn inability to rethink decisions before embarking upon a disastrous course of action. As Confucius remarked, "It is only the very . . . stupidest who do not change."[3]

> App. 2: Firm and white, the jade form
> Changes inside for the better.
> Fath. 2: Firm and white, the jade form
> Means: Changes are rightly made.

In this Appraisal assigned to the Middle of Thought, Yang Hsiung clearly refers to a *Changes* passage depicting the heart/mind of the noble man as "jadelike" and "firm as a rock."[4] However fine the basic stuff of humanity, it can always be improved, like jade, through polishing. Firmness must be offset by flexibility and mutability if self-cultivation is to occur.

> App. 3: Firmness is not pervasive.[5]
> Something leaks at its center.
> Fath. 3: Firmness not pervasive
> Means: It cannot maintain uniformity.

In the calendar year, we now face the first severe freezes, though the ice may not yet have frozen firm on rivers. Just as it is treacherous to walk over soft or thin ice, it is dangerous to be "mushy" or "soft" at center (that is, to waver in one's convictions). Typically, the petty person has both good and evil impulses. While he may initiate a good act, he lacks the inner strength to carry it through to completion. As thought yields to action, the reader is reminded of the hazards of weakness and inconsistency.[6]

> App. 4: Small bees, busy busy,
> Swarm at their hive[7]
> To make it firm not big.
> Fath. 4: Small bees, busy busy,
> Mean: The bees secure their base.

As in Western culture, in China bees symbolize productive community. The base of the hive stands for virtue; its chamber, for the state. Just as worker bees follow the direction of the queen, hardworking members of the community manage to build a firm basis for productive life after their ruler helps them realize an important lesson: contrary to the theories of the Legalists, true security does not depend upon the size of the community but upon its dedication to a common purpose in the Good.[8]

> App. 5: The hive is big, the swarm is small
> And so it hangs empty.
> Fath. 5: A big hive and a small swarm
> Means: The state is empty and hollow.

Appraisal 5 is the ruler of the tetragram; hence, its reference to politics and the Son of Heaven. The Legalist leader, preoccupied with aggrandizing his position and enlarging his territory, neglects to build up his "base" in virtue. As a result, there are few reliable allies in his inner circle. Soon the empire collapses due to the lack of good men.[9]

> App. 6: The swarm is fine, so fine,
> Suspended over the Nine Provinces.
> Fath. 6: The tiny swarm suspended
> Means: The people are thus at peace.

The professional beekeeper, knowing that bees are docile just after the swarm alights, picks that time to handle them. By analogy, the skillful ruler chooses the right time to effect change so as to retain his subjects' allegiance. In this way, his influence is greatly extended.[10]

> App. 7: The hardhead[11] smacks into the hill.
> Fath. 7: A hard head pitted against a hill
> Means: He knows not where he's going.

The bullheaded individual who fails to ascertain the proper moral course runs headlong into disaster.[12] Ironically, his very strength of purpose proves to be his ultimate undoing. Blind to the fact that he could easily circumvent many obstacles by changing direction, he stubbornly persists in error until it destroys him. To miscalculate one's own strength is tantamount to suicide.[13]

> App. 8: Confident and firm in calamity,[14]
> He uses only the *hsieh-chih*'s signs.[15]
> Fath. 8: Secure and strong in calamity
> Means: He uses the straight path.[16]

In Chinese myth, the *hsieh-chih* resembles an ox with one horn. Legend credits it with an uncanny ability to distinguish right from wrong. Therefore, in ancient legal trials it was purportedly employed to determine the guilty parties.[17] The good person uses his conscience and the

Classics to determine the Right, never wavering in his pursuit of it, even in calamity. Such steadfast service to the Good contrasts favorably with the bullheadedness depicted in Appraisal 7.

> App. 9: The bees burning their hive[18]
> Bring ruin to their forebears.
> Fath. 9: Bees burning their hive
> Means: What they rely upon is ruined.

Here, at the end of the cycle, supremely arrogant individuals destroy their own community. While the *Changes* likens this to "birds burning their own nest,"[19] the *Mystery* compares it to bees burning their own hive. All that has been built over generations is now lost in a general conflagration.

Ch'eng
No. 73. Completion
November 11–November 15 (a.m.)

Correlates with Human's Mystery; Yang; the phase Water; and the Yi ching Hexagram no. 63, After Completion; the sun enters the Tail constellation, 15th degree

HEAD: Yin *ch'i* is pure right now.[1] Yang is stored in a numinous [region].[2] Things, being rescued, complete their forms.

At this point in the calendar, yang *ch'i* has completely disappeared from sight. It now is stored away below the surface of the earth, though its vitality cannot be completely extinguished. From far below it provides enough life-giving impulse to rescue the myriad things from utter extinction. Pure yin for its part represents "pure" cold.[3] The tetragram title, Completion, then, refers to no fewer than three separate phenomena: (1) the fullness of wintry cold brought about by the complete separation of yin from yang *ch'i*;[4] (2) the various accomplishments that perfect the social order; and (3) the imminent closure of the cycle of eighty-one tetragrams. It is appropriate that all three phenomena are assigned to the realm of Man, for "it is Heaven that generates all the myriad things. And then it is Earth that nourishes them. But it is the sages [i.e., Man *par excellence*] who bring them to fulfillment."[5]

App. 1: Completion seems obstructed,
   Its use, though unending, is hidden.
Fath. 1: Completion like an obstruction
   Means: Thus it remains undefeated.

The *Lao tzu* writes, "Great completion seems deficient,/ Yet its use is not spoiled."[6] The Tao never draws attention to its own operations, yet nothing remains undone. By analogy, the noble man never parades his talents and virtues. Consequently, no one credits him with effecting great reforms. To some, he may even seem uncultivated or lax in his behavior. The advantage of this is that he does not inspire envy or dislike. As a result of his modesty, he is never harmed.[7]

App. 2: Tenuous achievements and constant change:
   Before it is done, he grows lax.[8]
Fath. 2: Tenuous achievements, continual change,
   Mean: He cannot keep up with himself.

Repeated change tends to disaster since it bewilders most people. Han philosophers proved this point by the dramatic example of the First Emperor of Ch'in (d. 208 B.C.). By contrast, the classic description of the ancient sage-kings shows them preferring subtle adjustments, incremental change, and natural inducements to overt change:

They [the sages] brought continuity to their changes, so that the people did not grow weary. . . . [Only] when one change had run its full course did they effect another.[9]

App. 3: He completes the leap by drawing back.
   Completing the flight, he is not caught.
Fath. 3: Completing leaps by drawing back
   Means: In completion, virtue is strong.[10]

Position 3 by Yang's schema correlates with advancement in rank or status. Here the individual knows enough to realize that he must curb his desires for elusive goals. Paradoxically, he makes tremendous progress precisely by shrinking back with humility. He is ultimately raised high, though he has never pursued wealth or fame. As the old proverb has it, "Contract the foot before you leap. Fold in the wings before you fly."

App. 4: On the verge of completion,
   He boasts and is thus defeated.
Fath. 4: Bragging when nearly done
   Means: Achieving the Way is impaired.

The unwise individual prematurely brags about his accomplishments. Such conduct hampers full attainment of the Way.

App. 5: If his center is complete,[11]
    He alone oversees all.
    Such is greatness.
Fath. 5: Singular oversight by a center complete
    Means: He can take the center position.

Position 5 corresponds to the Son of Heaven and is the ruler of the tetragram. Here, Yang Hsiung adapts the language of Legalism on strategic advantage to express a profoundly Confucian message: Ideally, the emperor is at center (that is, in his innermost self) a model of perfection, since he has All-under-Heaven in his care.

App. 6: In completion, so conceited and mean is he
    That completion only garners calamity.
Fath. 6: Arrogance in completing
    Means: He fails to employ modesty.[12]

Position 6 is past the halfway point of the tetragram. Paired with inauspicious Night, here it portends overweening arrogance coupled with high position, a combination that can only end in the individual's downfall.[13]

App. 7: Perfection marred, he repairs.
Fath. 7: Repairing defects
    Means: Surely it is hard to carry on.

Position 7 corresponds to the loss of ambition or to defeat. Here, however, it corresponds to auspicious Day. Even though his achievements are plagued by flaws and faults, the superior man works hard to correct them, despite the late hour. For that reason, the defects cannot persist.

App. 8: The time is perfect but he is not.
    Heaven rains down no good omens.[14]
Fath. 8: The time being perfect while he is not
    Means: He fails to strike it on his own.

Position 8 represents the inauspicious end of the cycle. When human beings do not avail themselves of opportunities for improvement, disaster is sure to follow. Heaven rains calamity down upon the unrighteous.

App. 9: With completion, exhaustion[15]
    Enters defeat: Destruction complete.
    The noble man does not complete.[16]
App. 9: In completing, exhausted and destroyed
    Means: The noble man by this achieves his ends.

Due to the cyclical nature of things, completion ultimately entails defeat. The superior man, realizing this, regards himself always as incomplete and imperfect. By focusing upon daily renewal and self-improvement, he maintains good fortune and high rank.[17]

Chih

No. 74. Closure
November 15 (p.m.)–November 19

Correlates with Human's Mystery; Yin; the phase Fire; and the Yi ching Hexagram no. 21, Biting Through; the sun enters the Winnower constellation, 1st degree

HEAD: As contact between yin and yang falters,[1] each closes in on itself so that it becomes a single entity.[2] Their ill fortune causes the myriad things to weep.

The tetragram title, which is a graphic pun apparently invented by Yang Hsiung, shows "a door tightly shut," a perfect symbol of contact that is completely "blocked off."[3] As yin flourishes, yang declines. With this reversal of their conventional values, yin and yang falter in their new roles, then finally retreat into separate spheres. This radical separation means ruin for the myriad things, whose continued existence depends upon their union, as Tetragram 16, entitled Contact, shows us.

> App. 1: Round peg and square socket:[4]
>   Inside is a bad fit.
> Fath. 1: Circle and square, peg and socket,
>   Mean: Inside, they miss each other.

These lines give a classic example of a lack of correspondence: the round peg in a square hole. Since Appraisal 1 is assigned to the Beginning of Thought, it is appropriate to apply them to the thought processes, which are viewed as successive attempts to fit external events into their proper categorical slots. Obviously, the heart/mind fails to function here. This failure in turn precludes the possibility of true community among men, since that must be based on shared moral perceptions.

> App. 2: Close with no intervening gap.
> Fath. 2: Close with no gap
>   Means: The two are as one.

True sageliness depends upon the ability to perfectly match external events with internal moral categories. Right thinking, then, is a kind of psychic union on which true union is based. The ultimate power of such unions is suggested by the *Changes*, which says:

> When two persons are of one heart
> They are sharp enough to cut metal.[5]

> App. 3: The dragon steals into[6] another's lair.
>   Its light is then lost to the house.
> Fath. 3: The dragon slipping into the wrong cave
>   Means: It fails in its constant rules.

Yang *ch'i* (aligned with the dragon, the east, and spring) retreats below ground, though the dragon generally prefers its natural habitat on high mountain peaks wreathed in rain clouds. Even the marvelous dragon can only flourish in the proper environment. Should it steal into the wrong type of cave, it not only endangers itself but it also deprives its dependents of its beneficent power. By analogy, the promising individual who accepts an unsuitable position risks disgrace to himself and harm to the community. Since Appraisal 3 corresponds to "Advance," Yang Hsiung's warning is timely.

> App. 4: To immerse the nose in fragrant fats
>   Is good for beauty and propriety.
> Fath. 4: The propriety of immersing the nose
>   Means: He sinks in what is fragrant.[7]

Because fatty meats, fragrant from cooking, nourish our bodies, the correspondent hexagram calls it a good omen to "sink our teeth in the tender meat until the nose disappears."[8] The good person also exudes a fragrance (a noble "reputation") that sustains while dulling the craving for less savory things.[9] As thought turns to action in Appraisal 4, we should consider how best to immerse ourselves in the model of the sages.

> App. 5: Gnawing bones, he breaks his teeth—
>   Enough to fill a crock.
> Fath. 5: Gnawing bones and breaking teeth
>   Mean: He greatly covets profit.

With Appraisal 5 the ruler of the tetragram, the petty person in high position is willing to inflict any sort of violence upon others in his ruthless pursuit of profit. In this, he is like the voracious diner who chews even the bones, lest the smallest morsel escape him. By his rapacious demands for taxes, he may even have inflicted famine, or worse—cannibalism, upon his subjects. Before long, the evil consequences of unrestrained greed become evident. Broken teeth will "fill the crock," a possible reference to funerary urns.[10] Harm inflicted upon others through greed soon comes back to haunt us; it is like "biting through dried meat to get poison."[11]

> App. 6: Lapping up sweat[12]
> To gain its glossy smoothness.[13]
> Fath. 6: Lapping up sweat, slurp slurp,
> Means: The Way is worth being relished.

By the sweat of one's brow one secures great good fortune. Oddly enough, the profuse sweating that accompanies hard work does not unduly tire the person, but instead lubricates the joints, massaging them with precious oils. In this way, sustained effort devoted to the Good ultimately provides refreshment and relief.[14]

> App. 7: Despite the breach, forcing a fit:[15]
> What's joined at first, later splits.
> Fath. 7: Forcing their faults together
> Means: Their union falls apart.

When the panels of a traditional Chinese gate are unevenly hung, the gate will not shut tight unless the panels are forced into place every time. Sooner or later, that forcing will ruin the panels. By analogy, defects in a union, initially glossed over, will resurface, causing an irreparable break.

> App. 8: He repairs the breaks,
> And covers the flaws.
> Such a person is dazzling and strong.
> Fath. 8: Repairing breaks and covering flaws
> Means: He is still capable of improvement.

So long as the individual dedicates himself to the task of self-cultivation, even at Appraisal 8 it is not too late to reform. The verses also work as a description of the faithful friend who encourages improvement.[16]

> App. 9: As yin and yang start to transform,
> They change to red and white.
> Fath. 9: Yin turning red as yang turns white[17]
> Means: Reaching their limits, they then reverse.

Though the exact significance of this color change is lost to us, the verses probably use an apparent anomaly in the traditional correlations of color magic to suggest an unhealthy disjunction in conventional values.[18] In China, the color white is always used for mourning while the red of the newborn babe is a sign of health, perfect potential, and virility. Also, the same system that correlates winter and *yin* with snowy white ties summer to red, to heat, and to yang *ch'i*. Thus, as summer yields to winter, red pales to white; as winter reigns supreme, what is fundamentally white glows with ruddy health.[19] With normal values reversed, a new cycle is about to begin. (This may even hint at a change in the dynastic mandate.)[20] Such dramatic disjunctions and metamorphoses are inherently dangerous. The wise man takes warning.

Shih

No. 75. Failure

November 20–November 24 (a.m.)

Correlates with Human's Mystery; Yang; the phase Wood; and the Yi ching Hexagram no. 28, Great Error; the sun enters the Winnower constellation, 6th degree; the Dipper points NNW; the musical note is B

HEAD: Yin on a grand scale acts like a bandit. Yang cannot gain anything. Things sink into the unfathomable.

With this tetragram we move past the Winter Onset solar period into full winter, when yang can no longer resist the repeated onslaughts of yin *ch'i*. In this unequal struggle between yin and yang, the myriad things will suffer greatly, sinking into decline and death until greater balance is restored in the cycle. In human life, the suffering occasioned by the internal struggle between good and evil can be mitigated by a return to balance and the reform of one's conduct.

> App. 1: Stabbing at the Void,
> > Plunging in the blade.
> Fath. 1: Stabbing the Void, sinking the blade
> > Means: Deeply he ponders his own first signs.[1]

In this Appraisal aligned with the Beginning of Thought, the Void refers to the mind. The noble man examines his innermost thoughts, intent upon destroying any traces of evil, however small. In an alternate reading, the Void symbolizes the emptiness and vanity of certain goals. Anyone who "takes a stab" at such goals finds them as ephemeral as the air. Because such misdirected activity often ends in tragedy, the wise man hopes to excise any sign of the petty within himself.[2]

> App. 2: Paltry virtue breeds small failures.[3]
> Fath. 2: Failures from paltry virtue
> > Mean: He knows too little to fear first signs.[4]

Appraisal 2, aligned with low position, coincides here with inauspicious Night. The petty person thinks his own paltry virtue sufficient for success. Persisting in his errors, he never acquires sufficient power to realize his goals. Minor errors multiply into major disasters.[5]

> App. 3: Persistent[6] and compliant,
>> Anxious[7] and attentive,[8]
>> In his heart, he advances.[9]
> Fath. 3: Persistent and compliant
>> Means: He is able to reform himself.

Appraisal 3, correlated with advancement, describes the best attitude for those who intend to progress: Each individual must persist in complying with the dictates of the conscience.

> App. 4: Trusting his faults, he does not eat,
>> So, like the sun, he sinks from sight.
> Fath. 4: Trusting faults and unemployed
>> Means: He forfeits salary due upright men.[10]

Position 4 corresponds to high officials or the aristocracy. Due to misplaced trust in himself or others, someone in high standing fails, losing rank and salary ("He does not eat.").

> App. 5: The yellow-haired and gap-toothed
>> Take to protecting the center.
>> By them, the noble man is cleansed of faults.
> Fath. 5: The aged taking center
>> Means: Faults are thereby cleansed.

The ruler as center of the community is assisted in his reforms by aged advisors who exemplify wisdom and experience (the "yellow-haired and gap-toothed" men mentioned in the *Odes*).[11]

> App. 6: Filling his granary but neglecting his fields,
>> He eats their fruits without tending their roots.
> Fath. 6: A full granary but neglected fields
>> Means: He is unable to cultivate the base.

Appraisal 6, past the midpoint of the tetragram, is also paired with inauspicious Night. The petty person, who only considers present benefits, makes no provision for the future. In his shortsightedness, he ignores the root of all happiness, virtue in community.

> App. 7: Sick men as a rule take medicine
>> While shamans pour libations.
> Fath. 7: Medicine for the sick, libations for shamans,
>> Mean: Calamity can be turned around.

Though Appraisal 7 generally describes loss, here it corresponds to auspicious Day. Plagued by physical or moral impairment, the individual applies every known cure in his attempt to improve. Such persistence is rewarded with a return to good health.

> App. 8: The hen cries at dawn.
> The female sports a horn
> And fish inhabit trees.
> Fath. 8: The hen calling at dawn
> Means: What is right for them is reversed.

The constant laws of the phenomenal world have been overturned. Erratic behavior in the animal world reflects disorder in the realm of Man. The crowing of a hen, for example, portends subversion of the family by its wicked females.[12]

> App. 9: With days and months passing,
> He changes at death's door.[13]
> Fath. 9: Changing at death's door
> Means: He is still not too far away.

Although the individual does not reform until death's door, he still is accounted a virtuous person.[14]

Chü
No. 76. Aggravation
November 24 (p.m.)–November 28

Correlates with Human's Mystery; Yin; the phase Metal; and the Yi ching Hexagram no. 28, Great Error; the sun enters the Winnower constellation, 11th degree

HEAD: Yin, coming to an end, weeps copiously that in yang it lacks a separate[1] partner. Such is the aggravation of parting.[2]

Even as yin's sway comes to an end, yang is still bereft of power. With no clear force in charge, the cosmic order approaches chaos; hence, the tetragram title, which conveys a sense of "aggravation," "scarcity," "extremity," and "intensity."

> App. 1: Bones bind[3] his flesh.
> Darkness.

Fath. 1: Bones binding his flesh
Mean: The thief within is at work.

Typically, bones support the flesh that binds the bones together. Here, the dramatic reversal of their usual roles suggests the degree to which internal dislocations affect external situations.

App. 2: An eclipse[4] with blood flowing
Is both bad omen and good.
Fath. 2: An eclipse with blood flowing out
Means: The noble man inside sees harm.[5]

The word "eclipse" comes from the Greek for "abandonment," which captures the sense of foreboding felt by many at the sun's vanishing. Like other ancient peoples, the early Chinese feared that the sun or moon would ultimately be devoured by total darkness during an eclipse. In lunar eclipses, the moon may turn blood-red. Here blood appears to pour forth, compounding the inauspicious character of the event. Such a dire omen could only portend the most dramatic of evils, for example, the usurpation of the imperial throne. Still, the noble man, recognizing the fearful implications of the eclipse, promptly resolves upon reform. In that way, a bad omen can inspire a change for the good. Good men even long for such signs. According to popular tradition, when disasters and prodigies ceased to appear in the Ch'u state, King Chuang (r. 836–826 b.c.) was far from delighted. "Am I not doomed?" he asked his courtiers. Thinking that an angry Heaven had abandoned its attempts to warn him against error, King Chuang responded with an ambitious program of reform.[6]

App. 3: Wine makes for loss of virtue.
Ghosts spy on his house.
Fath. 3: Wine causing virtue's loss
Means: He cannot take charge of himself.[7]

Both the *Odes* and the *Documents* specifically condemn intoxication, attributing to it a "loss of virtue" in the people and their leaders.[8] Although wine initially was created to bring men together in ritual acts,[9] drunken misconduct easily breaks communities apart. That ghosts are present suggests both the befuddled minds of drunken fools and imminent calamity.

App. 4: Eating in times of scarcity:
Parents are urged to take second helpings.[10]
Such is compliant behavior.
Fath. 4: Compliant though food is scarce
Means: He takes a salary so that he may comply.

Appraisal 4 usually refers to the bureaucracy. The superior man, ever mindful of his obligation to support his parents in their old age, accepts a less-than-ideal position so that his parents may eat their fill even when food is scarce. One popular tale from the Han dynasty concerns a certain paragon of filial piety named Tung Yung:

> Tung Yung was from a poor family;
> His elders left him no property.
> He took a loan to provide for his father.
> He labored for others that he might serve him sweets and meat.[11]

A similar story praises the filial nature of a young child who, "whenever he had some delicacy, would never eat it himself, but would first offer it to his father."[12]

> App. 5: Out into the wilds,
> He surveys the ruins.
> A tiger there is herding pigs.
> He hoists his pantlegs to his jacket.[13]
> Fath. 5: In the wilds, seeing ruin
> Means: No place is left to set his foot.

Unfortunately, Position 5 as ruler of the tetragram is aligned with inauspicious Night. The moral superior witnesses total disorder. A rapacious elite (the "tiger") takes charge of defenseless subordinates (the "pigs"). Knowing that there is no place for an honest leader at court, the good man hikes up his clothes in order to quickly flee the scene.

> App. 6: The Four States prosper.[14]
> He is their home.[15]
> Fath. 6: That the States fill his realm[16]
> Means: They seek a safe home.

In all four directions, the states look to the charismatic leader to protect them. They seek a just state, where they can prosper under his direction. Their attraction to him seems as natural as rivers running to the sea.[17]

> App. 7: How vigorous! how prosperous!
> Yet he carries the face of calamity.
> Fath. 7: Vigorous and flourishing
> Means: He wears clear marks of calamity.

The inner decay (moral or physical) of one in high position or in the prime of life is first betrayed by facial expression. Though superficially healthy, as the cycle approaches its extreme position, the individual is liable to calamity. As *Lao tzu* writes, even "the hard and strong" can be "comrades of death."[18]

App. 8: A flask secured by a well-rope
　　　Is a good omen and fine.
Fath. 8: Securing the flask
　　　Means: His duties are pressing.

The water flask is secured by a strong rope, so the benefits of fresh, clean water (a symbol for the cleansing heart/mind) are readily available without fear of loss. (Compare the same image in Tetragram 40.) The flask stands for the noble person, who is useful to the extent that he is restrained by the model of the ancients.

App. 9: Like the sea, flocks flying[19]
　　　Cover over Heaven's Barge.[20]
Fath. 9: Flocks flooding the sky
　　　Mean: The end is unspeakably bad.[21]

At the climax of the cycle, flocks of birds seem to flood the sky, obscuring the usual brilliance of Heaven's Barge (the Chinese name for the Milky Way). As one commentator writes, "This is an image of rain." That the inferior (i.e., the rain) hides the light of the greater (the Milky Way) portends ultimate calamity, with inferiors usurping the place of their superiors.

Surely the poem also alludes to the famous legend about the annual renunion (on the seventh day of the seventh lunar month) of the Oxherd and Weaver Girl, two star-crossed divinities who leave their homes in the Vega and Altair constellations to meet on a bridge of magpies in the clear light of the autumn sky. Since the Milky Way is intimately connected with the rivers, seas, and lakes of earth, including its circumambient ocean, this image may well portend great floods.[22]

Hsün

No. 77. Compliance
November 29–December 3 (a.m.)

Correlates with Human's Mystery; Yang; the phase Earth; and the Yi ching Hexagram no. 2, The Receptive; the sun enters the Dipper constellation, 3d degree

HEAD: Yin *ch'i* greatly conforms.[1] Undifferentiated like the primeval chaos and infinite in scope,[2] there are none who see its root.

Yin *ch'i*, nearing the end of its dominant phase, returns to primeval chaos.[3] Since it lacks all boundaries and distinguishing features (in contrast to yang *ch'i*, which is characterized by edges and sharp definition), yin's hidden source may not be located with any certainty.[4] Concerned not with heroic acts but with the repetitive aspects of the cycle, especially birth and death, yin is largely invisible, even as its labors.[5] Nevertheless, yin has the power to envelop all things in its womb. At this time, humans are urged to imitate yin *ch'i* by adopting feminine or motherly virtues,[6] including devotion, the capacity to nurture, modesty and forebearance, compliance, and receptivity, which are said to "bring sublime success, furthering through perseverance."[7] According to the *Changes*:

> Taking the lead brings confusion, because one loses his Way. Following with devotion—thus does one attain his permanent place.[8]

Quiet compliance with the rules of society and the laws of nature tends to produce good fortune in the end. For this reason, the wise person, in imitation of pure yin and Earth, chooses not to advertise his own merit; instead, he works to bring others' achievement to completion. In keeping with such prescriptions, this tetragram advocates the slow accumulation of good acts by devotion to the Way.

> App. 1: Yellow, the spirit of Earth,
>   Is profound: a good omen.
>   Such is compliance.
> Fath. 1: Yellow, numinous, profound, and true[9]
>   Means: Through compliance it corrects.

Black and yellow in combination often refer to the complementary powers of Heaven and Earth or of yang and yin respectively, as in tetragram 1.[10] Here, however, the poem talks only of yellow and what is profound (or dark). Yellow probably signifies the propensity of the heart/mind, the human center, to follow the Mean and respond with fairness and receptivity, while the profound (*yu*) may symbolize the good person's innate modesty. The attainment of such virtues invests the individual with divine powers.

> App. 2: Bearing the child[11]
>   Is the work of women.[12]
>   If she is not still, it will not live.
> Fath. 2: A miscarriage
>   Means: She could not keep pure and still.

In traditional China, the woman's primary responsibility was to bear male children to continue her husband's ancestral line. It was her solemn duty, then, to keep herself from physical harm while pregnant. Ideally, she also exposes herself to positive influences, such as soothing music and the proper books, so that the embryo might be educated in the womb.[13] Unfortunately, the mother in Appraisal 2 exposed herself to mental or physical disturbances. The results are predictably awful. This metaphor, of course, applies to any project that is "stillborn" due to its promoters' reckless behavior.

> App. 3: True women give constant care
> And so protect their roots.
> Fath. 3: True women give constant care.
> Meaning: They do not forget the base.

Appraisal 3 is aligned with Wood, whose characteristic virtue is all-encompassing benevolence.[14] A mother's ability to nurture her dependents selflessly is a strong force worth imitating. By practicing this virtue, males can easily secure the psychosocial base of individual, family, or state.[15]

> App. 4: Though boasting of his deeds,
> He is less heroic than Earth.
> Fath. 4: Boasting of his deeds
> Means: He brags of good acts.

Earth fosters all the myriad things without requiring gratitude in return. Similarly, the true gentleman cares for lesser mortals without insisting that they acknowledge his superiority.[16] In contrast, the petty man seeks to draw attention to his merits. Therein lies his downfall.[17]

> App. 5: The spirit sack[18] holds all in its embrace,
> Its virtue is precious as gold.[19]
> Fath. 5: The great embrace of the cosmic sack
> Means: It does not dare aggrandize itself.

Appraisal 5 as ruler of the tetragram outlines ideal behavior for the Son of Heaven. By receptivity toward others' suggestions, rather than by coercion, the emperor induces his subjects to contribute their talents to his government.[20] Ultimately, to govern effectively he must draw together the ideas of many loyal advisors, so that his own thinking comes to resemble a sack filled with marvels. In doing this, he comes to measure and to reflect the full complexity of the cosmos.[21]

> App. 6: The sack fails to hold,
> Leaking the precious tools.
> Fath. 6: A sack losing its hold
> Means: The subjects' mouths spill forth.

The basic virtue attributed to yin, Earth, and woman is silent devotion. But here Appraisal 6, past the midpoint of the tetragram, is paired with inauspicious Night, making an evil omen. Petty men in subordinate positions cannot be trusted to remain loyal to their master. (This, of course, may well be due to their leader's inadequacies.) Rumor and advice are offered to rival powers; for "as disorder develops, words are the first steps."[22]

> App. 7: To be square[23] and firm in opposing compliance
> Helps the subordinate prove his mettle.[24]
> Fath. 7: Square and firm in opposing compliance
> Means: He preserves correct principles.

The good subordinate is willing to risk his superior's anger, lest important principles be abandoned. When his superior commits to some wrong course, the loyal follower bravely points out the error of his ways. Since the wise leader values his advisors' outspokenness, he encourages them to demonstrate their worth in this way.

> App. 8: Compliant, he defies the Right.
> He fails to protect the Decree.[25]
> Fath. 8: Complying with what is wrong
> Means: He lacks the means to unite with the One.

Compliance with the rules of conduct laid down by the sage-kings of antiquity in conformity with Heaven can unify the hearts of men. To acquiesce in what is evil ultimately weakens community and undercuts the Way.

> App. 9: Complying with duty, he forgets life,
> Relying instead on Heaven's good omen.
> Fath. 9: Complying with duty and forgetting life
> Means: Receipt of the Decree is certain.

The verse plays upon various associations for the word "Decree," including "life" (given by one's parents), "fate" (sent by Heaven), and political "appointment" (mandated by the ruler). Taken together, these three decrees largely determine individual destiny. In recognition of the heavy debt owed to those who have given him physical and social life, the superior individual willingly performs all the duties associated with these decrees, even at the cost of his own life. When "the noble man lays down his life to follow his will,"[26] he may expect in return a reward, perhaps immortal fame or illustrious descendants.

Chiang
No. 78. On the Verge
December 3 (p.m.)–December 7

Correlates with Human's Mystery;
Yin*; the phase Water; and the* Yi
ching *Hexagram no. 64, Not yet
Complete; the sun enters the
Dipper constellation, 9th degree*

HEAD: Yin *ch'i* completes[1] things to the upper regions. Yang, extending, is about to return to begin them at the lower regions.[2]

Momentous changes are about to occur in the phenomenal world. Yin *ch'i*, which has nearly effected the completion of the myriad things, will soon depart. Yang is on the verge of returning to its initial position at the beginning of the cycle. Such reversals are the key to renewal, but given the potential danger inherent in times of great transition,[3] the noble man takes particular care to persevere in the course of moderation. As the *Lao tzu* says:

> The people always ruin their enterprises when they are on the verge of success. Be as careful at the end as at the beginning.[4]

App. 1: Almost off on a deviant course:
    Initial danger.
Fath. 1: About to embark on evil
    Means: Peril predominates.

In this Appraisal corresponding to the Beginning of Thought, the individual is about to set off on a mistaken course which ultimately will endanger him.

App. 2: Almost without a blemish:
    Initial purity.[5]
Fath. 2: Almost without blemish
    Means: Ease is what succeeds.[6]

Here the individual in low position has nearly purified himself of faults. This facilitates later success.

App. 3: With furnace and wheel not right,
    It would be good to stop.
Fath. 3: That furnace and potter's wheel are wrong
    Means: To transform the inside is harmful.

In early China the furnace and the potter's wheel signify the cosmological processes whereby undifferentiated stuff is fashioned into the fully articulated phenomena of Heaven-Earth Man.[7] Applied to creative thought, they suggest the processes by which raw sensory information is fitted into proper legal, social, and ethical categories. Here, however, fundamental flaws in the basic tools lead to the misuse of creativity. Like a good workman, the man of virtue must be careful to keep his tools (including his advisors and reasoning methods) in good working order if he hopes to build upon the model of the sages.

> App. 4: About to fly, he gets his wings,
>   Which help in rising to Heaven.
> Fath. 4: Prepared to fly on new-got wings
>   Means: Their support is strong.

Like a fledgling that has just discovered the use of its newly grown feathers, the good person on the road to advancement finds how useful good advisors can be. Without such support, all attempts to "fly high" prove futile.

> App. 5: The great sparrow, about to fly,
>   Plucks out its shaft feathers.
>   Despite a wealth of down, it cannot proceed.
> Fath. 5: Great sparrows plucking shafts
>   Mean: There it is not enough to rely upon.

Appraisal 5 as the ruler of the tetragram describes the Son of Heaven through a popular pun: "great sparrow" also means "great emoluments" (and by implication, high rank).[8] If the ruler of highest rank offends his strongest allies (the "shaft feathers"), he may find it impossible to continue despite the support of the masses (the "down").[9]

> App. 6: The sun slips down[10] in all its glory.
>   The noble man will soon decline and fall.
> Fath. 6: That the blazing sun slips down
>   Means: Self-generated light is great.

Position 6 is past the half-way point of the tetragram. The sun, still blazing with afternoon heat, begins its decline. The sun stands for the superior individual, especially the ruler, whose charismatic light is shed on lesser mortals. But in what sense can the noble man be said to be on the verge of decline? Three answers are possible: In the first reading, the superior man, recognizing death's inevitability, works hard to enlighten others before his own "light" is extinguished; in the second, he nobly declines a post in acknowledgement of his failing powers; and in the third, he condescends (i.e., "goes down") to meet with inferiors, like the setting sun as it sinks below the horizon.[11]

   App. 7: Hurrying the boat or rocking[12] the cart,
     Harmful effects are not far away.[13]
  Fath. 7: Hurried boat and rocked cart
     Means: He is not far from harm.

Boats and carts are two of the many tools invented by the sages to enhance human existence. As with all human inventions, their proper use implies a certain trade-off. Cart and boat are unwieldy, yet they carry great loads over long distances. Improper use of such tools destroys their advantages.[14]

   App. 8: A small child in a deep abyss:
     The adult men take out[15] their boats.
  Fath. 8: Adults out in boats
     Mean: They would save a drowning age.

A young child who has ventured too far out into deep water will surely drown unless rescued. Luckily, wise adults know how to employ the tools at hand to save him. By analogy, the worthy leader intent upon saving the common people in a benighted age must use the proper tools (for example, study of the Confucian Classics, ritual conformity, and good government).

   App. 9: Red silkworms cling to dry mulberries.
     Their cocoons will not turn golden yellow.
  Fath. 9: Not yellow on account of the dry
     Means: The silkworms' work is ruined.

Silkworms turn red when they are old or diseased.[16] The silkworms' problem is compounded because they have attached themselves to dry and leafless branches. (Since this is Appraisal 9, perhaps it is too late in the season for mulberry leaves?) Such a scant diet cannot produce healthy cocoons of average weight and value, let alone the highly prized silky golden threads used by connoisseurs in ritual activities.[17] Similarly, the potential for human productivity is ruined when bad timing and misdirected activity are combined with the wrong environment.[18]

Nan

No. 79. Difficulties

December 8–December 12 (a.m.)

Correlates with Human's Mystery;
Yang; the phase Fire; and the Yi
ching *Hexagram no. 39, Difficulty*
Walking; the sun enters the Dipper
constellation, 13th degree

HEAD: Yin *ch'i* makes difficulties on all sides.[1] Water freezes, the earth cracks. Yang drowns in the abyss.

At the end of the calendar year marked by the Great Snow solar period, the myriad things keenly feel the cruelty of wintry yin *ch'i* as it culminates. Yang *ch'i*, buried deep below the earth's surface in the watery netherworld, is so quiet that it seems dead, even though it will not be long before yang *ch'i* begins to reassert itself. After all, return or reversal is the movement of the Tao.[2]

> App. 1: Troubled am I in deep, dark places.
>
> Fath. 1: That I am troubled in deep, dark places
> Means: Its form is not yet seen.[3]

At the Beginning of Thought, the inner self, mired in doubt and confusion, struggles to reach the true light of understanding before its benighted ideas "take form" in action. In this it imitates yang *ch'i* in winter, struggling to escape its confinement below earth so that the myriad things can "take form."[4]

> App. 2: As solid ice thaws to slush,[5]
> A crazed horse escapes the whip.[6]
> Fath. 2: That a crazed horse escapes the whip
> Means: A reckless disregard for life.

Avoiding his master's whip, the crazed horse decides to escape across the frozen river. However, the ice has just begun to melt. As soon as the attempt is made, the horse will plunge headlong into the water to its death. Miscalculation combined with heedlessness brings disaster, not freedom.[7]

> App. 3: A center firm and hard
> Troubles the "inconstant."
> Fath. 3: A center firm and fixed
> Means: Finally, none are overturned.

Once again, the center refers to the individual's heart/mind, the seat of both the emotions and the intellect. So long as the *hsin* is firmly fixed upon the Good, the person has no difficulty repudiating evil impulses contrary to Heaven's norms.

> App. 4: When eggs break against stone,
>> The undeveloped die.[8]
> Fath. 4: Rotting embryos from broken eggs
>> Mean: The difficulties of the petty man.

The egg represents perfect potential. In the case of humans, this applies to the development of the innate capacity for Goodness. Two readings then follow: In the first, the petty man in the face of difficulties breaks as easily as an eggshell against a stone.[9] In a second reading, the petty man is like a stone and the good person is like an egg. Out of power, the virtuous individual cannot survive the vicious slander leveled by opponents.[10]

> App. 5: No gap between troubles:
>> No matter how great, he will not succumb.[11]
> Fath. 5: That troubles find no gap
>> Means: At center all is tightly blocked.

In both Appraisal and Fathoming, the first line is ambiguous. Either difficulties come in rapid succession with no gap (i.e., interval) separating them, or personal trials leave the individual largely unaffected, since no gap exists in the integrated self to allow evil an *entrée*.[12] As the ruler of the tetragram, Appraisal 5 reminds us that troubles cannot really defeat whoever rules by the conscience, no matter how often calamities plague this Job-like figure.

> App. 6: The great carriage lumbers on.[13]
>> Above, it is blocked by mountains;
>> Below, it runs into rivers.
> Fath. 6: The great carriage lumbering on
>> Means: Above and below, brakes are applied.

Appraisal 6, past the midway point of the tetragram, is paired here with inauspicious Night and so it portends ill. The individual who shoulders heavy burdens, like the great cart, meets with repeated delays and numerous obstacles. Just as the very size of the conveyance proves an added encumbrance, ironically enough, high rank or status may make maneuvering more difficult.

> App. 7: Extracting stones is difficult.[14]
>> His strength fades, still he persists.[15]

Fath. 7: Wresting stones free
   Means: He takes advantage of the time.

Appraisal 7 corresponding to loss is here aligned with auspicious Day. Clearing a field of stones is tough work even when the stones are smooth.[16] But the individual who intends to persevere will find his task much easier if he waits until rain or a thaw has softened the ground. Such are the benefits of acting at the right time. (Compare this message with Appraisal 4 of Tetragram 3.)

App. 8: Crashing against stones, snapping trees in two,
   He merely breaks his horn.
Fath. 8: Stone-crashing and tree-snapping
   Mean: This is no way to rule.

To overcome obstacles, this individual uses brute strength rather than charismatic virtue coupled with a calculating intelligence. Naturally, he is bound to fail.

App. 9: Leading the *hsieh-chih*[17] to use its horns[18]
   Offenders are finally set straight.[19]
Fath. 9: Making the *hsieh-chih* butt
   Means: By this in the end he straightens them.

When the true identity of an offender is unknown, Heaven may help right-thinking men to determine the criminal. While the marvelous *hsieh-chih* only appeared in the courts of the sage-kings of antiquity (see Tetragram 72), in the modern age there exist equally infallible guides to conduct, including the classics of Confucianism and the rituals sanctified by tradition.

Ch'in

No. 80. Laboring
December 12 (p.m.)–December 16

Correlates with Human's Mystery; Yin; the phase Wood; and the Yi ching Hexagram no. 39, Difficulty Walking; the sun enters the Dipper constellation, 18th degree

HEAD: Yin freezes firm as it is terrified of being wounded on the outside. Tenuous yang lodges in darkness, exerting its strength on the inside.

We are nearly now at the winter solstice, the point at which yang will start to wax and yin to wane. Yin has already rendered itself immobile, now that the myriad things are frozen; being immobile, it is particularly vulnerable to attack. Meanwhile, we detect the first hints of yang's latent strength gathering its force in the secret recesses of the Earth.

>App. 1: Diligence[1] of mind
>>Obstructs propriety.
>Fath. 1: Diligent but wrong
>>Means: The center is not upright.

At the Beginning of Thought, the heart/mind is set upon wrongdoing. Under such circumstances, the very diligence of the *hsin* is all the more frightening.

>App. 2: Laboring from a sense of duty,[2]
>>And tireless in diligence,[3]
>>The noble man has his center.
>Fath. 2: Laboring out of obligation
>>Means: Diligence is seated in emotion.[4]

By definition, the individual "has a [moral] center" once he acknowledges his obligations to a nested hierarchy of social relations, extending from parents to mentors to patrons to the state. Through ritual conduct designed to express his love and respect for those who have helped him, the individual becomes fully human.[5]

>App. 3: Babes[6] with "bridles" and "horns"[7]
>>Insistently weep *ku-ku*[8]
>>If unsupported by swaddling.
>Fath. 3: Babies with "bridles" and "horns"
>>Mean: They will not get to live.

"Bridles" and "horns" are the names given to the characteristic hairstyles once given female and male babies in imperial China; baby girls sported two small braids (the bridles) while the boys' hair was dressed in a single ponytail worn at the top, called the horn.[9] Newborns bawl incessantly until they are wrapped securely in swaddling clothes. Just as a child cannot survive to adulthood without the loving care of parents, our fragile conscience can only develop under the watchful eye of moral superiors.

>App. 4: Diligent in exerting his strength,
>>Doubling his efforts, he forgets to eat.
>>The great man has this ability.

> Fath. 4: In diligent labor, forgetting to eat
> Means: Such is the virtue of great men.

In tetragrams assigned to the end of the lunar year, the individual is often instructed to persevere in good conduct, even in the face of calamity. Here the good person redoubles his efforts so that nothing can stop his improvements. The sage Confucius was described by the *Analects* in comparable language:

> This is the character of the man: so intent upon enlightening the eager that he forgets his hunger, and so happy in doing so, that he forgets the bitterness of his lot, and does not realize that old age is at hand.[10]

> App. 5: Going forth,[11] he stumbles and stumbles.[12]
> Ill fortune is near and good far away.
> Fath. 5: That he stumbles in going forth
> Means: He keeps his distance from good fortune.

As ruler of the tetragram, these lines describe the individual who is prevented from achieving his goal by repeated missteps. Had he made sufficient preparations to advance, he could have proceeded with confidence.[13]

> App. 6: With labor comes success
> Nearly up to Heaven.
> Fath. 6: Success through labor
> Means: This is the help that Heaven grants.

Heaven aids the superior individual who has cultivated his original endowment to such an extent that his virtue nearly equals that of Heaven.

> App. 7: Working hard to drag it along,
> If not by the nose, then by the tail,
> He wearies.[14]
> Fath. 7: The weary work of leading
> Means: His way is contrary.

The oxherd leads his draft animal either by a rope strung from the animal's nostrils or by its tail. Due to its discomfort, the ox, increasingly angry, resists all efforts to be led. The oxherd fails to reach his goal, then, not because his strength is insufficient, but because he lacks the requisite skill and empathy. The way he has adopted is contrary to both reason and convention.

> App. 8: He labors at a breakneck pace,[15]
> With a heart at ease.[16]
> Crashing through thickets, he does not retreat.

Fath. 8: Working diligently
   Means: He sacrifices himself for the state.

The individual foregoes comfort, perhaps even sacrifices his life, in service to the state. This description recalls that of the sage-ruler Yü, who is said to have spent eight years selflessly laboring for the benefit of the common people of the Central Kingdoms at the time of the great flood.[17] According to Yang Hsiung, the true gentleman is one who "loves what is good for others, but forgets what is in his own interest."[18]

App. 9: So diligent, so diligent!
   Holding the cart, he enters deep pools.
   Bearing the boat, he climbs up mountains.
Fath. 9: How diligent, how diligent!
   Means: Such hard work brings no gain.

Without a basic understanding of the tools of civilization, the individual cannot hope to gain success through diligence. Misguided labors only end in utter weariness as Appraisal 9 depicts the height of folly.

Yang
No. 81. Fostering
December 17–December 21 (a.m.)

Correlates with Human's Mystery; Yang; the phase Metal; and the Yi ching *Hexagram no. 27, Providing Nourishment;[1] the sun enters the Dipper constellation, 22nd degree*

HEAD: Yin, like a bow stretched taut,[2] bulges out to the furthest reaches. Yang bathes[3] the myriad things [in its energizing solution], turning them red in the nether regions.

Together, Heaven and Earth provide physical nourishment for all the myriad things, endowing them with life. As the winter solstice approaches, yang *ch'i* from its unseen base below begins to imbue the roots of all the myriad things with renewed vitality, signified by the color red. On this model, the good person provides spiritual refreshment for lesser mortals. When in high position, he takes particular pleasure in sustaining worthies while providing for the physical needs of all.[4] Sustenance and support sought in the wrong places, however, only increases danger.

App. 1: Store the heart in a deep pool
    To improve[5] its marvelous roots.
Fath. 1: Storing the heart in a deep pool
    Means: Divinity is not outside.

The first Appraisal is aligned with the Water phase, which may have prompted the reference to a pool of great depth.[6] The pool signifies the "unmoved mind" of infinite capacity, which accurately reflects reality when functioning properly. Also, appropriate action in later Appraisals must draw upon depths of knowledge and moral courage. The noble person nurtures such divine aspects within (the roots of Goodness), rather than looking outside for good luck. In this way, he does not go astray in his thoughts and actions.[7]

App. 2: Silently, he fosters perversion,
    Harboring impropriety at the start.[8]
Fath. 2: In silence promoting evil
    Means: The center heart is defeated.

In an obvious contrast to Appraisal 1, Appraisal 2 depicts the wicked propensities of those who fail to nourish the roots of Goodness inherent in human nature. Even before taking action (when still silent), the inborn conscience is silenced.

App. 3: Manure and mulch enrich the hill,
    Nourishing its roots and stems.
Fath. 3: Fertilizing the hill
    Means: At center, the glory is great.

The center, of course, refers to the human heart/mind, the seat of both the emotions and the intellect. Just as the growth of vegetation depends upon repeated applications of fertilizer, full human development relies upon continued exposure to the nurturing qualities of ritual. Otherwise, the fragile human propensity for Goodness is stunted.

App. 4: Swallows feed everywhere[9]
    For they intend to steal.[10]
    This is good for seizing business.[11]
Fath. 4: Swallows feeding here and there
    Mean: The will is fixed on gain.[12]

The swallows swoop down to feed. Despite their insatiable appetites, they appear to have no fixed goal as they snatch others' food away from them.[13] In this, they are like greedy individuals who fail to pursue a single good with sufficient dedication. Adopting the philosophy that "more is better," they are like crass merchants who care less for community than for their own profit.[14]

> App. 5: With a heart of gold in the belly,
> Even old white bones grow flesh.[15]
> Virtue fostered[16] is not overturned.[17]
> Fath. 5: A golden heart in the belly
> Means: The highest virtue is Heavenly.[18]

The heart is golden yellow because it keeps to the Mean; yellow, after all, is the color assigned to the center. The virtue correlated with the center is good faith, without which true community falters. Here, the virtue that fosters sustains the noble man, perhaps the Son of Heaven himself, until he experiences renewed life (in the metaphor, dry bones growing flesh) and a fundamental kinship with the cosmic norms.

> App. 6: In quick succession,[19] in a single day,
> Three blood sacrifices, auguries from sacred oxen.
> Fattened animals bring no benefit.[20]
> Fath. 6: Repeated sacrifices
> Mean: Fat is of no benefit to the self.[21]

According to Yang's system of correlations, Appraisal 6 corresponds to the ancestral temple; hence, the references to sacrifices and Heaven-sent omens. The blood sacrifices associated with heterodox cults are offered repeatedly, which suggests the uneasy state of mind experienced by superstitious petitioners to the gods.[22] Frequent contact with the gods is itself a mistake: scarce human resources are wasted and the experience of the sacred is cheapened. Also, the claims of cult leaders are at best presumptuous and at worst a lie. For these reasons, the offering designed to please the gods, the fattened ox, does not augur well. It would be better to follow the ritual precepts strictly.

Several commentators, aping the style of Chuang tzu, consider this all from the viewpoint of the sacrificial ox, which comes to realize that it has been fattened only for the kill.[23]

> App. 7: A small boy leads an elephant.
> A woman ropes a fierce beast.
> Noble men care for the afflicted.
> Fath. 7: Leading an elephant, caring for the sick
> Means: They have no intrinsic connection.

The small boy symbolizes what is weakest; the woman, what is most gentle. Given these attributes, these two people are clearly unfit for their dangerous jobs.[24] In this they are like the petty man who does not measure his strength or who is unfit for his responsibilities.[25] In such cases, it is always left to the superior man, who pursues a different vision,[26] to resolve ensuing problems.

Another interpretation compares the small boy to nascent yang *ch'i*, which subtly leads the myriad things to fulfillment. In that case, the woman must signify "old yin," which still relies on force. The noble man chooses neither course of action rigidly, but flexibly and appropriately responds to each situation.[27]

> App. 8: The fishbone is not dislodged.
>> Its poisonous illness spreads.
>> Ghosts rise up on the tomb.
> Fath. 8: An outbreak of illness from fishbones
>> Means: He returns to the grave mound.

If the fishbone is not quickly dislodged from the throat, life-giving breath cannot reach the vital organs. Illness and death follow, with death envisioned as a return (*kuei*) to a ghostly (*kuei*) state.[28] Ironically, the subject of this verse only intended to nourish himself.

> App. 9: Like the fixed stars, like the Year,
>> Return and continue at the start.
> Fath. 9: The stars and the Year Star
>> Mean: At the end, they foster beginnings.[29]

In the final text of the final tetragram, with the end of the lunar year, we have come full circle. Yang Hsiung therefore reminds us of the constant cycles that rule our lives, especially the impressive revolving patterns of the night sky. Just as the heavenly bodies keep to their orbits, renewal ultimately depends upon our willingness to adhere to societal norms.

* * * * *

To provide for a leap year, Yang supplied two additional intercalary Leap lines, which together account for 3/4 of an additional day.

> "DEFICIT" (or "ODD")[30]
>> Freezing ice ascends to Red Heaven,
>> Swelt'ring heat enters the Mystery Spring.
>> The freeze mounting Red Heaven
>> Means: Yin makes a beginning.

Red Heaven refers to the point where yang is maximized, presumably in the highest heavens; Mystery Spring, to yin maximized in the deepest recesses of the earth. Freezing cold and blazing heat represent yin and yang respectively in their essential forms. Yin and yang alternate as they describe their cyclical path through the course of the year.

"SURPLUS" (OR "EVEN"):
>That one is empty and one overfull
>Is a state produced by unevenness.
>Uneven, uneven for empty and full
>Means: There is succession without an end.

As the days pass one by one, time marches inexorably on in an infinite succession of separate days. The annual discrepancy between the solar and the lunar calendars appears to account for the regular alternation between surplus and deficiency in a world ruled fundamentally by constant norms. If all distinctions were leveled, change would become impossible.

Autocommentaries of the *T'ai hsuan ching*

POLAR OPPOSITIONS OF THE MYSTERY 玄 衝
Hsüan ch'ung

*[This section is comparable to the "Sequence of the Hexagrams" (*Hsü kua)
section of the Changes Ten Wings.]*

If it is Center (no. 1), then yang begins.
If it is Response (no. 41), then yin is born.

With Full Circle (no. 2), a return to virtue.
With Going to Meet (no. 42), a counterturn towards punishment.[1]

With Mired (no. 3), great woe.
With Encounters (no. 43), small desire.

With Barrier (no. 4), isolation,[2] but
With Stove (no. 44), neighbors.

Keeping Small (no. 5) means the minute [first signs].
Greatness (no. 45) means battening.

With Contrariety (no. 6), internal contradiction.
Enlargement (no. 46) means external opposition.

With Ascent (no. 7), coming up against plainness.[3]
With Pattern (no. 47), increasing artifice.[4]

Opposition (no. 8) means recklessness.
Ritual (no. 48) means "squareness" [the correspondence between word
    and deed].[5]

If it is Branching Out (no. 9), it comes, but
If it is Flight (no. 49), it flees.

With Defectiveness (no. 10), selfishness and crookedness.
With Vastness (no. 50), fairmindedness and desirelessness.

Divergence (no. 11) means mistakes, but
Constancy (no. 51) is good.

With Youthfulness (no. 12), to have little, but
With Measure (no. 52), to have no lack.

With Increase (no. 13), the beginning of florescence, but
With Eternal (no. 53), what lasts to the very end.

With Penetration (no. 14), "grasping the one,"[6] but
With Unity (no. 54), the "Grand Accord."[7]

With Reach (no. 15), daily[8] increasing its kind.
With Diminishment (no. 55), daily depleting its type.

Contact (no. 16) means mutual compliance.
Closed Mouth (no. 56) means no contact.

With Holding Back (no. 17), to have fears.
Guardedness (no. 57) means to be impregnable.

As to Waiting (no. 18), it exits.[9]
As to Closing in (no. 58), it enters.

Following (no. 19) means dispersing, but
Massing (no. 59) means assembling.

With Advance (no. 20), many plans.
With Accumulation (no. 60), much wealth.

Release (no. 21) means a push forward.
Embellishment (no. 61) means a decline.

What Resistance (no. 22) approves is right while
What Doubt (no. 62) abhors is wrong.

With Ease (no. 23), a leveling, but
With Watch (no. 63), a collapse.[10]

With Joy (no. 24), raising high, but
With Sinking (no. 64), hiding below.

Contention (no. 25) means the *shih* are impartial.[11]
Inner (no. 65) means the women are partial.[12]

If it is Endeavor (no. 26), then joy, but
If it is Departure (no. 66), then sorrow.

With Duties (no. 27), esteem for activity.
With Darkening (no. 67), esteem for rest.

With Change (no. 28), alterations but sharing smiles.
With Dimming (no. 68), over a long time, increasing troubles.

With Decisiveness (no. 29), numerous affairs, but
With Exhaustion (no. 69), not a single happiness.

With Bold Resolution (no. 30), daring but
With Severance (no. 70), weakening.

With Packing (no. 31), a move home,[13] but
With Stoppage (no. 71), a failure to proceed.

With Legion (no. 32), gentle softness,[14] but
With Hardness (no. 72), cold firmness.

With Closeness (no. 33), no possible gap, but
With Completion (no. 73), no possible change.

With Kinship (no. 34), drawing close to goodness, but
With Closure (no. 74), closing out[15] feelings of obligation.

As to Gathering (no. 35), it is success.
With Failure (no. 75), loss of fortune.

With Strength (no. 36), untiring good.
With Aggravation (no. 76), unending evil.

Purity (no. 37) means the Way of the ruler.
Compliance (no. 77) means the subject's preservation.

Fullness (no. 38) means the prime of life, but
On the Verge (no. 78) means old age.

With Residence (no. 39), attaining to rank, but
With Difficulties (no. 79), meeting with demotion.

Law (no. 40) means to facilitate union with All-under-Heaven.
Laboring (no. 80) means to lack achievement despite strenous efforts.

Fostering (no. 81) receives all the rest.

The noble man fosters good luck.
That means the petty man fosters ill.

INTERPLAY OF OPPOSITES IN THE MYSTERY 玄 錯
Hsüan ts'o

*[This section is comparable to the "Interplay of Opposites" (*Tsa kua*) section of the* Changes Ten Wings.*]*

With Center (no. 1), it begins.
With Full Circle (no. 2), it wheels back.[1]

With Defectiveness (no. 10), the crooked.
With Bold Resolution (no. 30), the straight.[2]

The ways of Purity (no. 37) and Pattern (no. 47).
Some are simple and some are complex.[3]

As to Strength (no. 36), it is the solidly built.
As to Waiting (no. 18), it is the weak.

As to Accumulation (no. 60), it is the many, but
As to Keeping Small (no. 5), it is the few.

As to Watch (no. 63), it is the apparent.
As to Darkening (no. 67), it is the indistinct.

With Youthfulness (no. 12), having no knowledge, but
With Fullness (no. 38), having a surplus.

With Departure (no. 66), leaving the old, but
With On the Verge (no. 78), coming to a new start.

As to Greatness (no. 45), it is the outside, but
As to Closing In (no. 58), it is the inside.

As to Branching Out (no. 9), it is the advance.
As to Holding Back (no. 17), it is the retreat.[4]

With Joy (no. 24), calm and composure.
With Laboring (no. 80), hustle and bustle.[5]

With Reach (no. 15), thoughts that comprehend.
With Exhaustion (no. 69), thoughts that confound.

With Opposition (no. 8), at court, but
With Inner (no. 65), on the [sleeping] mat.[6]

With Divergence (no. 11), self-loathing.
With Embellishment (no. 61), self-love.

With Resistance (no. 22), intolerance, but
With Unity (no. 54), magnanimity.

With Increase (no. 13), daily additions, but
With Diminishment (no. 55), daily reductions.

With Compliance (no. 77), orders upheld, but
With Contrariety (no. 6), mutual opposition.

As to Release (no. 21), it is softness,[7] but
As to Hardness (no. 72), it is leathery toughness.

With Ease (no. 23), the level and smooth, but
With Difficulties (no. 79), the going up and down.[8]

With Decisiveness (no. 29), many decisions, but
With Doubt (no. 62), some hesitation.

With Flight (no. 49), there is what one avoids.
With Contention (no. 25), there is what one hastens towards.

With Advance (no. 20), the desire to proceed.
With Stoppage (no. 71), the desire for constraints.

With Enlargement (no. 46), no bounds.[9]
With Endeavor (no. 26), no duplicity.[10]

As to Response (no. 41), it is the present, but
As to Measure (no. 52), it is the past.

With Going to Meet (no. 42), one knows what preceded.
With Eternal (no. 53), one sees the later issue.

As to Following (no. 19), it is dragged along.
As to Guardedness (no. 57), it is secured.

With Mired (no. 3), plucked out from calamity.
With Aggravation (no. 76), lacking any pardons.

With Vastness (no. 50), the infinitely great, but
With Barrier (no. 4), the buried and blocked.

With Change (no. 28), creating the new.
With Constancy (no. 51), cleaving to the old.

With Failure (no. 75), great loss.
With Gathering (no. 35), small gain.

With Stove (no. 44), love of profit.
With Law (no. 40), abhorrence of the cruel.

As to Ritual (no. 48), it is the capital, but
As to Residence (no. 39), it is the home.

With Massing (no. 59), affairs emptying.
With Legion (no. 32), affairs filling.

As to Closure (no. 74), both are shut off,[11] but
As to Closeness (no. 33), all[12] use the One.

With Ascent (no. 7), high ambitions.
With Sinking (no. 64), low ambitions.

With Contact (no. 16), many friends.
With Closed Mouth (no. 56), few allies.[13]

With Penetration (no. 14), a sharp advance.
With Dimming (no. 68), an impeded walk.

With Kinship (no. 34), attachment between [even] distant [relatives].
With Severance (no. 70), offense to one's own [flesh and] blood.

With Encounters (no. 43), coming upon difficulties.
With Packing (no. 31), awaiting the proper time.

With Duties (no. 27), to exhaust oneself.
With Fostering (no. 81), to increase oneself.

As to Resistance (no. 22), it is contradiction, but
As to Unity (no. 54), it is conforming.

With Increase (no. 13), to have gains, but
With Diminishment (no. 55), to have losses.

What we term Completion (no. 73) is enduring achievements that cannot be changed.

EVOLUTION OF THE MYSTERY 玄 攤
Hsüan li

[Traditionally, this essay is compared with the "Appended Texts" (Hsi tz'u) commentary to the Changes. *The main idea of its first section is that the Mystery is both the entire sum of stuff from which all else derives and the fashioner of that stuff into the individual types of existence. Note that the term Mystery refers simultaneously to two related phenomena: the book of that name composed by Yang Hsiung and the cosmic Tao in its mysterious operations.]*

The Mystery of which we speak in hidden places unfolds[1] the myriad species,[2] without revealing a form of its own. It fashions the stuff[3] of Emptiness and Formlessness,[4] giving birth to the regulations.[5] Tied to the gods in Heaven and the spirits on Earth, it fixes the models.[6] It pervades and assimilates past and present, originating the categories. It unfolds and intersperses yin and yang, generating the *ch'i*. Now severed, now conjoined[7] [through the interaction of yin and yang *ch'i* the various aspects of] Heaven-and-Earth are indeed fully provided! As the heavens and the sun turn in their circuits [moving in opposite directions],[8] hard and soft [day/night, yang/yin] indeed make contact. Each returns [within the course of a single year] to its place, so that it is indeed a fixed rule that once ended, [the cycle] begins [again].[9] Now giving life and now giving death, human nature and the Decree are indeed illuminated [through the operations of the Mystery].

[The main idea of the following section is that the Mystery makes Heaven and Earth appropriate patterns for Man. The section ends with references to binary opposition.]

Looking up to contemplate the [starry] images, looking down to view [earthly] conditions,[10] [the sage] examines human nature and comes to know the Decree. He seeks the origin of beginnings and sees the final outcome.[11] The Three Reigns[12] share the same standard; thick and thin[13] intersect each other. Round [Heaven] as a rule wobbles unsteadily.[14] Square [Earth] as a rule conserves.[15] Exhalation [yang *ch'i*] as a rule makes the bodies flow out. Inhalation [yin *ch'i*] as a rule congeals forms. For this reason, what encloses Heaven we call spaces and what opens spaces out we call times.[16]

The sun and moon come and go so that now it is winter and now it is summer. As a rule, the pitchpipes complete things, while the calendar arranges the seasons. The pitchpipes and calendar meet in their paths. The sage uses them in planning. Day he regards as good. Night he regards as bad. Now it is day, now it is night, as yin and yang separately seek out [their respective realms].[17] The way of night is extreme yin. The way of day is extreme yang. For female and male, there are numerous orientations,[18] so there evolve [from these] good luck and bad. Then the ways of ruler and subject, of father and son, and of husband and wife are distinguished logically.

For this reason, the sun moves eastward while the heavens move westward. The heavens and the sun cross paths.[19] Yin and yang alternate in their circuits. Death and life are intertwined.[20] Only then do the myriad things become inseparably bound.[21] Therefore, the Mystery is what seeks to take the correspondent parts of All-under-Heaven[22] and string them together. It stitches them together according to their category. It prognosticates about them according to their norms. It clarifies the very dimmest parts of All-under-Heaven.[23] It illuminates the most obscure parts of All-under-Heaven. What else but the Mystery [can do all this]!

[The following section speaks of the unfathomable profundity of both the Tao and Yang Hsiung's neoclassical imitation of it.]

Now, as we know, the Mystery hides its position and conceals its boundaries. It stores its great expanse deep and obscures[24] its base. It thrusts aside its own merit and makes a secret of its motive force.[25] Therefore, the Mystery, itself surpassing, really shows man how far away he is. Itself vast, it really enlarges [the opportunities] for man to be great. Itself unfathomably deep, it really incites man to profundities. Itself infinite, it really cuts man off from insignificance.[26] The one that silently gathers all together, that is the Mystery. The one who with grand gestures[27] would disperse it,[28] that is Man.

> Knock on[29] its gate.
> Open its door.
> Rap its knocker.

Only later will the response come. How much less likely is [a response] for those who do otherwise?[30]

Good is "what people like and have too little of."[31] Evil is "what people dislike and have a surplus of." If the noble man daily strengthens what is deficient in him [i.e., the good], and eliminates what he possesses in surplus [i.e., the evil], then the Way of the Mystery is nearly approximated indeed! Looking up, he sees it located in the higher regions. Looking down, he spies it located in the lower regions. Standing on tiptoes [in eager anticipation], he watches for it to be located in front. Abandoning [it], he forgets[32] that it is located in back. Even if he would go against it, he cannot, for it is the Mystery that silently by rule makes each attain its proper place.

[The following section speaks of the man's relation to the Mystery. All human virtues are defined with reference to it.]

Therefore, the Mystery of which we speak is the ultimate in utility. To see and to know it is wisdom. To regard it with love is humaneness. To be resolute in deciding to practice it is courage. To rule without distinction,[33] broadly applying it, is fairmindedness. To be able to use it to correlate things is comprehension. To have no bonds or impediments is sageliness.

To be timely or not is the Decree.[34] What is empty of form[35] and the path of the myriad things, that we call the Way. Continuous development without abrupt change,[36] so that the internal order of All-under-Heaven is attained, that we call Charismatic Power. What orders living things[37] and unites the many so that there is all-embracing love, that we call humaneness.[38] What arranges matches[39] and measures what fits,[40] that we call the Right. Grasping the Way and its Power, humaneness and the Right, and then applying them, that we call the Task. What illuminates Heaven's achievements and enlightens the myriad things, that we call yang [*ch'i*]. What is dark, without form, and of unfathomable depth, that we call yin [*ch'i*].

Yang knows yang, but does not know yin. Yin knows yin, but does not know yang. To know yin, to know yang, to know stopping, to know proceeding, to know darkness, to know light—what else but the Mystery [can know all this]?[41]

As what suspends them, it is the balance. As what levels them, it is the steelyard beam. The polluted it purifies. The precipitous[42] it levels. Any departure from [true] conditions it invariably exposes as false. Any departure from falsity it invariably reveals as true. Whenever true and false push against one another,[43] the ways of the noble and mean man become relatively clear.[44] The Mystery of which we speak uses scales to measure.

> The elevated it lowers.
> The low it raises.
> The abundant it takes from.
> The depleted it gives to.
> The bright it tones down.[45]
> The doubtful it clarifies.[46]

To use it as compass is thought. To establish it is duty. To explain it is [true] disputation. To complete it is good faith.[47]

Now Heaven openly shows men the gods. And Earth grandly[48] shows men the spirits.[49] Heaven and Earth have their appointed places. The gods and the spirits make the *ch'i* communicate. There is one, there is two, there is three.[50] With each position a different generation,[51] [the *Mystery*] makes the circuit of the Nine Districts,[52] so that end and beginning are interconnected and interdependent [in a seamless cycle], so that above and below make a perfect circle.[53] Examine the patterns of the Dragon and Tiger.[54] Contemplate the lines of the Bird and Turtle.[55] Plot their revolutions[56] with regard to the Seven Regulators,[57] and tie them to the Culmen[58] of the Grand Inception.[59] By this comprehend[60] the system of the Jasper Template[61] and straighten the base line of the Jade Level.[62] As for the grinding of circle and square [Heaven and Earth] against one another, the mutual opposition between hard and soft [yin and yang]: By rule, abundance enters[63] decline and what ends is born again. There is filling up and emptying out. It flows or stops; there is no constancy.

[The following section describes the way in which each major pattern of human society derives from natural phenomena in the realm of Heaven-and-Earth.]

Now Heaven and Earth are placed; therefore, the noble and base are ranked.[64] The four seasons proceed [in order]; therefore, the son inherits from the father. The pitchpipes and calendar are set forth; therefore, relations between ruler and subject are orderly. Constancy and change are interspersed; therefore, the Hundred Affairs are hewn. Simplicity and embellishment take shape; therefore, what exists and what does not is made clear. Good luck and ill appear; therefore, good and evil are revealed. Emptiness and fullness propel one another; therefore, the myriad things are inextricably connected.[65]

If yang fails to culminate, then yin fails to germinate. If yin fails to culminate, then yang fails to sprout. Extreme cold gives birth to heat. Extreme heat gives birth to cold. The way of expansion induces contraction. The way of contraction induces expansion. In its active mode, [the Mystery] daily creates what it [the world] lacks and favors what it renews. In its quiescent mode, [the Mystery] daily depletes what it [the world] has and diminishes what it has completed. Therefore, we infer it by the waterclock; we further test it by the gnomon. Back and forth is its sequence; twisting and turning is its path.[66] By them we see the invisible form. By them we draw out the elusive thread.[67] Through it we become part of the continuum of the myriad categories of things.[68]

When above, it is suspended from the heavens. When below, it is submerged in the abyss. So fine is it that it enters a single blade of grass. So vast is it that it encompasses whole regions. Its Way is to wander in obscurity and to ladle out the full. It preserves what should be preserved and destroys what should be destroyed. It keeps hidden what should be hidden and manifests what should be manifested. It causes the beginning to begin. It causes the end to end.

Whoever approaches the Mystery will find the Mystery for its part approaching him. Whoever distances himself from the Mystery will find the Mystery for its part keeping its distance from him. It is like Heaven in its vastness. It is in the east, in the south, in the west, in the north. Look up and there is no place where it is not. But the moment someone bends down, then it is no longer seen. How could Heaven possibly leave Man? It is Man who leaves of his own accord.

Whatever comes after the winter solstice and midnight is an image of "approaching the Mystery." It advances but it has not yet culminated. It goes forward but it has not yet arrived. It is empty but it has not yet [begun to] fill. Therefore, we call it "approaching the Mystery." Whatever comes after the summer solstice and midday is an image of "distancing the Mystery." Once the advance culminates, it retreats. Once the forward movement ends, it goes back. Once it is already full, it is depleted. Therefore, we call it "distancing the Mystery."

As soon as the sun turns south,[69] the myriad things die.[70] As soon as the sun turns north,[71] the myriad things are born. As soon as the Dipper points north [that is, to the zodiacal sections signifying north-northwest and north], the myriad things empty out. As soon as the Dipper points south [that is, to the zodiacal sections south-southwest and south], the myriad things fill up. The sun in its southward path proceeds towards the right [that is, from the west], then returns in a leftward path.[72] The Dipper in its southward path proceeds towards the left, then returns in a rightward path.[73] Sometimes going left, sometimes going right; sometimes dying, sometimes living. The gods and the numinous[74] unite their plans.[75] Only then are Heaven and Earth aligned, so that Heaven is divine and Earth numinous.

ILLUMINATION OF THE MYSTERY 玄 瑩
Hsüan ying

[This essay also corresponds to the "Appended Texts" commentary to the Changes. *The opening paragraph describes the origin of the cosmos, tying the* Mystery *text to the mysterious Tao. Succeeding paragraphs outline the most important constant features of the Mystery, as it operates both in this text and in the universe outside the text. Finally, reference is made to certain organizing principles of human society.]*

When Heaven and Earth were severed,[1] spaces and times[2] broadened out and leveled.[3] The Heavenly Origin [midnight on the first day of the winter solstice in a *chia tzu* year][4] was spanned and paced;[5] the cycle of sun and moon was computed. Completing the [annual] revolution is the calendrical cycle;[6] grouping the social orders are the various ranks.[7] Sometimes there is conjunction, and sometimes separation; sometimes a surplus, and sometimes a deficit [when the solar and lunar years are aligned]. Therefore, I say: "Great indeed are Heaven and Earth, which engulf all development! As in a net, [all] is cloaked in the Mystery. The end and the beginning, the dark and the light, the Tables[8] and Appraisals [correspond to] Heavenly gods and Earthly spirits. As great yang rides on yin, the myriad things are held together. Making a circuit of the Nine Empty Positions,[9] calamity and good fortune are entangled in the net."[10]

Altogether there are twelve beginnings [one for each month of the calendar year]. With regard to the many orders [of existence], one draws out the end threads.[11] And so there exists 1, 2, and 3, which act to catch [the many orders] as in nets and snares.[12] The arts of the Mystery illuminate it.

The Five Phases of the Vast Base are set out repeatedly [in] the Nine Positions. Above and below they cleave to one another [in successive cycles, with the various] categories residing in their midst. The arts of the Mystery illuminate it.

Heaven is round and Earth is square. The Culmen [the Polestar] is planted in the exact center [of the cosmos]; the movements [of the stars around it] are fixed by the calendar.[13] Time rides on the twelve [zodiacal sections of the sky].[14] Thus the Seven Regulators [of sun, moon, and five visible planets] are established.[15] The arts of the Mystery illuminate it.

The Dipper, moving with the heavens, advances [toward the west].[16] The sun, going against [the westward spin of] the heavens, retreats. Some move with it and some go against it. Thus the Five Recorders [the Year star, moon, sun, stars, and calendrical calculations] are established.[17] The arts of the Mystery illuminate it.

One places the dial to have it give off a shadow. One drains[18] the clepsydra to figure the quarter-hour marks. [From] dusk and dawn, one empirically establishes the center [position of the circumpolar stars at noon]. Those who create [human institutions] are forewarned by [the information such instruments provide]. The arts of the Mystery illuminate it.

The bamboo of [Musicmaster] Ling-lun [i.e., the pitchpipe] is used to make a tube. Ash housed within [bamboo tubes] is used to make a "watch" device. By it are measured the Hundred Norms.[19] Once the Hundred Norms are in place, the legions of people[20] are no longer in error. The arts of the Mystery illuminate it.

East to west is the woof. South to north is the warp. When warp and woof are interwoven, the deviant and the upright are distinguished by it, while good luck and ill take form through it. The arts of the Mystery illuminate it.

Drilling a well supplies water; drilling for fire ignites wood. [Add to Water, Fire, and Wood] molten[21] Metal and moulded Earth to correctly apportion the Five Excellent Materials [i.e., the Five Phases]. The stuff of the Five Excellent Materials is used to endow the Hundred Corporeal Bodies. The arts of the Mystery illuminate it.

Odd numbers are used to enumerate yang [*ch'i*]. Even numbers are used to enumerate yin. Odd and even extended and expanded are used to calculate All-under-Heaven. The arts of the Mystery illuminate it.

The Six Beginnings make the male pitchpipes. The Six Intermediaries[22] make the female pitchpipes. Once the pitchpipes, male and female, are tuned to one another, the twelve are used to produce harmonies, and to number the solar conjunctions.[23] The arts of the Mystery illuminate it.

Region, Province, Department, and Family [yield] eighty-one places [i.e., tetragrams]. These are [further] delineated as lower, center, and upper to signify [all within] the four seas. The arts of the Mystery illuminate it.

There are 1 Ruler, 3 Dukes, 9 Ministers, 27 Councilors, and 81 chief Knights. The few by rule control the many; what lacks visible form [i.e., the Mystery][24] by rule controls what has form. The arts of the Mystery illuminate it.

[The following two paragraphs are extremely important. In them Yang Hsiung refutes the classic Taoist utopian vision, which celebrates the golden age of antiquity as a carefree time for the human race prior to the development of the discriminating mind. Yang Hsiung counters this vision by another, in which the ancient sage-king Fu Hsi creates divination so that Man might finally learn both to discriminate and to see connections. Through the proper use of sacred tools like divination, Man can hope to partake of divinity.]

In antiquity, humans were neither shaken by fear[25] nor worried.[26] They were sluggish in their thinking. They did not divine either by milfoil stalks or by turtle so good luck and ill seeped into one another [i.e., were indistinguishable]. It was then that the sage [Fu Hsi] created milfoil and turtle divination, drilling to get the essence,[27] and relying on the divine in the search[28] to understand favor and blame. The arts of the Mystery illuminate it.

For this reason, those who wish to know the unknowable estimate it by what is in the hexagrams and bone cracks. Those who would fathom the profound and probe the distant then tie them to what is in their thoughts. Are not the two [divination and thought] established by single-minded concentration?[29] When one divines with single-minded concentration, the gods prompt the changes [that reveal an answer to the inquiry]. When one deliberates [on this response] with single-minded concentration, one's plans are appropriate. When one establishes what is Right with single-minded concentration, no one can overturn it. When one maintains his principles with single-minded concentration, no one can snatch them away.[30] Therefore, to draw out the infinitude of All-under-Heaven, to dispel the confusion and chaos of All-under Heaven, what else but single-minded concentration can accomplish it?

[In another important paragraph, Yang Hsiung first describes the creative act, whether in the cosmos or in the human mind. Succeeding paragraphs describe the creativity and vitality of the Mystery *text.]*

Now, the act of creation honors its own precedents and prototypes[31] yet it gives physical form to the spontaneously generated [Tao]. When what it follows is great, then its embodiment will be vigorous. When what it follows is petty, then its embodiment will be meager. When what it follows is straight, then its embodiment will be coherent.[32] When what it follows is crooked, then its embodiment will be scattered. Therefore, it neither eliminates[33] what exists nor forces what is not. We may compare it to the physical body, in that any increase would be superfluous and any deletion would mean a deficiency. Therefore, the essential structure [of the creative act][34] rests in the spontaneously generated [Tao], while its external elaboration rests in human affairs. Can it really be diminished or increased?

Now all those in first position [Appraisals 1, 4, and 7, the first Appraisals in each of the three sets of three] are what patterns the beginning and fathoms the depths. All those in third position [Appraisals 3, 6, and 9] are what completes the endings and pushes the whole to extremes.[35] All those in the second position [Appraisals 2, 5, and 8] are what combines events and seeks the center. The Way of Man takes its image from them.

[The *Mystery*] focuses on its events but not on its phrasing. It multiplies its changes but not its patterns. Were [the *Mystery*] not economical [in its expressions], its points would not be detailed. Were it not compact, its responses would not have universal application. Were it not coherent, the events it describes would not be diverse.[36] Were it not deep, its ideas would not reveal anything. For this reason, pattern is used to see into the essential; and phrasing, to look into actual conditions.[37] If we take a close look at the phrases it lays out, then surely its heart's desire will be revealed!

[From the single Tao, there have evolved four kinds of change. Operating by turns, these four kinds of change provide models for human society. The concluding paragraphs of the essay define key terms for the reader. By means of such definitions, Yang Hsiung seeks to prove the ultimate utility of moral action.]

That Way has continuity and development,[38] [abrupt] change and [gradual] metamorphosis.[39] When continuity and development conform with the Tao, it makes them divine.[40] When change and metamorphosis are in accord with Time, it makes them fitting.[41] Therefore, though continuous [an entity] can still change. Only then is Heaven's way attained. And though changing, [an entity] can still be continuous. Only then is Heaven's way complied with. Now, if things did not continue [the model of their forebears], they would not be born. And if they did not change, they would not be completed. Therefore, to know continuity but not change is to have things lose their own rules. And to know change but not continuity is to have things lose their uniform aspects. When change goes counter to Time, things lose their foundation. And when continuity goes counter to internal pattern,[42] things lose their regulating principle. Continuity and change lead to [more] continuity and change. They are the very law and model for the state and family. Actions [in accord with this] model are most efficacious in success and failure.[43]

The warp that establishes Heaven is called "yin and yang." The woof that gives form to Earth is called "vertical and horizontal." Conduct that reveals Man is called "benighted or enlightened." We say of yin and yang, "They join their divided [selves to give birth to the myriad things]." We say of vertical and horizontal, "The woof threads its warp [to create significant pattern]." We say of the benighted and enlightened, "They differ in their essential qualities." Yin and yang hold all the limits together. Warp and woof function as meeting places. Benighted and enlightened refer to the substantive nature.[44] If yang had no yin, it would have no partner to join in its operations. If the warp had no woof, there would be no way for it to complete its fitting [pattern]. If the enlightened had no benighted, there would be no way he could distinguish his virtue. Yin and yang are the means to draw out the true conditions. Vertical and horizontal are the means to illuminate internal pattern. Enlightened and benighted are the means to shed light on affairs. When true conditions are drawn out, when patterns are illuminated, when affairs are made brilliant[45]—that is the Way of the noble man.

> Contact, back and forth,
> With fragrant smoke rising.
> This is the gate of gain and ruin.[46]

Now, what is gain and what is ruin? Gain is good fortune and ruin is calamity. In Heaven and Earth, good fortune is conformity [to prevailing trends], and calamity, going against them. In the mountains and riverways, good fortune is the low, and calamity, the high. In the Way of Man, good fortune is the upright, and calamity, the perverse. Therefore, the noble man is inwardly upright, and outwardly compliant,[47] always humbling himself before others.[48] This is why the outcome of his actions is good fortune and not calamity. If in good fortune one does no evil, [good fortune] cannot give rise to calamity. If in calamity, one does no good, [calamity] cannot become good fortune.

> Evil and good!
> Evil and good!
> Evil and good!

These are what ultimately reveal the noble man. Now, [for others,] when the joy of good fortune ends, the worry of calamity begins.

What Heaven and Earth value is called good fortune. What the ghosts and gods bless[49] is called good fortune. What the Way of Man delights in is called good fortune. Whatever is despised and abhorred is called calamity. Therefore, when there is too much vice in [periods of] good fortune, correspondent calamities rise up. In the daytime, men's calamities are few. At night, men's calamities are many. As day and night are interspersed, the good fortune and calamity associated with them are mixed.

NUMBERS OF THE MYSTERY 玄數
Hsüan shu

[This essay is comparable to the "Discussion of the Trigrams" (Shuo kua) section found in the so-called "Ten Wings" of the Changes. *The essay explains the entire system of correlations to be employed by the diviner when applying the individual texts of the* Mystery *to personal situations. We should remember always that such number correlations alert the reader to the profound order inherent in the universe.*

The autocommentary begins with several paragraphs which have been translated or summarized in the "Method of Divination" and "Interpretation after Divination" sections of the "Introduction" to this book. These sections, therefore, have been omitted here.]

Three and Eight correspond to:

> Wood
> East
> Spring
> the days *chia* 甲 and *yi* 乙
> the zodiacal periods *yin* 寅 and *mao* 卯
> the note *chüeh*[1] 角
> the color, green
> the taste, bitter
> the smell, sour
> the form, contracting and expanding

the Phase produced, Fire
the Phase conquered, Earth
the time to give birth
of the viscera, the spleen
the promotion of will
the nature, benevolence
the emotion, happiness
the duty, demeanor
the application, "reverence which makes for solemnity"[2]
the omen, drought
the emperor T'ai-hao
the god Kou-mang
the stars that attend its [the east's] position
the category, scaly creatures
thunder
drums
booming sounds
newness
bustling activity
doors
windows
heirs
those who inherit
leaves
main threads
pardons
expiations
many sons
going out
giving
bamboo
grasses
fruits
seeds
fish
drawing tools[3]
compasses
rice fields
carpentry
spears
green prodigies
nose ailments
wildness

Four and Nine correspond to:

> Metal
> West
> autumn
> the days *keng* 庚 and *hsin* 辛
> the zodiacal periods *shen* 申 and *yu* 酉
> the note *shang* 商
> the color, white
> the taste, acrid
> the smell, rank
> the form, violent change
> the Phase produced, Water
> the Phase conquered, Wood
> the time to kill
> of the viscera, the liver
> the promotion of the corporeal soul
> the nature, righteousness[4]
> the emotion, anger
> the duty, speech,
> the application, "compliance which makes for good order"
> the omen, rain
> the emperor Shao Hao
> the god Ju-shou
> the stars that attend its [the west's] direction
> the category, hairy things
> witchdoctors
> invocations by shamans
> fierce beasts [such as tigers]
> what is old
> metallic rings
> gates
> mountains
> limits
> borders
> [inner] city walls
> bones
> rocks
> bracelets and girdle ornaments
> head ornaments
> heavy jewels[5]
> metal buttons
> pounding of rice

mortars
strength
whatever is suspended
sparking fire by drilling wood
weapons[6]
shackles
teeth
horns
scorpions
poisons
puppies
entering
seizing
netting
plundering
thieving
ordering
the carpenter's square
metalworking
battle axes
white prodigies
muteness
slander[7]

Two and Seven correspond to:

Fire
South
Summer
the days *ping* 丙 and *ting* 丁
the zodiacal periods *szu* 巳 and *wu* 午
the note *chih* 徵
the color red
the taste, bitter
the smell, scorched
the form, what is above
the Phase produced, Earth
the Phase conquered, Metal
the time to nourish
of the viscera, the lungs
the promotion of the ethereal soul (*hun*) 魂
the nature, ritual
the emotion, joy
the duty, sight

the application, "clarity which makes for wisdom"
the omen, heat
the emperor Yen-ti
the god Chu-jung
the stars that attend its [the south's] direction
the category, feathered things
stoves
silk
nets
rope
pearls
patterns[8]
mixtures
seals
ribbons
books
whatever is light
whatever is high[9]
towers
wine
spitting
shooting with an arrow
dagger-axes
armor
thickets
the Commanding General[10]
string
working with fire
knives
red prodigies
blindness
laxity

One and Six correspond to:

Water
North
Winter
the days *jen* 壬 and *kuei* 癸
the zodiacal periods *tzu* 子 and *hai* 亥
the note *yü* 羽
the color, black
the taste, salty
the smell, rotted

the form, what is below
the Phase produced, Wood
the Phase conquered, Fire
the time to store
of the viscera, the testicles and kidneys
the promotion of sperm[11]
the nature, wisdom
the emotion, sorrow
the duty, hearing
the application, "perceptiveness which makes for [good] planning"
the omen, [undue] cold
the emperor Chüan-hsü
the god Hsüan-ming
the stars that attend its [the north's] direction
the category, things with shells
ghosts
sacrifices
temples
wells
caves
burrows
mirrors
jade
treading
making long trips
laboring
blood
ointments
coveting
containing
hibernating animals
hunting with fire
shutting
robbing
the Director of Public Works
laws
standards
water works
shields
black prodigies
deafness
urgency

On Five: Five corresponds to

> Earth
> Center
> the four seasons
> the days *wu* 戊 and *chi* 己
> the zodiacal periods *ch'en* 辰, *hsu* 戌, *ch'ou* 丑, and *wei* 未
> the note *kung* 宮
> the color, yellow
> the taste, sweetness
> the smell, fragrant
> the forms, verticality[12]
> the Phase produced, Metal
> the Phase conquered, Water
> the time to join together
> of the viscera, the heart/mind
> the promotion of the divine soul
> the nature, trustworthines
> the emotion, fear
> the duty, thought
> the application, "prescience which makes for sageliness"
> the omen, wind
> the emperor Huang-ti (Yellow Emperor)
> the god Hou-t'u
> the stars that attend its [circumpolar] direction
> the category, what is naked [i.e., human]
> tumuli[13]
> bottles
> palaces
> residences
> the center courtyard rainwell
> "internal" affairs[14]
> weaving
> clothes
> furs
> cocoons
> raw floss
> beds
> sleeping mats
> complying
> cherishing
> tools or vessels with bellies
> oils

lacquer
glue
sacks
pouches
carriages
hubs
sowing
harvesting
foodstuffs
flesh
coffins
calves[15]
thoroughfares
meetings
the capital
measures
weights
earthworks
bows and arrows
yellow prodigies
stupidity
benightedness

Among the Five Phases, the one in power is "the king." The one the king produces is "the minister." The "old king" is the one deposed. The one that [would] conquer the king is imprisoned. The one that is conquered by the [new] king dies.

Of the Musical Notes,

Kung 宮 is the ruler.
Chih 徵 is affairs.
Shang 商 is the minister.
Chüeh 角 is the people.
Yü 羽 is the common people.

Of Pitch Standards,[16]

Huang-chung 黃鐘 (middle C), the "Yellow Bell," produces *lin-chung* 林鐘 (G).[17]
Lin-chung produces *t'ai-ts'ou* 太簇 (D).
T'ai-ts'ou produces *nan-lü* 南呂 (A).
Nan-lü produces *ku-hsien* 姑洗 (E).
Ku-hsien produces *ying-chung* 應鐘 (B).
Ying-chung produces *sui-pin* 蕤賓 (F sharp).
Sui-pin produces *ta-lü* 大呂 (D flat).

> *Ta-lü* produces *yi-tse* 夷則 (A flat).
> *Yi-tse* produces *chia-chung* 夾鐘 (E flat).
> *Chia-chung* produces *wu-yi* 無射 (B flat).
> *Wu-yi* produces *chung-lü* 仲呂 (F).

[Of the Twelve Earthly Branches,]

> *Tzu* 子 and *wu* 午 count as 9.
> *Ch'ou* 丑 and *wei* 未 count as 8.
> *Yin* 寅 and *shen* 申 count as 7.
> *Mao* 卯 and *yü* 酉 count as 6.
> *Ch'en* 辰 and *hsü* 戌 count as 5.
> *Ssu* 巳 and *hai* 亥 count as 4.

Therefore, the sum of the "male" pitch standards is 42 and the sum of the "female," 36. The sum of the combined male and female pitches, with some "returning" and some "blocking," altogether is 78. The number of the Yellow Bell [which is 81] is set up by it. [In other words, 78 equals 81 once 3 is added to symbolize the triadic realms of Heaven-Earth-Man.] Their use as measures depends upon the fact that all are produced by the Yellow Bell.[18]

[Of the Ten Heavenly Stems,]

> *Chia* 甲 and *chi* 己 count as 9.
> *Yi* 乙 and *keng* 庚 count as 8.
> *Ping* 丙 and *hsin* 辛 count as 7.
> *Ting* 丁 and *jen* 壬 count as 6.
> *Wu* 戊 and *kuei* 癸 count as 5.

The notes are born of the days. The pitch standards are born of the zodiacal periods. The notes are used to express men's essential substance.[19] The pitch standards are used to harmonize the notes. When the notes and pitches are attuned to one other, the eight distinctive timbres [of various instruments] are produced.

Of the Nine Heavens,

> The first is made Center (no. 1 of the tetragrams).
> The second is made Defectiveness (no. 10).
> The third is made Following (no. 19).
> The fourth is made Change (no. 28).
> The fifth is made Purity (no. 37).
> The sixth is made Enlargement (no. 46).
> The seventh is made Diminishment (no. 55).
> The eighth is made Sinking (no. 64).
> The ninth is made Completion (no. 73).

Of the Nine Earths,

> The first is sand and mud.
> The second is marshes and pools.
> The third is small islets and banks.
> The fourth is low fields.
> The fifth is fields at the middle range.
> The sixth is high fields.
> The seventh is low mountains.
> The eighth is mountains of medium height.
> The ninth is high mountains.

Of the Nine [Types] of Men,

> The first is the low man.
> The second is the commoner.
> The third is the man who advances.
> The fourth is low rank.
> The fifth is middle rank.
> The sixth is high rank.
> The seventh is the man of lost ambitions.
> The eighth is the ill or infected.
> The ninth is the man in extremities.

Of the Nine Body Parts,

> No. 1 corresponds to hands and feet.
> No. 2 corresponds to [lower] arms and shin.
> No. 3 corresponds to thighs and upper arms.
> No. 4 is the waist.
> No. 5 is the belly.
> No. 6 is the shoulders.
> No. 7 is the throat.
> No. 8 is the face.
> No. 9 is the forehead.

Of the Nine Grades of Relations,

> No. 1 corresponds to great-great-grandchildren.
> No. 2 corresponds to great-grandchildren.
> No. 3 corresponds to grandchildren.
> No. 4 corresponds to children.
> No. 5 corresponds to the self.
> No. 6 corresponds to the father.
> No. 7 corresponds to the grandfather.
> No. 8 corresponds to the great-grandfather.
> No. 9 corresponds to great-great-grandfather.

Of the Nine Apertures,

> Nos. 1 and 6 correspond to the urethra[20] and the ear.
> Nos. 2 and 7 correspond to the eyes.
> Nos. 3 and 8 correspond to the nostrils.
> Nos. 4 and 9 correspond to the mouth.
> No. 5 corresponds to the anus.

The Nine Orders are ranked from 1 to 9.[21]

Of the Nine Affairs,

> The first is careful planning.[22]
> The second is hesitation in all directions.
> The third is self-assurance.[23]
> The fourth is outer-directed activity.
> The fifth is inner harmony.
> The sixth is abundance.
> The seventh is waning.
> The eighth is wasting.
> The ninth is total destruction.

Of the Nine Decades,

> No. 1 corresponds to the first decade.
> No. 2 corresponds to the second decade.
> No. 3 corresponds to the third decade.
> No. 4 corresponds to the fourth decade.
> No. 5 corresponds to the fifth decade.
> No. 6 corresponds to the sixth decade.
> No. 7 corresponds to the seventh decade.
> No. 8 corresponds to the eighth decade.
> No. 9 corresponds to the ninth decade.

[There follows a section which is quoted in the Method of Divination section in the Introduction.]

ELABORATION OF THE MYSTERY 玄文
Hsüan wen

[This corresponds to the "Wen yen" section of the Changes, *which treats the first two* Changes *hexagrams as a microcosm for the entire* Yi ching *system. The Elaboration autocommentary explains Tetragram 1 as a microcosm of the world of Heaven-Earth-Man, as well as of the* Mystery *text.]*

In regard to [the five mantic formulae],

Without (*wang* 罔),
Extending (*chih* 直),[1]
Covering (*meng* 蒙),
Completing (*ch'iu* 馗),
Hidden (*ming* 冥):[2]

Without refers to the north and to winter. It is whatever still lacks form. Extending refers to the east and to spring. It is whatever has substance but no pattern as yet. Covering refers to the south, to summer, and to things growing tall. It is whatever can be gotten and increased.[3] Completing refers to the west and to autumn. It is things all achieving [the potential implied by] their images and coming to completion. What has form then returns to the formless; therefore, it is called Hidden. Thus the myriad things are Without [form] in the north, are Extending in the east, are Covering in the south, are Completing in the west, and are Hidden in the north. And so,

Without [as primordial chaos] is the holding place for Being.
Extending is the plain background[4] for pattern.
Covering is the master of loss.
Completing is the repository of life.
Hidden is the storehouse of light.

Without lodges its *ch'i.*
Extending prods[5] its species [into life].[6]
Covering carries its growth to the limit.
Completing finishes its accomplishments.[7]
Hidden returns to its secret places.

Without and Covering push one another to the limit. Extending and Completing restrain one another. Coming out of Hidden, going into Hidden, the new and the old exchange places. As yin and yang [*ch'i*] succeed one another, the pure and the sullied depose one another. What is about to come advances. What has been achieved will retreat. What has already been used is generally despised. What is appropriate for the time generally is honored. Heaven is patterned and earth is plain. They do not change their positions.[8] Without, Extending, Covering, Completing, and Hidden![9]

Speech derives from Without. Conduct derives from Without. Calamity and good fortune derive from Without. The time that corresponds to Without is Mysterious indeed! Conduct as a rule leaves traces. Speech as a rule has sounds. Good fortune as a rule brings gifts of dried meat.[10]

Calamity as a rule has what takes form. This we call Extending. And once there is Extending there can be Covering. Once there is Covering there can be Completing. And once there is Completing then it can revert to . the Hidden. For this reason, the time that corresponds to Without can generally be controlled [meaning, we can forestall calamity in the early stage].

The eighty-one tetragrams evolve from Without. Heaven's dazzling light comes out of the infinite; its fiery brilliance comes out of the boundless. Therefore, the time that corresponds to Without is Mysterious indeed! For this reason, Heaven's Way is to:

Empty, so as to store them [the myriad things].
Move, so as to catalyze them.
Exalt, so as to make them approach.
Pare, so as to regulate them.
End, so as to seclude them.[11]

So profound is it that none can fathom it! So glorious is it that none can surpass it!

Therefore, [in imitation of the Tao] the noble man hiding in the profound is enough to embody[12] the divine. His first moves are enough to impress the masses. His lofty character and clarity of mind are enough to reflect on those below. His paring and cutting [i.e., his regulations and punishments] are enough to cause them to quake with fear and apprehension. His deep reclusion is enough to cause them to conceal or withdraw [from the world].[13] Because the noble man can [emulate] these five [attributes of the Mysterious Tao], therefore we describe [him in analogous terms] as Without, Extending, Covering, Completing, and Hidden.

Someone asks what is meant by: "Primal oneness encompasses all./ It is profound"? It says,[14] the worthy man is one with Heaven and Earth [insofar as his] thoughts embrace the many kinds [of being]. He unites them [his thoughts] at center before letting them take form outside [in action]. Living alone, he is happy. Thinking alone, he is concerned. Happiness [so great] cannot be borne. Concern [so great] cannot be overcome. Therefore it is said to be "profound."

What is meant by: "Spiritual forces war in darkness"? It says, the petty man's heart is impure.[15] When it is about to take form outside, yin and yang are arrayed in battle lines to fight over good luck and bad. With yang, [the heart] battles for good luck; with yin, for bad luck. "As with the wind, one knows the tiger./ As with a cloud, one knows the dragon."[16] The worthy man initiates action and the myriad categories are held in common.

What is meant by: "The dragon emerges at the center"? It says, the characteristic virtue of the dragon is apparent for the first time. If the yin has not culminated, then yang will not be born. If disorder has not culminated, then virtue will not assume form. The noble man cultivates virtue, thereby awaiting the proper moment. He does not rise up before the proper moment, nor draw back after it has already passed. Whether in action or at rest, whether obscure or eminent, he does not stray from the norm. Can this be said of anyone else but the noble man? Thus "head and tail are fit for use."

What is meant by: "Lowliness, emptiness, nothingness, compliance— Despite a full portion of nature and Decree, still he is blocked"? It says, the petty man cannot find it in his heart to embrace emptiness or to dwell in low places. Although he is debased, he cannot be approached. Although he is empty, he cannot be filled. When doing without would be appropriate, he is capable of possessing. When compliance would be appropriate, he is capable of striking out in an untried direction.[17] Therefore, "despite a full portion of nature and Decree," he lacks [the humility] to avoid [inappropriate action]. That is why "he is blocked."

What is meant by: "The sun centered in the sky"? It says, the noble man rides on [that is, takes advantage of] his position, making it serve as his carriage and as his horse. The frontboard of the carriage and the braided tail of the horse[18] can be put to use in making a circuit of All-under-Heaven. Therefore, [the sun] "helps him become master."

What is meant by: "The moon losing its fullness/ Is not as good as new light in the west"? It says, the petty man in the fullness of his powers[19] brings needless ruin upon himself. Water increases in the deep abyss [as] trees lose some of their limbs. In the mountains, the emaciated are killed off; in the marshes, the plump grow in number. The worthy man sees, but none among the masses understand.

What is meant by: "Repository of the fully ripe"? It says, the humane are afflicted by the inhumane. The just are afflicted by the unjust. The noble man is magnanimous enough to lead[20] the masses. He is gentle enough to make things secure. Heaven and Earth accomodate every single thing. Only inhumanity and injustice are not accomodated by [one allied with] Heaven and Earth. Therefore, "Water is the repository of rectitude."

What is meant by: "Yellow is not yellow"? It says, the small man fails to model himself on the center. By rule all of the first positions [in each set of three Tables][21] are beginnings; all of the threes are ends. The twos attain the proper center. The noble man residing in obscurity is upright. Residing in good fortune, he keeps himself humble. Residing in calamity, he turns [the blame] back on himself. The petty man residing in obscurity is perverted. Residing in good fortune, he is arrogant. Residing in calamity, he is at his wit's end. Therefore,

> When the noble man attains a position, he flourishes.
> When he loses it, he keeps his equanimity.
> When the petty man attains a position, he is tyrannical.
> When he loses it, he perishes.

At Appraisal 8, even if he attains a position still it "overturns the norms of autumn."

What is meant by: "When souls are overturned, *ch'i* and form revert"? It says, the excessive[22] culminates above. What culminates above then moves on in the cycle. The excessive goes below, where it is then overturned. The soul is overturned already, I daresay. The *ch'i* and form could not possibly remain and not revert. Does it mean that the noble man in his old age has reached the end of his time? Yang culminates above. Yin culminates below. The *ch'i* and form are at odds [with each other]. The ghosts and gods obstruct [one another]. The worthy man grows apprehensive [since he is aware that his demise is imminent], while the petty man grows presumptuous [since he uses his advanced age to excuse his self-indulgence].[23]

"Primal oneness encompasses all./ It is profound" refers to great receptivity. "Spiritual forces war in darkness" refers to mutual attack. "The dragon emerges at the center" refers to affairs proceeding smoothly. "Blocked to lowliness and emptiness" refers to not being fair-minded. "The sun centered in the sky" refers to all-pervasive light. "The moon losing its fullness" refers to depletion of the surplus. "Repository of the fully ripe" refers to taking the tried and true as model. "Yellow is not yellow" refers to losing the central thread. "Overturned souls reverting" refers to exhausting Heaven's conditions.

[The mantic formulae] Without, Extending, Covering, and Completing appraise the many [aspects of] the Hidden. [The phrase] "Primal oneness encompasses all./ It is profound" describes a situation where "the stuff embraced has no bounds." "Spiritual forces war in darkness" describes "good and evil in two rows." "The dragon emerges at the center" describes "laws and institutions that are civilized."[24] "Blocked to lowliness and emptiness" describes "subjects' ways that are unfit." "The sun centered in the sky" describes "riding on the firmness of *Ch'ien* [Hexagram 1 in the *Changes*, signifying pure masculinity]." "The moon losing its fullness" describes "the way to contemplate waxing and waning." "Repository of the fully ripe" describes "the ability to employ punishment and suasive virtue." "Yellow is not yellow" describes "the inability to proceed further in company with others." "Overturned souls reverting" describes "time by rule having its limits."

Without, Extending, Covering, and Completing—only then at last has one reached the limit of the spirit realm.

What is valued in Heaven and Earth is called "life." What is honored among things is called "human." The great organizing principle of humanity is called "good order." What good order depends upon is the ruler. Nothing else can compare to the ruler in exalting Heaven and broadening Earth,[25] in classifying the many and in pairing things, so that they do not lose their order. Now, Heaven rules in the regions above, and Earth, in the regions below. The ruler rules in the center. Looking up to Heaven, he finds that Heaven is not weary. Looking down to Earth, he finds that Earth is not indolent. The weary are not like Heaven. The indolent are not like Earth. It has never been the case—in the past or in the present—that the weary and indolent exhibit ability in their affairs. For this reason, the sage looks up to Heaven and takes constancy as [his] rule. He plumbs the limits of the divine; he mines the [possibilities for] change. He understands things completely; he exhausts [the potential] inherent in] natural conditions.[26] The sage would match his body with Heaven-and-Earth, aim for the numinosity of the ghosts and gods,[27] push his transformations to the limit with yin and yang, and participate in the integrity of the four seasons. Contemplating Heaven, he becomes Heaven. Contemplating Earth, he becomes Earth.[28] Contemplating divinities, he becomes divine. Contemplating Time, he becomes timely. Heaven, Earth, the gods, and Time, with all these he is in accord, so how could he enter into contradiction?[29]

REPRESENTATIONS OF THE MYSTERY 玄㮣
Hsüan yi

*[Tradition compares this essay to parts of the "Appended Texts" (*Hsi tz'u) *commentary to the* Changes. *The first two paragraphs list the component parts of the* Mystery *and suggest the conditions necessary to comprehend it.]*

The phrasing in the Appraisals of the *Mystery* sometimes is couched in terms of *ch'i* [according to the Five Phases],[1] sometimes in terms of category, sometimes in terms of the twists and turns[2] of [human] affairs. It ventures to ask questions about their natures; it examines their families [i.e., its tetragrams]. It carefully observes what they coincide with. It catalogs them by event, details them by number. In meeting with the gods, it sees them as Heavenly. In coming up against Earth, it sees it as fields to be sown. By rule, then, it attains the true conditions of the Mystery!

And so it is that the Heads refer to the Heaven-given nature. The Polar Oppositions refers to opposing the right [pairs of tetragrams]. The

Interplay refers to shuffling [them] together. The Fathomings are the means to know the true circumstances. The Evolution expands it. The Illumination clarifies it. The Numbers serves as a classificatory method. The Elaboration serves as a finely worked ornament.[3] The Representations refers to the likenesses. The Diagram refers to the images. The Revelation refers to its origin and ends.

[The following paragraph summarizes Yang Hsiung's ideas regarding the relation of human nature to fate.]

"Only Heaven takes the initative to send down life to the common people."[4] It sets their behaviors to acting, mouths to talking, eyes to seeing, ears to hearing, and minds to thinking. If they have good models, then they are perfected. If they have no proper models, then they are imperfect. With integrity, they have no reason to be in awe of anything.[5] The Representation likens[6] it to the canon.[7]

[The following five paragraphs stress the fundamental "naturalness" of various human institutions, correlating them with the number system of the Mystery. *In a sense, this section plays off part of the "Appended Texts" commentary to the* Yi ching, *which suggests that certain human activities find their sacred analogue in various trigrams and hexagrams of that divination manual.]*

Draping the lapel cloth makes the upper garments. Pleating lengths of cloth makes the lower garments. The regulations regarding upper and lower garments are used to inform All-under Heaven. The Representation likens it to the numbers three and eight.

Fitting together leather strips makes a breastplate. Capping the lance makes a halberd. Breastplates worn and halberds borne are used to inspire awe in the irreverent. The Representation likens it to the numbers four and nine.

Honored among the honorable is the ruler. Low among the lowly is the subject. The institution of ruler and subject is used to demarcate superior and inferior. The Representation likens it to the numbers two and seven.

The ghosts and gods are formless and scattered.[8] One thinks of them as having no fixed abode.[9] They have no winter or summer; there are no set intervals for sacrificing to them.[10] Therefore, the sages make them manifest through the ritual canon. The Representation likens it to the numbers one and six.

When the time is Heaven's time and the strength is the strength of Earth, there will be nothing but wine, nothing but food. "There one initates the sowing and the reaping."[11] The Representation likens it to the number five.[12]

Representations of the Mystery

[The following three paragraphs suggest the sacred models for Thought, Good Fortune, and Calamity, the designations given to the three successive sets of three Appraisals that belong to each Head text.]

The ancients treasured the turtle and used cowries as money. In later generations, the noble man exchanged them for metal coins and silk. These the kingdoms and royal houses circulated. The masses gained by it. The Representation likens it to Thought.

Principalities were established and kingdoms founded. Emoluments were dispersed and ranks distributed, in order to guide the Hundred Salaried Officials [of the state bureaucracy]. The Representation likens it to Good Fortune.

When the wicked are brought down only by the Five [Mutilating] Punishments,[13] the Representation likens it to Calamity.

Grasping the jade tablet, crowned with the jade circlet, he ranks in perfect order the many [feudal] rulers. The Representation likens it to the eighty-one Head texts.

[The final section explicates the Mystery *in terms of the parallel musical and astronomical systems.]*

Jujube wood makes a shuttle. Split wood makes a weaving frame. Once the shuttle and the frame are provided, people can keep warm with their help. The Representation likens it to warp and woof.

Carve and cut calabash, bamboo, leather, wood, earth, and metal [to make the musical instruments]. "Strike the music stone, pluck the silk strings"[14] to harmonize All-under-Heaven. The Representation likens it to the Eight [Musical] Airs.[15]

Yin and yang are interspersed. Male and female are attracted to one another.[16] Human after human, thing after thing,[17] each [develops] according to its category. The Representation likens it to the Deficit and Surplus [intercalary Appraisals].

The sun and moon succeed one another. The stars and planets do not crash into one another. The timbres and pitches are calibrated. Odd and even vary in *ch'i*. Father and sons have different faces. Elder and younger brothers are not twins. Lords and kings, none are the same. The Representation likens it to the yearly cycle.

Whatever roars[18] and bares its fangs has immature horns. Whatever flaps its wings[19] has [only] two feet. What has neither horns or wings [i.e., humankind] has the capacity to use the Way and its Power.[20] The Representation likens it to the equal apportionment of the nine-day period [among sets of two successive Appraisals].[21]

Dwelling in the seen, he comes to understand the hidden. Deducing from the near, he estimates the far.[22] [The sage] infers the outermost reaches of yin and yang. He examines the hidden aspects of divine light.[23] The Representation likens it to the gnomon and the quarter-hour marks [on the clepsydra].[24]

At one time it is bright. At one time it is dark. The firm and the weak continually alternate. To know yin is to go against the flow. To know yang is to go with it. The Represenation likens it to day and night.

Searching above, searching below, he honors the Heavenly norms. Transmitting the past, carrying it forward into the future, he honors the arts of Heaven. As he is without any [erratic] change or innovation, he honors Heaven's categories. The Representation likens it to the Heavenly Origin.[25]

Heaven-and-Earth acts as a divine womb for everything.[26] [Cosmic] models, being easy [to follow], last for all time.[27] The end is whatever is about to go away. The beginning is whatever is about to come. The Representation likens it to [the five mantic formulae] Without, Extending, Covering, Completing, and Hidden.[28]

Therefore, if we make water like a stream, then the water can flow freely. If we make our conduct like Virtue, then the conduct attains its Mean. If we make our speech like a model, then the speech attains a rightness.[29] When speech is right, then it has no equal.[30] When conduct attains the Mean, then it has no faults. When water flows freely, then it has no breaks. Because there is no break, it lasts long. Because there is no fault, it is fit to contemplate. Because it has no equal, it is fit to hear. What is fit to hear is the absolute perfection of the sage. What is fit to contemplate is the virtue of the sage. What is fit to last forever is the Way of Heaven and Earth. For this reason, the various sages long ago in initiating the affairs [of civilized society] likened them above to Heaven, likened them below to Earth, and likened them at center to Man.

Heaven and Earth form the container. Sun and moon are fixed sources of light. The Five Phases hold the categories together.[31] The Five Sacred Mountains act as masters to the other mountains. The Four Great Rivers act as elders to the other waterways. The Five Classics [of Confucianism] encompass all the normative patterns [in the cosmos]. If Heaven, Earth, and Man all oppose [a proposed action], the great affairs of All-under-Heaven are bound to go awry!

DIAGRAM OF THE MYSTERY 玄圖
Hsüan t'u

[This compares with part of the "Appended Texts" commentary (also called the "Great Commentary") to the Changes. *The first paragraph of the essay interweaves references to the structure of the* Mystery *text with refer-*

ences to the main structural features of the universe. The next three para-graphys speak of the order of the tetragrams as it relates to the yearly cycle of the seasons.]

The one *Mystery* like a capital[1] dominates the three Regions [of Heaven, Earth, and Man]. The Regions comprehend the Nine Provinces. Branching out, the Provinces are conveyed to[2] the various Departments, which are in turn subdivided and apportioned into the multitude of Families.[3] Affairs are managed in their midst. The darkness has the North-ern Dipper as its precise center[4] [in the night sky]. The sun and moon establish boundaries for their camps.[5] Yin and yang in deep secrecy make contact. The four seasons by stealth take their places. The Five Phases conceal their actions. Once the Six Directions [up, down, north, south, east and west] had cohered [with no visible separation],[6] the Seven Man-sions [assigned to each quarter of the sky] revolved in succession [around the Dipper]. One follows the profound to produce the calendar.[7] The six *chia* [of the sexagenary cycle used to mark time][8] then conform and the eighty-one [tetragrams of the *Mystery*] exist in full measure. The musical pitches and intervals penetrate the profound.[9] The calendrical calcula-tions obscure the regular cycles. The Diagram makes an image of the Mys-tery's form; it appraises, then conveys [the Mystery's] accomplishments.

The Beginnings are located in[10] Center (no. 1 of the tetragrams), De-fectiveness (no. 10), and Following (no. 19).[11] "The Hundred Plants be-gin to sprout."[12] Only then does report [of it] stimulate Heaven. Thunder hammers the deepest recesses [of Earth] so that many things are aroused on all sides. In the first month,[13] aid goes to[14] the weak and the unde-veloped, so that their roots are drawn out from the Origin.[15] In the east the Green Dragon[16] stirs. Rays of light are diffused [even] unto the deep abyss [below earth], prompting the myrial things to rise up. Heaven and Earth are all[17] renewed.

The Centers are located in Change (no. 28), Purity (no. 37), and Enlargement (no. 46).[18] They symbolize Heaven's twice-bright nature [which has both sun and moon],[19] and the brilliant flash of thunder and windstorms. All things proceed in timely fashion. Yin comes to comple-tion in the northwest. Yang rises up in the southeast. Despite the re-sponse inside,[20] [the response] outside is lofty and auspicious. As the dragon soars to Heaven, growing species know no bounds. A southern march[21] is not advantageous, as one encounters the dying light.

The Ends are located in [the tetragrams] Diminishment (no. 55), Sink-ing (no. 64), and Completion (no. 73).[22] As Heaven's Root[23] reverts to face [the north], mature *ch'i* draws in its essences. The many things are stricken,[24] so that all begin to cry out in their distress. Deeply conjoined with the Yellow Purity,[25] they broadly contain [the seeds of] all living things. The Great Handle[26] like "clouds scudding" [dispenses blessings along its path],[27] overseeing [each] quarter on earth at the proper time. Deviant plans, [however] high-flying, it reins in. Only then does [the universe] conform to the divine spirits [of Heaven and Earth]. On every side it encompasses the end and the beginning. The works of Heaven, Earth, and Man are all completed and true.

[The following paragraph opens with a contrast between Heaven and Earth, yang and yin. It goes on to relate these two powers to human society. The next two paragraphs return to the Mystery *text. In dividing the text into nine equal parts, they suggest that the text is comparable to the nine great divisions of Heaven of Earth.]*

Heaven governs[28] its Way. Earth disposes its tasks. Yin and yang are interspersed so that there are male and female. The Way of Heaven is a perfect compass. The Way of Earth is a perfect carpenter's square. The compass in motion describes a complete circle through the sites. The square, unmoving, secures things [in their proper place]. Circling through the sites then makes divine light possible.[29] Securing things then makes congregation by types possible. Congregating by types then makes riches possible. Divine light then makes the highest honor possible. Now the "Mystery" is the Way of Heaven, the Way of Earth, and the Way of Man. Taken together, these three ways are called Heavenly. [They are synonymous with] the way of ruler to subject, father to son, husband to wife.

The *Mystery* has one single Way.[30] The One gives rise [to things] by threes. The One gives birth [to things] by threes.[31] Those that have arisen by threes are the Regions, the Province, the Department, and the Family. As for those born by threes, thrice-divided yang *ch'i* makes up the Three Layers [of Thought, Good Fortune, and Calamity], which, squared, [in turn] make up the Nine Sites [of the Appraisals]. That is [a case of] having a common root but separate growth. It is the warp of Heaven and Earth. On all sides it pervades high and low; it is what joins the myriad things. With a complete circuit of the Nine Sites, the end [of the cycle] to the beginning is correctly oriented. [The calendar] begins in the eleventh month; it ends in the tenth month. In the net [of Heaven] the levels amount to Nine Courses, with each Course forty days long.[32]

Whatever truly has inner [force] is preserved in the Center (no. 1 of the tetragrams).[33] Whatever propagates and issues forth is preserved in Defectiveness (no. 10). "Clouds scudding and rain falling"[34] are preserved in Following (no. 19). Changing rhythms and altered measures are preserved in Change (no. 28). Precious light bathing the whole is preserved in Purity (no. 37). Whatever is empty within but great without is preserved in Enlargement (no. 46). Paring and retreating, waning and apportioning are preserved in Diminishment (no. 55). Descending, falling, obscuring, and hiding are preserved in Sinking (no. 64). "Coming to a good end"[35] in regard to nature and the Decree is preserved in Completion (no. 73). Do not the [Courses] 1–9 thus represent the [divine] plan for the waxing and waning of yin and yang?

[The concluding paragraphs explain the numerical system underlying the Mystery. *First, reference is made to the Chinese system of Heavenly Stems and Earthly Branches as it relates to the ancient Chinese lunar calendar. Then some of the more obvious correlations for Appraisal 1–9 are given. Finally, the divination method used in the* Mystery *is related to calendrical theories in vogue in Yang Hsiung's time.]*

Explaining it another way, if we are at *tzu* 子 [the first of the Twelve Branches, correlated with north], it is evident that yang is born in the eleventh month while yin ends in the tenth month. And if we are at *wu* 午 [the seventh of the Twelve Earthly Branches, correlated with south], it is evident that yin is born in the fifth month while yang ends in the fourth month. There is nothing so good as *tzu* for giving birth to yang. There is nothing so good as *wu* for giving birth to yin. *Tzu*, then, is absolute perfection in the northwest. *Wu*, then, is sheer perfection in the southwest.

Therefore, the thinking heart/mind is assigned to [Appraisal no.] 1. Turning it over [in one's mind] is assigned to 2. Completion of the idea is assigned no. 3. Branching out is assigned to 4. Shedding light is assigned to 5. Extreme greatness is assigned to 6. Defeat and diminishment are assigned to 7. Falling off is assigned to 8. Absolute destruction is assigned to 9. In bearing the divine, nothing takes priority over 1. In centering and harmonizing, nothing is superior to 5. In bowing to aggravations, nothing is as hampered as 9. Now, [Appraisal] 1 represents the first intimations of thought; [Appraisal] 4, the stuff of good fortune. [Appraisal] 7 represents the steps to calamity; [Appraisal] 3, the fullness of thought. [Appraisal] 6 represents the height of good fortune; [Appraisal] 9, calamity in the extreme. [Appraisals] 2, 5, and 8 are the centers of the three [sets of three Appraisals].

Good fortune by rule departs; calamity by rule succeeds [it].[36] Once the Nine Positions are set out, they become sites for the noble and petty man. In [Appraisals] 1–3 are the poor, the lowly, and the exercised in mind; in [Appraisals] 4–6, the wealthy, the honoured, and those in high position; in [Appraisals] 7–9, those suffering blame and meeting calamity. [Appraisals] 1 to 5 cause waxing. [Appraisals] 6 to 9 cause waning. The higher numbers may appear to be honoured but in fact are depleted. The smaller numbers may appear to be lowly but in fact are prospering. Waxing and waning are bound together. Honor and dishonor are conjoined.

As good fortune arrives, calamity departs. When calamity comes, good fortune flees. Hidden and immersed, the Way seems debased. High[37] and culminating, the Way seems lofty.

Night and day succeed one another. Husband and wife are tied to one another. Beginning and end produce one another. Father to son continue one another. Sun and moon join or separate.[38] Such is the duty of ruler and subject. From the eldest to the youngest, there is an order. This is the boundary between old and young. Two by two they go, [like] leaves of the gate.[39] Such is the meeting between friends. One day and one night make a single day. One yin and one yang give birth to the myriad things. More numbers correspond to day; fewer correspond to night.[40] [The *Mystery*] was made to reflect the moon's waning light in the face of the sun's over-whelming brilliance. When the ruler's course shines gloriously, the subject's [light] is extinguished. When the way of the noble man is complete, that of the petty man is seen as defective.

1 and 6 share the same ancestor.
2 and 7 share the same light.
3 and 8 become good friends.
4 and 9 keep a common way.
5 and 5 protect each other.

The *Mystery* has one compass and one square, one line and one level.[41] It uses the Way of vertical and horizontal, of Heaven and Earth. It makes the numbers of yin and yang conform. If we liken it to divine light, it elucidates it [the answer to the question] with regard to its obscure and dark places. Then the level and upright way of the Eight Directions can be ascertained.[42]

The *Mystery* works with multiples of six and nine.[43] The divining stalks use three times six (i.e., 18). The principles [of Heaven and Earth] use two times nine (also = 18).[44] The *Mystery* certainly does use eighteen [as a base], then! The Grand Accumulation Sum[45] begins with 18 divining stalks and ends with 54. If we add the numbers that correspond to the beginning and end [of the stalks, 18 + 54 = 72], we halve it to make the Grand Center [=36]. The 36 divining stalks of the Grand Center are used to regulate the 729 Appraisals. Altogether 26,244 stalks make up the Grand Accumulation, with 72 stalks per day for the 364 and 1/2 days [of the year]. The Deficit [Appraisal] fills it out, so as bring it into accord with the days of the year and the pitches and calendar in their course.

Therefore, [the Mystery] from *tzu* [the first of the Twelve Branches] goes to *ch'en* [the fifth in the same system], and from *ch'en* to *shen* [the ninth in the same system]. Then it goes from *shen* [back] to *tzu*, capping it off with [a return to] *chia* [the sign that marks the beginning of the cycle of the ten Heavenly Stems].[46] The concordance cycles of 19 years, of 513 years, of 1,539 years, and of 4,617 years[47] then coincide [at the beginning of their cycles] so that the number of [unexplained] lunar eclipses will all decline. Such is the Way of the Mystery.

REVELATION OF THE MYSTERY 玄告
Hsüan kao

[This essay compares with parts of the "Discussion of the Trigrams" (Shuo kua) commentary to the Changes. *As in earlier autocommentaries by Yang Hsiung, the term "Mystery" refers at points both to the cosmic Tao and to Yang's own neoclassic of that name.*

The first paragraph suggests the absolute perfection of the Mystery, *whose pages perfectly mirror all the component parts of the universe.]*

The Mystery gives birth to two divine images.[1] The two divine images give birth to the spherical [universe].[2] The cosmic sphere gives birth to Three Models [of Heaven-Earth-Man].[3] The Three Models give birth to the Nine Positions.[4] The *Mystery* in having the model "One" attains to Heaven. Therefore, we say of it that it "has Heaven [in it]." The *Mystery* in having the model "Two" attains to Earth. Therefore, we say of it that it "has Earth [in it]." The *Mystery*1 in having the model "Three" attains to Man. Therefore, we say of it that it "has Man [in it]."

[The following two paragraphs speak in terms of one paradox associated with the Mystery: both unity and multiplicity (symbolized by the threes) are subsumed in it. Man also is presented here as a full partner in the triadic realms of Heaven, Earth, and Man that make up the cosmos. Finally, the Mystery *book is shown to be an integral part of the divine system.]*

Heaven is complete only after it has three bases. Therefore, we call them Beginning. Middle, and End. Earth takes form only after it has three bases. Therefore, we call them Below, Center, Above. Man is revealed only after he has three bases. Therefore, we call them Thought, Good Fortune, and Calamity. What is united above and what is united below[5] go in and out of the Nine Sites.[6] The lesser rules and the greater rules[7] make the full circuit of the Nine Dwellings.

What we call the Mystery is the repository of the divine. In regard to Heaven, we take the unseen as the Mystery. In regard to Earth, we take the formless as the Mystery. In regard to Man, we take the heart and belly [i.e., the inmost reactions] as the Mystery. Heaven hiding away[8] in the northwest pens up the transforming essences.[9] Earth hiding away in the Yellow Springs secretes the flowering of the corporeal soul. Man hiding away in thought contains within the quintessential [power]. Heaven is arched and vaulted, but everywhere it reaches the lower parts. Earth in all directions thins out at the edges,[10] but it faces the upper regions. And Man in teeming multitudes takes his place at the center. Heaven turns in a circle[11] so its cycles are unending. Earth is stable[12] and quiet, so its growth is not delayed. Man complies with Heaven and Earth, so his operations do not deplete anything.

[Beginning with three rhyming couplets, the following two paragraphs demonstrate that the cosmos is filled with examples of complementary, yet opposing entities. They conclude from this that various distinctions in human society are not only necessary but fully natural.]

Heaven and Earth face each other.[13]
Sun and moon are in conjunction.

Mountain and valley flow into one another.[14]
Light and heavy float on one another.

Yin and yang succeed one another.
High and low rank do not defile one another.

For this reason, Earth is a pit while Heaven is high. The moon hurries while the sun tarries.[15] The Five Phases each in turn become king.[16] The four seasons are not all strong [at the same time]. The sun gives light to the day, while the moon gives light to the night. The Mane [constellation] as a rule rises up in winter, while the Fire Star[17] declines in summer.[18] North to south are fixed positions [set by the poles], the *ch'i* currents flow east to west.[19] The myriad things are interspersed in their midst.

The Mystery in a single act of virtue creates the Five Productions [Cycle].[20] In a single act of punishment it creates the Five Conquests [Cycle].[21] The Five Produced do not cut each other down. The Five Conquered do not oppose each other. That they do not cut each other down is the only reason that they succeed one another. That they do not oppose each other is the only reason that they can regulate one another. Succeeding one another provides a model for the way of father to son. Regulating one another provides a model for the treasured relation between ruler and subject.

[The following two paragraphs suggest that the true classic (like the true sage) investigates only the constants, since no useful conclusions can be drawn from anomalies in nature or in human society.]

The *Mystery* records the sun and [the direction of] the Dipper, but it does not record the moon.[22] It is by the constant and the full[23] that the irregular[24] are ordered.[25] When the lunar year is completed,[26] the solar year is off. For every 19 years [there must be] 7 intercalary months. This is Heaven's Compensation.

Yang is active and exhaling.[27] Yin is quiet and inhaling.[28] The way of yang is constant abundance. The way of yin is constant deficiency.[29] Such is the way of yin and yang. Heaven, being strong and virile, is active and creative.[30] In one night and one day, it makes one complete revolution, with some left over.[31] The sun has [its trip] to the south and [its trip] to the north. The moon has its goings and comings. If the sun did not move south and north, then there would be no winter and summer. If the moon did not go and come, then the lunar cycle[32] would not be complete. The sage investigates changes in the moon's appearance and location,[33] as well as departures from its orbit.[34] He [only] finds a norm in the [constant] sequence of sun and moon, and in the order of male and female.[35] He makes them the canonical model for all eternity.[36] Therefore, the *Mystery* in grand fashion comprises[37] Heaven's Origin,[38] binding and securing it to what is to come.

[The following two paragraphs summarize the mysterious power inherent in the text of the Mystery. *Though the* Mystery *focuses on the constant patterns in the universe, it should not be thought of as prosaic, but divine, for the* Mystery *teaches us how to extrapolate from the known to the unknown operating in the cosmos.]*

When the great has to borders and change has no [set] time, later it becomes the gods and ghosts, who wander in the Six Exalted Ones [Heaven, Earth, and the Four Seasons], infinite in number.[39] The myriad things, being moved [by them], are always pouring out.[40] In consequence, we have the phrasing of the *Mystery*, which sinks down to plumb the depths and floats up to reach the heights, [by turns appearing] twisted or straightforward, digressive or compact. So excellent is it that one never grows tired of its flavors. So great is it that one never exhausts its types. Joining above, joining below, it does not move in a single direction. Wide-ranging [yet] focused, without a constant rule, it proceeds by category; sometimes many and sometimes few, affairs are submitted to the light.[41]

Therefore, those who are good at talking about Heaven and Earth use human affairs [by way of comparison]. Those who are good at talking about human affairs use Heaven and Earth [by way of comparison]. As clarity and befuddlement push against one other, "sun and moon succeed one another."[42] As year upon year jostles one against the other,[43] Heaven and Earth continue to fashion ever more [things].[44] Of it we say, "The divine light goes on forever.[45]

Those who seek the origin find it difficult to trace, but those who follow out its secondary manifestations find them easy to follow. And so those with clans and ancestors are generally evaluated in terms of filial piety. And those who would order [relations between] ruler and minister are generally evaluated in terms of loyalty.[46] This is a real revelation and a great teaching.

Notes

INTRODUCTION

1. The primary source for information about Yang's life is the two-chapter biography found in Pan Ku's *Han shu*. Three chronologies detailing the main events of Yang's life are available: (1) CPL 1a–13b; (2) Tung Tso-pin; and (3) T'ang Ping-chen. The dates for certain key events in Yang's life are also discussed in Hsü Fu-kuan, II, 451–60. For a more technical discussion of this topic, scholars are advised to consult Nylan and Sivin (1987). (Note that the Nylan and Sivin article provides fuller annotation at many points.) Part I of this Introduction is an amalgam of that article, an earlier draft by Nylan, and later material by Nylan. The characters needed for Chinese terms and names used in the Introduction can be found in the appended Glossary, unless they appear in the Bibliography. For the debate regarding the proper written form for Yang Hsiung's surname, see Hsü Fu-kuan, II, 445–49. I use 揚, but both are found in the Bibliography, reflecting a lack of scholarly consensus on this issue.

2. Yang Hsiung in his *Fa yen* [hereafter FY] and "Dispelling Objections" prose-poem refers to the work simply as the *T'ai hsüan*. Probably Yang Hsiung's disciple Hou Pa or a later admirer elevated the work to the status of "classic" or "canon" (*ching*). The book is called the *T'ai hsüan ching* in Huan T'an's (43 B.C.– A.D. 28) *Hsin lun*, Wang Ch'ung's (27–?97) *Lun heng*, and Hsün Yüeh's (148– 209) *Han chi*. A more detailed discussion of the THC text, its major commentaries, and relevant secondary sources can be found in Nylan (forthcoming [b]).

3. Yang Hsiung presumably chose these two texts as prototypes for his own writings because the *Analects* represented the ultimate source for Confucian ethics and the *Yi ching*, the ultimate source of Confucian metaphysics. See Cheng, p. 283 on this.

4. Juan Hsiao-hsü (479–536), the Liang dynasty bibliographer, was apparently the first to specifically mention a "commentary by chapter and verse" attributed to Yang Hsiung. The Sui "Treatise on Literature" notes that this nine *chüan* edition has been lost. See Yi-wen, 3:71. Yang's biography tell us that he preferred wide reading to the "commentaries by chapter and verse" favored by the pedants. See HS 87A:3514 (Knechtges, 12); and HYKC 10A:130.

5. Pan Ku, cited in CPL 1/2a.

6. Some few of their laudatory comments about Yang Hsiung are collected in Chin Ch'un-feng, pp. 445–48. Chin, p. 445, argues that Eastern Han thinkers found Yang's writings useful in their "war against the spiritualists [associated with] the apocrypha."

7. Yang's feelings toward Wang Mang before and after his rise to power are not clear from the record. Prior to his founding the Hsin dynasty in A.D. 9, Wang Mang was widely admired by many Confucians professing a commitment to restoring the ideals traditionally associated with the Duke of Chou. Hans Bielenstein, the modern historian, argues persuasively that the usurpation initially represented for many a return to a stable form of central government administration. See Bielenstein, esp. pp. 82–92; 162–65. It is entirely possible, then, that

Yang's views changed as Wang's designs on the Han throne became more obvious. As court poet, Yang was expected to write encomiums to Wang as his patron, and he did so. On the other hand, Yang held only nominal office under Wang Mang, which suggests that he did not join the numerous sycophants who benefited from Wang's favor. For further information, see Knechtges (1978).

8. For Su Hsün's essay, see CYC 7:61–72. Chu Hsi's criticisms are scattered throughout his works. One of his most vituperative passages says, "Yang Hsiung is the most useless of all [scholars], a true rotten pedant. Whenever he gets excited, he throws in his lot with the Yellow Emperor and with Lao tzu [i.e., with Taoists]." See CTYL 137/4b. For a brief account of attacks on Yang Hsiung, see Forke (1934), pp. 78–83.

It should be noted that the objection to Yang Hsiung's revision of the Mencian theory is particularly unfair since Yang's warm praise of Mencius inspired greater interest in Mencius during the Eastern Han period. For Yang Hsiung on Mencius, see FY 2:6, 11:33, 12:37. A commentary to the *Mencius* is attributed to Yang Hsiung in the Sung "Treatise on Literature."

9. SKCS 108, *Tzu pu* 子部 21, pp. 1–3.

10. For a review of all recent secondary works on Yang Hsiung, see Nylan (forthcoming [b]).

11. By "early China," I mean the time that spans the age of the mature Confucius through the Warring States, Ch'in, and Western Han periods (ca. 500 B.C.– A.D. 8). Unfortunately, it is often difficult to date philosophical trends with greater precision; also, this formula allows me to avoid unwieldy phrases like "from the late Ch'un Ch'iu period until the end of Western Han."

12. For yin/yang and the Five Phases, see the Key Terms section. Derk Bodde, Frederick Mote, Joseph Needham, and others have commented on the apparent lack of a creation myth in Western Chou philosophical writings. (The *argumentum ex silencio* is always risky, however.) After the fourth c. B.C., cosmology began to attract greater intellectual attention. By Western Han, cosmogonic myth played an important part in the traditions associated with the *Yi ching* See CIS, IA, 21, 24, 25–27, for the four-stage cosmogonic sequence preserved in apocrypha to the *Changes*. There is no necessary conflict between the Han cosmogonic perspective, which emphasizes dynamic process, and the theory of continuous gestation presupposed by the *Yi ching*.

13. Translation by Nylan and Sivin, based partly upon a tradition attributed to Yang's own teacher, Chuang Tsun (better known as Yen Chün-p'ing) and partly upon later commentary traditions. See Nylan and Sivin (1987), pp. 55–56 (including footnote 20). Chuang Tsun's extant commentary to the *Lao tzu*, the subject of a recent article, suggests that he was more faithful to the Laotzuian vision than Yang Hsiung. See Wang Li-ch'i. Note also that Serruys would prefer that the last two lines be translated, "Equally we name them the 'Mystery.'/ Most mysterious of mysteries."

14. "Hsüan li" 7/5b (p. 1018b). Note that all references to the *T'ai hsüan* (THC) cite the WJL edition. For an early comparison of the *Lao tzu* and the *Mystery*, see YKC 15/8a–b (Pokora, 172).

15. THC "Hsüan t'u" 10/1b (p. 1032b). Cf. "Hsüan kao" 10/3b (p. 1034b).

16. FY 4:10.

17. *Ibid.*

18. Numerous passages in the FY and THC make this clear. The reader might begin with FY 4:10–11.

19. LT, ch. 18 (Lau, 165).

20. The translation for *wu wei* is that given in Graham (1969), on the assumption that *wu wei = wu so wei* 無所為 ("without preference or preconception for anything"). For Yang's objections to *wu wei*, see FY 4:11.

21. FY 7:19. Literally, "[What is called] 'discerning language' is for its part a paltry thing." In the case of the Rites, note the usual Han pun associating *t'i* 體 and *li* 禮 (GSR 597i = 597c). In the case of the *Odes*, note Yang's reference to the "Great Preface." Also, compare Yang's analysis of the Five Classics with SC 130:3296–98 on the Six Classics.

22. FY 11:33.

23. Perhaps here is the point to confess my discomfort with the use of masculine and feminine pronouns in this manuscript. Although classical Chinese usually does not indicate gender, there is no doubt that in most cases Chinese authors imagine both their subjects and their readers as male. In part this is simply because a majority of the literate population was male; in part this is because of Chinese attitudes regarding the "constant norm" of female submission. To pretend that the use of "he or she" is appropriate in all cases would be to distort. Accordingly, I use the standard terms Heaven-Earth-Man and refer occasionally to Man rather than "human." Of course, I believe that many lessons drawn from early Chinese philosophy apply to the lives of women as well.

24. THC44/A3.

25. For further information about Yang's life and poetry, consult Knechtges (1976) and Knechtges (1982).

26. TPYL 385:5b, citing Liu Hsiang's *Pieh lu* 別錄 identifies the son as the second of "two boys" or "two children" (*erh tzu* 二子). FY 5:15 talks of his son T'ung-wu 童烏, who at the age of nine was working with Yang on the composition of the *Mystery*.

27. HS 30:1720 attributes to Yang a work in one *p'ien* called *Ts'ang Chieh hsün tsuan* 倉頡訓纂 (*Compendium of Glosses on the Ts'ang Chieh*). For further information, see HS 30:1718, 1721; YKC 49/3b, which is translated in Thern, pp. 13–14; and Knechtges (1978), p. 1, n. 3. Fragments of this work have been collected in MKH, IV, 2228–29.

28. Though Yang did not compose any portent texts in support of Wang Mang, he did compose a poem ostensibly in praise of the Hsin dynasty founded by Wang. See Knechtges (1978). Cf. FY 13:43.

29. For further information, see Knechtges (1978).

30. Which include the *Yi lin* 易林 by Chiao Kan 焦贛 [=Chiao Yen-shou 延壽] (1st c. B.C.) and the *Ch'ien hsü* 潛虛 by Ssu-ma Kuang (11th c.).

31. Among the many modern studies which support this conclusion are four whose arguments are especially provocative: Li Ching-ch'ih; Waley (1933); Shchutskii; and Kunst.

32. We now know that the *Changes* came to be regarded as part of the Confucian canon only in late Warring States or Han times. See Uno Seiichi; and Matsumoto Masaaki, pp. 17–20.

33. Waley (1933), p. 125 ff., and Kunst, p. 57 ff., provide a number of examples, though they are not in complete agreement. For example, they give different explanations for the character *fu* 孚.

34. Of course, modern scholarly opinion presumes that the 64 hexagrams came first. The scholastic interpretation of each hexagram in terms of its two component trigrams seems to have occurred later.

35. For further information on the Han sponsorship of the Confucian Classics, see HS 30:1701; Shryock (1932); Uno Seiichi; and Wallacker. See Henderson (1990), ch. 1, on the requirements for religious canons.

36. There are two Ching Fangs 京房 associated with *Yi ching* studies in Western Han. The biography of Ching Fang the Younger specifically talks of his "apportioning the 64 hexagrams"; it also shows him correlating the hexagrams with the calendrical year. For further information, see HS 75:3160, 75:3164; Hulsewé (1986).

37. Yang Hsiung was not the first to do this, however. A generation before Yang, Chiao Kan had stepped outside the scholastic tradition when compiling his YL (*Forest of Changes*). For further information, see Nylan and Sivin (1982); Suzuki Yoshijirō (1963), pp. 431–593; and Kao Huai-min, pp. 126–38. The disputed attribution of this book is the subject of Suzuki Yoshijirō (1972).

38. See Key Terms.

39. This text was "not the product of a single act of creation, . . . but was accumulated . . . beginning approximately a generation before the Ch'in dynasty was proclaimed and hardening by the first century B.C." into canonical form. See Peterson (1982), 76–77. The Ma-wang-tui manuscript, buried 168 B.C., differs in some significant respects from the latter. See Report B; Mair (1990b), pp. 119–29; and Kunst, p. 452.

40. Note that the Ma-wang-tui LT manuscript (*terminus ad quem* 168 B.C.) divides that work into 81 chapters as well, unlike the previous standard text. The number 81, of course, is 9 squared. Nine was thought to be a sacred number because of the ninefold plan outlined in the "Hung fan" chapter of the *Documents* and the Nine Provinces of China enumerated in the "Yü kung" chapter of the same work. Perhaps the sacred character of 9 goes back to early Chou times. Shaughnessy (ch. II.2) suggests that 9 numbers altogether were originally used in the divination process.

41. The early commentator Fan Wang (fl. A.D. 265) originally assigned 5 days to odd-numbered tetragrams and 4 days to even-numbered tetragrams. This ignores Yang's own statement in one autocommentary calling for "equal apportionment of the nine-day period." See THC "Hsüan yi" 9/3b (p. 1030b). For further information, see CYC 7:61 ff.

42. For examples of Appraisals that do not accord with the table, see Part II of the Introduction. The quotation is from the THC "Hsüan ying" 7/9b (p. 1022b).

43. This rearrangement was first made by the early commentator Fan Wang in imitation of a similar rearrangement of the *Changes* text a generation before Fan. See T'ang Yung-t'ung, pp. 135–38.

44. This chart is said to have come down from Sung Wei-kan; it is repeated in Ssu-ma Kuang's preliminary remarks to his commentary to the THC. See 1/1a

in the SPPY edition. Note the omission of any reference in the list to the *t'uan* in the *Changes*. Note also the omission of any reference to the THC "Hsüan shu" in the WJL edition (a misprint?).

45. For the Grand Inception (T'ai-ch'u) calendar reform of 104 B.C., see Sivin (1969), esp. p. 10 ff.; and Loewe (1974).

46. For this, see Ch'ü Wan-li, pp. 82–98. Ching's was by no means the only arrangement of the *Changes* to be proposed in Han. The silk manuscript of the *Changes* contains still another order. See Liu Dajun; Report C; and footnote 39 above.

47. GSR 384a = 385a.

48. CYYT 46/Hsi B/3 (Wilhelm, 338).

49. I use "divine" or "godlike" to translate *shen* 神, a term that refers to (a) the gods themselves, (b) the depersonalized forces of Nature, and (c) the miraculous powers to be found in a person attuned with Heaven-and-Earth. "Spiritual" or "spirituality" to me suggests Christian impulses against the purely material and toward asceticism. Graham's "daimonic" doesn't work well, and Peterson's "numinous" leaves no convenient translation for *ling* 靈. However, Sivin (1990), p. 7, n. 8, prefers "spiritual" or "spirituality."

50. *Ch'ien* 謙 = *lien* 溓.

51. This alternation does not continue in later Heads as yang *ch'i* gathers strength.

52. CYCY 3/6a.

53. CYYT 32/52/*t'uan* (Wilhelm, 653).

54. See, for example, THC12/Head.

55. This is not a point that Yang Hsiung explains clearly, however.

56. In the *Changes* method, one stick is taken up from the right-hand pile after division.

57. THC "Hsüan shu" 8/5b (p. 1027b).

58. For detailed information about the mathematical aspects of the *Mystery*, see Nylan and Sivin (1987), p. 78 ff.

59. The notion of *ch'eng* 誠 was given a central place in the "Doctrine of the Mean." For further information about *ch'eng*, see Chan, ch. 5; and Tu.

60. For further information on *chen* 貞, see Key Terms in the Appendices.

61. For this reason, Yang compares divination to another invention by the sage-rulers of antiquity: coinage. If coins are to prove of any benefit to society, there must be unimpaired contact between the individual and others. Also, coinage can only benefit society if its value is undisputed.

62. THC "Hsüan li" 7/7b (p. 1020b), alluding to *Analects* 7/30 (Waley, 145 [renum.]).

63. THC "Hsüan wen" 9/2b (p. 1029b).

64. THC "Hsüan li" 7/6a (p. 1019a).

65. THC "Hsüan ying" 7/8b (p. 1022b). Cf. "Hsüan kao" 10/3b (p. 1035b).

66. THC "Hsüan shu" 8/1a (p. 1023a).

67. See FW 8/5a. Wang Mang is also said to have consulted the diviner's board (*shih*) when troubled. See HS 99C:4190 (Dubs, III, 463). Loewe (1979), pp. 75–79, discusses the Han diviner's board with reference to an excavated example from tomb 62, Mo-tsui-tzu, Kansu, as does Harper (1978).

68. See, for example, the biography of the statesman Lu K'ai 陸凱 in SKC, "Wu chih," 61:1400.

69. THC "Hsüan shu" 8/1a (p. 1023a). Material in brackets added on the basis of YTC 8/4a; FW 8/4b; and Hsü Han's commentary recorded in WJL, p. 1024a.

70. YTC 8/4a, on the basis of earlier tradition (?). This statement does not contradict FW 8/4b or Hsü Han's commentary (recorded in WJL, p. 1023a) but the commentaries in the latter two texts are too brief to serve to fully corroborate YTC's understanding.

71. Readers should note that China had a circle of 365 1/4 degrees, not 360, as in the West.

72. Cf. one passage in the *Mystery*, which suggests that a divination procedure yielding a tetragram corresponding to a date after the time of divination is considered generally auspicious, for then the user of the *Mystery* has time enough to adjust his conduct to coming trends: "Whatever is. . . "approaching the Mystery". . . advances but it has not yet culminated. . . ." See THC "Hsüan li" 7/7b (p. 1020b).

73. For example, associated with the annual cycle is the twelve-note gamut of mathematical harmonics, beginning with Yellow Bell at the winter solstice. The hours from midnight on are likewise assigned to groups of tetragrams.

74. HS 87B:3565 (Knechtges, 45).

75. For Yang on *tzu shou*, see FY 3:7; FY 4:12; and FY 8:22.

76. HS 87B:3583 (Knechtges, 59). In this section by "the *Changes*" I mean only the *Yi ching* proper, and not its later accretions.

77. That is, the assignment of successive numbers to specific hexagram titles and Line texts. Recent excavations suggest that several different orders were in existence in early Han. See Kunst, p. 452, for a summary of the Ma-wang-tui findings.

78. FY 5:13. Yang Hsiung was wrong, of course, when he argued that the *Changes* text had suffered few significant changes over time. See Part I.

79. For the Burning, see SC 6:244–45; and Bodde (1938). In FY 5:13 Yang comments that approximately half of the *Documents* was lost as a result.

80. By "verbal images," I do not refer specifically to the *hsiang* ("Image") texts included in the "Ten Wings" commentary. Instead, I refer to the single Line (*yao*) texts, accompanied by Image (*hsiang*) and Judgment (*t'uan*) texts, which depict a single situation.

81. See FY 5:14 for Yang on the inability of words to fully express reality.

82. The first sentence comes from THC "Hsüan li" 7/7b (p. 1020b); the rest, from THC "Hsüan ying" 7/9a (p. 1022a).

83. FY 2:6 characterizes a classic in this way.

84. HS 87B:3567, 3570 (Knechtges, 47, 49).

85. I recall here the example of Yang's beloved teacher, Chuang Tsun 莊遵 (better known as Yen Chün-ping 嚴君平), whose biography is given in HS 72:3056; HYKC 10A:129–30. According to these sources, Chuang Tsun used to sit in the marketplace and instruct the common people in morality under the guise of telling their fortunes. Chuang Tsun is often mistakenly identified as a recluse or hermit. The true recluse, however, according to Ssu-ma Ch'ien, "dwells in lowly

obscurity in order to avoid the masses and retires in order to avoid human relationships." See SC 127:3220 (Watson, II, 474). This eremitic ideal, which seems to have been present in Chinese culture since its inception, was not promoted by Yang Hsiung. Yang Hsiung's admiration for Chuang Tsun was consistent with his emphasis on the Five Constant Relations. Though Chuang dwelt in obscurity, he did so in order to teach the masses. And though he "hid himself" [in the sense of "did not advertise his powers"], he did so in order to promote better human relationships.

86. FY 5:12–13. The same phrase is used in THC "Hsüan wen" 9/2b (p. 1029b). See also FY 1:3; THC "Hsüan li" 7/6a (p. 1019a); and "Hsüan yi" 9/4a (p. 1031a), which talk of the sages becoming one with the triadic realms of Heaven-Earth-Man.

87. THC8/A1. Numerous other examples exist in the THC, for example, THC20/F2: "The model must be internalized"; and THC40/A4, which talks of internalized standards.

88. THC "Hsüan ying" 7/9a (p. 1022a) says that the divination process makes plain to the petitioner his own "heart's desire."

89. *Analects* 2/11 (Waley, 90). The German philosopher Schleiermacher makes much the same argument about the hermeneutical enterprise, when he compares it to the "reproduction of the original production" found in the fine arts. For further information, see Connolly, p. 11.

90. This may in fact be one of the few ways to teach virtue. See Nivison (1988), p. 414–15. The early Chinese assume that goals will change with increased understanding.

91. Hall, p. 213, objects to the terms "fate" and "destiny," arguing that those terms imply a "transcendental" force. Along with D. C. Lau (1963) and Graham (1967), I argue that *ming* means something beyond one's control. See below.

92. *Analects* 20/2 (Waley, 233). For various interpretations of the phrase *chih ming*, see Mori Mikisaburō, pp. 35–41; and Kanaya Osamu, pp. 136–66. Three translation possibilities exist: (1) "to understand [and obey] orders" of the ruler, (2) "to know [and accept] destiny as Heaven's Decree," and (3) "to know the Heaven-decreed [nature]," in which lie both the individual's orders and his potential from Heaven. Most commentators and intellectual historians take the phrase in the second sense, although some find the other senses more plausible.

93. CYYT 40/Hsia A/4 (Wilhelm, 295). The same phrase is used in FY 3:7. Traditionally, "understanding *ming*" is linked with freedom from certain kinds of worry and with inner contentment. More will be said about this below.

94. THC "Hsüan shu" 8/1a (p. 1023a). Compare CYYT 44/Hsi A/12 (Wilhelm, 324), which talks of "exhaustively presenting the circumstances of All-under-Heaven" through the hexagrams. Cf. *ibid.*, 41/Hsi A/5 (Wilhelm, 300), which defines "divination" as "exhaustively presenting the numbers and knowing the future."

95. An emphasis on the choice of an auspicious time for initiating activity is noticeable in most, if not all, aspects of divination and the consultation of oracles. I am indebted to Michael Loewe for this reminder.

96. See, for example, Hall, pp. 208ff., which talks of the fluidity of *ming* (p. 215); T'ang Chün-i (1962), p. 214; (1963), pp. 42, 48; Graham (1967), esp.

pp. 215, 255; and Moran (1983), p. 34ff. (esp. pp. 36, 41). Finally, note that Pankenier (1990a) associates *ming* with cyclical occurences in the sky.

97. Of course, we experience similar difficulties when we talk about fate. Early Chinese philosophy differs mainly in its presumption that the gods, even Heaven itself, are bound by cosmic norms. (Folk religion, in contrast, envisions gods who are as liable to change and corruption as their human counterparts; the gods of folk religion can be bought.)

98. Much of the work of Raoul Birnbaum speaks to this issue. I have put "schools" in quotation marks to indicate my own distrust of the attempt by many scholars to pigeonhole the works of various thinkers into different "schools," including Confucianism, Taoism, Legalism, and Mohism. Yang Hsiung himself was always careful to discuss individual philsophers; at no point in either the THC or the FY does he appear to envision close links between members of a "school." Lao tzu and Chuang Tzu, for example, are treated separately in the FY, though the two masters have often been lumped together as "Taoists." Mencius and Hsün tzu are also treated separately, rather than as "Confucians." At the same time, we must remember that well before Yang's time, thinkers had been identified as members of a particular philosophical "line" (*chia* 家, literally "family"), thanks to Ssu-ma T'an's 司馬談 (d. 100 B.C.) famous bibliography included in SC 130. My own work suggests that Yang was openly eclectic; he admitted to "taking" (*ch'ü* 取) numerous concepts from thinkers outside the Confucian "school" identified by Ssu-ma T'an. See FY 4:10, for example. For more on the erroneous appellation of "schools," see Sivin (1978), esp. pp. 312–16; and Loewe (1982), 7–11.

99. Mencius uses competing definitions of *ming*. See *Mencius* 1B/14; 5A/6 (Lau, 71, 145) for *ming* as just reward; *ibid.*, 5A/8 (Lau, 147) for *ming* as predestined; *ibid.*, 2B/13; 7B/38 (Lau, 94, 204) for *ming* as cyclical phenomena. This is pointed out in Fu Ssu-nien, pp. 150–4. For a single passage, see CCYT 165/Wen 13/3 *Tso* (Legge, 264), where the king speaks of *ming* as "vocation" while his counselors take *ming* in the sense of "lifespan." This passage is frequently cited in Han. See, for example, SY 1/9b.

Part of our confusion (and possibly theirs?) stems from the poverty of metaphors given for *ming* in Han and pre-Han texts. Metaphors help us determine the exact connotation of words like "Decree." In the early Sung period, for example, a new mercantile and banking mentality spoke of fate in terms of loans and reimbursements to the celestial treasury. For this information, I am indebted to Anna Seidel (private communication, March 1990).

100. HS 30:1721 states that the *Ts'ang Chieh* abecedarium that Yang studied contained "many old characters." Yang also, of course, studied surviving linguistic forms for the compilation of his famous dialect dictionary, the *Fang yen*, which in turn influenced the *Shuo wen*. See Serruys (1959); and Ma Tsung-huo.

101. MTYT 52/35/75 quotes ancient bronze inscriptions, though it is unlikely that people in Han times knew many Shang or Western Zhou bronzes. There are also passages in the *Documents* that appear to reproduce verbatim early bronze inscriptions. I am indebted to Laura Hess (presently at the University of Washington) for this reference.

The archaic form of *ling* shows a man kneeling down below a mouth turned downward. Cf. the character for "flute." See Serruys (1984), p. 667. The archaic pronunciation for *ling* was "mliang." From this, two separate pronunciations and characters evolved because the m was voiceless. SW2A/9a recognizes that *ming* came from *ling*.

102. T'ang Chün-i (1963), p. 195, makes this observation. As Mori Mikisa-burō, pp. 7–22, points out, however, the idea of an external mandate shaping the course of individual life appears in both the *Documents* and the *Odes* well before the term *ming* is employed for it. It is even possible that the formulation of the T'ien-ming doctrine by the founders of the Chou state was itself a response to the more popular view, sometimes preserved in the *Odes*, of Heaven as cruel and unpredictable (194/1, for example). See *ibid.*, pp. 10–11. The *Documents*, which originated at court, tends to be far more complacent in its belief that fate is tied to virtue. See *Documents*, "Chiu kao," par. 11 (Legge, 408–9; Karlgren, 45); and "Hsien-yi," par. 1 (Legge, 214; not in Karlgren), for example.

103. The oracle bone inscription form of *te* 德 ("virtue") shows a bulging eye looking downward under a straight line. Apparently the eye is a semantic element and the straight line is an etymon. The oracle bone character refers apparently to "visitations" designed "to look straight" at current conditions or "to look to straighten [rebellious situations]." In Chou times, the element "to straighten" comes to mean "to exert charismatic influence" or "virtue." For further information, see Hsü Chung-shu, pp. 168–69, 1385; Serruys (1981), p. 359 (greatly expanded in a private communication dated November, 1991).

104. Eno, p. 23 writes instead, until "the virtue of the ruling house . . . declined beyond a critical level."

105. I use Heaven or T'ien interchangeably in both these senses, since early Chinese philosophers never made it their chief concern to identify Heaven's character definitively, surprising as their relative indifference may seem to inheritors of the Western monotheistic tradition. (Eno, p. 5, mistakenly concludes from this that Heaven is not a key concept in Confucianism.) I find no clear indication in the works of Confucius, Mencius, Hsün tzu, or Yang Hsiung that Heaven is seen as an anthropomorphic, interventionist, or transcendent god. References to Heaven's acting, seeing, and so on fall into the category of conventional piety, just as a modern atheist may cry out, "Heaven help us" or "Oh, God" when witnessing a tragedy. Passages in Yang Hsiung's writings talk of gods and ghosts, but at one point Yang Hsiung admits that he is unsure whether to believe in them. See THC50/A8; THC52/A7; THC62/F7; FY 10:28. This skepticism is not necessarily true for the earlier period or for all thinkers. See, for example, Couvreur (1916), pp. xxii–xxvi; Kanaya Osamu, pp. 141–46.

106. CCYT 328/Hsiang 29/*fu* 8 (Legge, 551), for example, applies the concept of T'ien-ming to the tenure of the minister Tzu-ch'an 子産. By the time of the Confucian *Analects*, the term means the decreed lifespan, vocation, or innate purpose (in Aristotelian terms, the "final cause") even in the case of commoners.

107. Obviously, this kind of confusion exists as much in our tradition as in that of the early Chinese. The Protestant ethic tends to blur the distinction between moral goodness and material wealth. What's more, the term "the good life" is applied equally to Socratic inquiry and to consumerist yuppiedom.

108. Graham (1989), p. 107.

109.   Scholars disagree over the date when the character *hsing* is first used to signify "human nature." See Fu Ssu-nien, *passim*; and Mori Mikisaburō., pp. 12–13; 19–20.

110.   For one example of the confusion of the internal and external character of *ming*, see *Documents*, "Shao kao" par. 19 (Karlgren, 51; Legge, 431), where it is said that Heaven decrees wisdom, good or ill luck, and length of the individual lifespan.

111.   The Chinese use many different terms to describe the "good life." LHCC, for example, calls it the *ming* that is "generous" (*hou ming* 厚命) or that brings "riches" (*fu ming* 福命). See LHCC 17:362 (Forke, II, 11); and *ibid.*, 30:590 (Forke, I, 79).

112.   See *Analects* 12/5 (Waley, 163), where the disciple Tzu-hsia says, "Death and life are the decree of Heaven; wealth and rank depend upon the will of Heaven." However, Mo tzu (480–390 b.c.) already denounces the followers of Confucius as fatalists. See MTYT 62/*39*/10 (Watson, 126). The final list comes from CTYT 14/*5*/43–44 (Watson, 73; Graham, 80).

113.   This view corresponds with Wang Ch'ung's thesis, which, roughly summarized, states that human success (defined in conventional terms) depends upon two accidents: (1) the extent to which an individual is endowed with *ch'i*; and (2) successive accidents by which other, possibly better endowed entities are encountered. See LHCC, esp. *p'ien* 1–5 (Forke, I, 145–55, 313–317; II, 30–42). I am indebted to Michael Loewe for this neat formulation of Wang Ch'ung's philosophy.

114.   For Tsou Yen 鄒衍, see Needham, II, 232–44.

115.   For this, see THC18/A7 and THC57/A3.

116.   See Rubin, p. 96, on this point. Chuang tzu, of course, is the possible exception to this characterization.

117.   This slogan, implicit in the *Analects* but explicit in the *Mo tzu*, was soon taken up by many philosophers, including Hsün tzu. See Graham (1989), pp. 292–95.

118.   The most readable synopses in English on the debates over human nature are to be found in Schwartz, pp. 257–78, 295–302; Graham (1989), pp. 111–32; 235–67; Yearley; and Nivison (n.d.).

119.   See Kudō Toyohiko; and Ku Chieh-kang (1930?).

120.   For further information, see Mori Mikisaburō, pp. 203–19; and Fu Ssu-nien, pp. 179–80.

121.   The notion that Han represented a new dispensation influences many Western Han works.

122.   For the distinction between the documentary and rhetorical styles of argumentation, see Birdwhistell, pp. 9–10.

123.   Yang Hsiung uses the character *ming* in the following passages: THC1/A4; THC8/A2; THC26/A9; THC43/A7; THC59/A5; THC59/A9; THC 61/A6; THC "Hsüan li" 7/5b (2x) (p. 1018b), 7/6b (p.1019b); and THC "Hsüan shu" 8/1a (p. 1023a). The character unequivocally refers to the "king's commands" in THC8/A2; THC59/A5; and THC61/A6.

124.   *Analects* 9/1 (Waley, 138). Cf. 5/12 (Waley, 110). This explanation is given by most traditional scholars. See, for example, the commentaries by Ho

Yen and Chu Hsi. No commentary on this passage predating Yang Hsiung now survives. Yang Hsiung's exact contemporary, Pao Hsien 包咸, commented, "Since one can seldom reach it, therefore one talks little [of it]." On a parallel passage (7/20), K'ung An-kuo 孔安國 (fl. 128–91 B.C.) commented, "Perhaps it is of no benefit to moral transformation [to speak of it]; perhaps it is what he cannot bear to speak of." See MKH, III, 1606, 1574.

125.   See FY 5:13 for the "immersion into the mind" (*ch'ien hsin* 潛心) of the sage Confucius by his worthy disciple Yen Hui 顏回. An earlier passage (FY 5:12) promises that the individual's mind becomes divine (*shen*神) through this process of immersion.

126.   FY 6:17.

127.   THC1/A9. Cf. THC41/A9, which says that change "cannot be curbed."

128.   THC "Hsüan li" 7/6b (p. 1019b). Cf. HS 87A:3515 (Knechtges, 13). Cf. HTYT 83/22/6 (Dubs, 282; not in Knoblock), which defines *ming* as "what one meets at the time." See also Yang Liang's 楊倞 commentary ([SPPY] 16/2a). HNT 10/12b repeats this definition word for word. LSCC 2/11b, following CTYT 40/13/ 79, defines *ming* as "what cannot be changed." SY 17/2a defines *ming* as "what coincides [with present action] or not."

129.   Three Appraisals in THC24 (2, 7, and 8) reiterate the same message that "Heaven fixes the time."

130.   LHCC 1:3:13 (Forke, I, 148), which quotes the characters *yü pu yü, ming yeh* 遇不遇命也 taken from Yang's own biography (HS87A:3514; Knechtges, 13). However, Yang means, "Whether or not he [i.e., the gentleman] meets [the opportune time] is a matter of the Decree." Yang Hsiung concludes from this that humans should desire virtue, which is always attainable, rather than conventional goods, which may be unobtainable. (Cf. SY 17/2a.) Basically, Wang Ch'ung's citation out of context distorts Yang's view, in an attempt to justify Wang's quite different views on predestination.

131.   According to THC14/A4, "To be sharp about timing" leads to the situation where everything is done properly. Cf. FY 10:29, which describes "action being careful about Time" as the human contribution to success.

132.   See, for example, FY 10:34; THC41/F9; and THC "Hsüan wen" 9/2a (p. 1029a): "The noble man in old age has reached the end of his time." Certain healers and magicians in Han times would have disagreed. See Yü Ying-shih (1965).

133.   See THC16/A4, for example. Numerous other passages could be cited.

134.   THC23/A9.

135.   THC8/A9, for example.

136.   *Analects* 12/5 (Waley, 163). Confucius, after all, is not seen to dispute this view.

137.   My suggestion tallies with one made earlier by Ch'en Jen-hsi 陳仁錫 (1579–1634), who says in commentary to THC-SB 7/4a, "Master Yang liked to use unusual characters. If [the characters used] are not familiar to the ear and eye, an intensive light (*ching kuang* 精光) is born from them."

138.   Readers should not confuse these four factors (Virtue, Tools, Position, and Time) operating in human existence with the four aspects to consider in interpreting a divination result (stars, times, numbers, and phrasing).

139. "Virtue" and "ritual" are near synonyms for Yang Hsiung. See FY 4:10, which says that virtue cannot exist without ritual. FY 7:21 equates virtue, ritual, and Goodness. For more information about ritual, see THC48 and the section on ritual in Key Terms. For a synopsis of Chinese ideas about the relation of Goodness to hierarchy, see Fingarette; and Bauer, esp. pp. 21, 53.

140. For example, FY 10:29 defines man as duty-bound to "be cautious in his movements in regard to Time."

141. Ritual insists that even the good act can have disastrous effects if carried out under inappropriate circumstances. See, for example, THC8/A5, which says that virtuous remonstrance can do good only if the timing is right. (Eliade reminds us, of course, that certain rituals not only mark, but make time through the course of the year.) Many other examples could be culled from the THC. For one example from the FY, see FY 6:17, which talks of righteous action (in this case, the refusal of high office) in terms of timing. Mencius, of course, had tried to get at this disjunction between virtue and opportunity when he speaks of "proper destiny" as opposed to "destiny" (7A/2; Lau, 182).

142. *Analects* 6/22: "Seek for *jen* 仁 ; then you will get it" (Waley, 126). *Mencius* 2A/2 (Lau, 80), 3A/1 (Lau, 95), 4A/2 (Lau, 118), 4B/32 (Lau, 136), 6A/6 (Lau, 163), 6B/2 (Lau, 172), and 7A/4 (Lau, 182), for example, also presume that all humans have the capacity to become sages. For Hsün tzu, see HTYT 89/*23*/62-64 (Dubs, 307; not in Knoblock). Cf. FY 1:2–3.

143. CYYT 44/Hsi A/11–12 (Wilhelm, 318, 323) identifies "Tools" as what has forms (i.e., is visible on earth) available for man to use. FY 9:26 explicitly calls the Classics "great tools") (*ta ch'i* 大器). On the use of boat, oxen, and oars, see THC3/A7, A9; THC20/A8; on ministers as "props" to the ruler, see THC7/A8; on the torch, see THC12/A4; on acupuncture and medicine, see THC15/A7; on rhetoric as the "instrument (also *ch'i* 器) of speech," see THC30/A4. Conversely, the improper use of tools creates numerous problems. E.g., THC4/A3 speaks of the lock without the bolt; THC20/A5 speaks of the disadvantages of evil patrons. This talk of tools highlights Yang Hsiung's indebtedness to Hsün tzu. Still, I by no means want to imply that Yang Hsiung has what may be called an instrumental view of knowledge and wisdom.

144. THC "Hsüan ying" 7/8a (p. 1021a). Cf. THC62/A2-A3 on the need for divination; THC72/A8; and THC12/A2.

145. There exists a possible exception to Yang's vision of *ming*: men who lived prior to the time of the antique sages were denied access to the tools necessary for civilization, simply by virtue of timing. (Their position is in some respects comparable, presumably, to those who languished in Limbo prior to Christ's redemptive act.) For this reason, they are repeatedly characterized in Yang's work (in a twist on the primitivist vision of certain Taoists) as stupid and benighted. It is not at all clear, however, that Yang Hsiung can conceive of the truly amoral life. Graham (1989), p. 61, says this about Chinese thinkers in general.

For the primitivist vision, see, for example, HS 87B:3580 (Knechtges, 57); FY 4:10–11; and THC "Hsüan ying" 7/8b (p. 1021b). Of course, in the period prior to civilization, no ranks had been devised as yet, so Yang's explanation of Position can only apply to that period after the invention of basic social organization.

146. According to FY 4:11–12 and FY 7:21, the essence of practical wisdom

is to acquire through Virtue the Tools which will be needed once Time (i.e., opportunity) comes. See THC26/A6 on the timely use of Tools.

147. Sec, for example, THC71/A2, 8; and THC8/A1.

148. THC20/A8 and THC28/A6. See below.

149. FY 1:3 (2x) and FY 12:39. Numerous passages to this effect occur in the THC.

150. See THC2/A2; THC3/A5; THC9/A3,5 for example. Position is by no means synonymous with Virtue, as is made clear in THC32/A5 and THC67/A5, for example.

151. I view Position as a separate category from Tools (although at times it is hard to distinguish the two categories in Yang's work) on the basis of passages like THC3/A5, which shows strength residing in Position itself, regardless of practical wisdom and expertise.

152. Yang Hsiung, of course, incorporates the ideas of various Legalist authors here. Among the best treatments of Legalist writings on Position are Creel; Thompson; Rubin; Vandermeersch; and Hsiao Kung-ch'uan, pp. 368–468.

153. See FY 8:22–23; and *ibid.*, 10:30.

154. See THC5/A3 and THC46/A5, for example.

155. Readers unfamiliar with this term should consult the Key Terms section.

156. For such changes, see THC28/A2 and THC 51/A5; cf. FY 6:17–18.

157. Sivin (1990), p. 3; cf. Needham (1964).

158. THC "Hsüan wen" 9/2b (p. 1029b).

159. The example is my own, not Yang's.

160. The Greeks had two words for time: *chronos* (the successive passage of things in time) and *kairos* (the right time for things to occur). Yang Hsiung, following general Chinese usage, used the same word for both. It should be noted that "timeliness" does not appear in the early Line Texts for the 64 hexagrams of the *Yi ching*, but only later in the *t'uan*.The principle of timeliness becomes more important in the "Mean," par. 2 (Legge, 386).

161. THC24/A2 and THC24/A7 affirm that it is Heaven (or more accurately, the Mystery) that "imposes" time limits. Time and Heaven are shown to be inextricably bound in the THC "Hsüan li" and "Hsüan ying" autocommentaries.

162. See THC24/A2, for example. The emphasis, then, is not polytheistic (where different gods represent different goods) but polychronistic (where different times require different good acts).

163. CYYT 40/Hsi A/3; 45/Hsi B/2 (Wilhelm, 294, 328); THC41/A2; "Hsüan li" 7/6a (p. 1019a).

164. For Yang Hsiung, the single best proof of the identity of the triadic realms is ritual, which attempts to make each human activity no less emblematic of cosmic order than the regular succession of the seasons. Cf. Clark, pp. 21–26, on the integration of the natural and the sacred in religious tradition in general.

165. For the connection between virtuous acts and Position, see THC5/A3 and THC23/A6, for example. One's store of Virtue, however, may be inherited from ancestors. See THC60/A8, A9.

166. See, for example, FY 6:17.

167. For the phrase, "ready for use," see THC1/A3. Numerous passages sup-

port this view, including FY 4:11; FY 5:12–13; THC1/A5; THC4/A4; THC9/A7; THC26/A6; THC34/A7; and THC36/2.

168. FY 10:30. See also THC17/A5. Eno rejects the notion that the pre-Han Confucians were "devoted to seeking governmental responsibilities" (p. 31). Even if Eno is right, Han Confucians certainly were.

169. See Mori Mikisaburō, ch. 9, citing passages like CTYT 14/5/44; and *ibid.*, 41/16/14. In THC28/A2 Yang Hsiung affirms the links between Time and change.

170. THC 27/A3. Cf. FY 6:17–18, which laments Time's passing; and FY 9:25, which characterizes Time's passing as "quick as a flash." FY 6:17–18 probably borrows from Tung Chung-shu's prose-poem on the scholar's frustrations. See Pankenier (1990b), p. 443, fn. 58.

171. THC9/A7 shows a situation in which Time allows the man of Virtue who has the Tools at hand to gain a powerful Position. But even good Tools will not work if the Position is wrong. See THC33/A4 and THC36/A3, for example. THC10/A5, A9; THC30/A3; THC38/A9 show that high Position is not enough for security if the individual fails to follow the path of Virtue. THC61/A1 and THC78/A6 show that even the noble man can fail if other factors are against him. Under certain circumstances, however, the wise man can "ride out the time" until better days come. See THC79/A7.

172. This is why Yang Hsiung credits dramatic turns of fate to the interaction of T'ien and Man. See FY 10:29. The conventional "good life" in early China was equated with the Five Felicities of the *Documents*, as listed in "Hung fan," par. 33 (Legge, 343; Karlgren, 35).

173. THC36/A2; hence, the emphasis on "knowing Time" as one key to success. THC14/A4 and THC17/A1, for example, show the need to align oneself with cosmic forces. Cf. HS 87B:3572 (Knechtges, 51), where Yang lists various people who gained high Position because the Time was right. The flip side of this rule is Yang's dictum that no time is inherently good when the act is evil. See THC "Hsüan wen" 9/2a (p. 1029a); THC28/A9; THC29/A6, for example. THC60/A8 suggests that whenever Virtue and Time are in direct conflict, bad timing overcomes and ill luck ensues.

174. This is one explanation for Yang's phrases attributing bad luck to Heaven. See, for example, THC18/A1, A2, A3, A8, A9; THC24/A7; THC38/A6, A9; THC53/A5; THC57/A1; THC69/A9; and THC73/A8. (The other explanation, of course, is that Yang uses set phrases empty of religious content.)

175. Men of Han largely ignored the late 3d century B.C. *Ho Kuan tzu* 鶡冠子, which argues, "The seasons call up and cast down and take each other's places without uniformity; to imitate the seasons would be inconsistency." See Graham (1989), 215.

176. See THC24/A2; THC41/A2; and THC "Hsüan li" 7/5b (p. 1018b), for example.

177. CCFL 11/42/2b, translation from Needham, II, 250 (following E.R. Hughes). Such views are also attributed to Tung in his biography in HS 56.

178. For Han dynasty magicians, see Ngo; DeWoskin. Some of the more outrageous claims are associated with the apocryphal texts attached to the *Changes*. However, in the *Changes* to "*chih ming*" is to understand how to adjust

one's conduct to the fairly predictable cycles of Nature so as to ensure lifelong good fortune. Many students of the *Changes* recognized the crucial difference in approach between understanding the phenomena of transition through greater empirical or technical precision and comprehending those phenomena through the intuition or illumination characteristic of the sage. As Sivin writes, "Sagehood led to accurate knowledge about the world around us, not vice versa." See Sivin (1990), p. 16; and Mori Mikisaburō, pp. 154 ff., for details. We should not forget that these two views of the *Changes* parallel two very different views of Confucius promoted in Han. According to one view recorded in the *Tso chuan* and elsewhere, Confucius' powers are those simply of the farsighted and good person. In the other view, found in the *Kuo yü* and elaborated in the apocrypha, Confucius consistently displays superhuman powers of comprehension. See Durrant, p. 10ff. This, in turn, relates to the question of whether noble men ever need to worry. For more on this, see the "Illumination" autocommentary.

179. The relation of part to whole was one concern of the Sophists. See Graham (1989), p. 87.

180. FY 5:14. Cf. THC "Hsüan li" 7/5b (p. 1018b); "Hsüan ying" 7/8b (p. 1021b); "Hsüan wen" 9/1b (p. 1029b): "So profound is it that none can fathom it." THC4/A2 makes the point that whatever is most precious is hidden away, like jewels. THC33/A1 says that there is "no gap" by which man can effectively glimpse any aspect of the spirit world. That gap is associated with Time in THC27/A3.

181. For Yang's remark that Time somehow houses even space (which "encloses" Heaven), see THC "Hsüan li" 7/5b (p. 1018b). Cf. THC13/A3; THC28/A2.

182. THC "Hsüan kao" 10/4b (p. 1035b), in this context with reference to the divine. This argument differs from one that argues that Time in the natural world refers to physical regularities while Time as "human opportunity" depends at least in part upon the actions of inherently irregular beings, other humans.

183. FY 5:13; "Hsüan ying" 7/8b (p. 1021b). Whatever can be seen is liable to decay as it operates in the world of phenomenal change. See THC63/Head.

184. E.g., THC18/A2.

185. See Needham, II, 257–59 for this Principle of Masking by the Five Phases. THC49/A1 pictures the Tao acting like waves.

186. THC "Hsüan t'u" 10/1a (p. 1032a).

187. With a few Appraisals, it is hard to be certain of Yang's meaning, since the degree of compression in his four-character lines makes for occasional ambiguity. See, for example, THC9/A9; and THC17/A7. However, in the following cases, there is no doubt that an unfortunate intersection of personal and cosmic cycles, rather than a lack of Virtue, is to be blamed for poor luck: THC1/A9; THC18/A9; THC33/A9; THC35/A7; THC41/A9; THC49/A9; THC59/A9; THC59/A9; and THC80/F8. When this happens in the THC1/A9, the text may be imitating the last Line text in Hexagram 1 of the *Changes*, where the final yang line is said to be inauspicious. See CYYT 1/1/*shang* (Wilhelm, 375): "Arrogant dragon will have cause to repent./ For what is full cannot last."

188. See THC 1/A9 and THC24/A7, for example.

189. Yang indicates, however, that certain perceived disparities between conduct and fate are only temporary, rather than permanent. Men of Han im-

agined the cumulative weight of particular acts (both good and bad) eventually tipping the balance. Not every act will immediately elicit a response "swift as echo or shadow" (the typical Han phrase used to characterize Mutual Interaction between Heaven and Man), just as a single grain of sand added to a heavy weight might not tip a balance. The cumulative effect of good and evil acts by an individual, therefore, may not be felt until descendants inherit this "weight" in their patrimony of *ch'i*. See THC60/A8, A9. Cf. Pan Piao's 班彪 discussion on the destiny of kings in HS 100:4208-12 (*Sources*, 176–80).

190. THC39/A1 and FY 4:11 say that only constants are subjects fit for the study of emperors and kings. Cf. FY 8:23 ("The sages [only] speak of Heaven."); and FY 12:38 ("The sages' words are akin to Heavenly constants.").

191. FY 10:29 insists that Heaven depends upon Man for its completion.

192. For "human portents," see the Key Terms essay entitled "Yin-yang Five Phases Theory." The same term occurs in HTYT 63/*17*/33-35 (Dubs, 180; not in Knoblock), where it concerns the social welfare of the common people. This accounts for the focus on human roles in the *Mystery*.

193. FY 1:3 and FY 8:23, for example.

194. E.g., THC33/A5.

195. The phrase appears in FY 8:23 (2x); and *ibid.*, 13:40 (in a different context). Cf. Horace's *carpe diem*. In general, one finds remarkable similarities between Yang Hsiung and the Stoics in their respective writings on time and fate. I am indebted to William Mullen (Classics Department, Bard College) for this observation.

196. *Analects* 4/15 (Waley, 105). Cf. 15/24 (Waley, 98 [renum.]): "What you do not yourself desire, do not do to others." Graham (1989), pp. 20, 383, prefers to translate *shu* 恕 as "likening to oneself." His discussion is well worth reading.

197. Possibly the statement in the *Analects* most concerned with the precious character of time passing is *Analects* 9/17 (Waley, 142 [renum.]). HsinS 8/2b links the scholar's exertions with time's fleeting nature, but the passage appears to identify this association as Laotzuian. Similarly, there are numerous passages in the LSCC and HNT that mention Time, but most of these passages have a strongly Taoist flavor. See, e.g., LSCC 3:30, 14:153–56; and HNT 1:8–9, 2:31, 9:127–28, 10:162. I argue that the THC fully incorporates such notions in an integrated philosophy.

198. For *ai jih* in connection with filial piety, see FY 13:40.

199. THC 61/A6.

200. Ch. 1 of the FY and the prose poem "Dispelling Ridicule" both list frequent objections to Yang's view.

201. This attempt to argue by "the method of [discussing] advantages and disadvantages" (*ch'ang tuan* 長短) is typical of Han prose-poems, which inherited this device from the Warring States rhetoricians. See Kroll, esp. p. 124.

202. See FY 1:3; FY 3:7; FY 8:23; and THC50/A5, for example.

203. For Yang's emphasis on "greatness" over "smallness," see FY 4:12: "Whoever follows the great, acts the upright way. Whoever follows the small, acts the way of treason." Cf. FY 8:22–23; and THC "Hsuan ying" 7/8b (p. 1021b).

204. See, for example, THC24/A1.

205. Ch. 1 of the FY defines "study" as the dedicated pursuit of any particu-

lar course of action with the aim of achieving greatness and consequent happiness. FY 3:9 associates "singular practical wisdom" (*tu chih* 獨智) with sagehood.

206. On wealth, see FY 1:3 and FY 4:9; on factual knowledge, FY 7:19 and FY 12:38; on immortality, FY 12:39–40; on political power, FY 10:30–31.

207. FY 1:3–4 talks of the extension of charismatic power. Cf. numerous passages in the THC. Cf. *Analects* 20/2 (Waley, 233): "A gentleman can get work out of people without arousing resentment, . . . is proud but never insolent, inspires awe but is never ferocious."

208. THC "Hsüan wen" 9/2b (p. 1029b) shows the ruler acting this way, "pairing" analogues so that things "do not lose their order." Cf. THC "Hsüan li" 7/6b (p. 1019b). FY 2:6 and FY 5:16 both say the sage focuses upon only a few constant rules rather than the myriad details; FY 12:38 says that too much factual knowledge can make one muddleheaded. This argument, of course, draws upon the philosopher Chuang tzu's famous statement: "Your life has a limit but knowledge has none. If you use what is limited to pursue what has no limit, you will be in danger" (CTYT 7/3/1 [Watson, 50]).

209. *Analects* 7/22 (Waley, 127 [renum.]). Cf. THC12/A1, A2, A3; and FY 12:39.

210. Yang himself studied astronomy, yet FY 8:23 cautions against overconcern with the stars.

211. FY 1:2 explains that what distinguishes man from the beasts is "rites and duty" (*li yi*). Man becomes fully human only when he uses ritual.

212. See, for example, THC24/A6; THC33/Head; FY 3:7; and FY 5:13 (2x), which all describe this ideal state of "no gap." THC "Hsüan li" 7/7a (p. 1020a) also talks of the "myriad creatures bound together." FY 3:9 gives the rule: The wider the contact, the greater the entity. The phrase "no gap" is possibly borrowed from Chuang tzu, who uses it to describe the ideal stage before forms diverge. See CTYT 30/*12*/38 (Watson, 131). Yang Hsiung admits that he borrows from Chuang tzu the idea that Heaven-Earth-Man are a single system (FY 5:15). That separation is sign of regrettable weakness is the theme of THC66/Head; THC74/Head, A2;

213. THC13/A9.

214. THC "Hsüan li" 7/6b–7a (p. 1019b–20a). This description of the Tao recalls LT, ch. 77 (Lau, 139).

215. THC "Hsüan li" 7/6a (p. 1019a). Cf. THC36/A8; and THC41/A7, which use similar language.

216. For *kung* 公, see THC35/A7; THC39/A1; THC50/F6; and THC67/A9, for example.

217. Virtue's operation promotes a characteristic form of change, called "transformation" (*hua* 化), said to end in a thoroughgoing, lasting improvement accomplished without undue disturbance. For virtue's ability to bring about "continuous development without abrupt change," see THC "Hsüan li" 7/6b (p. 1019b); THC "Hsüan ying" 7/9a–9b (pp. 1022a–22b); FY 4:10; FY 12:38; and FY 13:40.

By definition, whatever is *shen* 神 ("divine") accomplishes major changes invisibly. For further information, see HTYT 7/3/27; *ibid.*, 84/22/35; CYYT 41/Hsi A/5; *ibid.*, 50/Shuo/5; and CCFL 6/19/7a. THC59/A1 and THC72/A2 are two of many THC passages to allude to these definitions of *shen* and *hua* 化. Cf. FY

5:12, which argues that the essence of *shen* is to "immerse oneself in Heaven and become it; to immerse oneself in Earth and become it; to immerse oneself in the sages' works and become a sage."

218.   E.g., THC1/A1; THC41/A3; THC77/Head, A5; and FY 3:9.

219.   Conflating two passages: THC "Hsüan li" 7/7a (p. 1020a) before the first break; after the break, *ibid.*, 7/5b (p. 1018b).

220.   THC "Hsüan li" 7/7a (p. 1020a) shows that all truly great entities are constant, while the phenomenal world is "without constancy" (*wu ch'ang* 無常).

221.   The concept of daily self-renewal is found repeatedly in the THC. The phrase *jih hsin* 日新 is related to good government in FY 9:25. Virtue "gets through" to Heaven in THC2/A6; there is a correspondence between Heaven's course and that of the virtuous in THC20/A4. Cf. THC26/A9.

222.   THC "Hsüan ying" 7/9b (p. 1022b). The possibility of continual, infinite accumulation of goodness is also expounded in FY 1:3; THC37/A9; THC57/A9; and THC "Hsüan kao" 10/3b (p. 1034b). THC60/A3–A4 contrasts the accumulation of virtue with other acquisitions, which are easily lost.

223.   These are the goals put forward in chapters 20 and 21 of the HFT, which purport to be commentaries on the *Lao tzu*. Yang Hsiung in FY 4:10 adopts the pun *te* ("virtue") = *te* ("to get") used by Han Fei, though he advises us to limit our getting to "getting Virtue." See below.

224.   For the phrase "snatch away," see THC33/A9 and THC52/A8. As to the second point, Yang usually regards lasting reputation as one of the sure gains of virtue. In FY 4:9 and 5:15, however, Yang Hsiung comments upon the unreliable rewards of fame's pursuit. The seeming contradiction can be resolved if we assume that Yang believes that good men will usually be vindicated by history.

225.   This is the argument of the first chapter in FY.

226.   THC10/A4.

227.   The attempt to define language more carefully in line with Confucius' call for the "rectification of names" is found throughout Yang's philosophical writings. FY 12:39, for example, argues that "advance should mean only advance in the Way, not in rank"; FY 4:12, that the word *fa* 法 should be reserved for the "model" presented by the sage kings of antiquity, rather than for Legalist theories or those of Chuang Tzu. The THC concern with this begins in Tetragram 1 (THC1/A7).

228.   Cf. *Analects* 2/18 (Waley, 92).

229.   E.g., FY 4:9 and FY 5:15.

230.   THC "Hsüan ying" 7/9b (p. 1022b). In the *Changes*' tradition, the claim that only moral action is truly auspicious dates back at least to the divination case of Nan-k'uai 南蒯 recorded for 530 B.C. in CCYT 378/Chao 12/8 *Tso* (Legge, 640). Note that good luck and virtue tend to be closely tied in the early tetragrams, which presume a generally favorable Time. See THC19/F8-F9, for example.

231.   FY and THC provide numerous examples showing that the individual harms himself by his own conduct. See, for example, FY 8:24; THC11/A3, A7; THC28/A7; THC29/A1, A6; THC34/A9; THC63/A7; THC71/A7, and so on. Contrast this with THC2/A3, which calls one's own conduct a "chief [i.e., not sole] determinant" of good luck and ill; and THC "Hsüan ch'ung" 7/3b (p. 1016b), which says that the sage "nurtures" good luck.

232. LSCC 20/8a.

233. THC11/A3; THC18/A1; and THC12/A8, for example. Cf. FY 6:17. Yang spoke from experience. His biography in HYKC 10A:130 particularly mentions his equanimity in poverty.

234. YWLC 35:628-89 (Knechtges, 106).

235. THC "Hsüan li" 7/6b (p. 1019b). Cf. FY 9:25, defining benevolent government as one that makes it profitable to be good; and FY 3:9, arguing the inherent advantages of following the Confucian Way of ritual. Here, of course, Yang Hsiung departs from Mencius, who objected to talking of Virtue and profitability in the same breath (*Mencius* 1A/1; Lau, 49). Yang Hsiung, in fact, borrows much from the Mohist logicians. See, for example, his definitions of good and evil reworking Mohist propositions A26, A27: "Benefit is what one is pleased to get. Harm is what one dislikes getting."

236. FY 3:7. Cf. the *Analects* 9/29 (Waley, 144 [renum.]): "He that is really good is not anxious; he that is really wise is not misled."

237. THC18/A8. Cf. FY 6:18.

238. This is the theme of Tetragram 24, which shows that real happiness is impossible without ritual. Cf. FY 1:1-2; FY 1:4; and THC7/A1, which tell of the joy that comes with goodness. For the same idea in the *Changes*, see Kao Huai-min, esp. p. 312.

239. See THC4/A6 for the phrase quoted. THC4/A8 associates violation with evildoing.

240. FY 1:2 links "being [completely] without worries" with the bestial state and with lack of learning. To be completely unafraid and unworried is also not a good thing because that description characterizes humans who lived prior to the sages in a world without social organization. See THC "Hsüan ying" 7/8b (p. 1021b) and notes to the translation. The earliest extant commentary to the *Analects* explains that the gentleman only does not "worry over [strictly personal] troubles." See MKH, III, 4:1578b, citing K'ung An-kuo 孔安國. FY 6:18 explains when the good person is worried. Cf. CYYT 48/Hsi B/6 (Wilhelm, 345): "Those [sages] who composed the *Changes* certainly had worries and cares."

241. FY 12:40.

242. FY 5:15 discusses the inability of some good men to win fame in their lifetime. FY 10:30 discusses the inability of the sage Confucius to become a dynastic founder since he had no feudal domain from which to build. Cf. FY 8:22 on the case of Confucius. FY 12:39 asserts that Yen Hui's 顏回 manifest virtue could not win him longevity. Cf. FY 11:36: "When the sage does not meet up with the proper time, he hides himself."

243. On the benefits of friendship, see FY 1:3.

244. Hence, the continual exhortations in the *Mystery* to yield. See also FY 3:7 and FY 6:7.

245. As THC "Hsüan wen" 9/1a (p. 1028a) says, only events that have not yet taken form "can generally be controlled." Numerous passages show "incurable" situations. See THC18/A9, for example. In certain cases, however, a change of heart can save the individual in the nick of time. See THC31/A9.

246. THC12/A1.

247. See THC18 devoted to "waiting."

248. THC25/A2.

249. THC "Hsüan shu" 8/1a (p. 1023a).

250. Yang Hsiung intentionally employs a divination manual on the model of that invented by the ancient sages in order to remind us of a simple truth: Divination with milfoil stalks started as an intuitive process that depended on the insight of the seer, not "an attempt to evade responsibility in the belief that mantic methods form a substitute for moral scruple and good judgment." See Loewe (1981), p. 48; and Loewe (1988), p. 23.

251. THC24/A2; THC21/A5, A7, A9; FY 1:4; and FY 3:7, for example, make the connection between "delight" and *"chih ming."*

252. See FY 8:24, where Yang argues that the sage seeks to know the larger patterns of the cosmos, rather than the details that delight the naturalist or pedant.

253. *Analects* 4/5 (Waley, 102). THC16 reckons "gain" and "loss" in terms of ritual.

254. *Analects* 2/11 (Waley, 90).

255. CYYT 39/Hsi A/2 (Wilhelm, 286). For further information, see Peterson (1982). Cf. LT, ch. 70 (Lau, 132).

256. The phrase comes from *Analects* 8/7 (Waley, 134).

257. FY 1:2.

258. FY 2:6 and FY 8:23.

259. THC "Hsüan ying" 7/8b (p. 1021b) defines a classic as a work "that cannot be added to or subtracted from." Cf. FY 5:13. HTYT 84/22/24–25 (Dubs, 292; Watson, 149) requires this of correct language: "The words of the gentleman are far-ranging and detailed, apt and to the point, varied and yet unified. . . . He makes certain that [his words and phrases] are sufficient to communicate his thoughts, and there he stops, for to try to force them to do more would be evil."

260. See FY 8:24; THC "Hsüan wen" 9/2b (p. 1029b).

261. FY 5:15.

262. See *Analects* 9/1 (Waley, 138); cf. *ibid.*, 14/36 (Waley, 189).

263. *Analects* 6/3 (Waley, 115 [renum.]); *ibid.*, 6/10 (Waley, 117 [renum.]); *ibid.*, 11/7 (Waley, 154); *ibid.*, 12/5 (Waley, 163); and *ibid.*, 14/36 (Waley, 189 [renum.]), all of which suggest that *ming* is "outside."

264. *Ibid.*, 16/8 (Waley, 206 [renum.]).

265. For early traditions that ascribe a preoccupation with time to Confucius, see Kao Huai-min, pp. 307–08.

266. *Mencius* 5A/6 (Lau, 145): *Ming* is "what happens though no person brings it about."

267. *Mencius* 7B/33 (Lau, 201). THC "Hsüan wen" 9/1b (p. 1028b) uses almost the same phraseology, but carefully adds that the individual awaits timely opportunity (*hou shih* 候時). On waiting, see THC18, a tetragram devoted to that theme. THC18/A8 emphasizes the cheerful equanimity with which the noble man regards his fate.

268. HTYT 83/22/6 (Dubs, 282). Cf. *ibid.*, 103/28/39 (not in Dubs or Knoblock).

269. Note that Yang Hsiung declared himself a disciple of Mencius, though apparently some contemporaries regarded Mencian doctrine with suspicion as

"heterodox." See FY 2:6 and FY 12:37. Yang Hsiung was far less admiring of Hsün tzu, though he appears to borrow often from him.

270. See Yearley. For Yang, see THC4/A5, for example.

271. Hence, the confusion over the significance of the term *li ming* 立命 ("establishing one's fate") in the *Mencius*. See Mori Mikisaburō, pp. 53ff.

272. See, for example, HTYT 103/28/37–41: "Noble men study broadly and plant deeply [yet] many do not meet with timely opportunity. . . . The noble man's study is not for [material] advancement. . . ."

273. Hsün tzu seems dimly aware of this, since his first chapter, entitled "Exhortation to Study," is the essay in which he most strongly links good fortune with right behavior. The Mohists clearly recognized this flaw in the arguments of certain Confucians. See MTYT, ch. 35–37 ("Contra Predestination").

274. It is also possible, of course, that he unthinkingly accepted prevalent ideas of his time, but this is unlikely in view of the critical way he assessed various philosophical texts. See FY 5:15 for Yang's statement that he has borrowed from Chuang tzu and Tsou Yen the idea of the unity of Heaven-Earth-Man.

275. FY 1:2 equates "seeing, hearing, talking, behaving, and thinking" with human nature, following the "Hung fan" chapter of the *Documents*. Yang apparently adapts this notion from CCFL 14/64/2b, which says the five human capacities are what the human receives as his individual *ming* from T'ien. Though the Mystery is the ultimate origin for human existence (and everything in the cosmos), there is no special stress in the *Mystery* on innate goodness in human nature. According to Yang Hsiung, both good and evil tendencies exist in the original endowment (See THC22/A1, A2; FY 3:7.). What matters is which tendencies one chooses to cultivate. For Yang, the original disposition is far less important than the "second nature," which may internalize the model of the sages, given proper teachers and books (FY 8:23). In FY 12:39, Yang links things to "natures" and humans to "goodness" (*jen*) in discussing their potential.

276. FY 3:7. FY 4:9 defines Tao as "connecting." FY 12:39 defines Confucianism in terms of "making connections between (*t'ung* 通) Heaven-Earth-Man." Cf. E. M. Forster's "Only connect."

277. FY 10:29.

278. CYYT 39/Hsi A/1 (Wilhelm, 280).

279. See, e.g., THC "Hsüan li" 7/7a (p. 1020a): "Now Heaven and Earth are placed; therefore, the noble and lowly are ranked." Cf. *ibid.* on the impossibility of things "changing their positions." See also THC "Hsüan kao" 10/3b-4a (pp. 1034b–35a): "Earth is a pit while Heaven is high."

280. See THC "Hsüan yi" 9/3b (p. 1030b) on differences in position, age, number, and responsibilities of humans.

281. THC "Hsüan yi" 9/3b (p. 1030b), which describes the natural order of Heaven-and-Earth as classifying things according to type so that things "do not lose their order."

282. See THC6/A7; THC14/Head; THC16/A9; THC32/A2; and THC "Hsüan ying" 7/9b (p. 1022b), for example.

283. FY 3:7 presumes an absolute correlation between preferring the great and doing the great. (This is a common way for early Confucian philosophers to discuss preferring the Good and doing the good.) Not to do the great shows that

one is confused about inherent greatness, according to Yang. See FY 10:26–27 on what is "true and false" (*chen wei* 真伪). See also a long passage in THC "Hsüan ying" 7/9a–9b (pp. 1022a–22b), which makes the the distinction between enlightened and benighted individuals.

284. Therefore, THC "Hsüan ying" 7/9b (p. 1022b) shows man to be *like* Heaven and Earth, the ghosts and gods, when he constructs a hierarchy of value.

285. Yang Hsiung concedes there may be some few innate sages. See FY 3:9, for example.

286. See FY 3:7 for the "mixed" endowment at birth. FY 8:23 defines the great man as one who "has no business with the small," then defines the "small" in terms of "whatever is not ritual and the Right (*li yi* 禮義)." Cf. THC "Hsüan ying" 7/8b (p. 1021b): "When what [an act] follows is great, then its embodiment will be vigorous. When what it follows is slight, then its embodiment will be meager." See THC "Hsüan yi" for a full catalogue of the most important civilizing inventions of the sages.

287. THC "Hsüan yi" 9/3a (p. 1030a).

288. Later Yang Hsiung would write more explicitly: "If I truly believe that life and death are equal, that poverty and riches are the same, that honor and debasement are comparable, then I take the sages' [teachings] as just so much noisy talk" (FY 12:38). Cf. FY 7:19, which portrays the debates of the Hundred Schools of philosophy as just so much "bickering."

289. FY 5:15, defending the THC. Cf. THC "Hsüan ying" 7/8b (p. 1021b), e.g., which states categorically, "The few by rule control the many; what lacks visible form [i.e., the Mystery] by rule controls what has form."

290. HsinS 1/8b associates this position with Yen tzu 晏子 (?–500 B.C.).

291. THC1/A9.

292. FY 12:40 before the break; FY 12:39 after.

293. *Ibid.*

294. FY 12:39.

295. *Ibid.*

296. HS 87A:3542 (Knechtges, 29).

297. HS57B:3571 (Knechtges, 50), followed by FY 3:7.

298. THC 10/A7.

299. I intend to devote a future article to comparing the views of Yang Hsiung, Liu Hsiang, and Wang Ch'ung on fate. For the Mohist critique of the Confucians, see footnote 273 above.

300. For the stars as directors of fate, see FY 8:23.

301. FY 10:28–30 considers dynastic change in this way.

302. For *li ming* 立命, see *Mencius* 7A/1–2 (Lau, 182), which is discussed in Mori Mikisaburō, pp. 53 ff.; Kanaya Osamu, pp. 98 ff.

303. Michael Loewe (private communication) points out that the Han claim to rule by T'ien-ming may have been comparatively recent in Yang Hsiung's time (50–40 B.C.?). During the reign of Emperor Ch'eng (ca. 12 B.C.), a certain Kan Chung-k'o 甘忠可 announced that the Han dynasty faced the need to receive a renewal of the Mandate of Heaven. See Loewe (1974), p. 278 ff.

304. Thanks to the excavated almanacs from Shui-hu-ti 睡虎地 (dated late 3d. c. B.C.), we have a good idea of the kinds of texts that Yang Hsiung argued

against. The two almanacs tabulate lucky and unlucky days of the month according to a 12-character standard formula. Many other Han texts talk of "days of avoidance" for certain activities, like planting fields and tailoring clothes. See Report A; Loewe (1988); and Kalinowski.

305. FY 12:39. The "technician" (*chi* 技) is skilled in only one specific art. In contrast, the "Confucian" (*ju* 儒) can lay claim to an integrated vision of the entire universe.

306. FY 8:23.

307. See YKC 15/2a (Pokora, 114).

308. CYYT 43/Hsi A/9 (Wilhelm, 315).

309. See above.

310. HS 87B:3577 (Knechtges, 54). Numerous passages in Yang's official biography, in an exchange of letters regarding his *Fang yen*, and in the *Hsin lun* (the work of his chief disciple, Huan T'an), testify to the vituperative attacks launched upon Yang Hsiung by Liu Hsin. On the other hand, Yang's biography in the *Han shu* says that Liu Hsin was one of the few contemporaries to respect (*ching* 敬) Yang Hsiung. See HS 87B:3583 (Knechtges, 59). Liu Hsin sent his own son to study "unusual characters" with Yang Hsiung.

311. FY 10:29.

312. For comparison, see PHT 8:327–29 (Tjan, II, 572–73) for three different types of *ming*. The same typology of *ming* appears in the apocrypha (based upon earlier folk beliefs?). See CIS, V, 49 (apocrypha to the *Analects*); and *ibid.*, IV(A), 55 (apocrypha to the *Ch'un Ch'iu*), for example. This typology was later criticized by Wang Ch'ung as unwieldy and self-contradictory. See LHCC, esp. *p'ien* 8–10 (Forke, I, 136–55).

313. See Peterson (1989); Hou Wai-lu (1957).

314. See THC10/A7.

315. FY 2:6; and THC "Hsüan yi" 9/4a (p. 1031a), based on CYTY 39/Hsi A/1 (Wilhelm, 286). Cf. THC "Hsüan wen" 9/2b (p. 1029b), which equates what induces weariness with lack of ability.

316. HS 87B:3585 (Knechtges, 60). For a complete list of commentaries on the THC, see Yen Ling-feng, V, 357–89.

Key Terms

1. The materials preserved in the Five Classics date from the 2d. millenium B.C. to Ch'in or even early Western Han (206 B.C.–A.D. 8). It also should be noted that these works were then revised and reworked later. Since at least the Sung, many scholarly works have focused on the difficult questions surrounding the Han redactions of all the Classics. In particular, the work of the 17th-century empiricists and the historiographical iconoclasts like Ku Chieh-kang in the early twentieth century have proven a valuable starting point in considering this messy business.

2. See Kennedy on this.

3. See, e.g., Hsü Shen, *Wu ching yi yi* (*Variant Intrepretations of the Five Classics*); Cheng Hsüan, *Po wu ching yi yi* (*Contra Variant Interpretations of the Five Classics*).

4. Powers (1978), *passim* believes that the swirling forms commonly identified as "cloud patterns" on Shang dynasty bronzes may refer to *ch'i*.

5. See GSR 517c. Cf. SW 7A:148a.

6. In Greek, *pneuma*; in Sanskrit, *prāna*; in Latin, *spiritus*; and in Hebrew, *neshamah*. All these words have the same "soulish" qualities as *ch'i*. By this comparison, I do not mean to imply the diffusionist view of culture. The comparison is drawn from Schwartz (1973), p. 44, n. 9; Libbrecht; and Mair (1990[b]), pp. 137–38.

7. All the characterizations of *ch'i* are drawn from *Mencius* 2A/2 (Lau, pp. 76–80), unless noted.

8. Much of this discussion is drawn from Sivin (1987), 46–53. Graham (1989), p. 314, prefers "Five Processes." Schwartz (1985), p. 181, objects to "energy," however.

9. Numerous articles and books are devoted to this topic. One of the best is that by Kurita Naomi.

10. For further information, see Hatton. This tendency to envision basic stuff and its transformation in a unitary way is also found in the Stoics. See Sivin (1987), p. 47.

11. Mencius calls *ch'i* "that which fills the body."

12. KT 16/49/3a–b (Rickett, 161).

13. See *Mencius* 2A/2 (Lau, 77); KT 16/49/6b (Rickett, 168).

14. KT, ch. 49 (Rickett, I, 151–79) discusses many of these arts.

15. See HFT 6:20:101–2 (Liao, I, 180–82), for example.

16. See *Mencius* 2A/2 (Lau, 80); 4B/32 (Lau, 136), for example.

17. Pankenier argues that an awareness of the causal relations between planetary phenomena, the cardinal directions, the seasons of observation, and their associated colors dates back to the 2d. millenium B.C., so that Five Phases theory won easy acceptance from the Han court and commoners. Five Phases theory is clearly the basis for the Shui-hu-ti *Book of Divination* (ca. 278 B.C.), though the theory was apparently incorporated somewhat later into Confucianism. See Kudō Motoo, 25–26; Ku Chieh-kang (1930); Loewe (1988).

18. Sivin (1987), pp. 72–80 explains why these other translations are not satisfactory.

19. LT, ch. 40 (Lau, 101).

20. *Documents*, "Hung fan," par. 5 (Legge, 325–26; Karlgren, 30).

21. Some of the most frequently cited correlations can be found in Needham, II, 262–63 (Table 12).

22. Yang, of course, makes continual reference to these systems in his Appraisals as well. See, for example, THC14/A6; and THC52/A6,8.

23. See Kroll, p. 125. Cf. Ricoeur's writings on "primary symbols."

24. Reding (1986a, b).

25. I have connected *Analects* 13/3 with *ibid.*, 12/11 (Waley, 171, 166).

26. HTYT 63/17/33-35 (Dubs, 180; Watson, 84).

27. See Robin Yates, cited in Ames (1987), p. 210.

28. See, for example, CCFL 1/4b (Gassmann, 13).

29. Ode 55/1 (Legge, 92)

30. *Analects* 4/6 (Waley, 103).

31. See FY 3:7.
32. I have connected *Analects* 1/5 (Waley, 85) with *ibid.*, 1/7 (Waley, 84).
33. HTYT 12/5/3 (Dubs, 67; Knoblock, 234).
34. FY 3:7.
35. Ode 65/1,2; 123/1,2; 145; 149; and 175/1–3, for example.
36. *Mencius* 3A/5 (Lau, 105). Cf. CTYT 18/6/75.
37. See, for example, *Mencius* 2A/2 (Lau, 76–80).
38. THC17/F7.
39. "Mean," par. 1 (Legge, 384). Cf. HTYT 85/22/60–61 (Dubs, 294–95).
40. Another definition of *chung*.
41. HTYT 80/21/34 ff. (Dubs, 267-8). Cf. *ibid.*, 81/21/67 (Dubs, 271).
42. See THC24/A6.
43. Fingarette, pp. 7–10.
44. Graham (1989), 20.
45. See FY 4:9–11 for these points in Yang Hsiung.
46. CCYT 69/Chuang 23/3 *Tso* (Watson, 57; Legge, 105). Cf. *Analects* 1/7 (Waley, 84–85).
47. However, the character for "cowrie" may be an abbreviation for "pledge," "offering," or gift." Consult SW 3B:69b, citing Ching Fang 京房; Nivison (1989). For a good summary of the early history of the character, see Kunst, pp. 200–11; Serruys (1981), p. 361; and *Shinjigen*, p. 144.
48. The stability of the tripod is the subject of several anecdotes recorded in early texts. This brings to mind the gloss of Chu Hsi 朱熹 (1130–1200), which equates *chen* with the "immovable." Chu Hsi's gloss reflects the influence of Chou Tun-i 周敦頤 (1017–73), who thought *chen* one aspect of cosmic creation.
49. Keightley (1978), p. 79; Takashima, p. 53; Kunst, 201. Similarly, the Greek sibyl used to sit on a cauldron.
50. For the reading of *chen* as "divine," see Shaughnessy, pp. 124–33. Serruys thinks that the early graph means (as verb) "to test" or (as adjective) "tested," "reliable."
51. The FW commentary to THC consistently glosses *chen* as *cheng*, presumably on the basis of CYYT 7/7/t'uan (Wilhelm, 421), which associates the two graphs. See also Nivison (1989), p. 124.
52. Kunst, p. 200.
53. *Ibid.*, p. 201. Shchutskii, p. 143, however, insists that *chen* in the *Changes* literature is a mantic formula whose real meaning has long been lost. *Chen* also functions as a technical term signifying the lower trigram in each hexagram.
54. See CYYT 1/1/yen. Cf. CTYT 89/32/26.
55. 貞 = 禎.
56. See, for example, Ode 268/1 (Karlgren, 146).
57. Waley, introduction to 1934; Kunst, p. 46.
58. HNT 16/22b.
59. See CCFL 4/9b, for example.
60. CYYT 45/Hsi B/1 (Wilhelm, 326)
61. *Analects* 15/36 (Waley, 200); HTYT 104/29/10, 13 (not in Dubs). HTYT 51/13/46 (not in Dubs or Knoblock) concedes that dramatic change may occasionally be necessary to achieve *chen*.

62. HTYT 8/3/44 (4) (not in Dubs; Knoblock, 180).
63. HsinS 8/4a, glossing it as *yen hsing pao yi* 言行抱一.
64. HsinS 8/4a.
65. See FY 6:17, for example, where Yang links *chen* with timely behavior. The same passage carefully distinguishes "correct" behavior from what "brings benefit."
66. THC *hsü* 序, recorded in WJL 1/1b (p. 947b).
67. See HNT 13/20a: "To be bound, manacled, or fettered, not to avoid [(literally, "taboo") situations giving rise to] his shame, this cannot be called *chen*." Cf. *Mencius* 7A/2 (Lau, 182).
68. For a general introduction to early Chinese poetic forms, see Hawkes (1959); Watson (1962); and Knechtges (1976).
69. For an example of what I call the classic form of the *Odes*, see Ode 1 entitled, "Kuan chü." The tetrasyllabic couplet form may also have been borrowed from a *fu* of Hsün tzu. Note that the political *fu* of Hsün tzu and Tung Chung-shu strictly coordinate change of topic and change of rhyme. See Pankenier (1990b), p. 437.
70. The same range of variation is found in the nearly contemporaneous YL. For further information, see Suzuki (1972).
71. See FY 2:5 and FY 3:8 for discussions on style.
72. In the *Yi ching*, certain hexagrams have extensive rhyme, the majority have some rhyme, and fifteen hexagrams have no rhyme at all (Kunst, p. 52). This variation is also found in the THC.

THE TETRAGRAMS

No. 1. Center

1. Often called the "Yellow Springs" in early literature.
2. *Hsin* 信 = *shen* 伸 ("to expand"), according to CYYT 46/Hsi B/3 (Wilhelm, 338).
3. *Ibid.*
4. The "center" is not only the tetragram title but the center in the Yellow Palace. See THC "Hsüan t'u" 10/2b (p. 1033b).
5. *K'un-lun* 昆侖.
6. THC "Hsüan li" 7/5b (p. 1018b).
7. CYYT 21/7/33 (Watson, 97).
8. Translation by A.C. Graham of CYYT 2/1/32: *p'ang po wan wu yi wei yi* 旁礡萬物以為一, in Graham (1981), p. 46. Cf. HS 87B:3576, following the annotation of Yen Shih-ku 顏師古.
9. Cf. THC "Hsüan kao" 10/3b (p. 1034b).
10. FW 1/4b–5a.
11. THC "Hsüan wen" 9/2a (p. 1029a).
12. CYYT 45/Hsi B/2 (Wilhelm, 328 ff.).
13. *Chen* 貞, which is usually glossed as *cheng* 正. See Key Terms. The term "mantic formulae" comes from Shchutskii, p. 143.
14. FW 1/5a.
15. CYYT 4/2/6 (Wilhelm, 15; Kunst, 243).

16. CYYT 4/2/*yen* (Wilhelm, 395) explains this in the following way: "When yin has aroused the suspicion of yang, the two are bound to fight because yang resents that [yin] lacks yang."

17. THC "Hsüan wen" 9/1b (p. 1028b).

18. SW 11B/245b.

19. CYYT 1/1/1 (Wilhelm, 7; Kunst, 241).

20. CCYT 132/Hsi 28/5 *Tso* (Watson, 60): "Young and old conduct themselves according to ritual. They are fit for use!"

21. THC "Hsüan wen" 9/1b (p. 1028b).

22. CYYT 2/1/1, 2, *yen* (Wilhelm, 379–80).

23. CTYT 59/22/45 (Watson, 241).

24. *Analects* 7/26 (Waley, 128 [renum.]).

25. THC "Hsüan wen" 9/1b (p. 1028b).

26. No two annotators agree about the message of this Appraisal; even the meanings of individual words become matters for debate. Probably this results from their basic disposition to read the Appraisal as either a Taoist or a Confucian document. Fan Wang, for example, sees the four aspects in the first line as yin (and therefore, evil), and so he gives a vaguely Taoist explication. Ssu-ma Kuang's reading draws on the "Elaboration," but in reading Sung Confucian ideas into the *Mystery*, it fails to capture the paradoxical flavor of Yang's original text.

27. For the phrase "nature and Decree," see Mori Mikisaburō, chapters 9 and 12.

28. Note that Earth specifically was the emblem of the Western Han dynastic house after 104 B.C.

29. FW 1/6a, possibly alluding to HsinS 9/11b. Cf. the same imagery in Ode 38/1 (Legge, 61).

30. For the same metaphor, see FY 9:27.

31. The spread of light obviously signifies the sage's "opening [the way] to enlightenment" for his fellow men. Yang Hsiung uses the same phrase *k'ai ming* 開明 in regard to moral enlightenment in FY 4:10.

32. For moon imagery, see Boltz.

33. For the same metaphor, see FY 8:24.

34. Serruys takes *k'uei* 魁 as "dominating," "heading over."

35. Literally, "The fully ripe, it he embraces."

36. Tentative translation. See below.

37. THC "Hsüan wen" 9/2a (p. 1029a).

38. For the "Great Plan," see Nylan (forthcoming).

39. THC "Hsüan wen" 9/2a (p. 1029a).

40. *Ibid.*

41. FY 4:10.

42. For this phrase, see *Analects* 13/3 (Waley, 171–72).

43. THC "Hsuan wen" 9/2a (p. 1029a).

44. For *ch'i*, see Key Terms. For early Chinese notions of the soul and the afterlife, see Yü (1987).

45. A yang Appraisal in general is supposed to be propitious. The picture is somewhat complicated here because the ninth Appraisal represents the final phase of the tetragram, which pertains to situations of extreme calamity. This

ambiguity brings to mind that of the final Line text to Hexagram no. 1 of the *Changes*, which Han commentators found unexpectedly baleful.

46. SMK 1/3b, citing *Documents*, "Hung fan," par. 33 (Legge, 340; Karl-gren, 35); and *Mencius* 7A/2 (Lau, 182).

47. THC "Hsüan wen" 9/2a (p. 1029a).

48. SMK 1/3b.

49. FW 1/6b.

50. THC "Hsüan wen" 9/2a (p. 1029a).

No. 2. Full Circle

1. I follow the punctuation of WJL. CPL 1/5a, however, reads *chou shen* 周神, meaning "divine in all directions." This is also preferred by Serruys because the scansion would be 4-4-4. That reading emphasizes the numinous quality of yang as it animates the myriad things. YTC 1/3a points to a pun here. The yang *ch'i* is not only "divine" (*shen* 神), but "unrolled" (*shen* 伸), as its circuit has come to an end.

2. For the early Chinese theory of suasive influence, see Knoblock, I, 177.

3. CYYT 46/Hsi B/3 (Wilhelm, 338). By analogy, the circle provides the model for the embryo in the womb, inside which the circulation of the breaths makes a closed circuit. See Kaltenmark, pp. 32–35.

4. The early Chinese, for example, took Heaven to be a perfect circle. For the early Greeks, I cite Parmenides, Fragment B5: "It is all the same from what point I begin, for I shall return again to the same point." Note that for the Han Chinese the circumference of the circle was 365 1/4 degrees (to match the number of days in the year), rather than 360 degrees.

5. For the importance of the concept of *kung* 公 ("fairness"), see Ames, p. 129 ff. For the Han association of the center with fairness, see Han glosses to the "Hung fan" chapter of the *Documents*, as discussed in Nylan (forthcoming).

6. LT, ch. 40 (Lau, 101); CYYT 16/24/3 (Wilhelm, 99; Kunst, 287).

7. CYYT 16/24/hsiang (Wilhelm, 505).

8. For this function, see *Documents*, "Shun tien," par. 8–9 (Legge, 36–37; Karlgren, 4–5); LC 5/21 (Legge, I, 216); 24/44 (Legge, II, 232); Geertz.

9. For this reason, many of the metaphors associated with the Return hexagram in Han *Changes* literature emphasize *t'ung* 通, which can be translated as "unblocking," "getting through," or "making contact." Cf. YL 2/14a.

10. *Mencius* 2A/2 (Lau, 76–80).

11. See, for example, YL 6/17b.

12. *Analects* 8/20 (Waley, 136-37). Cf. FY 4:9, which praises the Way practiced by King Wen of Chou as the "upright Way."

13. HS 87A:3516 (Knechtges, 13).

14. CYYT 16/24/t'uan (Wilhelm, 505).

15. Chih Yun 郅惲 letter to Wang Mang 王莽, cited in HHS 29:1025.

16. CYYT 48/Hsi B/6 (Wilhelm, 504).

17. Neither Legalist nor Taoist philosophers would agree that the mind or will of Heaven is revealed in tradition. Their position on the will of the people varies. To understand how extraordinary the early Confucian solution was, the

reader would do well to consider the contrasting case of Western philosophers. See Pocock (1984).

18. *Documents*, "T'ai shih, chung," par. 7 (not in Karlgren; Legge, 298).

19. *Analects* 4/15 (Waley, 105).

20. Reading *tu* 督 as *chung* 中, following SMK 1/3b. *Tu* literally refers to the center seam in the back of a cloak. See GSR 1031n.

21. See FW commentary.

22. CCFL 6/19/5b states that the emperor functions as "the pivot (*shu chi* 樞機) of all the myriad things [in creation]."

23. E.g., *Documents*, "Hsien yu yi te" and "Hung fan" chapters. FW 1/7a equates the phrase "without angles" and "having no [fixed] direction."

24. *Analects* 2/1 (Waley, 88).

25. See YTC 1/3a.

26. *Shih* 勢. For this, see Ames 65–107.

27. For the center seam, see CTYT 7/3/2 (Watson, 50).

28. *Documents*, "Hung fan," par. 14 (Legge, 331; Karlgren, 32).

29. Needham, III, 216–19.

30. Literally, "chief head."

31. This usage is attested for the pre-Han period in HTYT 32/10/20 (not in Dubs; Knoblock, 123). Alternately, it refers loosely to "comings and goings." See YL 7/21b.

32. Alternately, "A jade ring hangs down," reading GSR31g as 31a.

33. For the belt as symbol for self-restraint, cf. SY 19/3a.

34. Yang's focus on the waist, the center of the body, also implies the importance of the virtue of "centrality," for example.

35. For the association of belt and hook with officialdom, see *Analects* 5/7 (Waley, 108).

36. Ode 55/1 (Legge, 91). Cf. FY 12:27.

37. Ode 59/3 (Legge, 102), for example. If the girdlehook is also jade, that merely intensifies the auspicious character of the symbol. See Nagahiro.

38. For the seamless cycle of the cosmos, see THC "Hsüan li" 7/7a (p. 1020a). A classic metaphor compares the dynastic cycle to "running the finger along a jade circlet, for when [the cycle] is complete, there is a return to the base; when finished, a return to the beginning." See FSTY 1:4, for example.

39. The possessive pronoun *chüeh* 厥 is only used of a superior, usually Heaven.

40. Ssu-ma Kuang supports his analysis by alluding to passages in the "Doctrine of the Mean" that argue that few men will ever be able to attain, let alone sustain moral perfection. See "Mean," ch. 7, 14 (Legge, 388, 395). CF. CPL 1/6a.

41. For *lu* 廬 ("dwelling") as royal dwelling, see SY 12/4b. The "center of the country" (*t'u chung* 土中) is identified with the capital in numerous texts, including *Documents*, "Shao Kao," par. 14 (Legge, 428; Karlgren, 49); HsinS 3/7b.

42. See, for example, HFT 13:34:234 (Liao, II, 92). The carriage in the *Changes* symbol system also suggests great capacity and wealth. See CYYT 11/14/2(1), *hsiang* (Wilhelm, 459; Kunst, 267).

43. CYYT 29/47/4(6) (Wilhelm, 184; Kunst, 333) writes, "Troubled by the golden [or metal?] carriage."

44. CYYT 16/23/*shang*, *t'uan* (Wilhelm, 96).
45. The phrase is from CYYT 47/Hsi B/4 (Wilhelm, 341), cited by FW 1/7b. My reading borrows from YTC 1/3b.
46. "Mean," ch. 13/4 (Legge, 395). See also *Analects* 6/14 (Waley, 118); CYYT 32/52/*t'uan* (Wilhelm, 654).
47. YL 6/18a, for example, writes, "Eating the bread of idleness, . . . Salary not matched by [performance of] duties./ He will lose the carriage/ [And find] his dwelling torn down./ Quit the seat/ And move his residence. . . ."
48. Alternately, *chou* 周 can mean "to perfect" or "to sustain in every direction." See below.
49. See Neely, p. 15.
50. See the discussion on *hsin* 信 in Arthur Waley's "Introduction" to his translation of the *Analects*, pp. 43–44. Good faith was the patron virtue of the Han, since that dynasty was correlated after 104 B.C. with the center and the Earth phase.
51. See HTYT 7/3/26-28, 45 (not in Dubs; Knoblock, I, 177 translates it as "truthfulness"); "Mean," ch. 20/18 ff. (Legge, 413 ff.). See Knoblock, I, 166–67 for the importance of the term.
52. YTC 1/4a.
53. Following SMK 1/4a.
54. HTYT 8/3/45 (not in Dubs; Knoblock, I, 177).
55. Following CPL 1/4a; YTC 1/4a. FW 1/8a defines *feng* 豐 as *yin* 淫 ("excessive," "licentious").
56. The character *p'eng* 朋 depicts strung cowries, implying both similarity of type and near association. This interpretation differs from FW 1/8a, who glosses *p'eng* 朋 simply as "two." "Two," according to Fan, refers to the second appearance (after Appraisal 2) of agent Fire in Appraisal 7. The "great excess" (*feng yin* 豐淫) presumably then refers to an excess of Fire in the given situation. SMK offers no commentary for these lines.
57. E.g., FY 1:1, which credits friends with "polishing" the inborn nature. Cf. *Analects* 7/21 (Waley, 127), 4/1 (Waley, 102), 4/17 (Waley, 105); "Mean," par. 22/8 (Legge, 407); CYYT 16/24/*t'uan* (Wilhelm, 507): "Friends come. No blame."
58. The latter interpretation is given by CPL 1/6b.
59. This is like Adam running for cover from the sight of God when he realizes his own nakedness.
60. CTYT 53/20/40 (Watson, 215).
61. Reading *kuo* 過 instead of *yü* 遇, following SMK 1/4a, rather than FW 1/8a, assuming an internal rhyme.
62. CYYT 16/24/1 (Wilhelm, 98-99; Kunst, 287).
63. The phrase *ch'i chih hsing* 棄之行 is a pun. *Hsing* 行 can refer to either "walking" or "conduct." Those who leave the service of the ruler also "reject him [in regard to] conduct." Cf. YL 13/4b: *li ch'i wo tsou* 利棄我走.
64. My interpretation follows SMK 1/4a, which says, "When a state is about to rise, the people look to it as if to home; when it is about to end, the people leave it."
65. Such examples are frequently cited in Han texts, e.g. CCFL 6/19/6b. For an interesting discussion of this issue, see Keightley (1977).

No. 3. Mired

1. See GSR 368c,g; KYSH, pp. 808–10.

2. Most commentators read it as "to be in straits" (*chien hsien* 艱險), though some define it as "to be firm and strong" (*kang-ch'iang* 剛強).

3. *Pa* 扶.

4. The metaphor is well established by Han times. See, for example, "Mean," ch. 15 (Legge, 396).

5. HTYT 6/3/2 (not in Dubs; Knoblock, I, 174). CTYT 49/19/24 (Watson, 200) shows the sage looking with complete indifference on mountain and abyss. In FY, there are repeated criticisms of such relativistic outlooks (e.g., FY 3:7, 9:26). That real differences exist is also the theme of THC6/A8, which contrasts giving birth and taking life.

6. Literally, "at watery depths." This is a pun since *ch'ien* 潛 means "hidden" as well. See below.

7. Reading *tse* 嘖 as *yin* 隱. FW 1/8b glosses *tse* as *ch'ing* 情 ("conditions").

8. On an analogy with the state of primeval chaos.

9. Yellow is the color assigned to the center and to Earth. The Earth is also the location of the Yellow Springs. CPL 1/7b takes this to refer to the restoration of the Liu clan, since yellow is the patron phase of the Western Han Dynasty.

10. See YTC 1/4b. CPL 1/7b emphasizes that yang *ch'i* is still too weak to operate, but this interpretation is better suited to Appraisal 2.

11. Cf. *Analects* 12/19 (Waley, 168).

12. Or, "stunted"?

13. CPL 1/7b reads *shih* 適 as *ti* 嫡 ("legal wife" or "sons born of the legal wife." This seems unlikely.

14. FW 1/9a, citing CYYT 15/22/*hsiang* (Wilhelm, 496). For Fan, the character "impure" signifies the particolored flames of the Fire. Cf. CPL 1/7b, which goes on to argue that the lines portend the ruler's conquest by his *ch'en* 臣 ("subordinates").

15. Translation tentative, locus classicus of the reduplicative *fu fu* 扶扶. I follow SMK 1/4b, which glosses it as *pan yüan yi mu* 扳援依慕. FW 1/9a glosses it as *yu hsiao chih mao* 幼小之貌 ("appearance [of the baby] as young and small"). Since *fu* 扶 also means "to crawl," the reduplicative possibly conveys the sound of crawling.

16. Or, "great."

17. FY 4:9.

18. LT, ch. 40 (Lau, 116): "One who possessed virtue in abundance/ Is comparable to a naked babe." Cf. ch. 10 (Lau, 67); ch. 20 (Lau, 76).

19. See FY 4:10 for Yang's criticism of Laotzuian primitivism. For other images of the rosy babe, see THC9/A1; THC17/A4; THC22/A3.

20. In Chinese tradition, the mother teaches the child how to love; the father, how to respect. See FY 4:11.

21. *Mencius* 3A/5 (Lau, 105) and HTYT 35/10/83 (not in Dubs; Knoblock, 132) characterize the ancient rulers in this way. See FY 4:11 on the need for careful training of rosy babes. And FY 2:6: "If the sages are alive, study with the men; if the sages have died, study with [their] books."

22. CYYT 5/4/*t'uan* (Wilhelm, 407). Cf. FY 1:2, on the young ignoramus

who "entrusts his fate" to his teacher.

23. See below for an alternate interpretation.

24. Another pun. *K'an* 堪 also means "to vanquish."

25. FW 2/8a.

26. FY 1:2; 3:6–7 (translated in Ch'an, 289-90). Cf. THC22/A1,2.

27. Yang cannot mean that an individual's inner strength may be insufficient to reform his character, given the refutation of this view by Confucius in *Analects* 4/6 (Waley, 103).

28. FY 11:33.

29. YY 33:657 reads *ch'u* 出 ("out of") instead of *shan* 山. *Shan* is attested in several early editions, including FW and Wang Ya.

30. Deleting *ch'iu* 丘, on the assumption that it has crept into the text from Appraisal 7.

31. FW 2/9b.

32. Literally, "Someone leads for him an ox."

33. Following SMK 1/5a in reading *tai* 代 instead of *fa* 伐 (as in FW 1/9b).

34. HTYT 1/1/6–10 (Dubs, 32–33; Knoblock, I, 136–37). Cf. CTYT 57/21/59 (Watson, 231).

35. Or, in some texts, *hsien* 軒 ("carriage pole").

36. SMK 1/5a.

37. Literally, "Towering, towering are the high mountains./ Below there are river waves."

38. FY 1:1 until the break, then FY 2:5. The same metaphor appears in HsinS 3/2a.

39. Cf. *Analects* 15/30 (Waley, 193 [renum.]), where undirected thought is shown to be inferior to study of the classics and imitation of moral superiors. Also, *ibid.*, 2/15 (Waley, 53).

No. 4. Barrier

1. The character is that used for the preceding tetragram title.

2. FW 1/10b writes, "Although finished below, yin is still strong above. Therefore, it can hinder [yang] and hold it fast." CPL 1/9a envisions yang *ch'i* imprisoned in ice, like "a ruler who is controlled by his official."

3. LT, ch. 52 (Lau, 113); cf. ch. 56 (Lau, 117). On the importance of this theme, see Girardot, pp. 154–56; Ames, p. 210.

4. See YL 4/14a; 7/4b; 7/10b.

5. Graham (1989), p. 97.

6. CYYT 38/63/*hsiang* (Wilhelm, 711).

7. A pun here. *Ni* 泥 can also mean "to impede," "to obstruct." GSR 563d.

8. Or possibly, "none receive or confer." "Finally" is supplied by Nylan.

9. CYYT 2/1/*yen* (Wilhelm, 379).

10. CPL 1/9a calls the snake "a dragon without a horn." Cf. LHCC 16:344 (Forke, I, 365).

11. HNT 2/5a.

12. CYYT 6/5/3 (Wilhelm, 26; Kunst, 249).

13. Mauss (1990), vi–xvi. Following CPL 1/9a. SMK 1/5a, however, associ-

ates the phrase "none receive" with the line "none are males," implying that no heirs exist.

14. *Analects* 13/3 (Waley, 171).

15. HS 27A:1458, defining the significance of snakes as portents. CPL 1/9a suggests that the phrase "ruler not a ruler" most likely attacks the usurpation of Han imperial power by a woman (possibly the dowager Empress Wang?) or by the "womanish" catamite Tung Hsien. Hsü Fu-kuan, II, 542–56 also believes that this is one of many Head texts to reflect the political situation during the reigns of Emperors Ch'eng (r. 32–7 B.C.), Ai (r. 6–1 B.C.), or the regency, then interregnum of Wang Mang. Chin Ch'un-feng, p. 443, disputes this. In most cases, I hesitate to enter the realm of speculation by reading into the *Mystery* specific references to historical events.

16. This reading reflects Yang's use of the dragon as metaphor for the noble man in FY 5:13; 6:17; and 10:27.

17. Metal basins filled with water served at this time as mirrors. For this metaphor of the mirror, see LT, ch. 10 (Lau, 66). For the metaphor of the unmoved mind, see e.g. Mencius 2A/2 (Lau, 76-80). For daily self-examination, see e.g. CCYT 115/Hsi 19/4 Tso (Legge, 177); HTYT 4/2/19 (Dubs, 47; Knoblock, 154); *Analects* 1/4 (Waley, 84).

18. FY 1:2.

19. LT, ch. 8 (Lau, 64). Cf. ch. 78 (Lau, 140).

20. Reading GSR 48a as 48c (*she* 捨 as *she* 舍).

21. CYYT 42/Hsi A/7 (Wilhelm, 308), explaining 38/62/3 (Wilhelm, 707; Kunst, 241).

22. CPL 1/9b, however, says the verb *pa* 拔 means *t'ui erh chin chih yu ch'ien* 推而進之於前 ("to push to the front").

23. The FW commentary consistently glosses "our" (*wo* 我) as "the masses" (*wan min* 萬民), as in FW 1/11a. In his commentary, the lines celebrate the good officials' treatment ("removing the yoke") of the common people. It is difficult to see, however, why this would only provide a "small gain."

24. Sivin suggests, "honor in accord with good faith." "The good man" is supplied by Nylan.

25. *Analects* 2/22(15) (Waley, 93).

26. *Analects* 6/17 (Waley, 119).

27. Cf. CYYT 47/Hsi B/4 (Wilhelm, 342). Contrast Ode 26/3 (Legge, 39): "My heart is not a stone" [because "it cannot be rolled"—i.e., changed].

28. CYYT 47/Hsi B/4 (Wilhelm, 341).

29. FW 1/11a–11b defines *chih* 堞 as a wall 250 cubit measures in length.

30. Ode 254/7 (Legge, 503). This couplet is frequently cited in early texts, e.g., CCYT 94/Hsi 5/1 *Tso* (Legge, 144; Watson, 25). Golden walls are also associated with the sage in HsinS 2/7b.

31. HTYT 7/3/27 (not in Dubs; Knoblock, 175); and *Mencius* 4A/11 (Lau, 122).

32. THC "Hsüan shu" 8/3b (p. 1025b).

33. Two definitions are given for the reduplicative *chü chü* 趄趄: "to walk [and by a pun, to conduct oneself] crookedly" (*hsing pu cheng* 行不正); and "to

walk, but not advance" (*hsing pu chin* 行不進). Clearly, the reduplicative describes a stumbling or halting walk.

34. Literally, "Someone sleeps for him [i.e., in his place] at the lodge."

35. *She* 舍 could refer to either a relay station or a lodging. See below.

36. Ode 115/3 (Legge, 177). But see Karlgren (1964), p. 204.

37. SMK's reading is similar. Evil has been introduced into the [ruling] house, without its occupants fully realizing it. SMK 1/5b cites the famous (apocryphal?) anecdote concerning the downfall of the Ch'in dynasty. In response to a prediction that the Ch'in would be destroyed by Hu 胡, the wicked First Emperor launched numerous campaigns against the northern barbarians of that name, while ignoring the greed and ineptitude of his future heir, Hu-hai 胡亥.

38. FW 1/11b; YTC 1/7b; CPL 1/10a.

39. *Ch'ü ch'u* 遽篨 instead of *ch'ü ch'u* 籧除.

40. E.g., Ode 43/1–2 (Legge, 70). FW 1/11b is even more specific, pointing to evil slanderers at court on the basis of *Erh-ya*. See Karlgren (1964), 130, no. 121–22.

41. YY 33:658, citing Fang 5/37/34 which talks of "coarse straw mats."

42. YY 33:658–59 reads *fan* 燔 ("burns") for *po* 播, arguing that it is a sign of the battle between yin and yang (a parallel with THC8/A8). The change is unwarranted. *Po* could also mean "propagates."

43. If this is not read as a conditional clause, App. 8 appears to be inauspicious. My interpretation follows CPL 1/10a.

44. YTC 1/7b speaks of *o ch'i* 惡氣. The T'ang commentator Wang Ya identifies the Red Stench as the "killing *ch'i* which results from the yin and yang impulses at war." I suspect the phrase refers to some kind of plague, possibly anthrax. See Zinsser, p. 135. However, early Indian texts also speak of a "Crimson Breath," apparently some form of crop blight in India. CPL 1/16b, however, specifically identifies the Red Stench as Wang Mang, since Wang adopted Fire as the patron agent for his dynasty. In that case, the stench would emanate from the palace out to the border passes of the empire.

45. YY 33:659 deletes *chung* 終 because of scansion. "On an empty house" is supplied by Nylan.

46. Literally, "Til the end, it cannot be filled."

47. YTC 1/8a. Such a reading is supported by the association of the phrase "covetous and without virtue" with "It screens his home. . . ." See CYYT 34/55/6 (Wilhelm, 216; Kunst, 329), cited in CCYT 186/Hsüan 6/1 *Kung* (Legge, 299). For this, see also Smith, p. 13. It is also possible, the individual, in fear of appearing gullible, ends up doubting true teachings as well as false. This is a theme of the FY.

48. CCYT 94/Hsi 5/1 *Tso* (Legge, 144).

49. FY 3:7. Part of Yang Hsiung's answer is to be found in his prose-poem, "Refuting [Encountering] Sorrow," which has been translated in Knechtges (1982), pp. 13–16. While that poem begins by a sympathetic consideration of the poet Ch'ü Yüan, it goes on to emphasize the need for public commitment and political loyalty.

50. SMK 1/6a, citing CYYT 3/2/4 (Wilhelm, 14; Kunst, 243).

No. 5. Keeping Small

1. Reading *tan* 澹 as *shui-yao* 水搖 (Morohashi 18421), rather than as *pu-tung* 不動, as suggested by the FW 1/12a; Sung Chung; and SMK 1/6a, which follow usage in the LT. These commentators take "unmoving" as an adjective descriptive of yang above ground in early winter: "Yang *ch'i* calm [above ground but] spreading [its influence] through the deep pool [below the surface of the earth]."

2. KY, cited in Morohashi 17929, defines *chien* 潆 as "the large water breaking in the middle, the flow of the small emerges." SMK 1/6a; YTC 1/8a; and CPL 1/10b all read *chien* as *ch'ien* 謙 (here, "self-restrained"). This emendation is unnecessary, especially in view of the water imagery here.

3. Reading GSR 178o as 178i (*pien* 變 = *lüan* 欒).

4. CYYT 11/15/*t'uan* (Wilhelm, 462).

5. LT, ch. 77 (Lau, 139).

6. CYYT 11/15/*hsiang* (Wilhelm, 463).

7. For ritual imitating the Tao, see HTYT 73/19/63-5 (Watson, 100; Dubs, 232).

8. CYYT 11/15/*hsiang* (Wilhelm, 64–66).

9. LT, ch. 40 (Lau, 101).

10. The phrase comes from LT, ch. 52 (Lau, 113).

11. YL 4/13b. CWK, p. 22, n. 3 cites LT, ch. 38 (Lau, 99): "The highest virtue is not virtuous."

12. Or, "covered."

13. CYYT 11/15/1 (Wilhelm, 65). Contrast Kunst, 269.

14. *Analects* 1/16 (Waley, 87) before the break; 4/14 (Waley, 104–5) after it.

15. A pun. *Miao* 妙 for *miao* 眇 (GSR 1158c as 1158b).

16. Reading *ch'eng* 成 ("complete") rather than *ch'eng* 誠 ("integrity"), following FW 1/12b. The WJL edition gives the second character but offers no explanation for the substitution.

17. See YTC 1/8b.

18. Or, "His humility, [from] correct alignment."

19. CPL 1/11a takes *ch'ien* 籤 to mean *chien* 漸 ("little by little").

20. CWK, p. 22, n. 5, based loosely on FW 1/12b.

21. For this definition of *wu-wei* 無為, See Graham (1970). See FY 4:12 for criticisms of the *wu-wei* proponents.

22. FY 1:2.

23. SMK 1/6a, however, prefers "parading poverty," taking *p'in p'in* 貧貧 as *tzu ching ch'i p'in* 自旌其貧 ("display like a flag one's poverty"). However, that behavior has no necessary connection with the second line of Appraisal 4. Cf. Appraisal 8 below. It is also conceivable that Yang Hsiung wishes to indicate the dire poverty of the individual by his use of the reduplicative.

24. Literally, "Someone recklessly for him relieves [it]."

25. Literally, "Taking poor as poor, recklessly relieving."

26. FW 1/12b, however, talks of the man who knows himself to be "strong as Metal," despite low rank, then focuses on a disparity between talent and position.

27. FY 3:7, citing CYYT 40/Hsi A/4(15) (Wilhelm, 295).

28. E.g., FY 1:4.

29. This is Yang's argument in his prose-poem, "Expelling Poverty." See Knechtges (1976), 104–7.

30. *Analects* 7/11 (Waley, 125) before the first break; *ibid.*, 4/5 (Waley, 103) before the second break; after the second break, *ibid.*, 4/16 (Waley, 105). Cf. 4/5 (Waley, 102–3); 15/32 (Waley, 199); 16/1 (Waley, 203–4).

31. Literally, "What the Earth itself empties.

32. CYYT 20/31/*hsiang* (Wilhelm, 542). Cf. LT, ch. 61 (Lau, 121).

33. Literally, "Being small, [still] it holds on to being full." YY 33:659 argues that *ch'ih* 持 is a misprint for *shih* 恃 ("to rely upon"). The phrase would then mean that the small man is "arrogant and self-reliant." The emendation is unnecessary.

34. CYYT 47/Hsi B/4 (Wilhelm, 341).

35. LT, ch. 9 (Lau, 65).

36. FY 10:32 uses the same image. Cf. LHCC 1:14 (Forke, I, 149). For further information, see Lau (1968). For the same metaphor on a different point, see Graham (1989), p. 201.

37. *Ch'ih ying* 持盈, in Ode 248 (Legge, 75).

38. *Analects* 12/21 (Waley, 169) before the break; 9/24 (Waley, 143) after it.

39. *Analects* 12/4 (Waley, 163).

40. Following YTC 1/9a. Cf. CPL 1/12a.

41. However, Serruys prefers to read *ching* 靜 as *ch'ing* 情 ("quality").

42. *Jun* 潤.

43. *Ku* 谷 is a loan for "good" (read *yü*). See GSR 1202a.

No. 6. Contrariety

1. Or, "germinal." Following SMK 1/6b. FW 1/13b, however, glosses *fu* 孚 as *hsin* 信 ("truly"). An alternate reading, "The yang *ch'i* fosters what is small," stems from the root meaning of the character *fu* 孚, which shows a hand atop a child.

2. The root meaning of *ch'u* 觸 is "to butt against." From this come the extended meanings "to seek its target," "to go where it belongs." YTC 1/9b glosses *ch'u* as *kan* 感 ("to arouse").

3. CYYT 42/Hsi A/8 (Wilhelm, 313). For further information on the argumentation of the "Hsi tz'u," see Peterson (1982).

4. *Ch'i* 齊. Contrast the Western notion of "equality," which presupposes equal legal status for all. For further discussion, see Bauer, pp. 21–22.

5. For the *hsü* 虛 as "heart/mind," see HTYT 62/17/12 (Dubs, 179). Cf. HNT 2/11a. An analogy is made between the heart/mind and primal chaos since both are unseen catalysts of visible activity.

6. Glossing *ch'iu* 酋 as *chiu* 就, following FW 1/13b.

7. In many Warring States texts, the belly also symbolizes the animal nature with its desires for food and sex, as in LT, ch. 3 (Lau, 59). In that case, the back would stand for the visible expression of those desires.

8. SMK 1/7a.

9. Literally, "Each has what it takes care of."

10. CYYT 24/38/*t'uan* (Wilhelm, 575). Cf. 41/Hsi A/6 (Wilhelm, 343).

11. Karlgren says the character *shou* 首 depicts the head of a horned animal, although many scholars disagree. See GSR 1102a. FW 1/14a glosses *shou* as *hsiang* 向 ("direction").

12. KCTSCC 63:677 (top).

13. E.g., Ode 203/1 (Legge, 353); 262/6 (Legge, 555); FY 3:6. For the etymological relation between "straightness" and "virtue," see Hall and Ames, p. 218.

14. FY 9:26 calls the level, line, compass, and square *ta ch'i* 大器.

15. FY 10:26. Cf. HTYT 73/19/35 (Dubs, 225; Watson, 95); KT 10/30/16a (Rickett[b], 407).

16. FY 8:22 associates the use of these instruments with the employment of good advisors in government, for example. Cf. HTYT 48/12/99 (not in Dubs; Knoblock, II, 190). HTYT 39/11/43 (not in Dubs; Knoblock, 155) associates them with ritual.

17. HNT 9/11b (Ames, 146), added by Nylan. Cf. KT 6/16/7b (Rickett(b), 261).

18. This is a loose translation, reading *yü* 予 as *wo* 我, following FW 1/14b. *Hsin* 心 here functions as a verb ("to take to heart"), with *yü* as its object. See YY 33:659 for criticism of SMK 1/7a, which SYJ 8/18b upholds.

19. Following FW 1/14b; CWK, p. 26, n. 6. Instead of *hsü* 諝, Wang Ya reads *hsü* 謂, which he defines as *chih* 智 ("wisdom"). SMK 1/7a follows. SYJ 8/18b reads *hsü* 壻 ("son-in-law") instead.

20. Ode 189/9 (Legge, 317).

21. One thinks of Wen-chün, wife to Ssu-ma Hsiang-ju, whose tale is recounted in SC 117:3000–1 (Watson, II, 297–300).

22. *Ke te ch'i so* 各得其所.

23. HNT 9/7a–7b (Ames, 148).

24. FW 1/14b (under Buddhist influence?), reads *sha sheng* 殺生 as "killing living things," equating the "living thing" with the *ssu* of Appraisal 5 above. CPL 1/13b agrees, but I find this farfetched. Serruys reads: "Diminishing, growing, ..."

25. Reading *shih* 失 as *wu* 午, following YY 33:660. YTC 1/11a retains *shih* 失, arguing that the straight arrow symbolizes the appropriate Way of Chou, as in Ode 203/1 (Legge, 353).

26. THC "Hsüan li" 7/5b (p. 1018b).

27. See HFT 4:16:82 (Liao, I, 143) for this.

28. Literally, *shih* 失, meaning *shih ch'an* 失躔 ("to stray from orbit"). CWK, p. 24, n. 8, however, takes *li shih* 離失 as a compound verb.

29. For this term, see Schafer (1977), p. 79 ff.

30. HS 26:1285–86.

No. 7. Ascent

1. *Wu* 物 supplied by commentators.

2. Following YTC 1/11a; CPL 1/14a in reading *she* 射 as the verb "to shoot," which suggests the force of yang *ch'i* pushing upward. Alternate reading for *she* = *yi* ("to saturate").

3. If the alternate reading of "saturate" is used, growing things crowd the earth below until they saturate it, then climb up above.

4. *Documents*, "Hung fan," par. 5 (Legge, 325–26; Karlgren, 30).

5. FY 12:38.

6. CYYT 28/46/*hsiang* (Wilhelm, 179). Note that while the hexagram Pushing Upward is largely auspicious, Tetragram 7 associates Ascent with both good and bad luck.

7. FY 4:11.

8. Wang Ya reads *chian chian* 鏟鏟 as *jui chin mao* 銳進貌 ("appearance of sharp advance").

9. FW 1/15a says, "the pure heart suppressing itself" but this may show Buddhist influence. YTC 1/11a emphasizes the worries over social advance that lesser men experience; SMK 1/7b, the impatience of the petty man.

10. Note the etymological relation of the two characters *yüeh* 悅 and *jui* 銳.

11. LT, ch. 56 (Lau, 117). Cf. ch. 12 (Lau, 68).

12. Reading *chüeh* 谷 as *ch'üeh* 卻, following YY 33:660. YTC 1/11b; CPL 1/14b mistakenly read as *ku* 谷 ("valley").

13. Reading *huo* 活 rather than *chih* 治 ("to rule"), to rhyme with the last line of Fathoming 1. It is possible that *huo* here means *huan* 換 ("to moderate" [ill effects]), as in *Mencius* 2A/4 (Lau, 81), 4A/9 (Lau, 122).

14. E.g., *Analects* 1/2 (Waley, 83).

15. *Mencius* 7A/41 (Lau, 191).

16. LT, ch. 46 (Lau, 107).

17. Literally, *ku* 穀 ("grain"), and by extension, "nurture" or "nourishment."

18. Ode 165/1 (Legge, 253).

19. *Mencius* 3A/4 (Lau, 104) excoriates those who favor other doctrines over Confucianism by saying: "I have heard of coming out of the dark ravine to settle on a tall tree, but not of forsaking the tall tree to descend into the dark ravine."

20. *Mu* 木 = *ts'ai* 材 = *ts'ai* 才. It may even be significant that the bird alights on a luxuriant tree (*mao mu* 茂木), rather than the tall (*ch'iao* 喬) tree mentioned in the pre-Han classics. *Mao* is the standard adjective applied to "talent" even before A.D. 36, when the "Luxuriant Talent" (*mao ts'ai*) degree was awarded to scholars recommended by the commanderies and prefectures to the throne for service. For further information, see Bielenstein, pp. 133, 136.

21. FW 1/15b. Cf. Wang Ya, who equates them with delicacies.

22. E.g., FY 1:1–2.

23. Reading *fu* 孚 as "taking as cover." However, several commentators (including SMK 1/7b; CPL 1/14b–15a; and YTC 1/12a) seem unsure whether to read *fu* as *hsin* 信 ("truly") or to take it as "floating [like a cloud]," implying "without substance." Those commentators cite *Analects* 7/15 (Waley, 126): "Any thought of accepting wealth and rank by means that I know to be wrong is as far removed from me as the clouds that float above." FW 1/15b and CWK, p. 28, n. 6 ignore it.

24. Possibly, *chung* 中 should be read as *chung* 忠 ("loyalty"). For the second line of the Fathoming, cf. LT, ch. 21 (Lau, 78). There is another possible

allusion here. Ode 184 has the line *tsai yü chu* 在于渚 ("it stays on the islet"); here we have *yu chu chung* 有諸中.

25. YTC 1/12a.
26. Ode 184/1, 2 (Legge, 296).
27. FW 1/16a.
28. Literally, "do not find [it] felicitous."
29. Ode 100/1 (Legge, 154). Cf. FY 5:15, which repeats the metaphor, and YL 4/6b.
30. FY 4:9.
31. Reading *tien* 顛 as *tien pai* 顛敗 ("ruined," "toppled"), following CPL 1/15a. It could also mean "the highest."
32. Supplying the verb *te* 得, following SMK 1/8a.
33. Note the variant in FW 1/16b; Sung Wei-kan; and YTC 1/12b.
34. "On top of Stork-bird Tower" by Wang Chih-huan 王之渙 (695–?), translated in Turner, p. 97. The tower represented the nobility in early China, since only members of the aristocracy were permitted to construct such buildings.
35. Throughout *p'ien* 3 of HY (Ku, 79–82), good ministers are said to be the staff that props up government.
36. *Wei* 危 also means "precipice."
37. For the changing connotations of *shih* 士, see Hsü Cho-yün (1965), 7–8, 89–99, 150–51.
38. Ode 172/1 (Legge, 172).

No. 8. *Opposition*

1. The character *ch'i* 氣 is supplied from FW 1/16b and Wang Ya, on an analogy with other Head texts. For further information, see YY 33:660.
2. Supplied by YTC 1/13a.
3. Following WJL, rather than FW 1/16b and Wang Ya, in writing *ju* 如, not *erh* 而.
4. Literally, "spear-like." *Ke* 鈴 refers to the long spear. However, Sung Chung; FW 1/16b; and YTC 1/13a gloss *ke* as *hsien sheng* 陷聲 ("sound of falling down a shaft"). CPL 1/15b glosses it as *t'ou chien sheng* 透堅聲 ("the sound of penetrating what is hard"). This translation is also possible, when we consider that yang *ch'i* is pushing through the hard surface of the earth.
5. E.g., *Mencius* 5B/9 (Lau, 159); HTYT 92/25/2 (not in Dubs or Knoblock).
6. *Analects* 14/9 (Waley, 181).
7. SY 9/1a–25a.
8. LC 5/16a (Legge, I, 114).
9. PHT 5:193 (Tjan, II, 469).
10. See his assessment of the prose-poem *(fu)* as *feng* 諷 ("indirect criticism") in FY 1:4.
11. Taking *wan* 丸 as the verb "to turn round," following SMK 1/8a–8b. Alternately, *wan* means the round (i.e., blunt) tip of the drill, following YTC 1/13a: "The blunt [drill tip] boring." See below. For the round pellet with reference to debate, see CTYT 3/2/11 (Watson, 37).
12. Pan Ku 班固, "Ta pin hsi" 答賓戲, in YKC, II, 25/5a. The anonymous

Master of Ghost Valley uses the "turning bit" as chapter title for an essay now lost. See KKT B/13. For more information on disputation, see Kroll.

13. YTC 1/13a says that a probe ought to be pointed, while here it is rounded; hence, the clumsiness of the process. For the damage caused by a stone probe crudely applied, see FY 4:12.

14. SMK 1/8a–8b.

15. Morohashi 96.

16. Yang contrasts the term *wei* 微 with *chu* 著 ("what is obvious"). See FY 5:14. The evil is barely perceptible because it has just begun. Note that CPL 1/16a takes *wei* to refer to two additional conditions: the "lowly" station of minor officials and the "subtle" remonstrance aimed at the ruler by wise loyalists.

17. Following SMK 1/8b and CPL 1/16a. The phrase *kuei ming* 軌命 could also mean "to put on track the commands [of the ruler]."

18. LT, ch. 64 (Lau, 125).

19. The phrase "model decrees" can also refer to the "model speech" of the ideal official. YTC 1/13a and CPL 1/16a both read *wei* 微 as "minor [official]," rather than as "slight." CWK, p. 30, n. 4, follows.

20. However, Broschat understands the first verb (*ch'ien* 拑) as "to pinch," "to grasp between," equating GSR 606j with 606h 拑. He therefore explains the rhetorical device as "the rapid consolidation of any [rhetorical] advantage one is afforded" (p. 154, n. 34). The second verb (*chien* 鍵) is cognate with another term used in KKT. See Broschat, p. 145.

21. YTC 1/13a–b. Cf. CWK, p. 30, n. 5. The anonymous *Master of Ghost Valley* uses the gag to describe the rhetorical "art" (*shu* 術) of identifying the listener's desires while suppressing the expression of one's own. See KKT B/5/1a,2a,4a. CTYT 24/10/26 (Watson, 111); 54/21/6 (Watson, 222) show that the gag can be used both to silence others and to convey a disinclination to speak.

22. Ode 239/6 (Legge, 446).

23. KY 1/3. My translation is based on Hart, 44.

24. Alternately, "They go straight on their way"; or, "They straighten his way."

25. Cf. the early proverb, "Good medicine is bitter to the taste," cited in HFT 11:32:199 (Liao, II, 35).

26. FY 2:5 contrasts unusual delicacies with ordinary fare. YY 33:660 reads *ch'iu yi* 邱飴 as *ou yi* 甌瓵 ("earthenware pitcher"). See below.

27. See CCYT 121/Hsi 23/*fu* 2 (Legge, 186). Cf. HYKC 3:28 on the King of Shu's gift of dirt to King Hui of Ch'in (r. 337–311 B.C.).

28. SMK 1/8b.

29. Cf. FY 1:4, which mocks those who ignorantly hanker after vermilion and gold.

30. Pan Chao 班昭, "Nü Chieh" 女誡, in YKC 96/4a (Swann [1932], 83).

31. Or, "pole."

32. Literally, "knocks against."

33. Alternately, "It is proper to comply." FW 1/17b talks of complying with the ruler. SMK 1/8b, however, presumes that this means, "To comply with what is right [brings good fortune]." CWK offers no commentary.

34. Alternately, "[By] compliance it can be preserved."

35. Following FW 1/17b; YTC 1/14a; and CPL 1/17a for the definition of the reduplicative.

36. Adding "follow." See CWK, p. 31, n. 8.

37. A pun. My translation follows FW 1/18a; YTC 1/14a, but see below. Alternately: "They do not admit the Way" [into their thinking] *or* "They will not be admitted on the Way."

38. FW l/18a; SMK 1/9a.

39. Translation tentative. "In" is the more usual translation of the character *yü* 于, but it makes little sense in the context.

40. For information on Han exorcisms, see Berger.

41. There are many similar proverbs in Han texts, e.g., "The mouths of the masses smelt metal" (FSTY *yi-wen* 2:87) and "Long tongues work as battle-axes" (YL 5/14b).

42. This is still done by Taoist priests in Taiwan, as can be seen in Gary Seaman's films.

43. Ode 264/3 (Legge, 561) identifies slander and rumor as women's activities: "A wise man builds the city./ A wise woman overthrows it./ A woman with a long tongue/ Is like a stepping stone to disorder." Since women are to men as officials are to the ruler, officials may also be the subject of these verses.

44. *Analects* 7/15 (Waley, 126).

45. Proverb quoted in CPL 1/17b.

No. 9. Branching Out

1. Or "increase in size."

2. YTC 1/14b.

3. FW 1/18b; Lu Chi; and SMK 1/9a gloss this character as "advance." Wu Mi and Sung Wei-kan borrow from SW 14B:310b the equation of *shu* 疏 with *t'ung* 通 ("to get through"). I take my translation from the compound *fu shu* 扶疏 used in the Head, which is generally used of plants. Yang Hsiung's biography uses this same compound to describe the composition of the *Mystery*, which grew luxuriantly under his pen. See HS 87B:3566 (Knechtges, 46).

4. Reading *ming* 冥 instead of *yi* 宜, following WJL (1/9a) since *ming* is a quality repeatedly associated with Position 1. If *yi* is accepted from FW 1/18b, it means *mei* 美 ("excellent").

5. For crawling as a sign of one's willingness to exert oneself for the good, see Ode 35/4 (Legge, 57).

6. CPL 1/17b; SMK 1/9a.

7. YTC 1/14b. Cf. CKW, p. 33, n. 2. However, I doubt that a person could reach this level of perfection at the beginning.

8. Or "glinting," "flickering."

9. For this expression, see the *Fang yen* cited in *Cheng tzu t'ung* 正字通 (not in the present "Fang" index). See also CWK, p. 33, n. 3.

10. See FW 1/18b.

11. The single character *t'a* 姡 means "hounds devouring things."

12. See FY 3:7–8.

13. On this, see FY 4:12, where Yang admits his borrowing from Chuang tzu. Cf. FY 6:17.

14. CPL 1/18a reads *shu* 狩 as *shou* 狩. Cf. CWK, p. 33, n. 3. The bracketed material is added by the commentators.

15. CWK, p. 33, n. 3, reads this as, "They ought not to have what they pursue."

16. See YL 5/9b.

17. Reading *yen yü* 炎于 as a reversion of *yü yen*, following usage in the *Odes*. FW 1/19a; Wang Ya; and CWK, p. 33, n. 4, tie this to the spring, when the myriad things grow under the influence of yang *ch'i*. CPL 1/18a takes *yen* to refer to the hunt fires.

18. HTYT 1/1/10 (Dubs, 33; Knoblock, I, 137).

19. FY 8:23.

20. CPL 1/18a once again takes *shu* as *shou* 狩, adding addictions to the hunt to those of food and wine.

21. Or "method," following YTC 1/15a; CPL 1/18a.

22. Cf. *Mencius* 6A/17 (Lau, 169), which cites Ode 247/1 (Legge, 475) on "filling us with virtue" and "filling us with drink" but breaks the original parallel. Cf. Mencius 6A/14 (Lau, 168): "A man who only cares about food and drink is despised because he takes care of parts of smaller importance to the detriment of parts of greater importance."

23. Following Wang Ya in reading *ku* 轂 ("hub"). FW 1/19a reads *ku* 穀 ("grain").

24. The phrase "there is enough" was used in Han, for example, to describe the virtues of a famous chief minister in antiquity. See FSTY 2/9 (Nylan, 361–62). Note the relation between *tsu* 足 and and *shu* 疋, both meaning "foot" (see GSR 90a; 1219), one part of the title character *shu* 疏.

25. Reading *shih* 逝 as *shih* 逝 ("to leap"), following Serruys. FW 1/19b and Sung Wei-kan read *shih shih* 逝逝 as *hsi hsi* 晰晰 ("bright"). CWK, p. 34, n. 6, reads *shih* 逝 as *wang* 往 ("to go toward").

26. Reading *po jih* 白日 as "days of white [hair]" rather than as "broad daylight," as CWK, p. 34, n. 7, does. It seems unlikely that Position 7, well past the halfway mark in the tetragram, would speak of midday. YTC 1/15b identifies the time as sunset.

27. Reading *ch'en* 辰 as *shih* 時 ("the [right] time"), following the commentators.

28. Or, "finally able to get [his chance] to hear [the Way]," as suggested by YTC 1/15b; CPL 1/18a, who cite *Analects* 4/8 (Waley, 103): "In the morning, hear the Way. In the evening, die content." In that case, the verses describe the individual who reaches moral understanding only late in life.

29. Or, "taking [as model]." "Parasites" is supplied as subject by Nylan.

30. See HFT 19:49:339–50 (Liao, II, 275–97) for lice as symbols of social parasites.

31. Or, "[With] spreading out complete."

32. Because of rhyme, following FW 1/20a in reading *k'un* 困 instead of *hai* 害.

33. FW 1/20a ties the water also with return to the beginning.

34. LT, ch. 64 (Lau, 125).

35. LT, ch. 58 (Lau, 119). For similar injunctions to take great care, see

also, e.g., TTLC 4:52:24 on the Music Master Tzu-ch'un, who stubbed his toe; and Ode 195/6 (Legge, 333): "We should be apprehensive and cautious,/ As if on the brink of a deep gulf,/ As if treading on thin ice."

36.   *Analects* 26/8 (Waley, 206).

37.   *Chüan* 眷 (GSR 226c).

38.   FW 1/20a says simply that the "abyss" is "one."

No. 10. Defectiveness

1.   FW 1/20a assigns the tetragram to Hexagram no. 19, Approach. In that case, the character *hsien* 羨 must be translated as "extension" (*yen chin* 延進). However, the character refers more often to an error. Therefore, I follow SMK 1/9b.

2.   Literally, "assisting the hidden."

3.   Material in brackets supplied by FW 1/20a; SMK 1/10a.

4.   "The shapes of things" is understood, but unexpressed. YTC 1/16a, however, ascribes the distorted shape to yang *ch'i*. The title character *hsien* 羨 is used of shapes that are not perfectly round.

5.   YTC 1/16a.

6.   Or, "straighten."

7.   The passage preceding the ellipsis mark is drawn from the apocrypha attached to the *Changes*. See CIS, I(B), 31. A *li* is a Chinese mile, roughly equal to 1/3 the Western mile. The last sentence comes from CYYT 6/6/*hsiang* (Wilhelm, 417).

8.   KT 6/16/2a (Rickett[a], 91).

9.   See Graham (1978), pp. 227–28 for examples.

10.   Cf. CYYT 16/24/1 (Wilhelm, 98; Kunst, 287); 47/Hsi B/4 (Wilhelm, 342).

11.   CYYT 6/6/*hsiang* (Wilhelm, 417).

12.   Following FW 1/20b, reading *yü* 迂 for *yü* 于.

13.   Second possible translation for the literal line: "Defective in regard to the path."

14.   Literally, "The defective by pure circumstance is right." Alternately, "The defective balanced against the right."

15.   Cf. Ode 23/1 (Legge, 34).

16.   FW 1/20b defines *hsing* 幸 as *chiao hsing* 徼倖 ("lucky beyond one's expectations).

17.   SMK 1/10a, however, reads as, "Good [though] contrary to constants." See below.

18.   The material before the ellipsis marks comes from "Mean," ch. 14/4 (Legge, 396); the last sentence, from SY 10:344. Cf. *Analects* 6/17 (Waley, 117): "Man's very life is straightness. If he loses that yet lives, his escape from death is merely the effect of happy coincidence."

19.   See CCYT 322/Hsiang 28/*Tso* 6 (Legge, 542).

20.   CWK, p. 36, n. 5, citing FY 8:21–22.

21.   CPL 1/19a–20b; YTC 1/16b–17a.

22.   SMK 1/10a, citing SC 47:1923 (Chavannes, V, 335).

23.   Both *k'ung* 孔.

24.   For the same image, see FY 4:9.

25. LT, ch. 53, (Lau, 114). Cf. FY 2:6. The metaphor of "walking on by-paths" was also used by the Confucians. E.g., *Analects* 6/12 (Waley, 118).
26. Cf. THC6/A1.
27. Added by Nylan.
28. FW 1/21a, however, assumes the "void" implies the evil mind empty of all understanding of moral precepts.
29. Reading *ku* 故 as *ku* 古, following CPL 1/17b.
30. "Truths" supplied by YTC 1/17b.
31. Literally, "Danger, it [he] follows." CWK, p. 37, n. 8, prefers to read the line as "Dangerous[ly], it [he] relaxes, where "it" stands for the institutions associated with the sages. The ruler, then, institutes *wu wei* 無為, a governmental theory criticized by Yang in FY 4:11. Since *hsün* 訓 is often interchangeable with *chieh* 解, it is also possible to read the line as, "Dangerous(ly) it he explicates." For Yang's preoccupation with heterodoxy, see FY 4:9–12.
32. *Analects* 2/16 (Waley, 91).
33. E.g., FY 5:15. The innovative points in the *Mystery* were set within the framework of a received body of teaching, rather than in conscious competition with it.
34. *Analects* 7/1 (Waley, 122).
35. YTC 1/17b.
36. *Mencius* 3B/1 (Lau, 107).
37. Alternately, "to set the feet in a different ['deflected'] direction."
38. *Mencius* 1B/12 (Lau, 70).
39. SMK 1/10b believes that the individual in "twisting" "bends his principles to save himself from disaster." On the same assumption, YTC 1/17b criticizes Yang Hsiung (especially FY 8:22 on "bending the self in service of the Way").
40. Cf. THC9/A9 above.
41. Reading *k'ua* 括 as "entangled [in the traces]" (*chieh* 結), following SMK 1/10b. YY 33:661 reads *k'ua* as *kuai* 膾. In that case, the line would mean, "The four horses return to [their] stalls."
42. CPL 1/21a.

No. 11. Divergence
1. According to SMK 1/10b.
2. Tentative reading for *yung* 雍. SMK 1/10b; CPL 1/21a; and CWK, p. 38, n. 2, read it as "harmonies."
3. CPL 1/21a takes this as *wu kai ch'i jung* 物改其容 ("things change their appearance").
4. "Wriggling" (*ch'un* 蠢) is cognate with "spring" (*ch'un* 春).
5. Cf. SY 16/1a.
6. The term "lordly" is ambiguous. It can refer either to the emperor or to divinities.
7. YTC 1/18a glosses as *pu ch'i* 不齊.
8. FW 1/22a punctuates after *kung* 攻, reading "To attack [them] oneself/ Is principled." CWK, p. 37, n. 3, apparently follows.
9. Literally, "[If there] seeps through what he desires, . . ."
10. HFT 7:21:119–20 (Liao, I, 217–18).

11. For this usage, see CYYT 10/<u>12</u>/5 (Wilhelm, 55; Kunst, 263).

12. CYYT 47/Hsi B/4 (Wilhelm, 341). Cf. LT, ch. 58 (Lau, 119): "It is on disaster that good fortune perches; it is beneath good fortune that disaster crouches."

13. That is, "foregoing." SMK 1/11a reads instead as "to go too far in regard to." See below.

14. CYYT 47/Hsi B/4 (Wilhelm, 340–41) [text rearranged].

15. *Documents*, "Lü ao," par. 9 (not in Karlgren; Legge, 349–50).

16. Recorded in CTYT 82–83/<u>29</u>/43–74 (Watson, 334), for example.

17. Reading *che* 折 as *che hsüan* 折旋, following YTC 1/19a. Otherwise, it must mean "break."

18. Literally, "being near."

19. FY 2:5. Cf. *Analects* 11/15 (Waley, 156), which talks of "entering the door and ascending to the main hall."

20. See Stein.

21. Reading 中行 as *chung hsing* instead of *chung hang*.

22. Or, "stumbling."

23. *Analects* 1/8, 15/30 (Waley, 85, 199).

24. Alternately, "Having put oneself in danger, one acts to be safe."

25. See, e.g., HFT 3:10:54 (Liao, I, 96).

26. Following SMK 1/11a, which glosses *jang ts'ui* 躟趡 as *hsieh hsing pu yi* 邪行不已 ("deflected walk unending," meaning "he falters"[?]), probably on the basis of variant characters in the FW edition. I read this literally as, "When feet are fettered, and his steps stumble,..." Sung Wei-kan, however, reads this as "hurried" (*chi hsing mao* 急行貌).

27. YTC 1/19b, referring to CYYT 15/<u>21</u>/*shang* (Wilhelm, 89; Kunst, 281).

28. Reading *fu* 輔 ("bones of the upper jaw") as *fu* 甫 ("just up to"); taking *ming* 銘 ("inscribed," "branded," "marked") as *ming* 名 ("the area above the eye"). SMK 1/11a cites CYYT 18/<u>28</u>/*shang* (Wilhelm, 114; Kunst, 295): "In crossing the river at the shallows, he gets his crown wet."

29. Literally, "There are some shoots [of a fallen stump] which are verdant green."

30. For early Chinese walls, see Waldron, pp. 13–51; and Knapp, pp. 1–12; 54–63.

31. For the same metaphor, see Ode 304/6 (Legge, 642); CYYT 18/<u>28</u>/5 (Wilhelm, 113).

No. 12. Youthfulness

1. HTYT 24/<u>8</u>/106 (Dubs, 114; Knoblock, II, 81): "If an intelligent man is without teacher or precepts, he will surely become a robber."

2. CCYT 398/Chao 19/5 *Kung* (Malmqvist, 203), cited by CPL 1/22b.

3. FY 1:2. Cf. Yang Hsiung's disciple, Huan T'an, cited in YKC 14/5b (Pokora, 67): "Three years of [solitary] study does not equal three years with a selected teacher."

4. Cf. FY 6:17.

5. YTC 1/19b; CPL 1/22b equate *hui wo* 會我 with the *Changes* phrase, *ch'iu wo* 求我. See CYYT 5/<u>4</u>/*t'uan* (Wilhelm, 406). For further information on Han readings of this phrase, see Yen Ling-feng (1980), p. 71ff.

6. Reading *meng* 蒙 as its cognate with determinative 109 目.
7. The Chinese is ambiguous; either the teacher or the student could be ignorant and benighted. The *Changes* tradition, however, identifies the youth as the blind one. See Yen Ling-feng (1980), pp. 71–72. YTC 1/19b reads this "To meet with us [ie., teachers] on account of [his] benightedness." CPL 1/22b identifies the teacher as ignorant and benighted.
8. See FY 1:1.
9. For the pun, see HsinS 7/1a.
10. *Analects* 2/17 (Waley, 91).
11. 耆 = 老.
12. The turtle, of course, has itself "emerged from the muck" of its native habitat to the magnificent temple. Contrast Yang Hsiung's words with the famous *Chuang tzu* passage advising us to prefer the mud. See CTYT 45/17/82-84 (Watson, 188).
13. For *yi* 以 as *yi* 已, see SMK 1/11b. Compare Dobson (1976) 3.1.3 (p. 830).
14. *Analects* 4/6 (Waley, 103). A similar idea is expressed in FY 1:2.
15. *Analects* 7/3 (Waley, 123).
16. Reading *hsi* 錫 as *tz'u* 賜.
17. Cf. HS 58B:3579 (Knechtges, 56).
18. CTYT 36/13/70, 74. (Watson, 152).
19. FW 1/24a; YTC 1/20b; and CPL 1/23a read *te* 德 for *te* 得. In that case, the line means "His character is not fine."
20. YTC 1/20b.
21. FW 1/24a.
22. HsinS 6/3a; *ibid.*, 7/4b–5a; *Mencius* 1A/3 (Lau, 51–52).
23. This tradition is based upon the "Yao tien" chapter of the *Documents* (par. 26), which has the ancient sage-king Shun conferring with promising local candidates for office. Cf. *Analects* 3/5 (Waley, 95), and 5/5 (Waley, 108), where Confucius speculates that even barbarians might offer good examples. For further information, see Nylan (1991) on *feng su* 風俗 ("custom"). For the Chinese reformers' use of such traditions to sanction democracy, see Franke, p. 106ff. On the importance of the progress, see Geertz.
24. On the restorative quality of night air, see *Mencius* 6A/8 (Lau, 165).
25. Literally, "is equal to a runt."
26. For Yang, see FY 2:6.
27. The same argument is given in *Mencius* 6A/15 (Lau, 168).
28. CYYT 5/4/1 (Wilhelm, 22). Kunst, p. 247 translates differently.
29. LT, ch. 10 (Lau, 66).
30. Reading *lei* 纍 for *lei* 儡 (GSR 577f = GSR 577j). Alternately, "In return, it implicates [or binds?] itself."

No. 13. Increase

1. Literally, "abundantly waxing."
2. A play upon *Documents*, "Kao Yao mo," par. 4 (Karlgren, 8), which refers to *te* 德 ("charismatic virtue"). Note that YTC 1/21b and CPL 1/24a read

hsüan 宣 as *ta* 大 ("big"). CWK, p. 44, n. 2, reads it as *pu san* 不散 ("not to disseminate" [i.e., "spread out"]).

3. CPL 1/24a.
4. For alternate readings, see below.
5. Compare *Analects* 2/9 (Waley, 90).
6. FW 1/25a reads the final line as, "Recognized [only by] insiders."
7. SMK 1/12a reads the final line as, "His discernment is [kept] inside."
8. YTC 1/21b.
9. LT, ch. 33 (Lau, 95).
10. Literally, "But not to increase his squaring." FW 1/25a; and Wang Ya both gloss *fang* 方 as *tao* 道 ("Path"). In that case, the line should read, "Not to increase [the intensity] of his direction [towards Tao]."
11. Literally, "Not to increase his squareness./ But to increase his light-glory./ Is benighted. . . ."
12. HFT 6:20:100 (Liao, I, 178) defines "squareness" in terms of "the correspondence between the internal and the external, the agreement of word and deed."
13. See Peterson (1982), 102 ff., who translates *fang* 方 as "within conceptual bounds."
14. CYYT 4/2/*yen* (Wilhelm, 393).
15. CYYT 48/Hsi B/6 (Wilhelm, 597).
16. LT, ch. 44 (Lau, 105).
17. YTC 1/21b. Note the suggestion in FW 1/25a that the light imagery derives from the correlation of Position 2 with fire.
18. Following Wang Ya in reading *kai* 蓋 as *yen* 掩 (GSR 642q as 614b). Not following FW 1/25b in reading *yi* 益. If FW is followed, the verses allude to *Mencius* 2A/2 (Lau, 78), the famous anecdote about the idiot of Sung who pulls up his rice sprouts to "help them grow." Cf. YTC 1/22a; CPL 1/24b. 19. CYYT 26/42/ *t'uan* (Wilhelm, 597).
20. FY 1:2 characterizes wood in the same terms: "stationary below, [and so] gradually increasing above."
21. Literally, "There is someone who increases for him [the weight] carried on top." Following CPL 1/24b.
22. *Yao* 腰 = *yao* 要.
23. For the various meanings of *tse* 澤, see Bodde (1978) and Serruys (1955).
24. Literally, "The marsh, being low, is so capacious./ Where multitudes of moisturing [waters] come together./ The marsh, being low, is so capacious./ Means: It is what humble emptiness makes great."
25. LT, ch. 66 (Lau, 128). Cf. *ibid.*, ch. 32 (Lau, 91).
26. *Ode* 173/4 (Legge, 275); and 222/4 (Legge, 403).
27. Following Serruys in reading *chu* 燭 as "torch." CWK, p. 45, n. 8, reads *fen* 分 as *ming* 明 ("shine"). I can find no authority for this in Morohashi or GSR.
28. FW 1/26a, as usual, glosses *wo* 我 as *wan min* 萬民.
29. Literally, "What the petty man does not match."
30. See FW 1/26a; YTC 1/22b; and CPL 1/25a.
31. For further information, see Bauer, pp. 74–77.
32. In the "Preface" to the *Documents* (Legge, 8), King Wu's supporters are

numbered at 300 chariots; later texts also speak of 3,000 soldiers. See, e.g., *Mencius* 7B/4 (Lau, 195). For further information regarding these legends, see Allan (1981), pp. 103–21. In FY 10:26, Yang Hsiung speaks of holders of the Mandate of Heaven having 3,000 troops.

33. *Mencius* 7B/4 (Lau, 195) on King Wu. For the translation "no match," in the *Mystery*, *wu tang* 無當; in the *Mencius*, *wu ti* 無敵.

34. CWK, p. 45, n. 8, citing YTC 1/22b for support.

35. CYYT 48/Hsi B/6 (Wilhelm, 345).

36. FW 1/26a talks of the noble man's goodness to inferiors, allowing him to "walk together with them" because a rough parity holds among the group.

37. The oracle bone graph for *chien* 兼 shows two arrows grasped in the hand.

38. However, FW 1/26a glosses *t'i* 剔 as *yu* 憂 ("worries").

39. Literally, "Holding in hand [or, taking by the handful] cowries, thereby one is kept in service./ Past increases [make what comes] later be shaved off./ By taking handfuls of cowries thereby be kept serving./ Means: First felicitations and later ruination."

40. It is hard for modern readers to imagine the degree of this debasement. The early Chinese included shaving the head among the Five Mutilations. To them, the shaven head epitomized both unfilial behavior towards one's parents and antisocial (hence illegal) behavior in society. This is because the filial son was to return his body to his parents as received. For further information on Han dynasty notions of filial piety, see Hsiao; for the Five Mutilating Punishments, Hulsewé (1955), pp. 124–28.

41. Following Wang Ya. For the reduplicative *chiang chiang* 扠扠, see also THC36/A2. YL 2/22a associates the support of *shih* with the correspondent Hexagram 42.

No. 14. Penetration

1. Note that FW reverses the yin/yang values for the tetragrams 14 to 26 of *chüan* 2, which affects his reading of the Appraisals.

2. Commentary to *Mencius* 6B/1 (Lau, 171) defines *ts'en* 岑 as "tall and pointed like a mountain"; SW 9B:190b, as "a mountain which is small but high."

3. GSR 324a (*t'ui* 兌) means to "open a passage through." GSR 324f (*jui* 銳), more often "sharp" or "pointed," retains this meaning; hence, my translation.

4. Literally, "are not two."

5. FW 2/1b equates *jui* 銳 with *jui chin* 銳進 ("pointed advance").

6. See Chu Hsi's commentary to *Mencius* 7A/1.

7. HTYT 2/1/22 (Dubs, 34; Knoblock, I, 138).

8. *Documents*, "P'an keng," par. 45 (Legge, 247; Karlgren, 26).

9. HNT 9/4b (Ames, 174).

10. Cf. HTYT 25/8/110–11; 42/11/113–15; 53/14/22.

11. Following FW 2/1a.

12. HTYT 2/1/20–22 (Dubs, 35; Knoblock, I, 138).

13. Or, "Being sharp and singleminded."

14. For the phrase *chuan hsin yi chih* 專心一志, see HTYT 89/23/68 (Dubs,

313). For a longer discussion, see ch. 1 of the *Hsün tzu*.

15. *Ibid*. Cf. FY 1:1–2.

16. KT 16/49/3a (after Sivin [1990], p. 6).

17. Or, "advance."

18. Literally, "The agitated state of being wildly pointy."

19. *K'uang* 狂.

20. CYYT 22/<u>35</u>/4, *hsiang* (Wilhelm, 562). The *Analects* 17/16 (Waley, 213) castigates such erratic activity as typical "modern" behavior.

21. Alternately, "sharp at the time." YTC 2/1b reads this as *chin yi shih* 進以時 ("to advance according to timeliness"). Cf. FW 2/1b.

22. See FY 6:17.

23. Of course, Yang Hsiung borrows freely from earlier writers like Shen Tao (b. 260 B.C.), who regard the calculation of trends as the key to political and material success. With Yang Hsiung, however, the goal of the good man is moral authority, rather than conventional power. For Shen Tao's teachings, see Thompson.

24. Alternately, "to focus upon."

25. YTC 2/1b.

26. HTYT 78/<u>21</u>/1 (Dubs, 259; trans. after Watson, 121).

27. Reading *ch'ou* 醜 as *lei* 類, following FW 2/2a. CPL 2/2a; YTC 2/2a follow. SMK 2/1a reads as *chung* 衆 ("multitudes," "the masses"), following usage in the *Odes*. CWK, pp. 48–49, n. 8, follows. See below.

28. Serruys takes this to mean that he "aspires to."

29. *Kuei* 軌 describes the standard width between carriage wheels (8 Han *ch'ih*). By extension, it comes to mean standards in general. YTC 2/2a equates it simply with the "Great Way."

30. Each *chung* 鍾 measures 6 *hu*, 4 *tou* in Han times.

31. Literally, "emoluments."

32. SMK 2/1b reads this as, "Acute as to the masses' [hearts],/ [The sage-ruler] encompasses [a Way]/ [Broad as] Five Gauges/ [Bountiful as] Ten Thousand Measures. . . ."

33. See above. Regarding the first line of the Appraisal, FW 2/2a supports the first characterization; SMK 2/1b, the second.

34. CPL 2/2a assumes that the Gauges signify greatness in size; the Measures, greatness in number.

35. Following FW 2/2a.

36. YTC 2/2a; CPL 2/2a, citing CTYT 78/<u>28</u>/43 (Watson, 313). Cf. FY 3:8.

37. CPL 2/2a emphasizes that "the emoluments are not selfishly held to one himself."

38. See SC 6:239 (Yang, 168).

39. Literally, "Dishonor and hatred will arrive."

40. CYYT 29/Hsi B/8 (Wilhelm, 353).

41. *Mencius* 7A/44 (Lau, 192).

No. 15. Reach

1. Supplying the phrase "its full extension" on the basis of the Sung Chung commentary. FW 2/2b and Lu Chi read instead, "There is no thing which [yang

ch'i] does not reach," making yang *ch'i* the understood subject and "things" the topic operated on.

    2.   Contrast this with YL 6/8a, where evil branches out.

    3.   Ode 304/2 (Legge, 639).

    4.   Reading *tung* 迵 as *t'ung* 通, following FW 2/2b. However, FW is cited as authority in WJL for glossing it as *t'ung* 同 ("to make common"?), possibly a copyist's error. Perhaps *tung* means *tung* 洞 ("rapidly flowing"). See GSR 1176h. FW 2/2b reads *ch'ü* 屈 as *chin* 盡, so that the final phrase means "inexhaustible" rather than "undeterred." CWK, p. 50, n. 3, follows.

    5.   FY 5:12–13.

    6.   FW 2/2b.

    7.   SMK 2/1b.

    8.   Literally, "reaches.

    9.   YY 33:661 reads *yi pu tao ming* 以不道明 ("Seeing by what is not the Way").

    10.   For further information, see Girardot, pp. 266–68. Certain texts contrast fundamental needs (such as the belly's desire for food) with secondary objects of desire (such as jewels) that delight the eye. See Appraisal 8 below.

    11.   KT 16/49/3a (Rickett[a], 163).

    12.   FW 2/3a takes *wei liu* 維流 as a compound meaning "limbs and branches hanging down." I take *wei* 維 as a particle meaning "it is precisely."

    13.   Following SMK 2/2a in reading *pao* 苞 as *p'ao* 匏. Otherwise, *pao* means "shrubbery."

    14.   CPL 2/3a reads "to measure others." Cf. CYYT 27/44/5 (Wilhelm, 173; Kunst, 326) for the melons' association with what "drops down from Heaven."

    15.   FW 2/3a.

    16.   The secure home is the theme of Ode 156/3 (Legge, 236-37) talking of melons and gourds. Cf. the *Odes'* praise of southern trees: "With curved and drooping branches/ The sweet gourds cling to them." See Ode 4/1 (Legge, 10), 171/3 (Legge, 271).

    17.   Tentative translation. Literally, "Small sharpness [or, profit], small reach." CPL 2/3b clearly reads *li* 利 as "profit," arguing that an individual of limited talents survives only so long as he contents himself with minor profit; unfortunately, his very limitations lead him to pursue unattainable goals.

    18.   Or, "Greatly misled, [he is] narrow and small."

    19.   Literally, "not."

    20.   FW 2/3a; YTC 2/3a; and CPL 2/3b read *ku* 故 instead of *chiu* 救. If that reading is adopted, the individual "does not ascertain the true causes" behind events.

    21.   *Analects* 7/8 (Waley, 124).

    22.   *Ibid.*, 2/14 (Waley, 91).

    23.   For the Han depiction of "all-seeing," see Bodde (1975), p. 118 ff.

    24.   E.g., Chuang tzu's famous frog in the well, or *Mencius* 7B/29 (Lau, 200) on a certain P'en-ch'eng Kuo, "a man of limited talent who [knew] . . . just enough [of the Way for it] to cost him his life," cited by SMK 2/2a.

    25.   E.g., *Documents*, "Hung fan," par. 14 (Legge, 331–32; Karlgren, 32).

    26.   Or, following Serruys, "not being held back at the waist to stop."

27. Literally, "water channels" or "ditches" which direct the flow of water. Note that the same word also means "excess."

28. For alternate punctuation and reading, see below.

29. YTC 2/3b.

30. E.g., HTYT 25/8/124 (Dubs, 118; Knoblock, II, 83): "The noble man's discourse has an outer boundary; his conduct has an outer limit. . . ." See also HY *shang*/2a (Ku, 66) on the need for delineations, as recognized by the ancient sage Hou Chi 后稷.

31. CWK, p. 51, n. 7, reads *p'ien* 偏 as *pien* 徧 ("on all sides"). SMK 2/2a, however, argues, "Once the fields are [too] broad and large, if you follow this, you lose that." He therefore retains *p'ien*, leaving the final line unchanged.

32. This reading gains some support from Yang's criticism of the Taoist's propensity to ignore the basic human need for rules and regulations. See FY 3:10.

33. If the ruler is subject, the verses warn against the unfair distribution of favors.

34. *Mencius* 3A/4 (Lau, 102).

35. Or, "he is not done away with." The Fathoming translation adds "the affected spot."

36. Cf. HFT 11:32:199 (Liao, II, 35).

37. YTL 10/59/11a (not in Gale).

38. FW 2/3b; YTC 2/3b.

39. The examples are supplied by Nylan.

40. Meaning, "to retreat from evil," based on YTC 2/4a: "to diminish his faults."

No. 16. Contact

1. According to FW 2/4a.

2. Following CWK, p. 53, n. 2, for the translation of *yü yü* 喬喬; FW 2/4a talks vaguely of the sights and sounds of things growing in spring. Other commentators treat *yü huang* 喬皇 as the compound. Lu Chi reads it "good and beautiful" (*hsiu mei* 休美); Wang Ya, as "bright and flourishing" (*ming sheng* 明盛); YTC 2/4a as "harmonious and great" (*ho ta* 和大). CPL 2/4a combines the glosses of Lu Chi and Wang Ya.

3. FY 3:7.

4. For early Chinese notions of community, see e.g., Fingarette; Bauer; and Tu.

5. See Graham (1989), p. 20.

6. *Ming-t'ang* 明堂.

7. YTC 2/4a; CPL 2/4b. For further information, see Soothill; Steinhardt; and Allan (1991), pp. 92, 102, for example.

8. CPL 2/4b reads *ming* 冥 as *mo* 默, suggesting that all contact with the divine is achieved through silent communication.

9. FW 2/4b omits the character *chen* 貞 here. I follow WJL 2/2b.

10. FW 2/4b.

11. Cf. the arguments in FSTY 9:67 (Nylan, 520).

12. For this definition of "the divine (*shen* 神), see CCFL 6/19/5b–7b.

13. A pun: *Ming* 明 means "luminous" or "enlightened," but it also is used of the earth "spirits."

14. Or, "make others turn [towards him]" (?)

15. FW 2/4b.

16. SMK 2/2b, citing *Analects* 1/8 (Waley, 85). Cf. *ibid.*, 4/1 (Waley, 102); HTYT 1/1/16 (Dubs, 33; Knoblock, I, 137).

17. FW 2/4b.

18. Translation tentative. Cf. HS 87A:3532 (Knechtges, 22): "The pyre's smoke rises to august Heaven." As for the reduplicative, CPL 2/5a talks of visible signs of ritual. For the importance of fragrant smoke in contemporary Greek times, see Detienne, esp. pp. 7–8. Wang Ya glosses *hsün hsün* 熏熏 as *chung to* 衆多 ("multitudinous"): "Back and forth, many times [the exchanges]." CWK, p. 54, n. 6, follows. This emphasizes the repetitive nature of ritual action as well as the intimacy of contact. If the reduplicative is read with determinative 140, *hsün hsün* 薰薰 means "peaceful," "harmonious." That possibility, strengthened by the Fathoming, is adopted by YTC 2/4b. A similar pattern is found in THC57/A3, but it offers little help.

19. Literally, "Joining with the divine in exchanging activities." Note that Wang Ya replaces *shen* 神 ("the gods") with *fu* 福 ("blessings"), apparently on the basis of FW 2/5a.

20. FW 2/5a; YTC 2/5a. Cf. Ode 248/5 (Legge, 481), where the phrase *hsün hsün* 熏熏 describes the sated look of the ancestor's impersonator after the ritual feast. CPL 2/5a emphasizes the disastrous results of transferring this religious awe to the client-patron relation. Cf. THC20/A7, where Yang Hsiung deplores patronage.

21. CCYT 96/Hsi 5/*Tso* 9 (Legge, 146); and 347/Chao 2/*Tso* 3 (Legge, 584) also insist that men make their own fates.

22. For more on parrots, see Stern.

23. As LC 1/2b (Legge, I, 64) says, "The parrot can speak, but it is no more than a bird. The ape can speak, but it is no more than a beast."

24. *Ibid.*

25. SMK 2/2b, citing Ode 215/4 (Legge, 387).

26. CPL 2/5a.

27. YTC 2/5a.

28. Following FW 2/5a; YY 33:661; and CWK, p. 54, n. 8, in reading *chüan* 圈 as *kuo* 國. Wang Ya reads it as "bowls to hold delicacies" used in entertaining guests and diplomats; SMK 2/3a, as "animal pens" (a measure of the ruler's wealth).

29. CYYT 37/61/2 (Wilhelm, 237).

30. For the conventional antithesis of grain (as blessings, salary) to misfortune, see Ode 204/5 (Legge, 358); for bird and rat, see Ode 189/3 (Legge, 304); for the rat, see Ode 52/1–3 (Legge, 84–85).

31. FW 2/5b, however, takes the lines as criticism of lavish expenditure by the imperial household for the upkeep of exotic pets, to the detriment of the people's welfare. The most famous case of this is the obsession of Duke Yi of Wei with storks. See CCYT 83/Min 2/7 *Tso* (Legge, 129). This reading seems unlikely insofar as it ignores the parallelism with Appraisal 5.

32. CPL 2/6a reads *cheng* 征. CWK, p. 55, n. 9 follows. The WJL edition

(2/3a), however, reads *wang* 往 ("to go forward" or "away").

33.   Literally, "cannot be made to fail." Alternately, "[his propriety] cannot be forsaken."

34.   A loose paraphrase of CPL 2/6a. Cf. YTC 2/5b.

35.   A loose translation, punctuating before *fa* 伐 for scansion.

36.   Following FW 2/5b in reading *ch'eng* 城 ("city walls"). However, SMK 2/3a reads *fa* 伐 ("attack").

37.   YTC 2/5b. Literally, the Appraisal reads: "Engaging in battle,/ The attack is not right./ Overturned at attacks [or, city wall]./ Being violent, then he is devoured."

38.   See Shih.

No. 17. Holding Back

1.   Following SMK 2/3a. FW 2/12b assigns the direction and note to THC21.

2.   FW 2/6a reads *jui* 銳 as "advance" instead of the adjective "sharp."

3.   The analogy between moral and physical courage is made by Mencius in 2A/2 (Lau, 76–80). Cf. Mencius' discussion of Ox Mountain in 6A/8 (Lau, 164–65).

4.   CCYT 184/Hsüan 4/4 *Tso* (Legge, 296), cited by SMK.

5.   Literally, "Even though one is not allowed to stretch out, ..."

6.   Reading *fu* 拂 as *fu* 咈 (=*li* 戾), following Wang Ya.

7.   Or, "swing freely" (?)

8.   Both are *chieh* 節.

9.   FY 3:7 argues, "The superior man preserves [or, keeps to] himself." Cf. *ibid.*, 12:36: "If he does not meet with the proper time, the sage keeps to himself." CPL 2/6b; and YTC 2/6a tie this to Yang Hsiung's relations with Wang Mang.

10.   YTC 2/6b reads *szu* 肆 as *szu yung* 肆用: "Although he has never been used to the utmost [in service], he feels in no hurry to leave [government]."

11.   See SMK 2/3b.

12.   The character *wa* 哇 literally means "to spit out" or "vomit." It suggests something distasteful, possibly criticism of the ruler.

13.   Literally, "a peck." See GSR 1224n.

14.   *Analects* 16/6 (Waley, 205).

15.   SMK 2/3b specifies the *shih* 士 as subject of these verses, but this pre-occupation with gentry as "central" is anachronistic. See Nylan (forthcoming), ch. 3 on "Sung."

16.   See Yang Hsiung's "Shu tu fu" 蜀都賦, cited in YKC, I, 51/1a.

17.   *Ch'ing* 慶 = *ch'ing* 卿. Note that floating clouds are a symbol of unethical ministers. See Pankenier (1990b), 439.

18.   Translation tentative. Literally: "Someone/perhaps presents/assists/takes-over/follows him disaster." The WJL edition (2/3b) reads *ch'eng* 成 ("to complete") rather than *huo* 或, but this ignores the pattern borrowed from the *Changes*: *huo* verb *chih* 之 character. YTC 2/7a reads this as, "Some [or, In some cases this] advance(s) (*chin* 進) him [to] disaster." FW 2/7a and SMK 2/3b comment simply, "disaster follows" (*tsai ch'eng* 菑承).

19.   THC "Hsüan wen" 9/1b (p. 1028b).

20.   Translation tentative. The same characters could mean, "Bending at his

joints" as a sign of submission, or "bending his principles." But see below.

21. Reading *shu* 術 as *hsin shu* 心術. FW 2/7a; SMK 2/3b; and YTC 2/7a identify *shu* with the Tao.

22. Literally, "He offers [all] to what he dies for."

23. Citing a Chou bronze inscription after Eno, p. 212 (n. 28). Cf. SMK 2/3b and YTC 2/7a, which speak of dying for the right cause.

24. FW 2/7a–7b; YTC 2/7a, however, punctuate after "trees," taking *ting* 丁 as *tang* 當.

25. YTC 2/7a reads *k'uan* 寏 as *chih* 止 ("to stop").

26. Literally, "The impact [of wind] shakes its branches. . . ."

27. Cf. the comparison of the ruler to wind in *Analects* 12/19 (Waley, 168).

28. Following YTC 2/7b in taking *hui so* 悔縮 as verb object. However, SMK 2/3b reads the two characters as two equal verbs: the person "repents and draws back."

No. 18. Waiting

1. See CPL 2/8a.

2. Following FW 2/7b. Alternately, "When the time comes, it [brings] no felicity."

3. The term Heaven by Yang Hsiung's time is often used to mean simply the [inescapable] course of events.

4. Or, "brightening."

5. Following Sung Wei-kan. FW 2/8a reads as: "Prosperous days increase and magnify him" (*ch'ang jih yi ta chih* 昌日益大之); Wang Ya and SMK 2/4a as: "Prosperity in less than a day" (*chiang wu jih yeh* 將無日也).

6. THC "Hsüan wen" 9/1b (p. 1028b).

7. Literally, "grain."

8. Reading *ch'ih* 伎 as its cognate *chih* 忮 (GSR 864j = 864d). CWK, p. 59, n. 5, however, reads it as *shu* 舒 ("slow"), based on Ode 197/5 (Legge, 338): "The stag is running away/ But his legs move slowly."

9. Reading *la* 剌 as *li* 戾, according to SW 6B/128b.

10. CPL 2/8b, citing Ode 112/1 (Legge, 170): "eating the bread of idleness."

11. YTC 2/8b.

12. Reading *chüeh* 爵 as *ch'üeh* 雀; *yung* 庸 as *yung* 墉. This reading is preferred by SMK 2/4a; CPL 2/8b.

13. Following SMK 2/4a.

14. CYYT 25/40/6, *hsiang* (Wilhelm, 588; Kunst, 319); 47/Hsi B/4 (Wilhelm, 340).

15. Alternately, "with utmost propriety," or "being tried and true."

16. SMK 2/4a reads *fu* 服 (in my translation, "taken as tonic") as *fu hsing* 服行 ("to apply and carry out"). However, the phrase "eat of gold," is parallel to *yü shih* 玉食 ("eat of jade") in *Documents*, "Hung fan," par. 18 (Legge, 334; Karlgren, 32).

17. Translation tentative for the reduplicative *chieh chieh* 介介; reading it as *keng keng* 耿耿 (Morohashi 29026.11), defined as "not safe" (*pu an* 不安) or "unable to sleep because of anxiety." FW 2/8b reads it as "having harm" (*yu hai* 有害); SMK 2/4a and CWK, p. 60, n. 9, as "perverse and evil" (*p'i hsieh* 僻邪); CPL 2/9a, as "animals without a mate" (an ill omen).

18. SMK 2/4a, however, reads *yu* 邮 as the loan character for *yu* 尤 ("guilt") (GSR 997a = 996a).

19. YY 33:662, however, argues that the first line of the Fathoming repeats the Appraisal. I prefer the *textus difficilior*.

20. Taking the particle *chüeh* 厥 to imply a superior, Heaven or the ruler. Alternately, "It is not his fault."

21. *Analects* 12/4 (Waley, 163).

22. FW 2/9a; CPL 2/9a. For the proverb, "If calamity is not relished, then it cannot become a calamity," see Hart, p. 41.

23. CYYT 29/47/*t'uan* (Wilhelm, 625).

24. Literally, "Waiting [in the manner of] the *wang wang.*"

25. The *wang* illness is said to deform the body to such a degree that the victim's face permanently juts up towards the sky. Modern Chinese medical dictionaries give no equivalent for the *wang* disease; probably it describes a skeletal or neurological abnormality.

26. YTC 2/9a compares Heaven's strike to CYYT 18/28/6 (Wilhelm, 114; Kunst, 295). Perhaps Yang refers to the ancient practice of exposing a cripple in sacrifices for rain. For further information, see Schafer (1951), esp. pp. 161–62, citing CCYT 117/Hsi 21/*Tso* 3 (Legge, 180).

No. 19. Following

1. Literally, "raise their heels to stand on tiptoes," a phrase which conveys a sense of eager expectation of the profound transformations (*hua* 化) to be accomplished. The words "to follow" are supplied by FW 2/9b.

2. See HsinS 1/4b, e.g., for this imagery.

3. I.e., the moon. FW 2/9b explains *p'in* 嬪 (usually, "to marry") as *chi p'in* 羇嬪 ("to lodge temporarily [in a lunar mansion]").

4. "It" refers to the sun.

5. SMK 2/4b; CPL 2/9b.

6. For further information on the motion of sun and moon, see Tricker, pp. 40–41.

7. CPL 2/9b.

8. Literally, "Just emerging [in?] the faint light of dawn."

9. Reading *erh* 爾 as *jan* 然, despite CYYT 20/31/4, where *erh* 爾 may mean "your." Literally, "In pairs, following, they form categories."

10. See, for example, HsinS 9/11a, which compares the dawn to the superior man taking up his office. Cf. THC1/A6. Contrast this with sunset, as in CYYT 19/30/3 (Wilhelm, 120; Kunst, 299).

11. CYYT 39/Hsi A/1 (Wilhelm, 280), cited by YTC 2/9b.

12. FW 2/9b.

13. The commentators disagree on the identity of the pairs. SMK 2/4b compares the blurry outline of the sun at dawn to the unclear mind; once the mind chooses evil, ill fortune will come to pair it. CPL 2/10a says the pairs refer to dragons, the categorical analogues of the sun. According to Ch'en, the dragons' frustration mounts once they find themselves unable to leave their watery homes to join the sun in its daily round. Probably the pairs simply represent the full range of living things, as in Noah's ark, where the animals were paired two by two.

14. Literally, "Leading themselves, they follow him," following YTC 2/9b and CPL 2/10a. Serruys prefers, "Letting himself be led, he follows them." It could also mean, "Self-led to follow it," where "it" refers to the Right.

15. Literally, "Self-so, a witness [to charismatic power]." Not following the unnecessary emendation of SMK 2/4b, who reads *cheng* 正 for *cheng* 證.

16. Reading *k'uang* 匡 as *k'uang* 筐. Many commentators punctuate after *hsüeh* 血, but my scansion preserves the rhyme. See below for an alternate interpretation.

17. CYYT 33/54/6 (Wilhelm, 212; Kunst, 347).

18. CPL 2/10b.

19. YTC 2/10a.

20. Early Chinese literature associates harm from a blood sacrifice with a "military expedition without advantage." See CCYT 110/Hsi 15/*Tso* 14 (Legge, 169).

21. SMK 2/4b.

22. For the sexual metaphor, see Harper, 570 ff. Alternately, with different punctuation: "The woman [intends to] transmit her blood [as heir]./ Reform is lost." However, Li Yün, p. 33, understands *ch'eng k'uang* 承筐 as "shoulders."

23. FW 2/10a reads *k'o* 科 as *fa* 法 ("model"). But *Mencius* 7A/24 (cited below) shows that *k'o* means "pit" or "hollow." My translation attempts to capture both senses.

24. *Mencius* 7A/24 (Lau, 187).

25. CPL 2/10b. Cf. FY 1:2.

26. Literally, "Desires are excessively followed."

27. These needs are presumed by both Mencius and Hsün tzu. See, e.g., *Mencius* 2A/2; 6A/1–6.

28. Compare our own saying, "The eyes are bigger than the stomach," which accounts for many a stomach ache. The examples are supplied by Nylan.

29. Cf. HTYT 25/8/120 (Dubs, 116; Knoblock, II, 82): "If one indulges his . . . emotions . . . , he will become an ordinary man [rather than a superior]."

30. Reading *shu* 淑 (literally, "pure" or "clean") as *shan* 善 ("good"), following SMK 2/5a.

31. Reading *ts'ung* 從 as *ts'ung* 縱 (GSR 1191d = 1191h). Alternately, "[He] attends to his good," or, "[He] follows his good."

32. CPL 2/11a.

33. See App. 7 above for GSR 1191. Alternately, "Complying with the impure."

34. Literally, "is not caught [when pursued]."

35. Serruys conflates these two lines, reading, "Later and only then, climbing on the stairs [=his rise to success], he is brought to an end."

36. Or, "Later, he attains achievement."

No. 20. Advance

1. "Things" is added.

2. And, "makes [them] advance."

3. CWK, p. 64, n. 2, reads *chen chen* 溱溱 as *shu pu* 舒布 "expanding, unfolding."

4. Or, "[like] opening up the light." CPL 2/11b, however, reads, "as if the eyes are opened," defining *k'ai ming* 開明 as "getting rid of diseases in the eye."

5. FY 12:39.

6. FY 1:2 takes water as the model for "advance": "It never stops, day or night. . . ."

7. SMK 2/5a reads *ming* 冥 as *ch'ien* 潛 ("hidden").

8. Following YTC 2/11a, reading *p'i* 否 as *pu t'ung* 不通, following the rhymes for GSR 999e and 947a. SMK, however, reads *p'i* as *fou* ("wrong").

9. Alternately, "Initiatives [are] the mother of retreat."

10. Following Wang Ya, taking obstruction as the "root cause" of retreat. "Mother" also implies the all-enveloping nature (cf. the womb) of the retreat.

11. Alternately, following CPL 2/11a and Serruys, "The Great Man alone manifests [the Way]."

12. Literally, "The model cannot be kept on the outside [only]."

13. E.g., the "Doctrine of the Mean" and the "Great Plan" chapter of the *Documents*.

14. *Analects* 20/1 (Waley, 231–32). Cf. *Mencius* 7A/41 (Lau, 192). For Yang Hsiung, see HS 57B:3582 (Knechtges, 58): "In establishing government . . . nothing is superior to the harmony of the Mean."

15. Expanding the argument of FW 2/11a.

16. E.g., *Mencius* 2A/2 (Lau, 80); HTYT 21/8/41 (Dubs, 115; Knoblock, II, 82). This egalitarian claim of early Confucianism tends to be lost in later neo-Confucianism. YTC 2/11a takes the Fathoming to mean that model behavior cannot be attained "outside" [among the ordinary masses of people].

17. SMK 2/5a defines *chang chang* 章章 as *shih chü mao* 失據貌. The translation of the first lines of the Appraisal and Fathoming tries to reflect both possible meanings for the reduplicative phrase.

18. See, for example, *Analects* 5/21 (Waley, 113).

19. CPL 2/12a takes this as an evil omen: "The sun flies [away]; [in its place] the moon is suspended." However, this reading cannot possibly be squared with the emphatically positive notes sounded by the phrases "suffused with joy" and "flourishes."

20. Understanding *jung jung* 融融 as *ho le* 和樂. FW 2/11b reads as *mao chuang* 茂壯 ("flourishing, strong").

21. Literal translation.

22. Following FW 2/11b in reading *ch'ü shu* 欋疏 as *fu li* 附離 ("adherence" [as client or servant to more powerful interests?]). Couvreur (1947), p. 479 defines it as "what is near and far," "friend and foe" but I can find no support for this.

23. Following the WJL edition, reading *tsung* 宗 instead of *tsun* 尊 because of the rhyme. Literally, "He is trimmed by [his] protector's house."

24. Numerous articles have been written on this topic. See, e.g., Hsü Cho-yün (1965b); de Crespigny; and Powers (1987).

25. For further information on "Praising Hsin and Denigrating Ch'in," see Knechtges (1978).

26. CPL 2/12a, glossing the phrase *ch'ü shu* 欋疏 as *pi chieh* 篦梳 (two types of combs).

27. CPL 2/12a reads *chih* 制 as *chin* 禁 ("to prohibit")."

28. YTC 2/11b offers a still more unconvincing explication of the verses, in which a comb and walking stick represent two offerings made to the ruler, with the first gift rejected and the second accepted. According to Yeh, the poem criticizes the arbitrary nature of the ruler's whims.

29. Alternately, "great." See YY 33:662.

30. FW 2/12a.

31. Tentative translation, following CWK, p. 65, n. 9. Literally, "Advance, it is not what he uses." YTC 2/12a takes this to mean that the subject of these verses does not use remonstrance. Serruys reads instead, "The advance is perverted." Hence, the Fathoming translation below.

32. Following YTC 2/12a.

33. FY 2:5, 8:20 both employ the same metaphor. Cf. THC3/A9.

34. Contrast the phrasing with THC61/A9, an auspicious Fathoming. The first line of the Fathoming repeats the first line of the Appraisal.

35. *Analects* 5/6 (Waley, 108) on "feats of physical daring."

No. 21. Release

1. Following FW 6/12b. SMK 2/5b has the Dipper pointing due east in Head 17.

2. Reading *chen* 震 as its cognate *chen* 振. Most commentators gloss *chen* as *tung* 動 ("move," "shake").

3. "Casing of yin" supplied in a tentative translation. See below for an alternate reading.

4. The exact interpretation of the Head, then, hinges on the significance assigned to the character "round" (*huan* 圜). Sung Chung; FW 2/12b; and CPL 2/13a equate roundness with the "shape of yang" (presumably because of the sun), which envelops creatures with warmth and light, fostering their growth and plumping them up with health. It is also conceivable that "round" refers to the cosmic "sack of Heaven-and-Earth" that contains all the myriad things in its expanse. See KT 4/11/8b. My reading of KT follows Graham (1978), p. 367. My translation assumes the pattern topic 3-3-4-4. The alternative reading would be 4-4-4-4. Either is possible.

5. CYYT 25/40/*t'uan* (Wilhelm, 585).

6. Release is associated with "remiss" behavior (*chieh* 解 = *hsieh* 懈). See GSR 861a,b. Cf. the statement, "Release . . . often leads to loss," found in CYYT 53/*hsü* (Wilhelm, 584).

7. Following SMK 2/5b.

8. *Analects* 8/19 (Waley, 136). Cf. LT, ch. 1 (Lau, 57).

9. Following SMK 2/5b. As if to emphasize this point, FW 2/12b and CPL 2/13b offer this explanation: Appraisal 1 is assigned to Water; spring is allied with agent Wood (Appraisal 3). People seldom credit Water with fostering the beneficial growth, attributing it instead to spring's (i.e. Wood's) influence. Cf. LT, ch. 17 (Lau, 73): "The best of all rulers is but a shadowy presence to his subjects."

10. Literally, "Movement goes to echo and shadow."

11. Literally, "Not worth watching or listening to."

12. CYYT 43/Hsi A/9 (Wilhelm, 314); and HsinS 9/3b.

13. SMK 2/5b writes, "Their movement is not of their own accord" (*tung pu yu chi che* 動不由己者).

14. CPL 2/13b mentions those who are easily swayed by false rumors and unsubstantiated talk.

15. YTC 2/12b.

16. See, for example, Ode 178/4, 263/3 (Legge, 287, 557). Cf. *Analects* 12/19 (Waley, 168).

17. Literally, "mounds and hills." Cf. FY 1:3 for similar wording.

18. YY 33:662, however, reads *p'eng* 朋 as *peng* 崩 so that the line means, "To lose the lowlands. Collapse."

19. Literally, "Danger of losing the low."

20. FW 2/13a writes simply that the petty man "loses old," familiar ties.

21. YTC 2/13a–13b, after SMK 2/6a.

22. Literally, "Salves that harmonize and release." Alternately, "Harmoniously release for them the salves." I have supplied the topic.

23. Compare *ho shih* 和罦 with the phrase *ho yi* 和懌 in the *Documents*, "Tzu ts'ai," par. 7 (Legge, 432 [par. renum.]; Karlgren, 48).

24. The phrase "Four States" means all the states in the empire (since "four" covers every direction); it also refers to the various rebel or barbarian states, here brought into submission. For the phrase, see the *Odes* 153/4, 157/1–4 (Legge, 225, 238–40).

25. E.g., *Documents*, "T'ai shih," par. 5 (Legge, 285; not in Karlgren); Ode 258/3 (Legge, 530). For thunder imagery elsewhere in Yang's work, cf., e.g., FY 4:11.

26. FW 2/13b argues that the innovation concerns the ancestors since we are now in Appraisal 6, aligned with the ancestral temple. Apparently, the sacrificial duties have been neglected after the political successes outlined in Appraisal 5. As Fan Wang writes, "The gods are angry and the common people are resentful."

27. See YTC 2/13b.

28. Drawing upon Han political theory, SMK 2/6a gives an alternate interpretation, which distinguishes the techniques the ideal ruler uses within China's borders (suasive example, therefore "harmony") from those applied to the barbarian states (force, therefore "thunder"). Thunderclaps signify the use of awesome force in the Chinese court, which is inappropriate.

29. Literally, "Thunder thunder not disgraced./ Washing clean his insult."

30. For the last line, YTC 2/13b reads *wu fang* 無方 ("without direction") as *wu ting* 無定 ("not fixed [in evil ways]").

31. CYYT 31/51/*hsiang* (Wilhelm, 648–49).

32. *Ibid.* CPL 2/14b says there is still time to reform.

33. Following FW 2/13b; SMK 2/6a. Cf. YTC 2/13b, who says that the individual's angry outburst, however improper, does not merit final disgrace since reform follows.

34. Cf. CYYT 26/42/*t'uan* (Wilhelm, 597): "To walk together with time."

35. *Analects* 4/12 (Waley, 104).

36. *Analects* 4/16 (Waley, 105). Cf. *Mencius* 6A/10 (Lau, 166–67).

37. Or, "imprisoned."

38. The character *ku* 穀 refers literally to grain and by extension, to govern-

ment office (since salaries are paid in grain), to good luck, and to blessings in general.

   39. Cf. CYYT 5/4/1 (Wilhelm, 22; Kunst, 247).

   40. *Mencius* 7A/2 (Lau, 182).

   41. See CYYT 5/4/1 (Wilhelm, 22; Kunst, 247), where fetters originally needed for "discipline" are removed after moral development. For the same argument in the writings of America's Founding Fathers, see Takaki.

   42. Allan (1981), pp. 103–11.

No. 22. Resistance

   1. Or possibly, "Great Injury." See Kunst, p. 307.

   2. Literally, just "many yin."

   3. CYYT 21/34/3 (Wilhelm, 134). Cf. Kunst, p. 307 for a different reading.

   4. Following SMK 2/6b. Some commentators follow FW 2/14a–14b, which understands it to mean "[men] who are good inside."

   5. Literally, "Loses propriety and goodness," reading *lei* 類 as its synonym *shan* 善, following CWK, p. 69, n. 3. Sung Chung, however, reads *lei* 類 as *fa* 法 ("model"). Serruys reads *chen lei* 貞類 as "[all] sorts of good omens." FW 2/14a reads as, "To lose [touch with] men of propriety." It is also possible that *lei* means "categories." See below.

   6. Literally, "The center is not resembling," reading *hsiao* 宵, following Sung Chung and SMK 2/6b for parallelism with *lei* 類. FW 2/14a reads *hsing* 省, which he glosses as *hsün* 循 ("to follow" [the principles laid down by the ancients]). YTC 2/14a; CPL 2/15a also read *hsün*, with CPL defining it as *ch'a* 察 ("to examine" [the conscience].)

   7. *Mencius* 2A/6 (Lau, 83). HTYT 21/8/39–22/8/65 (Dubs, 99–104; Knoblock, II, 73–76); 89/23/53 (Dubs, 312; not in Knoblock) together suggest that Hsün tzu presumed the same. For Yang Hsiung's ideas on the mixed nature of the inborn nature, see FY 3:7, which has been translated in Chan, pp. 289–90.

   8. An alternate reading for the second line of the Appraisal.

   9. Following the alternate reading for the second line of the Fathoming. See *Analects* 12/4 (Waley, 163) on Master Confucius, who examined his conscience thrice daily. Cf. *ibid.*, 1/4 (Waley, 84).

   10. The FW edition adds the character *lei* 類 here in what is evidently an interpolation from the previous Appraisal.

   11. Literally, "Lower garments set off against belt and hook."

   12. Following FW 2/14b; and CPL 2/15b. Wang Ya; SMK 2/6b; YTC 2/14b; and CWK, p. 70, n. 5, however, read *yü* as "changed" (*pien* 變), meaning "to lose constancy."

   13. For the belt and hook, cf. THC2/A4.

   14. Punctuation tentative, following WJL. Literally, "The net wards off." Serruys prefers to make both Appraisal and Fathoming three characters long: "The net sets off the captive [birds]."

   15. Following FW 2/14b. Alternately, "to be in a position to use law to rectify," following SMK 2/6b. Serruys reads as, "to rectify lawful positions."

   16. YTC 2/14b and CPL 2/15b both argue that the net is "raised" as barrier but not spread out, signifying that no punishment is needed in the ideal state. This goes farther than the THC.

17. FW 2/14b.
18. See the discussion in Hulsewé (1955), pp. 103–09; 345–50.
19. FW 2/14b–15a.
20. CYYT 42/Hsi B/7 (Wilhelm, 307).
21. Poem 18 of the Nineteen Old Poems uses the same metaphor of glue and lacquer to describe the bonds of romantic love. For political applications, see SC 79:2421 (not in Chavannes or Watson; Yang, 112–13 [trans. as "close ties"]).
22. FY 9:25 characterizes a commitment to Confucianism in this way.
23. Or, "gold."
24. Following Wang Ya.
25. Metal mirrors were thought to produce water. For this, see Needham, IV, section 26g. Also, Camann and Bulling.
26. FW 2/15a.
27. Reading *t'i* 剔 instead of *t'i* 鬄. Alternately, "cut off."
28. Most of the commentators are clearly confused by the resistance to constraints exhibited by both the superior man (here) and the petty man (in Appraisal 3). FW's garbled interpretation (2/15a–15b) ignores the text, arguing that, "the noble man in position does not fear the strong control" associated with belting. SMK 2/7a passes over this poem without comment. CPL 2/16a mistakenly states that the petty man harms the superior man. However, the Appraisal is auspicious according to Yang Hsiung's yin/yang schema.
29. CPL 2/16a–16b talks of misrule at court.
30. *Huan* 還 can mean "in return," "as it turns out," or, if read as *hsüan* 旋, "everywhere."

No. 23. Ease

1. SMK 2/7a correlates it with Hexagram no. 16, "Enthusiasm." I follow earlier commentaries.
2. Sung Chung glosses *t'i* 鬄 as *ch'ü* 去 ("to rid"); Lu Chi and FW 2/15b, as *ch'u* 除 ("to excise").
3. Literally, "has no way to save itself from."
4. CPL 2/16b–17a: "Since yin has no time to save itself, how would it dare to oppress the common people?"
5. The original graph depicts a man with an arrow or an arrow with something wound around the shaft (㐱 and 弋). For the archaic forms, see GSR 551a.
6. However, YTC 2/16a takes *yi* 夷 (in my reading, "to ease") as "harm," arguing that self-cultivation entails an initial "trimming" of the self.
7. An alternate reading of "to rule" or "to cure" (*chih* 治) suggested by YTC 2/16a; CPL 2/17a.
8. *Ni* 貳. For the phrase "two minds," see *Analects* 12/10 (Waley, 165–66), 12/21 (Waley, 169).
9. FY 1:4, on Yen Hui's inner joy, as cited by SMK 2/7a.
10. *Mencius* 2A/2 (Lau, 76–80).
11. LT, ch. 73 (Lau, 135).
12. Reading *yu* 嚘 instead of *sha* 嗄, in order to preserve the rhyme. See YY 33:662–63.
13. LT, ch. 59 (Lau, 116).
14. Contrast FY 4:11, where the baby is not so strong.

15. Following YY 33:663, which reads *t'u* 土 ("dirt"). However, Wang Ya reads *t'u* 徒 as *k'ung* 空 ("in vain"). The line then means, "Those who would feed him try in vain." Contrast SMK 2/7b, which reads *t'u* 徒 as *t'u shu* 徒屬 ("adherents").

16. FW 2/16a. The second alternative is supplied by Nylan.

17. CPL 2/17a, however, reads this as criticism of those who swallow statements whole "without chewing" (i.e., without analyzing) them, but in that case the teeth would not necessarily be "leveled."

18. CYYT 39/Hsi A/1 (Wilhelm, 286). However, for other interpretations of the *Changes* as *chien* 簡, see Kao Huai-min, p. 283 ff.

19. Tentative translation. FW 2/16b; SMK 2/7b; YTC 2/16b; CPL 2/17b; CWK, p. 73, n. 8, read as, "Leveling his dwelling,/ His residence, the hills and ruins (Or, "a mound that is in ruin.")./ Leveling his dwelling/ Means: His virtue is lost." However, the particle *yu* 于 is superfluous in such a reading.

20. CWK, p. 73, n. 8, citing FY 3:7.

21. Since the trunk (*kan* 幹) by convention symbolizes strength, so the first part of the Appraisal could also mean, "What is [usually taken to be] strong is soft/ What is [usually taken to be] strong is weak."

22. Following CWK, p. 74, n. 9, in reading *li* 離 as *fu li* 附麗 ("to adhere to," "to make contact with"). Serruys prefers, "Apart from the wooden [handle], the cutting metal is evened out [i.e., no longer effective]." YTC 2/17a glosses *ai* 艾 as *chan* 斬.

23. *Documents*, "Hung fan," par. 5 (Legge, 325–26; Karlgren, 30).

24. LT, ch. 78 (Lau, 140). Cf. CYYT 21/34/3 (Wilhelm, 134). Kunst, p. 307, translates differently.

25. SMK 2/7b takes *li mu* 離木 as the bar over the well from which the rope and bucket are suspended; *ai chin* 艾金 as the whetstone sharpening the knife. I do not follow him since he supplies too many nouns. Also, his metaphors are mixed. No one wants the well railing to be split by the rope, but the whetstone is employed to sharpen knives.

26. Serruys reads as *li* 麗 ("It is destroyed.")

27. Taking a second meaning of the verb *yi* 夷.

28. FW 2/17a and YTC 2/17a read *yi* as "harm," but this Appraisal is auspicious.

29. I follow CWK, p. 72, punctuating after *li* 利 ("benefit"). Wang Ya, WJL (2/7b) and Serruys, however, punctuate after *k'ao* 考 ("old age"). The two lines would then read, "Finding ease in old age./ To benefit and respect the infirm and aged is a good omen."

30. Tentative translation. See above.

31. *Documents*, "Hung fan," par. 33 (Karlgren, 35; Legge, 340).

No. 24. Joy

1. However, Kunst translates as "Elephant." See Kunst, 271.

2. Following SMK 2/8a. FW 2/17a glosses *ch'u ao* 出奧 as "put out warmth." CPL 2/18b fancifully takes *ao* 奧 as the god of the soil, then interprets the entire Head text as a joyous ode similar to Ode 211/2 (Legge, 376–79). CWK, p. 71,

punctuates differently, taking *ao* as "southeast," the honored position where sacrifice to the gods takes place.

3. My tentative translation for *shu tieh* 舒疊. SMK 2/8b, however, talks of "unrolling out the things that have accumulated" (*shu chan tieh chi chih wu* 舒展疊積之物). FW 2/17a also reads *tieh* as *chi* 積 ("to collect"). Cf. YTC 2/17b; CWK, p. 75, n. 2.

4. Literally, "delighted and joyful" (*hsi le* 喜樂).

5. See fn. 2 above.

6. For the association of "genial airs," music, and luxuriant growth of the myriad things, see LC 19/3:3 (Legge, II, 115).

7. Huan T'an, cited in YKC 15/3a (Pokora, 118).

8. CYYT 53/16/3 (Wilhelm, 69–70; Kunst, 271).

9. Ode 114/1-3 (Legge, 174–75).

10. Translation tentative, following commentaries to SW 8B:179 defining *k'uan* 款 as *yi yu so yü erh yu sai* 意有所欲而有塞 ("in ideas, having what is desired is somewhat blocked"). See Morohashi 16107.18. FW 2/17b and CWK, p. 75, n. 3, unhelpfully define the reduplicative *k'uan k'uan* as "the appearance of solitary pleasure"; YTC 2/17b, as *yen an mao* 宴安貌 ("idle comfort"); CPL 2/18a, as *ch'eng* 誠 ("sincerity"), which would make this line contradict the inauspicious character of the second line.

11. Literally, "It makes his inner [state] excessive."

12. *Mencius* 1A/2 (Lau, 50), 1A/7 (Lau, 57).

13. LC 19/24 (Legge, II, 113).

14. See LC 19/18–21 (Legge, II, 112).

15. SY 5/3b makes the same point. Cf. the Wang Ya commentary to THC24/A6.

16. One such negative example is given in Ode 221 (Legge, 400–1), traditionally understood as a satire against King Yu of Chou (r. 781–771 B.C.), who purportedly kept his pleasures to himself.

17. Literally, "Joy cannot be [fully] known./ It is timed in Heaven."

18. YTC 2/17b.

19. Suggested by the statements of CPL 2/18b; CWK, p. 75, n. 4.

20. Lu Chi; SMK 2/8a; CWK, p. 75, n. 4. Similarly, CPL 2/18b talks of happy farmers so preoccupied with the spring sowing that they have "no time to be [consciously] happy."

21. LT, ch. 17 (Lau, 73).

22. Tentative translation. *Yen* 宴 could mean, "resting," "at repose," "feasting," or "having pleasure"; hence, the Fathoming translation, "Not at ease or refined." SYJ 8/19a–b reads as, "No longer carousing," following YTC 2/17b; CPL 2/18b. The participants in the feast, now thoroughly drunk, neither play music nor sing. SMK 2/8a reads, "not at peace, not upright."

23. Translation tentative. See below.

24. Morohashi 4076, 3454, 3935, 3488, 32726, 3559.

25. Wang Ya identifies the first four characters as "sounds of merriment and laughter," leaving the last two presumably as expressions of lamentation. YTC 2/17b takes all six as sighs of sorrow. CPL 2/19a takes all six as the raucous noises inevitable at a drunken feast. SMK 2/8a seems to agree, but his commentary is far

from explicit. FW 2/17b identifies the first and final sets of 2 characters (4 characters altogether) as "sounds of mourning," then talks of both "sorrow and joy having lost restraint," presumably because they are jumbled together in the individual's mind.

26. SMK 2/8a.

27. YTC 2/17b seems to suggest this.

28. CWK, p. 76, n. 5, citing SC 129:3274, which is not translated in Swann (1952).

29. Tentative translation for *chüeh*, in an attempt to capture the distinction between the third-person possessive *ch'i* 其, consistently used by Yang Hsiung to suggest a person of lower rank, relative to the third-person possessive *chüeh* 厥. *Chüeh* typically refers to the ruler or to Heaven. "Heaven-sent" is possibly the meaning here. "Godlike" comes from LC 19/23 (Legge, II, 125), which states that the individual who has mastered music and regulates his heart thereby is like the gods or Heaven in his repose.

30. Or, "The heart's integrity rejoices."

31. SMK 2/8a. See FY 4:12 for this description.

32. The phrase comes from *Mencius* 2A/2 (Lau, 77).

33. YTC 2/18a.

34. Literally, "Bell and drum sound in unison."

35. Following FW 2/18a; SMK 2/8a; and CWK, p. 76, n. 7. YTC 2/18a takes *chi chi* 喈喈 as "harmonious in sound"; CPL 2/19a, as the sound of flutes and pipes in unison.

36. Proverb cited by FW 2/18a.

37. SMK 2/8a.

38. Suggestion by Nylan, based on arguments in HTYT 77/20/35 (Watson, 115–16). CPL 2/19a, however, regards this as a description of crowds breaking up after sacrifices to the local god of the soil.

39. HFT 3:10:43–44 (Liao, I, 74–78; Watson, 53–56).

40. Literally, "[with] no gap"; cf. FY 5:13 and the Introduction. The character *ta* can either function as verb "make big" or as adjective modifying 大 ("great"). I use Appraisal and Fathoming to suggest both functions.

41. Literally, "Nothing not embraced."

42. SMK 2/8a–8b, which could have cited FY 5:13 in support.

43. Added by Nylan.

44. HTYT 77/20/35 (Dubs, 257; Watson, 119).

45. *Hsi* 嘻 is an exclamation, either of fear or of laughter. FW 2/18b regards it as laughter. YTC 2/18b and CPL 2/19b agree.

46. YTC 2/18b, however, reads *ch'eng* 稱 as *chü* 舉 ("to lift up" probably, but perhaps "to present" or "to promote"?).

47. Yü Ying-shih (1987). Cf. Yu (1987), which offers interesting insights on the later period. Note, however, that the ghosts are probably metaphorical. FY 10:28 shows Yang Hsiung doubting their existence.

48. See CYYT 23/37/3 (Wilhelm, 146; Kunst, 313).

49. Wang Ya, however, reads *hsi hsi* 嘻嘻 as "laugh laugh," arguing that "in the middle of laughter," the individual comes to realize he should be fearful."

50. Or, "Sigh, sigh, self[-made] fear," here and in the Fathoming. Alternately, "fearing [for?] the self."

51. Or, following FW 2/18b, "excessive joy."

52. The last two words are supplied by Nylan. If FW 2/18b is followed, the line reads, "He is lost [due to] excessive joy."

53. Or, "'Til the end."

54. *Analects* 5/26 (Waley, 114) talks of Confucius' search for a man "capable of seeing his own faults and bringing the charge home against himself." On the need to "turn the gaze within" rather than focussing on the faults of others, see *ibid.*, 1/16 (Waley, 87); 4/14 (Waley, 104–05); 4/17 (Waley, 105); etc.

55. Talk of *ch'i* added by Nylan.

56. Wang Ya; CWK, p. 77, n. 10.

57. YTC 2/18b cites Ode 114/1–3 (Legge, 174–75): "Let us not be wild in our love of enjoyment."

58. Omitting the translation of *tse* 則, meaning "as expected," "as a rule."

59. Literally, "the sighing and sniveling of weeping and wailing."

60. In fact, Lu Chi reads *chi* 幾 as *wei* 危, meaning "dangers."

61. CYYT 28/45/6 (Wilhelm, 177; Kunst, 329), cited by Wang Ya and YTC 2/19a.

No. 25. Contention

1. Literally, "contend and litigate" (*cheng sung* 爭訟). FW 2/19a adds, "Therefore, the myriad things, vying with each other, grow." CWK, p. 78, n. 1, glosses the same phrase as *cheng chin* 爭進 ("to struggle to go forward" or "to advance side by side").

2. CPL 2/20a gives a confusing explanation for the Head: Although yang *ch'i*, like a good ruler, wishes to bestow its beneficial presence upon all things equally, certain living things are by now developed enough to express their different natures ("their own models") by a range of reactions to yang's beneficence, from full acceptance to rejection.

3. *Documents*, "Hung fan," par. 14 (Legge, 331–32; Karlgren, 32).

4. LT, ch. 79 (Lau, 141): "It is the way of Heaven to show no favoritism."

5. Two lines from Ode 37 (now lost), cited by SMK 2/8b.

6. For further information, see Bauer, p. 21ff. Chuang tzu, of course, would have us regard all things and conditions as absolutely equal in value, but this extreme form of relativism was adopted by few in early China and specifically refuted by Yang Hsiung. See, for example, FY 12:39, when he equates relativistic thought with the loss of the evaluating mind.

7. For further information regarding the positive role of conflict in early China, see Lewis.

8. Alternately, following Lu Chi, "the plain essentials" (*su chih* 素質).

9. Tentative translation. See below.

10. Wang Ya commentary. Cf. e.g., LT, ch. 64 (Lau, 125): "It is easy to maintain a situation while it is still secure./ It is easy to deal with a situation before symptoms develop."

11. FW 2/19a, probably with reference to THC5/A9; and LT, ch. 22 (Lau,

50): "It is because he does not contend that no one in the empire is in a position to contend with him." Cf. LT, ch. 67 (Lau, 118); ch. 56 (Lau, 162).

12. SMK 2/8b.

13. YTC 2/19a.

14. Shakespeare, *Henry V*. Quotation supplied by Nylan.

15. Following SMK 2/8b. Alternately, "In [the misguided attempt to] shoo away the River, he becomes emaciated." However, FW 2/19a–b reads the first line of the Appraisal and Fathoming as, "[Attempting to] empty the [Yellow] River, he is exhausted," taking *ho* 嚇 as *hsü* 虛 ("empty"); and *ch'ü* 臞 as "exhausted, wasted." CWK, p. 78, n. 4, bases his reading on the Appraisal's alignment with Fire: "Drying the river is a waste [of effort and time]."

YTC 2/19a–b reads the lines completely differently. Identifying the first character of the text with a freshwater bird whose incessant honking drives away visitors to the river banks, Yeh reads the Appraisal as, "The *ho* bird [at] the river, worn out [presumably by its efforts?]." In that case, the bird symbolizes those with a taste for confrontation. CPL 2/20b borrows from both FW 2/19a and YTC 2/19a.

16. SMK 2/8b, citing Ode 35/6 (Legge, 56): "You are only angry with me."

17. Cf. the lines "Incensed against me,/ Though I go to do you good," from Ode 257/14 (Legge, 526).

18. Cf. CTYT 45/17/86ff. (Watson, 189).

19. *Analects* 7/10 (Waley, 124), making reference to Ode 295/6.

20. Following FW 2/19b, which clearly reads *yin yin* 齦齦 as *yen yen* 闇闇. This is the *locus classicus* of the reduplicative. The single character *yin* means "to gnash the teeth." Serruys prefers to retain that meaning.

21. *Analects* 3/7 (Waley, 95). For more on archery, see LC, ch. 45 (Legge, II, 446–53), entitled "She yi" 射義 ("The Meaning of Archery").

22. *Analects* 15/35 (Waley, 200).

23. Or, "good omens."

24. FW 2/19b reads *hun* 昏 (obscured) as *hun luan* 昏亂 ("dark and in confusion").

25. *Analects* 4/5 (Waley, 102): "Wealth and rank are what every man desires. . . ." Mencius comes the closest to leveling a blanket condemnation of profit, but succeeding scholastics were quick to explain it away. See, e.g., Ch'eng Yi, quoted in SSCS, "Shang Meng," p. 2.

26. SMK 2/9a says that Appraisal 5 represents *chung ho* 中和, a reference to the "Mean."

27. FW 2/19b.

28. Based on Han commentaries to the nine-part "Hung fan" chapter of the *Documents*. See Nylan (forthcoming).

29. CPL 2/20a.

30. Interestingly, the commentators disagree over whether "none of the things can compete [any longer because of the ruler's transforming influence]" (SMK 2/9a) or "each, wanting to compete for benefits, goes to its proper place" (CPL 2/20a).

31. FW 2/19b mistakenly writes 5 characters here *pi po ching ju ku* 辟膊脛如股, conflating the first lines of Appraisal and Fathoming. YTC 2/20a

takes *ching* 脛 as *tsu* 足 ("foot"). Compare YY 33:663, which reads *ching* as *chih* 直 ("straight").

32. Literally, "one who is great and high."

33. Alternately, "The subordinate greatly raised high." But Appraisal 6 typically discusses those on high (either the ruler or the ancestors).

34. HsinS 1/11b.

35. For the chief ministers as arms and legs of the ruler, see SC 130:3304.

36. HNT 9/16a, translated after Ames (1983), p. 196. Cf. *Mencius* 6A/14 (Lau, 168).

37. Cf. "ducal use offered to the king" in CYYT 11/14/3, *hsiang* (Wilhelm, 61). Kunst, p. 267 reads differently.

38. For the custom of "warning and prohibition" to clear the way for the imperial progress, see HCY 1/1a, cited in Goodrich.

39. Ode 62/1 (Legge, 105); 177/4 (Legge, 283).

40. SMK 2/9a–9b. The stretched bow typically stands for Heaven's justice. See LT, ch. 77 (Lau, 139).

41. Suggestion by Nylan.

42. HsinS 1/6b. Cf. CTYT 54/20/61–68 (Watson, 219), which tells the story of a magpie which does not see the hunter because it is intent on a mantis that itself has eyes only for a cicada resting in the shade.

43. Aesop, "The Ass, the Cock, and the Lion," p. 55.

44. CWK, p. 80, n. 11, takes it to mean each of the tigers has already sunk its teeth in the other. Serruys agrees.

45. Following FW 2/20b. Note the visual and aural pun, *chih* 制 and *chih* 掣.

46. The book *Maxims*, cited in CCYT 131/Hsi 28/5 *Tso* (Watson, 56).

47. LT, ch. 44 (Lau, 105).

No. 26. Endeavor

1. Not following Wilhelm for the translation of *ku* 蠱. In Han times, *ku* is glossed as *tsao shih chih tuan* 造事之端 ("the starting point for originating things") by Ma Jung 馬融; and as *shih* 事 ("affairs") by Hsün Shuang 荀爽. See MKH, I, 99(5b); 126(19a).

2. Material in parentheses added by CPL 2/22a. YTC 2/20b prefers Affairs for the tetragram title.

3. Literally, "bundle together in the hand."

4. THC "Hsüan ts'o" 7/4b (p. 1017b) defines the theme of "Endeavor" as *wu erh* 無二 ("without two").

5. See, e.g., HTYT 25/8/110–11, 125 (Dubs, 115; Knoblock, II, 81–82) on single-minded effort; and CTYT 3/2/9; 8/3/13 (Watson, 37, 52; Graham, 49, 64), for Heaven as a creative force that allows lesser creatures "to be unique."

6. This is the basis of the Mencian political program, of course.

7. Following SMK 2/9b. FW 6/20b and YTC 2/20b understand it to mean that the petty man is "benighted" or "stupified" (*wang mei* 罔昧) in the way he "uses" things. CWK, p. 81, n. 3, punctuates after *yung* 用, though his commentary simply follows FW and YTC. The parallel phrase is CYYT 22/34/3 (Wilhelm, 134; Kunst, 307). Kunst reads *yung wang* as "using [it], he will be without." Con-

ceivably, the line could mean, "although the petty person for his part uses it [hard work], he is left without [success or advantage]."

8. Literally, "It is not what a petty man [can] order."

9. CPL 2/22a identifies *shih wu* 始務 as the act of creation.

10. Literally, "He sheds light [or glory] on the self." For the last line, FW 2/21a reads *yü* as *yu* 由 ("from"), so that the light proceeds from the self.

11. See, for example, *Analects* 12/4 (Waley, 163); CYYT 17/26/*t'uan* (Wilhelm, 515); *ibid.*, 40/*Hsi* A/5 (Wilhelm, 299); and *Documents*, "Chung-hui chih kao," par. 8 (Legge, 182).

12. This is what Confucius meant by the injunction to "warm over the ancients" (usually translated as "reanimate the old"). See *Analects* 2/11 (Waley, 90).

13. Ode 235/6 (Legge, 431).

14. FY 9:25 makes daily renewal the key to both self-government and good government. The literary conceit associating the superior man with fragrant flowers may be found in poems attributed to to Ch'ü Yüan, especially the "Li sao." See Schneider, pp. 17–47, esp. 32–33.

15. Literally, "his," "hers," or "theirs."

16. General summary following CWK, p. 82, n. 5. The same argument may be found in the first chapters of HTYT and FY, both entitled "An Exhortation to Study."

17. YTC 2/21a talks of inner affecting the outer.

18. An allusion to the title of the correspondent hexagram.

19. CPL 2/22b.

20. *P'eng* 朋 (literally, "friends" or "friendship"). According to FY 1:3, "friendship" means "being of the same mind." Cf. SMK 2/9b.

21. Literally, "Seeing the arrow rise 'by itself,'/ Take as benefit the friendship of feathers."

22. Literally, "Their Way is thus."

23. Cf. FY 7:20. However, YTC 2/22a presumes both metaphors simply symbolize the need for interdependence between things.

24. SMK 2/9b. The canopy is metaphor for the ruler because it protects and shades all below. The chariot is metaphor for political office both because its has great capacity and because it can bear heavy burdens. See CYYT 11/14/2 (Wilhelm, 61; Kunst, 267). Contrast the Western "ship of state." The lower parts of the carriage often symbolize the common people.

25. See CPL 2/22b.

26. *Feng* 風 = *feng hua* 風化, from *Analects* 12/19 (Waley, 168). SMK 2/9b specifically mentions *feng hua* in his commentary.

27. See HSWC 6/27 (Hightower, 221); SY 8/1a.

28. Since the canopy and chassis are one Han metaphor for Heaven and Earth, the verses also hint at the government's role in keeping cosmic order.

29. Literally, "does not match." Alternately, "jacket," reading *yü* 褕 for *t'ou* 褕 , on the basis of Fang 4/27/6,9 (Serruys, private communication).

30. YTC 2/21b equates *t'ou* 褕 ("[the silkworm's] cloth") with the cocoon.

31. *Documents*, "Lü ao," par. 8 (Legge, 349; not in Karlgren).

32. Following YTC 2/21b; CPL 2/23b.

33.   YTC 2/21b; CPL 2/23a. Chinese convention also compares the ideal government with a potent fragrance. See the *Documents*, "Chün chen," par. 3 (Legge, 539; not in Karlgren).

34.   YTC 2/21b suspects that the character *li* 利 ("benefit") has dropped out of the text he uses for his edition, but this would ignore the rhyme. Most editions read *wu so wang* 無所往.

35.   YTC 2/22a.

36.   Or, "It is a good omen."

37.   *Ch'eng* 成 could also be read as *ch'eng* 盛 ("to fill the container").

38.   The possessive *chüeh* 厥 consistently indicates a superior power in Yang Hsiung's work. FW 2/22a acknowledges this. SMK 2/10a interprets the last line as, "It is because of his inability to fulfill his Heaven[-given] decree." YTC 2/22a says simply that it does not happen without something causing it. CPL 2/23b, however, emphasizes that it is the subject's own fault; it is not that he is fated to be ruined. CWK, p. 83, n. 11, says that the completion of the myriad things depends on Nature; the completion of the human nature, on the proper kind of endeavor (and so is not a matter of Heaven or Nature?).

39.   Wang Ya speaks of the inescapable failure when endeavors are made during inauspicious times.

40.   LT, ch. 9 (Lau, 65).

No. 27. Duties

1.   Reading *hsü* 勖, following the WJL edition (2/10a). Those commentators who follow FW 2/22b in reading *mao* 冒 understand it as *fu ch'ou* 覆幬 ("to cover"). See YTC 2/22a.

2.   SMK 2/10a reads *chao chih* 昭職 as, "[so that each is] clear about [its] tasks."

3.   Reading *hsin hsin* 信信 as *shen shen* 伸伸, following Wang Ya. FW 2/22b reads the reduplicative as *tzu hsin* 自信 ("to entrust oneself" [to the seasons so that there is growth]); YTC 2/22a, as *chin* 謹 ("earnestly").

4.   SMK 2/10a.

5.   E.g., LT, ch. 37 (Lau, 81), cited by YTC 2/22b.

6.   FY 4:11 discounts the usefulness of *wu wei* except in an already perfect society. Contra Wang Ya, who says that the lines refer to the sage who has nothing more to do once he has "rectified the base" (where the base means "ritual"). Such perfection seems premature in Appraisal 1.

7.   *Analects* 4/10 (Waley, 104).

8.   FW 2/22b. Cf. *Analects* 17/17 (Waley, 214): "Heaven does not speak, yet the four seasons run their course [by its command]; and the hundred creatures each after its kind are born by it"; *Mencius* 5A/5 (Lau, 143-4); and CTYT 21/7/32ff. (Watson, 97). That argument works well with the frequent mention in Appraisal 1 of "obscurity" and "the hidden."

9.   CYYT 39/Hsi A/1 (Wilhelm, 286) for the phrase "simple and easy" applied to moral action.

10.   Literally, "Affair at the pivot." FW 2/22b glosses *ch'u* 樞 as *shih* 始 ("at the beginning"); no doubt, Fan would emphasize that this Appraisal comes early in the set of nine. However, it is more likely that Yang refers to the Position 2 as

"center" of the first three Appraisals governing Thought. SMK 2/10a and YTC 2/22b clearly understand *ch'u* to mean "pivot" (and therefore, "critical juncture").

11. SMK 2/10a reads *fu* 符 as *jui* 瑞 , the jade tablet given at investiture symbolizing authority and rank. CWK, p. 85, n. 4, extends the meaning to *fu chu* 輔助 ("to assist").

12. YTC 2/22b and CPL 2/24a take the last line as, "to lose the clearest proof of good principles." SMK seems to think that the ruler ruins the expressions of his *potential advisors'* wit.

13. *Documents*, "Hung fan," par. 25 (Legge, 331; Karlgren, 33).

14. *Documents*, "Chung Hui chih kao," par. 8 (Legge, 187; not in Karlgren).

15. *Analects* 3/15; 10/15 (Waley, 97–98; 150 [renum.]).

16. CYYT 45/Hsi B/1 (Wilhelm, 326).

17. Cf. THC "Hsüan wen" 9/1b (p. 1028).

18. See my commentary to THC10/A1 above. For similar arguments regarding time, see THC9/A6; THC14/A4.

19. Literally, "Man serving [in] a womanly fashion."

20. Following FW 2/23a. Literally, "He does not replace her in suckling."

21. CCYT 45/Huan 18/1 *Tso* (Legge, 70). A century after Yang Hsiung, Pan Chao, a historian and lady-in-waiting, wrote her famous book on the proper role for women, entitled "Nü chieh" 女誡 ("Lessons for Women"). This has been translated in Swann (1932). However, numerous stories and even legal cases (e.g., CCCS, p. 1181 [2b–3a]) show that restrictions on women in Han times were far less severe than in later dynasties.

22. Literally, "Serving his service."

23. Following Wang Ya, defining *chia* 假 as *yü* 與. See Morohashi 835 for this definition. YTC 2/23a reads *chia* as "approaches," citing CYYT 28/45/*t'uan* (Wilhelm, 614).

24. Possibly the character *yü* 玉 (meaning literally "jade" and by extension, "rare") should be understood to modify "food." Cf. *Documents*, "Hung fan," par. 18 (Legge, 334; Karlgren, 32).

25. Literally, "Office is what he has as burden."

26. *Documents*, "Hung fan," par. 18 (Legge, 334; Karlgren, 32). On ritual exemptions and privileges, see Goodrich.

27. I take *fang lai* 方來 to mean "coming from all directions." However, YTC 2/23a reads *fang lai* 方來 as *chiang lai* 將來. CWK, p. 86, n. 8, similarly defines it as *chiang yao* 將要. Alternately, it means *shih chih* 始至 ("begins to come about"). See CYYT 7/8/*t'uan* (Wilhelm, 125).

28. Literally, "[Problems] coming from all directions, not rescue."

29. This is a synopsis of early Western Han arguments on *feng su* 風俗. See Nylan (1991).

30. In the last line, "knows what to do" can mean either "knows the proper direction [of the Way]" or "knows the method."

31. YY 33:633 reading *hu* 弧 for *ku* 孤, citing as proof a variant character in CYYT 24/38/*shang* (Wilhelm, 150).

32. Following the editions of Sung Chung, Lu Chi, and Wang Ya, not that of FW 2/23b, which apparently miscopies Appraisal 4.

33. Following Wang Ya, who notes that ten is the "completion number," so that in effect they will never be educable.

34. For the last line, reading *heng* 亨 as *hsiang* 享 ("to receive [Heaven's] blessings").

35. Or, "The matter is a good omen."

36. For the last line of the Fathoming Serruys reads, however, "To go against what one has heard [or learned] makes the act agreeable."

37. SC 55:2037 (not in Watson). Contrast the phrase, "incline [or lend] the ear" (*ch'ing erh* 傾耳) to "await commands." See SC 92:2618 (Watson, I, 218).

No. 28. Change

1. FW reverses yin/yang values for the entire chapter 3, which skews his interpretations.

2. WJL 3/1a, however, says the Net constellation instead.

3. The Sung Chung commentary says "flying to Heaven."

4. Tentative translation of the phrase *wu kai ch'i ling* 物改其靈. Literally, "they change what is 'numinous' (*ling* 靈) in them." The term *ling*, however, is used as synonym for "destiny" or "fate" (*ming* 命) in FY 11:35. FW 3/1a reads *ling* as *ling yao* 靈曜 ("sunlight"), so the phrase means, "Things alter [under the influence of] sunlight." CPL 3/1a says, things become numinous only if they change. CWK, p. 87, summarizes the meaning as, "Things all change their stupid and dull natures so that they become *ling* 靈 (in this case, "clever").

5. CYYT 49/Shuo/2 (Wilhelm, 264).

6. CYYT 50/Shuo/5 (Wilhelm, 272).

7. THC "Hsüan tso" 7/4b (p. 1018b). No doubt proper change is helped to grow by burgeoning auspicious yang *ch'i*.

8. The post-Han Ch'ing-ming festival was the possible inheritor of certain elements from the Han Lustration festival. See Granet, esp. pp. 129–36; Bodde (1975), pp. 273–289.

9. CPL 3/1a.

10. Literally: "Dark transformation, blocks propriety./ Seems like nature." CWK, p. 87, n. 3 reads *jo* 若 as *shun* 順 ("to follow"), rather than *ju* 如 ("like").

11. Alternate reading, "slightly."

12. CPL 3/1a.

13. Cf. the parable of Ox Mountain in *Mencius* 6A/8 (Lau, 164–65).

14. HsinS 5/3b, cited by SMK 3/1a.

15. Alternately, "To turn around on his path." The character *chen* 軫 (literally, the carriage-board and so metonymically "the carriage") may also be read as *li* 戾 (meaning "twist"). See Fang 3/23/37. SMK 3/1a talks of the carriage wheel, rather than the carriage-board, turning; hence, my translation.

16. FW 3/1b.

17. The same point is made in FY 5:13, cited by CWK, p. 88, n. 4: "The Tao is not something natural; [the gentleman] responding to the time creates [it]."

18. This seems to be the point of YTC 3/1a, which talks of "application and response without fixed numbers."

19. See, e.g., LH 2:34 (Forke, I, 374); *Analects* 17/7 (Waley, 211); HY 1/2b

(Ku, 68); or the opening lines of the *Hsün tzu*. Animals, in contrast to human nature, may be steeped in black mud without becoming dirty. See *Analects* 17/7 (Waley, 211).

20. Following SMK 3/1a. Cf. HTYT 1/<u>1</u>/16 (Dubs, 33; Knoblock, I, 137), which talks of the need for careful selection of neighbors after citing the *Analects* passage.

21. *Tsai* 淄 = *tsai* 甾.

22. Wang Ya adds six characters here, "Wo fou, fei ch'i yu ch'ih" 我否非其有恥. These characters apparently have been moved by mistake from THC29/A4.

23. According to CYYT 45/Hsi B/2 (Wilhelm, 328), the subjects of the sage-ruler do not fully realize his genius. They only realize that his policies seem "more natural" and productive, though they understand enough to gravitate towards him. Cf. SMK 3/1a.

24. See, for example, FY 7:21; 8:24; 9:27.

25. See CPL 3/1b. YTC 3/1b improbably suggests that the verses refer to the good official who could seize the empire for himself, but chooses instead to remain loyal to the throne.

26. Suggestion by Nylan.

27. Graham (1978), pp. 437–38 (B66).

28. According to SMK 3/1a, these lines may be making a more pointed political statement as well. A hornless ox is too immature to have its full powers. It may symbolize the individual who lacks the proper authority and strength to wield great power (either because he is too young or undeveloped in his heart/mind). SMK assumes that the regent Wang Mang was such a "hornless ox" at court.

29. Literally, "Fitting by kings it to reverse." Also this could mean, "The reverse of what is fit for kings." Since this Appraisal is auspicious, I give the more positive interpretation.

30. Or, "Their ways are reversed."

31. CTYT 38/<u>14</u>/35–37 (Watson, 159–60). The passage concludes, however, with a criticism of Confucianism: "To hope to practice the ways of Chou in the state of Lu is like trying to push a boat over land—a great deal of work, no success, and certain danger to the person who tries it. The man who tries to do so has failed to understand the turning that has no direction, that responds to things, and is never at a loss."

32. Following FW 3/2a; SMK 3/1b; YTC 3/2a–b; CPL 3/2a.

33. Or, "a crisis."

34. Following Wang Ya; SMK 3/1b; and CWK, p. 87, in supplying *pu* 不 before *neng* 能. Tentative translation. See below.

35. SMK 3/1b, citing HS 26:2505. For further discussion of the proposition "Changes does not change," see Louton, p. 113.

36. LSCC 15/33a–34a (translation after Louton, 111).

37. Translation tentative, following Wang Ya, who reads *chü chü* 趄趄 as *hsing pu chin* 行不進. FW 3/2a–b, however, reads the reduplicative as *pu t'iao* 不調 ("not adjusted"). In that case, the team of four won't pull together. CWK, p. 89, n. 10, follows FW.

38. Literal translation: "A team of four horses does not go forward./ And so

change its driver./ A team of four does not go forward./ Means: Changing the driver only then is good."

39. See, for example, FY 4:12.

40. SMK 3/1b seems to identify the "driver(s)" with the imperial ministers, but this interpretation reflects Sung claims regarding the importance of the *shih*, rather than Han thought. See Nylan (forthcoming), ch. 3, on the "Hung fan" in Sung commentaries.

41. Or, "He does not bring his virtue to final development."

42. Or, "Replacement caused by not persisting [in virtue]."

43. *Analects* 13/10 (Waley, 174).

No. 29. Decisiveness

1. Alternately, the verbs could be read as causatives. See below.

2. An alternate reading of the first sentence of the Head text. According to CPL 3/2b, yang *ch'i*, being strong within, now can soar above; being firm without, it can dispel yin *ch'i*. Cf. CYYT 10/12/*hsiang* (Wilhelm, 447).

3. CYYT 17/26/*t'uan* (Wilhelm, 515).

4. Literally, "What is within is self-ruled."

5. SMK 3/1b: "One can by means of norms and standards inside decide within the heart, but others will not see its traces."

6. FW 3/2b, e.g., says that the ax symbolizes the opposition between the Fire agent (patron of the tetragram) and the Water (patron of Appraisal 1).

7. Following YTC 3/3a.

8. FSTY *yi-wen* 2:87.

9. FW 3/2b; and CPL 3/3a find the ax a complimentary arm to the carpenter's line and square.

10. For this imagery, see FY 1:2.

11. Cf. the argument by America's Founding Fathers regarding "iron cages" in Takaki.

12. Literally, "goes wrong [or, is blocked]."

13. *Tsai* 在, however, conceivably is a loan for *tsai* 哉 ("begins [with]").

14. Alternately, "what centers the heart," following Serruys. I take the "center heart" to mean the inmost recesses of the mind. Cf. Ode 123/1,2 (Legge, 185); CYYT 9/11//4, *hsiang* (Wilhelm, 444); HTYT 62/17/12 (Dubs, 176), for examples of *chung hsin* 中心.

15. I include in the general term "Western philosophy" Buddhist philosophy, which sees sensory perception as one obstacle to appreciation of the illusory nature of the cosmos.

16. Such a relation between the senses and the mind is posited, for example, in *Documents*, "Hung fan," par. 6 (Legge, 326; Karlgren, 30).

17. See DeWoskin (1982), pp. 29–42.

18. Elaborating on SMK 3/1b.

19. CPL 3/3a reads *chüeh* 決 as *yüeh* 抉.

20. Literally, "deafness and nasal congestion." YTC 3/3a describes the ears and nose as *pu t'ung* 不通.

21. Alternately, "It will benefit those 'having plans.' See below.

22. *Documents*, "Hung fan," par. 11 (Legge, 329; Karlgren, 30).

23. Evil men are said to "stink," another reason for the reference to foulness. See FW 3/3a.

24. YTC 3/3a; CPL 3/3a.

25. Literally, "To eat what is not properly his is shameful."

26. FW 3/3a, as earlier, equates *wo* 我 with the "common people."

27. Ode 112/1 (Legge, 170).

28. Literally, the lower limbs.

29. Translation tentative. Alternately, *t'o* 脫 means "lets escape." See below. CPL 3/3b understands *t'o* as "unfettered." FW 3/3b mistakenly assumes that this Appraisal is inauspicious, so he describes a derelict or treasonous official (the "thigh") whom the the ruler exposes (*t'o* 脫) for the sake of the common people.

30. Or, "has what he cuts off."

31. CPL 3/3b, however, takes the lower limbs as symbol of the "little guy" (*hsiao jen* 小人).

32. "Great resolve" may or may not specifically refer to the wise ruler's decision to excise all treasonous men from court, as SMK 3/2a suggests.

33. CPL 3/3b emphasizes that it is the ruler's sense of justice that keeps his subordinates out of trouble.

34. YTC 3/3b.

35. That is, you will be attacked.

36. Or, "[Using] *keng* 庚 (Metal agent, symbol of social duty) to decide about *chia* 甲 (i.e., Wood agent, symbol of humaneness)."

37. Reference to Ode 259/8 (Legge, 540). Cf. Ode 209/3 (Legge, 370). FW 3/4a reads *shih* 碩 as *ta* 大 ("great"), following Fang 1/7/21.

38. Following YTC 3/4a.

39. Boodberg, pp. 38–39.

40. *Documents*, "Yin cheng," par. 7 (Legge, 169; not in Karlgren), cited by SMK 3/2a.

41. CWK, p. 92, n. 10, reads *mei* 侏 (=*mei* 昧) instead of *chu* 侏, however.

42. Literally, "Brave dwarfs them you attack,/ Highway robbers receive the favour of a decision to be released."

43. CPL 3/4a.

44. Translation tentative, taking *o-o* 蛾蛾 "as the blade polished until white," following CPL 3/4a; CWK, p. 92, n. 11. Alternately, *o* 蛾 means *o* 俄 ("curved").

45. Deleting *li* 利 on the assumption that it has crept into the text from the last line of the Fathoming. With *li* retained, the sentence literally means, "Beneficial to what has been tested for the artisan."

46. FW 3/4a, however, equates the tools with worthy officials, rather than with penal laws.

47. See Christopher, p. 158, on the curved or hooked blade.

No. 30. Bold Resolution

1. FW 3/4b reads *fang* 方 as "in all directions."

2. Literally, "good" or "skillful," if *liang* 艮 = *liang* 俍 (GSR 735a = 735f), as Serruys suggests.

3. Following SMK 3/2a in reading *hsin* 信 as *shen* 伸. FW 3/4b appears to

read *hsin* 信 as "faithful to," though he also mentions the "growth" of the myriad things. Similarly, CPL 3/4b glosses *hsin* 信 as *ch'iang* 強 ("strengthen").

4. Literally, "what they are intended for."

5. Following FW 3/4b.

6. CYYT 53/43/*hsü* (Wilhelm, 602).

7. *Analects* 13/27 (Waley, 178): "Imperturbable, resolute, treelike, slow to speak. Such is one who is near to Goodness." Cf. FY 1:2.

8. CYYT 27/43/*t'uan* (Wilhelm, 166): "One must resolutely make known the matter at the court of the king."

9. CYYT 27/43/*hsiang* (Wilhelm, 604).

10. FY 11:33.

11. *Wei* 威 refers to what is awesome. YTC 3/4b understands this to mean, "uniformly rely on awesome punishments" (*yi jen wei hsing* 一任威刑, i.e., the "love of intimidation"). CWK, p. 93, n. 3, equates *wei* with *pao li* 暴力 ("tyranny"). It could also conceivably refer to "delusions of grandeur."

12. YY 33:664, however, reads *man hsü* 滿虛 as "fills [i.e, preoccupies] the mind"; YTC 3/4b, as "fills the [entire] cosmos." Those meanings I have tried to reflect in the Fathoming.

13. FW 3/4b. YTC 3/4b talks of the (purportedly) megalomaniacal First Emperor of Ch'in.

14. FY 11:37.

15. For *chen* 貞 as "stability," see Shchutskii, pp. 142–43. Alternately, "propriety" or "good omen." "Model of" supplied by Nylan.

16. *Analects* 7/9 (Waley, 129).

17. Literally, "Wearing atop authority, it fills the head."

18. YTC 3/5a talks of *hua min* 化民.

19. *Analects* 20/2 (Waley, 232).

20. A pun on *man* 滿, translated above as "fills."

21. YTC 3/5a.

22. However, FW 3/5a takes the phrase "more than enough" to mean that there is more than enough violence and evil when the petty man rules. This works less well with the phrase "not enough" than my own reading, which follows SMK 3/2a–2b; YTC 3/5a.

23. CPL 3/5a, however, reads *shuo* 說 ("speech") as *yüeh* 悅 ("happiness"). Similarly, Serruys would read, "The superior man rejoices in the tool [i.e., in the talents he has]." The correspondent hexagram takes speech as one of its subjects; hence, my reading.

24. Following the WJL edition (3/2b). FW 3/5a says *ch'i jen* 其人 ("the proper man") instead of *ch'i yen* 其言.

25. SMK 3/2b.

26. See, e.g., PHT 2B/3a–4a (Tjan, 468); Kung 8/15b, Ho Hsiu commentary; KTCY 3/18b.

27. FY 2:4. Note Yang's injunction to have a "metal mouth but a wooden [i.e., plain-spoken] tongue" in FY 1:1.

28. *Analects* 13/23 (Waley, 177).

29. Reading *chien* 揀 as "to pick up," "to choose." However, YY 33:664–65 would read *tung* 棟 ("ridgepole," and by extension, "high position") here.

30. YTC 3/5b emphasizes that the individual may be unaware of his own inadequacies but this is no excuse.

31. *Analects* 15/38 (Waley, 201).

32. Ode 112/1 (Legge, 170).

33. Note the visual pun between "pillar" (*chu* 柱) and "master" (*chu* 主).

34. Literally, "It is the strength that bears the burdens of state." Alternately, "The kingdom is entrusted to the strong ones."

35. Following FW 3/5b, rather than SMK 3/2b, which would make both architectural features symbolize chief officials. SMK is rejected for his anachronistic emphasis on the *shih*. Cf. *Mencius* 1B/9 (Lau, 68).

36. YTC 3/5b reads *lei* 類 as *shan* 善 ("good"). I take it as "to type." CWK, p. 94, n. 9, reads *lei* as *fa* 法 ("proper model").

37. SMK 3/2b; YTC 3/5b–6a. Even in Shang oracle bone inscriptions, the *yang* 羊 ("sheep" or "goat") is associated with stubbornness maintained at the risk of one's safety (Serruys, private communication).

38. Added by Nylan.

39. Presumably this is the point of FW 3/5b.

40. Cf. E. M. Forster: "It is the vice of a vulgar mind to be thrilled by bigness."

41. *Analects* 1/10 (Waley, 86). CPL 3/5b, however, offers a very different interpretation.

42. FY 2:5: "What is not in accord with the model of the ancient sages, the noble man does not imitate."

43. For *chen* 貞 , see the Appendices. Alternately, "[equally] resolute in the face of calamity and good omens," following Paul Serruys.

44. Supplied by the CPL 3/6a; YTC 3/6a. SMK 3/2b instead supplies "his fame."

45. FY 3:7. Cf. CYYT 40/Hsi A/4 (Wilhelm, 295); *Analects* 2/4 (Waley, 88). The model of calmness in adversity, of course, is Yen Hui, the disciple of Confucius. See *Analects* 6/9 (Waley, 117–18).

46. See FY 6:17.

47. SMK 3/2b.

48. However, CWK, p. 94, n. 11, reads *fa* 發 as *she* 射 ("cause to shoot arrows").

49. CPL 3/6a insists they are "officers of Heaven."

50. See Kramers, pp. 236, 332.

51. YTC 3/6a; CPL 3/6a.

No. 31. Packing

1. FW 3/6a writes the Ghost 鬼 constellation instead of the Net, but this must be an error since the sun enters the lodge of the Ghost only after the summer solstice.

2. According to SMK 3/2b, but not FW 3/6a, the Dipper points SSE; the musical note is F.

3. Reading *wei* 微 as "very small." *Wei* is often used as antonym for *chu* 著 ("obvious"). Yin *ch'i* is nascent.

4. Serruys reads instead as, "Although yang *ch'i* is greatly pursuing affairs,

the small yin, relying on what is packed below, wants to depart." Serruys is right, of course, to carry over yin as subject, but the commentators unanimously talk of yang readying itself to depart in response to yin's actions.

5. CYYT 54/56/*hsü* (Wilhelm, 675).

6. The myriad things in the fourth month are also said to travel westward. See CWK, p. 96. The last sentence of the Head text does not specify which agent is preparing to leave. See above. In one sense, both yin and yang are preparing to change places. Both, then, are "packed" and ready to go, although auspicious yang is clearly regarded as the subject by the early commentators.

7. See the correspondent hexagram for these themes.

8. FW 3/6a, however, glosses *hsing* 行 ("go forth") as *shou* 首 ("the beginning").

9. CPL 3/6a.

10. SMK 3/3a.

11. FW 3/6b.

12. Fang 8/53/11 defines this as "wild goose that flies east from the passes." Modern dictionaries list it as *Leucoblepharon canadensish utchinsii* (the Canadian goose). Serruys notes that the very graph for the bird suggests its loud honking; hence my translation.

13. Following Wang Ya. Cf. CPL 3/6b. YTC 3/6b reads this as, "Takes wing on that south wind," arguing that it perversely flies north.

14. Literally, "Inside they cherish their mates."

15. Note that my translation varies from that proposed by YTC 3/6b. Yeh believes that the wild goose stands for yin *ch'i*, which moves from the south, hoping to displace yang. In that case, the last Appraisal line should probably be re-translated, "Within, it cherishes [the ambition] to succeed [to yang's position of ascendancy]."

16. FW 3/6b identifies them with yang *ch'i*; YTC 3/6b, with yin.

17. LC 18/38/13b (Legge, II, 392). Cf. HTYT 74/19/98–100. The wild goose is a conventional symbol for an absent mate in the *Odes*. See Wang, p. 77. Compare the frequent Han references to the wild swan as symbol of the faithful marriage. See, for example, FSTY 3:22.

18. SMK 3/3a disparages the goose for indecisiveness, comparing it with the petty man who can't dedicate himself to the Way. Contrast this with YTC 3/6b, which argues the bird's sensitivity to the cold symbolizes the exquisite sensitivity and predictive powers of the superior man.

19. SMK 3/3a says that the petty man so desires favors and high salary that he is reluctant to leave court at the onset of trouble. CPL 3/6b even speculates that Yang Hsiung here comments upon his own uncomfortable position at the court of the usurper Wang Yang.

20. CYYT 21/33/3, cited by SMK 3/3a. Wilhelm, p. 131, and Kunst, p. 305, translate differently.

21. YTC 3/7a adds "[and] obtain" (*te* 得).

22. Literally, "There are some cases following it joy." Alternately, "Some make the joy continue." CPL 3/6b reads as, "Some follow him joyously." YTC 3/7a reads as, "May promote his joy." This sentence structure, of course, is patterned after the *Changes*. Cf. THC24/A5.

23. Or, "He will meet [another] in whom he will find joy."

24. A pun for "[at] court."

25. Following YTC 3/7a, which says, "They do not stop to eat," making their case analogous to the self-endangering wild goose of Appraisal 2. Serruys follows. However, the line could conceivably read, "They never stop [looking for] food" since they are in the wintry north. SMK 3/3a says that they do not stop their search for food. CPL 3/6b comments that the birds have enticed others to share in their useless search.

26. Literally, "How could [this] be enough to rely upon?"

27. YTC 3/7a; CPL 3/6b.

28. Following SMK 3/3a. FW 3/7a, however, says that the *k'un* is a bird which "feeds nonstop" once it reaches the north where food is plentiful. After all, as a water bird the *k'un* should like the north (assigned to the Water Phase in the cosmic cycle.) FW, however, mistakenly assumes that Appraisal 4 is yang (auspicious) in value.

29. Ode 165/1 (Legge, 253) has birds making the *ying ying* 嚶嚶 call to locate their mates, suggesting some confusion.

30. CPL 3/6b.

31. Added by Nylan. The powerful Wang clan, for example, came from an area that corresponds to present Shantung province.

32. Literally, it "packs to go to the Tz'u [River]."

33. Alternately, "Drinking and feeding in great content." See CWK, p. 87, n. 7.

34. Cf. CYYT 33/53/2 (Wilhelm, 206): "The wild goose gradually draws near the cliff. Eating and drinking, in peace and concord. Good fortune."

35. FY 7:21 defines this as the essence of practical wisdom.

36. For this argument, see Wang Shu-min, 3:1375ff. who argues that Chuang tzu did not advocate the uninhibited lifestyle or promote withdrawal from the mundane world. FW 3/7a celebrates the lack of restraint, thinking these lines are assigned to (auspicious) yang.

37. YTC 3/7b.

38. SMK 3/3a, of course, emphasizes this.

39. Tentative translation, reading it literally as, "Is of benefit to attacking the blameworthy." I have added "unencumbered." However, YTC 3/7b reads, "Of benefit in campaigning [but] blameworthy." CWK, p. 98, punctuates differently and suggests the deletion of *li* 利 ("of benefit to"). See footnote 41 below.

40. SMK 3/3a offers no commentary at all.

41. YTC 3/7b says, "Though action is beneficial, to launch a punitive campaign without partners as a rule is blameworthy." CPL 3/7a repeats. CWK, p. 98, n. 9, also assumes that such deeds will be blameworthy.

42. The poem refers to the "younger sibs."

43. CPL 3/6b, however, says they are "packed in the carts." YTC 3/7b envisions the younger siblings running behind the carts.

44. Deleting *chih* 之 from the FW 3/7b text, following other editions. For these sacrifices, see Schindler; LC 6/2a (Legge, I, 314); and CFL 6:358.

45. Added by Nylan: "the worst."

No. 32. Legion

1. FW 3/8a writes, "the Net constellation, 12th degree." CWK, p. 99, n. 1, says it ought to be the 16th degree. SMK 3/3b gives the Triaster constellation.

2. "To" (*yü* 于) added by Nylan. Alternately, "truly high."

3. CWK, p. 100, n. 2, however, reads *ch'i* 齊 as *chai chieh* 齋潔 ("purifying"), citing CYYT 50/Shuo/4 (Wilhelm, 269).

4. Or, "manifest brightness." *Hsüan* may mean "everywhere-reaching," "make clear," or "propagate" here. See GSR 164t. "Spread [their] lights" is another possible translation. The commentators offer no help. This is also possibly an internal pun since Hsüan-ming 宣明 is the name of the God of Fire, an appropriate symbol for this season.

5. Lu Chi glosses *hu* 嫭 as *mei* 美; YTC 3/8a, as *ta* 大; CPL 3/7b, as *hu* 護 ("to protect").

6. CPL 3/7b, however, sees a problem in the aspirations of yang *ch'i*, which "hopes to be as high as Heaven," implying that it is overly aggressive. But the language of the Head recalls Hsün tzu's description of the good ruler. See HTYT 65/18/3 (Dubs, 187).

7. A loose translation of the line, "[Like] fire, it enters ears."

8. Following CPL 3/8a. FW 3/8a and the WJL edition (3/3b) punctuate after *ma* 馬.

9. Following YTC 3/8a. Alternately, the character *chiang* 將 may mean *chiang ma* 將馬 ("mares"). If it does, the presence of mares in the field suggests the desperation of the war, since mares would be used as battlehorses only after the more powerful stallions have perished on the battlefield. See HFT 6:20:106 (Liao, I, 188). Also, several commentators read *chiang* 將 as "general."

10. Literally, "be openly displayed."

11. The news is like "fire" because (1) it is terrifying; (2) fire is a symbol for any crisis; and (3) fire is particularly associated with war. For fire as symbol of a crisis, see FW 3/8a. For fire and war, see CCYT 10/Yin 4/4 *Tso* (Watson, 8).

12. LT, ch. 46 (Lau, 107).

13. See Nylan (1982), ch. 2.

14. Wang Ya reads as, "soldiers do not cross blades" (*ping pu chiao jen* 兵不交刃). See below.

15. An alternate reading has *lin* 隣 ("neighbors") for *lin* 鱗.

16. Following YTC 3/8b. SMK 3/3b reads *pin* 賓 as *tzu wai lai che* 自外來者 ("comes himself from afar").

17. Literally, "The unicorn may pledge itself to him,/ [Because of his] gentility."

18. LT, ch. 31 (Lau, 89).

19. The Cheng Hsüan subcommentary to Ode 11 says that the tip of the unicorn's horn is fleshy, signifying its potential to fight, but it chooses not to use it. See Shih 1:6.

20. LT, ch. 68 (Lau, 130). Cf. *ibid.*, ch. 46 (Lau, 107); ch. 69 (Lau, 131); ch. 80 (Lau, 142); and SunT 3/3 (Griffith, 77).

21. Literally, "a grown man." Some take this to be a general. SMK 3/3b takes this to be a family head as symbol for someone in authority. All assume that it refers to "someone in the army," as in the previous line.

22. Reading *t'ui* 推 instead of *ts'ui* 摧 ("to injure"). FW 3/8b reads *ts'ui*, but as "hastens on." In that case, the caring father pushes his family on, hoping they will escape enslavement at the hands of the conquerors. For *ts'ui nu* 摧弩 Wang Ya reads *t'ui nu* 推奴 ("push the slave"). Sung Chung and Lu Chi read [*t'ui*] *nu* 推弩 ("push the crossbow").

23. Tentative reading. Literally, "Inside, he/they tread(s) on it/them, making a flaw/rift/blemish."

24. Translation tentative. See above and below.

25. YTC 3/8b; CPL 3/8a read *lei* 纍 as *fu lei* 俘纍. FY 11:35 contrasts the rule by force (which ends in carts full of bloody corpses) and the rule by virtue.

26. CPL 3/8a.

27. Following SMK 3/3b–4a, which cites SunT, sec. 28 (Griffith, 71). The clan temple houses the strategy room.

28. Translation tentative. Literally, "shaking, arising." FW 3/8b glosses *chen hsin* 振廞 as "in appearance, full of anger." Wang Ya believes the tiger's roar rouses others to join the fray.

29. Reading *t'eng* 騰 for *sheng* 勝, following Serruys, who adopts this from CPL 3/8b. HS 87A:3548 (Knechtges, 34) shows the leopard "soaring."

30. Literally, "its selfish [impulses] blocked." CWK, p. 101, n. 6, understands this to mean, "overcomes its private mistakes."

31. Literally, "Like a hawk's rising." For the same metaphor, see Ode 236/8 (Legge, 436); HSWC 3/13 (Hightower, 90). Translation tentative. For variant characters, see below.

32. See Ode 263/4 (Legge, 557) for a similar description of victorious King Wu, founder of the Chou dynasty.

33. FY 5:15; 12:38. SMK 3/4a emphasizes that the two animals, though roused to anger by evildoing, refuse to let their passions rule their actions.

34. YTC 3/8b sees the leopard as enemy of the tiger. CPL 3/8b emphasizes the relative superiority of the tiger over the leopard (which symbolizes the courage of the ordinary fellow).

35. Following CPL 3/8b. Certain early editions read *t'eng ch'i pi* 騰其柲 for *sheng ch'i szu* 勝其私.

36. Reading *ch'u* 躇 as *chü* 虡, following YY 33:664.

37. Tentative translation. The reduplicative *chieh chieh* 喈喈 can mean, "the sound of bells and drums." See Ode 208/2 (Legge, 367). The single character *chieh* 喈 can mean "frantic in appearance" (*chi mao* 疾貌) or "numerous." Conceivably, the reduplicative might be used to emphasize those adjectives.

38. A loose translation, following SMK 3/4a. YTC 3/9a, however, reads *ch'u* 詘 as *chin* 盡 ("to exhaust"), citing FY 10:29: "Whatever exhausts others will win. Whatever exhausts the self will cause defeat."

39. Cf. Ode 263/3 (Legge, 557).

40. YTC 3/9a. Note that SunT employs the same metaphor.

41. Following SMK 3/4a. Cf. FY 4:12, which praises the man who overawes others less by his force than by his virtue. This strain of thought is clear in the early Taoist classics. For early Confucianism, see *Mencius* 7B/3 (Lau, 194), disputing a *Documents* claim that pestles floated in the blood shed by those fighting on behalf of a humane ruler.

42. YTC 3/9a says *wa lo* 絓羅 means *ju chih* 如織 ("as if interwoven" [like nets]); CPL 3/9a reads it as *p'o sui* 破碎 ("broken and tattered").
43. SMK 3/4a glosses *o o* 蛾蛾 as "the appearance of defeat and chaos"; CPL 3/9a, as "fleeing from the chaos of battle." Probably SMK 3/4a means that the weapons are "slanted" (*o* 蛾 = *o* 俄) rather than upright. That GSR 2x = 2h is attested by Yen Shih-ku, cited in HS 97B:3984.
44. SMK 3/4a and CWK, p. 102, n. 9, take *shih yün* 師孕 as "the troops' pregnant [wives]." Or, this could mean "the [survivors from the] army and the pregnant [widows]. . . . " Serruys, however, takes *yün* as the verb "to burst or let forth." YTC 3/9a–9b reads *shih* 師 as *mang* 盲 ("blind [ones]," i.e., the masses). According to Yeh, the common people, seeing the troops going out to battle, wail until blinded by tears, knowing the troops will fail.
45. Replacing *chih* 之 ("it") with the explanation "their loss." Following the latter part of FW 3/9a, who translates this as, "The blind and the pregnant condole with each other" (*mang yün hsiang yen* 盲孕相唁). The character 唁 means to condole with survivors or with those who have lost their states or fiefs. See CCYT 416/Chao 25/7 Kung (Malmqvist, 204–5).
46. Following SMK 3/4a and CPL 3/9a, who supply the ruler as object of the resentful stares.
47. Tentative translation.
48. Following FW 3/4a, Serruys reads as, "The weapons are laid down."
49. Or, "death-wagons." Literally, "carriages-full [of corpses]." Cf. FY 11:35.
50. CYYT 7/7/3, *hsiang* (Wilhelm, 423; Kunst, 253).
51. FY 11:35.
52. The ax blade is literally notched or blunted.
53. Alternately, "right to defend (literally, "to stop [the enemy]"), not right to attack."
54. Following FW 3/9b, which takes *chiang* 將 as the particle, "about to." CPL 3/13b, takes *chiang* as "general(s)."
55. Since the ax handle, if whole, is associated with pattern in Ode 158, the reader may conclude that ignoring fundamental patterns has led to calamity.

No. 33. Closeness

1. According to CPL 3/9b, "to join forces with it." Alternately, "is akin to," "associates with," "get close to."
2. FW 3/9b reads *wan-lan* 丸蘭 as *wan-mao* 完茂.
3. And, according to CPL 3/9b, "desirous of being equal [to Heaven]."
4. CPL 3/9b.
5. Wang Ya reminds us of the advantages for the myriad things of the conjunction of yin and yang *ch'i*. The things depend upon yin *ch'i* for their completion.
6. See FY 5:13.
7. CYYT 42/Hsi A/7 (Wilhelm, 307).
8. YTC 3/10a; CPL 3/10a read *wu fang* 無方 as *pu k'o ts'e* 不可測 ("unfathomable" [because infinite]), presumably a description of the Unknown; hence, the Appraisal translation.

9. Sung Chung speaks only of *shih-shih* 事事 ("every single affair"). FW 3/9b apparently takes this poem as a description of the watery mass below the surface of the earth. But I suggest tracing the metaphor to the "gate in the circle" discussed by Doeringer. The peering through the gate brings to mind CYYT 34/55/6 (Wilhelm, 216; Kunst, 349): "Peering through the door: Quiet it is without men." For another use of the metaphor of the "gap in the wall," see McMahon.

10. Following SMK 3/4b.

11. Following SMK 3/4b.

12. CYYT 42/Hsi A/7 (Wilhelm, 307).

13. FW 3/9b makes this point.

14. FW 3/10a takes *wo* 我 to refer to the common people.

15. CPL 3/10a glosses *tz'u* 次 as an "inn," a "wild place." Serruys takes it as "campsite [of war]." YTC 3/10a takes it as a hut exposed to the elements. For the imagery of the inn, see CYYT 34/56/2 (Wilhelm, 676–77).

16. Following FW 3/10a; YTC 3/10a.

17. FW 3/10a, citing CYYT 42/Hsi A/7 (Wilhelm, 307); CPL 3/10a.

18. SMK 3/4b, citing Ode 102/1 (Legge, 157): "Do not think of winning people far away./ Your toiling heart will be grieved." Nylan adds the conjecture that the "proper place" may stand for the conscience.

19. YTC 3/10a.

20. See D.C. Lau's discussion of "graded love" in his introduction to the *Mencius* translation (p. 41).

21. *Filial*, ch. 9 (Makra, 19).

22. YTC 3/10b, however, pointedly cites *Analects* 13/2: "Promote those you know, and those whom you do not know others will certainly not neglect."

23. Literally, "Close to the rancid stench./ In three days, he grows unaware. The mixture [or, confusion]." Nylan assumes the smell is *yao* 殽 ("mixed," "confused"). See SMK 3/4b. FW 3/10a reads *yao* 殽 as *hsiao* 效 ("to imitate"), which is also possible. See GSR 1167e.

24. YTC 3/10b, however, says, "[the subject of the poem] becomes one with it."

25. See SY 17/12b.

26. CPL 3/10b.

27. Wang Ya remarks, "The enlightened ruler draws close to those worthy of closeness" (*ming chün ch'in yü k'o ch'in* 明君親于可親).

28. SMK 3/4b.

29. Numerous passages in the *Changes* address this theme. See, e.g., CYYT 8/8/3, *hsiang* (Wilhelm, 428).

30. The last line of the Fathoming could also be read, "He pairs the unlike and the like." This would warn against the evils of of misapplied categorical logic. See Graham (1978), p. 473ff. (No. 6A).

31. FW 3/10b–11a, however, reads *sai* 鰓 as *nan* 難 ("obstruction"). YTC 3/11a and CPL 3/10b follow FW's lead and gloss *sai* as "a small fishbone that sticks in the throat," then see the poem as a description of loyal criticism addressed by a lower official to the good ruler: "Being close, and [with] a mouth [to remonstrate]./ [Straight talk is hard to swallow],/ [Like] a small fishbone sticking in the throat./ [Offered in] the presence of the great ruler; never behind his back."

The last line of the Fathoming could also be read, "The great ruler depends upon not going back on his word."

32. Literally, "The great ruler consists in having no reoccurence."

33. Following FW 3/11a in reading *feng* 逢 as *feng* 縫. If the character *ta* 達 given in many early editions is correct, the line reads, "To depend on the ruler's complete effectiveness [or, perspicacity]."

34. Interpretation by Nylan. SMK 3/5a offers no commentary. FW 3/11a takes the "fine opening" to refer to the leak of state secrets at court. YTC 3/11a assumes that the rift refers to the official who feels uncomfortable remonstrating with his ruler directly, though he may criticize him behind his back. The gill symbolizes "fear" according to CWK, p. 104, n. 9.

35. Following CPL 3/11a. FW 3/11a, however, glosses 齦 (read *k'en* or *yin*) as *shen* 哂 (GSR 594i), meaning "to smile" so that the line reads, "Having filed his teeth, he depends on a smile" (?). YTC 3/11b reads 齦 as "baby teeth."

36. Literally, "there will be no ruler."

37. See SY 10/2b–3a for a similar observation.

38. YTC 3/11b.

39. Wang Ya talks vaguely of "losing what is close." Cf. the proverb, "Cutting back the lips exposes the gums," from CCYT 88/Hsi 2/3 *Kung*; 96/Hsi 5/9 *Tso* (Legge, 145).

40. CPL 3/11b.

41. Tentative translation, reading *mi* 密 here as "closely packed." YTC 3/11b reads the phrase *mi huo* 密禍 as "calamity resulting from closeness" [referring to the loyal remonstrant punished for his forthrightness]; CPL 3/11a assumes the calamity results from secrets (*mi*) told. Serruys reads the first Appraisal line as, "Making close the nearness of disaster"; and the first line of the Fathoming, "Nearness of close [i.e., inescapable] disaster."

42. Tentative translation. See below.

43. SMK 3/5a takes *pi* 比 to refer to "closeness" between gentlemen who are of like heart.

44. After YTC 3/11b; CPL 3/11a. See above.

45. Added by Nylan, using Yang's own association of "calamity" with "moral failing." For further information, see the Introduction.

46. FW 3/11a, citing FY 7:21.

No. 34. Kinship

1. SMK 3/5a notes that the sun by Appraisal 8 enters the Eastern Well constellation.

2. According to FW 3/11b.

3. Reading *tun* 敦 as "kind," "benignant," "generous." CPL 3/11b reads *tun* as *chih li* 致力 ("to apply one's strength to"), so that the phrase *tun tu* 敦篤 refers to yang's ability to cover all things thickly and protectively.

4. This characterization of yang *ch'i* is interesting insofar as it shows the degree to which men of Western Han accepted the Mohist ideal of "ungraded love" as the foundation for a cohesive society, without explicitly rejecting the counter notion of "graded love" put forward by Confucius and Mencius. See Wallacker, p. 222ff. This conflatin of Confucian and Mohist teachings was made possible

perhaps by *Analects* 12/22 (Waley, 169), which associates *jen* 仁 ("humaneness") with *ai jen* 愛人 ("loving others"). I am indebted to Dr. Alan Chan for this observation. Note that Yang Hsiung pairs together the two characters for "graded" love (*jen* 仁 [in my translation, "humane"]) and "ungraded" love (*ai* 愛 [in my translation, "loving"]), as if they were a single concept.

5. Ode 223/2 (Legge, 405); Karlgren (1964), 154.

6. For the statement that Heaven only takes as "kin" men of virtue, see, e.g., CCYT 96/Hsi 5/9 *Tso* (Legge, 146); LT, ch. 79 (Lau, 141).

7. Not following FW 3/11b; Wang Ya; and YTC 3/12a. See below for an alternate reading.

8. See above. Following FW 3/11b; Wang Ya; and YTC 3/12a. For more on grating teeth, see Boodberg, pp. 397–98.

9. Following SMK 3/5a.

10. FW 3/11b writes of unrelated persons, "The goals are the same but the natures are different."

11. Reading *nei* 內 as *jou* 肉, following FW 3/11b. Cf. YTC 3/12a; CPL 3/11b.

12. Wang Ya says, "to choose." YY 33:665 would read this character as *tz'u* 咨, meaning "to consult."

13. FW edition (3/12a) mistakenly writes *chien* 間 as *wen* 問.

14. Alternately, "does not acknowledge [them] as dependents." Or, "fails to attach [its larvae properly]," following Wang Ya.

15. Tentative translation. Alternately, "The fly is utterly shamed," which requires reading *pu* 不 as *p'ei* 丕 and changing subjects back to "the fly." FW 3/12a reads *ya* 迓 as *kuan* 館 ("to lodge"): "Failing to lodge [is a] shame." SMK 3/5b also reads *ya wu* 迓侮 as *yü wu* 御侮, but he seems to mean, "It does not fend off shame" (?). CPL 3/11b reads the binome 迓侮 as *ni wu* 逆忤: "delinquent in filial piety." CWK, p. 107, n. 5, loosely translates the passage, "[The sphex teaches them goodness, so that] they are neither unruly nor lax."

16. *Ode* 196/3 (Legge, 334). Cf. Karlgren, "Glosses," p. 104, 586. What Karlgren dismisses as "an unnecessary loan speculation" on the part of Ma Jui-ch'en is clearly supported by this Han passage.

17. CPL 3/12a is equally critical of the sphex, who is happy to care for the young mulberry flies, though they are not its own kind.

18. See FY 1:1. For a citation of this poem as it bears on Han family law, see CCCS, p. 1180 (1b).

19. Following Wang Ya, who defines *chi chi* 几几 as *yu fa tu* 有法度 ("having [proper] measure"). The binome also means *sheng* 盛 ("replete, full"). YTC 3/12b glosses it as *chuang ching mao* 莊敬貌 ("stately and respectful in appearance"). CPL 3/12a thinks it describes ritual that is repeated and complete.

20. SMK 3/5b, citing LC 21/51 (Legge, II, 171).

21. Harper (1987), p. 572, n. 77, quotes Shirakawa Shizuka 白川靜 to the effect that in early religion "guest" (*k'o* 客) referred to the ancestral spirits summoned to sacrificial celebrations. This usage is preserved in several of the Odes.

22. An alternate reading for *wu fang* 無方 is "without remedy."

23. Ode 223/1 (Legge, 401).

24. *Mencius* 7A/44 (Lau, 192). Cf. *Analects* 8/2 (Waley, 132).

25. *Analects* 20/2 (Waley, 233).

26. *Analects* 2/1 (Waley, 88).

27. SMK 3/5b–6a reads *fei fu* 肺附 (literally, "lung and stomach") as "dependents among distant kin" on the basis of a commentary to the SC. See CWK, p. 108, n. 10. It is far more likely that the phrase refers to close kin, as lung and stomach are vital organs. See Morohashi 29328.2.

28. Literally, "[For] close kin, dried meat./ His being the trunk is completely good./ That which the superior man performs."

29. Taking *ts'ai* 材 to refer both to talent and to stuff (materials, wealth).

30. *Analects* 1/2 (Waley, 83).

31. YTC 3/13a.

32. *Analects* 8/2 (Waley, 132).

33. Ode 165/3 (Legge, 255), cited by Wang Ya. FW 3/12b–13a and CWK, p. 108, n. 10, read this as inauspicious, assuming that gifts of dried meat were paltry gifts bestowed by stingy rulers who failed to treat their advisors generously. THC "Hsüan wen" 9/1a (p. 1028a), however, specifically associates such gifts with good fortune. A gift of dried meat, while relatively humble, is hardly an insult. Confucius himself purportedly accepted such gifts from those who wished to become his disciples. See *Analects* 7/7 (Waley, 124). Cf. *Mencius* 6B/6 (Lau, 176), where portions of flesh are distributed at the solstitial sacrifice.

34. Or simply, "improper."

35. Translation tentative. Following Sung Chung, who reads this as, "Destroying their own roots by themselves" (*tzu chin ch'i ken kai* 自盡其根荄). Alternately, *kai* 荄 ("roots") can be read as its cognates *ai* 硋 ("to hinder") or *hai* 恔 ("to make suffer"): "As it turns out, it hinders [or, makes suffer] the self." YTC 3/13b reads this as, "to return to one's own roots" [presumably, in the ignorant, immature self]. CWK, p. 108, n. 11, follows. CPL 3/13a would translate as YTC, but he emphasizes the possibility of rebirth inherent in the cycle of the Five Phases.

36. Wang Ya commentary, cited in SMK 3/6a.

No. 35. Gathering

1. Wilhelm translates as "Taming Power of the Small."

2. Literally, *man* 滿 ("fills").

3. Because it is just starting to gain strength, yin *ch'i* is not yet obvious.

4. Lu Chi would tie this with the "roots" mentioned in THC34/A9. "It forces" supplied by Nylan.

5. CPL 3/13a.

6. E.g., *Mencius* 3A/3 (Lau, 97–100); Tung Chung-shu, cited in HS 24A:1137 (Swann [1950], 179).

7. Cf. FY 9:25, 9:27.

8. Following SMK 3/6a in reading GSR 918p as 918g on the basis of SW. CPL 3/13a, however, glosses *t'ai* 貸 as "to seek goods from others." CWK, p. 110, n. 3, follows. The line then reads, "When [additional] small taxes are not extorted [from the people]."

9. Mentioned by FW 3/13b.

10. Following SMK 3/6a, which glosses *mo* 墨 as *t'an* 貪. Literally, "black."

11. YTC 3/13b interprets this last phrase as "so that [eventually] not even an article a hair's-breadth in size is left [to others]." Such an extreme example of avarice probably belongs in a later Appraisal.

12. See, e.g., LC 6/10 (Legge, I, 256).

13. *Mencius* 2A/2 (Lau, 78).

14. Added by Nylan.

15. YTC 3/14a; CWK, p. 110, n. 5.

16. Yang Hsiung in effect interjects the notion of Time into the Chuang-tzuian argument about the ultimate utility of "uselessness" and "smallness." See CTYT 3/1/44–47 (Watson, 35).

17. After FW 3/14a, whose language is vague. CWK (p. 110, n. 6), however, believes *hsiao hsing* 小刑 is a technical term. The poem then describes a breach in ritual: punishments due to begin in the fall take place in midsummer. YTC 3/14a believes that the modifier *hsiao* for *hsing* shows that bad government "makes light of" its improper exactions.

18. Reading *cheng* 正 instead of *cheng* 政, following FW 3/14a.

19. Following CPL 3/13b. FW 3/14a reads *ch'u pan* 畜槃 as, "Gather wooden trays [for sericulture since it is time]. " YTC 3/14a prefers, "Suppress excessive pleasures" (reading *ch'u* 畜 as *ch'u chih* 畜止, and *pan erh yen* 槃而衍 as *pan lo yu yen* 槃樂游衍). I suspect Yang Hsiung chose *pan* as a verb to emphasize the close relation between the breeding of animals and the feeding of silkworms on trays. See STTH, "Ch'i yung," 9/15a for a picture of the silkworm trays.

20. Following YTC 3/14a. CPL 3/13b reads *ch'un* 純 as "silken." The graph could also be read as a causative verb, "to make pure white" (i.e., "to clean").

21. LC 4/9b (Legge, I, 227).

22. Chia Yi memorial, cited in HS 24A:1128 (Swann [1950], 152ff.). Cf. HsinS 3/3b–5b.

23. See, for example, *Mencius* 1A/1 (Lau, 49). Han ritual emphasized the ruler's duty to encourage agriculture, as the emperor himself yearly engaged in ritual "ploughing the fields." See Bodde (1975), 223–41.

24. Following CPL 3/14a. SMK 3/6b reads *min mien* 閔縣 simply as "small in appearance." The line could also be read, "Minor resentments." SMK 3/6b and CWK, p. 111, n. 8, read it that way. CPL 3/14a takes *mien* as "continuous," but his explanation is somewhat confused.

25. Literally, "What is sickly and small./ Makes the start of something big."

26. Sivin (1986), p. 156.

27. HFT 7:21:117 (Liao, I, 213).

28. After YTC 3/14b.

29. Possibly Yang means to imply that the husband and wife have been con-demned to penal servitude. See LC 30/3. In the second line, "for him" has been omitted for euphony.

30. Literally, the state.

31. CPL 3/14a.

32. Following Wang Ya.

33. Following YTC 3/15a. SMK 3/6b reads as, "How could it be criticized?", taking *chi* 幾 as *chi* 譏.

34. *Mencius* 1A/3 (Lau, 51).

No. 36. Strength

1. FW 3/15a reads *t'ung* 統 (meaning "rules" or "unifies") for *ch'un* 純. Cf. CPL 3/14b. I do not follow this reading.
2. Or, "completely masculine."
3. CYYT 1/1/*hsiang* (Wilhelm, 373), said of the gentleman who models himself upon Ch'ien.
4. "Overbearing" is a possible translation for *ch'iang liang* 強梁 (here, "strengthened"). See FW 3/15a on THC36/F2. CPL 3/15a says yang *ch'i* is "unbending."
5. This argument for flexibility frequently appears in Warring States and Han texts.
6. Or, "blocking the good omens," following Serruys. CPL 3/15a understands the phrase to mean, [yin allied with Water] "has strength [outside but] not right at the center."
7. *Analects* 15/40 (Waley, 201). Cf. THC1/A3.
8. THC58/A8 describes such a person.
9. For this point, see FY 6:16.
10. *Hsiu* 修 means both "to extend" [the wings] and "to cultivate" [the self]. FW 3/15a makes this pun explicit. YTC 3/15b has the phoenix preening (*hsiu shih* 修飾) its feathers, displaying its beauty. The pun on *feng* is noted by Nylan. For the association of *hsiu* 修 and *feng* 風, see Chung Hui 鍾會, cited in CWTT 805.67.
11. CPL 3/15a.
12. Yang Hsiung seems to take a small, but significant step away from certain Warring States philosophers who named the common people, rather than the chief ministers, as the primary "foundation" of the state. In doing so, Yang returns to still earlier traditions from the feudal period, such as the *Ch'un Ch'iu* attributed to Confucius.
13. For the particle *yüan* 爰 in this pattern, see Serruys (n.d.), pp. 50, 140.
14. Reading *ch'iang ch'iang* 彊彊, following SMK. If *chiang chiang* 橿橿 is read instead, the lines emphasize the number (*sheng to* 盛多) of attendants. See YTC 3/16a.
15. Literally, "Keen of eye and ear, there and over there," as in the Appraisal.
16. Wang Ya reads *yung* 永 ("forever") for *fang* 方 ("directions"), for reasons which are not clear to me.
17. *Documents*, "Hung fan," par. 6 (Legge, 326–27; Karlgren, 30).
18. YTC 3/16a.
19. See the discussion on *shih* 勢 ("political purchase") in Creel, p. 77ff.; and Ames (1983), pp. 65–107.
20. See FY 11:33.
21. SMK 3/7a reads it simply as "To overcome my strength"—in other words, to humble oneself when appropriate. Cf. FW 3/15b, who reads it as, "To overcome my overbearing nature." Serruys reads it as, "In overcoming myself I grow strong." I take it as, "[With] strength to overcome myself." All readings are possible. See below.
22. Serruys prefers, "In relation to Heaven, there is no limit."

23. Reading *wu chi* 無基 as *wu chiang chieh* 無疆界, following Sung Chung. FW 3/15b, however, reads it, "without a base [for evil]."

24. *Analects* 12/1 (Waley, 162) for the phrase *k'o chi* 克己. FW 10:27 talks of the dangers of *not* overcoming oneself.

25. SMK 3/7a.

26. CWK, p. 114, n. 8: he is "strong [after] overcoming himself."

27. See FY 10:27 contra "laws without limits." Cf. the argument against harsh or mutilating punishments in HsinS 9/1a–8a (esp. p. 2a); HS 23:1097–99 (Hulsewé, 334–35). For more information, see Shigezawa.

28. Legend cited by YTC 3/16b.

29. Both verbs *ch'iang* 彊 and *mien* 勉 mean (1) to make strong and vigorous, and (2) to make an effort. See GSR 710e, 22c.

30. FY 5:13; 9:25. Cf. "Mean," 20/9 (Legge, 407); and *Analects* 6/27 (Waley, 121).

31. Alternately, "'Til the end, [he lives] by violence."

32. FY 11:33 disparages the strongman Ching K'o in such terms.

33. YTC 3/16b comments that whatever is most hard is also most brittle and liable to break. FW 3/16b says that no help will be forthcoming for such a bully.

No. 37. Purity

1. The phrase "doubly illuminated" (*chung kuang* 重光) is explained by Sung Chung as referring to things high and low. CPL 3/16b, however, refers to the "rays of light from [the two light sources,] sun and moon." CWK, p. 115, n. 2, cites the *Erh ya* definition of *chung kuang*, which makes even less sense in the context.

2. Sung Chung commentary, with reference to THC31/Head.

3. Sung Chung commentary. Cf. FW 3/16b, which talks of the myriad things "becoming pure in their way."

4. See FY 5:15 for the phrase *wu tsa* 無雜, which ushers in a discussion on . "brilliance" (*kuang* 光) and virtue.

5. Alternately, "gazing at the inside." See below.

6. YTC 3/16b.

7. Serruys prefers this reading.

8. Reading *mao* 冒 as "feigns," following FW 3/16b and CWK, p. 116, n. 3. Cf. CPL 3/17a (commentary to Appraisal 4). Alternately *mao* means *ming* 冥 ("to cover up" or "to obscure"). Serruys prefers to read this, "If one hiddenly mixes up so as to cover up [i.e., annul] all candidness."

9. SMK 3/7b; CPL 3/16b.

10. FY 11:33 uses the same metaphor of a wolf preying on a sheep.

11. CWK, p. 116, n. 4, reads this as, "He reverently serves his superiors" (*ching shun shih shang* 敬順事上). Serruys prefers, "He will be respected." The Wang Ya edition leaves out the character *kung* 恭 altogether.

12. FY 6:16 credits the perceptive man with powers akin to Heaven's.

13. CYYT 45/Hsi B/2 (Wilhelm, 328–29).

14. The Li Kuei 李軌 commentary to FY 6:16 defines "looking up" as seeing the Classics; "looking down," as consulting with humble woodcutters and fodder-

gatherers. Cf. the statement by Tung Chung-shu regarding Confucius: "Confucius . . . with respect to what is above surveyed the ways of Heaven and with respect to what is below inquired of the feelings of men." See Tung Chung-shu, "Hsien lian tui ts'e," cited in HS 56:2515.

15. Serruys reads *chen* 貞 as "good omens." CPL 3/17a reads the line as, "The loss of rank is proper."

16. YTC 3/17b emphasizes that the petty person ought to have refused office in the first place.

17. Following SMK 3/7b.

18. Wang Ya defines *wu fang* 無方 as *pu k'o ming* 不可名 ("indescribable"). CPL 3/17a agrees.

19. Following Lu Chi in taking *tse* 則 as *fa* 法 ("model"). Literally, "Rectifying Earth, [it he] takes as model." Serruys reads, "The rectifying earth rules [in him]." Alternately, "Rectifying [himself by] the rule of Earth."

20. Cf. *Analects* 6/21 (Waley, 120), where the mountain "stays still."

21. Wang Ya commentary talks of "indescribable" brilliance. SMK 3/7b says that the superior man lives temporarily in obscurity and seclusion.

22. *Analects* 12/1 (Waley, 162).

23. Serruys reads as, "When gazing at time[-old] faults."

24. Adding "because." Literally, as in the Appraisal: "Pure time(ly?) seeing faults."

25. SMK 3/8a cites Ode 260/6 (Legge, 544): "Any defects in the king's duties/ Are supplied by Chung Shan-fu."

26. For this theory, see FY 3:7.

27. *Analects* 17/2 (Waley, 209).

28. Literally, "[as if at] the beginning."

29. Literally, "[Such is] propriety." Serruys prefers, "a good omen."

30. Eliade, *passim*. Added by Nylan.

No. 38. Fullness

1. According to SMK 3/8a, but not FW 3/18a, the Dipper points due south; the musical note is F-sharp.

2. Following Sung Chung. However, FW 3/18a and Wang Ya read *tien* 窴 ("stopping up") as *ming* 冥 ("hidden"). However, yang *ch'i* has little now to do with darkness or obscurity.

3. The pronoun *chüeh* 厥 indicates a superior, so it should refer to yang *ch'i* here. FW 3/18a and CPL 3/18a, however, specify that it is the myriad things that "complete their goals."

4. CPL 3/18a.

5. FW 3/18a.

6. CYYT 11/14/*hsiang* (Wilhelm, 458).

7. *Mo* 墨 refers to the inked cord used by carpenters in measuring. From this it comes to mean "rule," "principle," or "model." Therefore, SMK 3/8a reads *pu mo* 不墨 as "not according to the model"; YTC 3/18b and CPL 3/18a follow. FW 3/18a, however, takes *mo* as *ch'ien* 謙 ("modest"). Wang Ya takes *mo* as its cognate *mo* 默, meaning "silent." See below.

8. Literally, "dark." FW 3/18a and YTC 3/18b argue for "mysterious" (*hsüan*) 玄.

9. See the note 7 above on *mo* 墨.

10. Proverb quoted in SY 16:557.

11. "On reward" added by Nylan. However, FW 3/18b blames the individual who does not "rely on" (and so wait for) the proper time; the coincidence of Fire in the tetragram and in the Appraisal leads to precipitate action.

12. CWK, p. 118, n. 3, reads the line as, "[Then] can possess everything" (*neng wu so pu yu* 能無所不有).

13. LT, ch. 10 (Lau, 66), repeated in LT, ch. 51 (Lau, 112).

14. SMK 3/8a.

15. *Analects* 4/6 (Waley, 103) defines virtue in terms of the will to be Good.

16. *Analects* 2/18 (Waley, 92).

17. YTC 3/18b.

18. Or, "plans for."

19. Cf. THC35/A7.

20. Following SMK 3/8b, which reads *ch'en ch'en* 臣臣 as "self-abasement" (*tzu pi chien chih yi* 自卑賤之意). FW 3/18b, however, seems to read the reduplicative as "treating subordinates as subordinates [should be treated]."

21. Alternately, following Serruys, "Makes great the gate of [that] man."

22. Reversing "humane and worthy" in the Fathoming.

23. YTC 3/19a.

24. SMK 3/8b.

25. Wang Ya and CWK, p. 118 read *ch'an* 揮 as *hsiang ch'an* 相纏 ("tied up with it"). SMK 3/8b and YTC 3/19a read *ch'an* as *sui* 隨 ("following [inevitably after the other]").

26. Literally: "[He] bears good fortune, which fills [his] shoulders./ [He] raises up ill fortune, [and then] is entangled./ Bearing good fortune, raising up ill./ Means: It is the way of the petty man."

27. YTC 3/19a says the phrase "fills the shoulders" conveys "an arrogant attitude."

28. CPL 3/19a reads *yü* 于 as *yu* 由 ("from").

29. Literally, *ch'ing* 慶 ("[cause for] congratulations").

30. Taking *ta* 大 as a verb. However, the Fathoming conceivably should be read, "In modesty, greatly possessing," as Sivin suggests (private communication).

31. Cf. LT, ch. 40 (Lau, 88) on phenomenal existence as ruled by cyclical reversal.

32. Reading *yi* 挹 as *yi sun* 挹損 ("diminish"), rather than as *t'ui* 退 ("retreat"). CWK, p. 119, n. 9, reads as *yi* 抑 ("to suppress"). More literally, *yi* means "to ladle out from."

33. Punctuating after *ying* 熒 because of the rhyme.

34. Literally, "Nearing the later tumbling."

35. YTC 3/19b emphasizes that "even a sage or a worthy" can not escape from danger if the timing is wrong.

36. See Hsing 1/8a.

37. The character *ying* 熒 means "blazing," "dazzling," "deluding."

38. FW 3/19a.

39. See THC5/A6. Cf. HTYT 102/28/1–5 (not in Dubs or Knoblock) for the method of "maintaining the full."

40. Literally, "does not save."

41. The commentators cite LT, ch. 40 (Lau, 101). Cf. ch. 9 (Lau, 65). Alternately, "Heaven's Way is disobeyed."

42. See FY 8:23–24 for Yang's unequivocal discussion on this point.

No. 39. Residence

1. Certain commentators would supply *ch'i* here, on an analogy with other Head texts.

2. Lu Chi glosses *chü* 蹠 as *ch'ung shih* 充實 ("to fill"). In that case, the phrase *chü fu* 蹠膚 means literally "to fill the skin." This reading is supported by CPL 3/19b; YTC 3/20a. Cf. YY 33:665, where the same verb is glossed as "locked in incessant battle." In that case, the binome means something like, "takes its stand at the edge." SMK 3/9a, however, reads *chü fu* as *chü chü* 蹠蹠, a compound he glosses as *tung tso ch'iang liang mao* 動作強梁貌 ("to act with great [even overbearing?] strength" [so as to protect things].)

3. The single character *ho* 赫 can mean "awe-inspiring" or "frightening." See GSR 779a. At least two alternative readings are attested for the reduplicative *ho ho* 赫赫: (1) as *ho jan sheng ta* 赫然盛大 ("brilliantly flourishing"), following FW 3/19b; and (2) as "shining brilliantly," following FY 8:23.

4. Following Sung Chung; cf. CPL 3/19b, who refers to Ode 237/6 (Legge, 440); and SMK 3/9a, which says the character *tu* 度 means *chai* 宅 ("shelters"). Alternately, *tu* means "measure" (here, "to grow to full measure"), as in THC52. See FW 3/19b.

5. Sung Chung commentary.

6. CYYT 23/37/*t'uan* (Wilhelm, 570).

7. CPL 3/19b.

8. CYYT 23/37/*t'uan* (Wilhelm, 570).

9. Classical Chinese does not usually distinguish active from passive verbs. The line can then mean, "Neither praising nor blaming [others] or "Neither being praised nor being blamed." Hence, my translation. The commentators cannot seem to decide between the alternatives either. See below.

10. FW 3/20a: "He does not seek a reputation."

11. *Analects* 6/14; 14/26; 15/25 (Waley, pp. 118–19; 187; 198 [renum.]).

12. YTC 3/20a and CPL 3/19b explain these lines in terms of *wu wei* 無為 ("non-purposive activity").

13. Literally, "The woman receives them from the mother-in-law [or] paternal aunts." SMK 3/9a apparently reads as, "The young wife has her mother-in law serve her" since he says *chin fan shih ku ch'eng chih* 今反使姑承之. FW 3/20a; and YTC 3/20b read this as *fu shang ku shih* 婦尚姑事 ("The [young] wife supplants her mother-in-law in her tasks").

14. Reading *huo* 或 ("some," "perhaps") as a loan for its cognate *huo* 惑. Cf. footnote 1 on pp. 1, 3 in CYYT. However, it is also possible to read this as "in some cases" since the pattern *huo*-verb-*chih* 之 (3d. person pronoun)-noun fre-

quently occurs in CYYT. FW 3/20a reads *huo* 或 as *yu* 猶 ("akin to"), then says, "It is like being washed in mud." This is impossible phonologically.

15. SMK 3/9a, however, takes this to mean that the mother-in-law is assigned degrading tasks (*fu lao ju chih shih* 服勞辱之事) like "washing the paths." CWK, p. 121, n. 4 also reads *t'u* 塗 as *t'u* 途 ("pathway"). He says, however, that the young wife "washes [herself] on the path," making a public spectacle of herself.

16. CPL 3/19b.

17. See SMK 3/9a; YTC 3/20b.

18. Reading *k'un* 壼 for *hu* 壺.

19. SMK 3/9a emphasizes that his early training prepares him for that job. FW 3/20a refers to the filial interest that Yang Hsiung's second son displayed in the THC.

20. Following CWK, p. 121, n. 6.

21. Literally, "bodies."

22. For this reasons, dogs were often sacrificed when cornerstones were laid for major construction projects. For the early domestication of pigs and dogs in Neolithic times and the use of the dog in sacrifice, see Chang (1977b), pp. 95, 152, 261.

23. HS 27B(A):1398, which cites Ching Fang 京房.

24. The binome *chou lu* 舳艫 can also refer to a solid phalanx of warships lashed together to present a solid front to the enemy. Serruys reads, "If the *chou lu* 舳艫 boat all around is safely secured." This is possible here and in the Fathoming.

25. Wang Ya commentary.

26. SMK 3/9b; CWK, p. 122, n. 7.

27. Added by Nylan.

28. This is a common analogy in Chan-kuo and Warring States texts.

29. GSR 716a means "sacrificial offering," "feast," or "to enjoy." My translation of *pu hsiang* 不享 tries to reflect all three possible meanings. CPL 3/20b says *pu hsiang* means he "cannot get food or drink." CWK, p. 122, n. 8, seems to agree.

30. SMK 3/9b talks of petty persons who cannot get along with their betters in the clan.

31. CWK, p. 122, n. 8, seems to blame the head of household for this ill-judged decision. He then says all the family members rebel after basic food and water supplies suffer.

32. FW 3/20b is concerned with the effect on the ancestral temple offerings.

33. By putting himself in the shafts, according to SMK 3/9b.

34. CYYT 23/<u>37</u>/3(10) (Wilhelm, 146).

35. According to CPL 3/20b, the doubling of ladles shows that the first set of ladles has already been broken. I assume, however, that it shows ignorance of or disdain for the proprieties.

36. For further information, see Chang (1977a), pp. 62–66.

37. Suggested by Nylan.

38. SMK 3/9b.

39. YTC 3/21b, reads *pi* 枇 as *p'in* 牝, equating the doubling of ladles with an increase in the number of females (by this he means concubines).

No. 40. Law

1. FW 3/21b mistakenly gives 35 degrees.
2. As cover.
3. Ode 260/1 (Legge, 541).
4. For excellent discussions of the term *fa* 法, see Creel, 135–62; Bodde (1981), 171–94. In FY 4:10, 4:12, *fa* is reserved for "model."
5. *Analects* 2/3 (Waley, 88).
6. Cf. CYYT 30/48/*t'uan* (Wilhelm, 630). It is this equitability that the "well-field" economic system epitomizes. See *Mencius* 3A/3 (Lau, 97–100).
7. FY 1:2.
8. CYYT 45/Hsi B/2 (Wilhelm, 328 ff.).
9. Or, following YTC 3/22a: "[Hence, his] ability."
10. FW 3/21b and SMK 3/10a take the "Way of Centrality" preserved in the "Hung fan" chapter as the subject of this sentence. YTC 3/21a specifies the person as subject.
11. *Analects* 11/16 (Waley, 156): "To go too far is as bad as not far enough." The notion of centrality as it applies to politics is fully explored in the "Great Plan" chapter of the *Documents*, cited by SMK 3/10a. See Nylan (forthcoming), ch. 1.
12. FW 3/21b and YTC 3/22 gloss *pu* 甫 as *shih* 始. SMK 3/10a glosses it as *mei* 美 ("fine"); CPL 3/21b as *shan* 善 ("good"), so that the line says, "If level and line are no good." Serruys reads this line as, "If the level and line are not considered essential."
13. CIS, I, 13.
14. CPL 3/21b.
15. YTC 3/22a.
16. YTC 3/22b glosses the reduplicative *lu lu* 陸陸 as "short." If we follow YTC, the incapacity implied by the phrase "the well rope short" is repeated in the following phrase, "the well jar filled." YTC clearly follows CYYT 30/48/*t'uan* (Wilhelm, 630). SMK 3/10a thinks it describes "the rope coming down" (*so hsia* 索下). However, CPL 3/21b equates it with *lu lu* 碌碌, meaning "nothing out of the ordinary."
17. For the various claims made about the Confucian canon, including that regarding the profundity of the classics, see Henderson, ch. 4, esp. p. 130.
18. SMK 3/10a.
19. FW 3/22a, however, appears to equate the thread with the subjects and the rope with the ruler.
20. For the term *ta t'ung* 大統 see *Documents*, "Wu ch'eng," par. 5 (Legge, 311–12; not in Karlgren); SC 61:2121 (Watson[b], 11). For the sequence by which good rule is established, see "Learning," par. 5 (Legge, 359).
21. Is this why Confucius is said to have "fished with a line, but not with a net"? See *Analects* 7/26 (Waley, 128).
22. YTC 3/23a, however, reads this as, "Correcting by our blameless way."
23. *Documents*, "Ta Yü mo," par. 11 (Legge, 59; not in Karlgren).
24. I.e., over the sides.
25. Literally, "[Since] it is not a valley; it is not a gorge." Following FW 3/22b; YTC 3/23a; and Serruys. It is just possible that *fei* 匪 should be read as *fei* 騑 ("running unchecked").

26. A pun. For "flood" one could also read "error," "excess," or "loss." See GSR 197b.

27. Or, "Laws are reckless and unrestrained."

28. Added by Nylan. *Ku* 谷 ("valley") is a loan for "what is good." See GSR 1202a.

29. CPL 3/22b, following Wang Ya. Cf. FY 4:12; 11:33, for example, on the First Emperor of Ch'in.

No. 41. Response

1. SMK 3/10b alone of the commentators correlates this tetragram with Hexagram 31 ("Influence") of the *Changes*, arguing that Yang Hsiung's 81 tetragrams in the *Mystery* refer to only 60 hexagrams of the *Changes*, in imitation of the *kua ch'i* 卦氣 ("Hexagram/Solar Period") theory of Ching Fang (77–37 B.C.). While Tetragram 41 shows some connection with Hexagram 31 in its title and text, with greater frequency it alludes to the title and imagery of Hexagram 30 (See below.). There is also indisputable evidence that Yang's 81 tetragrams refer to all 64 hexagrams of the *Changes*. I therefore follow the majority of commentators in assigning Tetragram 41 to Hexagram 30. For further information on *kua ch'i* theory, see Ch'ü Wan-li, pp. 92–98.

2. According to FW 3/23a.

3. Following CPL 3/22b, which glosses the character *hsin* 信 as *pu shuang* 不爽. See below for other possible readings.

4. Literally, "to the low [regions]," but the blunted usage for *hu* 乎 must be used since yin is already below. See THC35/Head.

5. The summer solstice begins with Appraisal 5, according to FW 3/23a; with Appraisal 6, in the WJL edition. Tetragram 1, marking the winter solstice, is entitled Center.

6: Yang may wish us to recall the Triple Concordance calendar newly inaugurated in late Western Han. For further information, see Sivin (1969), 1–73.

7. LT, ch. 32 (Lau, 91).

8. The most important of such correlations current in Yang Hsiung's time are listed in Meng Hsi's (fl. 69 B.C.) "commentary by chapter and verse" to the *Changes*. See MH, 69. For the glosses, see CYYT 19/30/*t'uan* (Wilhelm, 536); 19/30/*hsiang* (Wilhelm, 537); 50/*Shuo*/4 (Wilhelm, 536); 54/*tsa* (Wilhelm, 536); 45/Hsi B/2 (Wilhelm, 336) respectively.

9. For *hsin* as a homonymic variant of *shen* 伸, see CYYT 46/Hsi B/3 (Wilhelm, 338).

10. *Sheng-chao* 聲兆 is his gloss for *hsin*.

11. Professor Ch'en Shun-cheng 陳舜政 of National Taiwan University, Chinese Studies Department made this suggestion (personal communication). The same phrase could also be translated either as "[its] sound commencing" or as "sound portent."

12. For the translation of the descriptive bisyllabic rhymes *lo ju* 羅如 and *li ju* 離如, I follow FW 3/23a, which glosses *lo* 羅 as *pu* 布 ("to spread out") and *li* 離 as *fu li* 附麗 ("to adhere to"). Cf. CWK, p. 127, n. 2, which glosses *lo ju* 羅如 as *lieh* 列 ("arranged"). YTC 3/23b takes both compounds simply as "intermixed"

(*pan pan erh sheng* 斑斑而盛). The poetic resonance of *lo ju li ju* is increased since *lo* and *li* are synonymous in two additional instances: First, both mean "to meet with a circumstance, " as in Fang 7/49/23. Second, both refer to woven enclosures, a definition which recalls the image of nets found in the correspondent Hexagram 30 of the *Changes*.

13. A pun, since the character *li* (here and in the first Appraisal line) means both "net[like]" and "to adhere."

14. No doubt this explains why SMK 3/10b offers no commentary here.

15. CYYT 42/Hsi A/8 (Wilhelm, 308).

16. CPL 3/22b-23a.

17. The Han "Treatise on the Pitch Standards" also says Heaven is 6 and Earth 5, since Heaven has six *ch'i* and earth Five Flavors. See HS 21A:981. A numerological system based on 6, rather than 5, is found in certain early Western Han texts, such as HsinS. Cf. on early *Changes* commentary, which says, "Heaven is six. Earth is five. That it is constant rule for numbers." See MKH, I, 53(1a).

18. Both the *Mystery* and the *Model Sayings* denounce whatever is *tsa* 雜. See, for example, FY 2:5-6.

19. YTC 3/23b.

20. Cf. LT, ch. 32 (Lau, 91), ch. 61 (Lau, 122), ch. 66 (Lau, 128).

21. Paul Serruys prefers, "It negates where they are correct." The translation follows a number of commentators (including Sung Chung, Lu Chi, Wang Ya, and SMK 3/10b) in reading *chen* 貞. FW 3/23b, however, reads *ken* 肯 ("to be willing") instead. Note that the phrase "union of spheres" is supplied by Nylan for the translation of the third line of the Appraisal above.

22. FW 3/23b.

23. For the theoretical correlation between the musical system and Earthly *ch'i*, see Bodde (1959).

24. CYYT 40/Hsi A/3 (Wilhelm, 294).

25. CYYT 40/Hsi A/3 (Wilhelm, 294).

26. Cf. LT, ch. 73 (Lau, 135), which speaks of its mesh "which is not fine, yet nothing slips through." Cf. THC40/A7.

27. See FY 10:26. Cf. THC40/A6.

28. FW 3/23b assumes "us" refers to "the masses." Clearly, "us" represents the targets hunted.

29. CPL 3/23b reads this as, "They cast the net over the wild reaches." SMK 3/11a, however, punctuates before *chih* 至, citing Ode 207/1 (Legge, 363). In that case, the character indicates that, "[incidents] are about to arise."

30. HsinS 7/4b-5a. Cf. *Mencius* 1A/3 (Lau, 51-52).

31. *Analects* 2/3 (Waley, 88); *ibid.*, 4/13 (Waley, 104).

32. The term *chen* 貞, which is glossed as *cheng* 正 by FW 3/24a. For further information, see the Appendix.

33. Or, "It makes shudder [i.e. ruffles?] its scales."

34. Or, "As the dragon soars, it shivers."

35. CYYT 47/Hsi B/4 (Wilhelm, 341).

36. The translation of the character *ch'eng* 承 is tentative. Wang Ya reads it as *cheng* 丞 ("to rise like steam"), a reference to the fact that "fire *ch'i* ascends."

Similarly, YTC 3/24b and CPL 3/23b gloss it as *chin* 進 ("advances"). The line would then mean that the blazing fire of yang *ch'i* ascends to heaven.

37. Cf. THC35/Head.
38. Literally, "to strengthen his decline."
39. FW 3/24a, however, reads *ying* 應 as *tang* 當 ("ought to"). For an alternate reading by SMK, see below.
40. Reading *lei* 類 as *shan* 善. See CWK, p. 128, n. 9, citing the *Erh ya*. Alternately, "They hate to defeat [their own] class [of men]."
41. Cf. THC 36/A8, whose language is almost identical.
42. Following FW 3/24a. For an early occurence of the compound *pai lei* 敗類, see Ode 257 (Legge, 526). For the use of *lei* 類 to signify "the [proper] type [of official]," see LSCC 20/8b–10b. The late commentators talk of "hating yin's defeat of [all] yang-type [things]." See CPL 3/24a and YTC 3/24b.
43. SMK 3/11a, reading the second line of the Appraisal as, "Those who respond will be numerous. Right."
44. CYYT 40/Hsi A/5 (Wilhelm, 299).
45. Wang Ya reads *wei* 微 ("minute") for *cheng* 徵 (here translated as "summons").
46. Taking *ying ch'i* 應其 as "in responding fashion." Wang Ya reads *shih* 時 ("timely"), instead of *ch'i* 其.
47. Or, "The great morning light, it reaches the limit." The character *li* 離 refers to the "trellis-like" appearance of morning light shimmering on the horizon (Paul Serruys, private communication).
48. Or simply, "stop," following Lu Chi.
49. FW 3/24b thinks the subject of this line is "yin *ch'i*." I take it as "change."
50. FW 3/24b, for example, brings up the case of Yao, who in his old age abdicated in favor of his wise official Shun. See *Documents*, "Yao tien," par. 14 (Legge, 32; Karlgren, 4).
51. SMK 3/11a. Cf. YTC 3/25a and CPL 3/24b.
52. CYYT 19/30/3 (Wilhelm, 120).

No. 42. Going to Meet

1. More literally, "go upwards against [yang]." See GSR 769d.
2. Added by Nylan, based on the root meaning of *su* 溯 ("to go upwards against"). YTC 4/1a talks of warning the myriad things against welcoming yin *ch'i*.
3. See also Needham, II, 232–91.
4. Following FW 4/1a, which omits the character *ying* 應, however. But SMK 4/1a reads GSR 579c as 579a, for he says that the meeting is not "according to the proper Way."
5. Literally, "has what he deviates in."
6. FY 1:3 says, "Pairs (*p'eng* 朋) that are not of one mind are [only] couples on the face of it."
7. Alternately, "hiding in." See below.
8. Literally, "Height eggs, [it] changes them."

9. FW 4/1a. Cf. HNT 12:349.

10. CPL 4/1a.

11. Cf. CYYT 37/<u>61</u>/2, 2 *hsiang*; 41/Hsi A/6 (Wilhelm, 701, 305): "A crane calling in the dark,/ Makes its young respond to it." Unaccountably, CPL 4/1a–1b talks of "bad people responding to bad people."

12. Taking *ching* 精 as subject, and *wei* 微 as adverb, following the suggestion of Paul Serruys. FW 4/1b clearly reads *wei* 微 as the adverb "subtly." However, SMK 4/1a seems to take *ching wei* as a binome, meaning "finest emanations" (*ching chin* 精祲); YTC 4/1b, as "the smallest, finest part" of things that respond with extreme sensitivity; and CPL 4/1b, as *yao fen* 妖氛 ("ominous exhalations"). FW 4/1b glosses *wang lai* 往來 (literally, "go back and forth") simply as *kan* 感 ("to stimulate").

13. Note that SMK 4/1a rearranges the word order, making it "Ill omens numinously precede awareness."

14. However, CWK, p. 130, n. 5, defines *cheng* 徵 as *chao* 召 ("[spontaneously] summon").

15. CPL 4/1b.

16. YTC 4/1b quotes the *Rituals* (*li* 禮) to this effect, but I have not been able to locate the exact citation.

17. Translation tentative. I read *sha* 睫 as *chieh* 睫 ("eyelashes"). FW 4/2a reads *sha kou* 睫鉤 as *ch'ü kou* 曲鉤 ("curved hook"), which can refer to the brows or to fishhooks. However, most commentators read *sha* as *ch'ieh* 唼, meaning *to yen* 多言 ("talkative") or *ni ni* 呢呢 ("sweet murmurings") which serve to "hook" the male. Cf. Wu Mi, who reads *sha* as *ti* 嗁. "Always" added by Nylan.

18. Neo-Confucianism, however, tends towards the prudish. Significantly, CPL 4/1b takes this as a scene of sexual seduction that ignores the proper rituals governing betrothal and marriage.

19. See *Mencius* 4A/15 (Lau, 124).

20. Cf. SY 8/3b.

21. CPL 4/2a reads *ch'eng* 乘 as *ch'eng yü* 乘輿 ("carriage"), then argues that the color of the carriage is insufficient reason to esteem it.

22. YTC 4/2a.

23. Literally, "Black and yellow mutually meet."

24. FW 4/2a argues that the use of the reduplicative emphasizes that both Heaven and Earth respond.

25. FW 4/2a.

26. Or, sky and earth?

27. CYYT 47/Hsi B/4 (Wilhelm, 342–43), cited by YTC 4/2a. For the possible origin of the contrast between black and yellow, see Allan (1991), pp. 30, 65.

28. See SMK 4/1a. Example by Nylan.

29. SMK 4/1b; YTC 4/2a; and CWK, p. 131, n. 9, take *hsieh hou* 邂逅 as "unexpectedly." FW 4/2b and CPL 4/2a read it as *chieh t'o* 解脫 ("to free oneself from worries"), which may be a misprint for *hsieh yüeh* 懈樂 ("relaxed and happy"). See Morohashi 39173.1; 35067.17; and 35067.185. I adopt the usage found in Ode 118/2 (Legge, 180), where the binome describes a happy meeting.

30. CCCS, p. 1181 (2b), where *kou fu* 詬父 ("to insult one's father") seems

to be a legal term. Perhaps Yang Hsiung offers a series of puns here, with GSR 112c and *hou* 詬 etymologically related both to 112e (the theme of "meeting") and to 112g ("insult"). Cf. YTC 4/2a.

31. CCCS, p. 1180 (1b).

32. CPL 4/2a–b.

33. Translation tentative. Following SMK 4/1b, which glosses *fu* 捬 as *han* 捍 ("to guard against," "to defend"). YTC 4/2b, however, reads *fu* as *fu* 俯 ("to bow the head"). See below.

34. However, YTC 4/2b and CPL 4/2b talk of the superior man confronting the trouble with bowed head, hoping that "softness" (ritual abnegation) eventually will defuse violent anger. Both commentators cite the "Mean" 10/3 (Legge, 389) in support of their interpretation: "To show forbearance and gentleness in teaching others, and not to revenge unreasonable conduct—this is the strength of the southern regions. The superior man makes it his study." They could also cite LT, ch. 22 (Lau, 79), which equates "bowing the head" with final preservation.

35. Reading *lei* 累 as *lei chi* 累及 (literally, "to involve"), following SMK 4/1b and CWK, p. 131, n. 11. *Lei* could also mean "to accumulate," so that the sentence reads, "It accumulates [to such a degree that it] goes to the adjoining room." FW 4/2b reads *fu* 罦 for *lei*, then glosses *fu* 罦 as *fu* 覆 ("overturn," "topple"). Along similar lines, YTC 4/2b reads *fu* as *kang* 綱 (a kind of bird net), then argues that the water is "trapped in" the walls of the adjoining room.

36. YTC 4/2b.

No. 43. Encounters

1. YTC 4/3a.

2. CPL 4/3a.

3. However, YTC 4/3a defines *yu* 幽 as *ching wei* 精微 ("what is essential and minute"). Note that SMK 4/1b and CWK, pp. 132–33 punctuate after *shih* 師 so that the Appraisal reads, "In darkness, to meet with gods and teachers./Dreams [display] propriety." CPL 4/3a believes that the phrase *yü shen* 遇神 describes yin *ch'i* meeting yang, and the phrase *chi shih* 及師, yang *ch'i* meeting yin. According to Ch'en, the two cosmic powers fight in the darkness; hence, the reference to dreams: "In dark obscurity, [yin] meets the god[like yang],/ [Yang] reaches the spirit [yin]./ Dreams [display] rectitude."

4. See YTC 4/3a. FW 4/3a and Serruys read *shih* 師 as *chung* 衆, so the line would read, "Many dreams [display] good omens."

5. The Han Chinese knew several incompatible theories of dream interpretation. Sometimes they argued that a dream apparition reveals the subject of the individual's recent thoughts, a perfectly acceptable explanation even today. Sometimes they spoke of the soul wandering outside the body during dreams in a fully conscious state akin to waking. And sometimes they envisioned the dream as a sort of telepathic communication between the dreamer and the spirit world. (Hence, the gloom with which Confucius reports his inability to envision the Duke of Chou in his dreams, in *Analects* 7/5 [Waley, 123].) See, e.g., *Documents*, "Shuo ming," par. 3 (Legge, 250–51; not in Karlgren); "T'ai shih," par. 5 (Legge, 291; not in Karlgren). For more on dreams, see Brown, C. The entire issue of *Asian Art* 3:4 (Fall, 1990) is also devoted to dreams in China.

6. KT 13/37/6b (Rickett[a], 169), cited by YTC 4/3b.

7. Reading *ch'ung ch'ung* 衝衝 as *chung chung* 尰尰 (GSR 1188j = 1188k). The Fathoming borrows from Wang Ya, who defines the reduplicative as *t'ung hun wu chih* 童昏無知; and from CPL 4/3a's gloss: *heng hsing wu chih mao* 橫行無知貌. Cf. FY 8:22 for similar usage. YTC 4/3a defines it as *wang lai pu ting chih mao* 往來不定之貌 ("unfixed in his comings and goings").

8. Following the argument of FW 4/3a–b, which text inserts *shou* 受, so that the line reads, "[He] will not accept instructions fixed for him." The WJL edition (4/1b) deletes *shou*, however, on the basis of scansion. Wang Ya reads the line, "[Lacking knowledge himself,] he does not ascertain it [that what he meets has knowledge and so can] teach."

9. *Analects* 1/2 (Waley, 83).

10. Following FW 4/3b, which reads: "Not to go, not to come, not to seek" (*pu wang pu lai pu ch'iu* 不往不來不求), following the *Li sao* (?). Cf. the description of the "good man" in Ode 257 (Legge, 525): "He does not seek it [office], nor does he push it [his career] forward." Other editions simply read, *pu wang pu lai* 不往不來 ("not going or coming").

11. SMK 4/1b–2a; CPL 4/3b.

12. FW 4/3b; YTC 4/3b. Cf. the figure of Liu-hsia Hui 柳下惠 praised in *Analects* 18/2 (Waley, 218), 4/14 (Waley, 104–5).

13. YTC 3/3b says, "exhausted from dancing for a long time." CPL 3/3b follows. Wang Ya reads as "courageous but impolite in appearance" (*yung erh wu li chih mao* 勇而無禮貌).

14. *T'ui jen* 兌人, which most commentaries equate with *(nu) wu* (女)巫. I use "opener" for *t'ui jen* since the term emphasizes the root meaning of the word and its association with the mouth (assigned to Appraisal 4 and west). For the controversy over the translation of *wu* as "shaman" or "shamaness," see Keightley (1989); Mair (1990a). Mair prefers "magus." Note, however, that YY 33:666 reads *t'ui jen* as "inhabitant of the wetlands." The Appraisal then reads, "Exhausted,/ A man of the wetlands meets with rain./ Danger." Too much of anything, even a good thing, is liable to be dangerous.

15. CPL 4/3b reads as, "No one to blame but oneself."

16. Schafer (1951).

17. FW 4/3b; CPL 4/3b.

18. YTC 4/3b.

19. FY 1:2.

20. However, FW 4/4a reads *pi* 俾 as *shih* 使 ("if").

21. YTC 4/4a.

22. "Eager to defend" supplied by Nylan. Following SMK 4/2a, which takes *fei* 匪 as *fei* 非. Cf. *Mencius* 7A/2 (Lau, 182), on the phrase *fei cheng ming* 非正命.

23. Contrast the unlucky account rendered in YTC 4/4a, however. YTC sees a case of the "ruler [or] father who treats [the man of honor] shamefully." Such a rejection is clearly undeserved; such mistreatment is not his "proper fate."

24. CYYT 28/44/6, *hsiang* (Wilhelm, 613; Kunst, 327).

25. Following SMK 4/2a.

26. YTC 4/4a, however, understands *pu sheng sang* 不勝喪 as *sang chih shen*

喪之甚 ("the extreme of destruction"), apparently taking *pu sheng* as "unparalleled."

27. It is possible that this stands for human combatants wearing horns. For such feats of strength, see Lewis, pp. 157–60; Loewe (1990).

28. SMK 4/2a, however, takes the horn as symbol of the *shih* 士 who resists an insult.

29. Reading *ti* 觝 as *ti* 抵 ("to push away"). It could also mean *ch'u* 觸 ("to butt against"). "The enemy's blow" supplied by Nylan.

30. Following YTC 4/4b; CPL 4/4a. However, FW 4/4b reads this as, "In some cases broken, his horn/ Hits below, wounding the foot." Note, however, that SMK in SPPY reads *pu* 不 ("not") instead of *hsia* 下 ("low regions") given in the WJL edition, which follows FW 4/4b.

31. Literally, "How can [the blow] be warded off [completely]?

32. YTC 4/4b.

No. 44. Stove

1. According to SMK 4/2a.

2. Reading 龢 as *ho* 和, following SMK 4/2a. CPL 4/4b reads *je erh ho* 熱而龢 as "roasts and boils." Note that I take *chih* 之 to refer to the collective unit of the myriad things ("them"). However, CPL 3/4 takes the first third-person pronoun to refer to yang, and the second, to refer to yin. CWK, p. 136, n. 2, seems to agree with me.

3. For example, see *Documents*, "Shuo ming," par. 2 (Legge, 260; not in Karlgren): "Do teach me what should be my aims. Be to me as the yeast and malt in making sweet spirits, as the salt and prunes in making tasty stew. Give me your help to cultivate me." Compare this with the figure of Butcher Ting in *Chuang tzu*. Contrast this with the comparison of the cooking stove to the evil ruler who employs his favorite (since a single person can effectively block the door of both the court and the stove). See HFT 16:39:295 (Liao, II, 196–97).

4. CYYT, 31/50/*t'uan* (Wilhelm, 642).

5. See Girardot, p. 180.

6. See SY 17/14b.

7. See YTC 4/5b. Cf. CCFL 3/5/10b (Gassmann, 65).

8. CYYT 54/*tsa* (Wilhelm, 641). Cf. THC/A4.

9. *Shih* 實 refers loosely to "contents." CPL 4/4b says there is water, but no uncooked rice (*mi* 米). CWK, p. 136, n. 3, agrees. Serruys takes the sentence to mean that there is no firewood, but see App. 3 below.

10. FW 4/5a emphasizes that he has no practical accomplishments.

11. CYYT 33/54/6 (Wilhelm, 212; Kunst, 347). Contrast the auspicious "tripod that has food in it," seen in CYYT 31/50/2 (Wilhelm, 195; Kunst, 339).

12. CPL 4/4b.

13. The word "golden" here and below probably refers to the color of polished bronze, rather than to the material used in making the tripod.

14. Literally, "outstanding." Fang 6/42/24 defines *chieh* 介 as *t'e* 特; Wang Ya defines it as *t'e li* 特立.

15. I presume that *yi* 裔 indicates a fundamental kinship found in posterity.

FW 4/5a glosses *yi* as *yü* 餘 ("having a surplus [capacity]" or "extra [food]"). CPL 3/4b glosses *yi* 裔 as *chung k'ung* 中空 ("[its] center empty").

16. Contrast Liao's translation of *lien chen* 廉貞 as "fidelity and integrity," then "merciful and faithful." See HFT 16:39:293; 19:49:346 (Liao, II, 193, 289).

17. SMK 4/2b (under Buddhist influence?) talks of not being desirous of external things, however.

18. FW 4/5a.

19. CPL 4/4b.

20. SMK 4/2b, though vague, seems to prefer this reading.

21. FW 4/5a; YTC 4/5a, and CWK, p. 136, n. 5, however, read *pin* 瀕 as brackish water; hence, "filthy."

22. *Hsin* 薪 = *ts'ai* 材 = *ts'ai* 才.

23. The *li* 鬲 is a tripod with hollow legs.

24. FW 4/5b, however, says, "The reward is not incommensurate with effort" (*shang pu shih lao* 賞不失勞). Compare the wording in FY 13:43.

25. Alternately, "Time, we uphold." FW 4/5b takes this to mean, "Timely is our being offered [to worthies]," where *wo* 我 refers to the "five tastes of the dish." SMK 4/2b says, "Worthy men at the proper time are employed." YTC 4/5b reads *shih* 時 as *shih* 是.

26. Added by Nylan.

27. Wang Ya notes that the steamer is a vessel with relatively small capacity as compared with the tripod. While this is true, the emphasis seems to be on preparation for achievement.

28. However, SMK 4/2b defines *shang* 鬺 as *chu* 煮 ("to boil or stew") so that the line reads, "The large tripod can be used for cooking" in ritual acts. CWK, p. 136, n. 6, defines *shang* as a small cooking pot.

29. FW 4/5b says the tripod symbolizes the emperor; the goblet, the feudal lords enfeoffed by him.

30. See SMK 4/2b; CPL 4/5a; and YTC 4/5b.

31. Added by Nylan.

32. FW 4/6a takes this as "a feast [offered by] the great man [i.e., the ruler]."

33. CYYT 3/1/yen (Wilhelm, 380). The term "great man" refers to anyone with the qualities needed to be an effective ruler.

34. By the time the *Ch'un Ch'iu* was composed, the word *tsai* 宰 (originally "butcher") was already used as title for a high official. See CCYT 5/Yin 1/4 *Kung*, 9 *Kung* (Legge, 6; Malmqvist, 71). For Han views on this, see FSTYCC, pp. 241–42, n. 1. For the analogous position of the butcher in early Greek society, see Detienne, pp. 11–13.

35. For a similar description of the duties of the prime minister, see, SY 2/2b; FSTY *yi-wen* 4:133, for example.

36. SMK 4/2b defines *ou wu* 歐歔 simply as vomiting. FW 4/6a and YTC 4/6a define *wu* 歔 as the sound of gagging.

37. See *Mencius* 5B/6 (Lau, 156), where gifts of meat to worthies are accompanied by cultivated expressions of humility on the ruler's part.

38. CPL 4/5b.

39. Translation tentative. FW 4/6a and others take *wei* 委 as salary "handed

over" to commissioned officials. CWK, p. 137, n. 10, takes *wei* as "stores" of grain, which symbolize government salary.

40. Or, "slander." See CPL 5/5b.

41. FW 4/6a and YTC 4/6a. CPL 4/5b loosely follows.

No. 45. Greatness

1. Note that the tetragrams clustering around the summer solstice do not add the word *ch'i* here.

2. CPL 4/6a, however, says, "Yin in silence wants to empty yang. Yang, unaware of its deceit, wants to make it flourish."

3. YY 33:666–67 shows that *p'eng* 蓬 and *feng* 逢 mean *feng* 豐 ("make abundant").

4. For the internal pun *yü* 與 = *yü* 舁, see GSR 89a. SMK 4/3a glosses *yü* 與 as *chieh [ju]* 皆[如]; CWK, p. 138, n. 2, as *ju* 如. Both apparently follow FW 4/6b, which compares the present flourishing state of the myriad things to "the canopy of a carriage." Cf. CPL 4/6a, who reads *yü* as *t'ung* 同. *P'an* 盤 can also mean) "to circle or revolve," as in YTC 4/6b.

5. CYYT 34/55/*hsiang* (Wilhelm, 672–74).

6. For further information, see Needham, III, 210ff.; Pokora, pp. 116–17, citing TPYL 2/6b–7a.

7. Following Sung Chung.

8. For example, *hsiao* 小, *shao* 少, *hsiao* 峭, and *hsiao* 削.

9. SMK 4/3a says, "being hidden, it is not yet seen." I take the "darkness" to refer to the "deeply mysterious" character of all Being.

10. SMK 4/3a; YTC 4/6b; CPL 4/6a. For Han usage, see HsinS 9/4b.

11. Following SMK 4/3a, reading *lü* 慮 as *mou* 謀 ("plans").

12. The reference here is to a bronze chisel used to polish or carve bone. Note the pun between the characters *lü* 慮 (here, "ambitions") and *lü* 鑢 (here, "grind down").

13. See *Mencius* 2A/2 (Lau, 76–80) on the causes of the needless fretting and frustration that impair bodily functions.

14. *Analects* 2/15 (Waley, 91).

15. "Learning," ch. 3 (Legge, 363).

16. Cf. Ode 102/1 (Legge, 157), cited by SMK 4/3a, which also criticizes overly ambitious thoughts, though with a different metaphor: "Do not try to cultivate fields too large./ The weeds will only grow more luxuriantly."

17. The characters *men hsiao* 門郊 normally refer to the suburbs just outside the city walls. See, for example, YTL 8/6b (not in Gale), where the binome clearly refers to the near suburbs, with relative ease of access. SMK 4/3a–3b, however, takes the gate as symbol of what is outside; the suburbs, as symbol of what is faraway.

18. See FSTY 2:20 (Nylan, 407) for one example.

19. Yang Hsiung may also be criticizing the official's failure to devote all his energies to court activities. This would make the ostentatious display particularly objectionable. See YTC 3/7a.

20. A pun since both meanings come from *li* 利.

21. CPL 4/6b glosses *tao* 刀 (here, "knife") as "knife money." He then goes

on to argue that the individual has spent all his capital in enlarging his house, taking no thought of the future, while boasting to others of his wealth.

22. *Pao* 包 literally means "to embrace in the arms." YTC 4/7a mistakenly reads *huang* 荒 as "weed-covered" or "filthy."

23. Literally, "overcomes." FW 4/7b, however, reads *k'e* 克 as *neng* 能 ("able to").

24. In Han terms, the ruler takes as "central" the teachings of the "Great Plan" chapter of the *Documents*, also called the "Way of Great Centrality." For further information, see Nylan (forthcoming).

25. YTC 4/7b.

26. Serruys reads as, "Being great, one fails in the small. Being many, one fails in the few."

27. SMK 4/3b reads these lines simply as criticism of the individual's failure to rectify himself at the first sign of wickedness.

28. Literally, a gift of food.

29. Following FW 4/7b and YTC 4/7b. Alternately, reading GSR 579h 悱 ("to make a painful effort").

30. The *ku* 觚 is reserved for wine-drinking, which is criticized in the *Documents*, "Chiu kao" (Karlgren, 43–46; Legge, 399–412).

31. For the same metaphor, see SY 7/1b. For walls of pounded earth, see Knapp, pp. 54–55.

32. YTC 4/8a reads *mieh* 蔑 ("denigration") as *wu* 無 ("emptiness").

33. Only after living out the natural lifespan can the quality of an individual's life be assessed. Compare the question asked of Socrates, "Can one be said to be truly happy if he has not yet died?"

34. Note that both FW 4/8a and CPL 4/7a think the Appraisal inauspicious. CPL reads *mieh* 蔑 as *mieh* 滅 ("destruction"). Such changes seem unnecessary. SMK 4/3b offers no commentary here.

No. 46. Enlargement

1. Following Sung Chung and Wang Ya, glossing *yi* 瘞 as *yi ni* 翳匿 ("to screen off and hide"). Literally, *yi* means "to bury." Alternately, "assisting" (*hsieh* 協), following FW 4/8a; "quieting [the process?]" (*ching* 靜), following Wu Mi (who cites the *Shuo wen*).

2. FW 4/8a; SMK 4/3b–4a and others read *shih* 佥 as *ho* 合 ("joining [with?]").

3. SMK 4/4a glosses *k'uo* 廓 as *k'uo chang* 廓張; YTC 4/8a, as *k'ai p'i* 開闢.

4. See, for example, CPL 4/7b.

5. See, for example, Ode 241/1 (Legge, 449).

6. HFT 7:21:123 (Liao, I, 225): "The largest vessel is slowly filled."

7. "Mean," ch. 1, par. 5 (Legge, 359).

8. YTC 4/8a. The foundation that needs to be straightened could conceivably refer to harmonious family relations as well. See *Analects* 1/2 (Waley, 83), 1/8 (Waley, 85).

9. Literally, "Many are those that aid and make upright." YTC 4/8b takes *fan fu* 蕃輔, however, as "chief ministers." CWK, p. 141, n. 3, reads *fan* as *li* 離 ("barrier," "boundary fence"). See below for SMK's rendering of the line.

10. *Chen* 楨 were the props (or stays or supports) holding the boards of the building frames into which the earth was pounded. (Note the visual pun on the character *chen* 貞, meaning "correct orientation.") From this, it comes to be used of those who make insubordinate princes "straighten up" ("keep in order"). See Ode 261/1 and Karlgren (1964), p. 128. For further information on these tapering supports framed on their long sides by lateral timbers, see Knapp, pp. 54–57 on the construction of *hang t'u* tamped walls.

11. YTC 4/8b.

12. SMK 4/4a applies the entire verse to self-cultivation, though FW 4/8b apparently takes the ruler as subject. SMK 4/4a then reads the last line of the Fathoming as, "Assisting [or, "flourishing" ?] and correcting, [such] is rectitude."

13. Literally, to "enchamber" (*shih* 室).

14. Specifically, a woman who lacks a uterine canal.

15. Following FW 4/9a and YTC 4/9a for the definition of *yü* 圉.

16. For the phrase *ching ying* 經營, see Ode 205/3 (Legge, 361).

17. YTC 4/9a.

18. SMK 4/4a says that the cultivated individual uses "righteousness and the rites" to enlarge himself in the Way.

19. Cf. the modern expression *hu k'ou* 戶口.

20. Conceivably, the gateways could also refer to the senses, often regarded in China as "gateways to the soul." CPL 4/8a mistakenly criticizes the individual for only attending to what is external. That is not Yang Hsiung's point here.

21. I take *k'uei* 恢 (GSR 950b) as "to extend [to]." Otherwise, it means "[make] great" or [make] complete." The character *t'ang* 堂 is supplied from the FW edition (4/9a).

22. For this reading, see YTC 4/9a. Cf. CPL 4/8b.

23. *Analects* 6/15 (Waley, 119).

24. Reading *ching feng* 經豐 instead of *wei feng* 維豐 on the basis of the SPPY edition. This is a case of *textus difficilior* supported by parallels in the *Odes*.

25. A stock phrase from the *Documents* signifying the chief feudal lords in the empire.

26. The reduplicative *p'ing-p'ing* 馮馮 may be read either as *p'ing* 憑 (=*yi* 依, "to rely or be relied upon"), following CPL 4/8b; or as *sheng-to* 盛多 ("numerous"), following SMK 4/4a and YTC 4/9a. I follow the first reading, on the basis of Ode 237/6 (Legge, 440).

27. In archaic Chinese, *yi* 伊 gives the flavor of "against all expectations." (Serruys, private communication). *Yi* comes to mean "this" only in late Warring States, with texts like the *Chuang tzu*. Given Yang Hsiung's archaizing tendencies, he may well mean us to read it in the older sense. In that case, the line should read something like, "Astounding, what virtue begets."

28. Following SMK 4/4b in reading *yi* 忔 as *hsi* 屹, meaning "great," "powerful," "sturdy." Wang Ya and Wu Mi read it as *k'ai* 棐 ("measure," "norm").

29. *Mencius* 6B/15 (Lau, 181).

30. See von Falkenhausen (1989) and (forthcoming). The same line could also be read, "Benefit to drum-bell assemblages." Following CPL 4/9a. See Ode 178/3 (Legge, 287).

31. Cf. the example of the canopy in the previous tetragram.
32. Reading 墉 (GSR 1185z) instead of 庸 (GSR 1185x).
33. LT, ch. 44 (Lau, 105).
34. SMK 4/4b and CPL 4/9a, alluding to *Mencius* 1A/3–4 (Lau, 51–52).
35. Following Wang Ya.
36. CYYT 2/1/*yen* (Wilhelm, 383).

No. 47. Pattern

1. According to commentators, Yang reads the hexagram title with the fire radical 火 (no. 86) instead of water (no. 85) 水.
2. *Analects* 6/16 (Waley, 119). A looser translation of this passage appears below.
3. FY 4:11, for example, talks of Heaven giving hearing and sight to man, so that man can use these faculties "to see ritual and to hear music." Cf. FY 7:19 on the relation between the sensory organs and discernment.
4. *Analects* 3/8 (Waley, 95–96).
5. *Analects* 6/18 (Waley, 119). Cf. FY 3:8 for a similar passage.
6. CYYT 30/49/5,6 *hsiang* (Wilhelm, 192). Cf. FY 2:5–6 (2x).
7. *Analects* 8/19 (Waley, 136).
8. *Mencius* 7A/24 (Lau, 187).
9. FY 5:15 defines *wen* 文 as *shun* 訓 ("to follow").
10. FY 3:5.
11. Note that one eminent scholar argues that Yang Hsiung's THC47 outlines the first detailed and coherent aesthetic theory in China. See Knechtges (1976), ch. 5, p. 90 ff. He goes too far. By equating "pattern" with "form" and "plainness" with "substance" or "content," he makes Yang Hsiung's verses sound at once more abstract and of more limited applicability than they are. His translation works against Yang Hsiung's predisposition to make concrete images function as multi-associational patterns.
12. Cf. FY 1:3.
13. See *Analects* 3/8 (Waley, 96).
14. "Mean," ch. 33/1 (Legge, 430–31).
15. Following SMK 4/4b, which reads *hui* 襀 as *hui* 繪 ("five-color embroidery"). The same character read as *kuei* can also mean the point where the collar meets in front, the belt cord, or even the buttons.
16. *Ch'ia* 袷 refers either to a lined garment without wadding or the rectangular lapel of a court robe.
17. *Analects* 5/9 (Waley, 109).
18. CCYT 357/Chao 5/*Tso* 3 (Legge, 604).
19. Reading *fu* 孚 ("truly") as *p'ei* 垺 ("great") (GSR 1233a = 1233h), contrary to the commentators.
20. CPL 4/9a takes "great pattern" (*ta wen* 大文) as the "pronouncements of the sage emperors."
21. LT, ch. 41, 45 (Lau, 102, 106), cited by YTC 4/10a–b.
22. *Analects* 2/9 (Waley, 90).
23. Literally, "Ornate-like, refined-like,/ The tiger and leopard are

patterned-like./ If does not please Heaven; they are bad./ The ornamentation and refinement, they are obstructing./ Means: How would it be enough to be praised?" See below for an alternate reading.

24. Cf. FY 5:14.

25. FY 2:6 says the beasts' markings are *yi chien* 易見.

26. Following Wang Ya in reading *hsiang* 享 as *hsiang* 嚮, since the two characters are often interchanged. See GSR 714j and 716a.

27. CPL 4/10a.

28. Following Wang Ya.

29. Knechtges reads *yung ju* 庸如 as "deserved."

30. *Documents*, "Yao tien," par. 20 (Legge, 37–38; Karlgren, 5).

31. CCYT 130/Hsi 27/5 *Tso* (Watson, 52). For further information, see Keightley (1990), esp. pp. 23–25. See HsinS 1/13a on the use of clothes to display status.

32. Cf. the Image of God motif in Christianity. For more information, see Pelikan, ch. 7.

33. FW 4/11a and CPL 4/10a talk of the river's flow.

34. A pun for *hung wen* 鴻文.

35. Fang 2/16/30 glosses *chin* 藎 as *yü* 餘 (GSR 381d =? 381e). In that case, the line means, "While chickens have more than enough grain." Otherwise, the line means, "Chickens are given grain." My translation attempts to capture both meanings.

36. Wang Ya offers no commentary on the final line, but given his equation of the pheasant with the man of purity, it could be read as, "In bad times (*nan* 難), [the hermit] feeds in secret."

37. FY 3:8 also condemns the mountain pheasant as too decorative.

38. See Wang Ya. Cf. YTC 4/11a.

39. SMK 4/5a, however, argues that it is better to retire from government service in times of decline.

40. Cf. the *ku-pi* 穀璧 ("grain-patterned" *pi* jade). The same argument is made in FY 2:4. The phrase, however, can also be read simply as "grain and cloth." See below.

41. Serruys reads as, "It is lost in time."

42. HS 24A:1128–32 (Swann [1950], 154–62). An alternate reading offered by many commentators makes much the same statement, though it is based on different punctuation: "Intricate carving,/ Grain and cloth are neglected at the right time./ Patterns as expected grow chaotic./. . . ."

43. By Han times, *fu fu* 黼黻 refers to the dramatically colored ceremonial garb reserved for the use of high officials participating in the most solemn ritual occasions at court or the ancestral temple. For further reference, see *Documents*, "Kao Yao mo," par. 12 (Legge, 80; Karlgren, 11); SY 19/1b. Serruys points out that in the bronze texts the term *fu fu* simply refers to figured embroideries in white and black, and in black and blue-green patterns respectively. This is supported by the "K'ao kung chi" section on figured embroidery in CL.

44. Various commentators, including CWK, p. 145, n. 10, read *tang* 當 as "should." The last line would then read, "Ought to use the essential."

No. 48. Ritual

1. According to FW 4/11b.
2. FW 4/11b.
3. FW 4/11b.
4. See Fingarette. FY 3:8 treats ritual as a balance between outer expression and inner substance.
5. *Li* 禮 = *t'i* 體 is a usual Han gloss.
6. HTYT, ch. 19 (Dubs, pp. 213–46).
7. See CCYT 27/Huan 2/*fu* (Legge, 40).
8. CYYT 52/*hsü* (Wilhelm, 435).
9. Literally, "grandfather and father" (*tsu ni* 祖禰), a term that often indicates the ancestral shrine.
10. *Li* 履 = *li* 禮 (GSR 562a = 597d). In archaic pronunciation, the two words are also homonyms.
11. SMK 4/5b.
12. SMK 4/5b. Similarly, CPL 4/11a says that walking on tiptoe focuses undue emphasis on what comes behind (the heel) and obscures or crushes what comes before (the toes). Classical support comes from LC 2/1 (Legge, I, 100). Numerous examples are found in Han portent literature. One anecdote drawn originally from the *Tso Commentary* equates "high-stepping" with the total abandonment of proper virtue. See HS 27B(A):1354–55, citing CCYT 39/Huan 13/*fu* 1 (Legge, 60).
13. See, for example, LSCC 9/9a.
14. Added by Nylan.
15. LT, ch. 24 (Lau, 81).
16. CPL 4/11a–11b says, "deferential, as if seeing their forms; solemn, as if hearing their words."
17. Ode 32/1 (Legge, 50–51), 174/2 (Legge, 276), for example.
18. CCYT 152/Wen 5/*fu* 1 (Legge, 241).
19. Commentary by Wang Ya to the following Appraisal.
20. Literally, "It is not its truth."
21. This possibly refers to the Mohist dictum: "Knowing is different from having a pictorial idea." See Graham (1978), p. 471. Han texts also attribute to Mencius the saying, "As stories circulate, they lose their point [of reference], just as painted images fail to capture a likeness." See Nylan (1982), p. 360.
22. SMK 4/5b. Cf. FW 4/12a; YTC 4/11b; and CPL 4/11b.
23. YTC 4/11b says that the "reality, not the form" moves other men.
24. CCYT 357/Chao 5/3 *Tso* (Legge, 604), cited by SMK 4/5b. It is also possible that the poem was composed to remind us of an additional truth: All types of likenesses (including the literary metaphor) can deceive. Cf. Plato in *The Sophist* (231a).
25. Cf. FY 5:12–13, which praises imitation.
26. The early commentator Yü Fan says that both are famous for their formations in flight (another pattern), but peacocks rarely fly. SMK 4/5b–6a credits the peacock with patterned plumage and the wild goose with a stately walk. Contrast the wild goose here with that in the previous tetragram. MTYT 64/39/47

talks of the "ceremonial gaits and wing-like gestures" of the Confucians it criticizes. My translation of the passage follows Eno, p. 53.

27. *Pi* 匕 can also mean "arrowhead." See below.

28. Alternately, "In error, he destroys the bestowed Nine Arrows." Following FW 4/12b; YTC 4/12a; and CPL 4/11b in reading *shih* 矢 ("arrows") instead of the *t'ien* 天 ("Heaven") in the WJL edition. If we accept the WJL variant, the line must mean something like, "Errors ruin the bestowals [from] the ninth empyrean."

For *kuo sang hsi chiu shih* 過喪錫九矢, Wang Ya reads *kuo ch'ang hsi* 過鬯錫, which means something like, "To overturn the gift of black-millet wine."

29. See FW 4/12b and CPL 4/11b, who take *pien* 貶 as *sun* 損 ("to diminish"). FW and Sung Wei-kan for *ch'i* 其 ("his") read *t'ien* 天 ("Heavenly"). I use "dignity" in the archaic sense, meaning "emoluments."

30. For further information on the Nine Conferrals bestowed upon the feudal lords by the Son of Heaven, see PHT 3A/8a–10b (Tjan, I, 504 ff.).

31. Following CPL 4/11b.

32. CYYT 31/51/*t'uan* (Wilhelm, 197).

33. CCYT 69/Chuang 23/3 *Tso* (Watson, 57; Legge, 105).

34. *Mencius* 4A/3 (Lau, 119), cited by YTC 4/12a.

35. CPL 4/12a takes *ch'a* 差 as "order."

36. Following the WJL edition (4/6a) in reading *ta* 大 ("greatly" bestow) for *shih* 矢 (a character which probably belongs in the previous Appraisal text). If *shih* is correct here, App. 6 reads, "Then set them [the ritual dishes] out [straight as] an arrow" (i.e., in an orderly fashion). See FW 4/12b; CPL 4/12a. YTC 4/12a reads *shih* 矢 as "simply," "straightforwardly," which presumably conveys the ease with which the ruler orders his kingdom with ritual.

37. SMK 4/6a reads instead, "The emperor uses [this] to mount to Heaven." CPL 4/12a reads *teng* 登 ("mount") as *heng* 亨 ("gain favor with"). For an analysis of the character *ti* 帝 as "going up," see Hentze.

38. This was a popular metaphor in Han. See SC 92:2622 (Watson, 224); HS 87B:3544 (Knechtges, 32), 3565 (Knechtges, 48).

39. *Analects* 11/16 (Waley, 156).

40. *Documents*, "Chou kuan," par. 19 (Legge, 533; not in Karlgren).

41. Reading *ch'üan* 全 instead of *chin* 金.

42. Following the FW edition (4/13a) in reading *ming* 明 ("clearly") for *chien* 賤 ("debased") and deleting *lu* 履.

43. For the same metaphor, see HsinS 2/5b.

44. See CPL 4/12a, which believes the compound refers to a mourning cap of coarse *chien* 菅.

45. Literally, "gold." CPL 4/12a reads *chin* 金 (defined as *chin* 錦) instead of *ch'üan* 全.

46. Reading *cheng* 正 instead of *shang* 上. Cf. FW 4/13a.

47. Taking "nine" to signifying the highest yang position, as in the expression *yung-chiu* 用九. See CYYT 1/1/*yen* (Wilhelm, 383).

48. Contrast this with CYYT 1/1/*yung* (Wilhelm, 10), which speaks of "So many dragons without heads. Felicitious."

49. CPL 4/12b.

No. 49. Flight

1. Or, "is manifestly forceful." FW 4/13b, however, reads *chang ch'iang* 章疆 as *ch'iang liang shang pai chih mao* 強梁傷敗之貌 ("overbearing and destructive").

2. Or, "stealthily."

3. Sung Chung talks of "minute yin in the inside wanting to come out from the earth."

4. CYYT 52/*hsü* (Wilhelm, 550).

5. Contrast CPL 4/12b, which reads *chuang* 創 as *shang* 傷 ("wound"). FW 4/13b reads it as *hen* 痕 ("scar").

6. Or, "remade." FW 4/13b would read this as the traces of the water's obliterating action leave "no scars."

7. Cf. LT, ch 27 (Lau, 84): "Good travelers leave no track." This entire paragraph added by Nylan.

8. FW 4/13b emphasizes that the present danger is only "small" (presumably because we are still at App. 1).

9. See, for example, SMK 4/6b; YTC 4/13a; and CWK, p. 149, n. 3.

10. SMK 4/6b, however, calls him "terrified."

11. Following Sung Chung.

12. LC 24/36 (Legge, II, 228–9).

13. Cf. YTC 4/13a.

14. *Analects* 2/24 (Waley, 93).

15. Tentative translation, drawing upon the root meaning of *ching* 兢 as "fearful," "cautious." SMK 3/6b clearly takes *ching ch'i ku* 兢其股 as "trembling, his thighs," and an indication of great fear, showing that it is the thighs of the owner that tremble; hence, my translation. FW 4/13b glosses *ching* as *tung* 動 ("to move"), but fails to ascribe the "movement" to either horse or owner. CPL 4/13a glosses *ching* as *ch'iang* 強 ("to force"), taking the first line as a description of the rider who, wanting to spur his horse on, digs his thighs into the saddle for a better grip before whipping the horse. In that case, the first line could also possibly mean "to press its [i.e., the horse's] rump." Therefore, in the Fathoming I translate as if the possessive pronoun *ch'i* refers to the horse.

16. Translation tentative, meaning: "As [the bandits] approach, [he] happens to see [them]." Sung Chung reads this as, "There approaches what he has seen," which emphasizes the imminent nature of the danger. Cf. CPL 4/13a.

17. *Ch'iao* 喬 refers to what is "tall and bent or pointed at top." With reference to trees, it refers to those whose upper branches are sparse.

18. The phrase *wei ts'ung* 維樅 comes from Ode 242/2 (Legge, 457), where its meaning is unclear. Karlgren (1964), p. 54 (item 852), says it means "dentated" in appearance. SMK 3/6b reads *wei tsung* 維樅 as *ch'ang mi chih mao* 長密之貌 ("long and fine in appearance"). YTC 4/14a says the upper portions of the tree are "flourishing." FW 4/14a is somewhat vague.

19. "Stop and then" added by Nylan. However, FW 4/14a presumes that the birds pass by the grove of trees, since they are "a place where birds do not gather." FW compares the tall trees to the ruler; the birds, to the petty men who "regard him and then go away." Unfortunately, FW ignores the clear sense of the passage. He is directly contradicted by SMK 4/6b and CWK, p. 149, n. 6.

20. See the "Cry of Sorrow" legend in FSTY 2:10 (Nylan, 363–70).
21. CPL 4/13a commentary.
22. SMK 4/6b.
23. Added by Nylan.
24. SMK 4/6b; YTC 4/13b.
25. Wu Mi, however, reads *ts'ui* 趇 as *t'a* 踢 ("to tread").
26. "Is imminent" added by Nylan.
27. Cf. the Line texts attached to the correspondent hexagram.
28. Sung Chung commentary.
29. This may explain why some of the commentators refer to one admirable trait associated with the otter: filial piety. See LC 5/28; 6/2 (Legge, I, 221, 251).
30. SYJ 8/19b reads *lu* 婁 as *lou* 耬 (=*li* 犁, "to plough"). CWK, pp. 149–50, n. 6, similarly reads it as "to hitch oxen," citing CCYT 415/Chao 25/7 *Kung* (Ho Hsiu commentary). Wang Ya reads *lu* as "to order" (*li* 理). FW 4/14b and CPL 4/13b think *lou* means *huo* 獲 ("to catch game" [for the ancestral temple?]), Serruys reads it as *lü* 摟 ("to carry off [any crops]").
31. Reading *hsi* 螇 instead of *hsieh* 膎, following the emendation, but not the entire argument of CPL 4/13b. (See below.) The character *hsieh* 膎 refers to "cooked or preserved food." FW 4/14b; Wang Ya; YTC 3/14a; CWK, p. 150; and Serruys therefore read this line as, "Wasting the result of our cooked [offerings]."
32. YTC 4/14a and CPL 4/13b read *jih* 日 ("time") for *li* 力 ("strength"). YTC also reads *wang* 忘 ("to forget") instead of *wang* 亡 ("to lose").
33. For the metaphor of sowing and reaping, see *Documents*, "P'an keng," par. 9 (Karlgren, 21; Legge, 227).
34. Added by Nylan.
35. SMK 4/7a.
36. CPL 4/13b reads the poem, "Many hunts, no catch./ Wasting the [farmer's] efforts [by] our [trampling] the footpaths. . . ." CWK, p. 150, n. 8, has the hunter's catch, which has not been securely tied, escaping; in the pursuit, the farmer's fields are ruined.
37. Sung Chung glosses *chi* 幾 as *chin* 近 ("to come near"), meaning that the bird has a narrow escape.
38. YTC 4/14a reads *tseng* 矰 as *tseng* 繒 ("silk string"). This emendation is unnecessary.
39. Alternately, "It is precisely the wings that it binds up." Following Wang Ya, reading *yi* 紉 as *yi* 翼. FW 4/14b and YTC 4/14a take it as *cho* 繳 ("string attached to the arrow").
40. Following Wang Ya and SMK 4/7a.
41. Alternately, "[until the feet grow] calloused [from walking so far]." YTC 4/14b and CPL 4/14a say that *p'ien p'ien* 跰跰 means that the hands and feet are bound (*chü lüan* 拘攣), making it difficult to walk. See GSR 824 p', q'.
42. Reading *tao te* 盗德 (a pun on *Tao Te* 道德?) as "thievish characters." However, CPL 4/14a (following Sung Wei-kan) reads *te* 得 ("to get") instead of *te* 德 ("character" or "power"). CWK, p. 150, n. 11 agrees.

No. 50. *Vastness*

1. Following Sung Chung.
2. Following Lu Chi, who says things are *k'ung chin* 空盡 ("empty and used

up in appearance"). Cf. CTYT 93/33/64 (Watson, 374).

3. Cf. English, where both "vast" and "wasted" are from a single Latin root, *vastus*, meaning "waste" or "empty."

4. CPL 4/14a glosses *tang tang* 盪盪 as "boundless, without a place to go."

5. See FW 4/15a.

6. See SMK 4/7a.

7. Following FW 4/15a, which explains *t'ang* 唐 as *wu so chü hsien* 無所拘限. Cf. SMK 4/7a, which talks of being "without fixed principles" (*wu so shou* 無所守). "Wavering" is another possibility. YTC 4/14b glosses *t'ang* 唐 as *k'ung k'ung* 悾悾 ("simple," "ignorant," "thoughtless").

8. Literally, "when unrestrained at the inside."

9. Following SMK 4/7a and CWK, p. 151, n. 3. Serruys prefers, "If you do not take the initiative [to follow the Way], there will be danger [or harm]." YTC 4/14b and CPL 4/14b read this as, "[Though] he does not [yet] act, it is [still] dangerous."

10. Literally, "benefits for [those] drifting in the dark."

11. Tentative translation, following FW 4/15b, who takes *su* 素 to mean *p'u su* 樸素 ("unadorned"). CPL 4/14b, in apparent agreement, reads *t'ang su* 唐素 as *le te tzu* 褦襶子 ("sloppily dressed"). However, YTC 4/15a seems to read *su* 素 as ("temperament"). CWK, pp. 151–52, n. 5, apparently agrees. As for the term *pu chen* 不貞, it could also mean, "He cannot be counted on," drawing upon the root meaning of *chen* 貞: "to test and ascertain [by the oracle bones]."

12. Following FW 4/15b. YTC 4/15a takes *lung ling* 瓏玲 to mean *t'ung ming mao* 通明貌 ("luminous in appearance"), on the basis of Yang Hsiung's "Sweet Springs" *fu*, recorded in HS 87A:3528 (Knechtges, 20). Knechtges says "glimmers and glistens."

13. Tentative translation. Alternately, "It is not your proper place." CPL 4/14b says, *fei erh so neng* 非爾所能 ("not within your capacities").

14. Tentative translation. CWK, p. 152, n. 6, takes *t'ang* 唐 as *kung erh wu yü* 公而無欲 ("fairminded and without [selfish] desires"), on the basis of THC "Hsüan ch'ung" (p. 1015a). Serruys, however, prefers, "Expending [energies] without predilections."

15. An alternate reading for the Fathoming, though it repeats the Appraisal graph for graph.

16. Note the misprint in the WJL edition, which reads *tzu* 子 for *yü* 予.

17. *Analects* 4/10 (Waley, 104).

18. *Documents*, "Hung fan," par. 14 (Karlgren, 32).

19. *Lu* 鹿 = *lu* 祿.

20. See, for example, SC 92:2629 (Watson, I, 231).

21. Cf. LSCC 15/4b; and HsinS 2/5a.

22. For the same metaphor, see SY 17/4b.

23. Following FW 4/16a.

24. Cf. CWK, p. 152, n. 8, which reads it as *pu tu hsiang* 不獨享 ("Not to enjoy by oneself").

25. Following FW 4/16a.

26. *Analects* 4/25 (Waley, 106).

27. *Mencius* 1A/2 (Lau, 50).

28. Literally, "Dawn's light shines forth on the march."

29. Literally, "In going forth, he does not have that which to follow."
30. YTC 4/15b.
31. HTYT 89/23/68 (Dubs, 313; not in Knoblock).
32. *Shou* 收 refers to the act of hooking in with a sickle.
33. SMK 4/7b; YTC 4/15b; and CPL 4/15b read *mu* 沐 as *tse* 澤 ("blessings"). FW 4/16b reads it as "wash," referring to purification (*chieh ch'ing* 絜凊). There may also be an allusion to the "washing" days allotted government officials since they imply "putting one's affairs in order."
34. Translation tentative. See below.
35. Literally, "the gain, no return." CWK, p. 152, n. 11, following FW 4/16b and the WJL edition (4/8a), takes *fei jou* 飛肉 as a binome. The next Appraisal line would then read, "His gain no return [for the outlay]."
36. Cf. HsinS 2/5a, where a valuable pot is thrown at a rat.

No. 51. Constancy

1. According to SMK 4/8a.
2. Or, generations.
3. CYYT 20/32/*t'uan* (Wilhelm, 546).
4. For the metaphor of the ink-line, see HNT 9/8b (Ames, 182).
5. Literally, "not decline [as the sun at dusk]."
6. YTC /16b reads as *t'i hsing yi yeh* 體形一也 ("The bodily form is one."). For the Fathoming, CPL 4/16a reads *li hsing* 禮刑 ("ritual [and] punishment") instead of *t'i hsing* 體形, then equates "divine measure" with ritual and "sacred model" with the penal code.
7. HTYT 108/32/1–2 (not in Dubs or Knoblock). Cf. LT, ch. 21 (Lau, 78). For the same term applied to cosmic principles, see LSCC 25/4b. Contrast *Mencius* 7A/26 (Lau, 188), which uses "holding fast to the One" to mean "holding one extreme view."
8. *Mencius* 7A/4 (Lau, 182).
9. Like Water, with which this Position is aligned, the ruler becomes an inexhaustible source of charismatic power.
10. CYYT 45/Hsi B/1 (Wilhelm, 326), cited by SMK 4/8a: "The movements of All-under-Heaven when aligned correctly become uniform."
11. The text says, "bearing aloft . . . treading. . . ."
12. CPL 4/16a offers another reading of the poem, which focuses upon the interdependent nature of the ritual and punitive arms of government. If the ruler upholds both ritual (the "ink-line of the gods") and the penal code (the "sacred model"), he will be able to rule the masses effectively so that his power is never eclipsed. Note the assumption that ritual (aligned with spring) takes precedence over law even at this point in the calendar year. CPL's reading depends upon a variant character, however.
13. *Wei* 微 (literally, what is "minute," "feeble"). CPL 4/16a says the inner apartments entirely lack virtue, reading *wei* as *wu* 無. FW 4/17a takes *wei* as *yu wei* 幽微 ("secluded"), the proper description of women's conduct.
14. Wang Ya, however, punctuates after *nü* 女, giving the reading, "[If] the "inner" chambers constantly [are occupied by] debased women,/ Propriety [or, "chastity"] in danger." Wang Ya faults the man for bringing low-class women into

the household. YTC 4/16b seems to think that women in general are debased since they are preoccupied with things of little value (*wei* 微), like cosmetics, rather than with the development of great "constants" like female chastity.

15. See Lu Hsün's essay "My Views on Chastity" in his *Selected Works*, II, 11–24.

16. Or, "The Way of the Ruler enlightens."

17. See HS 27C(C):1479-80.

18. See *Documents*, "Hsien yu yi te," par. 1 (Legge, 213–14; not in Karlgren), cited by SMK 4/8a. The same lines could conceivably refer to one who "daily makes his virtue constant/ For the three years [of mourning] he does not eat." This seems less likely in view of App. 4.

19. In Chinese, as in English, the term "course" can refer both to "orbit" and "course of conduct."

20. Brown, H., p. 67: "There are three . . . effects [on the moon] which are large enough to be detected with the naked eye. One of these, called variation, is a wobble in the moon's motion due to the fact that during part of each month the sun and earth pull it in the same direction and then in opposite directions. . . . A second effect, called evection, is due to the effect of the sun's gravitational attraction on the ellipticity of the moon's orbit. . . . Finally, there is a third effect, . . . called annual inequality, which is due to the fact that the sun's pull on the moon varies throughout the year because the earth's orbit is elliptical." That the Chinese noticed this wobbling is proven by SC 27C(B):1458.

21. YTC 4/16b.

22. Chin 12/1b (Ho, 121–22).

23. One possible translation for what literally reads, "his [or, their] verticality, his [or, their] horizontality." See below.

24. SMK 4/8b talks of the warp and woof.

25. See YTC 4/16b–17a; CPL 4/16b. Cf. CYYT 40/Hsi A/3 (Wilhelm, 294).

26. FW 4/17b says, "Having gotten 7, he grasps 9."

27. THC28/A2 uses the similar language.

28. CPL 4/17a regards this as an attack on insatiable greed or ambition. Having achieved at 7, the individual still wishes to push on to 9 to acquire greater benefits. Such moral weakness finally spells ruin to the individual. YTC 4/17a, however, sees this as symbol of the "inconstant" mind, unable to hold firmly to any fixed position (We might say he is always at "sixes and sevens.").

29. Reading *shuai* 衰 as *p'ou* 裒 in order to maintain the auspicious character of the line. For a reading which retains *shuai*, see YTC 4/17a and CPL 4/17a, who both interpret the constant flow of the water as an evil omen of the unfixed nature. CWK, p. 155, n. 9, agrees.

30. Taking *ch'eng* 承 as "to meet in battle." See GSR 896c.

31. *Mencius* 2A/2 (Lau, 76–80).

32. Added by Nylan. Note that SMK 4/8b offers no commentary here. This suggests the difficulty of the line.

33. Cf. HFT 7:21:120 (Liao, II, 215).

34. LT, ch. 71 (Lau, 133).

35. The commentators Wang Ya and SMK 4/8b see the magician healers as symbols of worthies come to advise the ruler about government policy.

No. 52. *Measure*

1. Following FW 4/18b, reading *jih* 日 instead of *yüeh* 曰.
2. Following FW 4/18b. Sung Chung says, yin now "moves" (*tung* 動) while yang *ch'i* "stores" (*tsang* 藏), a reversal of the usual values assigned to yin and yang *ch'i*.
3. FW 4/18b says that the reduplicatives are meant to convey the speed of the changes.
4. Following Wang Ya and YTC 4/17b. CPL 4/17b says that yang is forced to stop itself in the face of yin's increasing power.
5. CYYT 37/<u>60</u>/1, 4, 5, *hsiang* (Wilhelm, 696–97).
6. For further information, see Wheatley, pp. 411–75.
7. Following FW 4/18b, taking *tu* 獨 as "having a single characteristic." Several commentators take *tu* 獨 as *chi* 己 ("self").
8. *Documents*, "T'ai-chia," par. 6–7 (Legge, 202; not in Karlgren).
9. Following YTC 4/18a on the basis of *Analects* 9/16 (Waley, 142) and FY 1:2. Alternately, *tse* 澤 refers to "grace" or "blessings."
10. FY 1:2.
11. See Fang <u>13</u>/85/96, which defines *lai* 攋 (also read *lan*) as "ruin," "destruction."
12. Literally, "the errors from small measurements," following the *textus difficilior* in the FW edition (4/18b): *hsiao tu chih ch'a* 小度之差.
13. CIS, I, 13.
14. YTC 4/18a.
15. CPL 4/18b reads *ching ying* 經營 as *ch'ou mou* 籌謀 ("making plans").
16. FY 8:24 uses the same metaphor.
17. FY 9:24.
18. See THC42/A3 for the metaphor "timber" = "talent."
19. Following Wang Ya.
20. The reduplicative verb indicates that the action is carried out repeatedly, even continuously. FW 4/19b argues that the reduplicative form of the verb *chien* 檢 indicates that the superior man examines three areas: All-under-Heaven, himself, and others. SMK 4/9a, however, insists that the true gentleman doesn't take his own feelings as measure, but only looks to Heaven's images (for example, the starry patterns in the sky) for inspiration. Cf. YTC 4/18b and CPL 4/18b.
21. FY 4:9.
22. Added by Nylan.
23. CYYT 44/Hsi A/11; 4 (Wilhelm, 320, 294).
24. I take *kuei* 規 as the verb "to draw regulating lines." See GSR 875a. However, SMK 4/9a reads, "not to use laws and institutions to measure [or, advise?] oneself."
25. Alternately, "to loathe," "to fault." Note that the same graph also means "to measure."
26. Wang Ya contrasts the binome *ming ch'a* 明察 with ghosts, while YTC 4/18b and CPL 4/18a seem to think "those of keen insight" are "ghosts." I follow CCYT 360/Chao 6/*fu* 1 (Legge, 609). Cf. *Filial*, ch. 16; CTYT 83/<u>29</u>/84 (Watson, 336); and MTYT <u>49</u>/31/9.
27. FW 4/19b reads these as two separate aspects: stoniness and redness. For

him, the stone symbolizes firmness while redness stands for loyalty and integrity.

28. Literally, "The outstanding knight, him we take as a logical certainty." The term "knight" is an archaism by Han; *shih* 士 then refers, according to the eminent Han historian Hans Bielenstein, to "the pool of potential candidates for office plus actual officeholders" (private communication).

29. SMK 4/9a–9b reads as, "possible with him to have promises kept."

30. Note the pun between "stone" (*shih*) and *shih* 士.

31. See THC48/A2 above.

32. Added by Nylan.

33. Reading *tai* 貸 as *t'e* 忒.

34. Reading *shan* 善 as *ch'a* 差, following SMK 4/9b rather than FW 4/20a, because of the sense of the passage.

35. FW 4/20a reminds us that ten signifies completion.

36. Lu Chi glosses *tsao* 造 as "attain" (*chih* 至); CPL 4/19a, as "act" or "create" (*tso* 作). FW 4/20a gives the variant: "Accumulated good not enough./ For ten years, no return./ Accumulated good not enough./ Means: Cannot manage to complete [the rectification of affairs]." (Material in brackets supplied from FW's commentary.) This reading seems less likely, since Yang Hsiung follows Hsün tzu in assuming that accumulated acts of goodness work to strengthen a man's resolve to do good.

37. Wang Ya.

38. CYYT 16/24/6, *hsiang* (Wilhelm, 508; Kunst, 287).

No. 53. Eternity

1. The early commentators Sung Chung, Lu Chi, FW (4/20a), Wu Mi, and Wang Ya all assign Hexagram 32 here; CPL 4/19a and YTC 4/19a follow. SMK 4/9b correlates this tetragram with Hexagram 13, Fellowship with Men, however.

2. Following Sung Chung. An alternate reading given by CPL 4/19b (partly based on FW 4/20a) compares yin *ch'i* to a hegemon who forces yang to retire when its strength gives out. Therefore, yang *ch'i* "graciously" gives its position (an alternate, if forced reading of the phrase *yi wen yü* 以文與).

3. See Hulsewé (1955); Nylan (1982), 92–141.

4. CYYT 20/32/*t'uan* (Wilhelm, 546).

5. Following SMK 4/9b in reading *t'i* 替 as *fei* 廢. *T'i* can also mean "to change [for the worse]." Wang Ya has *chien* 僣 ("usurp") instead of *t'i*. FW 4/20a reads *shuang* 爽 as *ch'a* 差 ("to err [in appointing]").

6. Literally, "The eldest son, him he takes as constant." Alternately, "The constant rule of the eldest son."

7. See SMK 4/9b.

8. The controversy is recorded in WCYY 29–30, which cites CCYT 1/Yin 1/1 *Kung* (Malmqvist[a], 68–70). For further information on that handbook, see Miller.

9. An anecdote to this effect is given by Yang Hsiung's contemporary, Liu Hsiang, in SY 3/8b–9a.

10. YTC 4/20b, however, takes the verse as portrait of the model eldest son: "Neither neglectful nor at fault./ The constancy of the eldest son./ Neither neglectful nor at fault./ Meaning: He makes eternal the way of the ancestors."

11. FW 4/20b, however, appears to lay the blame on the son, who "inside harbors neglect and faults."

12. Deleting *wei* 未, both to repeat the length of the previous three-character line and to preserve better sense. However, if *wei* is retained, the line parallels THC36/A5: "Though he has not yet got [office,] [he] has no blame." FW 4/20b; SMK 4/9b; and YTC 4/20b read the line this way.

13. *Analects* 15/29 (Waley, 199).

14. See notes to the second line of the Appraisal. CPL 4/20a, however, gives a different explanation in the light of the Five Phases correlations.

15. Reading *pin* 賓 ("guest") as *p'in* 嬪 ("secondary wife"). However, all extant commentaries read the line differently ("That the guest leads is to forever lose the host."), making the first and second lines parallel examples.

16. FW 4/21a and SMK 4/10a both say that the establishment of the Three Guide Lines leads to the ruler being *huang chi* 皇極. For further information, see the *Documents*, "Hung fan," par. 9–16 (Legge, 328–33; Karlgren, 30–32).

17. Alternate readings: "The eternal [nature] of the Three Guide Lines," or "The Three Guide Lines, them [he] takes as eternal."

18. CCFL 12/53/6b. For further information on the history of the *san kang* 三綱, see Hsü Dau-lin.

19. For *chung chi* 中極, see Nylan (forthcoming), ch. 2. In pre-Han times, the related concept of *huang chi* 皇極 referred to that process whereby the ruler induces worthy candidates to contribute their talents to office so as to maximize his own power at the central court.

20. Tentative translation. Serruys reads as, "If greatness is made longlasting in regard to blessings."

21. Literally, "He enters in the darkness of what he has achieved." Note the deletion of the character *yü* 于 in YTC 4/20b. CWK, p. 160, n. 8, reads *ch'iu ming* 酋冥 as *shuai lo yu an ti ching ti* 衰落幽暗的境地 ("a decaying and dark situation"). SMK 4/10a attributes this darkness to the petty man's "not knowing regret or fear."

22. See THC39/A1.

23. Following SMK 4/10a.

24. CPL 4/20b.

25. Literally, "Forever thereby [i.e., by means of the new growth] they wind around its places which have nothing."

26. There is some confusion over the exact identification of this plant. The character *shih* 蒔 usually refers either to (1) rice seedlings newly bedded out, as in Fang 12/76/75, or to (2) *peucedanum anethum graveolus* ("East Indian dill" or cumin). Wang Ya says that *shih* means "side growth" (*p'ang sheng* 旁生). To me, it seems clear that the term "time plant" is chosen for the graphic components of the character: An element meaning "time" (*shih* 時) is topped by the "grass" radical.

27. Cf. THC39/A9.

28. Literally, "Making longlasting whatever is not on the right track will be ill-fortuned."

29. Meaning his lifespan, or possibly his appointment.

30. YTC 4/20b.

31.   Alternately, "For a long time, to rejoice and feel at ease." My translation tries to hint at the final stage of the cycle.

32.   The phrase "happy and at ease" is the typical characterization of the gentleman. See SY 6/8a.

33.   *Documents*, "Hsien yu yi te," par. 6 (Legge, 216). Cf. "Chung hui chih kao," par. 9 (Legge, 183); Ode 255/1 (Legge, 505); HSWC 10/13 (Hightower, 335).

34.   Suggested by Nylan on the basis of YTC 4/20b.

No. 54. Unity

1.   Note the two different uses of *shang* 尚 within the single Head text.
2.   CPL 4/21a defines *t'ung* 同 as "feeling sympathy for their troubles."
3.   See the Sung Chung and Wang Ya commentaries.
4.   FW 4/22a.
5.   See Wang Ya.
6.   CPL 4/21a.
7.   Cf. *Mencius* 2B/1 (Lau, 85).
8.   See especially *Mencius* 2A/6 (Lau, 82–83).
9.   See Sung Chung and SMK 4/10b, for example.
10.   FY 3:9.
11.   E.g., LT, ch. 38 (Lau, 85), cited by CPL commentary to THC54/F3. Cf. MTYT 29/17/12; 31/19/5; 45/27/72, for example, or HsinS 1/9a, which talks of matters "being as clear as black and white." FW 4/22a reminds us that black is the colour of water, the patron Phase for this position.
12.   YTC 4/21a.
13.   *Analects* 2/14 (Waley, 91).
14.   FW 4/22a and SMK 4/10b take *fei fei* 菲菲 as *tsa* 雜 ("mixed," "interspersed"). Wang Ya, however, writes that the white and black are "clearly separate" (*fen pieh ming pai* 分別明白). It is also possible that *fei* 菲 means *fei* 棐 ("to assist," "to help") or *p'ei* 斐 ("ornate," "elegant").
15.   *Analects* 13/23 (Waley, 177), cited by SMK 4/10b.
16.   SMK 4/10b.
17.   Also, SMK 4/10b directly contradicts numerous passages in the *Analects* that warn against association with evil men. See, e.g., *Analects* 4/7 (Waley, 105); 6/19 (Waley, 119); 7/21 (Waley, 127); 9/27 (Waley, 147); 15/7 (Waley, 195).
18.   YTC 4/21a.
19.   Proposed by Nylan. SMK 4/10b says the one beak stands for their united intention to combat insult; the same tail stands for their remaining intact at the end. FW 4/22a says that the beak stands for "harm," so that the beak and tail united means that no harm will be done.
20.   Also, Appraisal 2 corresponds to Fire, whose symbol is the Red Bird of the south (i.e., the sun, the ultimate source of auspicious yang).
21.   Tentative translation, based partly on FW 4/22a. Serruys reads *shih* 失 as *yi* 佚: "He idles [i.e., takes his ease] in not being black." YTC 4/21a–21b and CPL 4/21a talk of failing to fully understand that black is wrong since it is given little further notice (another kind of onesidedness). CWK, p. 163, n. 5, gives a confused explanation.

22. YTC 4/21a–21b and CPL 4/21a prefer *pu ch'u* 不除, "[he does] not get rid of [evil]." CWK, p. 163, n. 5, follows.

23. The same imagery may have had sexual connotations. See Li Yü's *Jou pu tuan* (Kuhn, 35).

24. *Analects* 16/1 (Waley, 203), cited in CWK, p. 163, n. 6.

25. Following the Wang Ya edition. FW 4/22b and YTC 4/21b read "grain" 穀 (a reference to official appointment) instead of "hub."

26. For the spokes metaphor used to show a poor fit, see CYYT 8/9/3 (Wilhelm, 42; Kunst, 257).

27. YTC 4/21b speaks of the "hub" as "[the ruler's ability to disperse] salary and rank by which he encourages worthies" at court.

28. For further information on the proper way to "utilize the masses," see Ames (1983), pp. 142–52.

29. Following Wang Ya and SMK 4/10b.

30. Compare other Han sayings, such as "Many mouths melt metal." CPL 4/22a agrees with this general interpretation of the verses, but objects to the apparent jump in subject from wheels to jade. Therefore, he reads the third line of the Appraisal as, "Numerous hairy [oxen] overturn the jade [carriage of the ruler]," taking oxen as symbols of petty men.

31. Literally, "sharing a single order."

32. *Documents*, "Yao tien," par. 19 (Karlgren, 4). Cf. CCYT 65/Chuang 21/2 *Tso* (Legge, 105); 66/Chuang 23/3 *Tso* (Legge, 112); 395/Chao 21/2 *Tso* (Legge, 671).

33. CYYT 45/Hsi B/2 (Wilhelm, 331).

34. Taking *chiu* 救 ("to save") as *hu* 護 ("to protect").

35. For alternate readings, see below. SYJ 8/19b-20a says *yen* 晏 means *hsing* 星 ("stars").

36. CPL 4/22a. SMK 4/11a says that evening rain is not equally beneficial to all types of plants in all situations. Note that Position 7 corresponds to the "evening" of one's life.

37. Punctuation unclear and the translation is tentative. Wang Ya takes "his person" as the object of the verb "to abandon" (*ch'i* 棄), then reads *yi k'ou* 遺寇 as "hand over to robbers." CWK, p. 164, n. 10, presumes an auspicious reading, citing *Analects* 15/8 (Waley, 195) in his support.

38. Taking *chüeh* 厥 to refer to a superior, such as Heaven.

39. SC 47:1909, the biography of Confucius, talks of "men . . . who put themselves in peril." They are those who criticize others and expose others' stupidity.

40. This may, of course, refer to Yang Hsiung's own suicide attempt.

No. 55. Diminishment

1. According to FW 5/1a.

2. CYYT 26/41/*t'uan* (Wilhelm, 590).

3. See the Line texts for Hexagram 41.

4. The single character *ming* 冥 carries the senses of "what is dark" and

"cover" (i.e., "what is hidden away" from the eye). See GSR 841a. FW 5/1a would add the phrase "[like Water]." SMK 5/1a talks of all this happening "in the hidden darkness where none can see."

5. Following Lu Chi.

6. LT, ch. 22 (Lau, 79).

7. Reading *hsing* 形 as 刑 (GSR 808d = b), following the earliest commentators, Sung Chung and Lu Chi. FW 5/1a–1b, however, takes *hsing* as *hsien* 見 ("to become visible"). The alternate reading would be: "That the heart is diminished and that it strikes itself/ Thereby takes form in his person./ The heart's diminution taking form in his person/ Means: He confines it at center."

8. Reflecting the two senses of *hsing* 形 (= 刑) in Line 2 of the Appraisal.

9. "Learning," ch. 6 (Legge, 367).

10. See SMK 5/1a, citing *Analects* 6/12 (Waley, 118 [renum.]).

11. See, for example, YTC 5/1b.

12. Or, "In desires, he restrains himself."

13. SMK 5/1a points out that Appraisal 3 is the "high point" for the lower triad. For the Western Han notions regarding the need to keep lines of communication open between superior and inferior without risk of *lesé majesté*, see Nylan (1991).

14. Literally, "A decrease in regard to good order."

15. *Mencius* 4A/1 (Lau, 117-8).

16. The "now" added by Nylan.

17. See Wang Ya. SMK 5/1b, however, takes the subordinate as subject for the verse, ignoring the "centrality" of Appraisal 5.

18. Contrast the phrase *ch'an yu* 闡幽 ("disclose the hidden") in CYYT 48/ Hsi B/5 (Wilhelm, 344).

19. Or, "are not even[ly distributed]."

20. SMK 5/1b talks of the stubborn ruler who does not distribute goods fairly.

21. See HFT, ch. 20 (Liao, I, 172), e.g.

22. CPL 5/1b.

23. Or, "faults."

24. CYYT 26/41/4, 4 *hsiang* (Wilhelm, 593).

25. Cf. Ode 58/2 (Legge, 98). CWK, p. 166, n. 9, however, reads this as "sap flowing down."

26. Cf. *Mencius* 6A/8 (Lau, 164–65) on Ox Mountain.

27. HTYT 1/1/7 (Dubs, 32; Knoblock, I, 136), cited by SMK 5/1b.

28. CYYT 13/17/6 (Wilhelm, 75; Kunst, 273).

29. See Loewe (1979), pp. 86–126; Wu Hung, pp. 108–41.

30. See, for example, CYYT 5/5/*t'uan* (Wilhelm, 411), 26/24/*t'uan* (Wilhelm, 505), and 37/61/*t'uan* (Wilhelm, 699).

31. See Needham, III, 210–16, describing the K'ai-t'ien cosmological theory.

32. See THC1/F9; FY 12:40, e.g.

33. YTC 5/2b discusses the inevitable cycles of rise and fall. However, CWK, p. 166, n. 10, talks of the noble man's willingness to sacrifice himself for the sake of others, as he equates the high mountain with extreme danger.

No. 56. Closed Mouth

1. HNT 3:35 says, "To exhale *ch'i* is to 'bestow.' To inhale *ch'i* is to 'transform.'" I therefore take "it" to refer to *ch'i*. SMK 5/1b says that the first "it" refers to yin's "form" (*hsing* 形) while the second refers to yang's "seminal essence" (*ching* 精). Serruys, however, offers an interesting alternative, which takes the character *chih* 之 as the verb "to get to." The Head text then reads, "Yin does not get to transform; yang does not get to bestow."

2. Alternately, "obstructed," reading *ho* 格 for *ko* 各 (GSR 766z for its cognate 766a).

3. LSCC 18/5a.

4. CYYT 10/12/*hsiang* (Wilhelm, 448).

5. Alternately, "not participating."

6. Literally, "The husband in wifely fashion takes [his] place."

7. Li Yün, p. 38 citing *Fang-nei*, 9a. For Han notions of sexuality, see also Gulik, pp. 55–90; and Harper (1987).

8. FW 5/3a.

9. CPL 5/2b suggests that he "bemoans" the possible exhaustion of his *ch'i*, so he is unwilling to share it with others.

10. Suggestion based on YTC 5/2b.

11. CYYT 37/60/2, *hsiang* (Wilhelm, 696; Kunst, 359), cited by SMK commentary to Appraisal 3.

12. Literally, "Closed off in regard to blood."

13. YTC 5/2b.

14. "Learning," vi.4 (Legge, 367), cited by SMK 5/2a.

15. Literally, "does not exchange" (*pu chiao* 不交).

16. Following FW 5/3a, *ch'i ni* 唭嶷 means, "there are sounds but no phrases" (*yu sheng erh wu tz'u* 有聲而無辭). CWK, p. 168, n. 5, takes this to mean "stammering" (*k'ou chih* 口吃).

17. For the literal translation, see the notes to the first line of the Appraisal.

18. The debate over the social consequences of eremitism became increasingly important in Eastern Han. For further information, see Nylan (1982), ch. 2, esp. p. 120 ff.

19. Literally, "Not to succour, not to be customary." CWK, p. 167, n. 6, reads *chen* 振 as "not to loan" (GSR 455p = 455r).

20. *Lei* 樂, which is translated above as "affect."

21. Based on FW 5/3a, though the commentary is too terse to be conclusive. Cf. CCYT 11/Yin 4/*Tso* 6 (Watson, 8).

22. CWK, p. 167, n. 4, deletes the *pu* 不, but this seems unnecessary.

23. Literally, "Rotten vermin, them he harvests." Alternately, "The miserliness of rotten vermin."

24. This is the point of FW 5/3b, which speaks of improperly high taxes.

25. Following SMK 5/2a.

26. CWK, p. 165, n. 8, however, reads this as, "closed off *from* the highlands."

27. Note the variant in the WJL edition of SMK 5/2a.

28. Cf. the "Mean," 27.ii, which talks of great virtue "full to overflowing" (Legge, 422).

29. The exile may be indicated. For the hill park in the *Changes* literature, see CYYT 15/<u>22</u>/5 (Wilhelm, 93; Kunst, 283).

30. Taking *t'i* 體 as *szu t'i* 四體, following SMK 5/2a. FW 5/3b associates *t'i* with one's kin.

31. CWK, p. 164, n. 9, simply equates it with "bones and flesh."

32. SMK 5/2a, however, suggests that they do not *reach* the appendages.

33. Added by Nylan on the basis of CPL 5/3b.

34. See FW 5/3b; SMK 5/2a; CWK, p. 164, n. 9.

35. This is possibly an attack upon the Mohist call for frugality.

36. Literally, "Truly it dries the dried meat."

37. YTC 5/4b.

38. SMK 5/2b.

39. FW 5/4a; YTC 5/4a; and CPL 5/4a contrast the dried meat with the generous sacrifice of the ox in Appraisal 8, arguing that paltry gifts cannot secure good fortune (including "good faith") either from the gods or from one's compatriots.

No. 57. Guardedness

1. CPL 5/4a. FW 5/4a talks of "above and below," presumably a reference to this.

2. CYYT 20/<u>31</u>/4 (Wilhelm, 124; Kunst, 301).

3. *Documents*, "Chün ch'en," par. 14 (Legge, 543; not in Karlgren), cited by SMK in commentary to the following Appraisal

2. Cf. LC 17/11 (Legge, II, 96), cited by SMK 5/2b.

4. FY 4:12 identifies "lessen desires" as a teaching of Chuang tzu that Yang Hsiung adopts.

5. *P'eng* 朋 can mean both "double" and "friends," since the original graph shows strung cowry shells.

6. FW 5/4a: YTC 5/4a; CWK, p. 171, n. 3. CPL 5/4a, however, takes "shutting the double windows" as a description of the Taoists, who in refusing to view through the world through the lenses of the Ancients retain their original possession.

7. Literally, "Is not as good as the One's being in one's possession."

8. Literally, "At center, he is without that which he uses." Sung Chung's commentary takes this to mean that he lacks the tools for self-preservation. YTC 5/4b follows.

9. The phrase comes from HTYT 108/<u>32</u>/1-2 (not in Dubs). However, CPL 5/4b takes this as criticism of the overly rigid personality which blindly "grasps at center, and so fails to recognize contingency and change."

10. CYYT 29/<u>48</u>/1 (Wilhelm, 185; Kunst, 335).

11. See, e.g., *Analects* 1/16 (Waley, 87): "He does not grieve that other people do not recognize his merits. His only anxiety is lest he should fail to recognize theirs."

12. Reading *ken* 哏 (GSR 416) with the mouth radical. YTC 5/4b disagrees.

13.   *Lien* 廉 originally refers to the perfectly aligned flanges of the ceremonial bronzes. Extending that meaning, CWK, p. 171, n. 6, wants to read *lien* a *ts'e yü* 側隅 ("side corner").

14.   The pun then reads, "the corner lacks an [adequate] defense," following Lu Chi in glossing *hu* 惆 as *chin yü* 禁禦 ("to prohibit and take precautions"), apparently reading *hu* as its cognate *ku* 固 (GSR 49x = 49f).

15.   Added by Nylan.

16.   Alternately, "Preserving centrality in order to harmonize."

17.   Serruys prefers, "a good omen." Alternately, "[For] marquises who covenant, [such is] propriety."

18.   CCYT 234/Cheng 13/2 *Tso* (Legge, 381–82).

19.   LT, ch. 80 (Lau, 142).

20.   Reading *pu* 不 as *p'i* 丕, following P'ei Hsüeh-hai, p. 243. For a different interpretation, see YTC 5/5a and CWK, p. 172, n. 9, where *pu shou* 不守 is taken to mean "do not keep to one place."

21.   YTC 5/5a.

22.   The character *tui* 碓 can refer either to the pestle or to the treadle (also called the tilthammer) in primitive threshing machines. For an early reference to the treadle for pounding grain, see Huan T'an, *Hsin lun*, cited in YKC 15/3b (Pokora, 120–21).

23.   Or, "to join with what the old ones hold to [as principle]."

24.   CWK, p. 172, n. 11, glosses *yü* 愈 as *sheng* 勝 ("surpass"), following Sung Chung and YTC 5/5b. *Yü* could also mean "to correct" or "to heal," a reading preferred by Serruys.

25.   *Documents*, "Ch'in shih," par. 4–5 (Legge, 628; Karlgren, 81), cited by SMK 5/3a.

No. 58. Closing In

1.   According to SMK 5/3b.

2.   For the very inexact usage of the terms *pien* 變 and *hua* 化 in early texts, see Sivin (1977) and Sivin (1990).

3.   Following Sung Chung. Sung Chung's characterization of yang, however, is not consistent with his remarks on yin.

4.   See CWK, p. 173, n. 2.

5.   See SMK 5/3b; CWK, p. l73, n. 2. for the first view; CPL 5/5b, for the latter. Note that the same verbs "heading against" and "acceding" are used of the political process, whereby the throne is transferred either through violence or by peaceful means (i.e., by accession or by abdication).

6.   This is the *Shuo kua* gloss for Hexagram 57, the counterpart of this tetragram.

7.   Wang Ya commentary glosses it as *ho* 合.

8.   Added by Nylan. CPL 5/5b would emphasize their impotence in the face of cruel yin *ch'i*.

9.   However, CPL 5/5b reads *ch'ung* 衝 (here, "to clash") as *hsü heng* 盱衡 ("to lift the eyebrow to gaze upward" [expressing high ambitions]).

10.   Tentative translation. SMK 5/3b treats *hsi* 翕 as *hsi lien* 翕斂 ("to

gather in"). Serruys thinks it refers to "concentrating" on their ambitions. Cf. FW 5/6a, which reads *hsi* as *shun* 順 ("to conform with"), so that the line talks of "following their intentions." See below.

11.   The term "free and easy wandering" appears often in early literature, with both positive and negative connotations. See Odes 79/2 (Legge, 131), 146/1 (Legge, 215), and 186/1 (Legge, 299), for example. Also see HSWC 5/2 (Hightower, 160) and the first chapter of *Chuang tzu.*

12.   Taking *tz'u* in the sense of "make grow or increase" and "be loving toward." Wang Ya reads *tz'u* 茲 as *tz'u* 滋 ("to increase," "to [make] grow"), so that GSR 996a = 966h. CWK, p. 173, n. 3 glosses *tz'u* 茲 as *chu* 助 ("to help"). However, FW 5/6a takes *tz'u* 茲 as *tz'u* 此 ("this"). Note also that FW 5/6a takes water, with its propensity to overflow, as the subject of the entire poem.

13.   SMK 5/3b.

14.   Or, "he aims for propriety." CPL 5/6a takes the verb *she* 射 literally as "to shoot an arrow."

15.   Following FW 5/6a. SMK 5/3b, however, reads *yü* 予 as *yü* 與 ("join with"), apparently on the basis of *Analects* 4/10 (Waley, 104). CPL 5/6a glosses *yü* as *shih* 施 ("to let out [the arrow]").

16.   This last line is somewhat puzzling. FW 5/6b says, *so li pu fang, ku ju wu yeh* 所利不方故如舞也 ("What he regards as profit is not square, so it is like dancing"). Wang Ya says, *yü li chih su ju wu chih fu chieh* 欲利之速如舞之赴節 ("The haste of his desire for profit is like the dance's going to the rhythm."). CWK, p. 174, n. 5, follows.

17.   SMK 5/3b.

18.   *Analects* 1/14 (Waley, 87).

19.   Following WJL 5/3b, rather than CWK, p. 173, in reading the *textus difficilior.*

20.   *Yü* 羽 = *yi* 翼. (GSR 98a = 954d).

21.   See, for example, Ou-yang Hsiu's (1007–72) famous essay, "On Factionalism."

22.   However, CWK, p. 174, n. 7, reads *pi* 辟 as *pi* 壁 ("to wall [up]") (= *tsang* 藏, meaning "to store away").

23.   Several editions read "gold and grain" (*chin ku* 金穀). I follow the earliest editions of Sung Chung and Lu Chi. YTC 5/6b takes *chin ku* as a compound meaning "excellent food" (*mei shih* 美食).

24.   SMK 5/3b clearly depends upon the pun between *chü* 舉 and *yü* 與 ("to give [others]").

25.   YTC 5/6a. CPL 5/6b follows.

26.   Literally, "yellow."

27.   For example, YTC 5/6b and CPL 5/6b, on the basis of FW 5/7a. Cf. SMK 5/4a, which talks of the gentleman and his aides.

28.   Serruys takes the verb as "confined," "tucked in," following Morohashi 28693. He points out the linguistic connection between *hsi* 翕 and *ho yü* 合羽.

29.   Following FW 5/7a; CPL 5/7a; and CWK, p. 176, n. 9.

30.   However, CWK, p. 175, n. 10, takes *sui* 遂 more emphatically as *yu ch'eng kung* 有成功 ("to have success").

31. YTC 5/7a reads *ti* 抵 as *chi* 及 ("to cause to come to"), so that the sentence reads, "It will merely prove useful in bringing [it, i.e., death] to your own clan." CWK, p. 175, n. 11, follows.

32. An apparent exception to the general rule that *chüeh* 厥 in the THC refers to Heaven or the ruler. Alternately, "exterminates its [i.e., Heaven's] types [i.e., good men]."

33. SMK 5/4a.

No. 59. Massing

1. SMK 5/4a says the Horn constellation instead.

2. Although SMK 5/4a reads *ch'ung* 崇 as a synonym for *chü* 聚 ("aggregating").

3. For the tetragram title glossed as *pi* 閉 ("to close"), see MKH, I, 115(7a).

4. See the "Introduction" for this. Cf. THC62/A7.

5. As noted by SMK 5/4a; YTC 5/7b.

6. CYYT 28/45/*t'uan, hsiang* (Wilhelm, 614–16).

7. Taking *wu* 無 as *wu hsing* 無形, following standard Han cosmological usage. Cf. FW 5/7b.

8. Following Wang Ya. Serruys prefers to read, "Ghosts and spirits are used by what is without [form] and numinous."

9. CCFL 6:19:62 defines *shen* 神 as perceptible change effected by an unseen cause. Cf. HTYT 7/3/27 (not in Dubs; Knoblock, 177), 84/22/35 (not in Dubs or Knoblock).

10. YTC 5/7a.

11. Literally, "In pleasure, they are excessive and in error."

12. Added by Nylan.

13. Serruys would read instead, "The many ghosts, it they regard as gateway," taking *men* 門 as a verb.

14. For further information, see Hsiao; Nylan (1982), pp. 175–209; and Schwartz (1985), 16–39.

15. The "elders" may also refer to worthy ministers, whose precepts reveal the cosmic patterns to men of virtue. This is apparently the understanding in FW 5/8a. This seems less likely in view of Yang's use of the pronoun "his" (*ch'i* 其), however.

16. The spirit of the *she* 社 , the god of the soil, resides in the thicket. See MTYT 81/46/65 (not in Watson). See also CWK, p. 177, n. 5.

17. Following early editions in omitting *pi* 辟. Note also that CPL 5/8a punctuates differently, reading *kuei hsin* 圭信 as "jade tablet and tally."

18. Reading *jung* 榮 instead of *lao* 勞 ("labor," "laborious"), as in FW 5/8a.

19. For the expression *tso pi* 左辟, see Ode 107/2 (Legge, 164), which, however, translates it as, "stand [or step] aside to the left." Cf. CPL 5/7b–8a.

20. CPL 5/7b.

21. CWK, p. 177, n. 5.

22. YTC 5/8a criticizes "leading the sheep to the thicket" as a symbol of the individual's overreliance upon the spirits, and "holding the jade tablet" as a symbol of his overreliance upon court position. However, there is no reason for the good minister not to rely upon his ruler.

23. The *yu* 蕕 refers to a stinking water plant, as FW 5/8b indicates. Its botanical name is *caryopteris divaricata, maxim.* I suggest three reasons for its use in certain rituals: First, its smell was said to last for ten years, according to CCYT 93/Hsi 4/*fu* 1 (Legge, 141). That would make it a good symbol for longlasting alliances. Second, it was popularly known as "horses' whip," so that it was appropriate to use it for various oaths of allegiance related to warfare. Third, the plant may have been chosen because of a pun; presumably its ingestion would make allies realize their fundamental likeness (*yu* 猶) with the king. This is speculative, however. Note that Wang Ya; YTC 5/8a; CPL 5/8a; and CWK, p. 177, n. 6, take *yu* as *yu* 楢 ("to pile firewood [for sacrifice]" (GSR 1096h). Most likely, the correct wording is preserved in the more difficult version.

24. The term refers to all relations in the patrilineal line from great-great-grandfather to great-great-grandson.

25. Alternately, "to extend."

26. YTC 5/8a seems to think that a stinky plant was chosen to show that the nine degrees of kin shared the same fortune, whatever it might be.

27. FW 5/8b, for example, talks of the oaths of allegiance made to the Son of Heaven. For the commensal meal in contemporary Greek society, see Detienne, esp. p. 13.

28. Alternately, "Excess and ruination."

29. Literally, "Fearing *his/their* (?) ghosts, upholding *his/their* (?) rituals./ Wantonly to cause benightedness. . . ." FW 5/8b omits the possessive pronouns in his commentary. CWK, p. 177, n. 7, equates the second *ch'i* with the "ancestral temple" on the basis of FW.

30. See, for example, ch. 9 of the FSTY.

31. CCYT 77/Chuang 32/*fu* (Legge, 120).

32. LC 2/22 (Legge, 116).

33. *Chiu* 鳩 means "pigeon," a bird said to usurp the magpie's nest. Alternately, *chiu* means "to collect [together]." See GSR 992h.

34. By screeching. See Morohashi 3458. Alternately, *fa* 吷 means "to attack."

35. FW 5/8b–9a.

36. In the "Owl" *fu* by Chia Yi, the owl symbolizes the slanderer in particular. See SC 84:2497 (Watson, I, 510). Note Wang Ya's more auspicious interpretation of the Appraisal: "The owl and the kite are in the forest./ Screeched at [by] those many birds./ The owl and the kite are in the forest./ Meaning: They are abused by the many." In that case, the line serves as a cautionary tale to those who use their present strength and vicious tendencies to destroy others. Eventually, they will receive their just deserts at the hands of those whom they have harmed. Cf. SMK 5/4b.

37. Following Serruys, I take *hui* 彙 to mean "to bunch together." FW 5/9a; Sung Wei-kan; and CWK, p. 178, n. 10, read *hui* as *lei* 類 ("category") so that the sentence reads, "[There] gather those in the category of family [i.e., friends]." Cf. YTC 5/8b.

38. CPL 5/8b, however, offers a different reading for the Appraisal text: "Snivel drips, coiling down [from] the nose./ The clan encircles [the corpse-like] hedgehog [spines]."

No. 60. Accumulation

1. Note that Wilhelm translates this as the "Taming Power of the Great," reading the character *ch'u* 畜 in a second sense.

2. "Everything" is implied in both sentences, since no direct object is specified for the transitive verbs.

3. SMK 5/5a talks of accumulating at their center.

4. See, for example, the argumentation of HFT, ch. 22–21 (Liao, I, 169–227). For a nuanced interpretation of Han Fei's theories, see Wang H-P.

5. Or, "what obstructs."

6. FW 5/9b reads instead, "To make a foundation for next [year]."

7. CPL 5/9a, however, gives another reading for *ming chi* 明基, saying that the petty man does evil in secret in hopes of achieving visible worldly success.

8. Following YTC 5/9a. *Chieh hsin* 介心 is the opposite of *hsiao hsin* 小心.

9. Or, "Accumulating what [others] hold to be useless."

10. Sung Chung and SMK 5/5a. Cf. FW 5/9b.

11. However, if we adopt the readings of the Sung Wei-kan and SMK 5/5a, *fan* 蕃 should be read with determinative 159 軬 (GSR 195m = 195g), referring to the covered carriage. In any case, note the visual and aural pun.

12. See FW 5/10a and CWK, p. 180, n. 5, for example.

13. See YTC 5/9b. SMK 5/5a argues instead that the carriage flaps indicate the fullness of his virtue.

14. Alternately, "[They] steal what is in short supply."

15. Cf. THC43/F4.

16. For this, see *Mencius* 3A/3 (Lau, 98).

17. SMK 5/5a talks of the Ao Granary belonging to the Ch'in dynasty falling into the hands of Hsiang Yü 項羽 and Liu Pang 劉邦.

18. YTC 5/9b; CPL 5/9b.

19. *Analects* 12/18 (Waley, 167). Cf. Ode 256/2 (Legge, 511).

20. LT, ch. 44 (Lau, 105).

21. Cf. LT, ch. 58 (Lau, 118); CCYT 333/Hsiang 31/1 *Tso* (Legge, 563).

22. Alternately, "Greatly full [and] broadly dispensing."

23. Following FW 5/10a; YTC 5/9b. Serruys prefers, "The men he gets are without peer."

24. "All" added by Nylan.

25. *Wang, wang che yeh* 王, 往者也.

26. "Learning," 10/20 (Legge, 379) before the break; after the break, 10/6–8 (Legge, 375).

27. Tentative translation. FW 5/10a reads this as, "The stores are apparent," taking *k'uei* 魁 as *ts'ang* 藏 and *yen* 顏 as *hsien* 見. YTC 5/10a reads this as, "To make the appearance seductive." SMK 5/5b takes *k'uei* 魁 as a synonym for *shou* 首 ("head"), implying that the situation just begins; then he says that *yen* 顏 ("face") means that it is apparent to all. However, generally following Serruys, I read the first *erh* 而 as *jan* 然; and the second as a final particle. Cf. Ode 98/1. Serruys would take *yen erh* more literally as "[his] demeanor."

28. Following CPL 5/10a. YY 33:667 reads *k'uai* 快 ("to indulge in) rather than *chüeh* 決, but this emendation is unnecessary.

29. FW 5/10a–10b, however, reads *shou* 收 instead of *chao* 招. "Only" added by Nylan.

30. The commentators cite the *Changes* lines, "If a man carries a burden on his back while riding in a carriage, he encourages thieves to draw near. . . . Carelessness about stored [items] tempts thieves [to steal]." See CYYT 42/Hsi A/7 (Wilhelm, 307–8).

31. Alternately, "It is simply [due to] what went before."

32. CYYT 4/2/yen (Wilhelm, 393), cited by SMK 5/5b.

33. For *wei* 訄, see GSR 163e. Serruys reads as, "This is what calamity [brings in] perverted [form]." CWK, p. 181, n. 10, reads *wei* as *wei* 委 ("delivers"? "collects"?) or *sui* 隨 ("follows").

No. 61. Embellishment

1. Following FW 5/10b; YTC 5/10b; and CPL 5/10b. But SMK 5/5b assigns THC61 to Hexagram no. 22, Ornateness. For comments on the unreliability of certain correlations proposed by SMK 5/5b, see the notes to THC41/Head.

2. According to FW 5/11a.

3. Note that two early editions write the archaic *chüeh* 厥 instead of *ch'i* 其 here. That usage would indicate high status.

4. Reading *yu* 有 as "most," as in the *Odes*.

5. Wang Ya commentary.

6. CPL 5/10b.

7. Note, however, that the Wang Ya edition omits the first two characters, so that the entire Appraisal reads, "[In] speech, he does not use speech." See WJL 5/5b.

8. *Mencius* 5A/5 (Lau, 143).

9. *Analects* 5/10 (Waley, 109 [renum.]). Cf. *Analects* 1/14; 2/18; 4/22; 4/24.

10. FW 5/11a.

11. Serruys reads, "Having no substance, he is ornamented."

12. Reading *fu* 服 as "clothing." However, YTC 5/10b and CWK, p. 182, n. 4, read *fu* 服 as *yung* 用 ("usage" or "function"). The line then reads, "With pattern put first, later loss of function."

13. Alternately, "loses good omens."

14. For the Taoists, see LT, ch. 80 (Lau, 142), for example.

15. YTC 5/10b.

16. *Analects* 3/8 (Waley, 95).

17. SMK 5/5b–6a.

18. Literally, "yellow." Omitting *ch'iu* 酋, following SMK 5/6a.

19. Alternately, "The yellow brush, it he considers of benefit."

20. FY 5/14, cited by SMK 5/6a.

21. CYYT 4/2/yen (Wilhelm, 395).

22. Several editions read *k'ou* 口 instead here.

23. My translation reflects both senses of *li* 利. For *wa wa* 哇哇, see FW 5/11b, which glosses it as *chan chuan chih mao* 展轉之貌. Cf. FY 2:4, where commentary by Li Kuei 李軌 defines *wa* 哇 as *yin sheng* 淫聲 ("illicit sounds") [in the context of music].

24. See *Mencius* 1A/1 (Lau, 49).

25. Literally, "they truly apply [the way of] the Heaven's Female." For the phrase "Heaven's Female," see LT, ch. 61 (Lau, 122 + Notes), where the metaphor is one of a "huge, boundaryless, bottomless, genital, . . . the vagina" that gestates all living things (Li Yün, p. 65). SMK 5/6a takes the binome to refer to the ocean, however.

26. Following FW 5/12a. SMK 5/6a, however, reads it, "Times when one should not speak." Serruys prefers, "If he is not fit to speak of the [present] times, . . ." The first Fathoming line repeats the first Appraisal line, though my own translation reflects two possible meanings.

27. Literally, "being subtle in wording makes the superior see suspected [points]." SMK 5/6a reads this instead as, "[Or you will] be doubted by the superior."

28. SMK 5/6a reads this instead as, "It is not time for straight-talking."

29. Adding "else" in order to make the meaning auspicious, to better accord with its yin/yang valuation.

30. FW 5/12a says that bluntness alone cannot clarify a matter. SMK 5/6a cites *Analects* 19/10 (Waley, 226): "A gentleman remonstrates only after he is trusted. If he does so before he is trusted, [his superior] will assume that he is being vilified." That suggests that SMK would have the good person say as little as possible here (another possible reading for *wei yü tz'u* 微于辭).

31. I take the reduplicative as a description of shrill cries. However, for SMK 5/6b and CWK, p. 183, n. 10, the reduplicative indicates "incessant cries."

32. Tentative translation. The reduplicative *yü yü* 于于 means "to belabor," both in the senses of "laboring to establish a point" and "belaboring a point." See FW 5/12b and CWK, p. 183, n. 11, which define it as *to nan mao* 多難貌 ("the appearance of many difficulties"). CPL 5/12a defines it as *wei wei* 娓娓 ("loquacious"); SMK 5/6b, as simply "the appearance of being pushed back." However, certain dictionaries gloss it as *wu so chih mao* 無所知貌 ("the appearance of having no knowledge"). See Morohashi 252.4.

33. Following SMK 5/6b; CWK, p. 183, n. 11. Alternately, "it can be judged superior."

34. SMK 5/6b and CWK, p. 183, n. 11, citing CYYT 29/47/t'uan (Wilhelm, 625).

35. See GSR 782a for the three related meanings of *po* 白: (1) white, (2) bare, and (3) clearly understand.

No. 62. Doubt

1. Note the dispute about the *Changes* correlate to this tetragram. Sung Chung, Lu Chi, and Wang Ya correlate it with no. 57, Laying the Offering. FW 5/12b correlates it with no. 51, Arousal; SMK 5/6b, with no. 22, Grace.

2. Or, "are harmed" [by yin's vigorous activity], following Lu Chi; FW 5/12b; and CWK, p. 185, n. 2.

3. Or, "disintegrate."

4. CPL 5/12a, however, reads this as, "[Yin finds yang at different times] seeming to be right, seeming to be wrong."

5. CWK, p. 185, n. 1, contrasts the external ornamentation of THC61/Head with the present decay, suggesting that this makes for doubt.

6. FW 5/12b.

7. Lu Chi; FW 5/12b; and SMK 5/6b.

8. CPL 5/12a.

9. Or, as Wang Ya reads it, "in a muddle."

10. Or, following Serruys, "good omens and straightness." CPL 5/12a, however, reads 乇 as one ancient form of *chih* 直, rather than *shih* 矢.

11. Or, "turn back [i.e., reverse] the self." See below.

12. Following CWK, p. 185, n. 4. Alternately, "Trustworthiness will not be far away."

13. LT, ch. 45 (Lau, 106).

14. *Mencius* 2A/2 (Lau, 76–77).

15. Literally, "Receives increasingly [or, 'this'] distressed distressed."

16. Reading GSR 46b' = 46i'. However, FW 5/13a reads *tsu* 祖 as *shih* 始 ("to begin"). This is impossible since the distress has been increasing. YTC 5/12b; CPL 5/12b; and CWK, p. 185, n. 5, read it as the noun "beginning." Note the internal rhymes, with *chao* 昭, *tzu* 兹, and *ch'i* 其, all ending in g with archaic Chinese. See GSR 1131m, 1115b, 952a.

17. SMK 5/7a; YTC 5/12b; and CWK, p. 185, n. 5, however, read as, "[Though] in doubt, to [wrongly] force [one's way to seeming] clarity." SMK 5/7a cites *Analects* 2/17 (Waley, 91): "To know when you know it, to know when you do not know it, that is [true] knowledge."; and LC 1/3 (Legge, I, 62): "Do not positively affirm what you have doubts about."

18. YTC 5/12b specifically ties "the old" to "elders."

19. *Analects* 16/10 (Waley, 206). Cf. *ibid.*, 1/10 (Waley, 85), 10/14 (Waley, 150).

20. *Documents*, "Chung Hui chih kao," par. 8 (Legge, 183; not in Karlgren)

21. *Hsiung* 䖝 means either "red," following FW 5/13a, or it is taken as a loan for 雄. I assume the latter. However, YTC 5/13a reads it as, "When yellow [dirt appears in] red [mud], it is mistakenly thought to be gold."

22. A very loose translation. The first line of the Fathoming repeats the entire Appraisal except for "gold."

23. Sung Wei-kan and CWK, p. 186, n. 7, emphasize its shine; hence, my belief that arsenic disulphide (realgar) is not the mineral described. However, it is possible that the text refers to hematite, as the Wang commentary suggests. Hematite is an iron oxide sometimes found in rocks that also bear pyrites ("fool's gold"). Yang Hsiung may have confused the two minerals in his mind. I am grateful to Nathan Sivin for this information.

24. The manufacture of false gold was sufficiently widespread to provoke an imperial edict in 144 B.C. against it. See HS 5:148 (Dubs, I, 323). On arsenic sulphides and early alchemy, see Needham, V:4, 295, 318. Mercury was combined with other metals frequently in the presence of arsenic sulphides. Arsenical sulphide was also used in the preparation of arsenical copper, which was included in a medieval list of "golds" discussed in *ibid.*, V:2, 252. Early recipes for the elixir (dating from A.D. 300 and 507) contain realgar and/or orpiment. See *ibid.*, V:2, 83: V:4, 217. Most elixirs were mixtures of mercuric and arsenical compounds.

For an early passage that apparently views realgar as a rudimentary form of gold, see HNT 4:17a–18b, as translated in Major (1991), p. 70.

25. SMK 5/7a.

26. Literally, "When one doubts, then he will [still?] have a way to verify," assuming that *so* 所 has been omitted after *yu* 有.

27. Alternately, "The enlightened king gives command." Or, following FW 5/13b and Wang Ya, "It illustrates the king's commands."

28. Wang Ya. For the institutions of *ming* 命 and *meng* 盟, see Dobson (1968).

29. SY 1/4a.

30. Reading *kuei hun yi* 鬼魂疑 as "ghostly souls [or, ghosts and souls] are doubted." All extant early editions add the characters *chen li* 貞厲, which have been deleted from most late editions, except for YTC 5/13a. YTC compares the ghosts to petty men, who mistrust proper authority. The sentence then reads, "As to ghosts and souls, they doubt the true, which is dangerous." If the THC follows the *Changes* for the binome *chen li*, however, then the phrase means "the determination is threatening."

31. SW 2A/11ba explains this compound as "a sigh of uncertainty." Serruys says, "With a sigh of doubt, one sighs," meaning that the sighs are doubled. Only CPL 5/13a takes this onomatopoeic compound to refer to the soughing of the wind through the trees and caves. YTC 5/13a–13b takes this to refer to the [evil] cry of crow and fox.

32. However, FW 5/12b ties the crow to the sun, so that this line would mean, "A stringed arrow [shot at] the sun in the trees."

33. SMK 5/7a, however, reads this as, "Exchanging eye for ear: Danger." Serruys would follow.

34. Following CWK, p. 186, n. 9. Alternately, following YTC 5/13a–13b, the onomatopoeic characters convey the cry of the fox and the call of the crow.

35. See Ode 41/3 (Legge, 68).

36. YTC 5/13b has the first line of the Appraisal symbolize how the petty man (associated with the ghosts) is suspected by the noble man; and the next lines, the noble person's being deluded by the petty man (symbolized by fox and crow). This may be overly schematic. CPL 5/13a gives a slightly different version in which the hunter is misled by the soughing of the wind into thinking that crow and fox (both ill portents) exist, when they do not.

37. Following YTC 5/13a; CPL 5/13a-13b; and CWK, p. 186, n. 9.

38. YTC 5/13b and CWK, p. 186, n. 10 read it as, "When one is overturned by [extreme] doubts, . . ." Cf. CPL 5/13b, which reads *chen* 顛 as *k'uang* 狂 ("crazed").

39. All early editions read *chiu* 九 here. The WJL edition (5/7b), however, deletes *chiu*, presuming a duplication of characters.

40. GSR 1209a = 1208h. Note also the puns GSR 598f = 598h ("to achieve") = 598e ("to delude").

No. 63. Watch

1. SMK 5/7b reads *pi* 妣 ("deceased mother") as *p'ei* 配 ("companion"); CWK, p. 188, n. 2, as *mu* 母 ("mother"). CPL 5/14a seems to say that as yin takes

over the corporeal, yang becomes ever more insubstantial, like a mother's corpse; YTC 5/14a, that yang is about to perish.

2. FW 5/14b talks of yang nourishing the roots of things below earth.

3. CPL 5/14a.

4. CYYT 40/Hsi A/4 (Wilhelm, 294), cited by CPL 5/13b. Cf. Peterson (1982), p. 100, for a different translation.

5. *Analects* 12/4 (Waley, 163).

6. FW 5/14b. YTC 5/14a emphasizes the latent power of his light.

7. SMK 5/7b emphasizes that thought has just begun; YTC 5/14a, "awaiting the proper time."

8. CPL 5/14a.

9. YTC 5/14a; CPL 5/14a.

10. CWK, p. 188, n. 4.

11. *Kan* 幹 refers to the posts in the framework used in building tamped earthen walls. From this derives the extended meaning of "to support."

12. SMK 5/7b.

13. YTC 5/14b.

14. Certain editions, however, read *ping* 頩 ("beautiful visage") rather than *pien* 頗 ("front part of the face"). See, e.g., CWK, p. 188, n. 6.

15. Following CPL 5/14b. YTC 5/14b, however, reads this slightly differently.

16. SMK 5/7b; CWK, pp. 188–89, n. 6. Of course, the man could simply have applied too much powder.

17. Chia Yi 賈誼, cited in SC 84:2495 (Watson, I, 511).

18. See CPL 5/15a.

19. Following FW 5/16a; CWK, p. 190, n. 11. Literally, "Ornaments [the sky] to the eastern quadrant."

No. 64. Sinking

1. FW 5/16a says Hexagram 58 instead. YTC and CPL follow.

2. Following FW 5/16a. CWK, p. 191, n. 1, says it should be 9 degrees.

3. Alternately, "thinks of [i.e., longs for]," following Sung Chung who glosses *huai* 懷 as *ssu* 思.

4. Sung Chung commentary. CPL 5/15a repeats.

5. FW 5/16a situates the Palace in the shadowy regions below the surface of the earth; CWK, p. 191, n. 2, follows. YTC 5/15b and CPL 5/15b, however, equate the Mysterious Palace with the northernmost regions of the earth.

6. SMK 5/8a believes that the title *ch'en* 沈 means *hsia shih* 下視 ("to gaze down"). CWK, p. 191, n. 1, follows, reading it as *ch'ien shih* 潛視 ("to look covertly"). FW 5/16a, however, explains the title in terms of the union of yin and yang far below the surface of the earth.

7. Serruys would say, "the good omen."

8. See, e.g., LC 1/12 (Legge, I, 454–55), and 2/13–14 (Legge, I, 470).

9. Consider the case of Pao-yü in the novel *Dream of the Red Chamber*.

10. LC 12/12 (Legge, I, 454).

11. Sung Wei-kan and CPL 5/15b define *mien* 眄 as *hsieh shih* 邪視.

12. Contrast these lines with the CYYT 33/54/2 (Wilhelm, 666; Kunst, 347): "the one-eyed man able to see."

13. LT, ch. 12 (Lau, 68).

14. CTYT 45/17/85–87 (Watson, 188).

15. The term refers to things still in the womb, or the very young unable to sustain themselves apart from their mothers.

16. CWK, p. 192, n. 7, takes *chou* 粥 as *yü* 育 ("to nurture"). Serruys reads the line, "They like to conceive but hate to rear [their young]," following Wu Mi and SMK 5/8b for the interpretation of the verbs. FW 5/17a reads it as, "They like to take in and hate to give out." YTC 5/16a reads *o chou* 惡粥 as a compound meaning "spoiled gruel."

17. For the same metaphor, see CTYT 45/17/87 (Watson, 188).

18. Following the earliest editions. However, FW 5/17a; Wang Ya; CPL 5/16a; YTC 5/16b; and CWK, p. 190, n. 8, read *p'iao* 票 ("fire spark") instead of *su* 粟 ("kernel"), then punctuate after *ming* 明. In that case, the "light" refers to the favorable reputation of the superior man.

19. Literally, "Seeing [or, making] clear the benefits-profits thereby rectifies [it] in (for?) the king."

20. Literally, "Nettedlike, boundlike." Reading GSR 123a as "[what] binds." Cf. THC41/A1. However, SMK 5/8b reads the phrase *li ju lou ju* 離如羅如 as a reference to Li Lou, the fabled official of the Yellow Emperor who purportedly could see the tip of an autumn hair at more than 100 paces. YTC 5/16b takes it, therefore, to describe "seeing clearly" (*shih ming mao* 視明貌). FW 5/17a and CWK, p. 193, n. 9, read the first line as a description of birds "forcefully staring" (*li shih mao* 力視貌), another possible reference to Li Lou (?). The verses then lament those of keen insight whose greed and bloodlust overcomes their better instincts. CPL 5/16b takes *li lou* to describe the skin of the prey "separated" (i.e., flayed or torn) from the muscle by the powerful beaks of the kites and owl.

21. Note the sound pun between *li* 離 and *li* 厲.

22. However, FW 5/17a; YTC 5/16b; CPL 5/16b; and CWK, p. 193, n. 10, read *p'an* 盼 as *mei mu* 美目 ("fine [i.e., clear] eyes"), implying that vision has been restored.

23. Literally, "bloodlike."

24. Curiously, SMK 5/9a assumes that the blood refers to *kao tse* 膏澤 ("what oils and moistens"); while *kang* 剛 means *kang* 岡 ("the ridge [of a hill or mountain]"). The individual is criticized for paring away too much from the common people. YTC 5/16b; and CWK, p. 193, n. 11, follow.

No. 65. Inner

1. According to SMK 5/9a, the Dipper points WNW; the musical note is A-sharp.

2. FW 5/18a.

3. CYYT 33/54/*hsiang, t'uan* (Wilhelm, 664).

4. Example added by Nylan. See footnote 20 below.

5. FW 5/18a, however, glosses *ch'iu* 朹 as *cheng* 正 ("uprightness"), rather than as a loan character for *ch'iu* 仇 (GSR 992p). Note the variation between what is recorded of FW in SMK 5/9a and in the FW edition.

6. Serruys: "He starts with what is attested in females."
7. This is the argument of the "Great Learning." CPL 5/17a reminds us that the *Odes* begins with the "Kuan chü" song, interpreted as a celebration of the faithful marriage.
8. YTC 5/17a–b.
9. Following WJL (5/9a), rather than FW 5/18a, in reading *hu* 乎 instead of *nai* 乃 to maintain the inauspicious character of the line.
10. Following FW 5/18a. CPL 5/17a takes it simply to mean the "bed in the room," since yellow signifies what is center.
11. Sung Wei-kan, quoted in SMK 5/9a.
12. The first suggestion is made by Nylan; the second, by CPL 5/17a.
13. Wang Ya, however, glosses *yi* 儀 as *p'i* 匹 ("match" or "mate").
14. FW 5/18a, however, glosses *k'an* 坎 as *yu* 憂 ("to worry"). YTC 5/17b; CPL 5/17b follow FW. I follow YY 33:668 and CWK, p. 195, n. 5, in reading *k'an* 坎 as *tz'u* 次 (=*chi* 即).
15. See LC 22B/4 (Legge, II, 431).
16. CPL 5/17b understands these lines as referring to Wang Mang's usurpation of the Han throne.
17. Wang Ya, however, reads *p'ao* 袍 as *pao* 飽 ("to be sated with food"). However, it is more likely that we have an allusion to "the shabby hempen gown" of *Analects* 9/26 (Waley, 144).
18. Literally, "The noble man profits [from the dragon's example], and uses [it] to marry a fine lady." *Hsi* 嬰 means "a fine lady." See GSR 960. Serruys prefers, "What the gentleman gains as profit, he uses to take a consort."
19. Literally, "And on meeting by customary law, they are equal," since the subordinate clause should not follow the main clause. The translation follows SMK 5/9a and YTC 5/18a, which read *yung* 庸 as "regular" or "customary"; and *yi* 夷 as *teng yi* 等夷 ("level," "grade"). For Han arguments on the equality of the wife, see SW 12B/259a; PHT 10:411 (Tjan, I, 261); and FSTY 3:22, all of which texts define *ch'i* 妻 ("wife") as "one who is equal (*ch'i* 齊) to oneself [the man]." However, FW 5/18b reads *yung* as *ta* 大 ("great"). CWK, p. 195, n. 7, wants to read this line as, "Treating [household members by the] Mean [produces] joy."
20. As FW 5/18b reminds us, in the traditional betrothal and nuptial ceremonies of ancient China, the bride introduced to the groom's house finds her future husband coming out to greet her personally. See LC 22B/2 (Legge, II, 429).
21. CPL 5/18a.
22. That is, toward the bedchamber. See FW 5/19a; YTC 5/18a.
23. YTC 5/18a.
24. FW 5/19a speaks of "the [proper] time being past."
25. Equally possible readings for *man kung* 滿宮 in the third line of the Appraisal. The first is given by CWK, p. 196, n. 8; the second, by YTC 5/18a.
26. FW 5/19a takes *ho* 皬 as "not purely white" (that is, a grizzled head). KYSH, however, suggests that *ho* refers to what is "shining and white" (a bald head?). The verb is *nei* 內.
27. Adding "soon" to clarify. SMK 5/9b, however, reads *yu* 有 as *fu yu* 富有 ("riches"). CPL 5/18b identifies *yu* 有 as "an expression of congratulations."
28. For *wu* 物 as "to give external or concrete form to," see CTYT 28/11/62

(3x) (Watson, 123): *wu wu* 物物.

29. SMK 5/9b reads instead as, "Things are delighted to get their [proper] category." CWK, p. 196, n. 9, follows.

30. CYYT 18/28/5 (Wilhelm, 527).

31. An alternate reading for *nieh* 孽 in the last line.

32. Ode 264/3 (Legge, 561).

No. 66. Departure

1. Both SMK 5/9b and FW 5/19b initially assign THC66 to Water, but this is wrong. See FW 5/19b commentary to App. 1 for a correction.

2. Reading the compound *wu-wang* 無妄 according to the Han commentators. See MKH, I, 101(8a). Wilhelm translates the hexagram title as "Innocence."

3. A number of glosses are offered for the compound *ch'ou ch'ang* 倜傽, whose *locus classicus* is this passage. FW 5/19b glosses it as "flourishing" (*ch'ang sheng* 長盛); Wang Ya, as *jou* 俩 ("lying," "exaggerating"); YTC 5/19a as *lei luo hsiang ch'ü* 磊落相去 ("to openly or greatly depart from one another); and CPL 5/19a as *huang huang wu so chih* 皇皇無所之 ("anxious, perturbed, not knowing where to go"). CWK, p. 198, n. 2, follows CPL.

4. See Ode 242/2, 3 (Legge, 457).

5. FW 5/19b–20a; Sung Wei-kan commentary.

6. See, e.g., HS 27B/A:2354–55. Cf. LC 2/1 (Legge, I, 100); CCYT 330/ Hsiang 30/5 *Tso* (Legge, 556).

7. *Yu lu* 有露.

8. SMK 5/10a. Cf. Ode 17/1 (Legge, 27). He may even have been implicated in shady dealings. See YTC 5/19b.

9. As noted by CPL 5/19b.

10. Following FW 5/20a–20b.

11. We know that this Appraisal should be auspicious, since it is correlated with lucky Day. CWK, p. 198, n. 6, assumes, however, that Yang Hsiung departs from his regular schema of alternating yin and yang lines. Following YTC 5/19b, CWK takes the lines as description of the unfortunate estrangement of father-son and ruler-subject. Typically, however, such departure from the schema only occurs in the later Appraisals associated with the decline of the cycle.

12. Reading *mi* 麋 as *mi* 蘪 (GSR 598m), following both FW 5/20b and SMK 5/10a.

13. He crosses the courtyard, then raises his hem, possibly to relieve himself outside the house.

14. SMK 5/10a. See also HS 27B/A:1396. GSR 598f = 598e?

15. Literally, "[by] his own person," meaning "on his own initiative."

16. LT, ch. 9 (Lau, 65). Cf. *ibid.*, ch. 77 (Lau, 139).

17. The most famous example of the official who readily leaves his position is Liu Hsia-hui (despite some critical remarks by Confucius). See *Mencius* 5B/1 (Lau, 150); 6B/6 (Lau, 175). For imperial cessions, see the stories collected by Allan (1981), pp. 27–54.

18. *Documents*, "Kao Yao mo," par. l4 (Legge, 60; Karlgren, 11).

19. More specifically, the term "three deaths" may have been selected to remind us of the three successive historians who chose death rather than fail to

record their ruler's misdeeds. See CCYT 304/Hsiang 25/*Tso* 2 (Legge, 514–15).

20.   Reading *chi* 機 as *chi* 幾, following FW 5/21a.

21.   Literally, it is "suspended." See CWK, p. 199, n. 10.

22.   The Hsin ("Heart") constellation is in Scorpio. The Fire Star is the "heart of the dragon" found in the Eastern Palace. See CCYT 352/Chao 4/1 *Tso* (Legge, 596).

23.   SMK 5/11a; CPL 5/20b. CWK, p. 199, n. 11, follows. FW 5/21a, however, takes this to refer to Wood's relation with Metal. For "seeking me," cf. the language of THC 12/A1, based on CYYT 5/4/*t'uan* (Wilhelm, 406).

No. 67. Darkening

1.   A tentative translation for the hexagram title based on Han commentaries. See MKH, I, 102(2b), which defines it in terms of *yi ming wei an* 以明為暗 ("to take the light as dark"). Other commentators associate it with "the [eye]sight's sideways glance" or with "inside cultivated and enlightened while outside gentle and compliant" or with light hidden away, "located in the earth." See MKH, I, 48(1b); 89(6b); and 131(3b). Kunst, p. 311, believes that the hexagram title originally referred to a "calling pheasant." But there are other indications that it represents an arrow, a bow, a wound, a place, and a tribe. See Kunst, pp. 77, 88.

2.   CYYT 23/36/*hsü* (Wilhelm, 564, 566).

3.   *Ibid.*, *t'uan* (Wilhelm, 565).

4.   Wang Ya.

5.   CPL 5/20b thinks "together" refers to the agents Metal and Water, which are bright within. This seems farfetched, however. CWK, p. 201, n. 3, cites LT, ch. 41 (Lau, 102): "The way that is bright seems dull."

6.   YTC 5/20b, however, reads *yu chen* 幽貞 as a description of the superior man, who is "profound [and] rightly oriented."

7.   Following Wang Ya.

8.   CWK, p. 201, n. 3.

9.   CPL 5/20b suggests that Yang Hsiung speaks of his own efforts to enlighten an age.

10.   Following CWK, p. 201, n. 4.

11.   Alternately, "He thinks it enlightened not to see the Way."

12.   FY 3:9.

13.   FW 5/22a and Wang Ya read *pi* 必 ("must") instead of *ta* 大 ("greatly"). According to FW, once there is good order in the family, it will always be extended to office. Therefore, it can be said to "go outside."

14.   CWK, p. 201, n. 5, following FW 5/21b–22a.

15.   Added by Nylan on the basis of FW 5/22a. However, CPL 5/21a and YTC 5/21a do not believe that the reversal of the usual yin/yang values can ever be good.

16.   However, CWK, p. 201, n. 6, wants to understand "categories" (*lei* 類) simply as "laws" or "models" (*fa* 法). FW 5/22a takes *lei* to refer to "[proper] types [of advisors]." The "Great Learning" is only one of many texts to link good advisors with "precious treasure." See "Learning," par. 10 (Legge, 376).

17.   FW 5/22a calls the "golden casket" a "beautiful treasure."

18. For the symbol of the metal-bound strongbox, see the *Documents*, "Chin t'eng" ("Metal-bound Coffer") (Legge, 351ff.; Karlgren, 35–36). SMK 5/10b, however, says that the metal casket more generally signifies the degree of security that good laws and institutions bring to the state. CWK, p. 201, n. 6, follows. CPL 5/21a sees in the metal casket a reference to events in A.D. 8, when a certain Ai Chang 哀章, an unscrupulous sycophant, tried to curry favor with Wang Mang by presenting a copper casket. See HS 99A:4095–96 (Dubs, III, 254–55).

19. That is, its position at high noon.

20. Chi tzu 箕子 is associated, of course, with the correspondent hexagram. See CYYT 23/36/5 (Wilhelm, 142). Hexagram 36 is tied to destruction and execution in CYYT 54/*tsa*; MKH, I, 147(14a).

21. See, e.g., Ode 303 (Legge, 636ff.). Cf. Wang Ya; CWK 202, n. 8. YTC 5/21b says the swallow symbolizes the approaching cold.

22. After all, the official with the surname "Dark-bird" (*hsüan niao* 玄鳥) was in charge of calendrical matters. See CCYT 392/Chao 17/3 *Tso* (Legge, 667).

23. SMK 5/11a. Hsün tzu bemoans the "light sinking into the earth" in the opening lines of his *fu*. See Pankenier (1990b), 451.

24. Reading this character as *hsiao* 艄, rather than as *miao* 胊, following Wang Ya rather than FW 5/22b.

25. Omitting *tsun* 遵, following Wang Ya. Otherwise, we should omit *te* 德, following the two earliest editions of Sung Chung and Lu Chi (rather than FW) to maintain the four character line. With no character omitted, the line reads, "Virtue is what they are about to follow and go forward to."

26. For the same metaphor, see KT 10/30/16a (Rickett[b], 407).

27. Following Sung Wei-kan, literally "one eye blind" (*yi mu mang* 一目盲). Cf. YY 33:668; FW 5/22b.

28. Following WJL (5/11a) in reading *chen* 真 rather than *chih* 直 ("straight"), so as to preserve the earliest reading. Literally, "looking at something that is not *his* (*ch'i* 其) [idea of] straight."

29. Serruys believes, however, that *yu* 右 describes the "assisting" eye rather than the right eye, since both eyes are needed for a balanced view.

30. FW 5/22b talks of his failing to distinguish worthy ministers from false.

31. Since *hui* 晦 refers to the last day of the lunar month, it is a clear symbol for a deteriorating political situation.

32. Alternately, "In a dark age seeing veils for what they are."

33. Taking *chen* 貞 as "to be tried and true." Serruys prefers, "It is beneficial to the omen-prediction [that takes place] in a not bright [age]."

34. Literally, "One does not gain [by] alone being bright."

35. Example cited by SMK 5/11a, which quotes CYYT 23/36/5 (Wilhelm, 142). Note that Kunst translates differently.

36. CPL 5/22a, however, cites the famous fisherman's query to Ch'ü Yüan asking, "When times are dirty, why not go with the crowd?" See SC 84:2486 (Watson, I, 505).

37. Following YTC 5/22a.

No. 68. Dimming

1. According to FW 6/1a.

2. Taking *chen* 貞 as *cheng* 正, following the commentators.

3. The Head text recalls THC67/A2, which speaks of "blindly forging ahead." In both cases, the verb *cheng* 征 is used.

4. CPL 6/1a associates the tetragram title ("Meng") with its homonym meaning "dream."

5. See the Wang Ya commentary.

6. FW 6/1a explains that the Water line conquers the Earth agent that rules the tetragram. Presumably this accounts for one's powers of perception being muddied.

7. CWK, p. 204, n. 4, cites HTYT 80/21/39 (Dubs, 268; not in Knoblock).

8. *Mencius* 7B/20 (Lau, 198).

9. Following FW 6/2a.

10. Following Wang Ya and CWK, p. 204, n. 7, in reading *p'an* 扳, rather than *pin* 頻 (=*p'in* 顰), as in YTC 6/2a. If the latter reading is adopted, the line means, "That which men frown upon." Consult Serruys (1984), p. 728, no. 412. Serruys, however, prefers to read *so* 所 as *so yü* 所於, so that the line reads, "It is where men collide with each other."

11. FW 6/2a.

12. Following Wang Ya, taking *li* 離 as *ming* 明. CWK, p. 205, n. 8, agrees. However, YTC 6/2a reads *li* as *tsao* 遭 ("to meet with"). An alternate reading is given in the Fathoming.

13. Tentative reading for *ying* 熒 and for *no* 妠, loosely following YTC 6/2a. FW 6/2a reads *no* as *hsiao* 小 ("small"); Wang Ya, as *jo* 弱 ("weak"). Alternate literal translation, "[He] does not find it fitting to flicker and be weak," follows Wang Ya. CWK, p. 205, n. 8, agrees.

14. FW 6/2a and Wang Ya read *ai ai* 薆薆 instead, so that the punch line reads, "The center does not obscure."

15. Following YTC 6/2a.

16. Following most editions in reading *hao* 好 ("good") instead of *chien* 奸 ("treachery"). If the alternate reading is adopted, the line means, "Dim-sighted as to treachery."

17. However, FW 6/2a punctuates after *meng* 瞢. FW assumes that the poem is lucky since what is unclear changes to clear.

18. Serruys prefers, "Dimming the good, it he abhors."

19. However, YTC 6/2a and CPL 6/2b both think the line inauspicious, assuming the dim "light" to be inadequate to the task.

20. Reading *chia* 嘏 for *chia* 珈 (GSR 15i = 15d). Cf. Ode 47/1 (Legge, 76), cited by YTC 6/2b.

No. 69. Exhaustion

1. CWK, p. 207, n. 2, reads *chü* 遽 as *wei chü* 畏懼 ("fearful") instead of "agitated."

2. CYYT 29/47/t'uan (Wilhelm, 624).

3. See the commentary by Sung Wei-kan, who reads *chü* 遽 instead of *chü* 據.

4. CPL 6/2b.

5. Alternately, "So people love centrality." FW 6/3a, however, reads *chung* 中 as *chung* 忠 ("loyalty").

6. This reading is supported by the main argument of the famous "Hung fan" chapter of the *Book of Documents*.

7. FW 6/3a.

8. See YTC 6/3a for this.

9. *Analects* 15/2 (Waley, 193).

10. FW 6/3a talks of the superior curbing his own desires so as to improve the common people.

11. Alternately, "So that the people become uncentered."

12. LSCC 14/6/15b–16a.

13. Presuming *Analects* 15/30 (Waley, 199). That is why the punctuation should not read, *ch'iung szu, ta* 窮思, 達.

14. Or, "are dessicated and diseased."

15. *Analects* 12/9 (Waley, 165), cited by SMK 6/2a.

16. *San* 糝 can refer to "rice gruel with meat." It also describes the rice hardened at the bottom of the pot (*kuo pa* 鍋巴).

17. Perhaps like Po Yi and Shu Ch'i, he sups on a stew of wild herbs only. For further information about the Han diet, see Yü Ying-shih (1977).

18. *Analects* 6/9 (Waley, 117) before the ellipsis mark; after, *ibid.*, 6/5 (Waley, 116). Cf. *ibid.*, 8/10 (Waley, 134).

19. Ode 233/3 (Legge, 423), cited by YTC 6/3a.

20. CPL 6/3b.

21. SMK 6/2a.

22. Alternately, "to stumble into." See, for example, the Wang Ya commentary.

23. Following the commentators, I take the "report" (*lu* 錄) as the written document granting him release. See, for example, CWK, p. 208, n. 9.

24. Following YY 33:668, reading *t'a* 他 as *t'o* 佗. Alternatively, "add to the burden." Wang Ya, however, takes the line to mean, "The blame is not another's deed" (*chiu fei t'a tso* 咎非他作).

25. A loose translation for, "S/he meets with what is coincidental bad luck."

26. The same metaphor appears in CKT 18:43 (Crump, 282).

No. 70. Severance

1. According to Wang Ya, this signifies that "it is not used."

2. Following Wang Ya. However, Serruys prefers to read *sha* 殺 *shai* ("reduced"). For this meaning, see GSR 319d.

3. CYYT 15/23/*t'uan* (Wilhelm, 501).

4. CPL 6/4b.

5. CYYT 15/23/*t'uan* (Wilhelm, 501).

6. CYYT 15/23/*hsiang* (Wilhelm, 501).

7. Following SMK 6/2b.

8. CPL 6/4b.

9. Suggested by Nylan.

10. CPL 6/5a. Cf. YTC 6/4b.

11. Alternately, "He can have what he perfects."

12. FW 6/5a talks of "being without selfish interest."

13. *Analects* 16/9 (Waley, 203 [renum.]), cited by CWK, p. 210, n. 6.

14. "The use of" added by Nylan. The term *fu ma* 服馬 refers to the inner two horses in a set of four that bear the main weight of the carriage. The word *fu* is used because the horses have "submitted" to the shaft.

15. Reading *p'eng* 朋 ("to pair with") instead of *ming* 明.

16. Note that the commentators cannot decide whether the rainbows and clouds represent good or evil omens. Wang Ya; SMK 6/3a; and CPL 6/5b take both as evil omens. YTC 6/5a–5b, however, takes the clouds (but not the rainbow) as a good omen. But HY 1/9b clearly shows contemporary metaphorical usage for Han: "Unethical ministers overshadow the worthy just as floating clouds obscure the sun and moon." (My translation follows Pankenier [1990b], p. 439, not Ku, p. 93).

17. It is possible that *wo* 我 is a mistake for *fa* 伐 since the two characters are very close in the oracle bone script. According to Serruys, the line reads, "He gets to axe the heart's disease." YTC 6/5b reads instead, "To get at what is certainly diseased" (*te pi chi* 得必疾).

18. HFT 19:49:339 ff. (Liao, II, 275 ff.)

No. 71. Stoppage

1. Wilhelm translates the hexagram title as Keeping Still; Kunst, 343, as Cleaving. The Han commentaries associate Hexagram 52 with stopping or with gatekeepers keeping the door shut. See MKH, I, 136(15b); 33(4a).

2. Serruys prefers, "Yin, being great, causes things to stand still in relation to what is above. Yang, being great, causes things to stand still in relation to what is below."

3. CPL 6/6a–6b.

4. FW 6/6a–6b.

5. Sung Chung commentary.

6. CYYT 53/*hsü*; 32/52/*t'uan*, *hsiang* (Wilhelm, 652–54).

7. For the phrase "know when to stop," see *ibid*. Cf. LT, ch. 44 (Lau, 105).

8. "Learning," par. 2–3 (Legge, 356–57), cited by SMK 6/3a.

9. Following the earliest editions, rather than the variant in FW 6/6b, for the first Fathoming line.

10. SMK 6/3a.

11. YTC 6/6a and CPL 6/6b assume that the age is unfavourable so that the driver awaits more favorable circumstances to proceed.

12. *Ku* 蠱 refers to poisonous vermin that cause madness and death when they are ingested. See Shryock (1935). Since the ingestion of *ku* ends in death or insanity, FW 6/6b takes *k'uang ku* 狂蠱 as "crazed licentiousness." SMK 6/3a–3b glosses it as *huo* 惑 ("delusion"). Cf. YTC 5/6a.

13. Cf. *Analects* 5/19 (Waley, 112).

14. See FW 6/6b; CPL 6/6a.

15. Reading GSR 90c tentatively as 90f. Otherwise, *shu* probably refers to "scattered" fruits. However, FW 6/7a equates *shu ku* 蔬穀 (literally, "vegetable-grain"?) simply with *kuo* 果 ("fruits"); Wang Ya, with "inedible grasses and plants"; YTC 6/6a, with *po* 薄 ("thin").

16. FW 6/7a.

17. Added by Nylan, since Appraisal 4 corresponds to ministerial rank.

18. Following FW 6/7a. Cf. Wang Ya, which takes *ch'iu* 酋 as *ting* 定 ("to fix").

19. YTC 6/6b also emphasizes the ruler's impartiality.

20. Reading *lien* 廉.

21. Reading *ch'ih* (㑦 or 儣) as *ch'uan* 輴 (GSR 168–1), a "funeral carriage with solid wheels."

22. Reading *lieh* 獵 as *lieh* 躐 (GSR 637e, f). CPL 6/7b reads *lieh* 獵 as *che* 折 ("cracked"). CWK, p. 214, n. 9, agrees.

23. YY 33:669 equates *lin* 鄰 with *lian* 遴, meaning "to walk with difficulty." See SW 2B/41a.

24. Literally, "To the end, does not stop [acting in this way]."

25. Cf. the metaphor of arrows that "return" in Ode 106/3 (Legge, 162).

26. CWK, p. 214, n. 10.

27. FW 6/7b; Wang Ya; SMK 6/3b.

28. This may refer to HTYT 107/31/35 (not in Dubs or Knoblock), cited by SMK 6/3b: "A bow is tempered before one seeks strength from it. A horse is domesticated before one seeks tameness in it. A *shih* is made trustworthy and honest before one seeks understanding and ability of him."

29. YTC 6/7a.

30. Following YTC 6/7a. However, CPL 6/7b glosses *chu* 株 ("tree stump," "roots that grow above ground," or "lower trunk of a tree") as *wang* 輄 (meaning "wheel rim"). This seems unlikely.

No. 72. Hardness

1. Wilhelm translates the hexagram title as Keeping Still; Kunst, 343, as Cleaving.

2. CPL 6/8a.

3. *Analects* 17/3 (Waley, 208).

4. CYYT 51/Shuo/10 (Wilhelm, 275). Cf. *ibid.*, 12/16/2 (Wilhelm, 69; Kunst, 271); 47/Hsi B.4(7) (Wilhelm, 342).

5. FW 6/8b; CWK, p. 216, n. 5; and Paul Serruys prefer to read *ling* 凌 as *ping* 冰 ("ice"), meaning "Firm, though not frozen." The Fathoming repeats this.

6. Following SMK 6/4b. CPL 6/8b reads this as a warning about the need to keep secrets so that no "leaks" occur.

7. Reading *ti* 螮 as the characteristic activity of bees akin to *chih* 滯 ("accumulating"), following Paul Serruys. Most commentators read *ti* as *ti* 蒂, meaning the "stem" or "base" of flowers or fruit.

8. Cf. SY 5:132 for the same argument.

9. HY (*p'ien* 1 and 3) develops this argument (Ku, 63–73; 79–82).

10. For this argument, see HS 4:116 (Dubs, I, 241), an edict of Emperor Wen of Han.

11. Following SMK 6/4b, which reads *tien* 顛 as "the crown of the head."

12. YTC 6/8b reminds us that hills are the "heads" of Earth.

13. To smash one's head against a rocky hill or a tree was a method of suicide in the pre-Ch'in period. See CCYT 139/Hsi 31/3 *Kung*; and *ibid.*, 181/Hsüan 2/4 *Tso* (Legge, 290).

14. Taking *ku* 怙 and *chien* 堅 as two adjectives, though SMK 6/4b–5a understands them as verb-object: "relying on [his] firmness."

15. *Chen* 貞 literally refers to the determination or omen verified by test.
16. Or, "method" or "direction."
17. For further information, see SW 10A:202a and HNT 8/16b.
18. Reading *yi* 蚓 with determinative 142 虫 instead of *yi* 朒, following SMK 6/5b.
19. CYYT 35/<u>56</u>/6 (Wilhelm, 219; Kunst, 351).

No. 73. Completion

1. FW 6/9b reads *hsiao* 消 ("dissolving") instead of *ch'ing* 清. This is followed by YTC 6/9a.
2. Following FW 6/9b.
3. See the commentary by Lu Chi. Its action is so fearsome that in some editions it is now apotheosized for the first time as Great Yin. See Sung Wei-kan and CPL 6/9b.
4. CPL 6/9b.
5. HY 1/1a (Ku, 63).
6. LT, ch. 45 (Lau, 106).
7. CPL 6/9b takes this as a description of yang *ch'i* hidden below the surface of the Earth. It seems that yang has no merit, since all things tend to wither and die at this time of the year. Nevertheless, in the unseen regions yang nurtures the myriad things so that they return to life in the spring.
8. Following YY 33:669, reading *tai* 怠 for *tai* 殆. Serruys prefers to read this line, "Though not yet achieved, it is nearly so." A third possibility advocated by Wang Ya is, "Though not yet achieved, it is perilous."
9. CYYT 45/Hsi B/2 (Wilhelm, 331).
10. Alternately, "The virtue that completes is strong." See CWK, p. 220, n. 5.
11. Serruys prefers, "If [his] centering is complete, . . ." or "If one is fully complete, . . ."
12. The FW edition (6/10b), however, reads *jang* 讓 for *ch'ien* 謙 ("modesty," "self-deprecation"). The meaning comes out much the same.
13. The phrase *k'uei so* 魁瑣 is apparently an alternate way of writing the *wei so* 鬼瑣, as cited in HTYT 15/<u>6</u>/1 (Dubs, 77; Knoblock, I, 222). Cf. *ibid.*, 23/8/88; 68/<u>18</u>/78. Knoblock translates the compound as "conceited and vulgar"; Dubs, as "paltry and insignificant."
14. Tentative translation. Serruys reads instead as, "What Heaven sends down ruins the good omens."
15. Or, "Completion is exhausted."
16. Alternately, "The noble man does not regard [it] as complete."
17. Following SMK 6/5b, which cites CCYT 242/Ch'eng 6/7 *Tso* (Legge, 397).

No. 74. Closure

1. Following SMK 6/6a, which glosses *tieh* 跌 as *kuo shen* 過甚. CPL 6/11a interprets *chiao tieh* 交跌 as "to square off in battle"; CWK, p. 222, n. 2, as *chiao hsiang yi wei* 交相易位 ("in mutual contact exchanging places").
2. CWK, p. 222, n. 2, however, takes this to mean that yin fully appropriates yang, so that there is now only one entity. Either description points to an im-

balance in yin/yang. Cf. THC "Hsüan ts'o" 7/5a (p. 1018), which talks of this tetragram in terms of "closing the two." Also, CYYT 52/*hsü* (Wilhelm, 489–90).

3. FW 6/11b defines *chih* 闔 first as *mi* 密 ("close," "dense," "fine," a reference to *tightly* woven cloth[?], = *chih* 緻), then as *tieh* 闔 ("to close the door"). Wu Mi equates the term with *chih* 窒 ("to block up").

4. Following YTC 6/10b, taking this as a symbol of "no fit." Alternately, "wobbling." FW 6/11b and CWK, p. 222, n. 3, define *wu ni* 杌捏 as *pu an chih mao* 不安之貌 ("unsteady").

5. CYYT 41/Hsi A/6 (Wilhelm, 306).

6. Following Wang Ya. YTC 9/10b reads *hsi* 襲 as *tsang* 藏 ("hides").

7. Reading *lao* 勞 as *fang* 芳, following Wang Ya; SMK 6/6a; CPL 6/11a; and CWK, p. 222, n. 6, rather than FW 6/12a.

8. CYYT 14/21/2 (Wilhelm, 492; Kunst, 281).

9. CWK, p. 222, n. 6, however, assumes that the good man covers his nose to curb his own desires. However, Han Chinese, as opposed to later Buddhists, seldom praised asceticism for its own sake.

10. Suggestion by Nylan.

11. YTC 6/11a also emphasizes the waste engendered by the wrong governmental policies.

12. CYYT 15/21/3 (Wilhelm, 88; Kunst, 281), cited by SMK 6/6a.

13. Taking *hang hang* 吭吭 as an adverb that describes the sound of lapping up liquid, following YTC 6/11a. FW 6/12a assumes that the "sweat" stands for *jun tse to* 潤澤多 ("abundant grace").

14. YTC 6/11a quotes lines by the historian Ssu-ma Ch'ien 司馬遷 (ca. A.D. 100): "To bathe in precious oils./ To sing of hard work."

15. Literally, "[Trying to] tightly fit [together] its (his?) faults-divergences." The metaphor is one of jamming the two sides of the gate together despite their lack of fit. Alternately (?), "shutting the door on his faults" (i.e., ignoring his faults). Or, following FW 6/12b, reading *chih* 闔 as *chih* 緻 (making "fine" or "dense").

16. CPL 6/12a.

17. Following the WJL edition (6/6b).

18. SMK 6/6b and CWK, p. 223, n. 11, however, assume that spring, with its red tips and white sprouts, is prefigured here.

19. FW 6/12b. Cf. YTC 6/11b and CPL 6/12b. There is a probable reference to Chinese alchemy (both chemical and physiological) here. Ko Hung uses cinnabar as one example of metamorphosis, for it is "naturally red" but capable of "whitening" so that it "looks like lead." See PPT 16/2a (Ware, 263), cited in Needham, V(2), 63; for a comparable Western example of the "albification" of cinnabar, see Connell, p. 21. Of interest also are Needham, V(3), 1–50 on "The Origins of Alchemy"; and *ibid.*, V(5), 239 for physiological alchemy. Many early alchemical recipes mention minium (red oxide) and white lead.

20. Pankenier (1990a).

No. 75. Failure

1. Or, following Serruys, "He deeply gives himself the subtle signs." Or, by a pun when *chi* 幾 is read as *chi* 譏, "He deeply criticizes himself." See FW 6/13a.

2. CPL 6/13a reads *mieh* 滅 not as "destroy" but as "submerge." Since Appraisal 1 corresponds to water, if we imitate the limpid and empty qualities of water, the knife blade plunges in without doing harm.

3. Assuming that *ling* 靈 has crept into the text, I have deleted it. Because of *ling*, Sung Chung, Lu Chi, and FW 6/13a read *wei* 微 as *cheng* 徵 ("omen"). YTC 6/12a; CPL 6/13a; CWK, p. 225, n. 4, follow here and in the Fathoming.

4. Or, reading *cheng*, "to fear omens." Literally, "He does not know to fear minute [signs]."

5. SMK 6/6b.

6. Literally, "going to the end." FW 6/13a–13b, however, takes *tsu* 卒 to mean *yu* 憂 ("worried," "at wit's end"?).

7. Following Wang Ya in reading *hsü* 郇 as *yu* 憂 ("to be concerned about").

8. Wang Ya reads *sung* 竦 as *ching* 敬 ("careful"); CWK, p. 225, n. 5, as "self-restrained."

9. Or possibly "practices." See Morohashi 24664. However, as in THC62/A3, YTC 6/12a; CPL 6/13a; and CWK, p. 225, n. 5, read *tsu* 祖 as "source" of the heart; Wang Ya, as "master."

10. Following the FW edition (6/13b) in writing *cheng lu* 正祿 rather than *lu cheng* 祿正. Otherwise, the final line reads, "He loses the right [amount] of income."

11. *Ode* 300/7 (Legge, 629). Cf. "Glosses," p. 184.

12. *Documents*, "Mu shih," par. 5 (Legge, 302; Karlgren, 29).

13. CWK, p. 226, n. 11, reads as, "Change [when nearly] in the coffin" [i.e., at death's door].

14. SMK 6/7a, however, has this describe the dying man who instructs his descendants from his deathbed.

No. 76. Aggravation

1. Alternately, *chieh* 介 means "special," "lacking a mate." See Fang 6/42/24.

2. However, some commentators, including CWK, p. 227, n. 2, say *li* 離 means *tsao* 遭 ("to meet").

3. But FW 6/14b takes *lei* 纍 as *huo* 禍 ("cause disaster").

4. YTC 6/13b and CPL 6/14b read the cognate *shih* 食 instead of *shih* 蝕, however.

5. For parallelism, following the Sung Chung, Sung Wei-kan, and Wang Ya editions in reading the variant *nei shang* 內傷 instead of *shang chih* 傷之 ("recognizes it as harmful"). CWK, p. 228, n. 4, agrees.

6. CCFL 8/30/11b; SY 1/10b; LHCC 14:295 (Forke, I, 119), where he is called King Yen in observance of an Eastern Han taboo; and FSTY 5:41.

7. If *chiang* 將 is read instead of *ch'ih* 持, it means, "He is unable to advance."

8. Ode 165/5 (Legge, 255); *Documents*, "Chiu kao" (Legge, 399–412; Karlgren, 43–46).

9. CPL 6/14b.

10. For *chün* 餕 see LC 12/10 (Legge, I, 453). It usually refers to food leftover after the first repast. It can also refer simply to cooked dishes. See GSR 468x, 436.

11. Tung Yung had lost his mother in childhood, so the poem only mentions his care of his father. For a Han dynasty depiction of the Tung Yung 董永 story, see Wu Hung, pp. 289–91. My translation closely follows p. 291.

12. See *ibid.*, pp. 303–4 for text and illustration.

13. Taking *yü* 與 as "level with"(?). Alternately, it means "and."

14. Reading *ssu* 斯 as the final particle, as in Ode 199/1. See Serruys (n.d.), Part II, on "The Verbs 'to be'. . . ."

15. Literally, "They regard him as home."

16. "Four" deleted by Nylan; "his realm" added by Nylan. This reading, which plays off a different sense of *man* 滿, is based on FW 6/15b, which compares the good ruler to the sea, the home to which all the lesser rivers hasten. Note that YTC 6/14a mistakenly writes *ssu hai* 四海 instead of Four States.

17. The metaphor comes from FW 6/15b.

18. LT, ch. 76 (Lau, 138).

19. Alternately, "Seawater in floods flying."

20. Following FW 6/16a in reading *pi* 敝 instead of *pi* 弊.

21. Or, according to FW 6/16a, ordinary people are so benighted in this age that they "cannot be made to understand. . . ." so that they stop the evil.

22. Also, see HS 26:1305, where comets (symbolized by the birds here?) reach to the Milky Way or the Weaver Girl (2x). For the legend of the Weaver Girl and Oxherd, see Loewe (1979), pp. 112–15. Both occurences portend violence.

No. 77. Compliance

1. Alternately, "harmonizes."

2. Literally, "without endpoints."

3. For the significance of *hun-tun*, see Girardot, p. 25ff.

4. For the association of *yang ch'i* with the square and with "edges," see Powers (1978).

5. Cf. the description of women given throughout de Beauvoir.

6. CYYT 4/2/yen (Wilhelm, 394); According to CYYT 51/Shuo/11 (Wilhelm, 274), "*K'un* means 'motherhood.'"

7. CYYT 3/2/t'uan (Wilhelm, 386).

8. CYYT 3/2/t'uan (Wilhelm, 388).

9. SMK 6/8a takes these as four virtues leading to upright behavior.

10. See CYYT 4/2/6, *yen* (Wilhelm, 395; Kunst, 243).

11. The character *kao* 膏 is the technical term for a "two month old fetus."

12. Serruys prefers, "The woman it burdens."

13. See van Gulik, pp. 132, 147.

14. For a change in the meaning of the term *jen* 仁 in Han times, see Wallacker, p. 221ff.

15. Cf. LT, ch. 6 (Lau, 62).

16. E.g., *Analects* 1/16 (Waley, 87); LT, ch. 22 (Lau, 79); and LT, ch. 24 (Lau, 81).

17. See CYYT 42/Hsi A/7 (Wilhelm, 306).

18. Cf. CYYT 3/2/4 (Wilhelm, 14; Kunst, 243).

19. Another pun, since *huang* 黃 refers also to yellow Earth.

20. Cf. CYYT 3/2/*t'uan* (Wilhelm, 388), and the argumentation of the "Hung fan" chapter of the *Documents*.
21. See Girardot, p. 150ff.
22. CYYT 42/Hsi A/7 (Wilhelm, 307).
23. Or, "on all sides."
24. A very loose translation. See the Appendix for *chen*.
25. The possessive *chüeh* 厥 signifies the Decree of a superior power, be it Heaven or the ruler.
26. Yü Fan 虞翻 commentary on the Images to Oppression (Hexagram 47), as cited in Sivin (1974), p. 52.

No. 78. On the Verge

1. Serruys prefers, "fords" or "crosses the stream." I follow FW 6/18a, which glosses *chi* 濟 as *ch'eng* 成.
2. Alternately, with 4-4-4 scansion, "Yang, extending, is about to return. It begins to go into the lower regions."
3. CYYT 39/64/*hsiang* (Wilhelm, 716).
4. LT, ch. 64 (Lau, 125).
5. The character *sui* 睟 refers to the countenance shining with virtue. See *Mencius* 7A/21 (Lau, 186).
6. Reading this literally as, "Ease on account of this follows." However, Serruys prefers: "Being at ease, it is made a later [worry]," where "it" refers to "attaining full perfection."
7. See the Wang Ya commentary. For differences between the Chinese and Western notions of creation, see Mote (1972).
8. *Ta chüeh* 大爵; however, *chüeh* normally refers to small birds.
9. A well-known anecdote regarding Duke P'ing of Chin (r. 557–532) employs the same imagery to lament the duke's lack of good advisors. See SY 8/1a, 8a.
10. Following several commentators, reading *shih* 失 as *tieh* 昳. Serruys, however, prefers to read it as "fails to be."
11. Cf. CYYT 26/42/*t'uan* (Wilhelm, 597), cited by SY 8/1a.
12. Or, "kicking" (?), since *pa* 跋 is sometimes glossed as *ta* 蹋.
13. Literally, "Their harm is not far away."
14. Cf. SY 8/1a. Following FW 6/19a; SMK 6/9a. However, CWK, p. 235, n. 10, regards this as metaphor for the sage who risks his own life when he hastens to save others.
15. Reading *po* 播 as "to spread out," "to bring forth."
16. FW 6/19a and CPL 6/19a think red silkworms are old. Wang Ya and YTC 6/17b say that diseased silkworms are red.
17. FW 6/19a.
18. YTC 6/17b: "Rotten abilities are placed in a ruinous situation."

No. 79. Difficulties

1. Alternately, *fang* 方 means "just now."
2. Sung Wei-kan commentary.
3. Following FW 6/19b in reading *wei chien hsing* 未見形 ("not yet seen the

form"); also, adding "its." However, most early editions, including Sung Chung and SMK 6/9b, read *chien wei hsing* 見未形 ("One sees that it has not yet taken form.") instead of *wei chien hsing*.

4. YTC 6/18b; CPL 6/19a; and CWK, p. 137, n. 3. FW 6/19b inexplicably takes *wo* 我 to refer to yin *ch'i*.

5. Literally, "Freezing ice from/in ice thaws," preferring the *textus difficilior* preserved in WJL 6/9b, based on early editions. Contrast FW 6/19b; CPL 6/19b.

6. Literally, "misses the wood." Following FW 6/19b in equating *ch'uai* 踹 with *ch'a* 差. Serruys reconstructs the text this way: *Ch'ui* 㯭 (=揣) = *chui* 箠 ("whip"), as CWK, p. 237, n. 4, shows (GSR 168q = 31j). Then *chui* = *ch'a* 𥫱 (GSR 31j = 5f,g). As Serruys points out, in the earliest forms both characters have the same top element 𥝌, apparently signifying "vegetation dropping down" (private communication). Cf. Serruys (1984), p. 699, no. 217. The SW therefore puts both characters in the same phonetic set. See SW 5A:99, 6B:129. Note the different solutions by YTC 6/17b and CPL 6/19b.

7. Alternately, the subject of the poem could be a man, who walks across the melting river of ice and is unable to discipline his horse.

8. Taking *tuan* 殿 as an "immature or infertile fetus" which "rots." See FY 9:27 for this.

9. CWK, p. 237, n. 6.

10. Wang Ya; YTC 6/18a.

11. CWK, p. 237, n. 7, reads *ch'in* 勤 as *ch'in* 廑 ("illness," and so "calamity" in general).

12. The latter reading preferred by FW 6/20a; Wang Ya; YTC 6/18a; and CWK, p. 137, n. 6. The former reading is reflected in the Appraisal translation; the latter, in the Fathoming.

13. This is the *locus classicus* for the reduplicative *ch'uan ch'uan* 川川. See Morohashi 8673.102. FW 6/20b glosses it as *chung ch'ih chih mao* 重遲之貌 ("the appearance of being heavily laden and tardy"). CPL 6/20a, however, thinks the reduplicative indicates a "flood" of carriages.

14. FW 6/20b takes *chen chen* 砼砼 as *nan chih chih mao* 難致之貌 ("difficult to cause to come out").

15. FW 6/20b and YTC 6/18b both read *chin* 盡 instead of *yin* 引. However, SMK 6/10a; CPL 6/20a; and CWK, p. 238, n. 9, prefer *yin*, meaning :"[Though his] strength is sinking, [he] takes it and pulls it [his strength] on." Both versions make sense. Both use the same rhyme. Both have a similar component in the top part of the oracle bone form (𠙴 and 𢎏). Probably the two versions have arisen because the top component of *chin* 盡 in an older form could be mistaken for the older form of *yin*.

16. For the equation of preparing a field for planting with clearing a place of evil, see HS 38:1992; there the phrase "deeply we till" signals the audience that the usurping Lü clan will be executed.

17. Some editions read *hsieh-chieh* 鮭鯱, one variant name for the marvelous animal. For more information on the beast, see THC72/A8.

18. Literally, "one makes the *hsieh-chih* butt with the horn."

19. Or, "In the end, thereby [the *hsieh-chih*] goes straight towards the offen-

ders." SMK 6/10a writes *fan* 犯. All other editions write *shih* 施, referring to those whose conduct is deflected (i.e., criminal). *Shih* is to be preferred since it preserves the rhyme.

No. 80. Laboring

1. Several early editions, however, add *mou* 謀 ("planning"). See SMK 6/ 10a; CWK, p. 238.
2. Serruys prefers, "Laboring [for] those with a sense of obligation."
3. Wang Ya reads *k'ung k'ung* 悾悾 as *k'uan k'uan* 款款 ("tirelessly," "with absolute sincerity"). CWK, p. 240, n. 3, defines it as *ch'eng hsin mao* 誠信貌 ("having integrity and honesty").
4. Literally, "Diligence, he has it in emotion."
5. For this argument, see, e.g., *Analects* 1/6 (Waley, 84), 1/7 (Waley, 84), 1/2 (Waley, 83). CPL 6/21a cites here Ode 155/1 (Legge, 233): "With love and with toil I nourished them."
6. See GSR 58; 37a.
7. See below.
8. This reduplicative suggests a high-pitched and insistent cry.
9. See FW 6/21b; Sung Chung; Wang Ya; and YY 33:669.
10. *Analects* 7/19 (Waley, 127 [renum.]).
11. Following FW 6/21b-22a; Sung Chung; and Lu Chi. Some other editions read *k'uang* 狂 ("crazed") for *wang* 往, however.
12. Cf. CYYT 24/39/1, 3, 4, 6, *hsiang* (Wilhelm, 582; Kunst, 317) for the same phrase. CWK, p. 240, n. 7, however, takes *chien* 艱 as *nan* 難("troubles"), and the reduplicative as "repeated obstacles."
13. YTC 6/19b.
14. Serruys prefers, "It will be defeating," which reads GSR 341a as 341e.
15. See SW 2B/46a, which defines *chi* 踖 as "a long neck walk." CWK, p. 241, n. 10, reads the reduplicative *chi chi* 踖踖 as *min* 敏; *chin k'uai mao* 勤快貌 ("diligent and quick"). Although the reduplicative can also describe "reverent demeanor," Serruys understands it as "with trepidation," taking the root meaning as "trampling." See GSR 798k.
16. *Shuang* 爽 means "clever," "bright," "active," "contented." CWK, p. 141, n. 10, reads *shuang* as *ming* 明 ("bright," "enlightened").
17. *Mencius* 3A/4 (Lau, 102).
18. FY 8:38, loosely translated.

No. 81. Fostering

1. Kunst, p. 293, has the hexagram title translated as "Jaws," however.
2. Literally, *p'eng* 弸; hence, the idea of "full." See CPL 6/22b. Cf. FY 12:37. Its cognate *peng* 崩 also means "to collapse," "to deflate." CWK, p. 242, n. 2, argues that both readings apply here.
3. Literally, "soaks," reading *ou* 蓲 as its cognate *ou* 漚. But Sung Chung reads *ou* 蓲 as *yin* 隱 ("hides"). In that case, yang hides the myriad things to protect them from culminating yin *ch'i*.
4. CYYT 18/27/t'uan (Wilhelm, 521).

5. FW 6/22b and CWK, p. 243, n. 3, define *mei* 美 as *mao* 茂 ("to make flourish").

6. See FY 5:12–13, as cited in YTC 6/20b.

7. Cf. KT 16/49/4a (Rickett [a], 163).

8. YTC 6/21a reads *yüan* 元 as *ta* 大 ("great"), but this seems less likely since this is an early Appraisal.

9. However, CPL 6/23a reads *p'ien p'ien* 扁扁 as *p'ien p'ien* 翩翩, meaning "to wheel around in soaring flight," apparently on the basis of FW 6/23a, which talks of swallows both flying and eating. Cf. MKH, I, 30(3a), where a similar gloss is found. CWK, p. 243, n. 6, follows.

10. Literally, "Their intentions are 'invasive'," following CPL 6/23a, which defines the reduplicative as "like occupying [another's] position." See GSR 778b. Cf. YTC 6/21a, which defines *chüeh* 傻 as "having gotten this, looking [greedily] at that."

11. Literally, "It is advantageous and useful in going on the attack and doing business," meaning the swallows provide a model or formula for such activity. Note the hedge rhyme in GSR 778 and 38b.

12. Following FW 6/23b. Cf. CWK, p. 243, n. 6, citing SW 6B/130b.

13. CPL 6/23a.

14. Since Appraisal 4 is correlated with the bureaucracy, perhaps those at court, like Tzu-shu Yi of old, care only for personal profit. See *Mencius* 4B/10 (Lau, 92), cited by YTC 6/21a: "Though his advice was not followed while in office, this did not prevent him from getting the younger members of his family into high office. . . . He was the only one who had his own 'vantage point' therein."

15. "Even" and "old" are implied in the original.

16. *Fu* 孚 means "to hatch."

17. SMK 6/11b, however, speaks of the myriad things' inability to requite (*pao fu* 報復) such marvelous virtue.

18. Following the *textus difficilior*, on the basis of a parallel in Ode 47/2. A second reading would be: "Rising, he attains," following FW 6/23b, which writes *te* 得 for *te* 德. Cf. CWK, p. 242, n. 7.

19. However, YTC 6/21b and CPL 6/23b read *tz'u tz'u* 次次 as *tzu tzu* 孜孜 ("never wearying"). FW 6/23b reads *tz'u tz'u* as *pu an chih mao* 不安之貌 ("insecure"), which describes the attitude of those offering sacrifice.

20. CPL 6/23b says that although the omen has been taken from a fattened ox, and the sacrificial meats eaten to fatten the participants' bodies, they do not realize that death is near at hand.

21. Following Lu Chi.

22. FW 6/23b. For the association of blood sacrifices with heterodox cults, see Stein (1979).

23. See YTC 6/21b and CWK, p. 244, n. 8, citing CTYT 90/32/47 (Watson, 360).

24. YTC 6/22a assumes that they symbolize the "illness" the gentleman must cure. Cf. Wang Ya.

25. The first characterization comes from SMK 6/11b; the second, from YTC 6/22a.

26. FW 6/24a, however, argues that it is the small boy and the woman who have nothing to do with one another.
27. CPL 6/23b. Cf. YTC 6/22a.
28. This is a popular Han pun.
29. See CWK, p. 244, n. 11.
30. See CWK, p. 245, n. 1.

AUTOCOMMENTARIES

Hsüan ch'ung

1. Note that FW 7/1a speaks of "giving birth to the country of killing."
2. Literally, "to be orphaned."
3. FW 7/1a says, "[because] things are newly born."
4. Following CWK, p. 248, n. 8. However, Serruys reads this as, "[preserves] many old [things]."
5. For one definition of "squareness," see CYYT 4/2/*yen* (Wilhelm, 393); 40/ Hsi A/4 (Wilhelm, 296); 48/Hsi B/7 (Wilhelm, 349). See also Peterson (1982).
6. An allusion to HTYT 108/32/1–2 (not in Dubs).
7. For this concept, see LC 9/1 (Legge, I, 364–65).
8. Reading the character as *jih* 日 not *yüeh* 曰, on the basis of FW 7/1b.
9. As FW 7/1b says, to wait for the right time to move.
10. Or, "Ease is equitable while Watch is biased."
11. However, CWK, p. 251, n. 26, reads *ch'i* 齊 as *chai* 齋 ("stalwartness").
12. Literally, *huai* 懷 ("what is harbored in the breast").
13. Or, "to the countryside."
14. FW 7/2b says, because it marks the Summer Onset solar period.
15. Tentative translation of the verb *chih* 閱 based on FW 7/2a; Hsü Han, cited in WJL, p. 1006b. However, CWK, p. 222, n. 1; p. 252, n. 35, reads as "join with." Since the tetragram is aligned with the hexagram "Biting through," one is tempted to read the meaning of "cut through" here.

Hsüan ts'o

1. Or, "revolves."
2. According to Hsü Han, this refers to timeliness and things.
3. Literally, "variegated."
4. FW 7/3b says, "seeing difficulty, to recoil."
5. Cf. Ode 114/2 (Legge, 175) for a comparable use of this reduplicative.
6. See the Hsü Han commentary, cited in WJL, p. 1017a.
7. According to FW 7/3b, "of things as they shed their dried husks."
8. For this meaning of *hsieh hang* 頡頏, see Ode 28/2 (Legge, 43). See Karlgren (1964), p. 109, n. 71.
9. Or, "no [preferred] direction."
10. Or, "no duality."
11. Tentative translation of *chieh ho erh* 皆合二. FW 7/4a takes it to mean, "All join the two [where 'two' refers to yin and yang *ch'i*]."
12. YY 33:670 reads *ch'eng* 成 as *hsien* 咸.
13. FW 7/4b takes this to mean "parsimonious," however.

Hsüan li

1. FW 7/5a glosses this *li* 攡 (the same character appears in the title) as *chang* 張 ("to expand"). The character is also related to *li* 離 (GSR 24), meaning "to be dispersed." My translation attempts to capture both meanings.

2. Literally, "categories."

3. Literally, "takes as stuff and fashions." YTC 7/3b says "gives birth to and nourishes."

4. Following FW 7/5a, which clearly assumes a reference to the primeval chaos. CPL 7/2b takes *hsü wu* 虛無 as a compound synonymous with *t'ai chi* 太極. YTC 7/3b says simply that this refers to Heaven.

5. Or, it "gives birth to what is round" [i.e., the sun]," following FW 7/5a. Sivin prefers, "[the things] are produced by its compass." Serruys prefers, "comes to life in the [Heaven-given] nature."

6. FW 7/5a, however, glosses *mo* 摹 as *shu* 數 ("numbers" or "calculations").

7. FW 7/5b takes "the severing" as the separation of pure yin from pure yang, and the "joining" as the admixture of yin and yang. CPL 7/2b follows.

8. The heavens move toward the left while the sun moves toward the right. They meet in their circuits at the Winter Solstice.

9. I am grateful to Paul Serruys for differentiating *chung shih* 終始 from *shih chung* 始終. According to FW 7/5b, this means, "None are tardy or hasty, nor do they stray from their orbits." CPL 7/2b follows.

10. Cf. CYYT 40/Hsi A/3 (Wilhelm, 294). For further information, see Peterson (1982). Serruys prefers "natural tendency" for *ch'ing* 情.

11. CPL 7/3a says that the sage seeks his origins in human nature so as to predict individual fate.

12. Heaven-Earth-Man, according to FW 7/6a; YTC 7/4b; and CWK, p. 267, n. 12; the sun, moon, and [other] heavenly bodies, according to CPL 7/3a. I follow FW.

13. FW 7/6a says this refers to yin and yang respectively, since yin is corporeal and "muddy" while yang is ethereal and "pure." CPL 7/3a believes the phrase "thick and thin" refers to the relative endowments given to different things by Heaven. If the endowment is "thick," man is born; if "thin," then a thing.

14. See CYYT 29/47/6 (Wilhelm, 184) for the definition of *wu nieh* 杌楗. Cf. YTC 7/4b.

15. This may also refer to the fact that yin is associated with harvesting, rather than dispensing. FW 7/6a cites CYYT 51/Shuo/11 (Wilhelm, 275) in support.

16. Tentative translation, based on certain passages where the binome *yü chou* 宇宙 unambiguously refers to spaces and times (e.g., HNT 11:178). Sivin comments that he "does not feel at ease interpreting *yü-chou* as two abstractions that can be identified with modern—or even Aristotelian—continua." He prefers "spaces" and "times" as translation "to keep them concrete" (private communication). However, Serruys thinks *yü chou* here describes the upper and lower worlds, with reference to the Kai-t'ien astronomical theory, which has Heaven like a huge domed vault perched on the flat plate of Earth. In that case, the passage says, "For this reason, what encloses Heaven, it we call the 'side eaves.'

What opens but from the 'side eaves,' it we call the 'canopy' [i.e., the vaulted dome of the heavens]."

17.   However, FW 7/6b reads *so* 索 as *shu* 數 ("numbers").

18.   Or, "omens."

19.   "The heavens and the sun cross paths" refers clearly to the angle (roughly 23°) between the equator, parallel to which the stars move, and the ecliptic, on which the sun move. I am indebted to Sivin (private communication) for this information.

20.   FW 7/7a reads *liu* 樛 ("to tie round") as *jao* 擾. He then takes "death and life" to refer to the moon's waxing and waning.

21.   Or, are "incessantly" produced. CWK, p. 269, n. 22, reads *ch'an* 纏 as *ch'an mien pu chüeh* 纏綿不絕, following FW 7/7a. CPL 7/5a attributes the unceasing production of the myriad things to the slight disjunction between the annual cycles of the heavens and the sun.

22.   Literally, "what All-under-Heaven has united."

23.   Including "benighted" members of the human race.

24.   Or, "renders mysterious."

25.   Literally, "makes a secret of that by which it is what it is." Compare the language of LT, ch. 34 (Lau, 93).

26.   Note how beautifully Yang Hsiung puns on the antonymic cognates *miao* 渺 and *miao* 眇.

27.   Translation tentative. Alternately, "bringing into full play." See CWK, p. 271, n. 31.

28.   CPL 7/4a takes "it" to mean "the phrasing [of the *Mystery*]."

29.   Following FW 7/8a. CWK, p. 271, n. 32, however, reads *chi* 稽 as *chih* 至 ("come to").

30.   Tentative translation of *k'uang ch'i fou che hu* 況其否者乎, based on YTC 7/6a and CPL 7/4b, who say, "It has never been the case that those who did not seek [the Mystery] were responded to." Hsü Han says, "How much more unlikely would it be the case [that there is a response] for those who do not do [this]?" (See WJL, p. 1019a.) Serruys follows. FW 7/8a, however, reads it as, "How much less would it be the case with what is not the Mystery?"

31.   The language is taken from HTYT 73/19/63 (Dubs, 306).

32.   FW 7/8a reads *wang* 忘 ("to forget"). All other editions follow, except CWK, p. 262, which mistakenly prints *wang* 亡.

33.   Taking *chien* 兼 as *chien ai* 兼愛. Serruys prefers, "to embracingly take control."

34.   I.e., fate.

35.   Hsü Han, however, reads *hsü hsing* 虛形 as *hsü wu hsing* 虛無形 ("empty and without form"). See WJL, p.1019b. FW 7/8b follows.

36.   Tentative translation. My translation of these terms is based on THC "Hsüan ying" 7/9a (p. 1022a).

37.   Tentative translation. CWK, p. 272, n. 46, reads this as *chih li yang yü* 治理養育 ("to order and to nourish").

38.   Note the typical Han confusion of "graded" and "ungraded" love (*jen* 仁 and *ai* 愛). See Wallacker.

39. Loose translation of the phrase *lieh ti* 列敵. The matches could presumably be made in society at large (for example, a man of talent "matches" a government post) and in categorical thinking. FW 7/9a apparently takes it in the latter sense.

40. CPL 7/5a takes "fitting" to refer to "proper timing."

41. CWK, p. 273, n. 50, argues that the character *chih* 知 ("to know") means *chu* 主 ("to be master of").

42. Or "dangerous."

43. Following the usage for *tang* 盪 in CYYT 39/Hsi A/1(3) (Wilhelm, 283). However, FW 7/9b reads *tang* as *cho* 濯 ("to wash"); Serruys reads it as "to spread."

44. Literally, "comparatively [or, 'measurably'] manifest." FW 7/9b adds *tzu* 子 here.

45. See GSR 833z, for the related meanings of "settles," "quiets," and "finishes."

46. YY 33:670 reads *t'i* 提 as *t'i* 題, meaning "to make clear." CWK, p. 273, n. 55, follows. For the whole passage, cf. LT, ch. 77 (Lau, 139).

47. YTC 7/8a says that "it" in each case refers to the Mystery.

48. YTC 7/8a reads *t'o jan* 他然 as *lung hou mao* 隆厚貌 ("amplitude"); FW 7/10b reads it as *t'ai jan* 泰然 ("greatness"). CWK, p. 274, n. 60, agrees with FW. CPL 7/6a, however, reads it as *t'o jan* 妥然 ("securely").

49. Most commentators take *shen* and *ming* to refer to the gods of Heaven and Earth respectively, and by extension, to yin and yang *ch'i*. See CPL 7/6a, for example.

50. That is, Heaven-Earth-Man, the triadic realms. However, an unnamed commentator to THC-SB 7/10a assumes that Yang refers here to LT, ch. 42 (Lau, 103).

51. FW 7/10b equates *pei* 輩 with *lei* 類 (category).

52. That is, the nine Appraisals. See FW 7/10b.

53. Literally, so "there are no hard corners."

54. These are constellations of the eastern and western quadrants of the sky.

55. These are constellations of the southern and northern quadrants of the sky.

56. Literally, "make them revolve" [in the mind or with astronomical instruments].

57. The 'Seven Regulators' refers to the sun, moon, and five planets. For the original use of this term, see *Documents*, "Yao tien," par. 16 (Legge, 33; Karlgren, 4). The Jasper Template and Jade Level (see below) also figure in the same passage of the "Yao tien."

58. Tentative translation. FW 7/10b reads *chi* 極 as *chung* 中 ("center"), meaning the circumpolar stars. CWK, p. 275, n. 64, agrees.

59. This phrase can refer to either the Polestar or the Calendar that was begun in 104 B.C. For further information, see Loewe (1974), pp. 17–36. The Han Chinese did not distinguish between true north and the Polestar.

60. Literally, "push through."

61. By Han times, scholars were confused about the exact nature of the *hsüan chi*. Some believed it to be an astronomical sighting tube; others, an armil-

lary sphere. For a modern solution, see Needham, III, 334 ff.; Ho Peng-yoke, pp. 59–66. Both the Jasper Template and the Jade Level (see below) also refer to certain stars in the Northern Dipper constellation. FW 7/11a takes both terms to refer to these stars, but it is unclear whether Yang Hsiung refers to certain stars in the night sky or to physical instruments used on earth in astronomical calculations.

62. If this refers to an astronomical instrument, it may be some kind of jade transverse tube.

63. The FW edition mistakenly reads *jen* 人 ("human") for *ju* 入.

64. Cf. CYYT 39/Hsi A/1 (Wilhelm, 280).

65. Or, "continue without end," following FW 7/11b. See above.

66. Note the two synonymous binomes here. The two syllables in the second binome share the same initial, final, and tone.

67. Literally, "the end thread that [can] not be drawn out." In other words, with the help of tools like the *Mystery* we move from seeing visible images to comprehending the underlying patterns of existence.

68. And so know them intimately as part of a single system.

69. From the summer solstice to the end of the year, because at the summer solstice the sun is in the Eastern Well, a southern constellation.

70. FW 7/13a says, "the cold burns old grasses."

71. From the winter solstice on. At the winter solstice, the sun is in the Oxherd, a northern constellation.

72. See Neely.

73. YTC 7/11a says that at the winter solstice the Dipper (now below the horizon) starts to travel from the east, whereas at the summer solstice the Dipper (now directly overhead in the sky) starts its return from the west.

74. According to FW 7/13b, this refers to the gods of Heaven-and-Earth.

75. CWK, p. 279, n. 85, however, says simply, "conjoin."

Hsüan ying

1. Taking *k'ai* 開 "to set free" (GSR 541a) or "to separate" (Morohashi 41233); and *p'i* 闢 as "to cleave" (GSR 853k = 853p). Serruys would read this, "opened up [i.e., begin to exist]." FW 7/13b, however, reads *ho* 闔 ("closed") instead of *k'ai* 開 in his commentary. For the philosophical implications of *ho*, see Broschat, pp. 131–33.

2. See THC "Hsüan li," footnote 16 for the compound *yü chou* 宇宙.

3. YTC 7/11b glosses *shih* 祐 as *k'ai* 開 ("open out"); CPL 7/8a follows. However, CWK, p. 283, n. 2 (apparently on the basis of FW 7/13a), glosses *shih* 祐 as *t'o* 拓, which he then defines as *kuang* 廣. It is possible, however, that *shih* 祐 refers to *t'o* 橐 ("sack," "bag," "bellows"), a reference to the bulging shape of Heaven's vault.

4. Midnight is considered the origin of day. The first day of the lunar month is the origin of the month. The winter solstice is the origin of the lunar year. The *chia tzu* 甲子 year is the origin of the sixty-year cycle.

5. The "span" is equal to 8 Han inches, while the "pace" is equal to 6 Han feet. See Loewe (1961). According to CWK, pp. 283–84, n. 3, Yang Hsiung refers to measurements by the gnomon. Serruys prefers to read the sentence,

"Heaven originated the span and pace [measurements]." The WJL edition (p. 1021a) moves the character *pu* 步 several lines down.

6. FW 7/13b reads *hun* 渾 as *yun* 運.

7. Translation tentative. FW 7/14a defines *p'in shu* 品庶 as *wu lei* 物類 ("categories of things").

8. Within the nine Appraisals, nos. 1–3, 4–6, and 7–9 make up the three Tables.

9. That is, the nine Appraisals in each tetragram.

10. FW 7/14a, however, defines *kua lo* 絓羅 as *liu li* 流離 ("flow into [one another]").

11. That is, whatever clues exist to the handling of things (*tuan hsü* 耑緒). The phrase *ch'ou hsü* 抽緒 also occurs in THC "Hsüan li" 7/7a (p. 1020a). However, FW 7/14b takes *ch'ou hsü* to mean *shou ch'i yeh* 收其業 ("settle up their work"). In that case, one "separates out [individual] tasks."

12. CWK, p. 285, n. 10, however, says, "which are interwoven."

13. Following CWK, p. 286, n. 12, in reading *ching* 靜 as *ting* 定. According to CWK, this says that their activity becomes predictable once calendars are established.

14. Each 30-odd degrees of the full sky. This could also refer to the twelve Earthly Branches.

15. For this phrase, see *Documents*, "Yao tien," par. 16 (Legge, 33; Karlgren, 4).

16. For this definition of *chen* 振, see GSR 455p.

17. See *Documents*, "Hung fan," par. 4 (Legge, 324; Karlgren, 30).

18. FW 7/l5a reads *yü* 榆 as *hsieh* 寫 (= 瀉).

19. For further information, see Bodde (1959).

20. Taking *chi* 濟 as "legion." See GSR 593o. Otherwise, the binome *chi min* 濟民 refers to "saving the common people."

21. Literally, "flowing."

22. However, CWK, p. 287, n. 19, reads *chien* 間 as *p'ei* 配 ("companions"), perhaps implying "alternates." For more on the music system, see THC "Hsüan shu," footnote 18.

23. This refers to the correlations of the twelve pitchpipes with the twelve months of the calendar.

24. Following Han cosmological accounts in taking *wu* 無 to mean *wu hsing* 無形, rather than absolute nothingness.

25. FW 7/16b reads *yü* 灊 as *shu* 恕 ("reciprocating," "compassionate"). He then goes on to say that they showed no emotions of any kind. My translation reads *t'ing* 霆, following CWK, p. 287, n. 22.

26. This statement, of course, agrees with the Taoist account of antiquity. As we shall see, however, Yang Hsiung soon goes on to disparage this stress-free society. Many passages in the FY and THC show the noble person "worrying." E.g., FY 6:18 says that the sage worries when his attempts at persuasion are not in accord with the Way, though he does not worry about what he cannot change (another's reception of his persuasions); THC11/A3, A7 show apprehensions leading to reform. Since LT, ch. 20 (Lau, 76) clearly ties the "extermination of

learning" to "having no worries," Yang Hsiung cannot describe the true sage as "unworried."

27. This could mean both that one drills to get at the essential substance [i.e., wisdom] of the turtle and that one bores into one's own soul to find essential answers.

28. FW 7/16b defines *ch'ien* 箝 as *ch'iu* 求. CWK, p. 287, n. 23, agrees. It is conceivable that *ch'ien* is a misprint for *hsiang* 箱, which should be read as *hsiang* 相 (GSR 731f as 731a), so that it means "taken together."

29. For *ching* 精, Serruys prefers, "intuitive sense." Basically, *ching* refers to the "quintessential," as in other passages.

30. More literally, "When single-minded concentration uses the bone cracks and milfoil, the spirits push for their changes. When single-minded concentration uses thought and deliberation. . ."

31. Literally, "its having what it follows." FW 7/17a quotes *Analects* 7/1 (Waley, 123), where Confucius says of himself that he "transmits but does not create on his own."

32. An attempt to capture the range of associations (including "undifferentiated" and "complete") for the cosmogonic term *hün* 渾.

33. Following FW 7/17b in reading *ch'üeh* 攫 as *ch'ü* 去. Otherwise, *ch'üeh* means "to seize." See GSR 778b. However, THC-SB 7/17a reads *chü* 懼 ("to be worried about").

34. Literally, "the trunk." Serruys would translate this as "capacity."

35. Reading *ch'ung* 崇 as "the whole." See GSR 1003h. FW 7/17b apparently takes it as a synonym for *chung* 終 ("the end").

36. Literally, "not spread around."

37. Or, "natural tendencies." FW 7/18a says, "If there were no patterns, there would be no way to see the essentials. If there were no phrasings, there would be no way to see actual conditions."

38. Literally, "has what adheres [or continues] and what complies [or conforms]."

39. The definition of the four key terms used in this paragraph is tentative. The commentators provide little help. FW 7/18a says, "*Yin* 因 is "when there are grasses that do not die in winter." *Hsün* 循 is "roots growing into a tree." *Ko* 革 is "burning or weeding out old grasses." *Hua* 化 is "falcons being metamorphosed into pigeons." However, YTC 7/16b says that *yin* means "being based on what exists from old"; *hsün* means "following their completed laws"; *ke* means "changing what is old or flawed about them"; and *hua* means "changing their old habits." For a discussion of similar problems translating comparable terms found in the "Great Commentary" to the *Changes*, see Sivin (1977) and Sivin (1990). In the second paper (p. 10), Sivin concludes that *yin* and *hsün* are adaptive change, that *ko* is change of something into its categorical opposite, and that *hua* is change that affects identity. Roth, p. 92, similarly translates *yin* as "adaptation."

40. Or, "we regard them as divine."

41. Or, "we regard them as fitting." Quite possibly, since *shen* 神 refers to Heaven, and *yi* 宜 refers to the god of the soil (i.e., Earth), we have here a more pointed reference to what is pleasing to the gods of Heaven-and-Earth.

42. Or, "reason."

43. Literally, "are synonymous with the efficacy of success and failure."

44. See the "Introduction" for Yang Hsiung's theory of human nature. As FW 7/19a writes, "[Man] receives them from Heaven; they cannot be changed."

45. See the minor change in wording proposed by YY 33:671.

46. A tentative translation. See THC 16/A4.

47. This description recalls the commentary to Hexagram 11 ("T'ai"): "Inside (referring to the lower trigram), it is yang and outside (referring to the upper trigram), it is yin; inside it is strong and outside it is compliant." This situation reflects the perfection that derives from balance. See CYYT 9/11/*t'uan* (Wilhelm, 441).

48. Or, "he can use being lower [than] others."

49. Or, "assist."

Hsüan shu

1. Such terms as *chüeh*, *kung*, and *shang* designate movable notes comparable to *do*, *re*, *mi*, etc. as used in the Anglo-American choral music tradition. For further information, see von Falkenhausen (forthcoming), p. 208ff.

2. For the duties and applications, see *Documents*, "Hung fan," par. 6 (Legge, 326–27; Karlgren, 30).

3. See KT 9/13b (not in Maverick or Rickett).

4. Taking *yi* 誼 as *yi* 義, on the basis of many Han puns.

5. Deleting the phrase *ta to* 大哆 on the basis of YY 33:671, who cites FW.

6. Alternately, "troops."

7. Or, with radical 9 instead of 149, "usurpation."

8. Or, "writing."

9. Or tall.

10. Deleting the phrase *wei li* 為禮 ("It is ritual."), because of repetition.

11. Literally, the "essence."

12. FW 8/11a; YTC 8/6b; and CWK, p. 320, n. 199, tie this to "planting" crops.

13. Or, according to FW 8/11a, "boundary walls."

14. That is, affairs having to do with women.

15. Or, with radical 75 instead of 93, "outer coffins."

16. These may be thought of as the names of tonalities. In the pre-Han period, there were various ways to indicate this system of pitch standards. Yang Hsiung adopts the nomenclature similar to that favored in the *Chou li*.

17. Falkenhausen (forthcoming), p. 212 ff., shows that the nomenclature and significance of the titles for the pitch standards varied over time. Therefore, I translate only the name of the important Huang-chung pitch standard. For all of these, see Pian also.

18. The implications of this are as follows: The six male pitches (also known as the Six Beginnings) join the six female pitch standards (also called the Six Intermediaries) in a single musical system covering the range of one octave. The six female pitches, as their alternate name implies, occupy the positions in between the six male pitch standards. Yang Hsiung refers to the "Subtracting or Adding a Third Method," a formula to generate a full set of tones in certain intervallic rela-

tions to one another (comparable to the famous Spiral of Fifths in Western musical theory). By this method, the entire series of twelve notes can be generated from the Yellow Bell pitch by a process of alternate subtraction and addition of a musical third (in Chinese terminology, producing a "superior" or "inferior" generation).

19. See, however, CWK, p. 327, n. 250.

20. Presumably because it releases Water, the patron phase aligned with no. 1.

21. Here I summarize the Chinese text, which ranks both siblings and bureaucratic scales from lower/lower to higher/higher in nine grades.

22. Literally, "compass-like planning."

23. Tentative translation. FW 8/17a says *tzu ju* 自如 means that "[the thoughts] have not yet been carried out [into action]." YTC 8/11a says it means, "already decided." CWK, p. 328, n. 256, agrees. Serruys says the phrase means, "to be true to oneself."

Hsüan wen

1. Translation tentative. CWK, p. 334, n. 4, defines *chih* 直 as *shen* 伸 ("expansion") on the basis of a passage from the *Mencius*. FW 9/1a equates it with its cognate *chih* 殖 ("to plant," "to flourish").

2. These five mantic formulae are treated as counterparts to four found in the *Changes*: *yüan* 元, *heng* 亨, *li* 利, and *chen* 貞. For further information on the Four Qualities, see Shchutskii, pp. 136–56.

3. See CWK, p. 334, n. 5, on this.

4. Literally, the white undyed stuff on which colors and patterns will be placed.

5. See GSR 1224g. CWK, p. 334, n. 14, however, defines *ch'u* 觸 as "to encounter."

6. A reference to CYYT 42/Hsi A/8 (Wilhelm, 313), where the phrase *ch'u lei* 觸類 is usually interpreted as "following [*ts'ung* 從] its own type" or "moving [*tung* 動] its own type." FW 9/2a equates this with "being born."

7. Reading *chiu* 就 instead of *ch'in* 親, following FW 9/2a. Cf. WJL, p. 1028a.

8. The last six sentences are omitted in THC-SB 9/2a.

9. Following FW 9/2b in taking this as an exclamation.

10. CWK, p. 337, n. 25, takes *po* 脯 as *fu* 脯 ("dried flesh," signifying great favor) on the basis of Hsü Han's 許翰 commentary in WJL 9/1a (p. 1028a).

11. Alternately, "Lasting to the end, it makes them hidden [or profound]."

12. Reading *t'i* 體 instead of *li* 禮, since *li* is seldom used as a verb. Otherwise, the phrase means, "to pay ritual courtesy [to] the divine."

13. Literally, "to conceal [himself] and shut [himself off from the world]. My reading follows FW 9/3a, which says of the noble man, "modeling himself on the hidden, he acts." Note that these actions correspond to the annual round of the seasons.

14. Or, "I answer, ..."

15. Literally, is "mixed."

16. Proverb based on CYYT 2/1/*yen* (Wilhelm, 382).

17. Literally, "initiating" or "creating" (*tso* 作).
18. This signifies that the horse is ready and of valuable stock.
19. Or simply, "in prosperity."
20. Or, "make grow."
21. There are 3 "Tables" in each Appraisal: the first, composed of App. 1–3; the second, of App. 4–6; and the third, composed of App. 7–9.
22. Tentative translation. *Chüeh* 絕 could also mean "cut off." See GSR 296a.
23. THC "Hsüan wen" 9/2a (p. 1029a), following FW 9/6b in interpretation.
24. Literally, "patterned and enlightened."
25. Through true understanding, to see the limits of both.
26. Or, "he plumbs the very meaning of conditions."
27. Or, "would make his soul approach [a perfection] with the ghosts and ghosts."
28. Cf. the language of FY 5:13.
29. That is, whatever "goes against" his good fortune.

Hsüan yi

1. Material in brackets supplied by FW 9/8a. I use FW, rather than WJL, as the basic edition.
2. Translation tentative. FW 9/8a takes *wei* 䐑 (=*wei* 委) to mean something like the "ins and outs" of affairs.
3. A loose translation for *tsao* 藻, as in *Analects* 5/17.
4. Cf. *Documents*, "Chiu kao," par. 2 (Legge, 399; Karlgren, 43).
5. This sentence may be garbled. For further information, see CWK, p. 349, n. 17.
6. In other contexts, *ni* 擬 means "to measure" or "estimate." Here, however, as in Yang Hsiung's biography and Chang Heng's assessment of Yang Hsiung, the verb is clearly used in another sense: "to make like," "to imitate." Cf. HS 87A:3515 (Knechtges, 13); HHS 59:1897.
7. Or, the warp of a cloth.
8. Following FW 9/9b in glossing *hao huang* 耗荒 as *k'ung hsü* 空虛, which might be rendered, "empty and formless" or "empty and barren." According to FW, this means they are not bound to place or form. Cf. YTC 9/7b. Serruys takes *hao huang* to mean, "reduced [in form] and scattered." There is a possible pun here since *hao huang* conceivably hints also at their vast age (=*mao huang* 耄荒) (See Morohashi 28909.8; CWTT 29550.13) and the "expending and wasting" of resources in sacrificial offerings.
9. Literally, "no direction." In other words, they can operate anywhere.
10. Serruys reads *chi* 祭 as *chi* 際: "Bordering them there are no rules."
11. *Documents*, "Hung fan," par. 5 (Legge, 326; Karlgren, 30).
12. For symmetry, Yang Hsiung here adds the phrase "and five."
13. For further information, see Hulsewé (1955), p. 103ff.
14. Cf. *Documents*, "Yao tien," par. 35 (Legge, 48 [par. renum.]; Karlgren, 7).
15. For this expression, which refers to the directional winds, see LC 19/3 (Legge, II, 93); CCYT 13/Yin 5/5 Tso (Legge, 19).

16. Literally, "do not dislike are another." Alternately, "do not become sated with one another" or "do not wound each other." *Yi* 射 gives a visual pun: the body is shot with an arrow, symbol of the penis.

17. Or, "Man acts as man; thing acts as thing."

18. SW 2A/34a defines *tse* 嘖 as *ta hu* 大呼. Therefore, the emendation suggested by CWK, p. 354, n. 46, is unnecessary.

19. Serruys prefers, "flaps and gathers [wings]."

20. Cf. the Ting Kuan 丁寬 commentary (Han) to the *Changes*, cited in MKH, I, 43(6a).

21. Presumably, because all the distinct potentials are evenly distributed among various living things, with no one thing monopolizing all of them. See FW 9/11b.

22. This is a proverb. See HTYT 12/5/32 (Dubs, 74; Knoblock, I, 207); HY 1A/4a (Ku, 74).

23. Possibly a reference to the Heavenly gods and Earthly spirits?

24. Or possibly on the sundial.

25. For this definition, see THC "Hsüan ying" 7/8a (p. 1021a).

26. Literally, "divinely enwombs [all]." Punctuating differently after *pao* 胞, in contrast to WJL or CWK (p. 346), which apparently read this as the "Heaven-and-Earth acts as the divine womb [gestating] norms and change." (However, CWK, p. 355, n. 54, somewhat contradicts this.) The change in punctuation provides a slightly better rhythmic scansion.

27. An apparent allusion to CYYT 39/Hsi A/1 (Wilhelm, 286), which associates "being easy" and "being longlasting." Cf. CYYT 41/Hsi A/5: "Being good at making it easy and simple matches that of the highest potent virtue." For more on this, see Peterson (1982), 91–94. However, Kao Huai-min, p. 283ff. proposes a different understanding for the CYYT passage. Note also that YTC 9/9b translates *fa yi* 法易 as "laws [or, norms] change."

28. See the "Hsüan wen" autocommentary for more on these five terms.

29. Literally, "get its rectification."

30. Literally, "there will be no [other, better] choice."

31. However, Serruys translates *kai* 該 as "arrange."

Hsüan t'u

1. Serruys reads *tu* 都 as *fan* 凡 ("generally," "altogether"); he would translate it as "to bring together," "to cluster."

2. Literally, "are carried [like a vehicle] to."

3. A synonym for tetragrams.

4. Literally, the bull's eye. Otherwise, the sentence must mean something like, "As a rule in darkness one orients oneself by the Northern Dipper," glossing *chih* 質 as *cheng* 正, following FW 10/1b; and CWK, p. 360, n. 4.

5. Just as the planets never travel outside the band of the zodiacal constellations, sun and moon have a band of the sky in which they appear to travel.

6. Following FW 10/1b.

7. Following FW 10/1b, reading *t'ui li* 推歷 instead of *li wei* 歷微. FW, however, reads the phrase as "plan to calculate the course of the stars."

8. Meaning the sequential order of the stems and branches used to indicate

the period, the day, and the cyclical year.

9. My translation refers to SW 12A/246b, where *k'ung* 孔 is glossed as *t'ung* 通. However, FW 10/2a understands this to mean, they are "extremely subtle [tools]." Possibly the phrase is a punning reference to the holes that pierce the pitchpipes. See below.

10. Reading *tsai* 哉 as *tsai* 在 (GSR 943v = 943i).

11. These correspond to a period of four months, from the 11th to the 2d months, according to the Han civil calendar.

12. TTLC 5/71/1b.

13. Following FW 10/2a.

14. CWK, p. 362, n. 10, glosses *tsan* 贊 as *chu* 助 ("to lend assistance"), after FW 10/2a, which glosses it as *tso* 佐. *Tsan* could also conceivably refer to the Appraisals of the THC.

15. CWK, p. 361, n. 10, equates the Origin with yang *ch'i*.

16. This refers both to yang *ch'i* and to a constellation in the eastern sky. Serruys prefers, "The east stirs the Green Dragon."

17. CWK, p. 362, n. 12, seems to read *yü* 輿 as *yü* 與. There is a vague graphic allusion to the astronomical theory by which the cosmos is compared to a carriage.

18. These correspond to the next four months (months 3–6) in the Han civil calendar.

19. Serruys prefers, "symbolize Heaven's renewing the light."

20. That is, yin is roused to germinate by the culmination of yang *ch'i*.

21. By yang *ch'i* to the southern regions. Contrast CYYT 28/46/*t'uan* (Wilhelm, 620).

22. These correspond to the last four months of the lunar year (months 7–10).

23. FW 10/3a defines the Heaven's Root as the winter solstice and the first degree of the Oxherd constellation.

24. See GSR 324p. FW 10/3a defines *yueh* 閱 as *chien* 簡, meaning "to inspect" or "to examine" by boring into.

25. FW 10/3a says this is the epithet for the tenth month. As yellow stands for the center, it may simply refer to the pure yang now hidden below the earth's surface. See YTC 9/12a; CPL 10/3a; CWK, p. 364, n. 22.

26. The Great Handle refers to the handle of the Polestar.

27. FW 10/3b supplies the "like" (*ju* 如). YTC 9/12a follows. For the expression, "clouds scudding," see CYYT 1/1/*t'uan* (Wilhelm, 370). The material in bracket supplies the Han association for the image.

28. Literally, "treats as domain." However, FW 10/3b reads *tien* 甸 as *t'ing* 挺 ("to straighten") while CWK, p. 365, n. 26, reads *tien* as *tien* 奠 (=*chih* 置), meaning "to position."

29. Following FW 10/4a, rather than the usual definition of *shen ming* 神明 in terms of "spirits of Heaven and Earth," since the THC often uses *shen ling* 神靈 in that sense.

30. Following the earliest editions in reading "one" rather than "two." FW 10/4a, for example, reads, "Heaven has a single way." YTC 9/13a follows. Cf.

THC-SB 10/3b. If there are two ways, they are presumably yin and yang (= Heaven and Earth), based on CYYT 40/Hsi A/4 (Wilhelm, 301): "A single yin and a single yang constitute the Way. What continues it is goodness; what completes it is the [moral] nature." CWK, p. 266, n. 32, however takes the two paths to refer to primal oneness and multiplicity. Cf. WJL, p. 1032b; CPL 10/2b.

31.　Here "three" stands for the entire multiplicity of things" in the triadic realms of Heaven-Earth-Man while "one" refers to the primeval Tao.

32.　Actually, each Course corresponds to 40 and 1/2 days. Yang Hsiung has rounded off.

33.　Serruys prefers "makes [it] preserved unto the Center."

34.　Literally, "being dispensed." See CYYT 1/1/*t'uan* (Wilhelm, 620).

35.　*Documents*, "Hung fan," par. 33 (Legge, 343; Karlgren, 35): "the achievement of a [naturally] ended life").

36.　See FW 10/6b for a slightly different explanation for this.

37.　Reading *k'ang* 亢 instead of *yüan* 元, following the WJL edition.

38.　Following YTC 9/15b; CPL 10/4a; CWK, p. 371, n. 71.

39.　This may refer to the Appraisals, which are grouped by twos according to direction, with numbers one and six aligned with the north, numbers two and seven aligned with the south, and so on. See FW 10/8a; CWK, p. 372, n. 73.

40.　In the 729 Appraisals assigned to 81 tetragrams there are 365 yang lines and 364 yin lines.

41.　The identification of these four is disputed. FW 10/8b equates the compass with Heaven; the square with Earth; the line with north-south; and the level with east-west. See the following sentence. CWK, p. 373, n. 77, equates them with Positions 3 and 8; 4 and 9; 2 and 7; and 1 and 6 respectively.

42.　Literally, "attained and examined."

43.　Literally, "has the numbers six and nine." Presumably Yang refers to the fact that 36 stalks are used in the divination process. 36 is composed of multiples of 6 and 9.

44.　This may refer to the two principles of Heaven and Earth, following CYYT 43/Hsi A/10–11 (Wilhelm, 308), where the number 2 is assigned to Earth and 9 is assigned to Heaven. However, FW 10/8b reads *yi* 儀 as *cheng* 正 ("to straighten").

45.　CWK, p. 274, n. 81, says this equals 729, the number of Appraisals, but that figure is disputed immediately below.

46.　One commentator suggests that each move sketched here corresponds to a passage of 1,539 years in the Grand Inception calendar.

47.　See Sivin (1969) for the various concordance cycles.

Hsüan kao

1.　I take *shen hsiang* 神象 as a compound phrase, based on FW 10/10a. CWK, p. 378, n. 2, however, argues that the "divine" refers to Heaven and yang, while the "imaged" (i.e, what has form) refers to Earth and yin. FW 10/10a identifies the two as Heaven and Earth. More likely they are yin and yang. As CYYT 42/Hsi A/8 (Wilhelm, 310) says, "Change has the Great Ultimate; this gives birth to two forms."

2. Or, "spherical [heavens]," according to certain commentators.

3. Represented by three different kinds of lines: the unbroken, once-broken, and twice-broken respectively.

4. The nine Appraisals attached to each tetragram that mirror the nine empyrean realms.

5. Reading *yü* 欲 as *ho* 合, following FW 10/10b.

6. CPL 10/7a, based on FW, takes this to mean that Appraisals 1 and 6 are to some extent parallel, as are 2 and 7, 3 and 8, and 4 and 9.

7. Where "lesser" indicates yin *ch'i* or the even-numbered Appraisals, while "greater" indicates yang and the odd-numbered Appraisals.

8. Reading *ao* 奧 as *ao ts'ang* 奧藏, on the basis of FW 10/11a.

9. Literally, "is what keeps pent up the transforming essence." The following three sentences are identifical in structure. Note that the northwest is said to be the direction of pure yin.

10. See THC 1/A1.

11. Tentative translation, taking GSR 458b = 458d. Serruys prefers, "Heaven turning gives a sign."

12. FW 10/11b reads *t'ui* 隤 as *an* 安, on the basis of CYYT 45/Hsi B/1(3).

13. FW 10/11b takes *kuei* 劌 as *hui* 會 (literally, to have a conjunction). YTC 9/19a takes as "to cut [each other]" because eclipses conceal part of either the sun or moon.

14. That is, the light material rises to the top, while the heavy sinks.

15. The daily course of the moon is 13 degrees, while the sun only moves 1 degree per day.

16. However, CWK, p. 381, n. 14, prefers to read *wang* 王 as *wang* 旺 ("to shine"), so the phrase would mean, "The Five Phases shine in turn."

17. Antares, part of the Heart constellation aligned with winter.

18. Meaning, the relative positions of the constellations are clear indicators of the seasons.

19. According to CPL 10/8a, this means the revolutions of the sun, moon, and visible planets take place in those directions.

20. The Five Phases in the Mutual Production Cycle. For further information, see Needham, II, 253ff.

21. The Five Phases in the Mutual Conquest Cycle. For further information, see *ibid*.

22. For similar language, see CCYT 1/Yin 1/*Kung* 1 (Malmqvist, 68).

23. Since neither the sun nor the Dipper wax and wane in appearance.

24. Literally, "empty" of constancy. For this translation, see CPL 10/8a. Cf. YTC 9/20a.

25. Alternately, the sentence could be read as, "The constant and the full are used to order the Positions," where *hsü* 虛 (as above) refers to the nine Appraisals, following the *Changes* usage.

26. However, CPL 10/8a reads *ning hsi* 甯悉 as *wu yu* 無憂 ("without worry"), meaning it "causes no worry" in calculating it.

27. That is, it disperses.

28. That is, it gathers in.

29. Shao Yung 邵雍 took "abundance and deficiency" to refer to more or less light in the course of the day. See CWK, p. 383, n. 23.

30. This binome *ch'iao chü* 僑躆 is only found in the *Mystery*. For its meaning, I follow FW 10/13a.

31. One complete revolution of the sun passes through slightly more than 1 degree of the sky. See FW 10/13a.

32. Yang Hsiung talks specifically of the first and last day of the lunar month.

33. Following WJL 10/4b (p. 1035b). SW 7A/141b defines *t'iao* 朓 as the moon appearing in the west on the last day of the lunar month; *niu* 朒 as the moon appearing in the east on the first day of the lunar month.

34. The term *ts'e ni* 側匿 means "to lose the regular course." This can refer to retrograde motions, to irregularities in speed, and so on.

35. The terms "male and female" are used to describe the longer and shorter months by the solar calendar, according to CPL 10/8b. However, FW 10/13b says the male is the sun and the female, the moon.

36. Literally, "in regard to whatever has no end." Or, for the "unending [processes]."

37. Reading *lun* 綸 as *kang* 綱, following CPL 10/8b.

38. For a definition of this, see the essay entitled "Evolution of the Mystery."

39. Reading *hun hun* 魂魂 as "many in appearance" (*chung to mao* 衆多貌). CPL 10/9a takes *hun hun* as *hun tun wu chih mao* 渾沌無知貌 ("confused, unknowing").

40. Following FW 10/14a. This refers to the fact that all things wane. However, CPL 10/9a reads *ch'ung* 沖 as "to crash against." He takes the sentence to mean that lucky men meet with good luck, while unlucky men meet with bad luck.

41. Literally, "Near and far, without constancy, by category proceed; sometimes many, sometimes few, affairs are accomodated to what is clear."

42. Tentative translation. See *Documents*, "T'ai shih," par. 3 (not in Karlgren; Legge, 627): "The days and months pass away." CWK, p. 384, n. 32, contradicts CPL 20/9b.

43. See GSR 720n'; 1124g. However, see FW 10/14b.

44. However, CWK, p. 384, n. 32, reads *erh t'ao* 遒陶 as *yi yü* 益育 ("increase the nurture").

45. Literally, "are not exhausted." Note than the binome *shen ming* can refer to the spirits of Heaven and earth as well. See THC "Hsuan t'u," footnote 27.

46. Here Yang Hsiung suggests that it is far less difficult to judge human conduct than it is to define the logically prior phenomenal patterns upon which these societal patterns are based.

Bibliography of Works Cited

Note: Most references to works in Chinese are cited in the following manner: *chüan* no., *p'ien* no. (if given), page no. Use of the slash (/) indicates Chinese-style pagination. Use of the colon indicates Western-style pagination. In the case of six of the thirteen Confucian Classics with standard paragraphing, I refer to chapter and verse or to paragraph number. For the transliteration of Chinese characters, references are generally given in Wade-Giles unless another romanization is used on the title page of the work cited.

Primary sources are indicated by their titles. In most cases, acronyms for part or all of the title have been adopted. In a few cases where the acronym might prove confusing, reference is made to the first character(s) of the title. Citation to an index follows the chosen format of the index.

Secondary sources are cited by author. Unless there are two or more Western authors with the same family name, I have listed authors of works in Western languages only by surname in the Bibliography. For authors of works in Chinese or Japanese, I give both family and personal name in the "main heading" (indicated by capital letters). In the case of authors who have more than one work cited, I indicate a specific work by the main heading and date of publication.

Translations are cited by author. Where multiple translations exist for the same Chinese work, I refer the reader to the translation(s) I consider most readily available. In the case of translations from the Chinese, I indicate the translator(s) and the appropriate page(s) in parentheses after the book title. Readers of classical Chinese will find that I have often modified the translations cited.

PRIMARY SOURCES AND COLLECTANEA

Analects (*Lun yü* 論語).
Documents (*Shu ching* 書經).
Filial = *Canon of Filial Piety* (*Hsiao ching* 孝經).
"Learning" = "The Great Learning" ("Ta hsüeh" 大學).
"Mean" = "Doctrine of the Mean" ("Chung yung" 中庸).
Mencius (*Meng tzu* 孟子).
Odes (*Shih ching* 詩經).

***

BSS: *Basic Sinological Series* (Taipei, 1968) (=*Kuo hsüeh chi pen ts'ung shu* 國學基本叢書), 400 vols.
CCCS: Tung Chung-shu 董仲舒, *Ch'un Ch'iu chüeh shih* 春秋決事, in MKH, II, 1180–81.
CCFL: Tung Chung-shu (?) 董仲舒, *Ch'un Ch'iu fan lu* 春秋繁露 (SPPY).
CCYT: *Ch'un Ch'iu ching chuan yin te* 春秋經傳引得 (Peiping, 1937) (HYISIS no. 11).
CES: *Centre franco-chinois d'études sinologiques de Pekin Series.*

CFL: Wang Fu 王符, *Ch'ien fu lun* 潛夫論, main commentary by Wang Chi-p'ei 王繼培 (Shanghai, 1978).

Chin: Fang Hsüan-ling 房玄齡, *Chin shu* 晉書 (Beijing, 1974), 10 vols.

CIS: *Chōshū isho shūsei* 重修緯書集成, ed. by Yasui Kōzan 安居香山 and Naka-mura Shōhachi 中村璋八 (Tokyo, 1971–), 6 vols.

CKT: *Chan kuo ts'e* 戰國策 (BSS no. 381).

CKTH: *Chung kuo tzu hsüeh ming chu chi ch'eng* 中國子學名著集成 (Taipei, 1977), 100 vols.

CL: *Chou li* 周禮, commentary by Cheng Hsüan 鄭玄 (SPPY), 2 vols.

CPL: Ch'en Pen-li 陳本禮, *T'ai hsüan ch'an mi* 太玄闡秘, in *Chü hsüeh hsüan ts'ung shu* 聚學軒叢書, comp. by Liu Shih-heng 劉世珩, XXI (Kuei-ch'ih, between 1875–1908; rpt., Taipei, 1970).

CTYT: *Chuang tzu yin te* 莊子引得 (Peiping, 1947) (HYISIS Supplement no. 20).

CTYL: Chu Hsi 朱熹, *Chu tzu yü lei* 朱子語類 (n.p., 1668; rpt., Kyoto, 1973).

CWK: *T'ai hsüan chiao shih* 太玄校釋, comp. by Cheng Wan-keng (Zheng Wangeng) 鄭萬耕 (Beijing, 1989).

CWTT: *Chung wen ta t'zu tien* 中文大辭典, ed. by Chang Ch'i-yün 張其昀 (Yang-ming-shan, 1973).

CYC: Su Hsün 蘇洵, *Chia yu chi* 嘉祐集 (BSS no. 292).

CYCY: *Chou yi cheng yi* 周易正義, commentary by Wang Pi 王弼, subcommen-tary by Han K'ang-po 韓康伯, in *Shih san ching chu shu* 十三經注疏, ed. by Juan Yüan 阮元 (n.p., 1816; rpt., Taipei, 1971–72), I.

CYYT: *Chou yi yin te* 周易引得 (Peiping, 1935) (HYISIS Supplement no. 10).

ESWSPP: *Erh shih wu shih pu pien* 二十五史補編 (Beijing, 1956), 6 vols.

Fang: *Fang yen chiao chien fu t'ung chien* 方言校箋附通檢 (Beijing, 1951) (CES no. 14).

FSTY: *Feng su t'ung yi fu t'ung chien* 風俗通義附通檢 (Peiping, 1943) (CES no. 3).

FSTYCC: *Feng su t'ung yi chiao chu* 風俗通義校注, commentary by Wang Li-ch'i 王利器 (Beijing, 1981), 2 vols.

FW: Yang Hsiung 揚雄, *T'ai hsüan ching* 太玄經, commentary by Fan Wang 范望 (CKTH no. 37).

FY: Yang Hsiung 揚雄, *Fa yen* 法言, commentary by Li Kuei 李軌, in HPCTCC, II.

GSR: Bernhard Karlgren, *Grammata Serica Recensa*, rpt. from *Bulletin of the Museum of Far Eastern Antiquities* 29 (1957).

HCY: Wei Hung 衛宏, *Han chiu yi* 漢舊儀, in *Han kuan liu chung* 漢官六種, comp. by Sun Hsing-yen 孫星衍 (SPPY).

HFT: *Han Fei tzu chi chieh* 韓非子集釋, comp. by Wang Hsien-shen 王先慎 (Changsha, 1896; rpt., Taipei, 1962), 2 vols.

HHS: Fan Yeh 范曄, *Hou Han shu* 後漢書 (Beijing, 1965), 6 vols.

HNT: *Huai nan tzu* 淮南子 (SPPY).

HPCTCC: *(Hsin pien) Chu tzu chi ch'eng* 新編諸子集成 (Shanghai, 1935; rpt., Taipei, 1978), 8 vols.

HS: Pan Ku 班固, *Han shu* 漢書, main commentary by Yen Shih-ku 顏師古 (Beijing, 1962 ed. primarily based upon the 1900 ed. of Wang Hsien-ch'ien's 王先謙 *Han shu pu chu* 漢書補注), 8 vols.

HsinS: Chia Yi 賈誼, *Hsin shu* 新書 (SPPY).

Bibliography of Works Cited

HSWC: Han Ying 韓嬰, *Han shih wai chuan* 韓詩外傳 (SPTK *so pen* no. 4).

HTYT: *Hsün tzu yin te* 荀子引得 (Beijing, 1950) (HYISIS Supplement no. 22).

HY: Lu Chia 陸賈, *Hsin yü* 新語 (SPPY).

HYISIS: *Harvard Yenching Institute Sinological Index Series.*

HYKC: Ch'ang Ch'ü 常璩, *Hua yang kuo chih* 華陽國志 (BSS no. 396).

KCTSCC: *Ku chin t'u shu chi ch'eng* 古今圖書集成, ed. by Ch'en Meng-lei 陳夢雷 (Shanghai, 1934; rpt., Taipei, 1964), 101 vols.

KKT: *Kuei ku tzu* 鬼谷子, commentary by T'ao Hung-ching 陶弘景 (SPPY).

KSP: *Ku shih pien* 古史辨, ed. by Ku Chieh-kang 顧頡剛, Lo Ken-tse 羅根澤, *et al.* (Peiping, 1926–37), 6 vols.

KT: *Kuan tzu* 管子 (SPPY)

KTCY: *K'ung tzu chia yü* 孔子家語 (SPPY).

Kung: Kung-yang Kao 公羊高 *Kung yang chu shu chi pu cheng* 公羊注疏及補正, commentary by Ho Hsiu 何休, subcommentary by Hsü Yen 徐彦, in *Shih san ching chu shu pu cheng* 十三經注疏補正 (Peking, 1816; rpt., Taipei, 1970).

KY: *Kuang yün* 廣韻 (n.p., 1704; rpt., Taipei, 1961).

KYSH: *Kuang yün sheng hsi* 廣韻聲系, ed. by Shen Chien-shih 沈兼士 (Beijing, 1960).

LC: *Li chi* 禮記, commentary by Cheng Hsüan 鄭玄 (SPPY), 2 vols.

LHCC: Wang Ch'ung 王充, *Lun heng chi chieh* 論衡集解, ed. by Liu P'an-sui 劉盼遂 (n.p., 1932; rpt., Beijing, 1967), 2 vols.

LSCC: *Lü shih ch'un ch'iu* 呂氏春秋 (SPPY).

LT: *Lao tzu* 老子 (SPPY).

MH: Meng Hsi 孟喜, *Chou yi Meng shih chang chü* 周易孟氏章句, in MKH, I, 59–73.

MKH: *Yü han shan fang chi yi shu* 玉函山房輯佚書, comp. by Ma Kuo-han 馬國翰 (Tsinan, 1871; rpt., Taipei, 1967), 6 vols.

MTYT: *Mo tzu yin te* 墨子引得 (Tokyo, 1961) (HYISIS Supplement no. 21).

PHT: *Po hu t'ung te lun* 白虎通德論, ed. by Pan Ku 班固 (BSS no. 68).

PPT: *Pao p'u tzu* 抱樸子, in *Tao tsang* 道藏, *ts'e* 1171–73.

Report A: *Yün meng Shui hu ti Ch'in mu* 雲夢睡虎地秦墓 (Beijing, 1981).

Report B: *Ch'ang sha Ma wang tui yi hao Han mu* 馬沙馬王堆一號漢墓 (Beijing, 1978).

Report C: Cheng Ch'iu-po (Zheng Qiubo) 鄭球柏, *Chou yi chiao shih* 周易校釋 (Changsha, 1987).

SC: Ssu-ma Ch'ien 司馬遷, *Shih chi* 史記 (Beijing, 1959), 10 vols.

Shih: *Mao Shih* 毛詩 (SPTK *so pen* no. 1).

Shinjigen: *(Kadokawa) Shinjigen* (角川) 新字源, ed. by Ogawa Tamaki 小川環, Nishida Taiichiro 西田太一郎, and Akatsuka Kiyoshi 赤塚忠 (Tokyo, 1968).

SKC: Ch'en Shou 陳壽, *San kuo chih* 三國志 (Beijing, 1959), 5 vols.

SKCS: *Ssu k'u ch'üan shu tsung mu ti yao* 四庫全書總目提要, comp. by Chi Yün 紀昀 (Peking, 1782; rpt., Peiping, 1934), 4 vols.

SKTYpc: *Ssu k'u t'i yao pien cheng* 四庫全書辨證, comp. by Yü Chia-hsi 余嘉錫 (Taipei, 1965), 2 vols.

SMK: Yang Hsiung 揚雄, *T'ai hsüan ching* 太玄經, commentary by Ssu-ma Kuang 司馬光, in WJL, IV.

SPPY: *Ssu pu pei yao* 四部備要 (Shanghai, 1927–35), 1372 *ts'e* 冊.

SPTK: *Ssu pu ts'ung k'an* 四部叢刊 (Shanghai, 1920 22), 2100 *ts'e* 冊.

SPTK *so pen*: *Ssu pu ts'ung k'an ch'u pien so pen* 四部叢刊初編縮本 (Shanghai, 1936; rpt., Taipei, 1967, with text reduced in size), 110 vols.

SS: Shen Yüeh 沈約, *Sung shu* 宋書 (Beijing, 1974), 8 vols.

SSCS: *Ssu shu chi chu* 四書集注, comp. by Chu Hsi 朱熹 (n.p., n.d.; rpt., Taipei, 1974).

ST: *The Shen Tzu Fragments*—see Thompson.

STTH: *San ts'ai t'u hui* 三才圖會, comp. by Wang Ch'i 王圻 and Wang Ssu-yi 王思義 (Huai-yin, 1609; rpt., Taipei, 1970), 6 vols.

SunT: *Sun tzu (ping fa)* 孫子(兵法) (SPPY).

SW: Hsü Shen 許慎, *Shuo wen chieh tzu fu chien tzu* 說文解字附檢字 (Hong Kong, 1966).

SY: Liu Hsiang 劉向, *Shuo yüan* 說苑 (SPPY).

SYJ: Sun Yi-jang 孫詒讓, *Cha yi* 札迻 (n.p., 1895; rpt., Taipei, 1964) [with *Cha p'u* 札朴, *Tung shu tu shu chi* 東塾讀書記].

THC: *T'ai hsüan ching* 太玄經, in WJL edition.

THC-SB: *T'ai hsüan ching* 太玄經, comp. by Chao Ju-yüan 趙汝原 (Wu-lin, 1626) [in the Rare Books Collection of Gest Library, Princeton University].

TPYL: *T'ai p'ing yü lan* 太平御覽, comp. by Li Fang 李昉 (Shanghai, 1935; rpt., Taipei, 1959), 12 vols.

TTLC: *Ta Tai Li chi* 大戴禮記 (SPTK *so pen* no. 4).

WCYY: Hsü Shen 許慎, *Wu ching yi yi* 五經異義; and Cheng Hsüan 鄭玄, *Po wu ching yi yi* 駁五經異義, in *Ts'ung shu chi ch'eng chien pien* 叢書集成簡編, ed. by Wang Yün-wu 王雲五 (Taipei, 1966), C.

WJL: *T'ai hsüan* 太玄, commentary by Ssu-ma Kuang 司馬光 and others, in *Chu tzu chi p'ing* 諸子集評, ed. by Wu Ju-lun 吳汝綸 (n.p., 1909; rpt., Taipei, 1970), IV.

WSTK: *Wei shu t'ung k'ao* 偽書通考, comp. by Chang Hsin-ch'eng 張心澂 (Shanghai, 1954), 2 vols.

YKC: *Ch'üan shang ku San tai Ch'in Han San kuo Liu ch'ao wen* 全上古三代秦漢三國六朝文, comp. by Yen K'o- chün 嚴可均 (Hupei, 1894; rpt., Taipei, 1963), 9 vols.

Yi-wen: *Hsin chiao Han shu Yi wen chih, Hsin chiao Sui shu ching chi chih* 新校漢書藝文志, 新校隋書經籍志, ed. by Yang Chia-lo 楊家駱 (Taipei, 1963).

YL: Chiao Yen-shou 焦延壽, *Yi lin* 易林 (SPPY).

YTC: Yeh Tzu-ch'i 葉子奇, *T'ai hsüan pen chih* 太玄本旨 (CKTH no. 92).

YTL: Huan K'uan 桓寬, *Yen t'ieh lun* 鹽鐵論 (SPPY).

YWLC: *Yi wen lei chü* 藝文類聚, ed. by Ou-yang Hsün 歐陽詢 (Shanghai, 1965), 2 vols.

YY: Yü Yüeh 俞樾, *Chu tzu p'ing yi* 諸子平議 (n.p., 1870; rpt., Beijing, 1954).

SECONDARY SOURCES

AESOP:

Aesop's Fables (New York, 1947), with illus. by Fritz Kredel.

Bibliography of Works Cited

AHERN:
Emily M. Ahern, *Chinese Ritual and Politics* (Cambridge, 1981).

ALLAN:
Sarah Allan
(1981): *The Heir and the Sage: Dynastic Legend in Early China* (San Francisco, 1981).
(1991): *The Shape of the Turtle: Myth, Art, and Cosmos in Early China* (Albany, 1991).

AMES:
Roger T. Ames
(1983): *The Art of Rulership: A Study in Ancient Chinese Political Thought* (Honolulu, 1983).
(1987): See Hall.

BAUER:
Wolfgang Bauer, *China and the Search for Happiness: Recurring Themes in Four Thousand Years of Chinese Cultural History*, trans. by Michael Shaw (New York, 1976).

BEAUVOIR:
Simone de Beauvoir, *The Second Sex*, trans. and ed. by H. M. Parshley (New York, 1974).

BERGER:
Patricia Berger, "Purity and Pollution in Han Art," *Archives of Asian Art* 36 (1983), 40–58.

BIELENSTEIN:
Hans Bielenstein
(1954): "The Restoration of the Han Dynasty, Part I," *Bulletin of the Museum of Far Eastern Antiquities* 26 (1954), 1-209.
(1980): *The Bureaucracy of Han Times* (Cambridge, 1980).

BIRDWHISTELL:
Anne D. Birdwhistell, *Transition to Neo-Confucianism: Shao Yung on Knowledge and Symbols of Reality* (Stanford, 1989).

BODDE:
Derk Bodde
(1938): *China's First Unifier: A Study of the Ch'in Dynasty as Seen in the Life of Li Ssu (280?-208 B.C.)* (Leiden, 1938).
(1959): "The Chinese Cosmic Magic Known as 'Watching the Ethers,'" in *Studia Serica Bernhard Karlgren Dedicata*, ed. by Soren Egerod and Else Glahn (Cophenhagen, 1959), pp. 14–35.
(1975): *Festivals in Classical China: New Year and Other Annual Observances During the Han Dynasty, 206 B.C.–A.D. 220* (Princeton, 1975).
(1978): "Marshes in *Mencius* and Elsewhere: A Lexicographical Note," in *Ancient China: Studies in Early Civilization*, ed. by David T. Roy and Tsuen-hsuin Tsien (Hong Kong, 1978), pp. 157–66.
(1981): "Basic Concepts of Chinese Law: The Genesis and Evolution of Legal Thought in Traditional China," in *Essays on Chinese Civilization*, ed. and

intro. by Charles Le Blanc and Dorothy Borer (Princeton, 1981), pp. 171–94.

BOLTZ:
William G. Boltz, "Evocations of the Moon, Excitations of the Sea," *Journal of the American Oriental Society* 106:1 (Jan.–March, 1986), 23–32.

BOODBERG:
Peter A. Boodberg, *Selected Works of Peter A. Boodberg*, comp. by Alvin P. Cohen (Berkeley, 1979).

BROSCHAT:
Michael Robert Broschat, "'Guiguzi': A Textual Study and Translation" (Ph.D. dissertation, University of Washington, 1985).

BROWN, C.
Carolyn T. Brown, ed., *Psycho-Sinology: the Universe of Dreams in Chinese Culture* (Lanham, Md., 1988).

BROWN, H:
Hanbury Brown, *Man and the Stars* (Oxford, 1978).

BULLING:
Anneliese Bulling, *The Decoration of Mirrors of the Han Period: A Chronology* (Ascona, Switzerland, 1960).

CAMMANN:
Schuyler Cammann, "Chinese Mirrors and Chinese Civilization," *Archaeology* 2:3 (Sept., 1949), 114–20.

CHAN:
Wing-tsit Chan, "Yang Hsiung," in *A Source Book in Chinese Philosophy* (Princeton, 1963), pp. 289–90.

CHANG:
Kwang-chih Chang
(1977a): *Food in Chinese Culture: Anthropological and Historical Perspectives*, ed. by K.C. Chang (New Haven, 1977).
(1977b): *The Archaeology of Ancient China*, 3d ed. (New Haven, 1977).

CHENG:
Cheng Chung-ying, "On Timeliness (*shih-chung*) in the *Analects* and the *I ching*: An Inquiry into the Philosophical Relationship between Confucius and the *I ching*," in *Proceedings of the International Conference on Sinology: Section on Thought and Philosophy* (*Chung yang yen chiu yüan, Kuo chi Han hsüeh hui yi lun wen chi: Wen hsüeh che hsüeh tsu*) 中共研究院國際漢學會議論文集, 文學哲學組 (Taipei, 1981), pp. 277–338.

CHIN CH'UN-FENG 金春峰:
Han tai ssu hsiang shih 漢代思想史 (Beijing, 1987).

CHRISTOPHER:
Thomas Christopher, *In Search of Lost Roses* (New York, 1989).

CHOW:
Fang Chow, "Han Dynasty Musicians and Instruments," *Journal of the American Musical Instrument Society*, 1 (1975), 113–25.

Bibliography of Works Cited

CHU HSI 朱熹:

Lun yü chi chu pu cheng shu shu 論語集注補正述疏, commentary by Chu Hsi, subcommentary by Chien Ch'ao-liang 簡朝亮, in *Shih ssu ching hsin shu* 十四經新疏, ed. by Yang Chia-lo 楊家駱 (Taipei, 1961).

CH'Ü WAN-LI 屈萬里:

Hsien Ch'in Han Wei Yi li shu p'ing 先秦漢魏易例述評 (Taipei, 1981).

CLARK:

Stephen R. L. Clark, *The Mysteries of Religion : An Introduction to Philosphy through Religion* (Oxford, 1986).

CONNELL:

Evan S. Connell, *The Alchymist's Journal* (San Francisco, 1991).

CONNOLLY:

Hermeneutics versus Science? Three German Views: Wolfgang Stegmüller, Hans-George Gadamer, and Ernst Konrad Specht, ed. by John M. Connolly and Thomas Keutner (Notre Dame, 1988).

COUVREUR:

F. S. Couvreur, S. J.

(1916): *Cheu king (Shih ching)*, 2d ed. (Hsien-hsien, 1916).

(1947): *Dictionnaire classique de la langue chinoise*, comp. by F. S. Couvreur, S. J. (Ho kien fu, 1911; rpt., Peiping, 1947).

CREEL:

Herrlee Glessner Creel, *Shen Pu-hai: A Chinese Political Philosopher of the Fourth Century B.C.* (Chicago, 1974).

CUA:

Antonio S. Cua, "Dimensions of *li* (propriety): Reflections on an Aspect of Hsün Tzu's Ethics," *Philosophy East and West* 29:4 (Oct., 1979), 373–394.

DE CRESPIGNY:

Rafe de Crespigny, "The Recruitment System of the Imperial Bureaucracy of Later Han," *Chung chi Journal* 6 (Nov., 1966), 67–78.

DETIENNE:

Marcel Detienne, "Culinary Practices and the Spirit of Sacrifice," in *The Cuisine of Sacrifice among the Greeks*, ed. by Marcel Detienne and Jean-Pierre Vernant, trans. by Paula Wissing (Chicago, 1989), pp. 1–20.

DEWOSKIN:

Kenneth DeWoskin

(1982): *A Song for One or Two: Music and the Concept of Art in Early China* (Ann Arbor, 1982).

(1983): *Doctors, Diviners, and Magicians of Ancient China: Biographies of Fang-shih* (New York, 1983).

DOBSON:

W. A. C. H. Dobson

(1968): "Some Legal Instruments in Ancient China: the *ming* and the *meng*," in *Wen-lin: Studies in the Chinese Humanities*, ed. by Chow Tse-tsung (Madison, 1968), pp. 269–82.

(1974): *A Dictionary of the Chinese Particles* (Toronto, 1974).

Bibliography of Works Cited

DOERINGER:
Franklin M. Doeringer, "The Gate in the Circle: A Paradigmatic Symbol in Early Chinese Cosmology," *Philosophy East and West* 32:3 (July, 1982), 309–24.

DONOGHUE:
D. Donoghue: "The Flight of Gerard Manley Hopkins," *New York Review of Books* 38:13 (June 18, 1991), 14–18.

DUBY:
Georges Duby and Phillippe Braunstein, "The Emergence of the Individual," in *A History of Private Life*, ed. by Phillippe Ariès and Georges Duby, trans. by Arthur Goldhammer, 2 vols. to date (Cambridge, Mass., 1988), II, 507–630.

DUHEM:
Pierre Maurice Marie Duhem, *Medieval Cosmology: Theories of Infinity, Place, Time, Void, and the Plurality of Worlds*, ed. and trans. by Roger Ariew (Chicago, 1985).

DURRANT:
Stephen Durrant, "Sima Qian's Confucius: A Discussion of *Shiji*, Chapter 47" (unpublished paper).

ELIADE:
Mircea Eliade, *A History of Religious Ideas*, trans. by Willard R. Trask (Chicago, 1978).

ENO:
Robert Eno, *The Confucian Creation of Heaven: Philosophy and the Defense of Ritual Mastery* (Albany, 1990).

FALKENHAUSEN:
Lothar von Falkenhausen (1989): "Shikin no onsei" 四金の音聲, *Sen'oku Hakkokan kiyō* 泉屋博古館紀要 6 (1989), 3–26.
(forthcoming): *Suspended Music: The Chime-Bells of the Chinese Bronze Age: Rites, Technology, and Political Matrix*, University of California at Berkeley Press.

FERRIS:
Timothy Ferris, *Coming of Age in the Milky Way* (New York, 1988).

FINGARETTE:
Herbert Fingarette, *Confucius: The Secular as Sacred* (New York, 1972).

FISHER:
Fred Fisher, "The Yellow Bell of China and the Endless Search," *Music Educators Journal* 59:8 (April, 1973), 3–33; 95–8.

FORKE:
Alfred Forke, *Geschichte der mittelalterlichen chinesischen Philosophie* (Hamburg, 1934).

FORSTER:
E. M. Forster, *Howards End* (London, 1910; rpt., New York, 1985).

FRANKE:
Wolfgang Franke, *China and the West*, trans. by R. A. Wilson (Oxford, 1967).

FRASER:

J. T. Fraser, *Time, The Familiar Stranger* (Amherst, 1987).

FU SSU-NIEN 傅斯年:

"Hsing ming ku shun pien cheng" 性命古訓辨證, in *Fu Meng-chen hsien sheng chi* 傅孟真先生集 (Taipei, 1952), III.

GEERTZ:

Clifford Geertz, "Centers, Kings, and Charisma: Reflections on the Symbolics of Power," in *Local Knowledge: Further Essays in Interpretive Anthropology* (New York, 1983), pp. 121–46 (ch. 6).

GIRARDOT:

N. J. Girardot, *Myth and Meaning in Early Taoism: The Theme of Chaos (huntun)* (Berkeley, 1983).

GOODRICH:

Chauncey S. Goodrich, "Some Ritual Privileges in Early Imperial China," *Journal of the American Oriental Society* 111:2 (April–June, 1991), 277–82.

GRAHAM:

A. C. Graham

(1967): "The Background of the Mencian Theory of Human Nature," *Tsing Hua Journal of Chinese Studies*, n.s. 6:1–2 (Dec., 1967), 215–74.

(1970): "Chuang tzu's Essay 'On Seeing Things as Equal'," *History of Religion* 9:2-3 (Nov.–Feb., 1969–70), 137–59.

(1978): *Later Mohist Logic, Ethics and Science* (London, 1978).

(1981): See Translations Cited.

(1989): *Disputers of the Tao: Philosophical Argument in Ancient China* (La Salle, Ill., 1989).

GRANET:

Marcel Granet, *Fêtes et chansons anciennes de la Chine* (Paris, 1929).

GULIK:

Robert Hans van Gulik, *Sexual Life in Ancient China: A Preliminary Survey of Chinese Sex and Society from ca. 1500 B.C. till 1644 A.D.* (Leiden, 1961).

HALL:

David L. Hall and Roger T. Ames, *Thinking through Confucius* (Albany, 1987).

HARPER:

Donald Harper

(1978): "The Han Cosmic Board (*shih*), *Early China* 4 (1978), 1–10.

(1987): "The Sexual Arts of Ancient China as Described in a Manuscript of the Second Century B.C.," *Harvard Journal of Asiatic Studies* 47:2 (1987), 539–93.

HART:

James A. Hart, "The Speech of Prince Chin: A Study of Early Chinese Cosmology," in Rosemont (1984), pp. 35–65.

HATTON:

Russell Hatton, "A Comparison of *ch'i* and Prime Matter," *Philosophy East and West* 32:2 (April, 1982), 159–75.

Bibliography of Works Cited

HAWKES:
David Hawkes, *Ch'u Tz'u: The Songs of the South: An Ancient Chinese Anthology* (Boston, 1959).

HENDERSON:
John B. Henderson, *Scripture, Canon, and Commentary: A Comparison of Confucian and Western Exegesis* (Princeton, 1991).

HENTZE:
Carl Hentze with Chewon Kim, "Göttergestalten in der ältesten chinesischen Schrift," in their *Ko- und Chi-waffen in China und in Amerika* (Antwerp, 1943), pp. 19–54.

HIGHTOWER:
James R. Hightower, "Review of Alfred Hoffmann, *Die Lieder des Li Yü (937–978); Frülingsblüten und Herbstmond.* Koln: Greven Verlag, 1950," *Harvard Journal of Asiatic Studies* 15 (1952), 204–13.

HO:
Ho Peng-yoke, *The Astronomical Chapters of the Chin shu, with amendments, full translation and annotations* (Paris, 1966).

HO YEN 何晏:
Lun yü 論語, comp. and annot. by Ho Yen (SPPY).

HOU WAI-LU 侯外廬:
Chung kuo ssu hsiang t'ung shih 中國思想通史 (Beijing, 1957–63), 5 vols.

HOWARD:
Jeffrey A. Howard, "Concepts of Comprehensiveness and Historical Change in the *Huai nan tzu*," in Rosemont (1984), pp. 119–31.

HSIAO:
Harry Hsin-i Hsiao, *Filial Piety in Ancient China* (Ph.D. dissertation, Harvard University, 1978).

HSIAO HAN 曉菡:
"Changsha Ma-wang-tui Han mu po shu kai shu 長沙馬王堆漢墓帛書概述, *Wen wu* 文物 9 (1974), 40–44.

HSIAO KUNG-CH'UAN:
A History of Chinese Political Thought, trans. by Frederick W. Mote (Princeton, 1979).

HSÜ CHO-YÜN:
(1965): *Ancient China in Transition: An Analysis of Social Mobility, 722–222 B.C.* (Stanford, 1965).
(1965b): "The Changing Relationship between Local Society and the Central Political Power in Former Han: 206 B.C.–8 A.D.," in *Comparative Studies and History* 7 (July, 1965), 358–70.
(1975): "The Concept of Predetermination and Fate in the Han," *Early China* 1 (Fall, 1975), 51–56.

HSÜ CHUNG-SHU 徐中舒, *Chia ku wen tzu tien* 甲骨文字典 (Chengdu, 1988).

Bibliography of Works Cited

HSÜ DAU-LIN:
"The Myth of the 'Five Human Relations' of Confucius," *Monumenta Serica* 29
(1970–71), 27–37.

HSÜ FU-KUAN 徐復觀:
"Yang Hsiung lun chiu" 揚雄論究, *Liang Han ssu hsiang shih* 兩漢思想史, (Hong
Kong, 1975), II, 439–562.

HSÜ HAN 許翰 (d. 1133) commentary cited in WJL.

HULSEWÉ:

A. F. P. Hulsewé

(1955): *Remnants of Han Law: Introductory Studies and An Annotated Translation of Chapters 22 and 23 of the History of the Former Han Dynasty*
(Leiden, 1955).

(1986): "The two early Han *Yi ching* specialists called Ching Fang," *T'oung pao*
72 (1986), 161–62.

IKEDA SUETOSHI 池田末利:
"Tendō to tenmei" 天道と天命, *Hiroshima Daigaku Bungakubu kiyō* 広島大
学文学部紀要 28:1 (1968), 24–39.

IKEDA SHŪZŌ 池田秀三:
"Hōgen no shisō" 法言の思想, *Nihon Chūgaku gakkaihō* 日本中國學會報 29
(1977), 32–46.

JUAN YÜAN 阮元:
Hsing ming ku shun 性命古訓, in *Yen ching shih ch'üan chi* 揅經室全集 (SPTK *so
pen* no. 98).

KALINOWSKI:
Marc Kalinowski, "Les traités de Shuihudi et l'hémérologie chinoise à la fin des
Royaumes-combattants," *T'oung pao* 72 (1986), 175–228.

KALTENMARK:
Max Kaltenmark, "The Ideology of the *T'ai-p'ing ching*," in *Facets of Taoism:
Essays in Chinese Religion*, ed. by Holmes Welch and Anna Seidel (New
Haven, 1979).

KANAYA OSAMU 金谷治:
Shi to unmei 死と運命 (Kyoto, 1986).

KAO HENG 高亨:
Chou yi tsa lun 周易雜論 (Chinan, 1979).

KAO HUAI-MIN 高懷民:
Hsien Ch'in Yi hsüeh shih 先秦易學史 (Taipei, 1975).

KARLGREN:
Bernhard Karlgren, *Glosses on the Book of Odes* (Stockholm, 1964).

See also "Translations Cited."

KAUFMANN:
Walter Kaufmann, "The Mathematical Determination of the Twelve *Lü* as Performed by the Prince Liu An in his *Huai nan tzu* (Second Century B.C.),"

in *Essays in Ethnomusicology: A Birthday Offering for Lee Hye-ku* (Seoul, 1969), 371–82.

KEIGHTLEY:

David N. Keightley

(1977): "Peasant Migration, Politics and Philosophical Response in Chou and Ch'in China," Berkeley, California, Nov., 1977 (unpublished paper).

(1978): *Sources of Shang History: The Oracle-bone Inscriptions of Bronze Age China* (Berkeley, 1978).

(1989): "Shamanism in *Guo yu*: A Tale of *Xi* and *Wu*" (unpublished paper, prepared for the Center for Chinese Studies Regional Seminar, April 7–8, 1989, University of California, Berkeley).

(1990): "Where have all the Heroes Gone?: Reflections on Protagonists, Art, and Culture in Early China and Early Greece," (unpublished paper dated April, 1990).

KENNEDY:

George A. Kennedy, "Interpretation of the *Ch'un Ch'iu*," *Journal of the American Oriental Society* 62 (March, 1942), 40–48.

KNAPP:

Ronald G. Knapp, *China's Traditional Rural Architecture: A Cultural Geography of the Common House* (Honolulu, 1986).

KNECHTGES:

David R. Knechtges

(1976): *The Han Rhapsody: A Study of the fu of Yang Hsiung (53 b.c.–a.d. 18)* (Cambridge, 1976).

(1977): "The Liu Hsin/Yang Hsiung Correspondence on the *Fang yen*," *Monumenta Serica* 33 (1977–78), 309–25.

(1978): "Uncovering the Sauce Jar: A Literary Interpretation of Yang Hsiung's "Chü Ch'in mei Hsin," in *Ancient China: Studies in Early Civilization*, ed. by David T. Roy and Tsuen-hsuin Tsien (Hong Kong, 1978), pp. 229–52.

(1982): See Translations Cited.

KNOBLOCK: See Translations Cited.

KROLL:

J. L. Kroll, "Disputation in Ancient Chinese Culture," *Early China* 15 (1990), 118–45.

KU CHIEH-KANG 顧頡剛:

(1930?) "Ch'in Han t'ung yi ti yu lai ho Chan kuo jen tui yü shih chieh ti hsiang hsiang" 秦漢統一的由來和戰國人對於世界的想像, in KSP, II, 1–10.

(1930): *Wu te chung shih shuo hsia ti cheng chih ho li shih* 五德終始說下的政治和歷史, *Tsing Hua Journal of Chinese Studies* 清華學報 6 (1930), 71–268.

KUDŌ MOTOO:

"The Ch'in Bamboo Strip *Book of Divination (Jih shu)* and Ch'in Legalism," *Acta Asiatica* 58 (1990), 24–37.

Bibliography of Works Cited

KUDŌ TOYOHIKO 工藤豐彥:
"Ryo-shi Shunjū Fujihen kō" 呂氏春秋不二篇考 Tōhōgaku 東方學 22 (July, 1961), 20–26.

KUNST:
Richard Alan Kunst, "The Original 'Yijing': A Text, Phonetic Transcription, Translation, and Indexes, with Sample Glosses" (Ph.D. dissertation, University of California, Berkeley, 1985).

KURITA NAOMI 粟田直躬:
"Jōdai Shina no tenseki ni mietaru 'ki' no kannen" 上代支那の典籍に見たる氣の觀念, in Chūgoku Jōdai shisō no kenkyū 中國上代思想の研究 (Tokyo, 1949).

KUTTNER:
Fritz Alexander Kuttner, "A Musicological Interpretation of the Twelve Lüs in China's Traditional Tone System," Ethnomusicology 9:1 (Jan., 1965), 22–38.

LAU:
D. C. Lau, "On the term ch'ih ying and the story concerning the so-called 'tilting vessel'," in Symposium on Chinese Studies commemorating the Golden Jubilee of the University of Hong Kong 1911–1961 (Hong Kong, 1968), III, 18–33.

LAUFER:
Berthold Laufer, Jade: A Study in Chinese Archaeology and Religion (Chicago, 1912; rpt., New York, 1974).

LEWIS:
Mark Edward Lewis, Sanctioned Violence in Early China (Albany, 1990).

LI YÜN 李雲:
"Ma-wang-tui fang chung shu yen chiu" 馬王堆房中書研究, forthcoming in Wen shih 35 (1992?), 21–47, ms. trans. by Keith McMahon (pages numbered 1–69).

LI CHING-CH'IH 李鏡池:
"Chou Yi shih tz'u hsü k'ao" 周易筮辭續考, Ling nan hsüeh pao 嶺南學報 8:1 (1947), 1–68.

LIANG CH'I-CH'AO 梁啟超:
"Yin yang wu hsing shuo chih lai yüan" 陰陽五行說之來源, KSP, V, 343–62.

LIBBRECHT:
U. Libbrecht, "Prāna = Pneuma = Ch'i?," in Thought and Law in Qin and Han China: Studies Dedicated to Anthony Hulsewé on the Occasion of his Eightieth Birthday, ed. by W. L. Idema and E. Zürcher (Leiden, 1990), pp. 42–62.

LIU:
James J. Y. Liu, The Chinese Knight-Errant (London, 1967).

LIU DAJUN:
"A Preliminary Investigation of the Silk Manuscript Yijing," Zhouyi Network 1 (1986), 13–25.

LO KEN-TSE 羅根澤:
"*Hsin hsü Shuo yüan Lieh nü chuan pu tso shih yü Liu Hsiang k'ao* 新序說苑列女傳不作始於劉向考, in KSP, IV, 227–29.

LOEWE:
Michael Loewe
(1961): "The Measurement of Grain during the Han Period," *T'oung pao* 49:1–2 (1961), 64–95.
(1974): *Crisis and Conflict in Han China, 104 B.C. to A.D. 9* (London, 1974).
(1979): *Ways to Paradise: The Chinese Quest for Immortality* (London, 1979).
(1981): "China," in *Oracles and Divination*, ed. by Michael Loewe and Carmen Blacker (Boulder, Colorado, 1981).
(1982): *Chinese Ideas of Life and Death: Faith, Myth, and Reason in the Han Period (202 B.C.–A.D. 220)* (London, 1982).
(1983): "The Term *kan-yü* and the Choice of the Moment," *Early China* 9–11 (1983–85), 204–17.
(1986): "The Manuscripts from Tomb no. 3, Ma-wang-tui," *Proceedings of Chung yang yen chiu yüan, Li shih k'ao ku* (Taipei, 1986), 181–98.
(1988): "The Almanacs (*jih-shu*) from Shui-hu-ti: A Preliminary Survey," *Asia Major* (3d. series), 1:2 (1988), 1–27.
(1990): "The *Juedi* Games: A Reenactment of the Battle between Chiyou and Xianyuan?" in *Thought and Law in Qin and Han China: Studies presented to Anthony Hulsewé on the Occasion of his Eightieth Birthday*, ed. by W. L. Idema and E. Zürcher (Leiden, 1990), pp. 140–57.

LOUTON:
John Louton, "Concepts of Comprehensiveness and Historical Change in the *Lü shih ch'un ch'iu*," in Rosemont (1984), pp. 105–117.

LU CHI 陸績 (d. 250) commentary cited in WJL.

LU HSÜN 魯迅 (pseudonym):
Selected Works of Lu Hsün (Beijing, 1956–59), 3 vols.

MA TSUNG-HUO 馬宗霍:
Shuo wen chieh tzu yin Fang yen k'ao 說文解字引方言考 (Beijing, 1959).

MAIR:
Victor H. Mair
(1990a): "Old Sinitic **Myag*, Old Persian *Magus*, and English 'Magician'," *Early China* 15 (1990), 27–48.
(1990b): "Afterword," in *Tao te ching: The Classic Book of Integrity and the Way*: (New York, 1990), pp. 119–53.
(1990c): "[The] File [on the Cosmic] Track [and Individual] Dough[tiness]; Introduction and Notes for a Translation of the Ma-wang-tui Manuscripts of the *Lao tzu* [Old Master]," *Sino-Platonic Papers* 20 (Oct., 1990).
(1991): "Tracks of the Tao, Semantics of Zen," *Sino-Platonic Papers* 23 (July, 1991).

MAJOR:
John S. Major, "Substance, Process, Phase: *Wuxing* 五行 in the *Huainanzi*," in Rosemont (1991), 67–78.

Bibliography of Works Cited

MATSUMOTO MASAAKI 松木雅明:
Shunjū sengoku ni okeru Shōsho no tenkai 春秋戰國にあける尚書の展開 (Tokyo, 1966).

MAUROIS:
André Maurois, *Illusions* (New York, 1968).

MAUSS:
Marcel Mauss, *The Gift*, trans. by W. D. Halls, foreword by Mary Douglas (Paris, 1950; rpt., New York, 1990).

MCMAHON:
Keith McMahon, *Causality and Containment in Seventeeth-Century Chinese Fiction*, Monographies du T'oung Pao, XV (Leiden, 1988).

MILLER:
Roy Andrew Miller, "The *Wu ching i-i* of Hsü Shen," *Monumenta Serica* 33 (1977–78), 1–21.

MORAN:
Richard Edwin Moran, "Explorations of Chinese Metaphysical Concepts: The History of Some Terms from the Beginnings to Chu Hsi (1130–1200)" (Ph.D. dissertation, University of Pennsylvania, 1983).

MORI MIKISABURŌ 森三樹三郎:
Jōko yori Kandai ni itaru seimeikan no tenkai 上古より漢代に至る性命觀 の展開 (Tokyo, 1971).

MOROHASHI TETSUJI 諸橋轍次:
Dai Kan-Wa jiten 大漢和辭典 (Tokyo, 1960; rpt., Tokyo, 1984), 13 vols.

MOTE:
Frederick W. Mote
(1972): "The Cosmological Gulf Between China and the West," in *Transition and Permanence: Chinese History and Culture*, ed. by David C. Buxbaum and F. W. Mote (Hong Kong, 1972), pp. 3–21.
(1990): "Review of *The World of Thought in Ancient China* by Benjamin I. Schwartz. Cambridge: Harvard University Press, 1985," *Harvard Journal of Asiatic Studies* 50:1 (1990), 384–402.

NAGAHIRO TOSHIO 長廣敏雄:
Taikō no kenkyū 帶鉤の研究, *Institute of Oriental Culture Monograph* (Kyoto, 1943).

NEEDHAM:
Joseph Needham
Science and Civilisation in China, ed. by Joseph Needham and others (Cambridge, 1954–), parts of 6 vols. to date.
(1964): *Time and Eastern Man*, the Henry Myers Lecture, 1964, rpt. in Needham, *The Grand Titration: Science and Society in East and West* (London, 1969), pp. 218–98.

NEELY:
Henry M. Neely, *A Primer for Star-gazers* (New York, 1989).

NGO:

Ngo Van Xuyet, *Divination, magie et politique dans la Chine ancienne: essai, Suivi de la Traduction des "Biographies des Magiciens" tirées de L'histoire des Han postérieurs*, Bibliothèque de l'Ecole des hautes études, Section des sciences religieuses, LXXVIII (Paris, 1976).

NIVISON:

David S. Nivison

(1985): "Review of *The World of Thought in Ancient China* by Benjamin I. Schwartz. Cambridge: Harvard University Press, 1985," *Philosophy East and West* 38:4 (October, 1988).

(1989): "The 'Question' Question," *Early China* 14 (1989), 115–25.

(n.d.): "Hsün tzu on 'Human Nature'" (unpublished paper).

NUSSBAUM:

Martha Craven Nussbaum, *The Fragility of Goodness: Luck and Ethics in Greek Tragedy and Philosophy* (Cambridge, 1986).

NYLAN:

Michael Nylan

(1982): "Ying Shao's *Feng su t'ung yi*: An Exploration of Problems in Han Dynasty Political, Philosophical, and Social Unity" (Ph.D. dissertation, Princeton University, 1982).

(1987): (and Nathan Sivin), "The First Neo-Confucianism: Yang Hsiung's *Canon of Supreme Mystery (T'ai hsüan ching)*, c. 4 B.C.," in *Chinese Ideas about Nature and Society: Studies in Honour of Derk Bodde* (Hong Kong, 1987), pp. 41–99.

(1991): "On the Changing Notion of *feng su* ("custom") in Han Times" (unpublished conference paper dated Nov. 1, 1991).

(forthcoming) *The Shifting Center: The 'Great Plan' chapter of the Documents and Later Readings*, Monumenta Serica Monograph Series, XXIV (Fall, 1992).

(forthcoming[b]): "*T'ai hsüan ching*," in *Early Chinese Texts: A Bibliographical Guide*, Early China Monograph Series (in press).

PANKENIER:

David W. Pankenier

(1990a): "Sandai (三代) Astronomical Origins of Heaven's Mandate," unpublished paper from the 6th International Conference on the History of Science in China, Cambridge, England, 2–7 August, 1990.

(1990b): "'The Scholar's Frustration' Reconsidered: Melancholia or Credo?," *Journal of the American Oriental Society* 110:3 (July–Sept., 1990), 434–59.

P'EI HSÜ-HAI 裴學海:

"Fourth Supplement to the *Ku-shu i-i chü-li*," trans. by Achilles Fang, *Monumenta Serica* 10 (1945), 239–308.

PELIKAN:
Jaroslav Jan Pelikan, *Jesus through the Centuries: His Place in the History of Culture* (New Haven, 1985; rpt., New York, 1987).

PETERSON:
Willard J. Peterson
(1979): "The Grounds of Mencius' Argument," *Philosophy East and West* 29:3 (July, 1979), 307–21.
(1982): "Making Connections: 'Commentary on the Attached Verbalizations' of the *Book of Change*," *Harvard Journal of Asiatic Studies* 42:1 (June, 1982), 67–116.
(1989): "Review of LeBlanc and Blader, eds., *Chinese Ideas about Nature and Society: Studies in Honour of Derk Bodde*. Hong Kong: Hong Kong University Press, 1987," *Journal of Asian Studies* 48:2 (May, 1989), 365–67.

PIAN:
Rulan Chao Pian, *Song Dynasty Musical Sources and their Interpretation*, Harvard Yenching Institute Monograph Series, XVI (Cambridge, Mass., 1967).

POCOCK:
J.G.A. Pocock, "*Ching* and *Ch'uan*, Virtue and Prudence: Policy and Innovation in Chinese and Western Political Thought" (unpublished paper dated January 12, 1984).

POKORA:
Timotheus Pokora, "The Life of Huan T'an," *Archiv Orientalni* 31 (1963), 1–79.
See also Translations Cited.

PORKERT:
Manfred Porkert, *The Theoretical Foundations of Chinese Medicine: Systems of Correspondence* (Cambridge, Mass., 1985).

POWERS:
Martin Joseph Powers
(1978): "The Shapes of Power in Han Pictorial Art" (Ph.D. dissertation, University of Chicago, 1978).
(1987): "Social Values and Aesthetic Choices in Han Dynasty Sichuan," in *Stories from China's Past: Han Dynasty Pictorial Tomb Reliefs and Archaeological Objects from Sichuan Province, People's Republic of China* (San Francisco, 1987), pp. 54–63.

REDING:
Jean-Paul Reding
(1986a): "Analogical Reasoning in Early Chinese Philosophy," *Asiatische Studien* 40 (1986), 40–56.
(1986b): "Greek and Chinese Categories: A Reexamination of the Problem of Linguistic Relativism," *Philosophy East and West* 36:4 (Oct., 1986), 349–74.

RONAN:
Colin A. Ronan, *The Shorter Science and Civilisation in China: An Abridgement of Joseph Needham's Original Text* (Cambridge, 1978), 2 vols.

ROSEMONT:

Henry Rosemont, Jr.

(1984): Henry Rosemont, ed., *Explorations in Early Chinese Cosmology*, Thematic Studies Series of the Journal of the American Academy of Religion Studies, L:II (Chico, California, 1984).

(1991): *Chinese Texts and Philosophical Contexts: Essays dedicated to Angus C. Graham* (La Salle, Ill., 1990).

ROTH:

Harold Roth, "Who compiled the *Chuang tzu*?" in Rosemont (1991), pp. 79–128.

RUBIN:

(1982): Vitaly A. Rubin, "The Concepts of *Wu-hsing* and *Yin-yang*," *Journal of Chinese Philosophy* 9 (1982), 131–57.

(1984): "Ancient Chinese Cosmology and *Fa chia* Theory, "in Rosemont (1984), pp. 95–104.

SCHAFER:

Edward T. Schafer

(1951): "Ritual Exposure in Ancient China," *Harvard Journal of Asiatic Studies* 14 (1951), 130–84.

(1977): *Pacing the Void: T'ang Approaches to the Stars* (Berkeley, 1977).

SCHINDLER:

Bruno Schindler, "On the Travel, Wayside, and Wind Offerings in Ancient China," *Asia Major* 1 (1924), 624–56.

SCHNEIDER:

Laurence A. Schneider, *A Madman of Ch'u: The Chinese Myth of Loyalty and Dissent* (Berkeley, 1980).

SCHWARTZ:

Benjamin Isadore Schwartz

(1973): "On the Absence of Reductionism in Chinese Thought," *Journal of Chinese Philosophy* 1 (1973), 27–44.

(1985): *The World of Thought in Ancient China* (Cambridge, Mass., 1985).

SERRUYS:

Paul L.-M. Serruys

(1955): "Aspects linguistiques de l'hydronomie chinoise," *Revue internationale d'onomastique* 7 (1955), 114–23.

(1959): *The Chinese Dialects of Han Time According to Fang yen*, *University of California Publications in East Asiatic Philology*, II (Berkeley, 1959).

(1981): "Towards a Grammar of the Language of the Shang Bone Inscriptions," *Proceedings of the International Conference on Sinology: Section on Spoken and Written Language* (*Chung yang yen chiu yüan Kuo chi Han hsüeh hui yi lun wen chi: Yü yen wen tzu tsu*) 中央研究院國際漢學會議論文集語言文字祖 (Taipei, 1981), II, 313–64.

(1984): "On the System of the Pu Shou (部首) in the *Shuo wen chieh-tzu* (說文解字)," *Bulletin of the Institute of History and Philology, Academia Sinica* 55:4 (1984), 651–754.

(n.d.): "Studies in the Language of the *Shih ching*," Parts I-III" (unpublished paper).

References to Serruys that are assigned no date refer to private communications over the years 1988–92.

SHAUGHNESSY:

Edward Shaughnessy, "The Composition of the Zhouyi" (Ph.D. dissertation, University of California at Berkeley, 1983).

SHCHUTSKII:

Iulian Konstantinovich Shchutskii, *Researches on the I Ching*, trans. by W. L. MacDonald and Tsuyoshi Hasegawa with Hellmut Wilhelm (Moscow, 1960; rpt., London, 1979).

SHIGEZAWA TOSHIO 重澤俊郎:

"Kan Gi ni okeru nikukei ron" 漢魏に於けの肉刑論, *Tōyō no bunka to shakai* 東洋の文化と社會 2 (1952), 103–119.

SHIH:

C. C. Shih, "Notes on a Phrase in the *Tso chuan*: 'The Great Affairs of a State are Sacrifice and War'," *Chinese Culture* 2:3 (1959), 31–47.

SHRYOCK:

John Knight Shryock

(1932): *The Origin and Development of the State Cult of Confucius: An Introductory Study* (New York, 1932).

(1935): and H. Y. Feng, "The Black Magic in China known as *ku*," *Journal of the American Oriental Society* 55 (1935), 1–30.

SIVIN:

Nathan Sivin

(1969): "Cosmos and Computation in Early Chinese Mathematical Astronomy," *T'oung pao* 55:1–3 (1969), 1–73.

(1974): with Kerson Huang, "The Earliest Principles of Interpretation of the *Book of Changes* (notes based on Ch'ü Wan-li)" (unpublished undated paper).

(1977): "Preliminary Reflections on the words *pien* 變, *hua* 化, and *t'ung* 通 in the "Great Commentary" to the *Book of Changes* (unpublished paper dated Dec. 31, 1977).

(1978): "On the Word 'Taoist' as a Source of Perplexity, With Special Reference to the Relations of Science and Religion in Traditional China," *History of Religions* 17 (1978), 303–30.

(1985): See Nylan and Sivin.

(1986): "On the Limits of Empirical Knowledge in the Traditional Chinese Sciences," in *Time, Science, and Society in China and the West: The Study of Time V*, ed. by J.T. Fraser, N. Lawrence, and F. C. Huber (Amherst, 1986), pp. 151–69.

(1987): *Traditional Medicine in Contemporary China*, Science, Medicine, and Technology in East Asia Series, II (Ann Arbor, 1987).

(1990): "Change and Continuity in Early Cosmology: The 'Great Commentary' to the *Book of Changes*" (unpublished paper dated June 4, 1990).

Bibliography of Works Cited

SMITH:
Sung Dynasty Uses of the I ching, ed. by Kidder Smith, Jr., Peter K. Bol, Joseph A. Adler, and Don J. Wyatt (Princeton, 1990).

SOOTHILL:
William E. Soothill, *The Hall of Light: A Study of Early Chinese Kingship* (London, 1951).

STEIN:
Rolf A. Stein,
(1957): "Architecture et pensée religieuse en Extréme-Orient," *Arts Asiatiques* 4 (1957), 163–86.
(1979): "Religious Taoism and Popular Religion from the Second to Seventh Centuries," in *Facets of Taoism: Essays in Chinese Religion*, ed. by Holmes Welch and Anna Seidel (New Haven, 1979), pp. 53–81.

STEINHARDT:
Nancy Shatzman Steinhardt, "The Han Ritual Hall," in her *Chinese Traditional Architecture* (New York, 1984), pp. 69–78.

STERN:
Jane and Michael Stern, "Parrots," *The New Yorker* (July 30, 1990), p. 55 ff.

SUNG CHUNG 宋衷 (d. 219) commentary cited in WJL.

SUNG WEI-KAN 宋惟幹 (d. 1151) commentary cited in WJL.

SUZUKI YOSHIJIRŌ 鈴木由次郎:
(1963): *Kan Eki kenkyū* 漢易研究 (Tokyo, 1963).
(1964): *Taigenkyō no kenkyū* 太玄經の研究 (Tokyo, 1964).
(1972a): "Shō shi *Ekirin* no sakusha ni tsuite" 焦氏易林の作者について, *Tōhō gakkai sōritsu nijūgo shūnen kinen Tōhōgaku ronshū* 東方學會創立二十五週年紀念東方學論集 (Tokyo, 1972).
(1972b): *Taigenkyō* 太玄經, Chūgoku koten shinso Series, LVI (Tokyo, 1972).

SWANN:
Nancy Lee Swann
(1932): *Pan Chao: Foremost Woman Scholar of China, First Century A.D.* (New York, 1932).
(1950): *Food and Money in Ancient China: The Earliest Economic History of China to A.D. 25*, trans. by Nancy Lee Swann (Princeton, 1950).

SWANSON:
Gerald Swanson, "The Concept of Change in the *Great Treatise*," in Rosemont (1984), pp. 67–93.

TAKAKI:
Ronald T. Takaki, *Iron Cages* (Seattle, 1979).

TAKASHIMA:
Kenichi Takashima, "Some Philological Notes to *Sources of Shang History*," *Early China* 5 (1979–80), 48–55.

T'ANG
T'ang Yung-t'ung, "Wang Pi's New interpretation of the *I ching* and *Lun yü*," *Harvard Journal of Asiatic Studies* 10 (1947), 124–61.

Bibliography of Works Cited

T'ANG CHÜN-YI:
"The *T'ien-ming* (Heavenly Ordinance) in pre-Ch'in China," *Philosophy East and West* 11 (1962), 195–218; 12 (1963), 29–42.

T'ANG LAN 唐蘭:
Hsi Chou ch'ing t'ung ch'i ming wen fen tai shih cheng 西周靑銅器銘文分代釋証 (Beijing, 1986).

T'ANG PING-CHENG 湯炳正,
"Yang Tzu-yün nien p'u" 揚子雲年譜, *Lun hsüeh* 論學 (April, 1937), 76–91.

THERN:
K. L. Thern, *Postface to the Shuo wen chieh tzu: The First Comprehensive Chinese Dictionary*, Wisconsin China Series, I (Madison, Wisconsin, 1966).

THOMPSON:
The Shen Tzu Fragments, ed. by P. M. Thompson (Oxford, 1979).

TING SHAN 丁山:
Chung kuo ku tai tsung chiao yü shen hua k'ao 中國古代宗教與神話考 (n.p., 1950; rpt., Shanghai, 1988).

TRICKER:
R. A. R. Tricker, *Paths of the Planets* (New York, 1967).

TU:
Tu Wei-ming, *Centrality and Commonality: An Essay on Chung yung*, Monograph of the Society for Asian and Comparative Philosohy Series, III (Honolulu, 1976).

TUNG TSO-PIN 董作賓:
"Fang yen hsüeh chia Yang Hsiung nien p'u" 方言學家揚雄年譜, *Chung shan ta hsüeh yü yen li shih hsüeh yen chiu so chou k'an* 中山大學語言歷史學研究所周刊 (June, 1937), 82–88.

UNO SEIICHI 宇野靑一:
"Gokyō kara shisho e" 五經から四書へ, *Tōyō no bunka to shakai* 東洋の文化と社會 (1952), 1–14.

VANDERMEERSCH:
Leon Vandermeersch, *La Formation du Legisme: Recherche sur la Constitution d'une Politique characteristique de la Chine ancienne* (Paris, 1965).

WALDRON:
Arthur Waldron, *The Great Wall of China: From History to Myth* (Cambridge, 1990).

WALEY:
Arthur Waley,
(1933): "The *Book of Changes*," *Bulletin of the Museum of Far Eastern Antiquities* 5 (1933), 121–42.
(1934): *The Way and Its Power: A Study of the Tao Te Ching and Its Place in Chinese Thought* (London, 1934; rpt., New York, 1958).

WALLACKER:
Benjamin Wallacker, "Han Confucianism and Confucius in Han," in *Ancient*

China: Studies in Early Civilization, ed. by David T. Roy and Tsuen-hsuin Tsien (Hong Kong, 1978), pp. 215–28.

WANG:

C. H. Wang, *The Bell and the Drum: Shih ching as Formulaic Poetry in an Oral Tradition* (Berkeley, 1974).

WANG LI-CH'I 王利器:

"Tao tsang pen 'Tao te chen ching chih kuei' t'i yao" 道藏本道德真經指歸提要, *Chung kuo che hsüeh* 中國哲學 4 (Oct., 1980), 337–360.

WANG SHU-MIN 王叔岷:

Chuang tzu chiao ch'üan 莊子校詮 (Taipei, 1988), 3 vols.

WANG YA 王涯 commentary cited in WJL (dated 809).

WATSON:

Burton Watson, *Early Chinese Literature* (New York, 1962).

WHEATLEY:

Paul Wheatley, *The Pivot of the Four Quarters: A Preliminary Enquiry into the Origins and Character of the Ancient Chinese City* (Edinburgh, 1971).

WU:

Wu Hung, *The Wu Liang Shrine: The Ideology of Early Chinese Pictorial Art* (Stanford, 1989).

WU MI 吳祕 (d. 1181) commentary cited in WJL.

YEARLEY:

Lee H. Yearley, "A Confucian Crisis: Mencius' Two Cosmogonies and Their Ethics," in *Cosmogony and Ethical Order: New Studies in Comparative Ethics*, ed. by Robin W. Lovin and Frank E. Reynolds (Chicago, 1985), pp. 310–27.

YEN LING-FENG 嚴靈峰:

(1973) *Chou Ch'in Han Wei chu tzu chih chien shu mu* 周秦漢魏諸子知見書目 (Taipei, 1973), 5 vols.

(1980): *Ma-wang-tui po shu Yi ching ch'u pu yen chiu* 馬王堆帛書易經初步研究 (Taipei, 1980).

YU:

Anthony C. Yu, "'Rest, Rest, Perturbed Spirit!' Ghosts in Traditional Chinese Prose Fiction," *Harvard Journal of Asiatic Studies* 47:2 (Dec., 1987), 397–434.

YÜ:

Yü Ying-shih

(1965): "Life and Immortality in the Mind of Han Chinese," *Harvard Journal of Asiatic Studies* 25 (1964–65), 80–122.

(1967): *Trade and Expansion in Han China* (Berkeley, 1967).

(1977): "Han," in Chang (1977a), pp. 55–83.

(1987): "'O Soul, Come Back!' A Study in the Changing Conceptions of the Soul and Afterlife in pre-Buddhist China," *Harvard Journal of Asiatic Studies* 47:2 (Dec., 1987), 363–95.

YÜ FAN 虞翻 (d. 233) commentary cited in WJL.

ZHAO:

Zhao Qi-gang, *A Study of Dragonology, East and West* (Ph.D. dissertation, University of Massachusetts, 1988).

ZINSSER:

Hans Zinsser, *Rats, Lice, and History* (Boston, 1934).

TRANSLATIONS CITED

BELPAIRE:

Le catechisme philosophique de Yang-Hiong-tse, trans. by Bruno Belpaire (Brussels, 1960).

CHAVANNES:

Les Mémoires historiques de Se-ma Ts'ien, trans. by Édouard Chavannes (Paris, 1967), 6 vols.

CRUMP:

Chan-kuo Ts'e: Intrigues, trans. by J. L. Crump (Oxford, 1970).

DUBS:

The Works of Hsüntze, trans. by Homer H. Dubs (London, 1928).

The History of the Former Han Dynasty by Pan Ku, trans. and annot. by Homer H. Dubs (Baltimore, 1938–55), 3 vols.

FORKE:

Lun heng: The Philosophical Essays of Wang Ch'ung, trans. by Alfred Forke (Berlin, 1907; rpt., New York, 1962), 2 vols.

GALE:

Discourses on Salt and Iron: A Debate on State Control of Commerce and Industry, trans. by E. M. Gale (Leiden, 1931).

GASSMANN:

Tung Chung-shu, Ch'un Ch'iu fan lu: Üppiger Tau des Frühling-und-Herbst-Klassikers, trans. by Robert H. Gassmann, Schweizer Asiatische Studien/ Études Asiatiques Suisses Monographie, VIII (Bern, 1988).

GRAHAM:

Chuang tzu: The Inner Chapters, trans. by A. C. Graham (London, 1981).

GRIFFITH:

Sun tzu: The Art of War, trans. and intro. by Samuel B. Griffith (Oxford, 1963).

HIGHTOWER:

Han shih wai chuan: Han Ying's Illustrations of the Didactic Application of the Classic of Songs, trans. by James Robert Hightower (Cambridge, Mass., 1952).

HO: See Ho Peng-yoke in Secondary Sources.

KARLGREN:

The Book of Documents, trans. by Bernard Karlgren, *Bulletin of the Museum of Far Eastern Antiquities* 22 (1950).

Bibliography of Works Cited

KNECHTGES:
The Han shu Biography of Yang Xiong (53 B.C.–A.D. 18) trans. and annot. by David R. Knechtges, Occasional Paper, Arizona State University Center for Asian Studies, XIV (Tempe, Arizona, 1982).

KNOBLOCK:
Xunzi: A Translation and Study of the Complete Works, trans. by John Knoblock, I (Books 1–6) (Stanford, 1988); II (Books 7–16) (Stanford, 1990).

KRAMERS:
K'ung tzu chia yü, trans. by Dr. R. P. Kramers (Leiden, 1950).

KU:
A Chinese Mirror for Magistrates: The Hsin-yü of Lu Chia, trans., annot., and critical intro. by Mei-kao Ku (Canberra, 1988).

KUHN:
Jou pu t'uan (The Prayer Mat of Flesh), trans. by Franz Kuhn [rendered into English by Richard Martin].

LAU:
Lao tzu, Tao te ching, trans. and intro. by D. C. Lau (Harmondsworth, 1963).
Mencius, trans. and intro. by D. C. Lau (Harmondsworth, 1970).

LEGGE:
The Confucian Classics, trans. by James Legge (Oxford, 1890s), 5 vols.
Li Chi, Book of Rites: An Encyclopedia of Ancient Ceremonial Usages, Religious Creeds, and Social Institutions, trans. by James Legge, The Sacred Books of the East Series, XXVII–XXVIII (Oxford, 1885; rpt., New Hyde Park, 1967), 2 vols.

LIAO:
The Complete Works of Han Fei Tzu: A Classic of Chinese Legalism, trans. by W. K. Liao (London, 1939), 2 vols.

MAKRA:
The Book of Filial Piety, trans. by Mary Lelia Makra (New York, 1970).

MALMQVIST:
(a): "Studies on the Gongyang and Guuliang Commentaries, I," *Bulletin of the Museum of Far Eastern Antiquities* 43 (1971), 67–222.
(b): "Studies on the Gongyang and Guuliang Commentaries, II," in *ibid.*, 47 (1975), 19–69.

NYLAN:
See Nylan (1982) in Secondary Sources.

POKORA:
Hsin lun: New Treatise and other Writings by Huan T'an, trans. by Timotheus Pokora (Ann Arbor, 1965).

RICKETT:
(a): *Kuan tzu: A Repository of Early Chinese Thought*, trans. by W. Allyn Rickett (Hong Kong, 1965), I.
(b): *Guanzi*, trans. by W. Allyn Rickett (Princeton, 1985), II.

Bibliography of Works Cited

SOURCES:
Sources of Chinese Tradition, comp. by Wm. Theodore de Bary, Wing-tsit Chan, and Burton Watson, with contributions by Yi-pao Mei, Leon Hurvitz, and others (New York, 1960).

SWANN:
See Swann (1932), (1950) in Secondary Sources.

THOMPSON:
See Thompson in Secondary Sources.

TJAN:
Po hu t'ung: The Comprehensive Discussions in the White Tiger Hall, trans. by Tjan Tjoe Som (Leiden, 1949), 2 vols.

TURNER:
A Golden Treasury of Chinese Poetry, trans. by John A. Turner, S. J. (Hong Kong, 1976).

WALEY:
The Analects of Confucius, trans. by Arthur Waley (London, 1938).
The Book of Songs, trans. by Arthur Waley (London, 1937).
The Nine Songs, trans. by Arthur Waley (London, 1955).

WARE:
Alchemy, Medicine, and Religion in China of A.D. 320: The "Nei P'ien" of Ko Hung (Pao p'u tzu), trans. and ed. by James R. Ware (Cambridge, Mass., 1966).

WATSON:
The Complete Works of Chuang tzu, trans. by Burton Watson (Columbia, 1968).
Han Fei tzu: Basic Writings, trans. by Burton Watson (Columbia, 1964).
Hsün tzu: Basic Writings, trans. by Burton Watson (Columbia, 1963).
Mo tzu: Basic Writings, trans. by Burton Watson (Columbia, 1963).
Records of the Grand Historian of China, translated from the Shih chi of Ssu-ma Ch'ien, trans by Burton Watson (New York, 1971), 2 vols.
Records of the Historian: Chapters from the Shih chi of Ssu-ma Ch'ien, trans. by Burton Watson (New York, 1958) [for selections from SC, cited as Watson (b)].
The Tso chuan: Selections from China's Oldest Narrative History, trans. by Burton Watson (New York, 1989) [cited for selections from CCYT]

WILHELM:
The I Ching or Book of Changes, trans. by Richard Wilhelm [rendered into English by Carl F. Baynes], Bollingen Series, XIX (Princeton, 1950).

YANG:
Selections from the Records of the Historian, by Szuma [sic] Chien, trans. by Yang Hsien-yi and Gladys Yang (Beijing, 1979).

***

Partial Index of Common Images

Note: This index is designed to help the reader become familiar himself with some images used by Yang Hsiung. Given the many-layered nature of Yang's poetry, it can in no way be comprehensive. However, study of this index may introduce the reader to the system underlying the *Mystery*. Images of death, for example, are largely confined to the late Appraisals in each tetragram; images of light, in contrast, tend to the be found in the early Appraisals.

abyss, THC3/5; THC4/2; THC7/2; THC9/9; THC19/Head; THC20/8; THC40/7; THC42/2; THC45/1; THC49/5; THC65/9; THC66/1–2; THC78/8; THC79/Head; THC80/9; THC81/1

aging, THC9/7; THC23/9; THC24/7; THC55/4; THC57/9; THC75/5; THC81/5

archery, THC25/3; THC50/7; THC58/7; THC62/7; THC68/3; THC71/8

architecture, THC30/6; THC40/3–4; THC46/1–2; THC52/4–5

arms and legs, THC25/6; THC29/5; THC56/7; THC70/5

arrows, THC6/5; THC7/Head; THC22/5; THC25/8; THC26/4; THC30/9; THC48/5; THC49/8; THC58/7; THC49/8; THC50/7; THC62/7; THC62/9; THC64/3

babies, THC3/3; THC9/1; THC17/4; THC22/3; THC80/3

backs, THC6/2; THC6/3; THC14/5

bandits, THC29/8; THC46/4; THC49/9; THC54/9; THC60/5; THC62/5; THC75/Head

barriers, THC4/1–9; THC15/6; THC20/1; THC29/2; THC29/3; THC67/2

bees, THC72/4; THC72/5; THC72/6; THC72/9

belly, THC6/2; THC6/3; THC15/2; THC15/8; THC19/6; THC29/5; THC30/2; THC58/5; THC68/1; THC68/2; THC69/5; THC70/1; THC81/5

belts. *See* restraints

bindings. *See* restraints

birds, THC7/5; THC18/5; THC22/4; THC31/2; THC31/4; THC31/5; THC32/4; THC36/2; THC47/6–7; THC48/4; THC49/4,5,7,8; THC50/7; THC50/9; THC54/2–4; THC58/4; THC58/6; THC59/8; THC61/8; THC62/7; THC63/5; THC63/6; THC63/8; THC64/4;

THC64/5; THC64/7; THC65/6; THC67/6; THC75/8; THC76/9; THC78/4–5; THC81/4

birth, THC6/8

blockage, THC2/1; THC56/7–8

blood, THC10/9; THC19/4; THC32/9; THC34/2; THC42/8; THC56/2; THC59/5; THC61/8; THC64/9; THC70/9; THC76/2

boat, THC3/9; THC20/8; THC28/6; THC39/5; THC78/8; THC80/9

bolt, THC4/3; THC8/1

bones, THC8/4; THC56/2; THC70/9; THC74/5; THC76/1; THC81/5

bow, THC62/9; THC71/8; THC81/Head. *See also* archery; arrows

carriages, carts, or chariots, THC2/5; THC3/5–8; THC9/5; THC10/9; THC13/6; THC26/4; THC27/2; THC28/6; THC28/8; THC23/9; THC32/3; THC32/8; THC39/7; THC47/5; THC53/5; THC54/5,7; THC57/6; THC60/4; THC63/6; THC71/2; THC71/5–7; THC71/8; THC79/6; THC80/9

center, THC1/Head; THC1/3; THC1/8; THC2/1; THC2/8; THC3/2; THC6/2; THC6/8; THC7/5; THC11/5; THC15/1; THC15/5; THC17/2; THC20/2; THC20/3; THC22/1; THC23/3; THC25/5; THC26/8; THC29/2; THC34/1; THC36/1; THC37/2; THC38/1, THC40/2; THC42/8; THC43/2; THC43/8; THC44/2; THC45/5; THC46/7; THC52/1; THC52/2; THC53/5; THC55/2; THC56/5; THC57/2; THC57/5; THC58/2; THC62/5; THC68/2; THC68/6; THC69/1; THC69/2; THC70/1; THC71/5; THC72/2; THC72/3; THC73/5; THC75/5; THC79/3; THC79/5; THC80/1; THC80/2; THC81/2; THC81/3 "center heart," THC4/2; THC6/2; THC23/3; THC29/2; THC34/1; THC55/2; THC62/3; THC81/2

chen, THC1/1; THC3/3; THC5/3; THC7/4; THC8/3; THC8/6; THC10/8; THC11/7; THC13/1; THC13/7; THC14/6; THC15/9; THC16/1; THC16/8; THC16/9; THC18/6; THC21/6; THC22/4; THC23/9; THC25/4; THC26/8; THC27/9; THC28/1; THC29/9; THC30/2; THC30/8; THC34/9; THC35/2; THC36/1; THC37/4; THC37/5; THC37/9; THC39/5; THC41/5; THC42/1; THC42/4; THC42/5; THC43/1; THC43/3; THC44/2; THC47/1; THC50/3; THC51/2; THC51/7; THC52/6; THC53/2; THC55/5; THC57/5; THC57/7; THC58/2; THC61/2; THC61/4; THC62/1; THC62/4; THC62/7; THC63/6; THC64/1; THC64/3; THC64/4; THC65/1; THC66/7; THC67/1; THC67/9; THC68/Head; THC68/4; THC68/8; THC71/7; THC72/2; THC72/8; THC73/8; THC76/2; THC76/8; THC77/1; THC77/3; THC77/9; THC81/2

child, THC12/1; THC43/2; THC46/3; THC78/8; THC81/7. *See also* babies

circle, THC2/1–9; THC74/1

city walls. *See* walls

clothing, THC2/4; THC7/6; THC22/3; THC22/7; THC22/8; THC42/4; THC47/1–4; THC47/5; THC47/8–9; THC48/8–9; THC49/2, THC61/2; THC65/4; THC66/5; THC76/5

clouds, THC8/9; THC17/5; THC70/7

contention, THC25/Head–9; THC32/Head–9

cosmic womb, THC3/Head

court, THC42/8; THC54/6; THC66/5

cowries, THC13/8

crab, THC14/1

crawling, THC9/1. *See also* babies; leaping

cries, THC23/3; THC24/3; THC24/9

cripples, THC18/9

crown, THC30/3

darkness, THC5/1; THC20/4; THC28/1; THC29/2; THC31/9; THC32/1; THC43/1; THC45/1; THC50/2; THC52/6; THC55/1; THC58/1–2; THC60/1; THC67/1; THC67/9; THC68/6; THC68/7; THC68/8; THC76/1; THC79/1

dawn, THC19/2; THC31/4; THC50/7; THC67/1

death, THC1/9; THC6/8; THC17/7; THC21/8; THC24/7; THC31/8; THC32/1; THC33/9;, THC43/8; THC45/9; THC54/9; THC59/7; THC68/9; THC75/9

ditches, THC10/8; THC49/2

divination, THC12/2

domestic animals, THC28/5; THC35/5; THC39/4; THC43/8; THC44/7; THC47/7; THC48/4; THC49/3; THC56/8; THC57/4; THC59/4; THC76/5. *See also* horses

dragon, THC1/3; THC4/1; THC41/5; THC42/2; THC65/5; THC74/3

drill, THC8/1

dwarfs, THC12/7; THC29/8

ears, THC20/7; THC27/9; THC29/2; THC29/3; THC32/6; THC37/3; THC62/7; THC64/1; THC70/1

earth, THC5/5; THC69/4; THC77/4. *See also* fields

echo, THC21/2

eclipse, THC51/3; THC51/4

eggs, THC11/7; THC42/2; THC79/4

eye, THC15/2; THC15/8; THC19/6; THC22/9; THC32/1; THC37/3; THC42/4; THC48/2; THC62/7; THC64/2; THC64/3; THC67/2; THC67/8; THC70/1

fabric, THC33/7. *See also* clothing

feasting, THC9/4; THC16/6; THC23/4; THC27/5; THC31/5; THC34/4; THC44/6; THC58/3; THC59/2

fields, THC19/Head; THC30/5; THC32/1; THC35/5; THC43/5; THC47/8; THC49/6; THC75/6; THC81/3

fire, THC8/8; THC32/1; THC38/7–8; THC41/6; THC44/9; THC66/8

fish, THC40/7; THC48/6; THC69/6; THC75/8; THC81/8

flowers, THC26/6; THC26/7; THC33/Head

food, THC44/1–9; THC64/5; THC69/5; THC70/4; THC76/4

foot, THC10/8; THC18/4; THC19/Head; THC43/9; THC48/1; THC48/2; THC49/2; THC49/9; THC69/7; THC69/8

fragrance, THC26/2; THC26/6; THC26/7; THC33/4; THC74/4

friends, THC2/7; THC19/2; THC19/4; THC26/4; THC43/5; THC58/4; THC70/7 fruit, THC7/3; THC26/6; THC26/7; THC70/6; THC71/4; THC75/6

gag, THC8/1
gate, THC4/3; THC11/5; THC33/1; THC38/3–4; THC42/8; THC45/4;THC46/4–5; THC57/Head; THC70/3
ghosts, THC24/7; THC50/8; THC52/7; THC59/1; THC59/3; THC59/6; THC62/7; THC76/3; THC81/8
gold, THC2/5; THC18/6; THC22/6; THC23/7; THC36/7; THC46/2; THC62/5; THC67/4; THC77/5; THC81/5
grasses, THC9/3; THC66/5

hall, THC7/6; THC16/Head; THC39/4; THC46/5; THC66/1
harvest, THC1/7; THC35/5; THC56/4
head, THC18/9; THC30/3; THC48/9; THC63/4; THC64/9; THC70/9; THC72/9
heart, THC2/1; THC6/2; THC7/1; THC14/5; THC17/2; THC24/4; THC26/Head; THC26/3; THC29/1; THC29/7; THC30/2; THC31/1; THC48/2; THC49/2; THC55/2; THC58/6; THC60/2; THC63/2; THC68/2; THC69/3; THC70/1; THC70/8; THC75/3; THC76/3; THC80/1; THC80/8; THC81/1; THC81/5
hills, *See* mountains
hinge, THC27/2
horn, THC18/4; THC22/9; THC23/8; THC30/9; THC43/7; THC43/9; THC54/2; THC54/3; THC58/9; THC75/8; THC79/8–9. *See also* wild animals
horses, THC28/5; THC49/3; THC71/2; THC71/5; THC71/7; THC71/8; THC79/2
house, THC2/5; THC4/7; THC4/9; THC6/9; THC20/5; THC23/6; THC39/1–9; THC67/8; THC71/5; THC74/3; THC76/6; THC79/2
hunting, THC9/2; THC12/5; THC43/5; THC50/5,7,9; THC58/7; THC62/7–9; THC64/7
husband/wife, THC6/4; THC6/7; THC32/3; THC35/7; THC56/1; THC65/5; THC65/7; THC65/8; THC68/9

ice, THC38/7; THC41/6; THC79/Head; THC79/2
illness, THC4/8; THC19/7; THC28/7; THC51/8; THC51/9; THC55/7; THC70/2; THC70/6; THC70/8; THC71/3; THC73/4; THC75/7; THC81/8
immaturity, THC12/1–9; THC28/1; THC31/8
inner/outer, THC6/3; THC9/Head; THC13/1; THC15/2; THC29/Head; THC35/Head; THC46/8; THC63/2; THC65/Head
innovation, THC10/7

jade, THC2/4; THC46/2; THC47/1; THC50/3; THC54/5; THC57/6; THC60/7; THC69/9; THC72/2
jar, THC40/5; THC74/5. *See also* vessels
journeys, THC3/5–7; THC31/1–9

leaping, THC9/6; THC52/3; THC73/3
light, THC9/2; THC11/3; THC12/3; THC13/2; THC19/2; THC20/Head; THC20/6; THC26/2; THC32/Head; THC35/2; THC37/Head; THC38/6; THC41/9; THC50/2; THC51/1; THC62/1; THC63/1; THC63/9; THC64/6; THC66/2; THC67/2; THC67/6; THC67/7; THC67/9; THC68/5–7; THC71/1; THC74/3; THC78/6

magic signs. *See* portents
magicians, THC43/4; THC51/9; THC75/7
male/female, THC4/1; THC6/4; THC6/7; THC27/4; THC27/8; THC32/3; THC35/7; THC42/4; THC43/3; THC51/2; THC55/1; THC61/5; THC64/1; THC65/1–9; THC68/9; THC75/8; THC77/2; THC77/3
marshes, THC13/5; THC21/4
measures, THC52/Head–9; THC54/6
medicine, THC15/7; THC19/7; THC21/5; THC64/8; THC75/7. *See also* illness
ministerial remonstrance, THC8/1–4
mirror, THC12/8; THC68/4
moon, THC1/6; THC19/1; THC51/4; THC66/8; THC67/5; THC68/8; THC75/9
mountains, THC3/5; THC3/7; THC3/9; THC9/3; THC13/7; THC13/9; THC14/9; THC20/9; THC21/4; THC36/9; THC55/9; THC56/6; THC59/7; THC60/Head; THC69/6; THC72/7; THC72/9; THC79/6; THC80/9; THC81/3
mouth, THC25/8; THC33/7; THC56/1,3,5; THC70/3; THC77/6

mud or muck, THC4/1; THC12/2; THC28/3; THC39/2
music, THC24/3; THC24/5; THC24/6; THC41/2; THC46/8

nets, THC22/4; THC23/2; THC40/7; THC41/3–4; THC58/7–8; THC64/7
new sprouts, THC11/9; THC17/1; THC39/9; THC41/6; THC53/7; THC65/7
noses, THC59/9; THC70/3; THC74/4

old age. *See* aging
omens. *See* portents
Oneness, THC1/1; THC14/Head; THC14/2; THC57/2; THC77/8

parasites, THC9/8; THC16/7; THC56/5; THC70/8
parent-child relations, THC27/7; THC32/3; THC33/3; THC39/2–3; THC39/7; THC42/7; THC53/1; THC53/2; THC53/4; THC65/3; THC66/4; THC76/4; THC77/2; THC81/7
pillars or posts, THC30/6; THC36/3; THC36/9; THC46/2; THC52/4; THC52/5; THC71/5
pivot, THC2/2; THC27/2
pools. *See* abyss
portents, THC17/5; THC42/3; THC68/8; THC70/7; THC73/8; THC76/2; THC76/8; THC771/; THC77/2; THC77/9
poverty, THC5/4; THC5/7
prison, THC21/9, THC69/7
probe, THC15/7
profit, THC14/7; THC17/1; THC21/8; THC25/4; THC28/4; THC43/6; THC58/3; THC64/6; THC74/5

rain, THC5/9; THC26/9; THC43/4; THC54/7; THC56/9; THC57/8; THC63/4; THC65/9
restraints, THC2/4; THC4/4; THC9/9; THC11/8; THC21/Head; THC21/9; THC22/1; THC22/2; THC22/3; THC22/4; THC22/7; THC22/8; THC24/4; THC26/3
retreat, THC17/2–3; THC17/6; THC17/9
river, THC3/9; THC20/9; THC47/6; THC55/9; THC60/Head; THC79/6. *See also* water
rope, THC40/5–6; THC76/8

roots, THC3/2; THC7/2; THC7/4; THC21/4; THC30/8; THC31/6; THC34/9; THC46/1: THC45/3; THC48/3; THC55/8; THC61/9; THC68/2; THC75/6; THC77/Head; THC77/3; THC81/1; THC81/3
ruler, THC1/5; THC4/1; THC5/3; THC20/4; THC21/5; THC43/7; THC51/3; THC51/5; THC63/3; THC64/6; THC65/2; THC66/4; THC78/1

sack, THC77/5–6
sacrifice, THC16/4; THC56/8; THC59/4; THC81/6
shadow, THC21/2
silk, THC28/3; THC35/5; THC47/1; THC60/7; THC78/9
souls, THC1/9; THC28/Head; THC42/3; THC63/Head
speech, THC61/1; THC61/3; THC61/4; THC61/5; THC61/6; THC61/7; THC61/8; THC61/9
spiders, THC26/5; THC43/6
stairs, THC19/9; THC46/5; THC55/3; THC66/3; THC69/7
stars, THC34/6; THC81/9
stone, THC4/5; THC16/3; THC22/6; THC48/2; THC52/8; THC55/6; THC60/3; THC71/9; THC72/1; THC79/4; THC79/5; THC79/7; THC79/8
storehouses, THC4/2; THC75/6
stove, THC39/6; THC44/1; THC44/3; THC44/9; THC69/9
strength, THC3/4; THC3/5; THC23/7; THC32/5; THC44/4; THC60/3
sun, THC1/5; THC9/7; THC13/6; THC19/1; THC20/4; THC41/9; THC51/3; THC63/9; THC67/5; THC70/7; THC75/4; THC75/9; THC78/6

teacher, THC12/1; THC69/3
teeth, THC23/4; THC25/9; THC30/9; THC33/8; THC34/1; THC74/5; THC75/5
thunder, THC21/3; THC21/6; THC21/7; THC21/8; THC32/6; THC61/6
time, THC1/9; THC8/4; THC14/4; THC17/6; THC18/1; THC18/2; THC22/8; THC24/2; THC27/3; THC28/2; THC35/5; THC35/9; THC36/2; THC68/9; THC73/8; THC79/7
tongues, THC8/8; THC61/3–4; THC61/9
tools, THC3/7; THC6/6; THC7/7; THC7/8?;

THC20/5; THC21/5; THC22/5; THC29/1; THC30/4; THC39/5; THC57/8; THC77/6; THC78/3; THC78/7
towers, THC7/7
tree, THC7/3; THC7/9; THC8/6; THC13/3; THC15/3; THC16/3; THC17/8; THC23/7; THC39/9; THC41/1; THC49/4; THC49/5; THC53/7; THC59/8; THC62/7; THC66/1; THC66/2; THC69/4; THC71/4; THC71/9; THC75/8; THC79/2; THC79/8

unicorn, THC32/2

valley, THC5/9; THC7/2; THC7/3; THC40/9
vessels, THC5/6; THC27/7; THC39/7; THC40/5; THC44/3-5; THC48/5; THC57/8
Void (= mind), THC6/1; THC10/6; THC75/1

waiting, THC18/3; THC18/7
walls, THC11/9; THC16/9; THC39/Head;

THC45/8; THC46/1; THC46/2;THC46/9; THC49/9; THC52/4-5; THC65/7
war, THC1/2; THC16/9; THC25/9; THC32/1-9
water, THC1/7; THC3/9; THC8/8; THC19/5; THC20/9; THC25/2; THC28/6; THC42/9; THC49/1; THC52/2; THC55/9; THC57/6; THC61/5; THC69/6; THC76/9
weapons, THC8/7; THC16/8; THC16/9; THC25/7; THC29/1; THC29/6; THC29/9; THC32/1-9; THC64/9; THC75/1
wells, THC39/6; THC40/5; THC40/9; THC54/6; THC76/8
wild animals, THC6/5; THC12/5; THC12/9; THC16/5; THC16/7; THC25/8; THC25/9; THC30/6; THC30/9; THC32/4; THC32/5; THC43/8; THC47/4; THC47/6-7; THC49/5; THC50/5; THC62/9; THC63/8; THC69/6; THC76/5; THC81/7
wind, THC21/3; THC31/2; THC61/6
wood. *See* tree

Index

Note: The correlations (astrological, directional, and musical, hexagramatic) assigned to each texagram may be found on pp. 80–83; therefore, they are not indexed here. The page numbers for tetragrams and autocommentaries may be found in the Table of Contents; to repeat that information here would be redundant. Tetragram and autocommentary titles are therefore indexed only when they are cited in other chapters.

Certain words, given their frequent occurrence, are indexed only as they relate to selected topics: Those words are: Appraisals, Fathomings, Five Phases, Heads, noble man, petty man, Tao, Virtue, Way, Yang *ch'i*, Yang Hsiung, Yin *ch'i*, Yin/yang.

Accumulation (THC60), 424, 426
"Admonition against Wine," 6
Advance (THC20), 182, 424, 427
Aesop, 118, 158, 205
aesthetic theory, 569n.11, 571n.21
age/aging. *See* old age/aging
Aggravation (THC76), 425, 427
agriculture, 95, 108, 163–64, 203, 205, 221, 229, 245–47, 300, 330, 550n.23
ai ("undifferentiated/ungraded love"), contrasted with *jen*, 239–40, 328, 431, 547n.4, 615n.38
Ai Chang (fl. A.D. 8), 600n.18
ai jih, defined, 46–48; importance in THC, 46–47, 480n.198
alchemy, 176, 360–61, 593n.24, 606n.19
almanacs, 486n.304
Analects, 1, 35, 40, 56, 302, 312, 487n.312; cited, 37, 90, 98, 109–10, 117, 135, 143, 150, 312–13, 324, 382, 417
ancestors, 11, 579n.10; temple of, 347, 420, 570n.43; ties with, 282, 293, 313; tombs of, 335; worship of, 259, 282, 293, 302, 304, 316, 346, 347–50. *See also* filial piety; ancestral line; patrilineal line
Ancients, 585n.6; as sages, 137, 182, 190, 313, 396, 409, 415, 482n.227; consulted, 149–50; imitating the, 287, 296, 303, 305, 406; love of, 254; teachings of, 115, 128; Way of the, 88, 143, 326, 366, 376. *See also* culture, invention of
Antares. *See* Heart constellation
antiquity. *See* culture, prior to; Taoists, primitivist vision of
Ao Granary, 590n.17
apocrypha, 62, 91, 478n.178, 487n.312, 507n.7
"Appended Texts." *See* "Great Commentary to the *Changes*"

Appraisals (tsan), anomalies in, 46, 94; as microcosm, 30, 84–86, 88; correlations of, 433, 459; phrasing in, 453; modelled on Line texts, 11, 73; read in divination, 13, 31; repeated in Fathomings, xii; related to direction, 625n.39; related to rank, 11, 459, 603n.17; related to time, 10–12, 27, 30–31, 45–46, 84–85, 246, 455, 598n.11; structure of, 11, 92, 94, 122, 183, 434, 459; Ying/yang Five Phases values for, 11, 131, 268. *See also* individual cosmic phases; Head texts
Approach (HEX19), 507n.1
Aquinas, Thomas, xi
archery, 122–123, 203, 379
architecture, 123, 243, 290, 292; as metaphor, 540n.35; courtyards, 146, 326, 336, 374; decoration of, 342; dedication of, 556n.22; palace structures, 171; structural supports in, 171, 225, 249, 258, 291, 320–21, 390–91. *See also* city walls; *hang-t'u*; sumptuary regulations
Aristotle, 614n.16
Aristotelian Mean, 183
arts, 303, 324; polite, 65, 69, 157, 198; technical arts, xi, 44, 60–61, 171. *See also* magic, occult arts; Mystery, arts of
Ascent (THC7), 21, 423, 428
asceticism, 283, 341, 345, 606n.9. *See also* "lessen desires"; sensory desire
astrologists. *See* cosmologists
astrology/astronomy, 8, 16, 97, 120, 125, 316, 455, 624n.17; Yang's interest in, 61. *See also* calendar; Grand Inception Calendar; Hun-t'ien astronomical theory; Kai-t'ien astronomical theory; Triple Concordance calendar
autobiography. *See* Yang Hsiung

autocommentaries, 3; related to "Ten
Wings," 8, 11, 14; cited, 173, 175, 214,
344. *See also* autocommentaries listed by
title
Autumn Equinox solar period, 327
Autumn Onset solar period, 26, 315
"awaiting fate" (*hou ming*), 38, 54, 56, 176–
77. *See also ming*
axis mundi, 86, 97–98, 134, 176, 287, 289,
325

barbarians, 288, 498n.37. *See also* Nine
Barbarians
Barrier (THC4), 19, 102, 423, 427
belly, symbolism of, 121, 162, 164, 181,
220–21, 224, 345, 367, 379, 385–86, 420,
461, 500n.7, 514n.10
benefit, maximization of, 48–49
benevolence. *See jen*
benevolent government. See just state
Bible, 63
biography. *See* Yang Hsiung
Bird constellation, 431
black. *See* color symbolism
Bold Resolution (THC30), 425, 426
Book of Changes (*Yi ching*), as best Classic,
8, 33–34, 465n.3, 470n.78; as Classic, xi,
4, 63, 467n.32; books imitating, 114,
467n.30, 468n.37; commentaries to, 11,
88, 108, 492n.45; Confucius studies, 7;
early core text of, 71–72, 88; different
arrangements for, 468n.43, 469n.46;
genesis of, 6–7; Han views of, 7–8;
method of divination for, 27, 72,
469n.56; prototype for THC, xi, 1, 6–15,
18–19, 21, 24–25, 27–29, 33–34, 73, 86,
88–89, 103, 108, 147, 258, 267, 326,
468n.43; tradition of, 108, 118, 141, 197,
482n.230; cited, 88, 95, 104, 109–10,
112, 114, 118, 122, 140–41, 146, 152,
155, 158, 169, 176, 179, 188–90, 195,
200, 210, 214, 219, 223, 227, 234, 252,
258, 270, 275, 282, 298, 306, 315, 321–
22, 332, 334–36, 341, 355, 358, 368, 371,
382, 385, 389, 393, 398, 407. *See also*
"Great Commentary"; hexagrams; Line
texts; "Ten Wings"
Book of Divination, 488n.17
Book of Documents. See Documents
Book of Odes. See Odes
Branching Out (THC9), 423, 426
bronzes, 281–82, 284, 349

Buddhism, 220, 283, 502n.9, 537n.15,
606n.9
bureaucratic selection, 5, 123, 136, 169, 220,
249, 284–85, 299, 313, 333, 353–54, 386.
See also career advancement; officials;
ministers; patronage; ruler
Burning of the Books, 33, 470n.79
butcher. *See* chef
Butcher Ting, 564n.3

Calamity (set of 3 Appraisals), 12, 185, 209,
217, 230, 234, 242, 246, 254, 257, 293,
355, 455, 458–59, 461. *See also* good
fortune/calamity
calendar, 44, 268, 423, 433–34, 457–58,
600n.22, 618n.13
canon. *See* classic
Canon of Supreme Mystery (*T'ai hsüan
ching*), as Chinese summa, xi, 1, 57–60;
as classic, 55–62, 97, 465n.2; as comprehensive, 4–5, 60; as divination classic/
manual, 11–14, 27–35, 71–72, 460,
469n.67; as tool, 617n.67; commentary
tradition to, xii; core text defined, 73,
88; date of compilation for, 31–32; innovation in, 8–13, 28, 62, 508n.33, philosophical importance of, 1–2, 5, 61–62;
structure of, 9–17, 73, 456–58; style of,
74–75; symbol system of, xi, 438–48;
underlying themes of, 46–47, 58–61. *See
also* Book of Changes
career advancement, 86, 89–90, 111, 125,
182, 220, 333, 353, 363
categorical thinking, 33, 55, 60–61, 65–68,
118, 140, 159, 165, 168, 187, 190, 252,
273, 295, 315, 355, 377, 546n.30,
616n.39. *See also* Key terms; Yin/yang
Five Phases theory
categories (*lei*), 67–68, 429–30, 432, 434,
450, 455; defined, 456, 599n.16
Catullus, 272
center, as auspicious, 91, 266; as creative
balance, 18, 84, 436; as Mean, 183, 289,
337–38, 342, 391, 450–51; associations
of, 95, 154, 266, 444. *See also* conscience; good faith; heart/mind; Mean;
Way of Centrality; yellow Center
(THC1), 18, 22–23, 25, 86, 423, 426,
446, 457, 458; as microcosm for Heads,
84–85, 92, 94, 267, 448–53
"center heart" (*chung hsin*), 69–70, 109,
111, 121, 194, 220, 240, 360, 537n.14.

Index

See also heart/mind; Key terms; Mean
Center Perfection (*chung chi*), 325
centering the self, 70, 87, 183, 253, 263, 459
chance. *See* coincidence
chang chü. *See* "commentaries by chapter
and verse."
Chang Heng, 1, 622n.6
change, 431, 481n.217; defined, 436–37
Change (THC28), 425, 427, 446, 457–58
"Change as the Only Constant" theory, 57
Changes. *See Book of Changes*
chaos, in present, 90, 435; primordial, 2, 58,
64–65, 68, 84, 86, 96, 235, 254, 287, 385,
406, 449. *See also* cosmogonic stages
charismatic Power, 8, 49, 65, 315, 351, 354,
382; defined, 431. *See also* Virtue, as
charismatic
chastity. *See* gender
chef/butcher, symbolism of, 282, 284, 386,
565n.34
chen, 28, 88; defined, 71–72, 469n.60,
489nn.48,50,51,53. *See also* Indexed
Themes
Ch'en Pen-li, 31, 111, 144, 176, 267, 305
ch'eng. *See* integrity
Cheng Hsüan, 487n.3
Ch'eng Keng-wang, 349
Chi Tzu, 377–78
ch'i, 335, 431, 449, 453, 455, 462; aroused,
198, 336; cycles of, 51, 96, 351; defined,
4, 63–65, 327; depletion of, 94, 107, 421,
452; Earthly, 559n.23; fiery, 559n.36;
"flood-like," 96, 194, 317, 338; generation of, 3, 130, 432; graphic form of, 63–
64, 488n.4; patrimony of, 60, 326, 335,
480n.189, properties of, 63–65, 185, 201,
332; related to *ming*, 37; ch'i, primordial. *See* chaos, primordial; ch'i, quintessential, 64, 274–75, 277. *See also*
collective reponsibility; cosmogonic
stages, Head texts for THC1–81;
yang *ch'i*; yin *ch'i*
Chia Yi, 204, 300, 589n.36
Chiao Kan, 467n.30; 468n.37
Ch'ien. *See* Creative (HEX1)
chih ming ("knowing ming"/"recognizing
fate"), 35, 44, 47, 65, 94, 116, 226, 238,
429, 471nn.92,93, 478n.178, 484n.251
chih yi ("holding fast to the one"), 157–58,
315, 341, 424; defined, 576n.7
Ch'in (dynasty). *See* Ao Granary; Burning
of the Books; First Emperor of Ch'in

Chinese philosophy, debates in. *See* philo-
sophical debates
Ching Fang, 8, 15–18, 558n.1
Ching K'o, 552n.32
Ch'ing-ming festival, 214, 535n.8
Chou dynasty, temple of 117; tombs of, 335.
See also cosmogonic myth; Duke T'an-
fu, King Wen; King Wu; T'ien ming
Chou Tun-yi, 489n.48
Chronicles (Ch'un Ch'iu), 4, 63, 487n.312,
565n.34
Chronicles of Mr. Lü (Lü shih ch'un ch'iu),
217
Chu Hsi (1130–1200), 2, 466n.8, 475n.124,
489n.48
Chu-jung, 442
Ch'ü Yüan, 498n.49, 532n.14, 600n.36
Chüan-hsü, 443
Chuang Tsun, 466n.13, 470n.85
Chuang tzu, 58, 86–87, 91, 103, 229, 297,
420, 472n.98, 473n.105, 481nn.208,212,
482n.227, 485n.274, 505n.13, 529n.6,
542n.36, 585n.4; *Chuang tzu*, cited, 87,
150, 203, 564n.3
cinnabar, 322, 606n.19
circle, defined for China, 470n.71, 492n.4
city walls, 148, 290, 319–21. *See also*
architecture; civilization; culture;
social order
clan. *See* family
classic, 57–62; defined, 55, 62, 462, 465n.2,
484n.259; Han views of, 7–9. *See also*
Five Classics
Classic of Filial Piety (Hsiao ching), 237
clepsydra, 434, 455
Closed Mouth (THC56), 424, 428
Closeness (THC33), 425, 428
Closing In (THC58), 424, 426
Closure (THC74), 425, 428
clothing, symbolism of, 99, 356–57,
570nn.31, 43
coinage/currency, 155–56, 455, 469n.61
coincidence, 141, 278–80, 385, 507n.18
Cold Dew solar period, 368
collective responsibility, 327, 346, 355
color symbolism, 356; of black, 34, 88, 183,
216, 328–29, 345, 355, 407, 443, 581n.11;
of golden, 110–11, 345, 412, 420; of
green, 93, 438; of red, 34, 105, 155, 400,
412, 440; of white, 34, 138, 216, 328– 29,
355, 358, 400, 440; of yellow, 88, 93,
103, 110–11, 253, 275, 333, 338, 345,

Index

color symbolism (*cont.*)
357, 369, 407, 412, 420, 444, 495n.9. *See
also* Yellow Center
Commanding General, 442
"commentaries by chapter and verse," 1,
465n.4
"Commentary on the
Judgments." *See* Judgments
"Commentary on the Images." *See* Images
community, 56, 129, 141, 148; breakdown
of, 97, 148, 194, 261, 265, 393, 399, 404,
420; creation of, 69, 71, 101, 108, 167,
182, 216, 237, 301, 303, 321, 328–30,
337, 351, 385, 394; ideal visions of, 47,
165, 207, 234–35, 369, 373, 398, 420;
need for, 49, 181, 195, 212, 298
Compendium of Annotations (*Ts'ang Chieh
hsün tsüan*), 467n.27, 472n.100
Completing (mantic formula), 449, 456
Completion (THC73), 425, 428, 446, 457,
459
Compliance (THC77), 425, 427
Confucian, defined. *See Ju*
Confucian Classics. *See* Five Classics
Confucian Way. *See* Way, Confucian
Confucianism, as state orthodoxy, 5, 8–9,
55, 62, 502n.19; as Tool, 42, 176, 195,
222; defined, 485n.276; focus on social
relations, 48, 165, 207, 229, 313, 387;
ideals of, 89, 322–23, 397; masters of,
198, 341; on education, 236, 290; on government, 243, 304, 319; on ritual, 41–
42, 113; tradition of, 4–5, 62, 65, 68, 94,
182, 222, 240, 253, 258, 316, 3?? 382;
vs. heterodoxy, 264. *See also* apocrypha;
Five Classics; greatness; Han Confucianism; human nature; independence; individual masters listed by name; punishments; ritual; Way, Confucian; Yang
Hsiung
Confucians, agreement with Taoists, 160,
206, 544n.41; debates among, 38–39, 63,
323–24; influenced by Legalists, 131; vs.
Legalists, 98, 245, 250, 304, 387; vs.
Mohists, 60, 486n.299, 474n.112, 547n.4;
572n.26; vs. Taoists, 90–91, 107, 237,
356, 536n.31. *See also* Han Confucianism; *Ju*; philosophical debates
Confucius (551–479 B.C.), 72, 146, 582n.39,
598n.17; anecdotes about, 141, 237,
524n.9, 529n.54, 549n.33, 562n.5;

author/editor of classics, 63, 129; student
of *Changes*, 7; supreme sage, 1, 5, 47,
53, 106, 142–43, 158, 417, 475n.125,
483n.242; "uncrowned king," 39; defining goodness, 90–91, 97, 162, 165;
Han views of, 479n.178, 553n.14; on
education, 69; on government, 269; on
ming, 33, 39, 56; on ritual, 301; cited,
35, 39, 47, 68–69, 91, 96, 110, 114, 116,
131, 142, 147, 149, 172–73, 189, 203,
210–11, 237, 242, 254–55, 287, 295, 297–
98, 307, 328, 354, 357, 360, 386–87, 393.
See also Analects; "reanimate the old";
Yen Hui
conscience, 8, 70, 97, 104, 142, 146, 183,
190, 193, 219, 236, 252, 254, 320, 332–
34, 338, 344, 351, 360, 366, 373, 377,
394, 416. *See also* heart/mind
consideration (*shu*), 47, 68, 162, 304. *See
also* reciprocity
Constancy (THC51), 24, 424, 427
constant norms, 51–52, 65, 93–94, 151, 215,
258, 315, 422; as proper subject of study,
46, 59, 480n.190, 481n.208. *See also*
cosmic law; Five Constant Relations;
pattern; ritual
constellations, correlations with individual
tetragrams, 80–83, 320–21
construction projects. *See* architecture, city
walls; *hang-t'u*
Contact (THC16), 424, 428
Contention (THC25), 424, 427
continuity, defined, 436–37
Contrariety (THC6), 20, 423, 427
correlative thought. *See* categorical thinking
cosmic balance, 88, 189, 243
cosmic harmony. *See* harmony
cosmic laws/norms, 44, 124, 159, 213, 257,
262, 269, 344, 350, 420; on retribution,
37, 174–75, 194, 200. *See also* Heaven's
Net; Tao; Yin/yang
cosmic order. *See* order, cosmic
cosmic origin. *See* cosmogonic stages
cosmic pattern. *See* pattern
cosmic process. *See* Tao
cosmic sack/womb. *See* Heaven; Tao
cosmic unity, 87, 200, 327, 425. *See also*
Tao, as one
cosmic way. *See* Way
cosmogonic myth, 466n.12, 609n.7
cosmogonic stages, 2–3, 10, 20, 22, 68, 84–

86, 88, 94, 118, 156, 161, 235, 410–11, 429; defined, 2, 90. *See also* chaos, primordial
cosmologists, 8, 38, 44, 46, 49, 57, 60–61, 588n.7
courage, 171, 173, 203, 221, 223–24, 226, 234, 307, 360, 419, 517n.3; defined, 430
Covering (mantic formula), 449, 456
creation. *See* cosmogonic stages
creation myth. *See* cosmogonic myth
creative act, defined, 436, 471n.89
Creative (HEX1), 15, 448, 452, 479n.187, 492n.45, 551n.3
Culmen, 431
culture, 306; invention of, 7, 41, 58, 121, 123, 185, 263, 268–69, 278–79, 317, 330, 391, 412, 434–35, 454–55, 469n.61; prior to, 435, 476n.145, 483n.240. *See also* pattern; sages; Tools

dance, 345
Dark Bird, 378, 600n.22
Darkening (THC67), 425, 426
death, 19, 27, 40, 48, 51, 58, 86, 106, 107, 111, 139, 143, 148, 173, 196, 200, 231, 233, 236, 238, 257, 272, 279–80, 302, 324, 332, 334–35, 349–50, 362–63, 368, 370, 374, 381, 388, 411, 429, 486n.288; defined, 94, 381, 421; defined as "good," 124, 290, 459. *See also* old age; rites; mourning; war
Decisiveness (THC29), 425, 427
Decree. *See Ming*
Decree of Heaven. *See* T'ien ming
Defectiveness (THC10), 424, 426, 446, 457–58
Deference (HEX15), 20
Deficit (intercalary App.), 455, 460
Departments (line of tetragrams), 10, 435, 457–58
Departure (THC66), 424, 426
desire, 136–38, 145, 162, 181, 194, 198–99, 233, 344, 367– 68, 423
destiny. *See ming*
development, 431, 481n.217; defined, 436
Diagram of the Mystery (*Hsüan t'u*), 14, 454
diet, in Han, 602n.17
Difficulties (THC79), 425, 427
Difficulty Starting (HEX3), 19, 107
Diminishment (THC55), 424, 427, 428, 446, 457, 459

Dimming (THC68), 425, 428
Dipper, 67, 97–98, 242, 321, 433–34, 457, 462, 617nn.61,73, 623n.4. *See also* Polestar
Director of Public Works, 443
"Discussion of Music." *See Hsün tzu*
Discussion of the Trigrams (*Shuo kua*), 14, 438, 461
Dispelling Objections *fu*, 6, 465n.2
Dispelling Ridicule *fu*, 6, 34
disputation, defined, 431
Divergence (THC11), 22, 424, 426
divination, 41, 71–72, 118, 150, 211, 435, 438, 455, 460, 482n.230; defined, 29, 34–35, 149–50, 469n.61, 471nn.88,94. *See also Book of Changes*; *Canon of Supreme Mystery*; yarrow stalks
divine (*shen*), 29, 34, 47, 155, 475n.125; defined, 19, 28, 158, 167, 201, 469n.49, 481n.217, 528n.29, 588n.9. *See also* gods; heart/mind; noble man; Virtue, as divine
diviner's board, 469n.67
Doctrine of Mutual Interaction between Heaven and Man, 45, 64, 269, 273–74, 480n.189
"Doctrine of the Mean" (*Chung yung*), 100, 291, 297, 469n.59
Documents (Shang shu), xi, 4, 63, 114, 404, 470n.79, 472n.101, 473n.102; cited, 146, 196, 208, 222, 299, 305, 343. *See also* "Great Plan"; "Yü kung" ch
Doubt (THC62), 424, 427
Dowager Empress Wang, 180, 497n.15
dragon, symbolism of, 85, 89–90, 108, 270, 273–74, 370–71, 450–52, 519n.13
Dragon constellation, 431
Dream of the Red Chamber, 595n.9
dreams, 277, 562n.5
duality, 65; of mind, 156–57, 193–94, 252
Duke Hsiao of Ch'in, 132
Duke of Chou, 374, 465n.7, 562n.5
Duke P'ing of Chin, 609n.9
Duke Tan-fu, 102
Duke Wen of Chin, 133
Duke Yi of Wei, 516n.31
Duties (THC27), 425, 428
duty (*yi*), 4, 35, 86, 92, 199, 210–14, 221, 256, 271, 279, 307, 341, 371; and rites, 117, 137, 195, 328, 568n.18; defined, 431, 460. *See also* family

Earth, 18, 84, 434, 454; as center, 91, 93, 116, 214, 245, 333–34; as divination result, 27–28; as model, 116, 333–34, 408; as patron phase for Han, 491n.28; as square, 429, 431, 434; as supreme entity, 42, 45, 437, 453, 486n.284; cosmic phase for Appraisals, 110, 245, 444–45; cosmic phase for Head, 266; graphic depiction of, 9, 27–28; numbers for, 267–68; Way of, 3, 113, 458. *See also* color symbolism, of yellow; Five Phases, enumeration orders of; Heaven-and-Earth, gods of; Heaven-Earth-Man

Earthly Branches, 459–60, 618n.14

Ease (THC23), 424, 427

Eastern Star, 150

Eastern Well constellation, 617n.69

eclecticism. *See tsa*

eclipse, 404, 461

education, 148–49, 207, 277–78; defined, 69, 104; in womb, 408; *See also* Confucianism; Confucius; family, as socializing agent; study; teacher

Eight Directions, 460

Eight Musical Airs, 455

Eight Trigrams, 252

Elaborated Teachings (*Wen yen*), 13–14

Elaboration of the Mystery, 13–14, 93–94, 454, 491n.26; cited, 87, 90–91, 93–94, 97

Embellishment (THC61), 24, 424, 426

emblem, 7, 46

Emperor Ai of Han, 1, 31–32, 497n.15

Emperor P'ing of Han, 305, 324

Emperor Ch'eng of Han, 1, 497n.15

Emperor Wen of Han, 604n.10

Emperor Wu of Han, 244–45, 294

Emperor of the Center, 86. *See also* Hunt'un

emptiness, 3, 90–91, 112, 283, 287, 294, 332, 357, 401, 451; *See also* humility

Emptiness, primal, 429, 433

Encounters (THC43), 423, 428

Endeavor (THC26), 424, 427

enfeoffment, 303, 385, 534n.11

Enlargement (THC46), 423, 427, 446, 457–58

equality, defined, 121, 500n.4, 529n.6; between sexes, 370, 597n.19; of experience, 237. *See also* moral relativism

equinoxes, 15, 22–24, 26, 182, 186, 189, 219, 355, 359, 362, 365

equitable treatment. *See kung*

eremitism, 101, 112, 337, 345, 570n.36, 584n.18

Eternity (THC53), 10, 424, 427

evil, defined, 430; solution to, 355

Evolution of the Mystery (*Hsüan li*), 14, 454, 627n.38

Exhaustion (THC69), 425, 426

"Exhortation to Study." *See* Hsün tzu

exorcism, 389, 505n.40

Expelling Poverty *fu*, 52, 500n.29

Extending (mantic formula), 449, 456

Fa yen. See Model Sayings

Failure (THC75), 425, 427

fairness. *See kung*

family, 302, 313, 338, 387, 403, 567n.8; as socializing agent, 69, 236– 37, 239–42, 278, 348–50; clan organization, 261, 337; elder-younger relations, 261, 302, 348–49, 455, 460; extended, 282, 428; feelings as "natural," 227, 235; husband/wife, 120, 124, 178, 180, 211–213, 246, 259, 273, 276, 316, 323, 325, 336, 368–72, 376, 381, 407, 429, 460; marriage, 368, 597n.7; parent/child relations, 29, 48, 65, 104, 124, 236–37, 240–41, 263, 275, 276, 279, 325, 404–05, 416, 429; father/son relations, 4, 259, 275, 373, 432, 455, 460, 462, 598n.11; property division within, 261; subversion of, 260–61, 403, 428. *See also* gender roles; hierarchy; law; patrilineal line; succession

Family line in tetragrams, 10, 28, 435, 457–58

Fan Wang, 87–88, 94, 105, 111, 117, 132, 136, 139, 291, 307, 317, 350, 468nn.41,43

Fang yen. See Regional Phrases

fate, 11, 35, 62, 201, 209, 382, 614n.11. *See also chih ming; ming;* predestination

"Fathomings" ("Ts'e"), xi, 13–14, 73, 454

favor/blame (*hsiu ch'iu*), 52, 435

feasting, 169, 212, 241–42, 284, 347–48, 589n.27

filial piety (*hsiao*), 41, 48, 68, 254, 277, 305, 348, 369, 404–05, 464, 574n.29. *See also* ancestors, family

"find their categories." *See* "follow its type"

Fire, 434; correlations of, 86, 88, 92–93, 125, 155, 202, 203, 215, 257, 344, 441–

42; cosmic phase for Appraisals, 2, 7, 86, 103. *See also* Five Phases, enumeration orders of

Fire Star, 374–75, 462, 599n.22

First Emperor of Ch'in, 251, 294, 396, 498n.37, 539n.13, 558n.29

Five Blessings, 94, 478n.172

Five Classics, 4, 33, 45, 97, 129, 259, 295, 311, 318, 487n.1, 552n.14; as inconsistent/flawed, 55, 63, 150; as infallible, 4, 202, 415, 557n.17; as orthodoxy, 468n.35; as supreme entities, 45, 137, 139, 142, 456; as Tools, 8, 106, 123, 130, 185, 262–63, 269, 395, 412; defined, 55, 63; study of, 8, 69, 106, 128, 146, 264; cited, 89, 110, 112, 157, 241, 265, 303–04, 320. *See also* Classics by individual title; sages, as authors of

Five Colors, 366

Five Conquests, 462, 626n.21

Five Constant Relations (*wu ch'ang*), 4, 15, 121, 471n.85; defined, 49, 191. *See also* Three Guide Lines

Five Excellent Materials, 434. *See also* Five Phases

Five Gauges, 159

Five Mutilations. *See* Five Punishments

Five Notes, 366

Five Phases, 16, 42, 44–45, 65–68, 84, 86, 214, 434, 453; as cosmogonic stage, 2; correlation with Heads, 16, 80–83, 266; enumeration orders of, 11, 66, 439–45, 462, 626n.20. *See also* cosmogonic stages; Five Gauges; Principle of Masking; Yin/yang Five Phases theory

Five Productions, 462, 626n.20

Five Punishments, 455, 512n.40

Five Recorders, 434

Five Sacred Mountains, 456

Five Tastes, 281, 284, 565n.25

Flight (THC49), 423, 427

"flood-like" *ch'i*. *See ch'i*

"follow its kind/model" (*ch'u lei*), 66, 118, 179, 202, 621n.6

Following (THC19), 424, 427, 446, 457–58

force, appropriate use of, 169–70, 523n.28; dangers of, 170, 173, 190, 196, 226, 233, 251. *See also* Virtue, war

Formlessness, primal, 3, 347, 429, 431, 449, 461

Forest of Changes. See Yi lin

Fostering (THC81), 25, 425, 428

Four Great Rivers, 456

Four Qualities. *See* mantic formulae

Four States, 188, 405, 523n.24

freedom. *See* independence

Freud, 307, 373

friends/friendship, 101, 109, 125, 130, 168–70, 187, 208, 211, 216, 237, 238, 241, 249, 260, 275, 313, 341–42, 345, 387, 400, 428, 460

Frontier Myth, 229

Frostfall solar period, 379, 388

frugality, 296, 585n.35

Fu Hsi. *See* Pao Hsi

Full Circle (THC2), 19, 423, 426

Fullness (THC38), 425, 426

gaps. *See* "no gap"

Garden of Sayings (*Shuo yüan*), 131, 361

Gate (between life and death), 236, 349

Gathering (THC35), 425, 427

gender roles, for females, 124, 211–213, 357, 407, 534n.21, 576n.13; importance of female chastity, 316, 366, 369, 371, 577n.14; male/female, 178, 180, 258, 316, 357, 366, 372, 403, 429, 455, 458, 463, 505n.43. *See also* "constant norms"; equality, of sexes; family; "rectification of names"; sex/sexual attraction

gentleman (*chün tzu*), defined, 162, 245, 295, 418. *See also* noble man; nobility

geomancy. *See* magic

ghosts, 29, 200, 277, 314, 347–50, 361, 404, 421, 438, 443, 452–54, 463, 473n.105

gnomon, 432, 455, 617n.5

god of Fire. *See* Hsüan-ming

god of the soil (*she*), 349, 528n.38, 588n.16, 619n.41

gods, 3, 29, 36, 61, 165–68, 200, 212, 235, 252, 274, 277–78, 282–83, 286, 293, 298, 301, 314–15, 339, 347, 349–50, 420, 435, 438, 452–54, 463, 473n.105; as supreme entity, 42, 453, 486n.284

Going to Meet (THC42), 423, 427

good, defined, 430. *See also* greatness; Virtue

good faith (*hsin*), 18, 68, 84, 101, 110, 167, 275, 322, 342, 345, 420; as patron virtue for Han, 494n.50; defined, 431

Good Faith at Center (HEX61), 18

good fortune, defined, 438

Good Fortune (set of 3 Appraisals), 12, 168, 187, 216, 455, 458–59, 461
good fortune/calamity (*fu huo*), 256, 417, 433, 449, 451, 460; defined, 51–52, 437–38
good life, 37–38, 44, 51, 189, 473n.107, 478n.172. *See also* luck
good luck/bad luck (*chi hsiung*), 52, 317, 429, 434–35, 450
goodness, 4, 8, 61, 101, 138, 195, 283, 320, 382, 425; as divine, 47, 49–51; as impartial, 142, 210, 250, 311–12, 360, 529n.4; capacity for, 61, 88–89, 104, 190, 215, 223, 258, 282, 296, 302–03, 328, 333, 341, 360, 419; commitment to, 68–69, 128, 136, 151, 158, 171, 178, 219, 224, 252, 255, 278, 332, 376, 394, 400, 414; constraints to, 56; habituation to, 65, 71, 145–46, 181, 190, 195, 215, 237, 244, 271, 323, 355; importance of models for, 454; promoting, 266, 338, 392; roots/trunk of, 153, 167, 236–37, 242, 348, 419. *See also* human nature; *jen*; single-mindedness
"graded love." *See jen*
Grand Accord, 424
Grand Accumulation Sum, 460
Grand Center, 460
Great Cold solar period, 21, 131
"Great Commentary" to the *Changes*, 9, 14, 55, 58, 245, 267, 428, 433, 454, 456; cited, 18, 58, 84, 88, 217
Grand Decline, 271
Grand Rule (*ta t'ung*), 264–65
Grand Inception (*t'ai ch'u*) calendar, 15, 30, 431, 469n.45, 625n.46
Great Handle, 458, 624n.26
Great Heat solar period, 300, 306
"Great Learning" (*Ta hsüeh*), 337, 389, 597n.7, 599n.16
"great man," 139, 143, 183, 256, 284, 313, 521n.11. *See also* greatness
"Great Oath." *See Documents*
Great Peace, 293
"Great Plan" (*Hung fan*) ch. of *Documents*, 92–94, 98, 154, 201, 211, 312, 468n.40, 567n.24; Han readings of, 342
Great Snow solar period, 413
Great Unknown, 236
Great Way, 513n.29
Greater Cold solar period, 21

Greatness (THC45), 423, 426
greatness, 45, 141–42, 297, 326, 485n.283, 506n.22; defined, 48–49, 51, 151, 154, 287, 294, 482n.220, 486n.286
Green Dragon, 457, 624n.16
Guardedness (THC57), 424, 427
Guide Lines. *See* Three Guide Lines

habituation to goodness. *See* goodness
Hall of Light, 165
Han chi. See Hsün Yüeh
Han Confucianism, 70, 100, 341; adherents of, 7, 14, 266; as synthesis of pre-Ch'in philosophies, 4–5, 8, 39, 67, 91, 131, 547n.4; debates in, 63; fundamental questions of, 118; masters/scholars of, 7, 61, 68, 215, 350, 354, 375, 396; Tung Chung-shu as "father" of, 39, 44. *See also* Confucians; Confucianism
Han court, 31–32, 90, 184, 231; legitimacy of, 7, 32, 34, 39, 45, 61, 486n.303, 491n.22; patrons for, 494n.50, 495n.9
Han Fei tzu, 65, 387, 482n.223
Han ruling house. *See* Han court
Han shu, 31
hang t'u construction, 148, 291, 320, 568n.10
Hardness (THC72), 425, 427
harmony, cosmic, 22, 184, 234–35, 266, 269, 325; in heart, 301; social, 269, 329, 342.
Head (*Shou*) text, as microcosm, 21, 26–27; defined, 10, 453, 455; related to Appraisals, 31, 42, 73, 162; structure of, 10, 15–16, 153, 450; dominion over time, 10, 15–16, 26–27, 30, 42, 273, 457, 468n.41; samples given, 18–26; *See also* THC1–81/Heads commentary
Heart constellation, 375, 599n.22, 626n.17
heart/mind (*hsin*), 112, 191, 277, 301, 345–46, 387, 444; as "godlike," 199, 450, 552n.12; as seat of emotions, 121, 162, 193, 379, 414, 419; as seat of goodness, 190, 407; as seat of intellect, 37, 58, 70, 121, 141, 159, 161, 164, 193, 219, 315, 328, 398, 414, 419, 435, 450, 459; as seat of will, 344, 416; as sensory receptor, 58, 162, 164, 220, 295, 361; as unseen ruler, 70, 236, 253, 383; development of, 296, 301, 390; functioning of, 56, 190, 263, 311, 359; failures of, 168, 307, 359, 536n.28; metaphors for, 103, 109, 152,

252, 287–88, 320, 372, 406, 497n.17, 500n.5. *See also* conscience; human nature; nature and Decree; self-cultivation; thinking; "unmoved mind"; Void

Heaven, 269, 345, 385; arts of, 456; as amoral, 37–38; as constant pattern, 100, 216, 296, 344, 414, 449, 456, 578n.20; as divination result, 27–28, 266; as model, 29, 96–98, 101, 237, 292, 409; as origin of bad, 298, 343, 397, 605n.14; as origin of Good, 56, 269, 341; as round, 429, 431, 434; as supreme entity, 42, 45, 437, 453–54, 486n.284; defined, 36, 38, 56–57, 175, 194, 356, 374, 473n.105, 518n.3; graphic depiction of, 9, 27–28; interventionist, 37–38, 60, 174–75, 259, 292, 343–45, 397, 417, 463, 605n.14; kinship with Man, 36–37, 56–57, 67, 101, 432; numbers of, 267–68; Way of, 3, 96, 101, 113, 209, 337, 458, 529n.4, 553n.14. *See also* Heaven-and-Earth; Heaven-Earth-Man; Time, as imposed; T'ien ming.

heavens, movements of

Heaven-and-Earth, 97, 287, 292, 438, 449, 458, 625n.44; as material entities, 64, 86–87, 170, 206, 335, 418, 429, 431–33, 437, 452, 456–57; as models, 57–58, 87, 93, 97, 113, 217, 247, 263, 266–67, 269–70, 292, 317, 432, 450, 453, 455–56, 463; as supreme entities, 42, 124, 161, 451, 453, 456, 625n.30; as womb, 275, 418, 623n.26; creative aspects of, 463; gods of, 3, 245, 429, 431, 433, 458, 616n.49, 617n.74, 627n.45; metaphors for, 532n.28; Way of, 3, 101, 209, 456, 460

Heaven-Earth-Man, 13, 50; as triadic realms, 5, 8–10, 13, 46, 51, 72, 120, 158, 164, 175, 266, 282, 292, 317, 319, 332, 457, 477n.164, 625n.31; in divination, 9, 13, 27; separate functions of, 392, 452, 458, 462. *See also* "no gap"

Heavenly Origin, 433, 456, 463

Heavenly Stems, 446, 459–60

heavens, movement of, 429, 434, 614n.8, 615n.19, 626n.19

Heaven's Barge, 406

Heaven's Compensation, 463

Heaven's Female, 357, 592n.25

Heaven's Mandate. *See* T'ien ming

Heaven's Net, 194, 269

Heaven's Root, 457, 624n.23

Heaven's Way, 113, 374, 437, 450, 555n.41

Heaven's will, 35, 53, 97, 101, 139, 257, 322, 492n.17

heir apparent. *See* succession

hermits. *See* eremitism.

Hexagram/Solar Period (*kua ch'i*) system, 15–17, 558n.1

hexagrams, 7, 9–10, 14–17, 435, 454

hexagrams, arrangements of, 28; related to tetragrams, 5, 9–10, 16, 18–23, 84, 107, 113, 127, 154, 174, 219, 223, 231, 239, 263, 279, 282, 286–87, 301, 319, 347, 372, 375, 379, 381, 385, 392, 399, 468n.34, 558n.1. *See also* Ching Fang

Hidden (mantic formula), 449, 456

hierarchy, 4; divine origin of, 48, 321, 432, 476n.139, 485n.279; in cosmos, 24, 433; in family, 4, 302, 315, 323, 373; in politics, 129, 232, 315–16, 373; in society, 71, 90, 121, 165, 211–13, 232, 259, 269, 278, 321, 416, 432; in THC, 10–11. *See also* pattern; rank, in society

Ho Kuan-tzu, 478n.175

Ho Yen, 474n.124

Holding Back (THC17), 424, 426

Holding Together (HEX8), 239

"holding fast to the one" (*chih yi*). *See chih yi*

Homer, 63

Horace, 480n.195

Hou Chi, 515n.30

Hou Pa, 465n.2

Hou-t'u, 444

Hsi tz'u chuan. *See* "Great Commentary" to the *Changes*

Hsiang Yü, 590n.17

Hsiang. *See* Images

hsieh-chih, 394, 415

hsin (good faith). *See* good faith

Hsin dynasty. *See* Wang Mang

Hsin lun (*New Treatise*). *See* Huan T'an

Hsü Han, 469nn.69,70, 613n.6, 615nn.30,35, 621n.10

Hsü kua. *See* Sequence of the Hexagrams

Hsü Shen, 487n.3

hsüan hsüeh. *See* "Mystery Learning"

Hsüan kao. *See* Revelation of the Mystery

Hsüan li. *See* Evolutions of the Mystery

Hsüan shu. *See* Numbers of the Mystery

Hsüan t'u. *See* Diagram of the Mystery

Hsüan ts'e. *See* Fathomings

Index

Hsüan ts'o. See Interplay of Opposites in the Mystery

Hsüan wen. See Elaboration of the Mystery

Hsüan yi. See Representations of the Mystery

Hsüan ying. See Illumination of the Mystery

Hsüan-ming, 443, 543n.4

Hsüan-niao, 600n.22

Hsün tzu, 56–57, 301, 472n.98, 473n.105, 474n.117, 490n.69; Yang Hsiung re, 103, 115, 146, 485n.269, 579n.36; *Hsün tzu*, "Discussion of Music," 197; "Exhortation to Study," 485n.273, 532n.16; cited, 69, 137, 157

Hsün Yüeh, 465n.2

Huan T'an, 1, 62; 465n.2

huang chi ("sovereign perfection"), 580nn.16,19

Huang-ti. *See* Yellow Emperor

Hu-hai, 498n.37

human, defined, 328, 416, 453, 481n.211

human nature, as distinct from bestial, 99, 104, 151, 168, 190, 306, 328, 536n.19; at birth, 37, 39, 58, 60, 65, 68–70, 125, 128, 296, 341; basic needs of, 41, 49, 57, 68, 162, 181, 195, 245, 345, 500n.7, 514n.10, 515n.32; defined, 37, 67, 485n.275, 614n.11; derived from Heaven, 453; development of, 38, 53, 416, 533n.38; metaphors for, 216; potential for perfection, 41, 49, 53–54, 56, 61, 65, 88, 104, 125, 166, 190, 215, 264, 393, 419; related to *ming*, 37; theories about, 2, 39, 56–57, 67, 466n.8; Yang Hsiung re, 2, 58, 68, 104, 454, 466n.8, 485n.275, 486n.286

human portents, 46, 49, 68

humaneness (*jen*), 92, 99, 165, 190, 193, 221, 224, 236, 239, 242, 244, 256, 263, 270, 289, 297, 303, 331, 354, 376, 451, 547n.4; defined, 430. *See also ai*; goodness, Virtue

humility, 91, 113–17, 154, 253–54, 256, 294, 297, 334, 357, 373, 396, 451; elevated to a major virtue in Han, 113–14; Way of, 373

Hun-t'ien astronomical theory, 87, 98

Hun-t'un, 385

Hundred Affairs, 432

Hundred Corporeal Bodies, 434

Hundred Lords, 292

Hundred Norms, 434

Hundred Salaried Officers, 455

Hundred School philosophers, 36, 38, 59, 129, 131, 142, 301, 354, 486n.288

"Hung fan." *See* "Great Plan"

husband/wife. *See* family

Icarus, 270

illness. *See* medicine/medical theory

Illumination of the Mystery (*Hsüan ying*), 14, 454, 479n.178

Images (*Hsiang*), 13–14, 73, 127, 375, 470n.80, 609n.26

immaturity, 104, 148–53, 194–95, 238, 242

"immersion" (*ch'ien*) in sage's mind, 34, 39, 61, 250, 475n.125

immortality, xi, 51, 172, 176, 322, 335, 345; seekers of, 57–59, 361

Increase (THC13), 424, 427, 428

independence, Confucian view of, 138, 172, 229–30

inheritance. *See* family; patrilineal line; succession

Inner (THC65), 424, 426

integrity (*ch'eng*), 28, 31, 65, 86, 88, 101, 107, 109, 112, 168, 190, 192, 219, 226, 282, 296–97, 301, 302, 304, 315, 317, 322, 341, 380, 454, 469n.59

Interplay of Opposites (*Tsa kua*), 14, 426

Interplay of Opposites (*Hsüan ts'o*), 14, 454

jade, symbolism of, 68–69, 99, 287, 311, 329–30, 342, 393, 493n.38

Jade Level, 431, 617n.61

Jasper Template, 431, 617n.61

Job, 414

Jou pu t'uan. See Li Yü

journey, metaphor of, 103, 141, 143, 157, 163, 215, 226–30, 351

Joy (THC24), 424, 426

Ju ("Confucian"), as orthodox, 2; "true Confucian" defined, 60, 328, 356, 487n.305. See also Confucians; Han Confucianism

Ju-shou, 440

Juan Hsiao-hsü, 465n.4

Judas Iscariot, 156

Judgments, 7, 14, 19, 25, 113, 154, 469n.44, 470n.80

just state, 91, 97, 121, 176, 192, 221, 260, 301, 328–29, 405, 524n.16, 544n.41; defined, 198–99, 243–44, 483n.235; metaphor for, 533n.33

just war. *See* war

Kai-t'ien astronomical theory, 286–87, 614n.16
Kan Chung-k'o, 486n.303
Keeping Small (THC5), 20, 423, 426
Key Terms, xi, 293
King Ch'eng of Chou, 361, 374
King Chuang of Ch'u, 404
King T'ang of Shang, 151, 261, 269
King Wen of Chou, 137, 189, 372, 492n.12
King Wu of Chou, 155, 511n.32, 544n.32
King Yu of Chou, 527n.16
Kinship (THC34), 425, 428
knowing ming. See chih ming
Ko Hung, 606n.19
Kou-mang, 439
Ku Chieh-kang, 487n.1
ku magic. See magic
"Kuan chü" ode, 597n.7
Kuan Chung (d. 645 B.C.), 142
k'un bird. See magical birds
kung ("equitable treatment"/"fairness"), 95, 121, 192, 202, 206, 230–231, 253, 256, 328, 330, 407, 424, 430
K'ung An-kuo, 475n.124

Laboring (THC80), 425, 426
laissez-faire. See non-purposive activity
language, 36, 48, 68, 72, 267, 337, 356, 449, 456; pattern in, 54
Lao tzu, 4–5, 91, 297, 472n.98, 480n.197; Yang Hsiung re, 3–5, 196, 466nn.8,14; Lao tzu, cited, 2–4, 107, 109, 113, 117, 142, 153–54, 194, 210, 231, 255, 318, 332, 342, 366, 374, 396, 405, 410; law, 151, 191, 202, 222, 263, 269, 276, 333, 346, 377, 394, 452, 482n.227, 538n.46; Han family, 548n.18. See also cosmic laws; Legalists; punishments
Law (THC40), 425, 427
learning, 158, 264, 313, 619n.26. See also study; teachers
Legalists, 8, 48, 98, 131, 319, 351, 394. See also Confucians; individual authors by name; just state; law; ruler; Yang Hsiung
Legion (THC32), 425, 428
legitimacy. See Han legitimacy; succession
"lessen desires," 341, 585n.4
Lesser Cold solar period, 107, 125
Lessons for Women (Nü chieh). See Pan Chao
Li Kuei, 591n.23

Li Lou, 596n.20
li ming ("establishing fate"), 60, 485n.271
Li sao. See Ch'ü Yüan
Li Yü, 582n.23
life, defined, 453
Line Texts (Yao), 7, 9, 11–12, 73, 470n.80, 477n.160, 479n.187, 574n.27
Liu Hsia-hui, 563n.12, 598n.17
Liu Hsiang, 1, 131, 579n.9
Liu Hsin, 1, 61, 487n.310
Liu Pang, 590n.17
Liu ruling clan. See Han court
logic. See categorical thinking
Logicians, 67, 103, 107, 216, 322, 479n.179
longevity. See immortality
Lu, 63, 117, 536n.31
Lu Chi, 23
Lü clan, 610n.16
Lu K'ai, 470n.68
luck, 33, 42, 71, 98–99, 207; related to Virtue, 52, 62. See also ming
Lun heng. See Wang Ch'ung
lunar lodge (constellation), 30, 125
Lustration festival, 535n.8
Luxuriant Talent degree, 502n.20

magic, 54, 71, 400; geomancy, 350; ku magic, 389–90, 603n.12; occult arts, 369. See also exorcism; numerology
magical birds, 249; k'un bird, 228; phoenix, 249; wan-ch'u, 366–67
magicians, 44–45, 278, 402, 440, 478n.178, 577n.35
male/female relations. See gender
Man (as triadic realm), 28, 55, 60, 96, 263, 266, 298, 301, 332, 336, 430; as divination result, 27–28; graphic depiction of, 9, 27–28; partaking of divine, 51–55, 87, 435; Way of, 3, 51–52, 59, 101, 113, 165, 204, 337, 436–38, 458. See also human nature
Man-ch'eng, 99
Mandate of Heaven. See T'ien ming
Mane constellation, 462
mantic formulae, of Changes, 88, 489n.53, 621n.2. See also chen
Massing (THC59), 424, 428
Master Huai-nan (d. 122 B.C.), 123
Master. See Confucius
Ma-wang-tui, 468nn.39,40, 470n.77
Mean, the, 93, 97–98, 124, 146, 163, 183, 204, 209, 241, 263, 289, 319–320, 337,

Mean, the (*cont.*)
357, 407, 420, 456, 597n.19. *See also*
Doctrine of the Mean
Measure (THC52), 10, 424, 427
median times, in divination, 12–13
medicine/medical theory, 120, 164, 181–82,
188, 214, 217, 285, 318, 336–38, 367–68,
402–03, 421
Mencius, 2, 60, 65, 70, 472nn.98,99,
473n.105, 476n.141, 517n.3, 547n.4; vs.
Hs1B011Cn tzu, 56–57; Yang Hsiung re,
484n.269; *Mencius*, cited, 65, 128, 143,
155, 181, 223, 231, 247, 313, 380,
571n.21. *See also* just state
Meng Hsi (fl. 69 B.C.), 8, 558n.8
merchants, 95, 229, 330, 357, 420. *See also*
profit
Metal, 434, correlations of, 192, 196, 221,
250, 262, 440–41; cosmic phase for
Appraisals, 116, 125, 191, 215, 224, 358;
cosmic phase for Heads, 191, 306, 392.
See also Five Phases, enumeration
orders of
metamorphosis, defined, 436
milfoil. *See* divination
Milky Way, 406, 608n.22
mind. *See* heart/mind
ming (Decree), and Virtue, 35, 37–38, 40–
41, 476n.141; as imposed, 35, 38–39, 56;
as king's command, 36, 39; as personal,
53, 60, 331, 409, 533n.38; defined, 409,
431, 472n.99, 487n.312; early notions of,
35–40, 53, 474n.110; questions about,
35–38; related to human nature, 37; related to Time, 430; Yang Hsiung re, 34–
35, 39–47, 54–56, 62. *See also chih
ming*; Confucius; fate; predestination
ministers, 70, 464, 517n.17, 588n.15,
603n.17; chief, 155, 282, 284, 387,
506n.24, 531n.35, 540n.35, 567n.9. *See
also* official; remonstrance; ruler
Mired (THC3), 19, 423, 427
miser, 337–39
misfortune. *See* good fortune/calamity
Mo tzu, 281, 474nn.112,117. *See also*
Mohists
Model Sayings (*Fa yen*), 1, 6, 35, 57, 115,
129, 131, 559n.18; cited, 93, 125, 127,
149, 210, 223, 263, 328
Modesty (HEX15), 113
Mohists, 60, 472n.98, 571n.21, 585n.35. *See
also* Confucians; Logicians; Yang Hsiung

monopolies, 245
moon, as changeable, 462–63, 577n.20;
movements of, 317, 429, 451, 455, 457,
462–63, 626n.19; symbolism of, 86, 92,
178, 316, 377, 603n.16
moral action, defined, 298
moral choice, 11, 35, 39, 58, 179, 334. *See
also* goodness; Virtue
moral integrity. *See* integrity
moral relativism, 9, 57–59, 529n.6
mourning rites. *See* rites, mourning
Mt. T'ai. *See* Tai-shan
music, 8, 63, 70, 197–99, 408, 470n.73,
527n.6, 528n.29, 559n.23, 569n.3,
591n.23, 620n.1; ancient masters of, 277,
376, 434. *See also* pitch standards
Musical Notes, 445
Musicmaster Ling-lun, 434
Musicmaster Tzu-ch'un, 507n.35
Mutual Conquest Cycle. *See* Five Conquests
Mutual Interaction. *See* Doctrine of Mutual
Interaction
Mutual Production Cycle. *See* Five Productions
myriad things. *See wan-wu*
Mysterious Power, 255
Mystery, active mode of, 432; approaching
the, 432, 470n.72; arts of, 434–45, characteristic activities of, 50, 428–33, 461;
distancing the, 432; *hsüan* defined, 2–4,
429–30; primal state of, 59, 86–87, 428;
quiescent mode of, 432; Way of the, 50,
430, 432, 461. *See also Canon of Supreme Mystery*; cosmogonic stages; Tao;
utility, Mystery as ultimate in; Way
"Mystery Learning" (*hsüan hsüeh*), 1–2
Mystery Palace, 365, 388, 595n.5
Mystery Springs, 421. *See also* Yellow
Springs

names. *See* "rectification of names"
Nan-k'uai, 482n.230
nature and Decree (*hsing ming*), 91, 429,
451. *See also* human nature; *ming*
neo-Confucianism, 2, 64, 521n.16, 561n.18
Nine Affairs, 448
Nine Apertures, 448
Nine Arrows, 303–04, 572n.28
Nine Barbarians, 288
Nine Cauldrons, 282, 284
Nine Conferrals, 303–04
Nine Courses, 458

Nine Decades, 448
Nine Districts, 431
Nine Dwellings, 461
Nine Earths, 447
Nine Empty Positions, 433–34, 459, 461
Nine Heavens, 446
Nine Orders, 448
Nine Positions. *See* Nine Empty Positions
Nine Provinces of China, 10, 394, 457
Nine Sites, 458, 461
Nine Tripods. *See* Nine Cauldrons
Nineteen Old Poems, 525n.21
"no gap," 55, 58–59, 70, 234–36, 414, 425, 479n.180; gap, defined, 47, 49, 200, 481n.212. *See also* harmony; union
nobility, defined, 69, 169, 258, 382
noble man, as godlike, 450; imitating Tao, 50, 255, 336, 396, 418, 450; vs. petty man, 190, 198, 203, 224, 245, 250, 272, 296, 304, 313, 353, 357, 363, 366, 382, 425, 431, 451–52, 460. *See also* gentleman; nobility
non-purposive activity (*wu wei*), 4, 97, 115, 187, 210, 467n.20, 508n.31, 533n.6, 555n.12
North Pole, 98
Nü chieh (*Lessons for Women*), 534n.21
numbers, as factor in intrepretation, 30–31
Numbers of the Mystery (*Hsüan shu*), 14, 27–31, 66
Numen Park, 372
Numen Pool, 372–73
Numen Terrace, 372
numerology, 2, 8, 44, 118, 215, 267–68, 434, 454, 459, 559n.17, 625n.44; correlations of, 438–445

occult arts. *See* magic
Odes, xi, 4, 63, 69, 73, 110, 114, 161, 402, 404, 467n.21, 473n.102, 597n.7; cited, 111, 117, 128–30, 133, 197, 205, 220, 224, 240, 242, 262, 295
officials, 99, 109, 111, 129, 155, 345, 374, 402, 538nn.29,46, 570n.43; assigned to App. 4, 99, 105, 128, 137, 162, 220, 224, 228, 256, 288, 308, 603n.17, 612n.14; in/near retirement, 100, 138, 196, 307, 570n.39; *shih*, 322, 537n.40. *See also* bureaucratic selection; career advancement; ministers; patronage; remonstrance; ruler
old age/aging, 149, 200, 363, 370, 405, 417,

425; App. 7 symbolizes, 138, 371; virtue in, 40, 70, 196, 349–50, 452
omens. *See* portents
On the Verge (THC78), 425, 426
oneness, 120, 156–58, 428; primal, 86–88, 315, 450, 453, 625n.30. *See also* cosmogonic stages; duality
onesidedness, 157, 159, 160, 162, 328, 330. *See also* goodness, as impartial
Opposition (THC8), 423, 426
oracle bones, 71. *See also* divination
order, 8, 453; divine cosmic, 28, 36, 71, 120, 277, 369, 438, 532n.28; integrated, 264, 296; social, 41, 62, 55, 68, 90, 108, 120, 122, 124, 207, 252, 295, 330, 333–34, 336, 395
Ou-yang Hsiu, 587n.21
"Owl" *fu*, 589n.36
Oxherd constellation, 30, 406, 608n.22, 617n.71, 624n.23

Packing (THC31), 23, 26, 276, 425, 428
Pan Chao, 534n.21
Pan Ku, 1, 465n.1. *See also Han shu*
Pan Piao, 480n.189
Pandora's box, 182
Pao Hsi (Fu Hsi), 252, 435
Pao Hsien, 475n.124
Pao-yü, 595n.9
patrilineal line of descent, 11, 241, 258, 262, 304, 316, 323–24, 365, 369–71, 407
patronage, 184, 299, 516n.20
pattern (*wen*), 125, 262–63, 436–37, 442; as eternal constant, 9, 86, 125, 269–70; cosmic/in Nature, 8, 65, 84, 88, 96, 101, 164–65, 181, 252–53, 266, 269, 277, 286, 295–96, 315, 323, 330, 391, 456, 588n.15, 627n.46; moral, 88, 181, 295; cultural, 54, 295–96, 299; divine derivation of, 186, 299, 321, 391; opposed to plain, 294–96, 298, 356, 423, 449, 619n.37; seasonal, 100, 315; societal, 181, 185–86, 266, 295, 432, 437. *See also* culture; Five Constant Relations; Heaven-and-Earth; language; ritual, as pattern; sages, imitating pattern; Virtue, as pattern
Pattern (THC47), 423, 426
Penetration (THC14), 424, 428
philosophical debates, 35–38, 48, 56–57, 60–63, 67–68, 89–90, 131, 304, 323–24, 356, 486n.288. *See also* Confucians; human nature; Yang Hsiung

phoenix. *See* magical birds
phrasing, as factor in interpretation, 30–31, 436, 453, 463, 619n.37
pitch standards, 268, 445, 455, 620nn.16,17,18
pitchpipes, 269, 429, 432, 434–35, 455, 457
Plato, 571n.24
pleasure, 198, 334, 348
Po Yi, 602n.17
Polar Oppositions of the Mystery (*Hsüan ch'ung*), 14, 453
Polestar, 98, 616n.59, 624n.26. *See also* Dipper; North Pole
portents, 72, 125, 129, 172, 188, 259–260, 269, 271, 274, 282, 295, 299, 316, 365, 381, 397, 399, 404, 406–07, 420, 605n.14; texts, theory of, 6, 44, 67, 571n.12. *See also* cosmologists; human portents; Yin/yang Five Phases theory
Position, 98, 106, 129–30, 208, 255; as factor in *ming*, 41–47, 58, 317; dangers of high, 130, 133, 155–56, 160, 185, 187, 242, 271, 333; defined, 42; related to Appraisals, 436. *See also* Nine Empty Positions
poverty, 52, 114–15, 134, 143, 343, 483n.233; advantages of, 52–53, 116–17
practical wisdom, 37, 42, 158, 175, 253, 288, 302, 353; defined, 430, 443, 476n.146
predestination, 57, 60–61, 474n.112, 475n.130, 485n.273, 533n.38. *See also ming*; Time, as imposed
"preserve oneself" (*tzu shou*), 31, 141, 181, 376–77, 470n.75, 517n.9
Prince Ch'ung-erh. *See* Duke Wen of Chin
Principle of Masking, 45, 479n.185
privacy, 256
profit, 101, 189, 244–45, 255–56, 278–79, 345, 367, 399, 427, 612n.14; Confucian view of seeking, 116, 160, 204, 229, 160, 313, 530n.25
pronoun usage, 493n.39, 519n.20, 528n.29, 533n.38, 553n.3, 582n.38, 609n.25
prose-poems (*fu*), 1, 5–6, 15, 35, 52, 137, 478n.170, 480n.201, 490n.69, 498n.49, 499n.29, 503n.10
proverbs, 135, 140, 145, 157, 164, 187, 199, 205, 209, 219, 231, 257, 263, 291, 308, 320, 357, 396, 505n.41, 519n.22
Provinces (line of tetragram), 10, 435, 457–58
punishments, 4, 60, 86, 92–93, 147, 152,
156, 164, 191, 202, 207, 212, 219, 221, 224, 231, 250, 254, 262, 265, 269–70, 304, 323, 337, 423, 450, 452, 524n.16, 576n.6. *See also hsieh-chih*; Confucians, vs. Legalists; Legalists; Yang Hsiung, vs. Legalists; law
Purity (THC37), 425, 426, 446, 457–58

Queen Mother of the West, 228, 335
quietists, 114. *See also* Taoists

rain, significance of, 118, 339, 371–72
Rainfall solar period, 156, 165
rank, in society, 11, 176, 221, 224, 285, 302, 304–05, 308, 313, 353, 364, 398, 414, 455. *See also* hierarchy
Reach (THC15), 424, 426
"reanimate the old" (*wen ku*), 35, 55, 62, 532n.12
Receptive (HEX2), 15, 448
reciprocity (*shu*), 97, 139, 162, 165, 213, 259, 271. *See also* consideration
Record of Ritual (*Li chi*), 350, 366; "Record on Music" (*Yüeh chi*) in, 197
rectification of names, 67–68, 86, 93, 108, 235
Red Bird, 581n.20. *See also* sun
Red Heaven, 421
Red Stench, 112, 498n.44
"Refuting Sorrow" *fu*, 498n.49
Regional Phrases (*Fang yen*), 6, 472n.100
Regions (line of hexagrams), 10, 435, 457–58
relativism. *See* moral relativism
Release (THC21), 22, 424, 427
remonstrance, 131–34, 142, 172, 176, 185, 224, 333, 358, 504n.16, 522n.31. *See also* ruler
Representations of the Mystery (*Hsüan yi*), 14, 454–55
Residence (THC39), 425, 428
Resistance (THC22), 424, 427, 428
respect/reverence, as factor in perfection, 252, 302, 305, 339, 350
Response (THC41), 23, 423, 427
Return (HEX24), 19, 96–97
Revelation of the Mystery (*Hsüan kao*), 14, 454
rhetoric, 131–34, 504nn.20,21. *See also* language; remonstrance
righteousness. *See* duty
rites, betrothal/marriage, 70, 368, 370,

561n.18, 597n.20; court, 299, 570n.43;
family, 259; mourning, 70, 143, 227, 351,
354, 363; imperial ploughing, 550n.23.
See also enfeoffment
Rites (Li), 4, 63, 467n.21. *See also Record of
Ritual*
ritual, 59, 123, 269, 300, 305, 339, 350, 360,
412, 569n.3; adherence to, 89, 253, 412;
as balance, 277, 571n.4; as ceremony,
241, 299, 303, 333, 570n.43; as con-
straint, 59, 164, 345; as courtesy, 70, 99,
202, 299, 306; as decorum, 303, 333; as
emotional outlet, 198, 265; as pattern,
70, 191, 249, 303–04, 516n.18; as repetition, 516n.18; as "root" of goodness, 59,
166, 304, 476n.139, 533n.6; as sacred,
47, 50, 59, 71, 96, 165, 167, 254, 284,
303, 325, 415, 576n.6; as Tool, 412; basis
of, 302; defined, 41, 47, 70–71, 164, 301;
forms of, 302–03, 326; graph for, 301;
internalized, 219; lapses in, 46, 166, 199,
305, 326, 348–50, 404; metaphors for,
321, 419; power of, 303; purpose of, 53,
70–71, 96, 121, 167–69, 180, 185, 198,
304–05, 342, 349, 477n.164; study of, 4,
47, 49–50, 412. *See also* Five Constant
Relations; "sumptuary rules"
Ritual (THC48), 423, 428
ritual dance. *See* dance
ritual feasts. *See* feasting
ritual gifts, 285, 304
ritual obligations, 4
ritual paraphenalia, 294. *See also* Nine Conferrals
ritual prerogatives, 304, 534n.26. *See also*
hierarchy, rank, in society
ritual prohibitions, 4, 70, 99, 150, 244, 278
romantic love, 525n.21
ruler, 67, 347, 376, 388, 405, 452; abdication
of, 272, 560n.50, 586n.5, 598n.17; as
center, 67, 97, 183, 221, 329–30, 333–34,
391, 397, 402; as dragon, 108, 270, 370;
as "father and mother," 236, 240; exemplary, 86, 92–93, 160, 172, 184, 213, 224,
231, 232, 237, 250, 262, 268, 270, 282,
293, 316, 323, 325; failures of, 100, 105,
236, 292, 300, 329, 388, 405; like sun, 91,
155, 184; like Tao/yang ch'i, 187, 201–
02, 206, 210, 245, 328, 529n.2; other
metaphors for, 100, 105, 108–109, 143,
160, 199, 204, 208, 211, 218, 225, 233,
242, 251, 321, 330, 338–39, 532n.24,

557n.19, 564n.3, 608n.16; ruler/advisor,
346, 376, 378, 386, 394, 402, 599n.16,
609n.9; ruler/commoner relations, 4, 24,
96, 211, 232–34, 239, 246, 268–70, 273,
279, 292, 294, 300, 305, 314–15, 323,
329, 334, 338–39, 353–54, 383–84, 391,
394, 399, 408, 411, 429, 432, 454, 460,
462, 598n.11; ruler/feudal lords, 204,
284, 292–93, 303–04, 342, 349, 405;
ruler/official relations, 96, 105, 142, 145,
156, 208, 211, 213, 221, 228, 235–36,
250, 268, 282, 285, 302, 309, 317, 319,
333, 345–46, 358, 364, 386–87, 464,
505n.43; ruler/minister relations, 124,
130, 172, 188, 204, 249, 284, 387, 464,
588n.22; techniques of, 38, 243, 246,
394; Way of the, 316, 425. *See also*
Grand Rule; remonstrance; ritual;
suasive example

sacrifice, 70, 72, 168, 170, 180, 212, 244,
298, 300, 303–04, 314, 316, 338–39, 342,
346–47, 349–50, 420, 454, 519n.26,
520n.20, 528n.38, 556n.22, 622n.8;
blood, 612n.22
sages, 9, 71, 104, 264, 454–55, 618n.26; as
authors of Classics, 150, 253, 483n.240,
495n.21; as models, 8, 34, 61, 71, 88,
183, 185, 225, 253, 264, 287, 296–97,
382, 399, 411; as divine, 29, 61, 139, 274;
as impartial, 216; as mediators, 88, 289;
defined, 2, 29, 162, 395, 430; identification with, 43, 137, 253; imitating pattern,
86–88, 262, 295, 321, 356, 409, 429, 453,
471n.86; like Tao, 186–87; like yang
ch'i, 227; mind of, 39, 87, 161; perfection of, 121, 159, 253, 372, 456; Way of,
284, 359. *See also* culture, invention of;
individual sages listed by name; Way,
the
sagehood, as goal, 65, 86; vision of, 7
sage-kings, as ideal rulers, 92, 123, 151, 155,
162, 164, 190, 200, 211, 214, 216, 265,
268–69, 293, 304, 313, 323, 330, 359,
415, 569n.20; study of, 8, 61, 69, 291
"schools," 472n.98
self-cultivation, 8, 35, 52, 57, 65, 70, 97,
115, 127, 136–37, 154, 214, 249, 251,
279, 282, 291, 300, 309, 344, 393, 400;
defined, 8, 68–69, 229; metaphors for,
99, 109, 287, 306. *See also* transformation

self-examination, 109, 145, 188, 270, 360, 363

self-preservation. *See* "preserve oneself"

self-sacrifice, 173, 233, 304, 331, 409, 418, 583n.33

sensory perception, 58, 121, 152, 277, 341, 366, 454, 537n.15, 568n.20

Sequence of the Hexagrams (*Hsü kua*), 14, 423

sericulture, 245

Seven Mansions, 457

Seven Regulators, 431, 434, 616n.57

Severance (THC70), 425, 428

sex/sexual attraction, 108, 165, 260, 274–75, 314, 336, 345, 370–71, 390, 561n.18, 584n.7

shamans/shamanesses. *See* magicians

Shang dynasty, 63, 71, 72, 96, 145, 155, 189, 377–78

Shang Yang, 132, 250

Shao Hao, 440

Shao Yung, 627n.29

she (god of the soil). *See* god of the soil

shen ("divine/divinities"). *See* divine; gods

Shen Tao, 513n.23

shih ("knight/official"). *See* official

shih. *See* Timeliness

Shu Ch'i, 602n.17

Shun (sage-king), 53, 275, 299, 510n.23, 560n.50

Shuo kua. *See* Discussion of the Trigrams

Shuo wen, 472n.100

single-minded concentration, 28–29, 99, 157–58, 195, 206, 258, 279, 313, 315, 341, 435

Sinking (THC64), 424, 428, 446, 457, 459

Six Beginnings, 435

Six Directions, 457

Six Exalted Ones, 463

Six Intermediaries, 435

solar periods, defined, 15–16, 30

solstices, 10, 15–16, 22, 26; summer, 251, 266–67, 271, 275–76, 433, 617nn.69,73; winter, 18, 22, 25, 30, 84, 95, 271, 418, 432, 617nn.71,73,4, 624n.23

Songs of Ch'u, 73

Sophists. *See* Logicians

souls, 70, 94, 289, 309, 318, 362, 440–41, 452, 461, 562n.5

spaces and times. *See yü chou*

speech. *See* language

spheroidal heaven theory. *See hun t'ien* theory

spirits. *See* divine; ghosts; gods

Spring and Autumn Annals. *See* Chronicles

Spring Equinox solar period, 26

Spring Onset solar period, 26, 144, 156

squareness, defined, 153, 409, 423, 511nn.12,13, 613n.5

ssu, 119, 122–23

Ssu k'u ch'üan shu catalogue, 2

Ssu-ma Ch'ien, 470n.85, 606n.14

Ssu-ma Hsiang-ju, 501n.21

Ssu-ma Kuang, 2, 24, 88, 94, 100, 305; commentary cited, 87, 91, 98, 104–105, 117, 128, 146, 163, 172, 175–76, 196, 267, 271–72, 307, 349, 373

Ssu-ma T'an, 472n.98

standard hexagrams (*cheng kua*), defined, 15

stars, as factor in interpretation, 30–31, 46, 60–61, 434, 439–40, 442–44

Startled from Hibernation solar period, 174

state, dissolution of, 102, 286, 330, 371, 378

state, just. *See* just state

Stoics, 480n.195, 488n.10

Stomach constellation, 205

"stone wife," 292

Stoppage (THC71), 25–26, 425, 427

Stove (THC44), 423, 427

strategic position. *See* Position; Shen Tao

Strength (THC36), 11, 425, 426

study, 4, 383, 495n.21; defined, 480n.205. *See also* Ancients, imitating the; constant norms, as proper subject of study; learning; ritual, study of; sage-kings, study of

Su Hsün, 2

suasive example, 103, 123, 151, 180, 184, 208, 210, 213, 221, 242, 244, 262–63, 274, 313, 323, 333, 354, 382, 452, 523n.28

succession, laws of, 323–25, 373; symbols of legitimate, 284. *See also* Han court, legitimacy of

Summa Theologica. *See* Aquinas

Summer Solstice solar period, 15, 18, 23, 280

Summer Onset solar period, 26, 226, 613n.14

sumptuary rules, 4, 70, 99, 137, 288, 299, 352, 356, 364, 570n43

sun, movements of, 429, 433, 435, 451, 455, 457, 462–63, 614n.8, 626n.19, 627n.31; symbolism of, 22, 91, 154–55, 163, 178, 184, 228, 316, 364–65, 377, 411, 519n.13, 603n.16. *See also* ruler, like sun
sundial, 434
Sung Chung, 1, 356
Sung neo-Confucians. *See* neo-Confucians
Surplus (intercalary App.), 455
"Sweet Springs" *fu*, 575n.12

Tables, 433, 451, 618n.8, 622n.21
T'ai-hao, 439
T'ai hsüan ching. See Canon of Supreme Mystery
T'ai-shan, 248–49, 251
tamped earth construction. *See hang-t'u*
Tao, 5, 101, 286, 387; apprehension of, 103; as cosmic origin/basis, 3, 68, 287, 315, 344, 433, 625n.31; as cosmic sack/womb, 102, 408; as eternal, 51, 53, 325; as goal, 55, 95; as immanent cosmic process, 23, 53, 61, 64, 68, 72, 84, 86, 360, 428, 436, 461; as one, 27, 63, 87–88, 195, 315, 436; defined, 3, 95, 535n.17; conformity with, 266, 291, 366; ineffable nature of, 51, 53, 61, 67, 70, 167, 186–87, 236, 287, 301, 306, 356, 428, 430, 450; model for, 59; "reversal" as Way of, 66, 95, 114, 160, 257, 413. *See also* cosmogonic stages; Mystery; noble man, imitating Tao; ruler, like Tao; sages, like Tao; Way
Taoists, 8, 104, 187, 202, 207, 352, 356, 374, 585n.6; primitivist vision of antiquity, 207, 435, 476n.145, 483n.240, 618n.26. *See also* Confucians; individual masters listed by name; quietists; Shen Tao; Yang Hsiung; Way, Taoist analysis of
Task, defined, 431
taxes, 243–247, 334, 399. *See also* just state
teacher, 162, 282, 379–80, 383; defined, 149. *See also* goodness, importance of model for; learning; study
technical arts. *See* arts
temporal associations. *See* Ching Fang
Ten Thousand Measures, 159
"Ten Wings" (*Shih yi*), 1, 7, 11, 13–14, 33, 423, 426, 438, 470n.80
tetragrams. *See* Heads
thinking, 287, 435; defined, 161, 295, 398–99, 431; metaphor for, 455. *See also*

categorical thinking; study
Thought (set of 3 Appraisals), 12, 127, 136, 140, 149, 150, 153, 166, 175, 183, 186, 190, 219, 227, 236, 263, 287, 334, 344, 393, 398, 401, 410, 413, 416, 455, 458–59, 461
Three Guide Lines, 322, 325–26, 580nn.16,17. See *also* Five Constant Relations
Three Models, 461. *See also* Heaven-Earth-Man, as triadic realms
Three Reigns, 429. *See also* Heaven; Heaven-Earth-Man, as triadic realms
T'ien
T'ien ming, 36–37, 40, 56, 60–61, 91, 209, 218, 305, 401, 473nn.102,106, 512n.32
Tiger constellation, 431
tilthammer, 340, 586n.22
Time, 434; as aspect of *ming*, xi, 40–47, 158, 350; as distinct from "times," 475n.138; as imposed, 43–46, 53, 56, 59, 94, 198–200, 272, 452, 477n.161; as supreme entity, 42, 45, 453–54; as unpredictable, 44–47, 53–54, 449; defined, 42–44, 211, 477n.160. *See also* Yin/yang Five Phases theory
timeliness/timely opportunity, 14, 35, 43–44, 57, 89, 93, 103, 158, 175, 208–09, 246, 249, 284, 428, 451, 535n.17; defined, 477n.160
times, as factors in interpretation, 30–31, 470n.72, 475n.138
Ting Kuan, 623n.20
Tools, 107, 150, 297, 386, 538n.46; as factor in *ming*, 40–47, 58, 412; defined, 41–42, 299, 476n.143; misuse of, 42, 217, 287, 343, 392, 411–12; utility of, 106, 260, 264, 435. *See also* Confucianism, as Tool; culture, invention of; Five Classics, as Tools; ritual, as Tool; Virtue, as Tool
transformation (*hua*) by virtue, 121, 183, 208, 214, 216, 273–74, 293, 303, 333–34, 400, 453, 481n.217, 519n.1
"Treatise on the Pitch Standards," 559n.17
triadic realms. *See* Heaven-Earth-Man
trigrams, 7, 454. *See also* hexagrams
Triple Concordance calendar, 558n.6
tsa ("mixed"/"eclectic"), 55, 143, 559n.18
Tsa kua. See Interplay of Opposites
Ts'ang Chieh hsün tsüan. See Compendium of Annotations

Tso commentary, 171, 212, 350, 571n.12
Tsou Yen, 38, 485n.274
T'uan. See Commentary on the Judgments
t'ui lei ("inference by analogy"), 66–67. *See also* categorical thinking
Tung Chung-shu, 217, 325, 478n.170, 490n.69, 553n.14. *See also* Han Confucianism, Tung as "father" of
Tung Hsien, 31, 497n.15
Tung Yung, 405, 608n.11
Turtle constellation, 431
Twelve Earthly Branches. *See* Earthly Branches
Tzu-ch'an, 307, 473n.106
Tzu-fan, 133
Tzu-hsia, 295–96, 474n.112
Tzu-shu Yi, 612n.14

uncrowned king. *See* Confucius
"undifferentiated/ungraded love." *See ai*
"unify the will" (*yi chih*), 313, 347
Unity (THC54), 424, 427, 428
"unmoved mind," 177, 199, 317, 360, 419
utility, 89, 352–53; Mystery, as ultimate in, 430. *See also* Tools

Vast Base, 434
Vastness (THC50), 424, 427
veiling one's light, 375–78
Virtue, 316, 365, 437, 456; as base/root, 354, 423; as charismatic, 56, 90, 98, 157, 159, 167, 176, 180, 208, 283, 293, 335, 364, 415; as divine, 101; as factor in *ming*, xi, 35, 40–47, 58, 138; as pattern, 59; as Tool, 250; defined, 41; "hidden," 175, 254; offenses against, 137, 237, 571n.12; pure, 251–52; pursuit of, 54, 136, 151, 174, 195, 250, 451; rewards for, 36–37, 42–43, 47–53, 60, 110, 130, 175–77, 185, 255, 279, 284, 299, 337, 351, 353, 363, 382, 409. *See also* charismatic Power; duty; filial piety; goodness; *jen*
Void, as metaphor for mind, 121, 142, 223, 401

Waiting (THC18), 424, 426
wan-ch'u. See magical birds
wan-wu ("myriad things"), effect of Yin/yang on, 15. *See also cosmogonic stages; THC1–81/Heads* and commentary
wang (disease), 177

Wang Ch'ung, 1, 465n.2, 474n.113, 475n.130, 487n.312
Wang Mang, 6, 29, 32, 305, 324, 469n.67, 536n.28, 597n.16, 600n.18; clan of, 542n.31; Yang Hsiung re, 2, 6, 31, 184, 465n.7, 467n.28, 497n.15, 498n.44, 517n.9, 541n.19. *See also* Dowager Empress Wang
Wang Pi, 18, 24
Wang Ya, 111, 380
war, 169–70, 202, 219, 222, 230–35, 323, 342, 347
Warring States, philosophical texts of. *See* Hundred Schools
Watch (THC63), 424, 426
Water, 30, 434; correlations of, 30, 84, 88, 92–93, 109, 181, 203, 276, 317, 344, 357, 406; cosmic phase for Appraisals, 86, 88, 192, 202, 252, 258, 268, 287, 306, 332, 338, 347, 372, 389, 419. *See also* Five Phases, enumeration orders of
waterclock, 432
Waxing and Waning Hexagrams (*hsiao hsi kua*), 15–17
Way, 185, 311, 373, 376, 387, 400, 460; advance in, 125, 136, 183, 333, 391; apprehending the, 153, 277; as cosmic origin, 327; as cosmic process, 8, 29, 59, 356, 436; as eternal, 59, 172, 258, 325; pursuit of the, 158, 181, 205, 296, 313–14, 341, 344, 407; as as one, 5, 8, 120, 268, 458; conformity with the, 143, 150, 199, 253, 263, 269, 292; Confucian, 55, 90, 106, 134, 151, 162, 311, 313, 325, 337, 356, 382, 483n.235; defined, 90–91, 141–42, 202, 431; departures from, 253, 263, 320; devotion to, 177, 238, 292, 407; King's, 247, 312; mastery of, 291, 337, 396; Taoist analysis of, 4, 90. *See also* Ancients, Way of the; single-mindedness; Tao
Way and its Power, 223, 431, 455
Way of Centrality, 342, 557n.10, 567n.24
Way of Centrality and Harmony, 342
Way of Chou, 536n.31
Way of Earth. *See* Earth
Way of Heaven. *See* Heaven
Way of Heaven-and-Earth. *See* Heaven-and-Earth
Way of Man. *See* Man, as triadic realm
Way of Spontaneous Nature, 59

Way of Unity, 5
Weaver Girl constellation, 406, 608n.22
Wei Sheng, 146
Well (HEX48), 263
"well-field" economic system, 557n.6
Wen-chün. *See* Ssu-ma Hsiang-ju
wen ku. *See* "reanimate the old"
Wen yen. See Elaborated Teachings
West Mountain, 335
Western Han (206 B.C.–A.D. 8), 5, 31, 39, 90, 231, 285
white. *See* color symbolism
White Tiger Hall Discussions, 131
Will of Heaven. *See* "Heaven's will"
Winter Dew solar period, 379
Winter Onset solar period, 26, 388, 400
Winter Solstice solar period, 15–16, 18, 22, 25, 30, 66, 107. *See also* solstices
wisdom. *See* practical wisdom
Without (mantic formula), 449, 456
Wolf constellation, 205
Woman constellation, 30, 102
Wood, 168, 434; correlations of, 86, 154, 221, 223; cosmic phase for Appraisals, 93, 104, 125, 154, 187, 196, 269, 372. *See also* Five Phases, enumeration orders of
Wooden Bow constellation, 205
Wu-liang-ts'e, 281
wu-wei. See non-purposive activity

yang *ch'i*, 4; as master of myriad things, *see wan-wu*; associations of, 12, 165; characteristic operations of, 4, 26; perfection of, 144, 239, 247; like Tao, 223. *See also* Yin/yang
Yang Hsiung, 473n.105; academic studies on, xi, 2, 465nn.1,2; admired, 1, 40, 465nn.2,6; apologists for, 2, 31–32; as classicist, 39, 54–62, 97, 143, 197, 231, 268; as Confucian master, 1–2, 41, 56–57, 465n.2; as innovator, 28, 56, 61–62, 143; attacks other thinkers, 32, 43, 45–46, 49, 55–57, 101, 112, 324, 387; biography of, 1, 5–6, 40, 622n.6; attributed works of, 465n.4, 466n.8, 467n.27, 472n.100, 498n.49, 575n.12; attacks on, 2, 466n.8, 508n.39; eclecticism of, 3–5, 45, 55–56, 61; influenced by Legalists, 477n.152, 513n.23; influenced by Mohists, 483n.235; influenced by Taoists, 194, 202, 267, 306, 466nn.8,14,

481n.212, 485n.274, 505n.13, 585n.4; vs. Taoists, 4, 41, 90– 91, 103, 115, 150, 207, 237, 297, 435, 515n.32, 529n.6, 618n.26; vs. Legalists, 41, 48, 98, 170, 216, 250, 387, 394, 397. *See also* also human nature, Yang Hsiung re; Hsün tzu, Yang Hsiung re; Mencius, Yang Hsiung re; ming (Decree); poverty; Wang Mang
Yao, 186, 560n.50
yarrow stalks, 9, 27–28, 149, 460, 484n.250. *See also* divination
Year Star, 421, 434
Yeh Tzu-ch'i, 111
yellow. *See* color symbolism
Yellow Bell musical mode, 18, 445, 470n.73, 621n.18
Yellow Center, 209
Yellow Emperor, 444, 466n.8, 596n.20
Yellow Palace, 18, 20, 22, 84
Yellow Purity, 457
Yellow River, 54, 129, 203
Yellow Springs, 103, 157–58, 165, 257, 461, 495n.9
Yen Chün-p'ing. *See* Chuang Tsun
Yen Hui, 298, 383–84, 475n.125, 540n.45
Yen tzu, 142, 486n.290
Yen-ti, 442
Yi lin (Forest of Changes). See Chiao Kan.
Yi ching. See Book of Changes
yin *ch'i*, as round casing, 140, 186; characteristic operations of, 4, 26, 605n.3; acts on myriad things, *see wan-wu. See also* Yin/yang
Yin/yang, 453, 456; as models, 277; as cosmogonic stage, 2, 437; as Hard and Soft, 19, 24, 238, 429, 432; characteristic operations of, 342–43, 453, 455, 458; comingling of, 282, 335–36, 429, 458; complementarity of, 271; dominant characters of, 4, 7, 12–13, 26–27, 42, 65, 86, 342–43; graphic symbol for, 66; in opposition, 66, 85, 88, 339, 355, 388–89, 395, 450; related to Head texts, 10, 18–27; reversal of usual values for, 23–25, 212, 336, 376, 379, 400, 578n.2; waxing and waning of, 10, 15, 18, 42, 44, 96, 318, 331, 432, 451–52. *See also* cosmogonic stages; Head texts; Line texts; Yang *ch'i*; Yin *ch'i*

Yin/yang Five Phases theory, 8, 15, 45, 51, 60, 65–68, 221, 355–56, 466n.12, 488n.17, 580n.14. *See also* Appraisals, Yin/yang Five Phases values for; Five Phases; Principle of Masking; yang *ch'i*; yin *ch'i*
Ying Shao, 1
Youthfulness (THC12), 424, 426

yu water plant, 349
Yü, 164, 283, 418
yü chou ("spaces and times"), defined, 429, 433, 614n.16
Yü Fan, 609n.26
"Yü kung" ch. of *Documents*, 468n.40
Yü Yüeh, 111, 213, 378

Made in the USA
Middletown, DE
19 September 2024

61158343R00411